HIGHWAYS AND BYWAYS
ROUND
KINCARDINE

Also by
ARCHIBALD WATT, J.P., M.A., M.Ed., F.E.I.S., F.S.A.Scot.
Honorary Sheriff in the Sheriffdom of Grampian, Highlands and Islands,
ex-Deputy Rector, Mackie Academy, Stonehaven.

HIGHWAYS AND BYWAYS
ROUND STONEHAVEN

A unique aerial picture showing a two-mile section of the Deer Dyke stretching across Arnbarrow Hill from near the Clatterin' Brig. The length of the Deer Dyke, surrounding what was once the mediaeval King's Deer or Hunting Park of Kincardine Castle, had been not less than eight miles, enclosing a Hunting Park of about five square miles. In the background are the white buildings of Glensaugh; in the centre is the small Loch of Muchrae, nestling in the minute Glen of the same name. On this side of the loch and quite near the track is an unenclosed settlement comprising three hut circles some 2,400 years old, and in the foreground can be seen the remains of a mediaeval farmstead to the right of which is an area of rig-and-furrow cultivation.

Highways and Byways Round Kincardine

By

Archibald Watt

GOURDAS HOUSE PUBLISHERS
ABERDEEN
1985

First published by Gourdas House, Publishers,
5 Alford Place, Aberdeen 1985

ISBN 0 907301 09 6

Printed in Great Britain
by W. M. Bett Ltd., Tillicoultry

To
Christopher and Sarah

Foreword

by

THE RIGHT HON. THE VISCOUNT OF ARBUTHNOTT
D.S.C., J.P., M.A.

The history of Kincardineshire and the Mearns is the history of Scotland. To the discerning the traces of the influence of man on the old county, its towns and its parishes will tell of the earliest people, food gatherers and pastoralists, down the succeeding generations of settlers to the present day. Place names or a family link often give an indication of past events and the people involved. Pictish settlements are revealed in the hill-top farms of Pitcarry, Pitcarles and Pitforthie. Parish names, themselves sometimes derived from Celtic thanedoms, as at Arbuthnott and Crathes, still retain the feudal bounds set by William The Lion for his favoured servants. A thousand years of administrative change has not erased this evidence of ancient local government areas!

We are fortunate to live in a time of comparative prosperity in North-east Scotland. I have a theory of there having been three previous areas of peace and development in our turbulent history. One included the period of the Scoto-Norman kings when local government first took its form before the Wars of Independence. The second spanned the period of the rulers of James I to James V when art and architecture flourished in castle, cathedral and university and the third ran from 1750 to 1850 – the great period of agricultural improvement which gave our countryside the scenery it largely retains to this day.

Not only the visitor to Kincardineshire, but also the serious student of Scotland and its heritage can find all this and be guided to learn more by reading this book of 'rural rides' around the county. Archie Watt is a dedicated teacher and would have us all benefit by and enjoy his search for an awareness of our history in Kincardineshire and the beauty of our land.

Arbuthnott House
By Laurencekirk
Kincardineshire

Honour the Countryside Code

Inclusion of a route in this book does not imply that every part of it is a right of way. Similarly inclusion of a site does not necessarily mean that there is a right of public access.

As many sites mentioned are on farm land, often in rural areas, it is essential that walkers respect the rights and interests of landowners and of farmers for they will otherwise not only involve themselves in immediate unpleasantness but also prejudice for the future the good relations which exist – no-one is entitled to enter any farm land without the owner's permission unless a public right of way is being followed.

Walkers should keep to the paths across farm land, being careful to avoid trampling growing crops or saplings and damaging fences, hedges and walls. In forests they should keep to forest roads and rides and, when visiting archaeological sites, should not disturb the ground or structure in any way.

Readers of this book will find it most helpful to possess the Ordnance Survey map entitled 'Stonehaven'. This is Sheet 45 of the Landranger series of Great Britain, about 1¼ ins. to the mile. A compass on occasion may also be found useful.

Contents

Introduction

Greatly encouraged by the success of my first book, *Highways and Byways Round Stonehaven*, I am now delighted to present what is in effect a complementary volume, dealing with the history of Kincardineshire in the form of exploratory car tours, very often by quiet roads off the beaten tourist track. There are nine roughly circular drives in all, covering 420 miles of county highways and byways, 380 of them by car, the remaining 40 on foot. Extra excursions are suggested for the more enthusiastic wayfarer, totalling a further 20 miles by car and 18 on foot. So that round trips may begin at suitable starting points, in five of the journeys it has been necessary to retrace a total of 120 miles of main roads radiating from Stonehaven.

My book, I hope, will hold many attractions for the reader – historical associations, legendary lore, castellated buildings and prehistoric remains. There is, to the best of my knowledge, no book of this kind dealing with the history of Kincardineshire and certainly none dealing with its noteworthy prehistoric features now that the science of archaeology has advanced immeasurably and doubtful antiquarian discoveries have long ceased to be labelled merely Roman. In a sense the book is an embodiment of Sir Walter Scott's lines,

> *Of ancient deeds, so long forgot;*
> *Of feuds whose memory was not;*
> *Of forests, now laid waste and bare;*
> *Of towers which harbour now the hare;*
> *Of manners, long since changed and gone.*

I am most anxious that my researches should find permanence on paper, and yet I would not have my work considered solely as local history. 'Give me a companion by the way', said Sterne – and this is how I prefer to regard my book as we follow in leisurely fashion various paths of adventure, absorb the historic atmosphere of a castle or contemplate the peace of the lonely hills.

For there is a great deal of truth in the fact that most readers will probably be astonished at the number of precious things they have not seen – not because they are so distant but because they live so near to them. It's like the man who spent all his working life in London who confessed that he had never been inside the Tower. It was not because he was lacking in interest – he had been to St Peter's in Rome and to Granada to see the Alhambra. If the Tower had been on the other side of Europe, I think he would probably have made a pilgrimage to it, but as it had been within a stone's throw of him all his life, he had never found time to visit it. Have you been to Fasque, for example, full of precious treasures, or to see what remains of Cowie Castle, 1,725 yards as the crow flies from the middle of Stonehaven Square? You are always going but 'never get' as they say in Lancashire. It is too handy.

You may, if you care, select any starting place in the nine tours provided according to the paragraph heading that takes your fancy – you need not necessarily start at the beginning. And this, I am told, has proved one of the attractions of *Highways and Byways Round Stonehaven*. You are tied to no timetable. If you like the road or the optional excursion, you follow it. What liberty is there like this? You will have temporarily cut your moorings from the world, alone with the wide sky and elemental things that have been from the beginning. When you stand on the summit of Clochnaben or on the battlefield of Corrichie or by the Neolithic long barrow at Capo, a thousand years older than the first Pyramid, it will be as though you have passed into eternity where a thousand years are as one day. There is no calendar for this dateless world.

We shall then no longer, it is hoped, look upon Kincardineshire as a kind of Bradshaw's Guide – we should find it as fascinating as a fairy tale, as full of interest as a Canterbury Pilgrimage. Haulkerton will again resound with the screeching of birds in the royal mews, we shall visualise the lumbering figure of Johnson at Monboddo, and the Cairn o' Mounth will again echo to the tread of the army of Malcolm Canmore, driving ahead the fleeing Macbeth.

My principal aim is, however, to stimulate public interest in the history, character and beauty of Kincardineshire, to further knowledge of and interest in our local heritage and to encourage the preservation of various ancient historical sites and buildings that mean so much to us and are of aesthetic and environmental importance. For many years discerning citizens have been alarmed by the destruction and decay of old buildings and landmarks and by the ever present threat to close those that remain (witness the desecration of the ancient Water Yett in Stonehaven) for all communities are prone to take for granted what their forefathers have left them. The few precious remains we have of the past are vanishing like snows before the south wind, going without a murmur so pre-occupied are we with more urgent matters. These buildings and sites are an essential part of our heritage and a part which, once gone, can never be replaced.

As we wander around the county, may we find enrichment by the discovery of new kingdoms for our inheritance. May wider horizons be opened for us – worlds presently outside our experience.

'Call that a sunset?' said the lady to Turner as she stood before the artist's picture. 'I never saw a sunset like that.'

'No madam', replied Turner, 'don't you wish you had?'

Perhaps the world of some of us is limited because we are near-sighted. Perhaps we miss the vision of our heritage not because the vision is not there but because we darken the windows inadvertently.

Archibald Watt

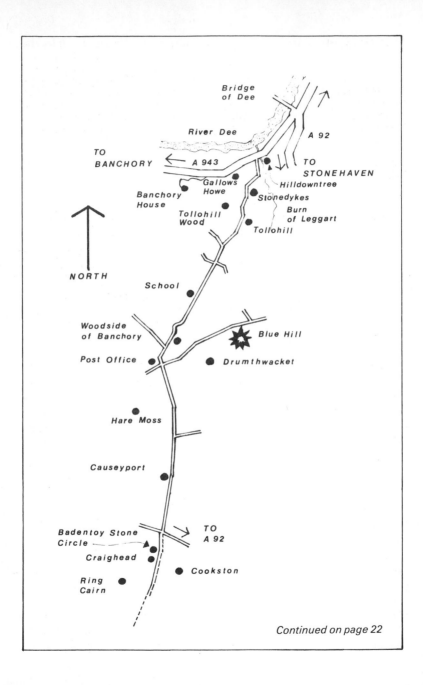

Bridge
of Dee

River Dee

A 92

TO
BANCHORY

← A 943

TO
STONEHAVEN

Gallows
Howe

Hilldowntree

Banchory
House

Stonedykes

Tollohill
Wood

Burn
of Leggart

Tollohill

NORTH

School

Woodside
of Banchory

Blue Hill

Post Office

Drumthwacket

Hare Moss

Causeyport

TO
A 92

Badentoy Stone
Circle

Craighead

Cookston

Ring
Cairn

Continued on page 22

Route One

Stonehaven Square – Bridge of Dee – Hilldowntree – Banchory House – Banchory-Devenick Schoolhouse – Moor of Drumforskie – Drumthwacket – Blue Hill – Hare Moss – Causeyport – Craighead – Cairnwell Ring Cairn – Old Bourtreebush – Stone Circles of Aquhorthies – Berryhill House – Chapel of Elsick – Gillybrands – Windyedge – Elsick House – Nether Cairnhill – St Ternan's Episcopal Chapel – Muchalls Castle – Blackbutts – Bridge of Muchalls – Cowie House – Stonehaven Square.

Distance: 32 miles, 24½ by car and 7½ on foot if all suggested diversions are followed.

Round the Causey Mounth and Muchalls Castle

in which we see a unique coat of arms and a bridge unique in Britain, the Old Pretender's bed and a type of stone circle unknown elsewhere in the world – not forgetting a battle-field where Highlanders once fled at the sound of cannon. We also read of the first Civil War engagement, of an Aberdeen provost whose shirt front was drenched by his rivals with wine and of whisky smuggling in a horse-drawn hearse!

Would you care to traverse one of the most historic roads in the north of Scotland, a road that for 700 years ran through history as the straight highway and the only direct means of land communication between Aberdeen and the great centres of the country in the south, a road that, avoiding swamp and moss as far as possible, kept Aberdeen in living touch with the outer world and can still be traced in portions that have escaped absorption in cultivated land?

The Cowy or Causey Mounth

I refer to the road known throughout the centuries as the Cowy Mounth because it was the roadway by Cowy near Stonehaven (or Cowie as it is now), the principal pass over the mountainous Mounth or extreme eastern slopes of the Grampian range to Aberdeen, a road protected (or obstructed) at its Stonehaven entrance by the ancient Castle of Cowie a few hundred yards from it. Mounth is the ancient name of the range of hills that forms the watershed on the right bank of the Dee from Ben Nevis in Lochaber to the Hill of Cookney between Stonehaven and Aberdeen. Named from the Gaelic 'monadh' (pronounced mōn-a), meaning a heath or

1

moor, the formidable mountain barrier was a dreaded obstacle to any who ventured to penetrate beyond its vast limits, and in early times the thought of crossing the 'Mounth' was sufficient to fill even the stoutest heart with apprehension. There were eight main routes or passes across it, all distinguished by different names, generally with the affix, 'Mounth'.

The Cowy Mounth pass was also known as the Causey Mounth because originally it was a very rugged and ever difficult track over an extensive moss which during the winter season would have been quite impossible for such conveyances as were in use in olden times, and even for foot-passengers, but for two man-made 'causeys' (from the French 'causie', now 'chaussée'). These raised or paved roads or highways were constructed through the flooded parts of the morass.

A Highway Used Since William the Lion

How early this highway existed it is quite impossible to tell. Probably there was some kind of road there when Aberdeen got its first royal charter from William the Lion, granting certain trading privileges to the burgesses of Aberdeen and all other burgesses *north of the munth*. Certain it is that the Causey Mounth is the best evidence of the character of the country in remote times, but its importance did not develop until Aberdeen emerged from its obscure position as a wayside hamlet situated at the mouth of the Don. The importance of the western or Cairn o' Mounth road decreased just as the importance of the Cowie Mounth grew.

The highway was marched by the forces of Wallace, Bruce and, in 1296, of Edward I, the Hammer of the Scots, but that great king did not use the northern end of it. And the Gausey or Cowie Mounth is still in use for several miles today from Aberdeen over Cran Hill to Causeyport. Except for a short stretch over Portlethen Moss one can follow it from Aberdeen almost to Muchalls. And that is just what we propose to do.

To reach the road we must travel by bus or car from Stonehaven to the traffic lights at the end of the dual carriage-way at the Bridge of Dee, Aberdeen, a distance of just under 13 miles. Let us do this, turning immediately left into Leggart Terrace, the first part of what is known as the South Deeside Road, distinguished now as A943. We must stop a few yards round the corner at the pillar-box and opposite the gap in the wall which is the entrance to an attractive public garden by the river.

The Bridge of Dee

You are advised to enter this small garden to view at closer quarters the Bridge of Dee, one of five first-class ancient, historic bridges of Scotland. Its history and construction are alike so remarkable that it may well be regarded as our best example of this class of public structure. Still continuing admirably to fulfil its work, it was exactly 450 years old in 1977 as Gavin Dunbar, Bishop of Aberdeen, began to build it in 1520, finishing it in 1527. It was projected by an even greater prelate, Bishop William Elphinstone, founder of King's College and Chancellor of Scotland. He, however, while providing the means for the bridge, did not live to see the building begun.

It is certain that there was a bridge of some kind over the Dee, perhaps made of timber, nearly 150 years before the erection of the Bridge of Dee. This we learn from an entry in the oldest register of Aberdeen, the Register of the Bishopric, relating to the maintenance of a bridge over the water of Dee in 1384. It is clear, however, that there was no bridge at this spot in the years prior to 1520. The 'Foords of Dee' were in use 500 or 600 yards down river and a little above the railway bridge where one can still easily see the shingly bed of the river at low water.

Three Remarkable Features

As we stand looking at the Bridge of Dee, there are three remarkable features to be noticed. To begin with, it is practically a level bridge, a very unusual thing among mediaeval bridges of Scotland. Very unusual, too, is the fact that all the seven arches are beautifully ribbed on the under side. A third remarkable feature of the bridge is its wonderful series of inscriptions and coats of arms – twenty-eight of them in all. There is nothing like it on any bridge in the whole of Britain. Let me advise anyone interested in such matters to walk over the bridge and spend a half-hour examining these inscriptions: most of them are on the west side, easily seen from the recesses in the pavement above the piers.

The Bridge of Dee was widened by the Town Council in 1841-42 in a most skilful and interesting way. Before then it was only 14½ ft. wide, too narrow for traffic even in those days. What the Council did was to dismantle the whole western face of the bridge with all its sculptures, insert the additional 11½ ft. of width and then replace the western face with the inscriptions and coats of arms as they were before. Accordingly we have the Bridge of Dee today presenting in the main the same external appearance as it has done throughout the 450 years of its history.

Let us continue our walk of exploration to the little round pillar or turret at the south-west or nearest corner of the bridge, the oldest part. This pillar was heightened by three courses of masonry – easily distinguishable from the original smaller courses – when the roadway and parapets at the ends of the bridge were heightened in connection with the widening operations. Here near the water's edge one can easily distinguish, too, the new work in the ancient structure of the bridge itself.

The west side of the Bridge of Dee, showing some of the twenty-eight inscriptions and coats of arms that make the bridge unlike any other in Britain.

The Arms of Bishop Dunbar

It is, of course, quite unnecessary here to detail the remarkable series of twenty-eight sculptures on the bridge. Mention should be made, however, of the coats of arms on the south-west corner pillar by which we presently stand. On top are the arms of Bishop Gavin Dunbar standing out in relief from the sandstone block. The details of this early and plain sculpture are fairly clear, doubtless due to the fact that it has been considerably sheltered by its position. Nevertheless, the motto on the scroll or band under the shield has been weathered out. Clearly visible on top is Dunbar's mitre (but without fibulae or ribbons) with on either side the initials G.D. in raised Gothic capitals. The shield contains, in heraldic terms, what are known as 'three cushions within a double (royal) tressure', that is, a double border running parallel with the sides of the escutcheon.

The Coat of Arms of Scotland

Below this is the coat of arms of Scotland – a lion rampant on a shield surmounted by a crown, *circa* 1520. It, too, stands free on the block, carved in the same yellowish grey sandstone as that of the bridge. The extremely interesting feature of this coat of arms is the absence of the double tressure on the shield. The curious Act of James III's Scots Parliament of 1471 which decreed that in future there should be no tressure about the lion in the national arms was not obeyed, and Sir James Balfour Paul, the Lyon King, is quoted as saying just before World War I,

> *I am not aware of even a solitary instance of the Scottish arms without the tressure either at or after this period.*

The coat of arms at which you are looking would therefore seem to be unique.

The coat of arms of Scotland on the south-east corner pillar of the Bridge of Dee. It is unique because there is no double tressure (or border) on the shield.

Bishop Elphinstone's Coat of Arms

On the south spandrel of the seventh arch (i.e. the triangular space between the curve of the arch and the enclosing right angle) can be seen the coat of arms of Bishop William Elphinstone, his mitre above the shield with at either side the initials V.E. in raised Roman capitals. Under the shield is a scroll with the motto, *Non Confundar* (I shall not be confounded). This coat of arms is interesting on two counts. Firstly, it has for some reason the chevron represented 'humetty', that is with the ends cut off instead of extending, as they ought, to the edge of the shield. Secondly, it is the only piece of sculpture in the main wall of the bridge. The explanation seems to be that this is one of the two coats of arms ordered to be erected in the stone port (from the French porte, a gate) above the roadway of the bridge in 1679. When the port was removed in 1774, the likelihood is that the coat of arms was carefully inserted in the wall of the bridge itself in a position as near as possible to its original one.

The Port on the Bridge of Dee

The fate of this interesting stone port was decreed in the following Act of the Town Council:

> *14th August, 1773 – The said Day, the Council having visited the Bridge of Dee are unanimously of opinion that the Port and Stone Walls upon the south end of the Bridge are a great obstruction and hindrance to the free and easy passage of all carriages passing along the Bridge and therefore agree that the said Port, and Walls on each side thereof shall be removed and taken down as soon as possible, and that the entry on that end of the Bridge shall be made open betwixt the said two parapets; as also that the corner of the West Parapet Wall without the Port should be removed as far as possible so as to make the passage on that end of the Bridge still more easy and commodious for carriages; and recommend to the Magistrates to cause the same to be done as soon as convenient, and to defray the expense thereof out of the Bridge of Dee Charge.*

The idea of striking off the corner of the west parapet wall was to round off the sharp angle at which the Causey Mounth road, coming from Leggart's Den, turned on to the bridge.

But the port was not just presently removed. Some difficulty seems to have arisen, but on 22nd July, 1774, on the occasion of another visitation, and having resolved on certain repairs to the bridge itself, the Council went on:

> *The Council further recommend to the Magistrates to employ proper tradesmen to cause take down and remove the Port upon the south side of the Bridge, and to Open and Enlarge the Passage from the high road upon each side agreeable to the Council's Act of last year during the visitation of the Bridge, and to meet and settle with the Doers* (agents) *of Mr Menzies of Pitfoddels as they shall think proper for what ground may be necessary belonging to them for enlarging the said Passage.*

Covenanters' Faulds

On the south-west face of the sixth pier you can just see a block with the oldest date on the bridge, 1520, with immediately under it another coat of arms of Gavin Dunbar . . . but it is time we continued our journey. Before we re-enter our car, however, cast a glance at the high ground behind the Stonehaven road on which is now built the housing estate of Kincorth. Beyond rises the eastmost ridge of the Grampians, only 300 ft. high, a sad falling-away from the soaring mountains of Ben Macdhui, Mount Keen and Lochnagar. Kincorth, you will be interested to know, has the alternative name of 'Covenanters' Faulds' (sheep-folds) because in 1639 the Covenanter army, under the Earl Marischal and the Marquis of Montrose, crossed the Grampians by the Causey Mounth into Deeside. Estimated at 9000 strong and declared to be *weil-armit both on horss and futt*, the Covenanters occupied the heights in bombarding the Bridge of Dee at which we have been looking. It was the very first engagement in the Civil War that cost King Charles his head and gave Britain for the first time in history a Commonwealth government. The name, 'Covenanters' Faulds', is preserved in several street-names – Covenanters' Drive and Row, and Faulds Crescent, Gate, Row and Wynd.

Now let us proceed towards the Causey Mounth road which after all is our main objective. We must continue along the South Deeside Road which was first properly laid out as a turnpike road in 1837-42 and which was formerly nearer the river than it is now. After some 780 yards we arrive at the bridge over the tiny Burn of Leggart with, beside it, the ruined corn-mill, the Mill of Leggart, last used in November, 1926, and just under 13⅓ miles from Stonehaven Square. The narrow hill road immediately on our left is the one we must take.

7

Hilldowntree

The few houses here where the suburbs end at the Aberdeen boundary are called Hilldowntree, traditionally named according to Jervise's *Epitaphs*

> *from a huge tree which long ago had been floated down from the hills where it took root and grew to an enormous size. It was blown down by the storm of 3rd October, 1860, but its root is still visible.*

Or, rather, it was – just where the Burn of Leggart enters the Dee. Public executions are believed to have taken place here in ancient times – a belief borne out by the name, 'Gallows' Howe', given to a hollow in a field 350 yards farther along the south side of the main road between the cottage which is visible there and Tollohill Wood. Here too, for many centuries, there was a roadside hostelry near the meal-mill at which travellers could regale themselves. This former inn is now seen as Elm Cottage, an 18th century building and the only building on the south side of the main road. From here, we are told, whisky used to be smuggled to Aberdeen in horse-drawn hearses! At Hilldowntree a few years ago was a wood-carving workshop in the now derelict saw-milling buildings by the roadside. Here handsome wooden articles were created.

Visit of Prince Albert

Ready for the two-mile climb? Off we go. Just under 600 yards up the old road and past a rough piece of moorland on our right, part of the policies of Banchory House, is the farm of Stonedykes. Near it at Cotcraig in Tollohill Wood stands a massive roughly dressed granite obelisk, about 12 ft. high, commemorating Prince Albert who, presiding at the British Association meeting in Aberdeen in 1859, spent the night in Banchory House nearby. On a sunk panel in the dado of the monument is the inscription:

In Remembrance of the Visit of

H.R.H. Albert, Prince Consort,

To this Spot

XV September MDCCCLIX.

Banchory House

Banchory House, situated on the rising ground on the west side of the road, is a charming building in the Elizabethan style, the foundation stone of which was laid with great ceremony on 21st January, 1840. It was designed and built by John Smith (Tudor Johnnie), City Architect of Aberdeen, for Mr Alexander Thomson, the last and most venerable of the Thomson family who had owned the estate of Banchory since 1743. The massive new mansion, erected on the site of an earlier 17th century house, is virtually identical with the massive extensions to old Balmoral Castle, also designed by Smith and closely similar in style. In its fabric is incorporated a date stone of 1621 from the old mansion.

Banchory House, re-named Beannacher, is now a Camphill-Rudolf-Steiner community school with a new approach to agriculture.

Dr Chalmers and Other Distinguished Guests

Prince Albert was a guest in Banchory House while attending the meetings of the British Association, as we have noted. His bedroom still exists, his visit being commemorated by an engraving on the mantelpiece, and when he died, Queen Victoria sent to Mr Thomson handsomely framed lithographs of herself and her consort.

Another famous visitor was the great Dr Chalmers, the Scottish divine who, when he visited Aberdeen at the time of the Disruption on September 10th, 1843, preached on the lawn to an immense congregation, drawn from many miles around, including Aberdeen. Mr Thomson, his host, took a very prominent part in the Disruption controversy, sparing neither time nor money in advancing the cause of the Free Church. He was the means of forming a congregation and procuring a minister for the Free Church of Banchory-Devenick which was built entirely at his own expense.

Stanley, the great African explorer (1890), and many other distinguished men have been guests at Banchory House.

Owners of Banchory House

In 1743 the lands of Banchory-Devenick were bought by Alexander Thomson, Advocate in Aberdeen and a descendant of John Knox, and in 1872 the estate was bought for £76,000 by Mr John Stewart, the Aberdeen comb manufacturer who had made Aberdeen Combworks the largest comb-making centre in the world. One of the most remarkable figures in the mercantile history of Aberdeen, he pioneered the Great North of Scotland Railway Company and transformed the Aberdeen and London Steam Navigation Company. A later owner, Sir David Stewart, LL.D., Lord Provost of Aberdeen, who succeeded to the estate in1887, entertained the Marquis of Lorne, later the Duke of Argyll, when he visited on a political mission.

A more recent chatelaine of Banchory House, Mrs David Stewart, was a descendant of the Thomson lairds, and her husband, Mr David Stewart, O.B.E., brought to their lovely home many reminders of close links with the municipal and cultural history of Aberdeen. William Dyce, R.A., perhaps the greatest painter Aberdeen ever produced, was a great-grand-uncle of Mr David Stewart, and there used to be many fine Dyce pictures in Banchory House, the most notable being 'David in the Wilderness' and 'The Man of Sorrows'.

Pictish Stones and Motte and Bailey

Into the garden wall of Banchory House are built the Pictish

The Pictish symbol stones from Dunnicaer built into the garden wall of what was Banchory House. On top is a roughly-dressed stone on which is incised a fish. On the left the familiar crescent and V-rod can be discerned, while on the largest stone are seen the conventional 'spectacle' figure, with dots in the centres of the circles, together with variants of the abstract z-rod design.

stones found in the middle of the 19th century by the rock of Dunnicaer.[1]

Still conspicuous on the left of the approach to Banchory House is the great earthen mound of the motte and bailey castle of Alan Durward of Coull, still clearly defined like the sister mottes at Durris and Strachan. To Alan Durward, who became Regent of Scotland, a charter of the lands of Banchory-Devenick had been given in 1256 by the monks of Arbroath. These lands Alexander III later converted into a *free barony* and conferred them on Durward as *the most accomplished knight and best military leader of his time.*

A Kirk Road and a Parish Church

Resuming our journey up the Causey Mounth road for 300 yards, we presently, on the high ground 125 yards before the farm of Tollohill and by a fire notice, see steps in the dyke on our right, leading up to a path along the edge of the high field and of the wood, thence through a gap in the trees. It was a Kirk Road, a short cut to the road leading to the U.F. Church of St Devenick-on-the-Hill (now no longer used) and, farther on, to the parish church on its ancient site far down near the river. It is supposed to stand over the grave of St Devenick, one of the missionary disciples of St Columba. He had a chapel here and carried on his missionary work along the north-east coast as far as Caithness till his death when his remains were brought back to the banks of the Dee and buried near his chapel. From St Devenick the parish took its name, Banchory-Devenick. The farm of Tollohill stands where Montrose's soldiers looked down on Aberdeen before the Battle of the Bridge of Dee.

A Panorama of Aberdeen

We are now well up the southern slope of the Mounth towards the ridge of the Grampians and, if we look back, we shall see a panorama of Aberdeen that takes the breath away and enjoy the same view as Burns saw on his way home from his Highland tour in 1787 when, having crossed the Dee and ascended the high ground, he looked back on Aberdeen lying in its sleepy hollow in the September sunshine. Of the sky-scrapers and twenty-five or so tapering spires now in evidence he saw, of course, only the spire on the old Tolbooth at the Castlegate and, if he carried his eye over to Old Aberdeen, the crown and tower of King's College and the twin spires of St Machar's Cathedral. We are amused at his remark characterising Aberdeen as *a lazy town*. Probably he was right

[1]See *Highways and Byways Round Stonehaven*, pp. 127-129.

although even a supreme genius could scarcely hope to discover all the sparkle and wit of a town in the course of a three-hour visit.

Gradually ascending to Banchory-Devenick schoolhouse and the adjoining school, we obtain another splendid view on our right before we enter the delightfully wooded slack at the crest of the road. The elevation is about 400 ft. Here Aberdeen is best seen from the south side, and here is a commanding outlook over the magnificent sweep of Aberdeen Bay and the wide landscape to the west and north. Over the valley of the Dee and beyond the rugged hilly ridges of Countesswells and Skene we may be able to make out, if the day is very clear, something of the great fort on the Mither Tap of Bennachie, 20 miles away, the flat mass of the other remarkable fort on the Tap o' Noth and, a little farther west, the fine peak of the Buck of the Cabrach almost 40 miles in the distance.

The Moor of Drumforskie

At last, in just short of half a mile we are at the top of the rise with Woodside of Banchory farm on the left and, on the right, the remains of the heathery Moor of Drumforskie, a skrunt of waste moor which extended down the hill to what are now the policies of Banchory House behind the farm of Stonedykes. The Moor of Drumforskie and the Causey Mounth were to pass into literature in September, 1796, when Sir Walter Scott as a young advocate attended the Circuit Court on his only visit to Aberdeen as far as we know. Struck by this wild bleak moor beyond the Grampians, he reproduced it in his novel, *A Legend of Montrose*, as the Moor of Drumthwacket, the paternal *natural heritament − that fertile and pleasant spot* of Dugald Dalgetty, soldier of fortune, who plays a great part in the stirring episodes of that story. About his *heritament* the celebrated soldier of the great Gustavus never ceased to boast − and with no cause or excuse for a poorer patrimony never kept knight from starving. He would not have so very far to trudge to the Marischal College he was so fond of calling to mind.

It is interesting to know that only a little over a century ago Sir David Stewart, proprietor of the lands of Banchory-Devenick, changed the name of one of his farms here from Banchory Hillock to Drumthwacket to preserve the interesting association with Sir Walter Scott. It lies only three-tenths of a mile south-east of Woodside Farm where we are.

The venerable Causey Mounth road was beginning to lose its supremacy even at the time of Scott's visit when steps were being taken by Kincardine County Council and Aberdeen Town Council to have a new road laid out between Stonehaven and Aberdeen under the new Turnpike Road Acts (1751) which proved a civilizing influence in the North of Scotland. The Aberdeen authorities were eager for a new access. Although the new coast road cost them £12,000 before they were done with it, they and their successors alike felt that the expenditure was justified.

The Blue Hill

At the cross roads at Banchory-Devenick Post Office let us depart for a short time from our journey along the Causey Mounth road by turning left to visit the Blue Hill which commands extraordinary views of land and sea. Passing the farm of Drumthwacket only 240 yards away on our right, we need travel only three-quarters of a mile downhill. Just before the house on our left we reach the rusted remains of a gate on the right-hand side. Through it we must go. After a walk of 290 yards we presently reach the summit of the Blue Hill, an eminence of only 467 ft. (for it has little of the appearance of a hill). It is one of the best view-points in the immediate neighbourhood of Aberdeen, covering a wonderfully varied and characteristic panorama of about 90 miles from the sea horizon about 27 miles distant on the east to the Cairngorms on the west. The name, Blue Hill, is merely an English form of the Gaelic 'carn', a cairn or hill, and 'gorm', blue, a descriptive designation applied to a hill as seen in the distance as faint purple in colour.

Clochandichter and Views to South and North

Two and a third miles away to the south-west you see the bare, brown crest of Clochandichter (545 ft. above sea level), a type of Scottish place-name that never fails to tickle the fancy of the Sassenach. Though to the Celtic ear the name may sound poetic, it has a shaggy, cacophonic ring. Could Burns, do you think, ever have been moved by passion for a Bonnie Mary o' Clochandichter?

A few miles beyond Clochandichter rises the hill-ridge of Fetteresso across which you can trace easily the route taken by the Roman armies 1800 years ago as they marched northwards from Raedykes[1] to the camp at Culter on Deeside. Beyond a splendid view of Aberdeen Slains Castle is visible to the north, as are the sands of Forvie, the coast-guard houses at Belhelvie, Tarbathie (or Strabathie) Hill and Buchan Ness lighthouse near Peterhead about 50 miles away. The distant objects that can be distinguished towards the south are Dunnottar Castle[2] with the striking War Memorial of

[1] *Highways and Byways Round Stonehaven*, pp. 181-189.
[2] Ibid., pp. 130-153.

13

Stonehaven erected on the hill nearby[1] and, about 20 miles farther on, Johnstone Tower on Garvock Hill at Laurencekirk standing almost 1000 ft. above sea level.

View to the West

But always the most alluring view is to the west, away beyond the valley of the Dee to the multitude of hill and mountain tops that give such character to the upland scenery of Aberdeenshire and Kincardineshire. The great mass of the Hill of Fare is only 15 to 20 miles away in the near distance, but beyond on either side one can pick out easily the summits of the Corrennie range, Clochnaben with its stone mass on the top (1963 ft.), Mount Battock (2555 ft.), Mount Keen with its fine conical summit (3077 ft.), Lochnagar (3786 ft.), Beinn a' Bhuird (3924 ft.) and, to the north-east of it, Ben Avon at the head of Glen Avon nearly 60 miles away, Beinn a' Bhuird recognisable by its grand eastern corries and Ben Avon by its rocky pinnacles. The most distant mountains, less readily noticed, are Cairn Toul near the source of the Dee and Beinn Bhrotain just south of it. The following more or less familiar hills are also seen: Cairn-mon-earn, Kerloch, Peter Hill, Scoltie, Barmekin, Buck of the Cabrach, Bennachie and Brimmond Hill. It is astonishing, indeed, that so many distant objects of interest can be picked out with the naked eye from a hill not quite 500 ft. high.

The summit of the 467ft. high Blue Hill, showing the view to the west, away beyond the valley of the Dee to the mountains beyond.

[1] *Ibid.*, pp. 125-126.

Causeways Necessary from Ancient Times

And now let us return to Banchory-Devenick Post Office, turn left
and continue on our way. In half a mile we see on the right Hare
Moss and become vividly aware of why the road on which we are
travelling was known in history as the Causey Mounth. It was so
named because in the old days the flat piece of country where we are
now was low, boggy moorland known as the Moss of Aberdeen. So
it was that, because of morasses and boulders, this region across
which the old highway stretched its stoney way was fraught with
discomfort as well as danger until it was superseded after 1795 by
the present road along the coast. So flooded and broken up was it
that causeways, paved and bottomed with trees, stones, etc., were
necessary from very ancient times to render the highway passable
for man and beast and for such conveyances as were then in use.
You are standing on one of these causeways now, and it is fascinating to see that to this day the road surface is still high above the land
through which it passes. Fascinating, too, to see that the moss has
still not been completely drained although a great extent of moor
was reclaimed in Banchory-Devenick and Fetteresso towards the
latter half of the 19th century.

*The Causey Mounth road just past Banchory-Devenick Post Office, clearly showing
part of the causeway still high above the land through which it passes. Originally the
road would have been bottomed with trees, stones, etc., necessary to make the highway
passable across Hare Moss, seen on the right. Causeyport Farm is marked by the trees
in the middle of the skyline in the extreme distance, a third of a mile beyond the farm
seen in the picture.*

15

There were two 'causeys', one about three-quarters and the other about quarter of a mile in length. In ancient days it is not unlikely that a footing for men and cattle was necessary between Causeyport and Muchalls as well. Not without reason was the road described as it was.

A Bleak, Miserable Country

Captain Francks, a caustic observer who journeyed from Aberdeen to Stonehaven in 1658, says in his *Northern Memoirs* with reference to the causeways,

> *But what have we here? Cawses uncartable, and pavements unpractical, pointed with rocky, stumpy stones, and dawb'd all over with dingy dirt, that makes it unpassible; and the fields as I conceive, are ten times worse, because o'erspread with miry clay, and incumbered with bogs that will bury a horse.*

George Kinloch, also, who became the first post-Reform M.P. for Dundee, remarks in the following century,

> *I never saw a more bleak, miserable country – bogs and heather and not a hedge or tree to be seen, And this continues till within a mile of the town.*

This bleakness, of course, is nothing like so apparent as it once was although, even now, there are not many trees to be seen. As late as 1733 the whole barony of Ury was declared to be entirely destitute of planting, and in that year directions were given to the tenants of the estate for embellishing it in this way.

Town Council Maintenance

For the causeying and maintenance of this part of the road the Town Council of Aberdeen were held responsible for, indeed, the periodic inspection and state of repair of the Causey Mounth were matters of vital interest to the city. From an early date the town called on owners of lands through which the Causey Mounth passed to help in defraying the cost of upkeep, but they were not always successful in getting payment. Among records in Aberdeen Town House is a *summons by the burgh for a feu-duty granted 9th April, 1378, for supporting Calsey at Cowie Month.* Again, on 3rd October, 1632, the Town Council summoned a meeting of the neighbouring lairds relative to the repair *of the calsies' of Month Cowye*, for the roadway was then evidently in bad condition. But these expedients having failed, the Council took the effectual step of presenting to the Privy Council of Scotland, on 17th July, 1634, a *Supplication* for authority to exact a toll on the Causey Mounth to pay the cost of mending and upholding the same. They set forth that:

> *The Calsies in Cowymonth are now so worn and decayed as there will be no possibilitie of passage in this approaching winter, and the supplicants hes done alreadie all that lyes in thame for the mending and up holding of these Calseyis, bot the work is so great, and the manie other burdeins lying upoun the said burghe presseth thame so hardlie as it lyis not in their power to outtred and perfytee that work – there being none within the Kingdome more important and necessar.*

The Privy Council, after hearing some barons and gentlemen of the north anent the matter, found it to be for the weal of the country and good of the people that the prayer of the Aberdeen magistrates should be met. Not only did they grant the Aberdonians the right to exact a toll as they requested; it also granted them *for the better collecting and ingaddering of this custom and dewtie* authority

> *To caus big ane port at suche pairt and place of the calseyis as they from tyme to tyme sall think expedient, and to close the port and suffer none to have passage that way bot such as sall pay the dewtie foirsaid, debarring all otheris frome passage who sall refuse to pay the same.*

This authority the Privy Council granted on 17th July, 1634, for the space of 19 years. But it was renewed, again with limit of duration, as an Act of the first Scots Parliament after the Restoration on 22nd February, 1661, and again in 1699.

To meet the expenses of upholding the calseys of Cowie Mounth, then, tolls were charged from all who passed, as follows: foot passengers 2d, horsemen 8d, ten sheep 8d, a cow or ox 4d, a cartload 2s Scots.

Stone Gateway or Causey Port

Now where was this stone gateway or port of which we speak? Let us proceed for only half a mile farther until we reach the next farm on our right, still named Causeyport Farm and still keeping the memory of the ancient Causey Mounth green. Here, just short of a mile from the Banchory-Devenick Post Office cross roads and exactly three miles from the South Deeside Road, the old causeway ended. Exactly where the port stood and what its exact character was we do not know, but that it was erected across the road fairly near this historic spot is certain. Here was maintained a burgh guard, and here the magistrates of Aberdeen were authorised to prevent the passage of any of the above-mentioned traffic unless the tolls were paid.

And here was a stopping place for horsemen on their way south, a place where on their return they loaded up their carts with peat from the marshy land at the east of the farm. The stoney road which they used through the marsh, now used to reach cultivated fields, is still visible.

The exacting of tolls was not by any means, of course, the first occasion on which the authorities of Aberdeen supported the causeways. A feu-duty of some sort was granted as early as 9th April, 1378, for supporting the *calseys* at Cowie Mounth. The lairds who were concerned with the causeway at the Cowie end were the lairds of Ury, Cowie, Muchalls and Elsick.

Macfarlane in his *View of the Diocese of Aberdeen* of about 1725 tells us,

> *To the North of Auchorties 1½ mile is the Caulsay port, with a large Caulsay, which pass throw a large moss, and the port was built and the Caulsay laid in 1634 by the City of Aberdeen, and the said towne setts in tack the said port to a man who gathers up from every horse that passes throw the port eight pennies Scots. At the north end, the said caulsay passes throw the Grampian hills, which goe straight to the sea, and there is a large highway passes from Aberdeen to Edinburgh along the caulsay.*

Liberal Benefactions

The minutes of Aberdeen Town Council show the importance attached to the gate and keeping open the route across the swamps, hollows and rocks of the Cowie Mounth. They received grants to keep in repair the causeway and the service roads connected with it. In 1384 a notable burgess of Aberdeen, John Crab, proprietor of Kincorth on the south side of the ferry of the Dee, left to his son, Paul Crab, an annuity of 40 shillings

> *for the use, necessity and maintenance of the Causey Mounth and the Bridge of Dee.*

Some of the more opulent citizens of Aberdeen also made liberal benefactions. In 1463 Andrew Alanson granted a foundation of 16s

8d, and the burgh records tell us that during the year 1612-13 the sum of 6s 8d was given

> *at the prouest's command to ane calcimaker to meet my Lord Mershell in Monthe Cowie to mend the calcies,*

and that in 1633-34 £20 6s was received for

> *ane warrand to big ane port upon the calcies of Mounth Cowie.*

Throughout the first half of the 18th century the Town Council continued to acknowledge ancient obligations on them to maintain the Causey Mounth, but the upkeep of the highways was passing into other hands, and the Council became less and less willing to share responsibility for a trunk road that was clearly passing beyond their jurisdiction. On 26th March, 1759, they granted £15 sterling out of the Bridge of Dee funds *for repairing the Stonehyve Road*, but resolved at the same time *that no more* (is) *to be given for that purpose in time coming.* Yet were they rather better than their resolution for they contributed £10 sterling towards the same object in 1775, which was probably the last contribution made towards this ancient highway under the old conditions.

The Causey Port Removed

For new conditions were now arising. Mail coaches were beginning to revolutionise travelling throughout the country. People were beginning to move about from place to place with the mere object of travelling, and the pleasantness of the new means of transport was a surprise and a delight to the whole countryside. Although it was 1787 before the first mail coach-run between Edinburgh and Aberdeen was made, the roads were being more and more used for the new wheel traffic, and the Causey Port on the old Stonehaven highway was found to be in the way. On 15th April, 1760, accordingly, the Town Council

> *agreed to consent to the taking down of the Causey Port in order to streight and widen the king's highway.*

It had done its duty here by Causeyport Farm for 125 years and more.

The Badentoy Circle

But to continue our walk. The old highway can still be used for another 740 yards to the T-junction from where, if you turn left along the Maryculter-Findon road, the main road to Stonehaven can be reached in just under a mile. Before you do so, however, you should walk only 280 yards along the good, serviceable farm road to Craighead Farm straight ahead of you where the Badentoy stone-circle stands on the right-hand side. Only three of its original seven stones now remain, and these have been moved to stand on a mound 2 ft. 6 ins. high, a wall having been built round the edge. In the centre of the circle were found charcoal and half burnt bones.

The 'Husbandtowne' of Cookston

Opposite Craighead Farm and 120 yards to the west stands the farm of Cookston which reminds us that the inhabitants of Aberdeen as well as the men of the Mearns once had an interest in seeing that the approaches to the Causey Mounth road would always be of such a satisfactory character as to make the passage through the hills a permanent one. It is said that the old *husbandtowne* (farmstead) of Cookston was *given out* for the maintenance of the causeys and that the *gentlemen of the Mearns* made a general contribution towards the upkeep. For the same purpose a fine was occasionally imposed by the Baron of Ury in his court.

The Parting of the Ways

And now comes the parting of the ways. Your car can proceed no farther – and we presume that you have most probably arrived at this point by car. If you have, your driver must return to the cross roads by Craighead Farm and proceed down the hill to the east. The first turn on the right will take him in three-quarters of a mile to Roadside of Cookston on the main Stonehaven-Aberdeen road, the A92, and another 3¾ miles southwards to the cross roads where the Cookney-Muchalls road intersects the main trunk road quite near the bus shelter at the Muchalls road end. There the driver must patiently await his more adventurous passengers who have 3¾ miles to walk and several interesting things to see before they appear in 2 hours or more. Alternatively, of course, he might walk back to meet them halfway!

As far as we are concerned, our nostalgically attractive walk continues past Craighead Farm on the remains of the old road for some miles farther as we have said, almost all the way to Muchalls through fields in some places, through woods here and there, across bridges long disused and now hidden from the public eye, past standing-stones of great size, indicating significant events in pre-historic times, and sometimes through farm steadings. It will be found a quietly exciting excursion.

Ring Cairn of Cairnwell

First of all let us follow the track past Craighead Farm for 580 yards to the point where it veers sharply to the left to join the main Aberdeen road. 425 yards to your right from this point, across the moor to the edge of the belt of trees and on a line which, as it were, is an exact extension of the track to the left are the remains of the very degenerate ring cairn of Cairnwell in an inconspicuous position in a hollow of agricultural land and now partly obscured by field-gathered stones. A ring cairn[1] is a burial cairn with a ring of large stones round its outer edge to keep loose stones from rolling away, with a burial chamber in the centre of the cairn and with a surrounding stone circle. The cairn is sometimes removed, leaving only the ring of uprights. Ring cairns belong to the late Neolithic or early Bronze Age.

This is a very curious site which must surely represent the last flicker of the ring cairn tradition. The interior setting has been carefully built with a diameter of 14 ft. 9 ins. The cairn kerb, which can be traced only intermittently, lies only 3 ft. to 4 ft. outside it with its slabs set on their long sides and 1½ ft. to 2 ft. high. A particularly long slab, 5 ft. 10 ins. from end to end, is set in the kerb on the south-south-west side. Some of the slabs are somewhat displaced, but originally the setting had been carefully constructed in an accurate circle. The circle of free-standing stones stood only 3 ft. to 4 ft. farther out again, but of this circle of monoliths only three remain, 2 ft. 4 ins. to 3 ft. high. The overall diameter of the ring is 30 ft.

The narrowing of the ring of cairn material reducing the relative diameter of the stone circle is a feature taken farther at Cairnwell than in other ring cairn sites, and the extreme compression of the three concentric circles is unique. The site was excavated by an archaeologist named Alexander Thomson on 30th September, 1858, when, incidentally, it had thirteen monoliths although some even then were missing. The centre, we are told, was full of black mould with fragments of bones and charcoal and, what was specially interesting, a central arrangement of five coarse earthenware urns in a quincunx, that is with four at the corners of a square or rectangle and the fifth at the centre. All these have been subsequently lost.

The ring cairn is now extremely ruined and barely recognisable. As in addition the moss is treacherous, you may prefer to continue straight on.

---

[1] Ring cairns and stone-circles are described in *Highways and Byways Round Stonehaven*, pp. 191-198.

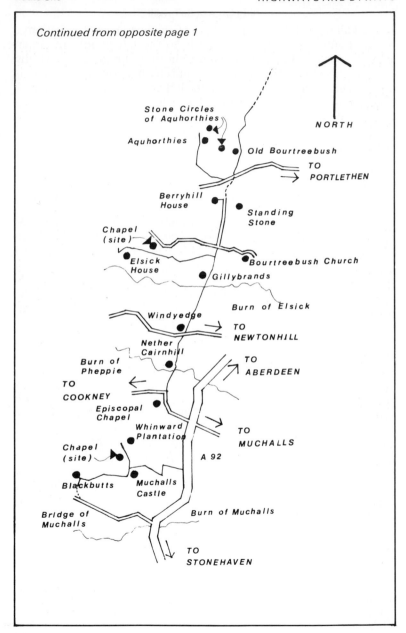

Continued from opposite page 1

Stone Circles of Aquhorthies

NORTH

Aquhorthies

Old Bourtreebush

TO PORTLETHEN

Berryhill House

Standing Stone

Chapel (site)

Bourtreebush Church

Elsick House

Gillybrands

Burn of Elsick

Windyedge

TO NEWTONHILL

Nether Cairnhill

Burn of Pheppie

TO ABERDEEN

TO COOKNEY

Episcopal Chapel

Whinward Plantation

TO MUCHALLS

Chapel (site)

A 92

Blackbutts

Muchalls Castle

Bridge of Muchalls

Burn of Muchalls

TO STONEHAVEN

Hill of Auchlee

Before you do so, have a look at the Hill of Auchlee, 1⅓ miles to the west, prominently surmounted by the tall Boswell's monument, a massive circular tower rising from an octagonal base and a well-known landmark, approached by a rhododendron walk on the hillside now having a hard struggle for existence.

The tall tower was erected in 1862 by Mrs Irvine-Boswell of Kingcausie in memory of her husband, John Irvine Boswell of Balmuto and Kingcausie, the son of Lord and Lady Balmuto and a former notable laird of Kingcausie who fought with the Coldstream Guards at Talavera and who died in 1860, aged 75. He was a relative of James Boswell, biographer of Johnson, and a scion of a distinguished family which originally came to this country with William the Conqueror. In addition to the possession of virtues set forth in the manner of the time which called forth Johnson's epigram, *In lapidary inscriptions men are not upon oath*, John Irvine Boswell, we are told, *transformed the natural barrenness of the estate into luxuriant fertility* – no extravagant claim. It is of interest that Boswell of Balmuto fought the last duel on Scottish soil near Auchtertool Toll in Fife against the son of the laird of an estate near Burntisland. Boswell was mortally wounded.

Old Bourtreebush

For the next 590 yards we keep to the line of the dyke across the moss because for the first time our road has temporarily disappeared: the Causey Mounth here is merely a strip of enclosed grass-covered, boggy land.[1] Ultimately we pick it up again, and a further 600 yards takes us on to higher ground and to the farm of Old Bourtreebush, named from the clump of elders ('bour-tree' in Scots is an elder tree) that once stood at the side of the new road from Stonehaven to Aberdeen. There remains evidence, nevertheless, of boggy ground on either side, particularly in the second field before the farm: we are still noticeably on a causeway, the road being built up with stones.

The Lands of Aquhorthies

About 270 yards to the right of Old Bourtreebush can be clearly seen on an eminence the remains of the two stone-circles of

---

[1] The walker who wishes to avoid fences and 600 yards of grass-land skirting fields may, of course, do so. He must proceed by car to Roadside of Cookston with the rest of his party and travel south along the A92. A walk of 260 yards along the first road to the right will enable him to rejoin the route.

Aquhorthies with the farm of the same name beyond. The lands of Aquhorthies, including Auchlee and Bourtreebush, extend to approximately 850 acres and were in 1390 owned by one Thomas Kennedy. An Alexander Annand is mentioned as owning *Auchirtie* on June 24th, 1620, and it was his son who sold the estate fifteen years later to Alexander Irvine, 6th of Kingcausie. Although the Irvine line ended in a daughter, Anne (1763-1841), who married Lord Balmuto (the great-great-great-grandparent of the present Mr James Irvine-Fortesque of Kingcausie), the lands of Aquhorthies have continued in the unbroken possession of this family since 1635.

Recumbent Stone-circles

The stone-circles of Aquhorthies are good examples of a special type of stone-circle, found in the counties of Banff, Aberdeen and Kincardine, which is a feature of North-east Scotland, unknown in any other part of the world. In these counties eighty have been recorded, many unfortunately wholly or partially destroyed and fewer than thirty now retaining any notable features. I refer to a complex structure called a recumbent stone-circle which derives its name from its most distinctive feature, a massive block of stone lying flat, roughly speaking east to west, and far greater in bulk, ordinarily, than any of the standing-stones. It is flanked by two tall uprights which may be as much as 10 ft. in height. These are always in the southern and usually in the south-west sector.

These three stones are the major feature in an eccentric circle of stone uprights which remarkably decrease in height and size the farther they are away from the flankers of the recumbent stone. The average diameter of this type of circle is about 70 ft., but it may exceed 100 ft.

Another characteristic of this class of monument is that the recumbent stone-circle is normally fairly closely set round a low, flat ring cairn, sometimes kerbed with stones, and contains a central hollow or open space about 10 ft. in diameter which was used for cremations. Normally some burnt matter remains buried. Usually this ring cairn does not occupy the precise centre of the circle but approaches near to the recumbent stone. Both the outer edge of the cairn and that of the central area show signs of paving.

Recumbent stone-circles are usually in bad condition, but the great size of the recumbent stone and its flankers tends to keep them in position so that this type of circle can be identified. It has been suggested that such circles are developments from the Clava passage-grave and that the recumbent stone is a counterpart of the original lintel stones over the passage entrance. The graduation of stones in height (unusual outside this type of circle) is a trait probably designed to emphasise the passage-grave entrance and points to the circle's being either contemporary with or subsequent to the earlier chambered tombs.

And the dating of these sites? It may be seen as roughly the same as for North-east ring cairns – late Neolithic to Early Bronze Age. Beaker, urn and other pottery finds indicate a date within the first half of the 2nd millenium B.C. for these recumbent stone-circles. Probably a period from 1800 B.C. to around 1500 B.C. would be acceptable.

The Circle of Easter Aquhorthies or Bourtreebush

Both the recumbent stone-circles of which we speak are somewhat difficult of access, necessitating as they do the crossing of fields. If these are, of course, in cultivation, approach to the circles will be impossible; even if they are not, and if it is desired to visit the actual sites instead of viewing from afar, it will be essential (and only courteous) to ask for permission at the farm-house. The fields near the circles, as a matter of interest, are some of the best on the whole estate. Could this be associated in any way, we wonder, with the old story, mentioned by Mr George Robertson in *The Agricultural Survey of Kincardine, 1813*, of an annual tribute of as much earth as a man could carry on his back being brought to the stone-circles?

To reach the circle of Easter Aquhorthies or, as it is commonly known, Bourtreebush, the slightly larger of the two with a diameter of 27 yards, one must proceed straight through the steading of the farm of Old Bourtreebush, turning along the front of the old courtyard and passing through the gate on the right. A walk of some 210 yards diagonally across the field will take you there.

The circle, now completely ruined, was possibly, when entire, the finer of the two. Neither of the two inner concentric circles remains and, whereas in 1858 there were seven large stones placed at irregular intervals round the circumference of the circle, now only three stones in the outermost circle are still standing, two of them 9 ft. high and 6 ft. broad. A third stone, 9 ft. high, lies overturned amid a vast number of boulders now so lacking in order that it is difficult to visualise the concentric circles that probably once existed here. When we read that out of one stone which had fallen down a workman cut a big millstone and 40 ft. of pavement we are not surprised!

Stone-circle of Aquhorthies

The neighbouring stone-circle of Aquhorthies is, of course, the one really to visit, the largest, the most entire and the most remarkable of the several circles of unembellished stones in Kincardineshire, well seen from east, south and west. To reach it we must make a diversion of 1 $^1/_{10}$ miles there and back.

Return in the first place to the steading of Old Bourtreebush and continue southwards alongside the trees on the old Causey Mounth road for some 370 yards until you meet the Portlethen road. This you must follow to the right for only 140 yards until you reach on the right what used to be a private drive to Kingcausie House. But we may walk there for we are turning off after 460 yards, again to the right, to the farm of Aquhorthies 350 yards farther on. Just beyond the farm a gate leads us into a field on the right (if the land is fallow and if we have been granted permission) which will take us to our circle 200 yards away. Or you may prefer merely to carry on up the farm track until opposite the circle 40 yards off in the field.

The stone-circle of Aquhorthies consisted originally of three concentric circles, enclosing an area some 23 or 24 yards in diameter. In the external circle eleven large stones remain, placed end

The stone-circle of Aquhorthies, dating from between 1800 and 1500 B.C. The large recumbent stone, weighing about 10½ tons, is seen at the south side of the circle, flanked by one of its uprights, 5ft. high.

to end and 22 ft. apart, the largest being some 8 ft. or 9 ft. above the ground while most are 3 ft. or 4 ft. high. Stones lying on the ground, 9 ft. to 10 ft. long, once brought the total of stones standing in the outermost circle to sixteen.

An inner circle, 15 or 16 yards in diameter and some 8 yards or more within the outer ring of great stones, is composed of smaller stones, some 3 ft. high, similarly set on edge and touching one another end to end. It is remarkable in having a large, recumbent stone, 9 ft. 9 ins. long, 5 ft. high and about 1 ft. wide across the flat top. This weighs about 10½ tons and is placed so as to fill the space between the two uprights on the south side of the circle. In this case only one of the uprights remains, 5 ft. high and 3½ ft. thick, and a cavity shows where the corresponding upright had stood. The circumference of the outermost circle runs many feet outside the recumbent stone group.

There have also been found traces of a platform in front of the recumbent stone, an integral part of the original structure in this type of circle. This being so, we may fairly conclude that the great low-set slabs which spring out of the ends of the platform and then expand into the circumference of the inner setting are part and parcel of the original design.

The smaller of the interior circles, some 4 yards in diameter, is made of low, flattish stones about 2 ft. high, really big boulders, similarly set on edge, end to end.

Aquhorthies, excavated on September 30th, 1858, produced charcoal, half-calcined bones and black, greasy earth. In the ring was evidence of *three or four bodies having been laid out so as to form the perimeter of a circle* with at the centre a cist or coffin of boulders about 3 ft. long and 1½ ft. wide, containing black mould and fragments of an urn containing a deposit of pieces of calcined bones. As there are several other smaller circles in the neighbourhood, it is to be concluded that in these far-away days the population of the area was considerably greater than one would normally expect it to have been.

Bronze Age Circles

It is hardly a matter of surprise that early observers, content to examine superficially and seeing a great ring of pillar stones guarding, as it were, a semi-prostrate one within, fancifully filled their imaginations with scenes of sacrifice and of so-called Druidical ceremonial. For what would particularly catch the eye of the antiquary would be the one peculiarly placed stone – the recumbent stone – which it pleased our forefathers to call the altar, with its two pillars forming an isolated group well within the boundary stones of the circle.

This great stone must have attracted immediate notice because, the interior of the circle being grassy all over, scarcely anything of the inner setting would be visible, and it would not be until after a good deal of attempted excavation had occurred that the true structural connection between the recumbent stone and the inner setting was even partially revealed.

Circles of standing-stones, of course, have no connection with the Druids whatsoever as is so commonly believed. Nor are they places of elaborate sacrificial rites.

Lunar Observations

It has often been noticed that the upper surface of the recumbent stone tends to be flat and horizontal. Professor Childe in his *Ancient Monuments (Scotland)* thus conjectures that this *would provide a good 'artificial horizon' for observing astronomical phenomena, such as the heliacal rising or setting of a star, that were used by the priestly astronomers of oriental antiquity for the correcting of the calendar.*

Similarly, Professor Thom suggests that stone-circles could have been used for lunar observations and for their ability to forecast the future in the sense that the angle of the moon from certain points on the circle would automatically predict various phases of the moon, eclipses, and so on.

Dramatic Props for Moonlight Rituals

The theory, however, that the stones of Bronze Age circles are precisely aligned to the stars so that ancient Pictish priests could draw knowledge from the heavens has fallen into disfavour: every astronomical alignment towards the moon, it is said, would be too crude to be of any use to any astronomer priest. One of the problems of inferring things astronomical in the circles is that the siting and alignment of the stones would have to be very accurate indeed. And they're not. In any case, there are so many stars that astronomical alignment with something is almost inevitable.

A new and perhaps more convincing theory about the stone-circles of the North-east has been advanced by archaeologist Aubrey Burl who suggests that they were nothing more than props

for an effective dramatic piece of stage management during moonlight rituals: the chief effect sought by the designers and builders of
the circles may well have been one of fearsome drama as the light of
the moon blazed down on the centre of the circle, illuminating the
solemn ceremonies being enacted, flanked all the time by the imposing silhouettes of the upright stones.

On ten per cent of all stones is a small circular hollow, probably
made by grinding with a hard pebble or lump of granite, and within
some circles crescent-shaped arrays of stone are just visible. Those
who follow Burl's hypotheses maintain that the former represents
the power of the full moon and the latter the growing might of the
new moon. Fascinating – but entirely inconclusive and in the
realm of the imagination. But what is quite clear, states Burl, is that
fire, death and the moon are the quintessence of the circles. Quite
clearly, he says, the moon *was as vital* to the ancient Picts *as the sun
was to other communities in Britain.*

It is certain that recumbent stone-circles were places of interment: almost invariably do they contain burials in the central area.
Whether they were only tombs or ritual circles as well remains
debatable. It seems beyond doubt, however, that the purpose of
these monuments was religious, but what secret and ancient ceremonial was involved therein we shall perhaps never know.

Berryhill House and Bourtreebush Kirk

And now we must return to the Portlethen road and retrace the 140
yards until opposite the Old Bourtreebush farm road we meet again
attractive evidence of the old road on the right. We must cross the
dyke and follow it for just short of 200 yards: it is quite clearly
marked between the rotting tree stumps of this little wooded patch,
a bank on one side of it, a ditch on the other and whins everywhere.
Again it is significant that, although rushes appear on both sides of
it, the road itself is dry.

So we continue for another 240 yards until the entrance to Berryhill House, an imposing red-brick mansion, is reached. It was here
at Berryhill, before a parsonage was built about 1840, that a cottage
was rented from 1828-41 for the incumbent of Muchalls Episcopal
Chapel – sadly at a considerable distance from his church.

With some surprise we find that for the next two-fifths of a mile
the old road has assumed again the modern tar macadam surface of
a fine service road until the drive to Elsick House with its trim
hedges appears on the right just beyond the cross roads. Elsick
House (which we shall later see) is the home of His Grace the Duke

of Fife and of his ancestors, the Bannerman family, who for long were intimately connected with the civic life of Aberdeen. Notice, however, before you leave Berryhill House, the standing-stone some 200 yards across the field on your left.

Opposite the drive to Elsick House is, on the left, Bourtreebush kirk, built in 1848 on the land of the farm of Gillybrands. In the spring of 1843 meetings to prepare for the Disruption of Church from State were held in Kidd's Barn, Bourtreebush. In May of the same year the General Assembly of the Free Church resolved that a missionary should do duty at Bourtreebush for the south side of the parish of Banchory-Devenick. After 1844 Bourtreebush was worked from Aberdeen and later was a joint charge with Maryculter. In 1876 the General Assembly reduced it to a preaching station but six years later granted leave for the congregation to call a minister, the first time a minister was inducted to the full charge.

The Importance of Cammachmore

Beyond Bourtreebush kirk is Cammachmore Hotel on the site of which there stood in 1870 Cammachmore Post Office on the main Aberdeen-Stonehaven road. It was, and had been for some time previously, a most important place. It marked the end of the first stage or the beginning of the last, according to whether you were journeying north or south by coach, and for some years after the railway reached the city of Aberdeen, it retained a considerable measure of importance. It was not, of course, only a Post Office for within the walls of this modest one-storeyed building was a general merchant's store, a thriving trade being done with the then flourishing fishing hamlets on either side, Dounies and Skateraw.

The Chapel of Elsick

At the cross roads we speak of let us deviate for a moment to view what remains of the ancient Episcopalian Chapel of Elsick, only some 430 yards from the mansion-house of Elsick. Turn up to the right for just under half a mile and stop at the right-angle bend before the farm of Chapelton the name of which is obviously derived from the ruins of the chapel we are to see.

Now pass through the gate at the corner and proceed along the side of the field adjoining the piggery for 120 yards until you come to a wall which you must climb. Once there was a gate here and a footpath through the field we have traversed. Alas, these days have gone with the passage of time although I am told that in the ploughing season the line of pathway stones may still be recognised.

Traces of the chapel still remain within the burial-ground, a small building indeed, only 28¼ ft. long by 11½ ft. broad, with a stone wall reduced to its lower courses. It is not to be confused with the ruined cottage on its south side ('Francie's hoosie' although who Francis or Frances was remains a mystery). Little is known about the Chapel of Elsick. Dr Eeles' book on the bells of Kincardineshire states that the chapel had no bell while Jervise in his *Epitaphs and Inscriptions* refers to it as a mediaeval building. And that is about all. There is a tradition of the chapel's having been used as a place of worship prior to the '45, but there is no written evidence of this. It is traditionally believed, too, to have suffered the same fate as the chapels of Stonehaven and Drumlithie in 1746 at the hands of the Duke of Cumberland and never to have been rebuilt.

Nevertheless, it would seem that the chapel, once the burial place of the Bannermans of Elsick House, prominent among the Episcopalians and Jacobites of the district, continued to be used for interments for some time after the estate passed out of the hands of the family in the middle of the 18th century. In the burial-ground half a century ago several tombstones remained; now only one is visible in the middle of the enclosure. It bears the usual symbols of skull and hour-glass and is thus inscribed:

> *Here lyes GEORG HEPBURN, indweller was at Gilibrans who departed this lyfe on 2d day of November, 1702, and was of age 67 years, who lived in the foresaid place since the year 1680.*

A holly bush in the burial-ground is, I am told, still lovingly pruned nearly every year. Incidentally, do notice before you leave, the old manse 100 yards away towards the road between the site of the chapel and the farm of Chapelton.

Gillybrands

And so back to the Causey Mounth and down the hill for just over quarter of a mile, past the curiously named Gillybrands Farm until you reach the old piered bridge over the Burn of Elsick. This, with other burns to come that trickle down to the sea, the Muchalls Burn and the Limpet Burn, must have formed but a small obstacle to the spurred and booted traveller compared with the knolls and morasses which succeeded one another on the earlier part of the journey between here and Kingcausie in the neighbourhood of Aberdeen. Gillybrands Farm derives its curious name from 'Jeally Bran's' Inn which stood nearby in the middle of the 18th century.

Part of the Causey Mounth road as it might originally have been. The picture is taken from Gillybrands Farm where 'Jeally Bran's' Inn once stood. On the skyline is Windyedge; in the middle of the picture, at the beginning of the half-mile climb, is the old piered bridge over the Burn of Elsick.

The remains of the old bridge over the Burn of Elsick on the Causey Mounth road. In the background can be seen Gillybrands Farm, once an 18th century inn where coach horses were changed on what was one of the most historic roads in the north of Scotland.

The Climb to Windyedge

The climb from here for the next half-mile, up the hill to the farm of Windyedge, the road to Newtonhill and the sharp ridge 125 ft. above us which catches every breeze that blows, must surely constitute the most attractive part of our present walk. Here between the hedgerows the road is more or less in its original state. And how easy it is, amid the pleasant, rolling countryside, far removed from what Milton calls *the busy hum of men*, to visualise the steaming stage horses of old restively breasting the hill or old Dr Johnson with his faithful Boswell in the gathering dusk of a Saturday evening in August, 1773, approaching Aberdeen in the leisurely fashion he liked so well. He found the country south of Aberdeen naked and hard – so generally ploughed that he found it difficult to imagine where grass would be found for the horses that tilled the fields.

As they were both *somewhat drowsy*, however, after an exhausting visit to Laurencekirk and the home of Lord Monboddo, they are unlikely to have taken much interest in the country through which they were driving.

Windyedge

According to local tradition it was here at Windyedge (what a fit name for a bleak spot constantly assailed by biting blasts and ocean spray) that James Walker, appointed a minister at Muchalls in 1780, taught a school and, according to the Dean Christie manuscripts, apparently set up a rival chapel to the old-fashioned building some 240 yards from Muchalls Castle (see pp. 38-39). This was the result of an unfortunate schism in the local congregation of hereditary Episcopalians as a result of which another pastor, George Garden, was appointed to serve the 'regular' congregation while James Walker, the only minister of religion resident in the district for seven years, continued in the role of what can only be called a hedge-priest, recognised neither as a Scottish Episcopalian nor a member of an established congregation. Whatever the rights and wrongs of the case, one cannot but pity Mr Walker spending the best years of his life under conditions of spiritual isolation and material destitution. No wonder he is alleged to have tried schoolmastering here. If the 'regular' congregation at Muchalls could provide a stipend of only £15 per annum, the poverty in which he and his family lived must have been dreadful indeed.

Elsick House

From Windyedge another short deviation to the right of between a tenth of a mile and half a mile (dependent upon the season and the resultant visibility through the trees) will enable you to catch a glimpse of the interesting, historic House of Elsick half a mile to the north and something of the chief estate in the hinterland of Newton-hill.

There is thought to have been a building at Elsick as early as the last decade of the 13th century, and certainly the oldest part of the House has enormously thick walls and low-ceilinged chambers. The present mansion is, however, a complex structure of various periods with a predominating 18th century character. It is a long, rectangular building with, at the west end, an addition covering a former courtyard and, at the east, a modern wing.

Early on Sunday, January 20th, 1754, the House of Elsick took fire and, according to the *Aberdeen Journal*, *without any possible Assistance was consumed to Ashes by the Carelessness of the Servants who were left to keep the Rooms in order*. It was after this fire that some lovely hinged panelling of around 1750 in date was installed in the upstairs rooms when the House of Elsick was largely rebuilt.

After World War I the Earl of Southesk, then Lord Carnegie, made many improvements to the House and estate, and even as late as 1971 the Duke of Fife was undertaking some very interesting alterations. On the north front, for example, from where a gable interestingly projects, a battlemented porch built in 1937 was removed and a new porch built with a pediment bearing an interleaved motif surmounted by the ducal coronet.

Descent from the Standard-bearer of Scottish Kings

The Duke of Fife is descended from the Bannermans of Elsick who claim their descent from the ancient banner-man of the Scottish kings. They first appear in the history of the North-east in 1364 when Donald Banyrman, physician of King David II, was granted an annual fee of 20/- and the Thanage of Aberdeen. It was a few years later that his son, Alexander, who became Provost of Aberdeen in 1382, acquired from Sir Alexander Fraser of Philorth and Cowie an important part of the ancient Barony of Cowie – the lands of Elsick.

In 1608 Margaret Bannerman of Elsick married George Gordon of Haddo, ancestor of the Earls and Marquesses of Aberdeen, and in 1682 the laird of Elsick, another Alexander, was created a baronet by King Charles II in recompense for his loyalty. Patrick, the fourth son of this first baronet, became Provost of Aberdeen during the Jacobite Rebellion in 1715, elected as he was without opposition

by Jacobite burgesses who had doubtless been impressed a week or
more previously by the entry to the town of the Earl Marischal at the
head of a troop of county gentlemen and retainers to proclaim
James VIII with great ceremony at the Mercat Cross. During his
term of office Patrick raised money through taxes and loans to aid
the Jacobite cause and was knighted at Dunnottar in December,
1715, by the Old Pretender who had landed at Peterhead. When the
Rebellion collapsed, however, he narrowly escaped with his life at
his trial at Carlisle.

By failure in the direct line of succession the sixth baronet of
Elsick was Sir Patrick's grandson, Professor Alexander Bannerman
of the Chair of Medicine at Aberdeen University. He lacked, however, both House and lands: these had been sold out of the family by
the fourth baronet in 1756. The lands, sold to Aberdeen Town
Council, had been feued out in lots; the House by a strange irony
had been bought by James Morison, the famous 'Provost Positive'
of Aberdeen who only eleven years before, having refused to drink
the health of the Pretender, had had the wine poured down his shirt
front by the indignant supporters of Prince Charlie! The estate
passed to his son, Dr Thomas Morison, to Dr George Morison,
minister of Banchory-Devenick Church and builder of the 'Shak-
kin' Briggie', and eventually to the nephew of the latter, Captain
Robert Farquhar of the Madras Infantry.

It was Sir Alexander Bannerman, the ninth baronet, who bought
back Elsick House. On his death in 1877 the baronetcy and properties went separate ways. Sir Alexander's only child, his daughter,
Ethel Mary Elizabeth, inherited the properties of Elsick, Crimon-
mogate, Cairnhill and Kirkhill and in 1891 married the tenth Earl of
Southesk. Their son, Charles, the eleventh Earl, who as Lord
Carnegie had married Princess Maud, granddaughter of King Edward VII, then took occupation of Elsick House in 1923, and it is
their son, born 1929, who is the third Duke of Fife and the present
laird. He spent much of his boyhood at Elsick House, and there is a
familiar picture of him there with the present Queen and Princess
Margaret when they were all children together. The Duke of Fife
has added considerably to the acreage which he inherited. He is now
farming 1300 acres with a substantial commercial herd, a large
acreage of barley and some fine woodlands.

Episcopal Chapel of Muchalls

From Windyedge the old road carries on for just over half a mile
past the farms of Nether Cairnhill and Burn of Pheppie until it

meets the road from Cookney to Muchalls. This we follow for 200 yards until, just at the corner where it turns at right angles to the coast, we find ourselves with some surprise at the famous Episcopal Chapel of Muchalls, a picturesque little church hidden away behind hedgerows and the thick clump of trees on rising ground which surround it.

The church, situated on high ground overlooking the village of Muchalls and about half a mile inland from the rock-bound coast, has been the place of worship for many generations of Scottish Episcopalians. Only from 1864 onwards has it been associated with St Ternan, a name derived from the 5th century Celtic missionary who is traditionally connected with the district. The history of St Ternan's, Muchalls, stretches back to the preaching of St Ternan on the braes of Findon in the 5th century. Their chapel never being a parochial church, the fisher folk of Skateraw and the now extinct village of Seaton of Muchalls never came under the influence of Presbyterianism but worshipped together according to their ancient faith in various places.

The original Muchalls Chapel, indeed, was an integral part of Muchalls Castle. After its destruction by the Duke of Cumberland in 1746 three other chapels were erected before the end of the 18th century on a site less than 300 yards across the field from where we are now. This site we shall see later.

The first portion of the church, the middle part, was built in 1831 and consecrated by the Bishop of the Diocese. The date can still be seen on the coping-stone under the cross on the east gable of the nave. As available funds were very limited, the original edifice was probably a humble one: it was nearly square and provided with a gallery.

By 1858 the gallery was no longer in use (the seating capacity being thereby reduced from 216 to 175), and in 1865 the beautiful apse and chancel were added, a bottle containing current coins of the realm, a Book of Common Prayer and other contemporary papers being deposited under the foundation stone. A vault was constructed under the chancel to serve as a burial-place for future incumbents and their families, but it has never been used. The entrance, walled up with rough masonry, is under a stone in the exterior east wall inscribed with the initials of Bishop Penrose Forbes and of the incumbent, Rev. William H. B. Proby.

1870 saw further improvements: because of an increasing con-gregation the nave was enlarged (the older building reached only as far as the middle of the present south porch). The seats were so close, we are told, that kneeling was impossible and sitting very difficult. Further restorational work was carried out in 1881, 1884 and 1892, the old narrow seats being replaced by more commodious ones, choir stalls being provided, and the stonework and tinted glass of the four windows on the south side of the church being renovated.

The Bell

In 1847 the Church became possessed of *a canonless ship's bell* which F. C. Eeles tells us in his *Church and Other Bells of Kincardineshire* was fished up from the bottom of the sea by Cowie line-fishers. Taken down from the old belfry when the church was lengthened in 1870, it was 'temporarily' hung in a wooden frame on the north side of the chancel for 80 years, awaiting hanging in its new, arched belfry over the west end of the Church where it is today! In the mid-19th century £1 per annum was paid the ringer! With this belfry and its long, narrow roof St Ternan's, Muchalls, used to present itself as a striking feature on the landscape: it formed a well-recognised and important landmark for fishermen in the daily pursuit of their hazardous calling.

The Parsonage

The incumbent of the new chapel for the first nine years appears to have lived in a house constructed nearby (perhaps the house now called Muchalls Cottage situated to the south-west of the church). The present parsonage was built about 1840 and enlarged in 1878. A heraldic shield surmounts the bay-window, and a stone above the enlarged window of the room on the right gives the date and is inscribed with the initials, 'H.W.J. epis, W.H. sac'. (i.e. Hugh Willoughby Jermyn, Bishop; William Hatt, Priest). The adjoining plot of land, described in the 1860's as the parsonage drying ground (the annual feu duty was one shilling), is now occupied by the little wood at the back of the church and house.

The Chapel a Stronghold of Episcopacy

The Episcopal congregation at Muchalls, one of the oldest country congregations in the Kingdom, has a continuous history from the Middle Ages onward. The congregation was partly composed of the descendants of those who worshipped at St Mary's, Cowie, and those who worshipped at St Ternan's, Findon. They joined together and worshipped in Muchalls' earliest chapel about 1624. When Episcopacy was disestablished in favour of Presbyterianism about 1690, Muchalls became one of the local strongholds of the Episcopal Church, remaining so through the years that followed.

Almost the whole of the population of the fishing villages was Episcopalian then. Changing conditions, however, at the end of the century caused most of the community to move to new districts when the old-time 'fisher touns' lost their original role as white fishing havens. During the present century there followed the introduction of the steam trawler and the development of the fishing industry at Torry. A large number of the fisher congregation departed to Aberdeen where, alas, there were far fewer prospects of making a living.

The Causey Mounth Road Disappears

Our retracing of the old Causey Mounth road is not with convenience to be taken much farther than St Ternan's Church. The road is seen to continue for a short distance in the direction of Whinward Plantation, the whinny enclosure around the copse of trees seen on the skyline to the east of Muchalls Castle but is soon indistinguishable where cultivation has eradicated all trace. True, a ditch alongside the first two fields might indicate where the old causeway once existed – but that is all.

You must therefore follow the main road for the quarter of a mile from St Ternan's Church to the main Aberdeen road where your car awaits you by the Muchalls road end. From the cross roads before Craighead Farm we have followed the old road on foot for just under three and a half miles and nearly seven miles in all if we include the whole journey from Hilldowntree. Certainly four and a half miles remain to the point where the Causey Mounth road joins the present Aberdeen road at Cowie, but only at very occasional points is it recognisable at all.

En Route to Muchalls Castle

One of these points is where the road passed within two or three hundred yards of the delightful Castle of Muchalls. Let us go there. You must drive southwards along the dual carriage-way towards Stonehaven for only half a mile or less, turning off at the first road on the right. (You'll see a signpost). Another half mile along a rather rough road will take you there. Before we explore the castle, let us visit the site of the three Episcopalian chapels which preceded St Ternan's and of which we spoke earlier.

Site of Three Earlier Chapels

Walk only 60 yards down the hill from the castle entrance and you will come to a gate on your right through which you must pass.

Don't worry: you're on a right of way and – it may well be – on the Causey Mounth road again! A further walk of only 176 yards up the side of the field will take you to the site of the chapels – ten yards before the third telegraph pole and more or less in a line with the dyke round Whinward Plantation – a very inconspicuous spot, out of sight of the main road and concealed by the fold of the hill and probably at the time by a growth of thick trees. Here a temporary dry-stone chapel was erected about 1748 after the castle chapel had been destroyed. In the same place another 'stob-thatched' chapel was built in 1770 (one, that is, thatched with 'stobs' or stakes to keep down the thatch) while a third and last chapel to occupy the site, tiled this time, was built in 1795. It was *of ancient appearance* and was removed in the early 19th century.

Ministries of John Troup and Alexander Craig

It was in the first two chapels on this site that the Rev. John Troup of Tolbooth fame[1] ministered during his later years, probably with the connivance of the authorities, for active persecution began to die down within a few years of the '45 so that in most districts Episcopalian congregations met with a certain degree of unofficial toleration after the accession of George III in 1760. Mr Troup was a man of mature years at the time of his coming to Muchalls, and the influence of his powerful personality continued to be felt far beyond the lifetime of those who had been in contact with him. After Mr Troup's death in 1776 we may suppose that the chapel was served during a vacancy of four years, as far as circumstances would permit, by Mr Alexander Greig of Stonehaven.[2] One must admire the conscientiousness of this ageing priest (he was then a septuagenarian) in his attempts to provide some religious ministration at Muchalls by means of periodic visits to the chapel, making the five-mile journey on foot or on horseback or in an open conveyance in the bitter days of the 1780's.

Like Swinburne's Forsaken Garden

A ground-rent of £3 3s per annum was paid for the chapel, house and garden on this old site, and these payments were continued for the house and garden until 1833 together with a payment of £3 per annum for the new site. If no vestige of the chapel remains, the *ghost of a garden* may be seen only 90 yards to the east and just inside the boundary wall of the plantation. Part of a thick wall,

[1] *Highways and Byways Round Stonehaven*, pp. 33-37.
[2] Ibid., pp. 33-36.

perhaps 20 yards long, and the presence of a very ancient laburnum, together with honeysuckle, rowans and a few daffodils, make it likely that this is the authentic site of the parsonage of two centuries ago and more. Pieces of pottery and of broken clay pipes found nearby confirm this view.

> *The fields fall southward, abrupt and broken,*
> *To the low last edge of the long lone land.*
> *If a step should sound or a word be spoken,*
> *Would a ghost not rise at the strange guest's hand?*
> *So long have the grey bare walks lain guestless,*
> *Through branches and briers if a man make way,*
> *He shall find no life but the sea-winds, restless*
>   *Night and day.*

This is also the only spot in the immediate vicinity where there is a supply of water, and it is probably not without significance that a laburnum stands opposite the door of St Ternan's.

Muchalls Castle

Muchalls Castle, hidden in woodland overlooking the sea on a commanding site in the midst of rather bare countryside, is one of the most interesting castles in the North-east both for its own excellence and because it has been so little altered and added to. It is an architectural gem of great charm and a well-preserved and typical specimen of the defensive architecture of a Scottish laird's baronial mansion of the beginning of the 17th century. There is reason to think the castle of today is built on top of the basement vaulting of an earlier 13th century castle.

Lands, Barony and History

The lands and barony of Muchalls, originally part of the Barony of Cowie, were conferred by King Robert the Bruce on his chamberlain, Sir Alexander Fraser. Afterwards they came into the possession of the Hays of Errol, passing on June 24th, 1606, into the hands of Alexander Burnett of Leys. Details of the building of the castle are given on an inscribed stone over the gateway of the courtyard:

THIS   WORK . BEGVN . ON . THE
EAST & NORTH . BE . Ar BVRNET . OF LEYIS 1619;
ENDED . BE . SR. THOMAS BVRNET . OF LEYIS . HIS
SONNE . 1627

Alexander Burnett, father of the first baronet (who also built Crathes Castle) built much of the present work, and the rest was finished in 1627 by his son, Sir Thomas, who was created a baronet of Nova Scotia in 1626. In 1714, on the death of the fourth baronet of Leys, the barony of Muchalls was sold to Thomas Fullerton of Gallery in Angus for £6673.

Muchalls Castle was the scene of some stirring events of the Covenanting days. It entered national history in 1638 when the pillars of the Covenant, Henderson, Dickson and Cant, retired thither as the guests of Sir Thomas Burnett to compose their reply to the Aberdeen doctors – the theological professors of the University who claimed that the Covenant ought not to be forced on those people in Aberdeen who did not accept its teaching. A year later, after Montrose and Leslie, the Covenanting generals, had entered Aberdeen and seized the Earl of Huntly, his son, Viscount Aboyne, raised an Aberdeenshire force which encamped at Muchalls.[1]

Renaissance Features

The castle with its roughcast walls has fine internal decorations in the Renaissance style which had just begun to assert itself in Scotland early in the 17th century when the castle was in course of erection. With a range of massive chimney-stalks a feature, it has the handsomest ceilings in Scotland, a secret staircase, a Green Lady, a wishing-well in the courtyard and a mysterious (and now 'lost') underground passage to a smugglers' cove at 'Gin Shore', a name suggestive of practices common enough in days past.

Courtyard and Curtain-wall

Designed on the favourite L-plan with a slight extension, it is one of the few mansions remaining with buildings still surrounding an old flagged courtyard, the north, the east and part of the west side being occupied by the house, and the remaining fourth and part of the third side enclosed within a low and handsome curtain-wall few specimens of which exist in Scotland at the present time. The southern face of this interesting curtain-wall has been ornamented rather than fortified with four formidable-looking open bartizans or corbelled roundels, a fashion which had outlived the necessities of the time. These are separated by a parapet, also crenellated, and the existence at one time of a parapet walk was proved a century and a half ago with the discovery of a built up doorway leading to it. On each side of the gateway are triple shot-holes of a type consistent with the period of the building.

[1] *Highways and Byways Round Stonehaven*, p. 99.

Turrets, Roof and Basement

There is a semicircular stair turret in the main re-entrant and charming single-storey angle turrets at all main gables except for the slightly extending wing at the east end which contains the door and the main stair to the first floor and which has crow-steps and a richly elaborated belt of corbelling above which a watch-tower has been formed. The roof levels have been slightly altered, and originally

Muchalls Castle which possesses the most handsome ceilings in Scotland. Clearly shown are the L-plan and the low curtain-wall surrounding the courtyard. Notice the single-storey angle turrets, the massive chimney-stacks, the elaborate belt of corbelling and the triple shot-holes on each side of the gateway.

there was almost certainly a further attic storey. The plain, groined and vaulted basement chambers on the ground floor include the kitchen and a number of cellars, with extra thick walling in areas taking the place, it would seem, of the barrel vaults of an earlier fortalice on the site, owned by the Frasers. Originally the cellars had small loopholes.

The Great Hall Ceiling

The first floor of the main block, reached by a particularly wide and handsome wheel stair, contains the large, elegant Great Hall, dated 1624, the special feature of which is a magnificent painted ceiling such as enriched Scottish castles of the third decade of the 17th century. It is one of the showpieces of the county and among the finest examples in Scotland of this kind of craftsmanship. It is richly ornamented with delicate white stucco plaster-work of a kind found also at Glamis, Craigievar, Pinkie near Musselburgh and Winton near Tranent. But this amazing ceiling is the finest of them all. Its design includes six coats of arms of the Burnett and allied families, fully tinctured, four medallions depicting the heads of Roman emperors, classical heroes and Old Testament characters (David, Joshua and Alexander) and three knops with hooks for hanging lamps, all joined with a pattern of straight and curved ribs bearing floral designs in relief.

Almost rivalling the ceiling in splendour is the fine sculptured and coloured overmantel, also dated 1624, above the enormous fireplace, and flanked by the fashionable caryatids of the period. The fireplace is worthy of mention because of its great lintel-stone and panelling embellished with the royal coat of arms as borne in Scotland following the Union of the Crowns in 1603 with the collar of the thistle inside the garter and surmounted by the Scottish crest. The explanation seems to be that the ceilings and overmantel were the work of a London craftsman.

The fireplace and ornamental work of the Hall ceiling are almost exact replicas in miniature of those in the Great Hall of Glamis, done by the same craftsman soon after Muchalls Castle was built. The late castellated mansions of the North-east (where there is a veritable galaxy of them) are, of course, the work of a vigorous school of native master-masons, the Bells and the Leipers and doubtless others whose names we know not. But for the internal decoration of Scottish baronial masterpieces like Allardyce, Balbegno and Muchalls Castle in the Mearns artists were imported from south of the Border, and it is to them that we owe such beautiful plaster ceilings as we find here.

'Nobles' in the Drawing-room

There are similar overmantels in the withdrawing-room (now the dining-room) and the laird's study leading off it, both excellent public rooms on the first floor of the west wing with fine plaster ceilings and heraldic decorations. The withdrawing-room has also a spectacular ceiling of white pargetted plaster even more beautiful than and not quite so flamboyant as that in the Great Hall. Here there are also 'Nobles', sculptured portrait medallions of Hector of Troy, King David with his harp and the Emperor Jovian whose sole distinction was that he replaced Julian the Apostate and so restored the Empire to Christianity. Above the fireplace are the arms of Sir

Thomas Burnett of Leys, the first baronet, with their holly leaves and the famous Horn.

Mysterious Cupboard Panels

In the Great Hall is a cupboard fronted by mysterious panels from the pulpit of the old kirk of Fetteresso, panels alive with animals, birds and grotesque figures. They were acquired by a joiner at a fairly remote period and might have been destroyed but for the vigilance of an apprentice who was impressed by the excellence of the workmanship. He was allowed to keep them to form a decorative front to the cupboard.[1]

The Old Pretender's Bed

There is ample bedroom accommodation above. The bedroom at the west end of the main block was evidently the laird's for from a wall-chamber therein a listening device or 'laird's lug' aperture communicated with the ingoing of the huge open fireplace of the Hall directly below. In this bedroom is the handsome canopied bed from Fetteresso Castle (now demolished)[2] in which James Stuart, the Jacobite Old Pretender claimant to the throne of the United Kingdom, spent nine nights while passing through the Mearns in the campaign of 1715.

The Chapel – an Exception to the Rule

Before we leave the castle, let us look outside on the terrace on the south side where stood until 230 years ago and more, as we have already noted, a chapel which had been used for Episcopalian services by the whole community. Castles of the 17th century did not normally contain a chapel, but Muchalls was an exception to the rule: it was in 1624 that the Burnetts of Crathes, though not themselves Jacobites, built a chapel at their castle.

After the Revolution of 1688 the Episcopal Church in Scotland had been disestablished and disendowed when William of Orange supplanted King James. The majority of local inhabitants, however, never came under the Presbyterian establishment: they held fast solidly to the Church of their fathers and were loyal to the Stuart dynasty, and the chapel at Muchalls Castle came to be recognised as an Episcopal stronghold. Not being a parish church, it was therefore less directly under the control of the party in power than it would otherwise have been and thus provided a sphere for the ministrations of such of the dispossessed clergy as remained in the district.

[1] *Highways and Byways Round Stonehaven*, p. 117.
[2] Ibid., pp. 118-122.

When the '15 broke out, for example, Mr William Cruickshank, minister at the time, observed the thanksgiving for the safe arrival of the Pretender and prayed for him *under the style and title of King James*. This leads us to imagine that he may have been one of those who went to pay their respects to the Stuart heir during his short sojourn at Fetteresso Castle near Stonehaven.[1]

During the period between the two Jacobite Risings (and, indeed, from 1708 onwards) the Muchalls congregation is mentioned more than once in the records of the Presbyterian Kirk Session of Fetteresso – a body whose members exercised almost dictatorial powers as guardians of public morals, besides administering all the charitable funds of the district, and who were thus in close contact with all the inhabitants, whether Presbyterian or not.

The End of the Chapel and the Rev. J. Troup

But the end of the chapel came with the march northwards to Culloden of the Duke of Cumberland in 1746. While staying in Stonehaven with John Young of Stank (near Kinneff), sheriff of the county, he burned the church of Drumlithie, sacked that of Stonehaven and gave orders for the chapel of Muchalls to be *razed to the ground*.

The minister of Muchalls at the time, the Rev. John Troup, was with the loss of his church driven like so many of his fellows to preach in whatever accommodation he could find. Furthermore, with the imposition of the ban on Episcopalian clerics preaching to more than five people at a time, his ministry became increasingly difficult, and the law was for ever at his heels. Finally, along with his colleagues from Drumlithie and Stonehaven, he was brought before Sheriff Young and confined in the Tolbooth at Stonehaven.[2]

On his liberation from prison Mr Troup returned to Muchalls and continued to preach in circumstances which were still far from easy. Tradition says that one Sunday morning in the autumn of 1749 he and his flock were interrupted at service in a corrie between Scarths Craig and Goudie, two precipitous rocks at no great distance from the Loch of Blackhills, and had to disperse hurriedly in the face of English soldiers who came over the hill of Aquhorthies.

Three traces of the castle chapel remain today. What is now the south window of the Hall of the castle was at one time a doorway which gave access to the private gallery in the place of worship, and above the entrance to the castle was the priest's room where the

[1] *Highways and Byways Round Stonehaven*, p. 120.
[2] Ibid., pp. 34-35.

private chaplain of the Burnett family lived. Finally, the entrance to the barrel-vaulted crypt of the chapel, now a cellar, is still visible in the garden at the side of the castle. The doorway has been altered.

The castle is open to visitors on Sundays and Tuesdays from 3 to 5 p.m. between May and September. It is now the home of Mrs Maurice Simpson who has filled it with antique treasures.

The Hill of Muchalls an Impassable Bog

As we start our journey homewards, let us follow what is almost certainly a small portion of the old road, the extension of our right of way down the side of the boundary wall. Did the Causey Mounth continue straight on through the trees towards Muchalls School? Or did it follow more or less, as is more likely, the Muchalls Castle road which we are to take, inland to Blackbutts and Montgatehead where the causies or calsies come to an end. Certainly it was this part of the road southwards from Montgatehead that was for centuries known as the calseys. For at Muchalls, on the line of the causeway (as at Banchory-Devenick and Nigg) were once briggs or what the Irish call floating bogs, huge passages formed through the moss by cart-loads of boulders and lumps of heathery moss heaped together and consolidated by the bosky growth of ages before the road was made across the bog. The name is still seen today in the farm of Heatherybriggs, Glithno, Fetteresso. For the entire region between these briggs at Glithno and a line drawn to the east of them by Kempstonehill to the sea and north to the Dee was until about 1863 a track of bog quite as impassable as the Causey Mounth to the east would have been had there been no causeway. Stretching westward from the height on which Muchalls Castle stands, the moss was 8 or 10 miles in circumference including Star Moss, Cowie Moss, Redmoss, etc., all generally called in modern times the Hill of Muchalls.

The Causey Mounth from Muchalls to Stonehaven

After three-fifths of a mile from the castle we arrive at the Bridge of Muchalls-Netherley road. We turn left here and in about a mile arrive at the dual carriage-way at Bridge of Muchalls itself. Here the old road crossed the Burn of Muchalls, ran parallel to it for quarter of a mile and ascended towards the farm of Wellhead, seen quite clearly on the skyline. You may walk a portion of it through what was once a wood until you are about 500 yards above the burn. The road then passed through the farm of Aquhorthies, and the bridge, long disused and hidden from the public eye, that carried it over the

Limpet Burn is still there although between the Limpet Burn and Muchalls Burn the old road is mostly out of existence. A quarter of a mile south of the Limpet Burn, on the farm of Logie, it is also still in being, used as a service road.

The Causey Mounth then kept to the higher ground alongside the Hill of Megray, the battlefield where Highlanders once fled at the sound of cannon, a new weapon in their experience,[1] climbing the high ground above the Den of Cowie, westwards by a tortuous path by Wester Logie (where we find it running along the entire breadth of that farm). It then ran southwards along the eastern fringe of what used to be Cowie Common, commencing the descent on the south side of Megray Hill through the site of the now obliterated town of Cowie and along the west side of the grounds of Cowie House until it joined the present main road just below and on the north side of Mains of Cowie Farm. It then skirted the beach in the centre of Stonehaven Bay and left Stonehaven by a ford about 30 yards east of the present Bridge of Cowie.[2]

As, however, we can follow the Causey Mounth no longer, we simply drive along the dual carriage-way homewards. 3¾ miles will take us to Stonehaven Square.

Part of the old Causey Mounth road beside the Mains of Cowie farm where once stood the Candida Casa Inn. In the background the road is seen skirting the wall of Cowie House towards Megray Hill in the distance.

[1] *Highways and Byways Round Stonehaven*, pp. 99-100.

[2] Further details concerning the Causey Mounth road, the historic old inn of Candida Casa, the ancient Royal Burgh of Cowie and of the ancient Castle of Cowie which protected or obstructed the entrance to the Causey Mounth road are to be found in *Highways and Byways Round Stonehaven*, Route Four.

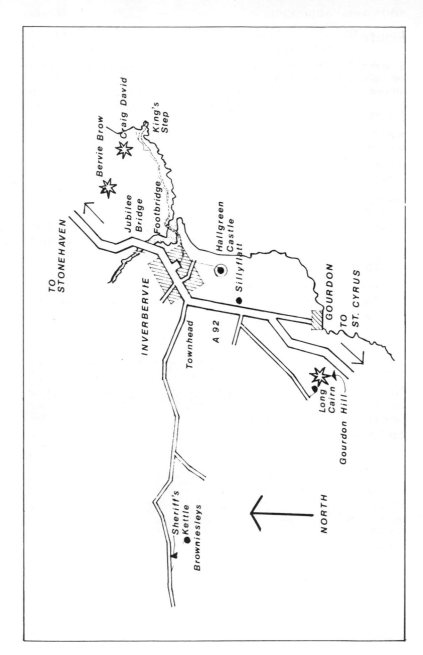

TO STONEHAVEN

Bervie Brow

Craig David

King's Step

Jubilee Bridge

Footbridge

Hallgreen Castle

INVERBERVIE

Sillyflatt

Townhead

A 92

GOURDON

TO ST. CYRUS

Long Cairn

Gourdon Hill

Sheriff's Kettle

Browniesleys

NORTH

48

Route Two

Stonehaven Square – Roadside of Catterline – Roadside of Kinneff – Inverbervie – Sheriff's Kettle – King's Step – Gourdon Hill – Inverbervie – Stonehaven Square.

Distance: 34.82 miles, as follows:

Round trip from Stonehaven to Inverbervie by car – 20 miles.
In Inverbervie – 0.13 miles on foot.

Suggested excursions:
Sheriff's Kettle – 7.87 miles (7.76 by car and 0.11 on foot)
Long Cairn, Gourdon – 3.58 miles (1.68 by car and 1.90 on foot)
Iron Age Fort – an extra 0.53 miles on foot
King's Step – 1.78 miles on foot
Hallgreen Castle – 0.93 miles (0.86 by car and 0.07 on foot)

Round the Ancient Royal Burgh of Inverbervie

in which one reads of the first spinning-mill in Scotland, the hardship of eating oatcakes, a sheriff boiled in a kettle and 'supped in bree', a barrow built a thousand years before the Pyramids, and the gutting of three haddocks!

As we shall see, King David Bruce met with such kind treatment from the inhabitants of Inverbervie which so gratified and pleased him that he granted a *charter of erection in une free burgh*, conferring many privileges on its inhabitants. It seems not inappropriate, therefore, since Bervie is the only royal burgh in Kincardineshire, that we visit it on its own to see what it has to offer us.

A Royal Burgh with a Long History

Let us therefore follow the A92 for 10 miles exactly from Stonehaven Square until we reach the Square of Inverbervie (known also as Bervie). Originally a small fishing town where coastal vessels found anchorage at the mouth of the River Bervie, it can boast a long and interesting history. Its shelving beach and tidal pool have proved a convenient landing place for marauding bands of Frisians, Saxons and others who for about 700 years infested our shores and settled in the coast lands. Even in the reign of William the Lion the names Bervyn, Glenbervyn and Inverbervyn appear frequently in charters in association with the name of the Mearns and generally connected with the principal land-owners of the district, the De

Montforts of Kinneff Castle, the Barclays of Mathers, the Fitzber-
nards of Catterline, the Raits of Hallgreen and the early Arbuthnotts, one of them Hugh the Blond who was popularly believed to
have gained his estate for killing a monster in the Den of Pitcarles.

The Oldest Extant Charter, Granted by David II

As far back as the 12th century, in a document relating to Arbroath
Abbey, we read that a certain Simon of Inverbervie witnessed a
charter transferring the lands of Balfeith to Arbroath Abbey.
About 1219 David, Earl of Huntingdon, brother of King William
the Lion, held the lands of Inverbervie as part of his inheritance,
and a castle is recorded here in the first half of the 13th century.

The earliest known charter was granted in the reign of Alexander
II (1249-85) when the Scottish kings, journeying to and from their
royal palace of Kincardine (see page 339), were in the habit of
landing and embarking at Bervie. But the charter which elevated
the town to a Royal Burgh (a position which the royal place of
residence, Kincardine, never achieved) was granted in gratitude by
that unfortunate monarch, King David II, on 22nd June, 1342. On
his return after an adventurous voyage from La Rochelle in France
where for seven years he had been sent for security during the
second War of Independence with his Queen Consort, Johanna,
and Court, the King made a spectacular forced landing on the rocks
below the headland of Bervie Brow on 2nd June, 1341, his ship
having been driven ashore in a violent storm. He had been escaping
from the English fleet which was pursuing them. A rock, The King's
Step, is believed to mark the exact spot where the king set foot in
Scotland, and the *Statistical Account* of 1792 states that the ruins of
St David's Chapel, erected in gratitude of landing safely from a
stormy passage, stood near the spot.

Hospitality 'with a Shovit Trowel'

Along the boulder-strewn shore they made their way to Inverbervie
to receive a warm welcome. An apocryphal story tells that His
Majesty, being very hungry, entered a fisherman's cottage at King-
hornie, near the mouth of the Bervie Water, and asked for food. 'I'll
gut twa haddocks', cried the fisherman's wife. 'Gut three!' said her
good man. This so gratified the king that he replied, 'Gut three your
name shall be'. So was Guthrie afterwards adopted as the name of
the fisherman, and thus does tradition explain the origin of the
name!

Be that as it may, in the words of an old writer, the king was
dined, wined and flattered and, in the words of Disraeli, the

hospitality was *put on with a shovit trowel*. It is thought that the king afterwards proceeded by old stepping-stones, now demolished, to David Street in Inverbervie where he resided, and was so well pleased with the reception and royal welcome he received from the inhabitants that he granted the burgh a charter, signed at Aberdeen on June 22nd, 1342:

> *Know ye that we have granted, and by this our present charter confirmed, to our burgesses and community of Inverbervie, that they and their successors have, hold and possess for ever the aforesaid town of Inverbervie as a free burgh with suitable liberties, commodities, easements, free customs and all just pertinents that belong or can of right in any wise belong to a free burgh.*

Among the advantages which the charter conveyed was the right to form a Town Council, the right of trial, the right to hold markets, to sell certain goods and to fish on both sides of the river and in the bay for salmon and white fish alike. King David's charter was lost when the Tolbooth and much of the town were destroyed in 1567 by a disastrous fire which took place during the Civil War, following on the deposing of Mary, Queen of Scots. The order to burn the town was given by the Regent Moray because of the inhabitants' loyalty to Queen Mary and the Roman Catholic cause. The burgh's royal status was subsequently renewed by King James VI in 1595 in a charter of confirmation even more explicit and elaborate.

A Seaport Rendezvous of the Well-to-do

During the Middle Ages Bervie was a moderately sized town and a favoured rendezvous of the neighbouring young gentlemen and well-to-do farmers, and sometimes brawls ensued. On one occasion in 1570 a Rait of Hallgreen Castle nearby with some companions slew William Sibbald, brother of the laird of Kair at Gilbert's Hill, Auchenblae (see page 298). (There was a lady in the case.) The laird with nine others retaliated three months later, killed a Peter Rait of Tipperty and cut off both his brother's hands. Not to be outdone the Raits and their company, seventeen in all, illegally gathered under the pretence of carrying out the ancient performance of Robin Hood and the Abbot of Unreason (a kind of carnival, the parties being disguised, strictly forbidden by law since the Reformation) with the intention of making a mass attack on the Sibbalds. Nothing further has been recorded of the outcome except that at several trials no verdict of guilty was obtained.

The Presbytery Driven off with Divots

During the latter centuries of the Middle Ages down even to recent times Bervie was quite an important town and seaport. On one occasion the people of Stonehaven complained how much their trade was being hindered by the excessive dues payable by their harbour managers or Town Council in Bervie which as a Royal Burgh had this privilege, and the Privy Council took steps to mitigate this grievance.

The 18th century brought many changes, social, economic and political. In 1707 by the Act of Union Inverbervie lost its right as a Royal Burgh to send a commissioner to represent her in the Scottish parliament, which it had done since 1612 at least, and was then included in a group of burghs – Aberdeen, Montrose, Arbroath, Brechin and Inverbervie – which elected one Member to Westminster.

Following the 1688 Rebellion it was with great difficulty that Presbyterian ministers could be settled in the parishes, and it was not until 1714 that an attempt was made to settle a Presbyterian minister in Bervie. When the Presbytery came there, they found that the church had been barred up so that they could not enter the building: they had to travel to Benholm to ordain the minister there. After the ordination the people of Bervie pulled the minister off his horse and took him to Gourdon. There the members of the Presbytery tried to rescue him but were driven off with stones and divots.

A Flourishing Fishing Burgh

At Inverbervie there was once a flourishing fishing population, herring fishing being carried on in the latter part of the 18th century. In the middle decade of last century, however, only some five or six boats belonged to the village, and about seventy men worked at the white fishing. The large quantities of cod and ling then caught were salted by curers for the London market, and about 100 barrels annually were shipped to England from Montrose. Bervie haddocks were sent regularly as far as Glasgow as were turbot and skate, caught from May to July. In summer cod was dried for home consumption. Later, however, the draft of water at the mouth of the river was progressively reduced by the formation of a gravel bar which prevented its proper use as a harbour and ultimately rendered impossible its use by locally based fishing boats. As a consequence the neighbouring harbours of Gourdon and Johnshaven were developed.

Industrialisation and the First Scottish Spinning-mill

Perhaps more important than Inverbervie's ancient renown is the fact that the town has been an industrial one since 1750 when, as it continued its association with coastal trade and fishing, sail-cloth manufacturing was introduced in the Haughs of Birnie, situated inland behind the town and stretching for a considerable distance alongside the River Bervie. In 1778 the making of coloured threads was introduced to Bervie, and in 1790 there was erected the first spinning-mill in Scotland with the first machine of its kind, powered by water, for spinning linen yarn. Known as the 'Auld Mill', it employed sixty workers and survived till 1919 when it was destroyed by fire. At the end of another 100 years there were four flax and tow mills, a chemical works and wincey and sacking factories. Considerable industrialisation and resultant prosperity continued until the end of the 19th century when several mills, first actuated by water and thereafter by steam, were established for the weaving of flax.

After the 1914-18 War due to difficulty in the supply of raw material and setbacks caused by fire damage one mill after another failed, bringing much hardship to the town and reducing its prosperity. Today, apart from agriculture, the eleven factories which Bervie once possessed have dwindled to five, and even if a hundred Bervie folk commute to work elsewhere each day, there is still a strong manufacturing tradition evident. Flax, tow and rayon are spun in Inverbervie at the Craigview Mill which, using up-to-date machinery, continues the original processing which is their staple industry. They employ about forty workers for whom an excellent canteen has been built. A very important second Bervie industry is sited in the old Lint Mill in the Burgh Haughs, originally a flax-spinning factory and later simply a store. It was taken over in 1854 by St Clair Fisheries, and in 1968 was acquired by Highland Seafoods Ltd. with their flourishing fish processing plant. In 1971 part of the old building was demolished and a modern extension, doubling the available space, was embarked on with a view to providing fifty more jobs. Highland Seafoods employs between thirty and a hundred workers (dependent on the season), processing and deep freezing crab and lobster meat in season and other sea foods. By ideal up-to-date methods the meat is made into packs which are quick-frozen and retained in that condition until sent off in containers to markets in the south. Visitors to the factory are welcome. Bruce Plant and Elsashire, Ltd., an engineering firm, employ between them a further eighty workers.

The Duke of Cumberland and Other Notables

A native of Inverbervie was John Coutts (born there in 1699), the father of Thomas Coutts, the famous London banker. Several famous personages have visited the town. In 1504 King James IV passed through the burgh in the course of a pilgrimage, and Daniel Defoe in 1724 in his tour of Scotland. The next visitation of special interest was in 1745 when the Duke of Cumberland was side-tracked from his customary practices by the diplomacy of the parish minister. The troops of 'The Butcher' on their way to Culloden were causing fear and consternation in the district by pillaging and laying waste Johnshaven four miles south, knocking down houses and burning the boats of fishermen.

Mr Thomas Dow, the minister, fearing a similar fate for Bervie, hurriedly set out on foot to meet Cumberland in person to put in a good word for his flock. He is reputed to have met the Royalist army at or near Bridge of Benholm and to have been invited into the ducal carriage, conveyed back to his own door and permitted to act as host to Cumberland who spent the night in the manse which was at that time situated in King Street, probably on the site of the present manse. In the course of dispensing hospitality Mr Dow was able to assure his guest of the parishioners' loyalty to the House of Hanover and that the Bervie folk were well affected towards him: their immunity from the fate of most coastal burghs with strong Jacobite leanings was therefore spared by diplomacy.

A volunteer who accompanied the Duke left this record:

> *Here we put up at the Provost's house, a good, honest old fellow whose face showed what he loved. His wife told us she had brought out wine to present to the Duke and his officers when they passed by, but she could get none of her neighbours to support her actions, We were here first obliged to eat oatcakes on the journey which was a great hardship to several of our inexperienced travellers.*

A Roving Privateer is Hoodwinked

John Wesley visited Inverbervie in 1786 during a tour of Scotland, and ten years later James Burness, writer in Montrose and first cousin to Robert Burns, was appointed Town Clerk of the burgh. There was also the instance of the French privateer which appeared in the bay of Bervie in 1800 during the French Revolutionary War and gave chase to several merchant vessels which took refuge at the mouth of the Bervie Water and in Gourdon harbour. There were fears that the Frenchmen would not only take the ships as prizes but also plunder Inverbervie as well. This time it was the Provost, Mr Hudson, who took charge of the situation. Calling together a small band of volunteers, he divided them into two groups and marched them off to repel the invaders. Although small arms were their only rather ineffective means of defence, they made a brave show. One party went to the beach on the north bank of the Bervie Water and another to the beach by Hallgreen Castle. The first party were fired upon by the vessel, but her cannon balls happily did no damage. Hallgreen Castle, however, though unfortified, had all the appearance of a stronghold, and it was presumably suspected that the second muster of local folk were in reality artillerymen stationed there who would repay the privateer's gunfire with interest. At any rate the privateer, deciding that discretion was the better part of valour, made off at speed over the horizon.

Queen Victoria Makes a Brief Halt

In 1848 Queen Victoria, who had been on holiday in Balmoral, halted briefly outside the King's Arms Hotel (where later the old primary school was built) to allow the horses to be changed when, accompanied by her husband and three children, she travelled to Montrose by coach. The *Stonehaven Journal* remarks:

> *From the shortness of the notice, preparations such as the magistrates could have wished could not be made. A number of special constables were appointed, and flags of every colour were displayed on the main streets. At fifteen minutes past four the Queen arrived in the Burgh to the accompaniment of three cheers from the people. During her stay a band played the National Anthem, and a Loyal Address from the magistrates was handed over to Sir George Grey by Baillie Watson.*

The Market Square

Towards the end of the 17th century the Burgh was contained by the four streets forming the original rectangle round the Market Square where our car is parked now. These were the Fishergate (or 'Seygait' – Seagate) which is now David Street, the Kirkburn (now King Street) – street names doubtless mementoes of that ill-starred monarch, David II – the Cowgate, the only one remaining of four ports or gates referred to in the Minute Book of the old Town Council, and the High Street. At one time the Square extended beyond the present road.

About 1559 the Townhouse was built in the middle of the Market Square, consisting of a hall and small council room above with a chamber for prisoners and with the flesh and meal markets below. In olden days it was a common thing for the county gentry to do their shopping at the fish market, flesh market and booths for the sale of all kinds of merchandise which were situated in the Market Square, but changing customs saw these open-air markets disappear. The Townhouse was restored in 1720, and a mansion belonging to the Marischal family, which became the town house of the Arbuthnotts, was sited here too. A stone bearing the date 1569 is set in the east gable of the present Town Hall in Church Street.

A Picturesque Mercat-cross

Standing where the old Townhouse once stood is the interesting old mercat-cross, Inverbervie's silent and visible link with its ancient historic past and a picturesque relic of the days when Bervie was a busy market town. It was one of the rights contained in the charter granted to the burghers by James VI in which power was given

> *for the choosing and creating of a provost, baillies, treasurer, fiscal, councillors, burgh officers and all other members whatsoever within the said burgh for the ruling and governing thereof*

together with the right to have a court-house, to hold a weekly market on Thursdays and to have a market-cross. It is not known if the cross is the original one or (as is more probable) a replacement of the original at the time the charter was granted. It is a slender pillar of stone, about 14 ft. high, surmounted by a ball, dated 1737, and surrounded by a flight of seven steps at its base from which royal proclamations are read. Exposed to the blasts of countless storms, the cross has suffered from the ravages of time and has been repaired several times at the ratepayers' expense.

The stocks which once stood at the mercat-cross may be seen in Montrose museum. They are unusual in that they have holes for seven feet. Perhaps the seventh hole was for a one-legged man!

A Convent of Carmelite Friars

And now let us view one or two of Inverbervie's more interesting sights. Let us cross the Cowgate and take the road almost diagonally opposite and a little to the north. The area at the corner, only some 50 yards away and now occupied by several cottages, is the site of a convent of a contemplative order of Carmelite friars which was established in 1443. They held lands in the vicinity with regard to which the name, Friars' Dubbs, occurs in old charters. The monastery was dissolved about the time of the Reformation in 1567, and no visible remains survive.

Hercules Linton and Nannie, the Witch

Opposite, in an even more prominent corner, is a charming little memorial garden, with flagged pathways, seats and borders of shrubs. It commemorates a very illustrious son of Scotland as well as of Inverbervie, Hercules A. Linton, designer of the famous *Cutty Sark*, launched at Dumbarton in November, 1869, and one of the finest and most graceful ships the world has ever seen. It is now preserved at Greenwich where it attracts thousands of tourists. He was born in 4 The Square, Inverbervie, in 1836 and attended Arbuthnott School under the famous Dr Chrystal. When he returned to Inverbervie, he interested himself in the Town Council and local matters and died on 15th May, 1900. He lies buried in the old churchyard.

The principal feature of this attractive memorial is a handsome half life-size bronze sculpture of the figurehead of the *Cutty Sark*, designed by Mr R. Scott Sutherland, at one time head of the sculpture department at Dundee School of Art. The figurehead, of course, which projects with striking flourish from a stone monument over a central pool, shows the comely young witch, Nannie, in Burns' *Tam o' Shanter* after whom the clipper was named. She wears only her cutty sark and stretches forward her left hand to cling to the tail of Tam's mare as he flees. The memorial was unveiled on 23rd October, 1969, by Sir Francis Chichester, the famous yachtsman who circumnavigated the world single-handed, and in the old Council Chamber is a superb model of the *Cutty Sark*, heavily insured.

The Fabulous Cutty Sark

Linton designed the fabulous *Cutty Sark* for one John Willis, a canny Scots ship-owner who cherished a burning ambition to win the coveted Blue Riband of the sea, the prize awarded to the winner of the great annual race to bring the first cargo of China tea into port. This award the *Cutty Sark* never did win for winning meant beating the fastest ship of them all, the rival *Thermopylae* of Aberdeen with its brilliant timing. On the one occasion in 1872 when the ships raced to Australia in company, the *Cutty Sark*, after 26 days and when she was some 400 miles ahead of her rival, lost her rudder in a heavy gale in the Indian Ocean, the *Thermopylae* romping home a week ahead. (The *Thermopylae* refused to show her log, and the *Cutty Sark* was held to be the winner). The finest and most glorious years of the *Cutty Sark*, however, were from 1885 to 1895 when she made the fastest passage time home annually from Australia, beating her old rival *Thermopylae* every time they competed in the wool trade after the dwindling clipper tea trade had ended. Certain it is that we shall never see again anything to match the sight of this wonderful ship battling across the oceans, her sails filled and her sharp prow slicing through the waves.

The handsome, half life-size bronze sculpture of the figurehead of the famous Cutty Sark *which projects from the Inverbervie memorial, commemorating the ship's designer, Hercules Linton. The sculpture shows Nannie, the comely witch in Burns' 'Tam o' Shanter', clinging to the tail of Tam's mare as he flees.*

The Jubilee and Old Bervie Bridges

If we continue some sixty yards farther down the hill, we arrive at a
vantage piont from which we can see the handsome Jubilee Bridge
by which we entered Inverbervie, the old bridge beside it and the
whole extent of the valley of the Bervie Water stretching away to
the north-west. The Jubilee Bridge is so named in honour of twenty-
five years' reign by King George V. Opened in August, 1935, by
Viscount Arbuthnott, this dominating and massive bridge with its
graceful lines is a revelation even to many who have crossed it often.
It has seven spans with a total length, including approaches, of 1700
ft. Constructed of reinforced concrete and designed to withstand
the heaviest loads, it took three years to build. Sealed in a cavity in
the base of the towering 80 ft. central pier is a bronze tube containing a number of Jubilee silver coins and specimens of spun flax.
These articles, when they next see the light of day, will be relics of a
past age and will tell posterity something of Bervie, of Kincardineshire and of the Scotland of 1935.

Situated in close proximity is the old Bervie bridge, a single span
structure, 80 ft. high, which dates from 1799, the foundation stone
being laid by Hercules Ross of Rossie two years earlier. The arch is
reputed to be one of the highest single arches in Scotland. Despite
the occasional floods to which the river is subject, the bridge has
never been damaged. It had large stone chambers incorporated at
the north and south ends, with barred windows and doors. Although these might suggest prisons, the new *Statistical Account* of
1837 stated they were for storing coal and lime.

Curious and interesting facts regarding stratae came to light when
the foundations of the new bridge were being laid. Beech and hazel
nuts were found among the debris, indicating the former presence
of vegetation, while other finds formed clues to happenings as far
back as the Ice Age. It is thought that the valley was at one time
much wider than it is now and that the ground on which the town is
built is of a later period.

The Beattie and Stratton Bridges

There were two other bridges across the Bervie Water. In 1695
William Beattie, a baillie of the burgh, constructed at his own
expense a bridge of two arches which crossed the river where the old
bridge now stands. In the same year Beattie successfully petitioned
the Estates (the Scottish Parliament) for the vacant stipends of
certain churches to be paid to him to recompense him for his outlay,
and in his will he left the sum of 300 merks Scots for its upkeep. This

sum was left in trust in the keeping of Aberdeen Town Council, part of it being used in the 1950's to effect repairs on the present old bridge.

The first important bridge at Bervie (and perhaps the original) is believed to have been built in 1474 by Alexander Stratton of Knox, and its central pier is still clearly visible in the bed of the river under the arch. Jervise records that the town of Aberdeen held a fund which was mortified for the support of the bridge, a vital link in the old Causey Mounth road (q.v.) over the mosses of Findon and Portlethen, down Megray Hill and through Stonehaven to the school of Kinneff and over Wardhead and Kinghornie to Bervie and Montrose.

From the vantage point where we stand can be seen almost under and on the seaward side of the Jubilee Bridge the old Lint Mill, now used by Highland Seafoods, Ltd.; on the landward side of the old bridge the Elsashire engineering works. Perhaps more interesting – we are just able to pick out the site of the first spinning-mill away at the end of the Haugh in front of the cottage which is beside the windmill.

The old single-span bridge at Inverbervie which dates from 1799 with reputedly one of the highest single arches in Scotland. Notice the barred windows of the large stone chambers incorporated at both ends. In the background is the massive Jubilee Bridge constructed of reinforced concrete and opened in 1935.

Four Possible Inverbervie Excursions

Four greatly differing optional excursions from Inverbervie may be
of interest if time permits, one to Hallgreen Castle, one on foot
along the cliffs with their striking rock scenery north of the town to
the King's Step, one to the top of Gourdon Hill, and the fourth by
car to a hollow by a stream, known as The Sheriff's Kettle, where
took place one of the most dramatic incidents in the history of the
county. The return journey for the last is one of 7¾ miles and, such
has been the recent denuding of the countryside, little is to be seen
once you arrive there. Yet, as it is not every day that you can visit
the place where a sheriff of the Mearns was allegedly barbarously
stripped and boiled in a cauldron, your curiosity may require satisfaction!

A Grave and a Railway Line of the Past

The first excursion to the remains of Hallgreen Castle includes en
route one or two further points of interest. We leave Inverbervie
Square and proceed southwards along King Street for 150 yards to
the first cross roads where stands the 100 ft. high Gothic tower of the
parish church, a splendid structure which, architecturally, is the
dominating feature of the town and a notable landmark in the
surrounding country. The church was opened on January 1st, 1837,
and the bell came from the former parish church at Kirkburn, built
in 1781, the remains of which, a ruined gable, can be seen behind
the Bervie fire station. In Church Street on the right can be seen the
Town Hall nearby with, high on the gable and just below the
guttering, the inscribed stone already mentioned.

Let us turn down the Kirkburn opposite. 75 yards away is the
entrance to the kirkyard. The second stone along from the top of the
steps marks the grave of Hercules Linton, previously commented
upon. When we continue down the hill for another 300 yards or so,
we arrive at the site of the railway station for the old Inverbervie –
Montrose line which played a great part in the economy of the
district and was busy with both passenger and freight traffic. At the
beginning of the century passenger trains usually consisted of four
coaches, and at one time there was almost an hourly service. It was
at 5.45 on an October evening in 1951 that the last passenger train
was flagged off from Inverbervie. It carried fourteen passengers.
The service was uneconomic in view of competition from the buses.

Prehistoric Remains

In 1927, during excavations in the children's recreation ground
nearby a Bronze Age stone cist was found, containing a skeleton. It

is now in the Anthropological Museum, Marischal College, Aberdeen. In January, 1937, a gravel bed was discovered in the garden at Craigwellbank, suggesting it had been specially laid there. Farther down was found a stone urn (which, unfortunately, was destroyed), a stone hammer and another stone which had a hole in the centre, all dating back to the Stone Age.

Hallgreen Castle a Typical Laird's House

Our route, however, takes us along Hallgreen Road to the right (parallel to the line of the old railway track) at the end of which, 350 yards away, is a bay where we can leave our car. On the prominent rocky eminence above, and overlooking Bervie Bay, stands Hallgreen Castle. A walk of a hundred yards or so will take us there – up the hill and alongside a ravine where a gushing burn cascades. The castle is an L-shaped stronghold with very thick walls of the late 16th century, pitted with arrow holes and possessing some good specimens of the architecture of this period. The north and west fronts of the building were later added to and modernised, and the castle was ultimately remodelled as a more Elizabethan style mansion. The setting in which it stands was at one time quite romantic, and its park had a number of tofts and crofts.

The three-storey castle, built of local red-brown sandstone, was a fairly typical medium-sized laird's house, with its hall on the first floor, the bedrooms above, and with its vaulted basement. The oldest parts of the building, the south and east frontages (although the latter is partly rebuilt) retain the wide splayed gun-loops of what had been in all likelihood an earlier castle, those on the east being of the double aperture type. At the south-east corner, where the ground slopes away to the burn, a peculiar buttress projects to strengthen the wall. Unaltered despite the many later additions and alterations are the steep attic roofs, the crow-stepped gables, dormer windows and corner turrets at the angles. Many of the early windows have been enlarged, while others have disappeared altogether.

Inside the castle, before it fell into a state of dilapidation from about 1973 onwards, were still to be seen on the wooden panelling of the walls two landscape paintings and a flower piece, supposedly of Dutch origin. The dining-room showed an example of wood-graining on plaster with elaborate stylished friezes, and two of the bedrooms still had Victorian wall-paper depicting a hunting scene and the months of the year.

The Castle Owned by the Raits in the Reign of Robert III

The earliest portion of the castle is said to have been erected by the Dunnet family in 1376, and it apparently passed to the Raits in the reign of Robert III (1340-1406) although the family was found in the Mearns at least half a century before that. Tradition tells that they first settled in what is now Moray and Nairn under Malcolm IV (1141-65) and that, in consequence of a Sir Alexander Rait's having killed a thane, he fled to the Mearns and, receiving the protection of the Earl Marischal, married the heiress of Hallgreen. The castle was rebuilt in 1683-87, and the coat of arms of the Rait proprietor of the time with the words, Spero Meliora (I hope for better things), and the date 1683 could still be made out quite clearly until the turn of the century on the stucco ceiling of one of the principal rooms. Above a door in the court the date 1687 with Rait's initials was at one time visible. Sir Alexander Rait's descendants, one of whom was Captain of the Guard in the time of James IV, held the barony until the end of the 17th century, being responsible for many additions to the castle.

In 1724 the Hallgreen estate was purchased by Thomas Coutts of the famous banking family, and in 1767 by the Hon. Thomas Lyon, brother of the Earl of Strathmore. It changed hands again in 1779 to Robert Barclay of Urie, and in 1795 to David Scott of Dunninald. The Farquhars who purchased the estate in 1806 were a distinguished local family in whose hands it remained until 1926 when the estate was broken up and sold. James Farquhar was for twenty years prior to 1818 M.P. for the royal burghs of Montrose, Brechin, Arbroath and Aberdeen. A lectern to the memory of Major Farquhar of Hallgreen, one of the family killed on active service, was presented in 1916 to Bervie Parish Church where it may still be seen.

The Horrible Murder at the Sheriff's Kettle

To visit the Sheriff's Kettle – our second excursion from Inverbervie – you must drive along King Street for 450 yards or so, forking right at the end to Townhead of Inverbervie.[1] Continue for two miles, keeping to the right at the road fork. After a further two-tenths of a mile fork left and continue for just under this distance again until you reach the road-end to the farm of Browniesleys. Here leave your car and walk towards the farm for just over

[1] Four-fifths of a mile after leaving the main street of Inverbervie one passes Dendoldrum farm on the right. 300 yards west of the farmhouse and just to the right of the road to Peattie farm is the cropmark of a circular enclosure about 66 ft. in diameter within its ditch. On the north there is a possible entrance.

100 yards. The hollow on the left by the stream (sadly disfigured by rubbish) is known as The Sheriff's Kettle or Brownies' Kettle or Brownies' Hollow or Fairies' Hollow. Here tradition states that about 1420 in the reign of James I of Scotland John Melville, Sheriff[1] of the Mearns and a member of the early Glenbervie family mentioned on page 283, was plunged in a boiling cauldron and horribly murdered. The story is as follows.

Melville being something of a martinet in the execution of his duties, the neighbouring barons made repeated complaints to the king whose patience was finally exhausted. So it was that to this undistinguished piece of ground in what was then the well-known hunting Forest of Garvock was decoyed the unsuspecting Melville. A grisly murder took place, and the unpopular sheriff was flung into what the Rev. Mr Charles, minister of Garvock from 1831 to 1868, calls *a large kettle* from the boiling water of which the barons each took a spoonful of the ghastly devil's soup made from his bones. The chief actor in this godless deed was David Barclay, laird of Mathers, and concerning the gruesome demise of the sheriff there appear the names of many prominent Kincardineshire lairds of the period.

'Sodden and Supped in Bree'

It may be of interest to record what Sir Walter Scott has to say of the abrupt and unceremonious end of the unfortunate gentleman in his *Border Minstrelsy*:

> *Extraordinary cookery was actually practised ('horresco referens') upon the body of a Sheriff of the Mearns. This person, whose name was Melville of Glenbervie, bore his faculties so harshly that he became detested by the barons of the county. Reiterated complaints of his conduct having been made to James I (or, as others say, the Duke of Albany), the monarch answered in a moment of unguarded impatience, 'Sorrow gin the Sheriff were sodden and supped in bree!' The complainers retired perfectly satisfied. Shortly after, the lairds of Arbuthnott, Mathers, Lauriston and Pitarrow decoyed Melville to the top of the hill of Garvock under pretence of a grand hunting party. Upon this place, still called the Sheriff's Pot, the barons had*

Coincident with the substitution of thanes for Maormors, the first Sheriffs appeared. The office became hereditary subsequently and was held successively by the Keiths (afterwards Earls Marischal). In later times the Sheriff exercised his prerogative of appointing a depute to act on his behalf.

> *prepared a fire and a boiling cauldron into which they*
> *plunged the unlucky Sheriff. After he was 'sodden', as the*
> *King termed it, for a sufficient time, the savages, that they*
> *might literally observe the royal mandate, concluded the*
> *scene of abomination by actually partaking of the hell-*
> *broth. The three lairds were outlawed for the offence, and*
> *Barclay, one of their number, to screen himself from jus-*
> *tice, erected the Kaim (i.e. the fortress) of Mathers which*
> *stands upon a rocky and almost inaccessible peninsula*
> *overhanging the North Sea. The Laird of Arbuthnott is said*
> *to have eluded the Royal vengeance by claiming the benefit*
> *of the law of the Clan Macduff. A pardon, or perhaps a*
> *deed of replegiation, founded on that law, is said to be still*
> *extant among the records of the Viscount of Arbuthnott.*

King James, when he heard of the incident, was not very pleased, and the wheels of 15th century justice were set in motion. These were leisurely times, however, and Barclay was able to protect himself from the royal wrath by building his Kaim on a perpendicular rock 60 ft. above the sea in the parish of St Cyrus (see page 484).

The Law of the Clan Macduff, referred to above, is an ancient Teutonic custom which Sir Robert Sibbald and other Scots historians have written about. In case of homicide, it allowed a pardon to anyone within the ninth degree of kindred to Macduff, Thane of Fife, who fled to his cross which then stood near Lindores, near Newburgh in Fife, and paid a fine. Cramond comments that it would be interesting to know if the letter of remission of 13th September, 1421, is still in existence, or if it ever existed. It is said to set forth that

> *Hugh of Arbuthnott, George Barclay, Alexander Fal-*
> *coner, William Graem, Gilbert Middleton, Patrick Barclay*
> *and Alexander Graem (are) received into the clan for the*
> *deid of whilom John Melville of Glenbervie.*

The fate of the other conspirators is not known.

Considerable doubt has been thrown on the authenticity of this not very pleasant story, highly dramatic though it is. Dr Cramond, for example, enumerates various objections in his *Annals of Fourdoun*, thinking it improbable that any laird of Glenbervie was ever a sheriff of Kincardine and that such vengeance would be taken for the strict rule of law and harshness to the poor, not much of a sin in days when the country was not very easily shocked.

Alexander Arbuthnott's Version

Cramond quotes the following version as being probable in all respects. It was written by Alexander Arbuthnott, Principal of King's College, Aberdeen, in 1569, less than a century and a half later:

> *Melville, puffed up with riches and a sense of power, chiefly because he had a great number of Highlanders at his command, bore himself haughtily towards his neighbours of whom Hugh Arbuthnott, being nearest, suffered most. Not being able to deal with him alone, Arbuthnott entered into a league with others of the Kincardineshire notabilities with the result of increasing rather than of allaying irritation. At last a meeting is arranged — a hunting party, Melville being of the number. They fell out on the Hill of Garvock, and Melville was killed.*

Principal Arbuthnott adds that Hugh of Arbuthnott, having had matters smoothed down by the intervention of judges and friends, built a chapel at Drumlithie which he richly endowed, a priest being appointed to pray daily for John Melville's soul.

However it happened, the slaughter of Melville would seem to have taken place at or near the spot where we now stand, the event being perpetuated in the name of Browniesleys Farm 340 yards farther on at the end of the road because the field where the murder took place was long supposed to be haunted by brownies or goblins after the perpetration of the deed. Fairies bulked largely in the life of the time, and elves, kelpies and fairy arrows were dreaded (cf reference to Beattie's *John o' Arnha'* on page 463). In 1875 a cinerary urn containing a cremation was found in a gravel hillock on the farm of Browniesleys.

The King's Step Below Historic Bervie Brow

A third possible excursion takes us on a delightful cliff and seaside walk round the foot of the high slope of the historic eminence of Bervie Brow (or Craig David as the headland was later called) which towers 451 ft. above sea-level on the north side of the Bervie Water and shelters Bervie on the north-east side. From the top on a clear day Lochnagar is visible with the Cairngorms in the distance. The massive leonine form of the two-stepped headland, yet another of the sea-washed promontories that figure so largely in Mearns history and one of the finest on the Scottish coast, ends in a shoulder of rounded cliff which bars the river's way when it reaches the coast.

The headland contains first of all a layer of conglomerate or pudding-stone; then there is volcanic rock. Craig David marks the end of the high cliffs which form the natural wall of protection to most of the Kincardineshire coast.

If the day is a pleasant one and time permits, we might walk to see what purports to be The King's Step, a journey of only 1¾ miles in all, there and back. We must begin by crossing the Square and walking down High Street until, after 140 yards, it joins David Street. Here we turn left, descending the slope to the foot bridge across the Bervie at the Cruives, built in 1934 to replace stepping-stones farther up stream. It is interesting here to see issuing forth from the rise across the river and below, as it were, the roof-tops of the farm of Kinghornie opposite, the path of the old coast road. And it is also of interest that cropmarks east-south-east of King-hornie farmhouse reveal what may be the site of at least one circular timber house.

It may be noticed that a 'platform', submerged at high water, runs for miles along the coast. The absence of this platform opposite the park adjoining the Recreation Ground indicates that the Bervie Water once entered the sea at a different spot from the present estuary. It is safe to infer that the former channel was about the centre of the bay before the Ice Age; after the pre-glacial valley was blocked up, the present gorge was formed through which the Bervie Water forces its way from the haughland of its lower slopes to the sea. The land sank, leaving the lower raised beach which is a feature of the bay today and a high raised beach on the south bank of the Bervie Water on which Inverbervie stands.

A walk of a further third of a mile through the war-time concrete blocks and beyond takes us to a grassy bay which is the site of the Chapel of Kinghornie (the rusting winch may well roughly mark the spot!). It is said to have been visible at the end of the 18th century, but nothing now remains. At the end of a further third of a mile we find ourselves on an eminence immediately below Craig David and looking down upon a deep rocky inlet of the sea. The rocks which project out to sea on the south side of this inlet mark The King's Step where King David II traditionally set foot in Scotland in 1341.

A Neolithic Long Cairn

Before we continue our journey, it would be a pity if we did not undertake a fourth excursion and avail ourselves of the opportunity of seeing one of the five Neolithic long cairns and barrows which are to be found in Kincardineshire, especially when it is so near. We must travel by car south along the A92 for just over three-quarters of a mile and, a few yards past Sillyflat Farm, turn up the road on the right to Hallgreen Mains. Seventy-five yards up this farm road we can leave our car and tackle the track leading off to the left on foot as a car is not advised unless there is good clearance and the road conditions are exceptionally dry. Nine-tenths of a mile long, this track, known as Long Rigg, leads to the summit of Gourdon or Bikmane Hill (447 ft.) in a field on the summit of which, 85 yards away to our left, is a Neolithic long cairn, well worth a visit. On the way one passes Shakil Hill on the right on the summit of which is a possible cairn 18 ft. in diameter and 1 ft. in height.

A Prehistoric Relic Older Than the Pyramids

The long cairn on Gourdon Hill is an example of the first regular and visible burial mounds to be found in Britain, introduced not long after 4000 B.C. by the farming people of the Neolithic or New Stone Age who brought to us the basis of our civilization and left us these striking monuments of which there are about 200 examples surviving in Britain. Long barrows are therefore between 5000 and 6000 years old and quite the most ancient prehistoric relics to be found in the county. Indeed, these barrows have the distinction of being the oldest form of field monument known in Britain. An example at Dalladies near Northwater Bridge (no evidence of which now remains) was carbon dated 4000 B.C. by Professor Piggott of Edinburgh University in 1971. This informs us with no little surprise then that the Gourdon and other Kincardineshire barrows were built 1000 years before the first Pyramid!

The idea of long barrows may have been brought from Northern Europe whence many of the settlers came, but barrows may have originated in Brittany. Certainly this type of monument is distributed throughout the North European plain and thence to Scotland. They are the collective burial-places of Neolithic dead, and there is good reason for regarding them as family graves. It has been estimated that the Dalladies barrow took 5750 man-hours to build, a long time indeed. This reveals, if nothing else, the very strong sense of duty of these New Stone Age men towards their dead.

Long barrows are long, grass-covered mounds of earth, turf, rubble or stone, piled up directly over a number of bodies. Generally aligned east and west, they vary between 100 ft. and 300 ft. in length and between 30 ft. and 100 ft. in breadth. Often they are as much as 10 ft. or 12 ft. in height. The sides of most long barrows are usually bounded by dry-stone walling, and most have a flanking ditch along each of the long sides, these ditches normally continuing round both ends of the mound to join up in a curve or horse-shoe or being broken by one or more causeways. As seen in the field, however, these details are usually obliterated.

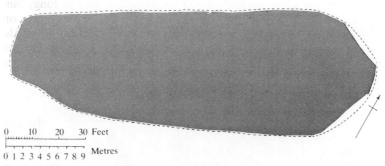

0   10   20   30 Feet

0 1 2 3 4 5 6 7 8 9 Metres

Plan and elevation diagram of the Neolithic long barrow on Gourdon Hill.

Gourdon long cairn is a characteristic one, 151 ft. long, 46 ft. across near the east end and (where it is about 8.2 ft. high) 26 ft. across near the west end with ends rounded in plan. The main axis is east-north-east by west-south-west. It is composed of small rounded boulders and angular stones with some earth and is covered with turf. The cairn has been much robbed at the east end and in places along the sides, but still stands about 5½ ft. high for much of its length although it is lower towards the west end.

Fluidity of Burial Rites

Prehistoric burial rites of the disposal of the dead in long barrows, and their contents, were marked by great fluidity and variety as though personal ideas of what was fitting were allowed free play. Most burials were by inhumation, and they might range in number from two to more than twenty. Sometimes, indeed, the remains of as many as fifty persons have been found in one barrow although they contain on average only six bodies of all ages and both sexes. Buried, too, were bones of young animals, horses, cattle and sheep.

Well-attested Mortuary-houses

Internally, long barrows reflect a rather curious ritual. Excavation has shown that they contain timber features in the form of mortuary-houses which, taken with the condition of the skeletons,

69

The long barrow on Gourdon Hill – built 1000 years before the first Pyramid.

indicates that the barrow is only the last stage of a process. First, an open space was set aside and fenced off as a 'mortuary-enclosure', the dead being laid out at one end, sometimes on a low platform. The Dalladies barrow, thoroughly excavated by Professor Piggott during the summers of 1970 and 1971, revealed (and let us assume that the interior of the Gourdon cairn is roughly the same) that there had been a pre-existing timber building 26 ft. 2 ins. by 11 ft. 4 ins. and 4 ft. 9 ins. high, supported by nine posts, arranged in the pattern 1, 3, 3, 2, roofed in pointed fashion with birch bark and with a timber rail along the outer side. Nine post holes for large tree trunks were discovered, and there had been an imposing entrance façade of boulders at the east end together with a crude boulder wall surrounding the whole structure (see page 433).

The mortuary-house was presumably used for a considerable time for usually a proportion of the remains in long barrows belongs to people who had died some time before: in many cases the flesh on the bones had obviously rotted away before the bones were buried. These individuals are therefore represented by more or less complete parcels of bones, reserved until a suitable occasion had arisen to inter them with other relatives who had just died. Later bodies were normally added until sufficient numbers made it expedient to close the mortuary-enclosure. This was done with ceremonial, often including a funeral feast if one is to judge by the large numbers of animal bones which are often found nearby. Burning of the mortuary-house at this stage is a well-attested feature of the period, the boulder wall at Dalladies revealing that the stones were scorched. Finally, over the burnt mortuary-enclosure the tribe or family piled a long mound of earth – and this is what we see as a long barrow.

An Iron Age Fort with a View

Some 450 or 500 yards to the south-south-west of the long cairn on a steep-sided spur there is an oval Iron Age fort, measuring about 86 yards by 39 yards internally. On the north-east and north-west, where there are traces of an outer rampart, the main rampart survives as a mound of rubble 10 ft. thick and 2 ft. high, but elsewhere it has been reduced to a low scarp along which several stretches of outer facing-stones are visible. There is a possible entrance midway along the south-west side.

And now, our excursions completed, it remains only to return home. A mile and three-quarters takes us back to Inverbervie Square whence the journey to Stonehaven is ten miles exactly.

The clipper ship Cutty Sark, *as she was in the wool trade from Australia.*

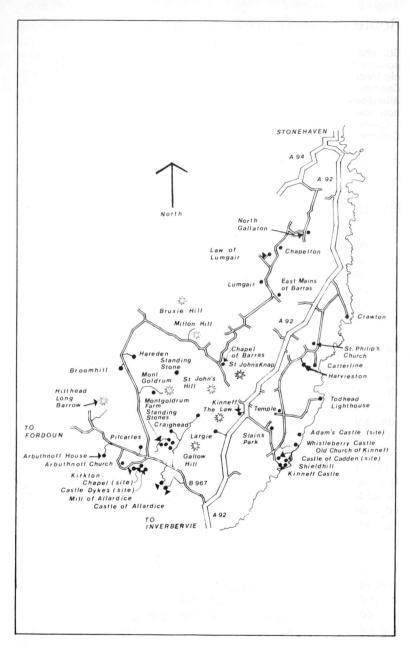

STONEHAVEN

A 94

A 92

North

North
Gallaton

Law of
Lumgair

Chapelton

Lumgair

East Mains
of Barras

Bruxie Hill

Mitton Hill

A 92

Crawton

Hareden
Standing
Stone

Chapel
of Barras
St John's Knap

St. Philip's
Church

Broomhill

Mont
Goldrum

St John's
Hill

Catterline

Harvieston

Hillhead
Long
Barrow

Montgoldrum
Farm
Standing
Stones
Craighead

Kinneff
The Law

Temple

Todhead
Lighthouse

TO
FORDOUN

Pitcarles

Largie

Slains
Park

Adam's Castle (site)

Whistleberry Castle
Old Church of Kinneff
Castle of Cadden (site)
Shieldhill
Kinneff Castle

Arbuthnott House
Arbuthnott Church

Gallow
Hill

Kirkton -
Chapel (site)
Castle Dykes (site)
Mill of Allardice
Castle of Allardice

B 967

A 92

TO
INVERBERVIE

Route Three

Stonehaven Square – Crawton – Fowlsheugh – Catterline – Todhead Light-
house – Whistleberry Castle – Adam's Castle – the old Church of Kinneff – the
old Manse of Kinneff – St Arnty's Well – Kinneff Castle – Shield Hill – Castle of
Cadden – Temple – Roadside of Kinneff – The Law of Largie – Castle of
Allardice – Chapel of Allardice – Castle Dykes – Church of Arbuthnott – Arbuth-
nott House – Plantation of Hillhead – Mont Goldrum – Bloomfield – Mitton Hill
– Chapel of Barras – Place of Barras – Lumgair – Law of Lumgair – North
Gallaton – Smiddymuir – Stonehaven Square.

Distance: 46½ miles, 40 by car and 6½ on foot, if every suggested deviation is
followed.

Round Kinneff and Catterline, Arbuthnott and the Lands of Barras

*concerning the Hogmanay Crawton Ball and the first steam
plough, Papal gifts buried under paving stones and half a
lighthouse underground, a sword-belt in a garden wall and
sermons in a milk churn, the oldest effigy of its type in
Scotland and the only Scottish book of its kind, the inventor
of John Bull and 'the voice of the Scottish earth'.*

Leave Stonehaven Square and follow the Stonehaven-Dundee
coast road (A92) towards the South. After 1⁴/₅ miles we pass the
lodge of Dunnottar Castle. This is followed by Gallaton Farm and
the road-end to the farm of Uras.

When we have travelled 3¾ miles in all, we arrive at a road
junction where there is a signpost for Crawton: here we turn left. In
a further four-fifths of a mile (carrying straight on at the T-junction)
we arrive at the car park near the remains of the village of Crawton.
Even if we have not the time to linger for a picnic on the beach
(perhaps a return visit can be made?), we must at least walk the 35
yards to the gate and the further 110 yards to the viewpoint at the
edge of the rise from which we can see the whole of Crawton Bay
beneath the almost perpendicular cliffs. We shall find it worthwhile.

Crawton Village
Houses which have now crumbled to decay and ruined gables
standing gaunt against the skyline are the only reminder that only a
little over 100 years ago (about 1860) there was a thriving little
village here on the west side of Crawton Ness. In its heyday it
consisted of sixty-one houses the inhabitants of which, with their

fleet of twelve boats and twenty to thirty fishermen, depended for their livelihood on the harvest of the sea. Even at the turn of the century Crawton was described in guide-books as a picturesque village, and at that time there were still six yawls and three drifters here, together with thirty fishermen, for the village was then still of considerable importance and not without its social attractions as well. Believe it or not, the 'Crawton Ball' was in those days a great annual social occasion and one of the highlights of the Hogmanay season on the Mearns coast, never considered complete without the presence of Sandy Mackie and his fiddle from Stonehaven.

Decline and Ruin

By the early years of this century the decline of Crawton had begun. White fishing was in the doldrums as fish were no longer plentiful inshore, and the death knell was sounded when motor power began to be introduced to the fishing fleets along the coast. With life becoming more and more difficult for this little fishing community families began one by one to break up their homes and to drift away, most of them to Stonehaven, with no one to take their places. Once started, the decline was rapid and, when the 1914-18 War broke out, Crawton as a village was non-existent. The last fisherman left in 1912.

Silence and Scenic Beauty

A path leads down to the shingly beach, but it is now grass-grown. The strange silence of this deserted village on its rocky promontory has been broken now for very many years only by the plaintive cry of the sole occupants, the sea birds, and the breaking of the waves on the rocks below. Not least of the scenic beauties to be discovered is the inlet called the Trollochy, to the east of the car park, with its well-nigh perpendicular bulwarks and rock fissures where the Crawton Burn tumbles over the face of the cliff into the wild seas which crash in fury on the rocky outcrops below.

A Mecca with a View

Each year Crawton is the Mecca of hundreds of tourists who come to admire such scenic beauties and doubtless to ponder over the doubtful values of a civilisation that has denuded the coast of many such colourful little communities. Crawton has not been forgotten, and this desolate little spot will amply repay the trouble spent in reaching it. The view that can be obtained seawards is magnificent, and it is possible on a clear day to trace shipping from the bay of

Aberdeen away past Todhead lighthouse on Todhead Point a mile and three-quarters to the south to well beyond Montrose.

Fowlsheugh, a Towering Wall of Rock

By far the most magnificent sight to visit, however, and outstanding on a coast-line famed for the grandeur of its rocky scenery is the forbidding bulk of Fowlsheugh, one of the most remarkable cliffs in the British Isles and only 700 yards away to the north from where we stand.

There are two ways to visit it – on foot from above or by sea from a boat hired at Stonehaven. For the moment let us view it from Crawton. To reach it you must walk 70 yards northwards from the car park to a small swing gate in the fence on your right beside the notice for the Royal Society for the Protection of Birds. 90 yards down the hill is the Crawton Burn which must be crossed (a relatively easy operation), and a stile will help you farther on your way. Now follow the footpath up the hill and along the cliff-top for another 490 yards and you will arrive at an awe-inspiring inlet of the sea with a promontory known as Henry's Scorth before you, a rock-face 200 ft. high with breath-taking fissures and caves at its base. Round this and a further 60 yards to the cliff edge and you have arrived at the top of Fowlsheugh, a towering wall of sheer rock, a full 200 ft. high as you have seen, falling perpendicularly to and in some parts overhanging the North Sea the waters of which, even at low tide, never recede from its base. It extends over a mile towards Trelung Ness to the north.

The rock itself is a conglomerate of the Lower Old Red Sandstone System of Scotland, composed of a mass of outsize pebbles joined together by a strong natural compacting element. As in appearance it resembles a mammoth plum-pudding, the conglomerate is in consequence popularly termed pudding-stone.

Spectacular Sea-bird Colony

It is not, however, solely on account of its awe-inspiring aspect that Fowlsheugh attracts visitors by land and sea but also because, due to the inaccessibility of its sides and the rock of which it is composed, it houses perhaps the most spectacular sea-bird colony on the mainland of Britain. Atmospheric action and constant weathering throughout the ages have caused many of the surface pebbles to loosen and fall away, leaving the face of the rock pitted with innumerable cavities and crevices which, with the rock ledges, form natural nesting and resting places for myriads of appreciative sea-birds.

The magnificent cliffs of Fowlsheugh, one of the reserves of the Royal Society for the Protection of Birds.

Fowlsheugh is one of the well-known breeding stations of the East Coast for all kinds of sea-bird, migratory and otherwise, and a marvellous sight it is to see this great cliff in the nesting season in early summer with clouds of wings with accompanying bedlam of squawks and screeches: the spectacle of myriads of birds on the rock face is most interesting and instructive and will well repay a visit from others besides bird lovers. Many thousands of guillemots, kittiwakes and herring gulls nest here. In smaller numbers are pretty and perky tammy-nories, known also as the Greenland parrot or puffin, razor-bills, fulmars, shags, rock-doves, crows and jackdaws. Although cormorants are numerous along the coast throughout the year, none breed on Fowlsheugh, and greater and lesser black-backed gulls nest only sporadically.

Fulmar Petrels

It is believed that about 1930 the first pair of fulmar petrels came to Fowlsheugh. Said to be natives of lonely St Kilda, these birds have been common in the Orkney Islands, but it was only in the early 1920's, say bird authorities, that they first began to come farther south to establish themselves as part of the bird life along the East Coast. A distinctive point about the bird is the straight wing compared with the curved wing of the gull, and the egg is about the size of a hen's, in shape of course having the non-roll characteristic of most cliff birds' eggs. As the fulmar petrel lays only one egg per year, increase in numbers is slow.

Peregrine Falcons

It is asserted also that each season a single pair of that noblest bird of prey, the peregrine falcon, have their nest on the rocks of Fowlsheugh amid an abundant food supply. A peculiar feature of these birds is that they suffer no others of their kind near their nests so that, in consequence, never more than one pair frequent the area in any one year. A further peculiarity is that if one of a pair is killed, its place is taken without fail the succeeding year.

Birds' Eggs and Kittiwakes

At one time the Earl Marischal of Dunnottar Castle employed a tacksman or lessee all summer with the privilege of taking seabirds' eggs and young kittiwakes, *a delicious meat*, from the fastness of Fowlsheugh. As once on St Kilda, men were lowered from the cliff-top by a rope to reach the nests. This practice was in vogue in the early years of the last century, and it has been recorded that no accident ever happened although on one occasion some person or persons maliciously cut the rope almost through overnight. The interference was fortunately discovered before the next day's operations, the tacksman being saved from a watery grave in the twelve fathoms over which he was accustomed to dangle.

High Guillemot Mortality

The birds themselves have not always been immune from accidental death in the waters around the cliff, and considerable alarm was occasioned among bird lovers at the turn of the century by the high mortality among the divers, or 'queets' as they are known locally, which frequent its rugged face. These birds obtain their food beneath the water, and from their perch of perhaps 100 ft. high dive down till near the water they change their direction into a beautiful curve and pass far out with the impetus thus gained. The trouble began when in 1896 the Crown let the right of salmon fishing, by stake-net, at the rock foot. There were placed in the sea at Fowlsheugh three nets with consequences disastrous in the extreme. As the birds sought their food, they either became enmeshed or followed the leader, as fish do, into the bag of the net in which they were able to rise to the surface but could not escape. Thousands were thus slowly drowned or hanged in the meshes, and many would-be rescuers related how the birds' bodies were torn to pieces in their struggles since the nets cut deeply into their flesh. Altogether it was a most painful sight, and this destruction occurred daily during the hatching period. Since the total revenue obtained by the Crown amounted to only £70 per annum, it was felt by people in and around Stonehaven that fishing should be prohibited in the immediate vicinity of Fowlsheugh. Strong representations were made to the authorities in London who had not foreseen the consequences of their action in letting the fishing. As a result the conditions of the lease were revised, and no nets were permitted on the mile of water here until August 1st by which date the rearing of the young birds was completed and many of the denizens of the rock had disappeared.

Fowlsheugh from Stonehaven by Sea

As mentioned earlier, Fowlsheugh can also be reached by leaving the main Stonehaven-Inverbervie road at the farm of Gallaton, but in order to derive full advantage from a visit all this part of the coast from Stonehaven past Dunnottar Castle to what was once the red-roofed little fisher town perched on Crawton Ness is best visited by boat from Stonehaven. A boat for hire is sometimes available during the summer months, and few more interesting stretches of cliff than this are to be seen on the east coast of Scotland.

A Rewarding Experience

During the season, when the young birds are fledged but have not yet reached the stage when they forsake their birthplace, a gunshot, or even a sudden hand clap, will result in the scaring from their rocky hiding-places of an unbelievable mass of birds. An excursion to the foot of the rock is an experience that no visitor to Stonehaven should miss. One is rewarded by a spectacle which gives some idea of a peep into a long past geological epoch before the balance of nature was disturbed by the coming of man.

Cliffs, Crags and Caves

As one's boat emerges from the lee of the quaint, green-snouted Downie Point, there opens southwards a striking panorama of cliffs and bays all of which bear witness to the gigantic power of marine erosion that prevails for several miles along the coast. This picturesque succession of precipitous sea-cliffs and crags that seem ready to topple into the sea is worn into the strangest shapes, into tunnels and single stacks, into 'bullers' with turf-bound slopes on top, into many interesting creeks and caves in which the sea moans. From Downie Point to a little beyond Dunnottar Castle the conglomerate rock occupies an almost vertical position. The beds belong to the Old Red Sandstone formation, making in all the enormous thickness of 8000 ft.

On rounding Downie Point, we come to Strathlethan Bay with its rock of Dunnicaer[1] beyond which appear the Bowduns with the 'Deil's Kettle' (a blow-hole) at the base. Between Bowdun Head, just south of the War Memorial on the Black Hill above, and Fowlsheugh there are some ten caves, inhabited in several instances by flocks of rock-pigeons, and many interesting nooks and crannies well worth a visit. A magnificent view is obtained of Dunnottar Castle,[2] standing menacingly high overhead, and one can appreciate to the fullest extent the wisdom of the choice of such a commanding site and the difficulties to be surmounted before an enemy could reach the summit of the rock.

The striking grandeur of Dunnottar Castle, as seen from the sea. Built on a nearly inaccessible promontory, it is one of the most exciting castles in Scotland.

[1] See *Highways and Byways Round Stonehaven* p. 127.
[2] Ibid. pp. 130-153.

The Lang Gallery

Just over a mile south of the castle stands in the sea the mighty rock
called Gull's Crag. And between the grey towers of the old stronghold of the Earls Marischal and Fowlsheugh there are four subterranean passages. The most remarkable of these is one named from
its great length the 'Lang Gallery' under a promontory three-
quarters of a mile south of Dunnottar Castle, a natural subterranean passage 40 ft. in height and 30 ft. in width in the face of a
perpendicular rock 150 ft. high. With a favourable tide a small boat
is able to pass in at one opening of this navigable cavern and emerge
again into daylight about 200 yards from the point of entry, being
enveloped in total darkness when about the middle of the gallery
which has gradually narrowed.

As one sails farther south for a fourth mile, the cliffs rise into the
remarkable mile-long straight wall without any deep indentations
that is Fowlsheugh itself with its many tens of thousands of swarm-
ing, clamorous sea-fowl during the breeding season. The quaint old
lines of Dunbar are irresistibly recalled,

> *The air was dirkit with the fowlis*
> *That cam' with yammeris and with yowlis,*
> *With shryking, skreeking, skrymming scoulis,*
> *And meikle nayis and showtes.*

The traveller by road is apt to pass unsuspecting by all this for
little or nothing can be seen from the inland side as we have
discovered.

The Turbulent Beauty of Catterline Waterfall

But we digress: we must be on our way. We return along the road we
have come for only half a mile until we reach the fork to the left
which we are to follow straight on to the village of Catterline. You
may not have the time or consider it worthwhile, but if you wish to
visit the entrancing Catterline waterfall and pool, you must leave
your car at the fork here by the Mill of Uras bridge and walk
southwards along the busy A92 for 350 yards. On the top of the rise
a gate is reached on the left. When you cross into the field here, you
should already hear the minor roar of the cascading waters of the
Catterline Burn, and a descent of some 90 yards by a path through
the gorse will take you to where you will almost immediately catch a
glimpse of a splash of white between towering tree-lined slopes. A
few more steps and the almost turbulent beauty of the place is
revealed in all its green and leafy glory. During the last War vibra-

tion from the explosion of a German bomb which fell in the area caused a landslide on one of the steep sides of the Catterline Burn.

Returning to our car, we pass the farm of Cloak in two-fifths of a mile and, in a further 400 yards or so, when we see the gleaming whiteness of Todhead lighthouse and of the village ahead of us, St Peter's Episcopal School with what was once Catterline Episcopal School adjacent to it. Here is a joint reminder that, as is usual on the Mearns coast, the fishermen were Episcopalians.

St Philip's Episcopal Church

From 1690 for more than a century and a half there was no Episcopal Church on account of the Penal Laws, but in 1848 the present beautiful little church of St Philip was opened and consecrated by Bishop A.P. Forbes of Brechin. This followed the build-up of the fishing village after its small harbour had been erected. In 1842 a group of nineteen male communicants from Catterline, speaking for a community of 132, petitioned the Diocesan Synod, showing their need of a church since the Episcopal Chapel at Drumlithie was seven miles away. In 1843 they elected their first pastor, the Rev. James Stevenson from Stornoway. From the inception of St Philip's to 1928 the Church had its own minister resident at Catterline – in the eighty-five years there were seven rectors – but from 1928 to the present day it has been served successively from Inverbervie and Stonehaven. Since 1931 the rectors of St James' in Stonehaven have also been rectors of St Philip's. Services are presently held once a month.

The Old School

A school followed alongside the church, and it remained Catterline Episcopal School until what the Education Committee rather ponderously called 'undenominationalisation' on December 5th, 1955. This was a prelude to the building of the present fine, modern Catterline School in 1956 with a roll of forty-one. This school has fallen heir to three schools – Catterline Episcopal School, Brackmuirhill School and Barras School – most of the pupils coming from the large farming area in the hinterland. The roll presently varies between fifty and sixty.

The Old Episcopal Church

And now let us carry on to Catterline Bridge – late 18th or early 19th century – only 350 yards farther on. On the brow of the brae on our right on a not undesirable site overlooking Catterline Burn with its many linns between Birdiesknap and the sea are relics of the old pre-Reformation Episcopal kirk of Katerin surviving in the old kirkyard. Given to the Abbey of Arbroath by William the Lion, it was confirmed by Turpin, Bishop of Brechin, between 1178 and 1198 and dedicated to Catherine, probably a companion of Bridget on her Pictish tour or, it may be, St Cathan. The church probably went out of use when the parishes of Kinneff and Catterline were united in 1719. Evidences of the building survive in a few place names, and we know the Knights Templars were here, the religious and military order founded at Jerusalem about 1118. A rude, carved ogival-headed ambry or sacrament house, probably of 16th century date, and the fragment of a mediaeval coffin slab bearing an incised cross and sword are built into the south kirkyard wall, and the graveyard contains the burial-place of the Douglasses of Barras. The gate piers are dated 1817.

A Delectable Village Show-piece

But our road is to the left, and we should carry straight on to the end and up the hill to the car park of the Creel Inn before us. Let us leave our car here.[1] If we walk a mere 40 yards along the road from the car park towards the row of fisher-type cottages, we can begin to see, perhaps, what a delectable little fisher village Catterline is, the showpiece of the parish. Perched on a long, wedge-shaped bluff of land and forming an elevated half moon ridge above towering Old Red Sandstone cliffs with fine, natural arches in the rocks below, it stands above a picturesque, rocky bay with temptingly irregular curves. Down below us is the little harbour 300 or 400 yards away (you can take your car) with its jagged and tumbled rocks behind it and a steep, grassy cliff rising up in the background. Crowning this cliff in splendid isolation is the Watch House, the oldest structure there (it dates from about 1750) which was built as a 'look-out house' for the detection of smuggling for the remoteness of this little haven made it a favourite resort of smugglers in the 18th century. The Watch House is now used as an artist's studio.

[1] There used to be a favourite walk on a right of way between Catterline and Todhead Lighthouse which is just under ¾ mile distant as the crow flies. The walk begins at a stile across the fence opposite the foot of the steps from the Creel Inn car park to the road below. On this right of way an 'Auld Briggie' across the Catterline Burn was erected about 1930 by public subscription and frequently repaired thereafter by subscribers. Unfortunately, as the footbridge is now in a state of dilapidation, the walk can no longer be recommended unless the intrepid adventurer with time on his hands is prepared to ford the burn. In case any reader wishes to assess the situation, perhaps I should say that the 'Auld Briggie' is only 160 yards away.

Neolithic and Bronze Age Finds

Like most of the area through which we are touring today, Catterline was well populated in Late Neolithic and Bronze Age times from 2000 to 1400 B.C. if we are to judge by the number of burials and finds discovered in a relatively small area. Rather an important contribution was made to archaeological knowledge in the Northeast when a valuable cist was unearthed at Catterline around 1924. A more recent excavation of the same kind was made in the village when a garden was being landscaped and a new lawn prepared: in this case grains found in a beaker were sent to a laboratory in Denmark for dating and identification. A third short cist was unearthed at Upper Mains of Catterline on March 17th, 1923, and a fourth in 1958 in a fluvio-glacial deltaic deposit of sand and gravel 140 yards north-west of Purlicknowe on the A92, an area just four-fifths of a mile west of Catterline where previous cists are recorded. This last cist was built of sandstone flags and measured 30 ins. $\times$ 16$\frac{1}{2}$ ins. $\times$ 13 ins. It contained the bones of a child about five years old and a beaker with, inside it, a fragment of glass, the stem epidermis of grain and the pupae of flies. In the early 1920's a discovery was made at Roadside of Catterline when the occupant of a cist was a man who had received a severe head injury, while 1$\frac{1}{10}$ miles farther south and just off the A92 to the east further stone cists and urns have been found.

A surface find of a different kind was made in 1971 when a large polished stone axe was found on the shore of Catterline Bay immediately below the line of cliff-top cottages known as South Row. The axe of pale brown, fine-grained quartzite is 7$\frac{9}{10}$ ins. long with a maximum breadth of 3 ins., tapering to $\frac{1}{2}$ in. at the flattened butt, and a maximum thickness of 1$\frac{3}{5}$ ins. The finely ground cutting edge shows no sign of wear, indicating that it has never been used. Nor does the tool appear to have been finished as some rough parts of the surface suggest that the final polishing was not done. The axe may be seen in Dundee City Museum. Finally, 640 yards due south of the Creel Inn and 200 yards north of Millhill, a barbed and tanged arrow-head was unearthed. Retained by workmen, it is now lost.

Scanty Historical Records

Historical records concerning the old-fashioned village of Catterline are scanty, but it seems to have evolved as a fishing settlement around its bay and small harbour formed by a stone pier projecting south. It first appears on record in the 12th century as Katerlin (a spelling which we have already met), and about 1206 the green 'Reath' of Catterline from the Mill of Catterline below us on our west side to Braidon's Bay, two-fifths of a mile south of where we now stand, was granted to the monks of Arbroath Abbey by the Norman family of Fitz-Bernard who had been introduced among the people of the Mearns by King William. They were ancestors of the Sibbalds of Kair. 'The Reath' begins in the field behind the South Row cottages and can be clearly seen from the top of the hill after a walk of only 140 yards along their frontage.

The word 'reath' or 'raith' really signifies a circular earthwork mound or place of defence as does, indeed, the name Catterline itself, derived from 'cathair', a fort, and 'linn', a waterfall. Another rath used to be beside the old churchyard upon which we have already commented. It was not much more than a fortified farm-house which had been a place of defence at one time. The rath was quite traceable a few years before the turn of the century.

Catterline was once a parish in its own right, but in 1719 was joined to Kinneff at the instance of the Presbytery of Fordoun. By 1793 the village was a 'sea-town' in a very small way, but a very rapid build-up came when the tiny harbour was constructed by the then superior, Viscount Arbuthnott.

'Primitive Frontier-style Impact'

The nucleus of the village is its fisher-type cottages, set in rows facing the cliffs. And it is this cliff-top housing arranged around the wide sweep of the bay which gives Catterline its considerable character. Most important, of course, are the early 19th century South Row cottages, stepped to the slope, *a rare and possibly unique example of an authentic early fishing village settlement not yet neutralised by subsequent development* as was expressed by the official reporter appointed by the Secretary of State when conservation (now in being) was discussed. *It would be a pity*, he continued, *to reduce its primitive frontier-style impact without a compelling reason*. The second section of the housing consists of what one can see from South Row of the rest of the wide-sweeping bay, and the third section consists of the Coastguard Cottages with the central part of the village behind on the left. All is on a simple scale appropriate to the unsophisticated primitive pattern it is desired to conserve.

Fishing

At no time in its history does Catterline seem to have been a very important fishing station. Neither the old nor the new *Statistical*

Account has more than a passing reference to it beyond an allusion to *drunkenness, theft and perjury* and the fact that *smuggling has been suppressed*. In 1845 no more than nine boats, with twenty-two fishermen, fished from here. By the 1880's the number of yawls and drifters had increased to twenty-eight while the fishermen mustered thirty. Every summer eight boats, all engaged by a local curer, left Catterline for the herring fisheries, while during the other months of the year twelve yawls or so went to the line-fishing. So did the importance of Catterline fisheries increase until about 1900 when the prosperity of the village began to decrease.

In the early years of this century the village possessed six or seven whitefishing boats, and there was actually a boom during the War years. But by 1930 only some half-dozen boats sailed from the harbour, and only some twenty elderly fishermen were left to find a more or less profitable occupation catching lobsters or, in the winter, fishing with hand-lines. In 1926 only two whitefishing boats remained alongside the busy salmon fishing coble. Now one white-fishing boat and the salmon coble have gone so that only one redoubtable vessel and two fishermen still survive to operate from the tiny harbour where once, in the words of Robin Munro, Catter-line's poet, *all men were fishermen*. Latterly only water-skiers have found the pier-sheltered little bay a perfect amphitheatre for their sport. It is not easy to explain the decay of Catterline as a fishing centre: the principal reason was possibly the high cost of transport and the distance of the village from any large town.

Joan Eardley

Today Catterline is famous for its colony of artists, past and present. James C. Morrison 'discovered' Catterline and for a time made his home here, exploiting the visual inspiration which he found; Mrs Annette Stephen over three decades has depicted it in works of great delicacy; Miss Lil Neilson, who has lived for many years at No. 2 South Row, continues to paint the sea and its wildness. Best known, however, is the late Joan Eardley (1921-63), a leader of a modern Glasgow School who was already an artist of great achievement before she came to the North-east in 1950. In Catter-line she lived first in the Creel Inn, then at No. 1 South Row (the top house) and finally in No. 18 Catterline where she died. In Catterline she was to discover sombre grandeur in the wildness of the sea and the menace of storms in the dead of winter with a pale, yellow sun scarcely breaking through the heavy storm-clouds and the cottages of South Row reeling almost drunkenly under the impact of the

85

weather on their exposed cliff-top. These South Row cottages have featured in so many of Joan Eardley's pictures that the terrace has been made famous and become a shrine visited by many.

Original Primitive Perfection

By the force of her intense impressionism she etched upon many minds at home and abroad the uniqueness of the Catterline scene. And this stood her adopted community in good stead when the issue of conservation arose. It is true that up and down the east coast of Scotland havens with an obvious resemblance to Catterline still survive in some sense: in this corner of the country Muchalls, Skateraw and Cove Bay are examples that spring to mind. But not one of them has been left in its original primitive perfection as Catterline has been, and it is obvious that the visual factors which Joan Eardley so glowingly interpreted lend it a special dimension of drama.

This was very well brought out in the Aberdeen Art Gallery introduction to the exhibition of her works there some years ago:

> *We are helped to see, looking at her work, the straggle of low cottages along the cliff-top against the sky, the sheer drop to the little bay with its tiny fishing harbour between the jagged rocks, the marvellous fluctuating fusion between the two, and the high hinterland of fields in summer and autumn luxuriance, with hay and oats and wild flowers in profusion in the bright bee-laden air, or bleak with snow and stubble in the hard brittle cold of the North-east winter.*

Because of Joan Eardley's celebration of Catterline in paint, and also because of its significance as a precedent, the official conservation of a coastal strip of Kincardine, including both Catterline and Crawton and extending as far inland as the Church of St Philip and its rectory, is an event of national importance. It will save from mutilation a small but perfect example of the Scottish cliff-top fishing haven as it was in the heyday of man's partnership with nature in this unique and now abandoned form of economic adventure. It is visionaries like Joan Eardley who have shown to the world what this pattern of life really means, its hidden poetry and splendour, its openness to a terrible beauty on the lip of the land, quite separate and remote from the industrial life that is the lot of modern man.

The famous early 19th century South Row cottages on the cliff-top in Catterline which have featured in so many of Joan Eardley's pictures and which became a shrine visited by her admirers. They are now conserved by the Secretary of State. Joan Eardley originally lived in No. 1, the far-away top house in the picture.

'Winter Sea IV', a picture of Catterline harbour painted in 1958 by Joan Eardley when she was 37. It is in Aberdeen Art Gallery. The full drama of an angry and relentless North Sea has been reconstituted in thick paint on board, applied by the force of her intense impressionism with an almost sculptured vigour. Viewed from South Row is the little harbour with its jagged and tumbled rocks behind and the steep grassy cliff crowned by the Watch House.

En Route to Todhead

Now we must be on our way. We return to Catterline Bridge, take the left fork up the hill past the site of the old church and in some 250 yards thereafter reach a T-junction at Mains of Catterline Farm where a stone axe (now in Edinburgh) was found. Here we turn left, taking a last excellent view of the South Row cottages and the Reath. In some 400 yards or so we pass on our left the road to the farm of Harvieston where the steam plough was first tried in the North. Notice the stook or corn-sheaves sign. In another 360 yards we take the left fork at the Give Way sign, and now it's straight on past the farms of Bellfield and Fernyflatt until in $1^3/_{10}$ miles we turn left for Todhead lighthouse exactly a mile away.

Todhead Lighthouse

The lighthouse of Todhead (literally, the promontory frequented by foxes – and they are still there!) is the most powerful light between Scurdy Ness at Montrose and Girdleness. It was built by the Northern Lighthouse Commission, the engineer being one of the family of Stevenson of whom the best known to posterity is Robert Louis Stevenson, the writer. It first sent its rays flashing out to sea on December 20th, 1897. The lighthouse with its entasised (or convex) column and corbelled gallery stands prominently on the lip of huge cliffs which fall sheer to the ocean bed below and is said to be the shortest in the British Isles, being 42 ft. from the top of the dome to the base of the tower above ground.

But herein lies its secret for, although to the naked eye Todhead seems from ground level stumpy in appearance, half of the lighthouse is underground, hewn by manual labour out of the solid rock upon which it stands. In order to counteract the shortness of the tower sufficiently to give play to the drop weights operating the clockwork mechanism of the powerful light overhead it was found necessary to excavate as far down as the tower went up. It is recorded that such were the difficulties in the construction of Todhead that no fewer than three firms were engaged on it in turn before the work was actually completed.

The light flashes four times every thirty seconds with an intensity of over 300,000 candle power. The beam can be seen nearly seventeen miles out to sea in clear weather. Since the lighthouse became automatic, two 3,500 watt bulbs have replaced the paraffin light, and if the main power fails, there is a generator which goes on automatically twenty-five seconds later. The weight on an endless chain which once drove the machinery is still there, lying idle, a reminder of days when the keeper had to wind it up to the top every fifty-five minutes.

The Fog-horn

The present fog-horn is the third in use, two previous horns having been placed on the rocky promontory nearer the sea on the point of a headland overlooking a 100 ft. drop. The original fog-horn was installed on August 26th, 1898, less than a year after the lighthouse itself was opened. To its left was sited the larger and more substantial fog-horn tower which came into use just before the War. Now the electric horn is placed slightly behind the main light in line with the balcony of the lighthouse. It has four blasts of 2.5 seconds' duration every sixty seconds, the signal having a range of four miles through the murk, day and night, when the mists hang over the rocky coast.

Wrecks and a Spy

The rugged nature of the coast on either side of the lighthouse claimed many ships before and after it was erected. In November, 1917, for instance, the London steamer, *Reindeer*, was driven on the rocks at the Muckle Shield just south of Todhead. All her crew perished, and the cargo of pit props was lost. In 1933 another ship with a similar cargo, the Norwegian steamer, *Granero*, went to her doom north of the lighthouse at Crawton.

During World War I a small garrison was stationed at Todhead. It was the scene of an incident which created much excitement in the district. A sentry on duty in front of the storehouse, which served as a guardroom, saw a suspicious looking figure. Getting no satisfaction in reply to his challenge, he was satisfied that he had surprised a spy and opened fire. The figure escaped, but the bullet marks on a dyke from the only shots of the War in the Mearns were pointed out by local inhabitants long afterwards.

Whistleberry Castle

We must now retrace the mile of our original road where we turn left. In ³/₅ mile we take the farm road, again to the left, noticing as we turn the old church of Kinneff in the trees in front of us. In a quarter of a mile we reach the farm of Whistleberry. If we proceed through the steading and get out of the car at the end of the road where it overlooks the sea, we shall see precariously perched on a narrow point of land the ruin of Whistleberry Castle. Only one gaunt fragment of wall face remains and this is probably of 16th century date. There are traces of a curtain-wall enclosing the promontory, and within it are remains of at least two buildings. Entry to the castle was through a gatehouse, and the abutments for a drawbridge are visible in the ditch which bars the landward approach. Most of the walls have been reduced to their lowest courses. This fortalice or manor as it was sometimes called was associated with the Lindsays of Edzell and was once occupied by Sir Alexander Lindsay of Glenesk who fought at Otterburn (1388) and fell at Verneuil (1424). The castle was inhabited up to the middle of the 17th century. In 1633 it is referred to in a document *cum maneriei loco vocato Qwhissilberie* (the estate along with the manor-house called Whistleberry), relating to the heritage of Sir Robert Arbuthnott.

Wild Wall-flower

During the earlier part of the month of May the promontory on which Whistleberry Castle stands is a most attractive sight, covered as it is by wild wall-flower (cheiranthus cheiri), a cruciferous plant, that is one with four equal petals arranged crosswise, which was introduced to Britain about 1573 from southern Europe. Some say it was brought for the first time to the garden of Dunnottar Castle by a traveller from abroad. At any rate it is now naturalised on old walls, rock cuttings and castles such as Dunnottar and Whistleberry here.

Adam's Castle

Of similar construction to but larger and stronger than Whistleberry Castle was Adam's Castle, a *stronghold* which stood some 600 yards to the north. Tradition is silent about it, but it was probably a maiden castle (that is, a fortified, defensive site, presumably impregnable) for it is called by Christison a *maiden kaim on the coast*. A kaim is a pinnacle resembling a cock's comb and hence a fortress. From Whistleberry Farm the flat-topped coastal promontory on which Adam's Castle stood can be seen quite clearly less than half-way towards the farm of Hallhill on the skyline and more or less below the cottage which stands midway.

The Old Church of Kinneff

We must now be on our way to visit the old church of Kinneff which we saw earlier. Some of our party may wish to walk there by the right of way from Whistleberry Farm. You'll see it quite clearly across the fields, and it's only half a mile distant. But the car must return to the main road, turn left and travel the 230 yards to Kirkcorner where we turn left again down the steep brae to reach the gate of the church in another 350 yards.

Although in bygone days at least four castle strongholds stood within its bounds, the parish of Kinneff might well have occupied a very insignificant place in the pages of history had it not been for the long history of its church and the men who ministered therein. For this church overlooking the rocky sea-shore was the place where, during the siege of Dunnottar Castle by Cromwell's troops, the Regalia of Scotland, Crown, Sceptre and Sword of State, were conveyed from the castle in March, 1652, and given into the charge of the minister here, Rev. James Grainger or Granger, while General Overton and his successors were besieging that fortress and endeavouring to obtain possession of them.[1]

Derivation of the Place-name

Although it is quite possible that, linguistically, the place-name of Kinneff is derived from one of the kings named Kenneth who is alleged to have built the castle here, or to have had a residence in the area, there are no historical data available to confirm or refute the legend. Rather is it almost certain to have come from Ceinnech or Cainneach or Kenneth, born 517, who, like Kieran of Fetteresso, was one of the Irish saints and a co-disciple of Columba in Ireland before he came among the Picts in this region, content to live, it is said, on the sunless braes at the foot of the Monadhliath Mountains in Inverness-shire. Next to Bridget and Columba he was the favourite Irish saint in Scotland, and the record of his miracles in the calendars reads like a fairy-tale.

The Original Church

The church you see is, of course, not the original building which played its part against the usurping power of the Cromwellian soldiery. For the kirk of Kinneff, dedicated to St Arnty or Arnold or Anthony, patron saint of the parish who settled here in 700 A.D., is almost certainly a Celtic foundation. It is likely that the parish was not fully established and endowed until the 13th century when the kirk became a foundation belonging

[1] See *Highways and Byways Round Stonehaven* pp. 144-145.

to the Priory of St Andrews. It was consecrated on August 5th, 1242, by the famous Bishop David de Bernham, Bishop of St Andrews and Chancellor of Scotland.

Of the original church of Kinneff few vestiges remain, and nothing that recalls its architectural proportions. All the more welcome, therefore, is the brief description which occurs in Macfarlane's *Geographical Collections* where a writer at the close of the 17th century informs us it was

> *a very old fabrick, the walls thereof being supported by eight strong butrishes of stone and the roof by pillars of wood, so that probably it is the oldest countrey church presently possess'd and in use of any in Scotland.*

The mediaeval church of Kinneff would have been a simple, rectangular building with an altar placed against the east gable but with few other furnishings. It would have been easy to rearrange for Reformed worship. The altar would be removed and a pulpit placed against the south wall. There would be no pews, but a long table and benches would be brought in when the Sacrament of the Lord's Supper was observed.

The old church of Kinneff. In the original building on the same site the Regalia of Scotland were safely concealed during the time of the Commonwealth. The building, no longer used as a church, has now been restored by a Trust formed in 1979 under the chairmanship of the Right Hon. the Viscount of Arbuthnott.

Theft of a Silver Chalice

In the 15th century the church was broken into by one Straiton, proprietor of the Knox of Benholm and a notorious thief of the period, who made off with one of the most sacred altar utensils. He was caught and charged with *the wrangwis spoliacioun of a silver chalice out of the Kirk of Kyneff*, and the theft was proved against him. It was a case, however, of other days other ways, and the penalty imposed was to restore the chalice

> *als gude as it was tane, or the avale thereof, as it ma prefit it was worth the tym it was tane.*

The kirk of Catterline was annexed by Kinneff in 1709, and King-hornie near Inverbervie, famous as the landing place of King David II, which, likewise, had been an independent entity in the diocese of Brechin, also came under the jurisdiction of Kinneff. Bervie, on the other hand, is believed to have been before the Reformation part of Kinneff parish and later to have achieved ecclesiastical independence.

It appears that in the early days there was a chapel attached to the old church of Kinneff, and several chroniclers consider it to have been that which stood at Barras. The site we shall pass later in our journey.

Building of the Old Church

The original church survived into the first quarter of the 18th century but was demolished and superseded in 1738 by the old parish church we are now visiting the west wall of which is probably the only part known by Mr Grainger whom we shall meet in a moment. It is probable that the 1738 kirk retained the original two south doors which, together with windows set in the finer masonry of the earlier kirk, could be quite easily traced when the harling was removed during the restoration of 1981. Then it was seen that the 1738 kirk was merely a modification and heightening of the old walls of the original building.

There have been various restorations from time to time, the north aisle and internal staircase being added in 1876 when fragments of the 13th century building were found and when the church assumed its present T-plan. This was during the ministry of Dr William Mearns whose coat of arms appears over the entrance. In the east gable is a small Norman window, and there are five Gothic windows in the south wall. Over the 1876 north-east porch can be seen traces of the door which led from an entrance stair to the gallery or loft of the 1738 kirk. The picturesque, ancient classic belfry contains one of the two bells in Kincardineshire made in Holland, the other being in Banchory. Round the rim is inscribed the name of the maker, 'PIETER OSTENS TE ROTTERDAH – AO: 1679'. The initials 'M.J.H.' on the west side of the bell may refer to one of the Honymans four of whom were ministers of the parish as we shall see.

Some Early Ministers

When William the Conqueror came from Normandy, there came with him Hugh de Montfort who fought at Hastings and afterwards received from his Prince lands in Kent, Suffolk and Norfolk. A century later his descendants had penetrated to the Mearns, and the manor of Kinneff was granted to them by William the Lion.

Around 1211-14 a member of this de Montfort family became parson of Kinneff, and in 1296 *Magister Robertus, persona, Ecclesiae de Kynef*, with the clergy of the kirks of Glenbervie, Garvock and Dunnottar, did homage to Edward I during the great struggle for the independence of Scotland after the unfortunate death of Alexander III.

When we pick up the threads once more around 1567, we find Alexander Keith, the first post-Reformation cleric, with a stipend of £26 Scots,

> *holding the parishes of Katerling, Barvie, Arbuthnott, Garvott and Kinneff.*

Under his supervision, James Simpson was reader at Kinneff, Bervie and Catterline with an annual salary of £33 6/8. Mr James Raitt, who succeeded Keith, died in 1620, and the church was taken over by Mr James Strachan. In 1639 came the Second Reformation, and Strachan was removed from his charge by the Covenanters. It is interesting to know that, after the Restoration, the Estates of Parliament granted him the sum of £100 Scots out of the vacant stipends in the northern shires in consideration that he

> *hes bien put to great sufferings these many yeeres by gone, and always given constant testimony of his loyaltie and affection to the King's Majestie, and injustly deposed from his service at the kirk of Kinneff for the same.*

Rev. James Grainger and the Honours Three

As far as is known, Strachan's successor was the Rev. James Grainger whom we have already mentioned and who was admitted minister on the orders of the General Assembly. Mr Grainger is possibly the most famous of all the ministers of Kinneff for it was by him and his wife that, wrapped up in linen cloths, the 'Honours Three' were safely concealed during the time of the Commonwealth.[1] These precious articles were carried by the minister's wife from Dunnottar Castle through the very ranks of the besiegers and by her own well-managed plans and those of the lady of Governor Ogilvy were buried at night under the clay floor of the ancient parish church. Let James Grainger speak for himself in his authentic account of the secret disposition of the Regalia, dated 31st March, 1652, and given to the Countess of Marischal:

> *I, Mr James Grainger, minister of Kinneff, grant me to have in my custody the Honours of the Kingdome, viz. the Crown, Sceptre, and Sword. For the Crown and Sceptre, I raised the pavement-stone just before the pulpit, in the night tyme, and digged under it ane hole, and layed down the stone just as it before, and removed the mould that remained, that none would have discerned the stone to have been raised at all; the Sword, again, at the west end of the church, amongst some common seits that stand there, I digged down in the ground betwixt the foremost of these seats, and layed it down within the case of it, and covered it up, as that removing the superfluous mould it could not be discerned by anybody; and if it shall please God to call me by death before they be called for, your Ladyship will find them in that place.*

The risk of detection was not yet over. Once every three months they dug up the Regalia at night to air them before a fire to preserve them from damp and injury. Having wrapped them in fresh cloths, they buried them again. So did they remain hidden but not uncared for for a period of eight stormy years until the Restoration while an English army searched for them in vain. If, at the services on Sundays, Mr Grainger's eyes occasionally wandered towards two particular spots on the floor, he kept his thoughts to himself. It would have been hard for a strict Presbyterian minister not to admire the Sceptre and Sword – even though they were gifts from a Pope!

[1] See *Highways and Byways Round Stonehaven* pp. 144-145.

The Belt of the Sword of State was retained by the Governor, Sir George Ogilvy, and was discovered nearly a century and a half later built into the garden wall of the family's house at Barras. It was presented to the nation by the Rev. S. Ogilvy Baker in May, 1893.

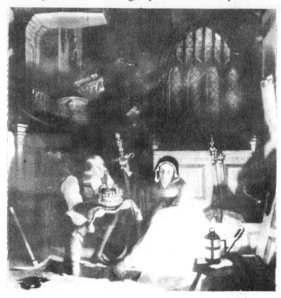

'The Concealment of the Scottish Regalia in the Kirk of Kinneff, 1652.' A painting by A. Chisholm.

The Honours Restored to the Nation

In 1660 the 'Honours of Scotland' were restored to the former Governor of Dunnottar Castle, Sir George Ogilvy of Barras, and handed back to the nation at an impressive ceremony in Edinburgh Castle. When the Parliament of Scotland was finally dissolved, they were locked up on March 26th, 1707, in an oak chest in the Crown Room there and for many years lay neglected and almost forgotten, the key lost, until Sir Walter Scott rescued them from obscurity. Following efforts made by him, the Prince Regent, afterwards King George IV, issued a warrant, dated October 28th, 1817, to the Scottish Officers of State and to Sir Walter himself to open the Crown Room and search for the Regalia. So on February 14th, 1818, the Honours were found. Sir Adam Ferguson, friend and neighbour of Sir Walter Scott, was appointed their Keeper, and since then, except during the two World Wars, they have been on view in the Crown Room at Edinburgh Castle, the oldest remaining Crown Jewels in Europe.

The Rewards

The rewards for the important service of preserving the royal insignia were dealt out in inverse ratio. John Keith, brother of the Earl Marischal, who knew nothing of the matter, having been himself abroad during the whole transaction, but whose name had been used in a letter for the sole purpose of misleading the usurpers, got (as Sir Walter Scott has well expressed it)

> *the Earldom* (of Kintore), *pension, etc.; Ogilvie only inferior honours; and the poor clergyman nothing whatsoever or, as we say, the hare's foot to lick.*

Testimony of Mrs Grainger's Services

In consideration of Mrs Grainger's services the following Act was passed on 11th January, 1661:

> *FORASMUCH as the Estates of Parliament Do understand That Christian Fletcher spous to Mr James Granger minister at Kinneth wes most active in conveying the Royall Honors his Maties Croun Sword & Scepter out of the Castle of Dunnoter immediately befor it was rendered to the English Usurpers. And that be her care the same wer hid and preserved Thairfor the Kings Matie with advice of his Estates of Parliament Doe appoint two thousand merks Scots to be forthwith payed unto her be his Maties Treasurer out of the readiest of his Maties rents as a testimony of their sense of her service aforementioned.*

A cynic might add the comment that there is no evidence that the money was ever paid!

The Honyman Association — and Dr Mearns

On the death of Mr Grainger in 1663 there began a wonderful family association, lasting in all 118 years. James Honyman, brother of the Bishop of Orkney and of the Archdeacon of St Andrews, succeeded to the charge which he held until his death thirty years later. This first James Honyman was, incidentally, the author of the Scottish song, *Hie, bonnie lassie, blink ower the burn.* He was succeeded by his son, Andrew, who is described in the call inserted in the Session records, dated March 19th, 1693, as a preacher of the gospel. Although he apparently officiated right away, it was not until 1702 that he was ordained. He continued as a fully fledged clergyman until 1733. His son, James, succeeded on his death and ministered until 1780, being in turn succeeded by his son who bore the same name as himself. This last of the Honymans died a year later and brought the 'hereditary succession' to an end. It was during the ministry of the third Honyman that the church was rebuilt in 1738. A monument in the church commemorates this remarkable dynasty of ministers.

In 1782 Mr Patrick Stewart was settled in the charge, and two years later the church was renovated. He remained in the church until 1818 when his son, Allan Stewart, was made his assistant and successor.

As a tailpiece one might note that one of Kinneff's ministers was the Dr Mearns of whom we spoke earlier. He kept his sermons in a churn and took one out every Sunday. One particular Sunday the sermon he extracted was somewhat tattered so that, turning to the congregation, he said,

> *The mice, I'm afraid, ha'e been at my text so we shall ha'e to begin where the mice left off, and ye can gather as ye gang.*

He was extremely fond of toddy and, cycling home one evening, far from sober, he ran into two horses and a carriage and was killed.

Handsome Memorial Tablets

The Visitors' Book bears witness to the hundreds of pilgrims who view the several interesting 17th century monuments and stones in the church and churchyard. Among these is a handsome memorial tablet inscribed in Latin to the Rev. James Grainger who buried the Regalia under the spot where he had most authority and security in a troubled world, and one to Sir George Ogilvy of Barras who as Governor of Dunnottar Castle had discharged his trust by denying the Honours to the invader. It is built into the south wall of the church, on the left of the pulpit, adorned with the arms of Ogilvy of Barras.

The translation of the epitaph is as follows:

> *Sacred to the memory of Sir George Ogilvie of Barras, knight baronet, who, being governor of Dunnottar Castle, for some time vigorously defended it against the forces of the English parricides but was at length compelled to surrender it; not, however, until, with the assistance of his wife, Lady Elizabeth Douglas, the Scottish regalia, namely the crown, sceptre and sword which had been there deposited, had been secretly removed from it and placed in safety in the*

church of Kinneff. For these distinguished services to his country and his constant and untainted loyalty to the royal family he received the rank and title of knight baronet by letters-patent, granted by the king the 5th day of March, 1660, his family arms, which his descendants still use, being added to those of his forefathers. Moreover, by a charter under the Great Seal of Scotland the right granted him of holding his lands by the tenure which is commonly called Simple Wardship was changed into White Land (tenancy secured by a nominal payment). *In both of these royal documents his unswerving fidelity and distinguished services to his sovereign were mentioned with the highest praise. Sir David Ogilvie, baronet, great-grandson of the above mentioned, died the 5th day of December, 1799, aged 70 years. Lady Ogilvie, his wife, died December 20th, 1800, aged 53. Both are buried in this church.*

A tablet on the west wall of the church on which are the initials 'M.J.G., C.F.' eulogises the share which Mr Grainger and his wife, Christian Fletcher, had in saving the Honours of the kingdom. The epitaph, also in Latin, reads as follows:

Here lie the remains of Mr Granger to whom Scotland is indebted for the preservation of her royal regalia. During the siege of Dunnottar, when these were on the point of being captured, he carried them off and concealed them in the sacred ground in which he is interred. He enjoys his reward above: the heroic preserver of his country's honour now wields a sceptre amid the celestial choirs.

So it is that this picturesque little church was not just an ordinary site of parochial worship. On its walls are written some of the most glamorous passages in the history of the Mearns. Services were held in it until 1975, but the church is now pensioned off. A Trust was formed in 1979 under the chairmanship of the Right Honorable the Viscount of Arbuthnott to restore the building, and an appeal was launched to try to preserve for all time a part of our heritage irreplaceable in the Scottish scene.

The Old Manse

In the old manse, dated 1738, which stands beside the old parish church (now a private dwelling) a room still bears the name of the

Regalia Room. For, although it is the old church itself that is usually associated with the memorable incident of the saving of the Scottish Regalia, one accepts as reasonably authentic the fact that the precious relics must have been hidden in the manse for some time before being actually buried in the church, and the minister's bedroom is pointed out as the apartment in which they were secreted. The picture is incomplete unless due recognition is also given to the part played by the manse and its courageous mistress, Christian Grainger.

St Arnty's Cell

Almost opposite the church, either in the very small dell on the west side of the road or 130 yards south-west of the church, opposite the old manse, stood the *old building* known as *St Arnty's Kill* or *Kiel* as it was curiously called, perhaps on the site of the cell of St Anthony or Arnold. It was said to have been a *religious house* and was still visible in the 18th century when it was referred to as *St Arnold's bell*. But it had been removed by 1842, and nothing now remains. His Well, which supplied the original manse with water, is still to be found some sixty or seventy yards up the bed of the stream, but you are advised because of boggy conditions to avoid walking beside it, reaching the waterfall and the pool below rather by crossing the shoulder of the slope.

Who St Arnty of Kinneff was it is vain to speculate although the name may be a form of Adamnan who is commemorated in several places in North-east Scotland. The only authority for calling Kinneff Church St Arnold's or St Anthony's is that there was a cell of this monk close by. At the church (or St Arnty's if you like) at the beginning of the century was found in a heap of stones the fragment of a late Celtic slab cross which may date from about the 8th century and is believed to have been taken from the north wall of the church when a transept was being built in 1876. It is in the National Museum.

Kinneff Castle

And now walk past the old manse and round the corner to the left. At the fork do not turn to the right past the disused outhouses and towards the white, modern bungalow but rather follow the rough, grass-grown pathway to the left through the trees and alongside the stream. In only 290 yards from the gate of the church, as you walk along the north side of a small ravine, you will see opposite you on the other side all that remains of Kinneff Castle, a huge block of masonry some 9 ft. or 10 ft. long by about 3 ft. high, occupying a steep-sided promontory. On the north-west and south-west there is a prominent scarp which is probably all that remains of a substantial earthwork defence.

Kinneff Castle was destroyed in 1337 and never rebuilt. As late as the 18th century one high wall was described as standing *so strongly cemented that stones may be easier won out of quarry*. The castle, alleged to have been built by King Kenneth as we have said, belonged to a branch of the Scottish de Montforts. Buchanan says it was repaired and garrisoned by the English when they overran the country during the minority of David Bruce, son of King Robert, who succeeded his father as David II in 1329.

Just before the middle of the 19th century, while digging a grave for Lady Ogilvy of Barras in Kinneff churchyard, workmen found an earthen pot containing about a pound and a half of old silver coins. These bore the impressions of Alexander of Scotland and Edward of England and were believed to have been a relic of the Sassenach garrison in Kinneff Castle.

All that remains of Kinneff Castle, destroyed in 1337 and never rebuilt. It belonged to a branch of the Scottish de Montfort family. On the left of the picture can be seen the remains of a fisherman's cliff-top cottage in the derelict village of Shieldhill.

The Derelict Village of Shieldhill

A further 130 yards takes us past the ruins of several fishermen's cottages on the cliff-top. (Note the mussel midden outside the last cottage above the gate!). Here, below the church, is all that is left of the derelict, tiny village of Shieldhill, once a famous fishing centre, perched above two very small coves from which salmon and crab fishing-boats once put out.

In the middle of the 19th century the fires burned brightly in nine homesteads in this village, and a small but hardy colony of twelve fishermen pursued their calling in five boats from the rocky inlet more than 100 ft. below. There is no real harbour, and small boats in olden times were pulled up the beach for safety. Employment for thirty-one persons was found in this once prosperous little community which, although not large, was definitely part and parcel of the fishing industry of the county. As recently as 1871 the complement of the cove was four yawls, two of which carried a crew of three men and the remaining two (of smaller dimensions) two apiece; just before the outbreak of the 1914-18 War the Shieldhill fleet still consisted of four small boats.

The backbone of the industry was, of course, line-fishing, but in the summer months the men of Shieldhill drew up their boats and sailed from Stonehaven or Gourdon to the then thriving herring fishing. Catches landed at Shieldhill were sent to Gourdon for disposal or were sold by the men themselves in the surrounding countryside. Indeed, most of the fishermen possessed, in addition to their boats, horses and carts for the disposal of their wares. There used to be a fishing station here where salmon, trout, etc. were brought to the top of the cliff by 'chairlift'.

An Unequal Struggle for Fishermen

The drift to larger centres of activity which has sounded the death knell of so many of our fishing villages began at Shieldhill about 1887, and several factors have contributed to its continuance. The shore is reached by a steep and tortuous path down the cliffs, and stout hearts in addition to stouter bodies were needed to face the task of manhandling gear and catches by such a route. Towards the end of World War I nature put a further obstacle in the path of the fishermen. The shingle which had hitherto been one of the characteristic features of the cove began to shift southwards to a neighbouring bay, and nothing could be done to stay its departure. The men, however, did not give way to this latest development without a fight and, indeed, on two occasions they carted the entire lot back again by land and by sea and replaced it in its original position. The struggle was an unequal one, however, and today there is not a vestige of shingle at Shieldhill. Yet there is a charm in the very desolation which is evident to the least impressionable among us.

The Castle of Cadden

Let us now proceed northwards across the shoulder of Shield Hill itself, which can be seen rising above the sea in front of us, to the cliff-top beyond. A walk of a further 265 yards will take us there, and we should follow the rough path on the seaward side of the fence from which is visible magnificent cliff scenery with turbulent seas dashing on the rocks below. From our vantage point it is possible to see Montrose far to the south with its gleaming lighthouse on the point; immediately to the north we look down on a rock-girt inlet with perpendicular cliffs frequented by countless gulls and on the left below us a mighty 'triumphal' archway of rock.

On your way back you will find it of interest to follow the fence behind the ruined cottages northwards along the cliff edge for only 160 yards. This will take you to the corner at the top of the field from where you will see a precipitous peninsular neck of land jutting into the sea in the middle of a cove. On it once stood what was probably a mediaeval fortification known as the Castle of Cadden. The promontory is enclosed by a low bank, and the only possible line of approach, from the west-north-west, is cut off by a ditch, broken only by one entrance-causeway. From descriptions published while the remains were yet distinct the castle had a drawbridge to protect it from attack by land. Along the cliff edge on the south-west a short stretch of lime-mortar masonry is visible, and on the north-north-east side of the interior there are possible traces of a range of buildings.

The Castle of Cadden and the three neighbouring castles of Kinneff, Whistleberry and Adam's Castle, all within four-fifths of a mile of one another on the top of isolated and all but unapproachable neighbouring cliffs, and all obviously important places in ancient times, must have been quite small keeps belonging to the 14th century. Probably on account of security against baronial strife and attack lands on the coast became favourite possessions for numerous castles were built on the rocks and cliffs extending from Cowie[1] to Mathers: Herbertshields at Kinneff and Dunnottar[2] are, of course, others.

[1] See *Highways and Byways Round Stonehaven* pp. 55-58.
[2] Ibid. pp. 130-153.

Numerous Shipwrecks

In the days when wrecks around our coastline were more numerous
than they are today, Shieldhill had its share of that form of excitement. The 'Muckle Shield', a huge, rocky promontory which pro-
tects the cove on the north, stretches farther seaward than Todhead
Point on which Kincardine's lighthouse stands, and many years ago
the authorities seriously considered the establishment of some
warning there. Happily, however, it has not been found necessary.
The last wreck of note took place there in October, 1917, when the
Reindeer, an ammunition ship, sailing light, was cast on the rocks
during the hours of darkness. The wreckage streamed into Shieldhill cove at seven o'clock the next morning, and the entire crew of
twenty-five were lost.

The Farm of Temple

We must now resume our journey, returning to the old kirk of
Kinneff on foot and thence proceeding by car to Kirkcorner up the
hill. Here we must turn left, turning right again almost immediately.
In two-fifths of a mile we pass the farm of Slains Park. A quarter of a
mile after this, and opposite a farm road on the left, we see through
an opening into a field on our right the farm of Temple 600 yards
away.

Here is a reminder to us that Kinneff, like Inverbervie, had at one
time a close connection with the Knights Templars who had a
settlement here. Temple or Teampull meant a sacred enclosure or
church. Vestiges of the Order remain also in the farms called
Temple of Barras and Temple of Fiddes although one must remember that some places were so named because of services held there
by dispossessed Episcopalian clergy who called their meeting-
houses temples after the Revolution of 1688.

Kinneff a Place of Importance

In another two-fifths of a mile we reach the A92 at the village of
Kinneff, a district which at one period of history – the Bronze
Age – seems to have been of very considerable importance. From
time to time numerous finds have been made by excavators in the
area. At Kinneff have been found small, leaf-shaped rivetted
spearheads with moulding down the sides of the socket and with
rivet holes in the socket. These products of the first phase of the
Late Bronze Age are now in the Museum of Antiquities, Edinburgh. There, too, is a pair of circular bronze rings, nearly cylindri-
cal in section but slightly flattened on the inner circumference with

the ends fitting together without being joined. When ground was being trenched, these and two 'buttons' (one of bone, the other of jet or shale) were found in 1831 about 330 yards south-south-east of Kinneff parish church together with an unburnt burial and a low wide-mouthed urn of the food vessel type, a feature of burials in the centre of standing stones around 1500 B.C. The urn is now also in Edinburgh. A Late Bronze Age spearhead, said to have been found 2 ins. above the food vessel, was probably a later deposit. At Kinneff, too, flint arrow-heads have been found.

In more modern times, the manor of Kinneff was granted to the de Montfort family by William the Lion, as we have seen (page 101), and from charters we learn that the priests of the Altar of the Blessed Virgin in Inverbervie possessed houses and gardens in Kinneff as did also the Carmelite Friars. It is of interest to note that at one time Kinneff was the only coast parish which was not within the jurisdiction of the Archbishop of St Andrews. As sailing on summer seas was a much easier mode of moving about than scampering over rough and naked country, it was more convenient for the Episcopal authorities to sail in and out amongst the Kincardineshire coves to administer their spiritual office in comfort.

The Law of Largie

We must now turn left to continue our journey. In just half a mile is a short 500-yard farm road on the right to the farm of Largie. Here, just to the right of the farmhouse where the silcage pit is once stood a castle of which no trace now is visible unless a low overgrown wall almost on ground level by the fence and behind the small trees is mute evidence of the foundations. From this castle several dressed stones have been dug up by the farmer. One interesting sculptured stone remains, a dormer-window-pediment inset high up in one of the walls of the farm steading and bearing the initials 'I.A.' (Abercromby?) and the date 1611. Report has it that in the neighbourhood a Battle of Largie was once fought.

Perhaps equally interesting are two natural sandy knolls, now sadly spoilt by ploughing and the ravages of sheep and cattle over the centuries. The larger, marked on the Ordnance Survey maps as 'The Law' (or conical hill) and designated 'tumulus', is a prominent mound, quite visible some 380 yards to the north of the farmhouse and 50 yards inside the field with the wooden shed. St John's Hill can be seen in the background to the right. Originally it must have been about 120 yards in circumference. A similar, but smaller, knoll can be clearly seen in a field to the north nearby.

In the Law was discovered a considerable time ago, when what may have been a cairn was removed from the top, a *large number of stone coffins containing black, unctuous matter and ashes but no urns*, *boxes* of stone slabs possibly containing the remains of importantly related persons in tribe or clan. Here was obviously a prehistoric burial place of some sort, probably belonging to Beaker or Bronze Age settlers who originally crossed the Channel about 1800 B.C. and lived in these parts 4,000 years ago. But there is nothing specific to suggest this.

Further evidence of Bronze Age settlers in the area is provided by the fact that another two stone cists were found nearby, one some 520 yards due west of the Law, between the Law and the farm of Auchindrich to the left, and the other 570 yards to the north-west on the mound called Grieve's Knap (or hillock) to the right of the Water Hill behind Auchindrich. At Auchindrich itself was found a bronze spear-head $7^3/8$ ins. long with a projecting loop on each side of the socket. It is now in the Museum of Antiquities, Edinburgh. Furthermore, beside the site of the castle there used to be a standing-stone.

The Parish of Arbuthnott

And now we follow the A92 for $1\frac{3}{4}$ miles, turning sharp right along the B967. We are now about to enter the parish of Arbuthnott which was probably brought into being as a result of the Norman influence that pervaded all Scottish affairs during the reigns of Queen Margaret and her sons from 1153. Although but a small parish, devoid of any modern feature of note, Arbuthnott has many claims to distinction in the pages of Mearns history.

We know that even about 3,000 B.C. New Stone Age man settled where Pitcarry Farm is now (the road to it is only a little over 700 yards along the B967) for a stone axe, an essential part of the equipment of the first Neolithic settlers, was found there and is now to be seen in the Museum of Antiquities, Edinburgh. Indeed, these axes continued to be used until bronze axes became common about 1,500 B.C.

A Bronze Age flanged axe from Arbuthnott, together with one from Bogs of Arnhall, is to be found in Montrose museum.

The Castle of Allardice

Most famous families have had their roots in Kincardineshire but few retain their association with the lands of their fathers, and equally few of the ancient and historic edifices of the county have defied sufficiently the ravages of time to be in use today. One of these is, however, the delightfully attractive Castle of Allardice the unpretentious and unheralded drive to which we pass on our left only three-quarters of a mile along the B967. Just short of 1¾ miles north-west of Inverbervie the deep valley of the Water of Bervie sweeps round and, forming almost a complete circle, encloses a terraced park of about ten acres. In this picturesque natural setting amid sheltering trees the castle stands. Centuries ago the park formed the garden of the castle, and in their season two clumps of lilies still nod.

The Allardice Family

This ancient castle is the original home of the Norman family of Allardice who with the Arbuthnotts settled in Kincardineshire around 1165 in the reign of William the Lion or earlier, one of them being clerk to the King. Their names appear frequently in very old charters. It was at Allardice Castle here that Walterus de Allardyce (Allardas) took the oath of fealty to Edward I of England in 1297, signing the notorious Ragman Roll. Soon afterwards the property of 'Alrethes' was granted by a charter of Robert the Bruce to one Duncan Judicii who, with his descendants, adopted the name Allardice of that Ilk and retained possession for many centuries. In 1656 Thomas 'Ardes' was nominated by Cromwell a justice for Kincardineshire, and six years later Sir John Allardice married the granddaughter of the Earl of Airth. In 1800 the estate passed by the marriage of the Allardice heiress to the ancient and powerful family of the Barclays of Ury who held it until 1854 when, upon the death of Captain Barclay-Allardice, the long line of Allardice of Allardice became extinct.

The Castle a Structure of Interest

The castle with its white harled walls rises to four storeys and an attic and, although it has, as usual, the Hall on the first floor with bedrooms above and a vaulted basement with kitchen premises below, it is a structure of considerable architectural interest. Fairly unusual, for example, is the fact that an attractive narrow and low vaulted passage or pend through the main block gives access to what had been a curtain-walled courtyard two sides of which were formed by the angle of the L-shaped castle itself. Highly unusual, too, is the re-entrant angle, and most pleasing are the finely intricate and elaborate label mouldings supporting the corbelling of the stair-turret which forms at the top a gabled watch-chamber reached

107

by a secondary stair-turret and flanked by a slender angle-turret. Notable also is the offsetting of the walling to the west, and the tall chimney-stack above this front.

The peculiar formation of cornices and turrets in the angle of the building was part of the old-time architects' methods of getting as much accommodation as possible into the smallest possible floor-space. The design is peculiar to the North-east, this being the most southerly example of it. An apparently unfinished design at one part suggests that it had been the intention to build an additional wing parallel to one of the existing wings.

Although this interesting castle, possessing some good specimens of the architecture of the middle of the 16th century, was rebuilt about 1541, most of the present mansion dates from about the time of the marriage of Sir John Allardice to Lady Mary Graham in 1662. The west wing of the L-plan, for example, was very considerably extended about this time, and possibly the other wing about thirty years later. At any rate, a stone built into part of the extention is dated 1695. It may be, too, that further additions were made about 1714.

Allardice Castle, a structure of considerable architectural interest. Notice the unusual yet attractive narrow, vaulted pend through the main block giving access to what had been a curtain-walled courtyard. Highly unusual, too – and most pleasing – is the peculiar formation of cornices and corbelled turrets in the angle of the building.

A Beautiful and Impressive Picture

Surrounding the castle are some fine ash and beech trees, interspersed with gean or wild cherry trees. The delicate tints of the ashes and beeches and the ruddy glow of the decaying leaves of the gean with the turreted castle towering on the heights above form a beautiful and impressive picture.

Brooding Standing-stones – Et Cetera

And now let us continue along the road to Fordoun with the top of Gallow Hill (465 ft.) on our right some three-fifths of a mile away. On the west side of this hill and just 130 yards from the top was found in 1971 a polished stone axe of pale green, fine grained metamorphic rock. The axe, donated to Dundee City Museum, is 4 ins. in length with a maximum width of $1^4/5$ ins. across the cutting edge which, although fairly sharp, is rough, having been chipped both recently and in antiquity. The surface of the axe is smooth but bears the marks of grinding, lacking as high a polish as the type of material would take. The edges of the axe are slightly flattened and about $1/10$ in. in width, and the straight sides taper to a width of $4/5$ in. across the straight butt. Maximum thickness is $3/4$ in., and the weight is 145 gms.

From the same field was recovered a red sandstone spindle wheel $1^1/2$ ins. in diameter and $1/2$ in. thick with the hole $1/4$ in. in diameter at its narrowest, drilled from both sides. An irregular shaped stone with a hole in it was also picked up. This and the whorl were donated to Bervie School.

At the moment, however, we are interested only in viewing a large Bronze Age standing-stone. If you think it merits it, you may drive your car the requisite half-mile along the shoulder of Gallow Hill until you reach the junction of the Auchindrich and Craighead farm roads. The standing-stone can be seen on your left 240 yards away, a conglomerate mass $9^1/2$ ft. by 2 ft. and $5^1/2$ ft. high. It may be all that remains of a cairn. 190 yards farther on in the same direction and on the crest of a spur are the remains of a large cairn measuring about 69 ft. in diameter by up to 2 ft. in height. On the south-west perimeter amid the broom at the edge of the field there is a standing-stone, $4^1/4$ ft. by 2 ft. at the base and $5^1/4$ ft. in height, the last remnant of a stone-circle which once stood there.

In themselves these stones are perhaps of only minimal interest and, you may consider, not worth a visit, but the writer has in mind Lewis Grassic Gibbon whom we shall meet later in this narrative.

There are standing-stones, a cairn, recumbent stone-circles and a long barrow within a mile or two of Allardice Castle and of his childhood home, and doubtless it is these and other stones on the moorland around which feature in his works.

More Bronze Age Cists – and a View

290 yards farther along the B967 is a road to the right to the farm of Millplough where once existed the solitary recumbent stone of a circle. Sixty yards farther on again is a farm track to the left, leading to the Mill of Allardice. Two more Bronze Age cists were discovered in this area, the first 345 yards down the road (some 20 yards before the end of the concrete car run-way) and just inside the field on the right, the second 135 yards farther on inside the sharp V-shaped corner. There is nothing whatsoever to see – except for the first time an excellent view of Allardice Castle: this may justify the deviation.

The Chapel of Allardice

Back to the B967, and in two-fifths of a mile we reach the road to Arbuthnott Church. This we follow, stopping, however, in only 390 yards in the hollow just before the cottages on the right. If it is possible, let us enter the field by the gate on our left and follow the streamlet for a little more than 100 yards until we are exactly opposite the deserted cottage with its three trees and abandoned garden. We are now standing on the actual site of the mediaeval Chapel of Allardice, probably the baronial chapel of the Castle of Allardice, and perhaps near the castle's outer defences. Nothing now remains.

The Camp or Fort of Castle Dykes – a Bronze Age Earthwork?

Some 160 yards farther on to the south-east is the crest of a field known as Castle Dykes, bounded on the east side by the Chapel Den, on the south by the River Bervie and the precipitous 'Kirkton's Rocks', and on the west by another steep slope. The field forms a flat promontory the north side of which was at one time cut off from the adjacent field by twin ditch and earth ramparts, the soil from the ditches having been thrown to the inside of the camp, thus forming strong ramparts of over 120 yards long and between 20 ft. and 30 ft. wide, including the ditches, and enclosing a fort or camp of two and a half acres in extent. It is very probable that the rampart was surmounted by palisading, and the camp may possibly have been the principal tribal stronghold of the locality. Around the middle of the 19th century the site was brought under cultivation: the ditch was filled up, the rampart levelled and the ground added to the adjacent field. The remains of a number of hut circles were found (in and around which was a considerable quantity of charcoal) and numbers of flint flakes and arrowheads. Also discovered was a small cannon with a portion of its muzzle missing which lay about the farm of Kirkton for years. Its ultimate fate is unknown.

There is little doubt that the site of Castle Dykes is prehistoric,

An aerial photograph, taken in 1976, of the prehistoric camp or fort of Castle Dykes. Crop marks of two ramparts are clearly seen extending across the 'promontory' of field overlooking Chapel Den on the east and the precipitous 'Kirkton's Rocks' and the water of Bervie on the south. The site of the Chapel of Allardice can be seen in the angle of the field at the top left of the picture where stand three trees and a deserted cottage.

probably originally belonging to the Bronze Age – a stone[1] with unusual markings found on the site and examined by the Museum of Antiquities, Edinburgh, may well prove the point – although it was possibly occupied at different periods later: the broken cannon may have belonged to the time of the Marquis of Montrose. I am told by the farmer of Kirkton that the defences of bank and ditch are still noticeable as cropmarks: whenever a ditch has been dug into the ground, it fills with soil looser than that around it so that cereal and leguminous crops over the disturbance grow darker and higher due to greater humic and moisture content. The converse effect occurs over buried walls or dykes.

The Parish Church of Arbuthnott

A further half-mile up the valley, in a remote and naturally beautiful hollow on a quiet loop of the road that follows the left bank of the Bervie Water to the sea, nestles the attractive old parish church of Arbuthnott, undoubtedly one of the finest and most interesting historic pieces of mediaeval architecture in Kincardineshire. It is situated on a slope overlooking the Bervie Water where, incidentally, the parish priests obtained their supplies of fish during Lent.

The church, which dates back to a period before the 12th century, is one of the few remaining pre-Reformation kirks in Scotland which escaped destruction during the period of transition and is the only such church in the county of Kincardineshire and one of the few in Scotland still in use for public worship. It was built in 1242 and consecrated on August 3rd of that year by David de Bernham, Bishop of St Andrews, four years before he performed a similar function for the old church of Fetteresso. From very early times it was dedicated to St Ternan, said to be a Pictish native of the Mearns and of noble origin. After training in his native country, he went to Ireland, became a follower of St Ninian, Scotland's first missionary, and then Abbot of a monastic settlement in Leinster. Thereafter he returned to Kincardineshire and probably settled in Banchory where his religious community was an important missionary centre.

Originally, of course, the church was a prebend of Kirkheugh

---

[1] About 1976 a sandstone block (12.2 ins. by 9 ins. by 5.1 ins.), bearing cup-and-ring and other markings on three faces, was found during ploughing. On the upper face are three small cups linked to a central cup-and-ring by three radial grooves. The lower face bears a cup-and-ring together with three plain cups from which three parallel grooves (crossed by a fourth groove) run on to the narrower end of the block where two terminate in cups.

Church, St Andrews, and a Roman Catholic chapel. As is usual with Catholic buildings, it faces east (symbolic of the star which rose there).

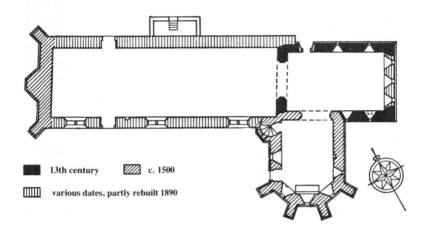

13th century   c. 1500

various dates, partly rebuilt 1890

The plan of the parish church of Arbuthnott, showing in black parts of the original fabric and, on the south side of the chancel, the Arbuthnott Aisle.

The Chancel

The first part to be erected was the sharply pointed chancel, built in the early English style and dedicated in 1242, a beautiful little sanctuary now considerably restored and the only part of the original fabric extant. Later an aisleless nave was added, dedicated to St Mary, and at present these two parts are divided by a beautiful Norman arch, semi-circular and with heavy mouldings which, before the nave was built, had been the western window of the chancel. Historians have it that this window was dedicated in honour of St Ternan. Three fine, stained glass lancet windows adorn the east gable of the chancel, and three tall square-headed lights in the east end are now fitted with stained glass. Under the eastmost south lancet is a lovely piscina or stone basin with pointed arch, still in perfect condition. This would have been located on the south side of the altar and used by the priest during and after services when water for ritual cleaning was required.

From earliest times the chancel has served as a burial-place for the family of Allardice.

The evidence of the Norman arch on the south side of the chancel (at the entrance to the Arbuthnott Aisle) and an incomplete wall on the north side indicate other buildings that could have been earlier than the chancel itself. As can be seen, too, the lancet windows and the top part of the east gable have been considerably altered at some later date.

The Nave

The nave of the church is long and narrow, measuring 60 ft. by 18 ft. It had two circular-headed doors, exactly opposite each other in the north and south, and on the east side of the south door are the mutilated remains of a small stoup which would have once contained holy-water to 'cleanse' the visitor as he entered the building. The west gable is of peculiar interest with its corner buttresses and central turret surmounted by a stone-roofed belfry. To all appearance it is the same age as the Arbuthnott Aisle. It would seem, in fact, that a scheme of reconstruction of the whole church was at one time in progress as is shown by the projecting bond-stones at the east end of the north wall of the nave. The intention evidently was to erect a new choir in keeping with the rest of the edifice, but with the intervention of the death of Sir Robert Arbuthnott and the Reformation the ancient chancel was allowed to remain.

On the 2nd of February, 1890, the greater part of the nave, then the only part in use, was destroyed by fire, the fire removing the plaster partition which had been fitted into the gap between the nave and the chancel and so revealing the archway which can be seen today. In the extensive work of renovation galleries which had been added to three sides of the nave, including the Laird's Loft, were dispensed with and, the chancel arch being opened up, the chancel itself was reroofed and restored to its fitting place in the worship. The church bell made by Mowat at Old Aberdeen in 1736 was broken by its fall but, recast, continues to announce Sunday services. The first nave was built probably soon after the chancel and then rebuilt on the eve of the Reformation.

The Arbuthnott Aisle

Between 1450 and 1500 Sir Robert Arbuthnott of that Ilk, an ancestor of the present Viscount, had a transept added on the south side of the chancel in the form of a round tower in two storeys with a curious and almost unique bell-turret.

*The Arbuthnott Aisle, a transept added between 1450 and 1500 by Sir Robert Arbuth-
nott on the south side of the chancel of Arbuthnott Church. It includes a round tower in
two storeys with a curious and almost unique bell-tower. The upper part of the Aisle
was originally used as the living quarters of Sir Robert's priest, and it was here that the
famous Missal, finished in 1492, was penned. Notice the Norman arch which is the
entrance. The Arbuthnott Aisle is the burial-place of the Arbuthnott family.*

He also gave two bells to be rung for the services and offices. Sir Robert used the lower part of this tower, heavily buttressed outside and vaulted and groined inside, as a private chapel or chantry for the purpose of holding a portable altar which he had obtained under licence from Pope Innocent VIII. It is 23 ft. by 16 ft., terminating in an apse at the south end. The fact that the Aisle had contained an altar is indicated by the presence of a piscina near the circular-headed door at the south-west. An ambry or wall recess for keeping the sacrament utensils and the host (bread, water and wine) is to be seen in the east wall. At the entrance to the Aisle is another holy-water stoup.

For this chapel, dedicated to the Virgin Mary and known as the Lady Chapel, the church of Arbuthnott is especially notable, and it is certainly the most striking feature of the exterior of the building. The Aisle, 50 ft. in height in all, and built of finely hewn ashlar (square, hewn stones), is a beautiful example of exquisite late Scottish Gothic architecture. It is the only structure in the district at all entitled to the name of mausoleum for it is the only family burial-place of the Arbuthnotts.

The centre window in the apse is a finely cusped lancet (that is, with a small projecting ornamental point in the tracery); the others having circular headings peculiar to the Scottish style. The four buttresses supporting the building are exceptionally massive and contain graceful niches adorned with richly carved canopies and corbels, while the whole masonry is of excellent polished stone. The Arbuthnott Aisle was probably built on the site of an older building as it is of a later period than the archway that divides it from the church.

Recumbent Effigy of a Knight

In the chapel apse, on the probable site of the altar, lies a full-length monumental effigy of a knight in full armour, helmet and sword, the face looking upwards and the feet resting on the figure of a dog. The Arbuthnott arms are figured on the shield. It probably represents James Arbuthnott, son of Sir Robert, who died in 1521, or else it is a memorial to Hew or Hugo de Arbuthnott, a 13th century figure, distinguished in charters from two similarly named forebears by the name of Blundus or Le Blond and the reputed founder of the family of Arbuthnott. Fable says that he had large additions made to his estates in consequence of killing a wild boar that frequented the Den of Pitcarles two-thirds of a mile away greatly to the danger and annoyance of the neighbourhood. A cannon ball preserved in

Arbuthnott House is the stone with which Sir Hew killed the animal! It was in fact fired at Inverbervie by a French privateer during the Napoleonic war! One does not want, however, to discount the story altogether: there must surely have been some basis for this traditional 'St George and the Dragon' legend applicable to this district.

The effigy is clearly of the same age as the building in which it is preserved, and it is much more probable that the hitherto unnoticed and uncared for slab, embellished with a beautiful cross, two shields and a sword and used at one time as a door-step to the kirk, had been the tombstone of that hero. Certainly its style corresponds more with that of the coffin slabs of the century during which Sir Hew flourished. The effigy is interesting as being the oldest of its type in Scotland. The tomb beneath the effigy is of a later period, probably mid-16th century, and in all likelihood contains the remains of James Arbuthnott of that Ilk, son of Sir Robert, the builder of the Aisle. The side of the base of the tomb is ornamented with four armorial shields, bearing the coats of Stewart, Arbuthnott and Douglas, all connected with the family.

The Priest's Room

The upper storey of the Aisle, reached by a narrow, winding stair in the tower, was originally designed for and used as the living quarters of Sir Robert Arbuthnott's parish priest. The apse here has only two small, square-headed windows, but there is a larger one looking towards the west and protected by a strong iron grill. The western window and the one in the middle of the apse are fitted with stone seats at the sides. There is a small recess at the east wall, decorated with a single trefoil, but no sign of any fireplace. The existence of wooden dooks in the walls would suggest that the room had originally been panelled.

The priest's room or sleeping apartment at one time contained a library which was bequeathed by Principal Arbuthnott (and the Rev. John Sibbald of Kair, near Fordoun, who also endowed the parish school) to the clergy of the Mearns. But the books have long since disappeared.

Disrepair and Fire

Right up to 1560 Gothic art continued to flourish in the North-east with unabated vigour as may be studied in such a fine example as Arbuthnott Church here, but by the time of the Reformation the church had fallen into a sad state of disrepair. Neglect of churches was a common failing about that period. Due to the very strong influence of the Arbuthnott family, however, it did not suffer deliberate damage at the hands of the iconoclasts or image breakers. The only alteration made was the removal of the images around the Arbuthnott Aisle. About this time the roof of the chancel collapsed, no attempt being made to repair it, and the church remained in this condition until the nave was accidentally damaged by fire.

Skilful Restoration

The church was skilfully restored in 1890 to something like its pre-Reformation state under the direction of Sir Marshall Mackenzie, the architect who designed Marischal College, Aberdeen. The roof of the chancel was repaired, and the old earthen floor was laid with stone. Great care was taken, however, to preserve the design of the building and to retain the relics of mediaeval days. It may have been at this time that the lancet windows were altered. Probably the bell-tower and the Arbuthnott Aisle are the only two constructions that remain in their original state exactly.

James Sybbalde's Service-books

Towards the end of the 15th century the vicar at Arbuthnott was James Sybbalde, one of the Sibbalds of Kair, examples of whose calligraphy have been preserved by the Arbuthnott family. In the priest's room already mentioned Sybbalde penned and illumined three Church service-books to which the name of Arbuthnott is attached. First is his Psalter which was completed in 1482 at the express desire of Sir Robert Arbuthnott and presented to the Chapel of the Virgin Mary. In this chapel was placed for use another of Sybbalde's books, a Prayer Book or Book of Hours, written in 1482-83, in which appear illuminated drawings of 'St Ternan in his Robes', 'The Salutation by the Angel', 'The Virgin and Her Child', 'The Rich Man and Lazarus in Hades', 'The Crucifixion' and 'The Sacrament of the Supper', while at the end appears an obituary of the Arbuthnotts from 1314 to 1507. The Book of Hours is designated *Office of the Blessed Virgin which was used in Her Chapel of St Ternan of Arbuthnott in the diocese of St Andrews*. Sybbalde's own death which occurred on September 11, 1507, has been added to the volume.

The Arbuthnott Missal

The third of Sybbalde's service-books is the famous Arbuthnott Missal, *Liber Ecclesiae Beati Ternenani de Arbuthnott* (the book of the church of the blessed St Ternan), used in the Parish Church. The missal, beautifully penned in large letters, ornamented with flowers and fruits, and in many places with splendidly illuminated designs of the highest order, contains complete services of the Mass for every Sunday and Saint's Day throughout the year. Although following mainly the recognised English Prayer Book, it possesses some distinctively Scottish features such as the substitution of Scottish for English saints in the Calendar. Indeed, it is now treasured as the only Scottish book of its kind. The quaint volume, finished in 1492, is bound in old oaken boards covered with brown leather and still retains the original brass clasp.

These historical and interesting specimens of early craftsmanship with their beautiful design, colours and illumination were in the possession of the Viscounts of Arbuthnott until 1897 when they were bought by Archbishop Coates of Paisley and presented by him to his native town where they are now carefully preserved by the Renfrew District Council Museum and Art Galleries Service.

Parts of two pages from the Arbuthnott Missal, the only Scottish book of its kind. On the left, beautifully penned and ornamented, is an excerpt from the Nativity story; on the right is pictured St Ternan. Being in black and white and not in colour, these small pictures, of course, give little idea of the splendid craftsmanship of the volume.

Dr David Sibbald and Family

Through the 16th and 17th centuries the long association between the church and the family of Arbuthnott continued. One finds records of a Dr David Sibbald who apparently married a daughter of John Arbuthnott of Mondynes. Tutor to the Duke of Gloucester, son of Charles I, he was imprisoned in London because of his attachment to the Royal cause, and his estates were declared forfeit. With the Restoration, however, came happier times, and he died in his own House of Kair in 1661. Sibbald apparently had two sons both of whom were clergymen. Dr James Sibbald, a stout opponent of the Covenant, was minister of St Nicholas, Aberdeen. On the death of Charles I he laid down his charge and fled to Ireland where he ministered until about 1650. His brother, John Sibbald of Kair, minister of Arbuthnott, was noted

> *for his pious and religious life, his great painfulness in his calling, his learning and charitable work; for he was instrumental and contributed liberally for building an edifice for training of youth, and mortified considerable sums of money for maintenance of a school-master and the poor of the parish; and also bequeathed his books to the Aisle of Arbuthnott, worth more than a thousand merks, for the use of his successors, incumbents in that place.*

A large plaque in the north wall of the church above the centre of the nave is a memorial to him.

Grave of Lewis Grassic Gibbon

Outside the church to the west a slight depression in the churchyard marks the original boundary of the burial-ground. (Beyond this depression stood the original school of Arbuthnott which was destroyed after the new school at the top of the hill was constructed).It is here, at a corner of the wall surrounding Arbuthnott kirkyard in his beloved Mearns that the ashes of the great Scottish writer, Lewis Grassic Gibbon – or, to give him his real name, James Leslie Mitchell (1901-35) – were laid to rest on Saturday, February 23rd, 1935, in the heart of the countryside where he was reared and about which he wrote in his *Sunset Song* and *Cloud Howe*. Many outstanding men have been produced in North-east Scotland, but it is doubtful if there have been many more talented than he. His gift for describing the Scottish rural scene unequalled, he has aptly been described as *the voice of the Scottish earth*, and what a tragedy that that eloquent voice should have been silenced a week before his thirty-fourth birthday.

His interment followed a short service in the church of Arbuthnott, the company mainly comprising crofting and farming folk with a sprinkling of notable literary friends including Eric Linklater, Cuthbert Graham, Helen Cruickshank, Nan Shepherd and members of the Scottish PEN Club, all come to pay their last respects to 'Bloomfield's loon' and to do honour to the greatest Scottish writer of the century. Brilliant sunshine lit the silent land so vividly portrayed in *A Scots Quair*. White cumulus clouds raced across a blue sky, and from the lower slopes of the distant Grampians billowing smoke rose from the moor-burn. The whins were in bloom, and an early lark carolled above the Bervie Water where Leslie played as a boy. His widow carried the casket to the grave and, turning to the assembled mourners said, 'A great man is dead'.

His tombstone is a simple grey granite pedestal supporting an open book. On one page are the author's name, pen-name and dates; on the other is an inscription from the final chapter of *Sunset Song*, *The kindness of friends, the warmth of toil, the peace of rest*. And beneath on the base, *And I will give you the Morning Star*.

The tombstone marking the grave of Lewis Grassic Gibbon, a simple grey granite pedestal, supporting an open book. His ashes are buried at a corner of the wall surrounding Arbuthnott Kirkyard in his beloved Mearns.

121

Irreverent Satirical Description

In Arbuthnott churchyard, too, can be seen the graves of most of those from the farms on the wooded braes above, people in Gibbon's *Scots Quair*. If his spirit ever stops to think, it may quietly chuckle at the thought that even this churchyard and the church itself are described rather irreverently in his story, even the recumbent statue of the Lord of Kinraddie in the old tower not being proof against the shafts of his devastating wit:

> *'Hidden away among these yews'*, he wrote, *'were kirk and manse. Next door the kirk was an olden tower, built in the time of the Roman Catholics, the coarse creatures, and it was fell old and wasn't used any more except by the cushat-doves and they flew in and out the narrow slits in the upper storey and nested all the year round and the place was fair white with their dung. In the lower half of the tower was an effigy-thing of Cospatrick de Gondeshil, him that killed the gryphon, lying on his back with his arms crossed and a daft-like simper on his face . . . the real kirk was split in two bits, the main hall and the wee hall, and some called them the byre and the turnip-shed, and the pulpit stood mid-way . . .'.*

Anyone who visits Arbuthnott will immediately recognise the point of this highly satirical description which must have caused shock and heartburning in the 1930's. The *main hall* and the *wee hall* are the nave and the chancel, the *olden tower* the Aisle.

As Mitchell grew older, he became fascinated by this fine church and the plaques on its ancient walls which evoked so many memories of the past. One of the oldest of these, recording the

> *burial-place of the family of Allardice of that ilk, the lords of the barony of Allardice from the reign of King William the Lion in the 12th century,*

provided a starting-point for the prelude to *Sunset Song*. Readers of that book will be able to discover for themselves many other correspondences, and indeed one could spend days of well-rewarded pilgrimage in Glenbervie and Arbuthnott parishes which represent a complete cross-section of the 'old Scotland' that Gibbon both mocked and yet deeply loved.

Principal Alexander Arbuthnott

In the course of long centuries it was inevitable that many offshoots of the parent tree should make their marks in the country, and it may be of interest to mention only three of the more notable personages with the same name as that of the ruling house (two of them ministers) because they had an ancestor who came from Arbuthnott itself or at least from the parish. Perhaps the most famous of those to hold the charge of Arbuthnott was Alexander Arbuthnott, second son of Andrew Arbuthnott of Pitcarles and Elizabeth Strathauchin and a grandson of the Baron of Arbuthnott. Alexander Arbuthnott was born in the parish in 1538, studied at St Andrews University and at the age of twenty-three went to France where he spent five years in the study of the civil law under the famous Cujacius at the University of Bourges. Having obtained his degree, he returned to his native land in 1566 with the intention of following the legal profession. The fever of Reformation being, however, in the air, he quickly espoused and championed the new doctrine. After a twelve-month study of theology he was appointed minister in the parish which bore his name.

He proved such an able cleric that in 1568, as a member of the General Assembly, he was appointed to examine a work entitled *The Fall of the Roman Church*. Objections which had been raised to the work because in it the king was styled *the Head of the Church* were upheld by Mr Arbuthnott, and he ordered the publisher, Bassandyne, not only to recall all copies and expunge the passage but also to delete a *profane song* printed at the end of the Book of Psalms. He also prevented Bassandyne from printing any further books without a licence from the supreme magistrate, and in the matter of religious books made him consult the Assembly and have the works revised by its Commission. In 1569 he was appointed first Protestant Principal of Aberdeen University.

A Moderator in Disfavour with the King

Three years later he was a member of the General Assembly at St Andrews which strenuously opposed a scheme put forward by the Regent Morton and his party to restore the old titles of the Church. In 1573, 1577 and 1578 he was Moderator of the Assembly, his work in shaping the government of the Church of Scotland bringing him into disfavour with James VI. The rift increased when in 1582 he superintended the publication of Buchanan's *History of Scotland*, and he was transferred from Aberdeen to St Andrews by an Act of Assembly. This the king, suspecting an ulterior motive, forbade by royal mandate and refused to listen to the petitions of the Church. Further dispute was averted by the death of Arbuthnott on October 16th, 1583, at the age of forty-five. Four days later he was interred in the chapel of King's College, Aberdeen.

While he held the charge of Arbuthnott, the Principal was also minister of Logie-Buchan, but despite the obvious calls on his clerical duties, he found time to write what has been described as an elegant and learned work, entitled *Orationes de Origine et Dignitate Juris*. The manuscript of an account of the Arbuthnott family, begun by him, was later translated and continued by another Arbuthnott, minister of the parish. A memorial stone with the Arbuthnott arms and the inscription 'A.L., A.R. 1573' in the north wall of Arbuthnott Church near the pulpit commemorates his first occupacy of the Moderatorial chair.

An interesting poem written by Principal Arbuthnott and kindly sent to me by the Viscount of Arbuthnott gives yet another sidelight on the Principal's remarkable character:

On Luve

He that luifis lichtliest
Sall not happin on the best.
He that luifis longest
Sall have rest surest.
He that luvis all his best
Sall chance upon the gudliest.
Quha sa in luifis trew and plaine
He sall be lufit weill againe.

Alexander Arbuthnott – Translator

Alexander Arbuthnott, the translator mentioned above, was also a near relative of the laird and was rector of the parish during the post-Restoration era. In 1690 his anti-Presbyterian ideas, unpopular since the Revolution two years previously when it was introduced by William III, caused him to resign his charge

for not reading the proclamation of his estates nor praying
in terms thereof, not keeping the fast,

and to retire with his family to his old castle of Hallgreen which stood close to the sea just outside the town of Inverbervie and which was by then a decaying ruin which housed a number of squatter families.

Dr John Arbuthnott

Alexander had two sons of whom John, the elder (1667-1735), born at Kinghornie near Inverbervie, is said to have had his early education at Arbuthnott. He graduated M.A. at Marishcal College, Aberdeen, and, seeking fame and fortune in London, for some time earned a living there as a teacher of mathematics. He later graduated M.D. from St Andrews, began practising as a doctor and had the good fortune to become physician at the court of Queen Anne. Quickly establishing himself in the fashionable society of the time, he is likely to be remembered as a prominent figure in the famous literary coterie of the Queen Anne period and the intimate friend of Pope, Swift and others who, according to Swift, *knew his art but not his trade.* Yet *the Doctor*, said Swift, *has more wit than we all have, and his humanity is equal to his wit.* He has left his mark in the field of literature with his *History of John Bull* (he was the inventor of the name and character of John Bull as typical of England and Englishmen) and he was the chief editor of the *Memoirs of Martinus Scriblerus.*

Arbuthnott House

We are now ready to resume our journey although it is not yet towards Stonehaven. For a short deviation is necessary if we are to see something of historic Arbuthnott House, the home of the Viscount of Arbuthnott and the third notable edifice which we have had cause to mention during this car run because it has defied the ravages of time to be in use today. Continuing along our present road, we rejoin the B967 in 700 yards. Thence we proceed to the left for only another 530 yards to reach the entrance drive. I am told by the Viscount of Arbuthnott that both House and gardens are open to the public by private arrangement.

Arbuthnott House, a castle or mansion house on the left bank of a stream derived from the Bervie Water across the haugh, is the ancestral home of the ancient family of Arbuthnott which has held the surrounding 2,700 acres of estate land continuously since the 12th century, the family name appearing on records even before then. Originally the lands from which the family takes its name formed a Celtic thanage. As far back as the end of the 11th century they were held by the Norman family of Oliphant, the present house of Arbuthnott springing from the union of Helen Hasse and Duncan Oliphard or Olifard as we have seen (page 290). Late in the 12th century the Oliphant heiress married Hugh of Swinton from Dunbar whose family is derived from the princely earls of Dunbar of

March. It was he who, taking to himself the name Arbuthnott, founded the present family.

Derivation of the Place-name

What the word Arbuthnott means is not too clear. Considerable light is, however, thrown on the early forms of the name by documents in the possession of the family of the Viscount, and it is possible therefrom to make a pretty accurate guess at its derivation. In the years prior to the 12th century the name was spelt 'Aberbothenoth', by 1282 the word had become 'Abirbuthenoth' or 'Aberbuthenot', and around 1335 it became corrupted to 'Aberbuthnott'. The final evolution to its present form occurred about 1443. 'Aber', very common in this part of Scotland, denotes the influx of a river into the sea or of a small stream into a larger one. 'Bothenoth', according to W. J. Watson in *Celtic Place Names of Scotland*, is the name of a stream and means 'little one of virtue' or, literally, 'little triumph, little virtue'. In other words, it was a holy stream possessed of healing power such as we shall see at St Mary's Well near Tipperty (page 184). When one puts these derivations together, one finds that Arbuthnott means 'the place where the holy stream with healing power joins (in this case) the Bervie water'.

From Fortified Tower-house to Georgian Frontage

There has been a house on the present site since about 1170, but nothing remains of any building before 1420 except for parts of a fortified keep or tower-house with walls 5 ft. 9 ins. thick, built by Hugh Arbuthnott at that time, which can be seen within the east wing of the present building. The original vaulted cellars also remain. Hugh Arbuthnott's great-great grandson, Robert, completed the castle between 1470 and 1500, adding a baronial hall, kitchens and a courtyard with entrance gateway and battlemented containing wall. It has been stated that the ancient Arbuthnott Castle was destroyed by fire in 1555 although the present Viscount doubts if there is any evidence for this assumption. At any rate, after further alterations in the 16th century the drawing-room wing (the first purely domestic residence) was erected by Sir Robert Arbuthnott, father of the 1st Viscount, probably in the 17th century, magnificent plaster ceilings being added by his grandson who also laid out the gardens between 1660 and 1670. (The viscountcy dates from 1641 when Sir Robert's son was raised to the peerage by Charles I with the titles of Viscount Arbuthnott and Baron Inverbervie). In 1754 were added the north wing and the notable, symmetrical west front with its pedimented classic centre bay. These, with the further addition of the front door and main Adam-style staircase sixty-six years later, obliterated most traces of the original old courtyard type of castle. The front door stands where an opening originally led through a pend under the first floor into the castle courtyard at the back, the original front door being in the 15th century wing where it can still be seen. To the rear, north and south ranges are vaulted, and the skewput[1] of a corner watch-house is dated 1588. The ancient manor is very evidently a very old family home that has just grown with the times.

Notable Plaster Ceilings

Of particular artistic and historic merit are the 17th century plaster ceilings in the Italian style, already mentioned, perhaps the most notable feature of Arbuthnott House. These are to be seen in the drawing-room and two of the bedrooms. For their restoration a Historic Buildings Council grant was given. Interesting is the fact that one of the plaster casts of a lady (probably Queen Margaret of Scotland) is repeated at Muchalls Castle. Such plaster casts, it is said, were jealously kept by the craftsman who made them, later to be broken up at the end of the craftsman's working life so that they might not again be used.

Magnificent Avenues of Trees

Arbuthnott House is well worth a visit if only to see the drive with its tall stately trees (constructed by the 8th Viscount). Around the House, indeed, the trees are old and majestic on both sides of the valley, in autumn their tints lovely, varied and pleasing to the eye. Here in the high trees beside the Bervie is a very old recorded heronry, and from the foliage of the higher branches, at certain seasons, numerous slender necks may be seen protruding. It is, however, with the magnificent avenues of stately trees that visitors are always particularly struck, one in particular richly deserving fame. This is one of Nature's masterpieces – a 400-yard carpet of green sward enclosed by parallel lines of ancient beeches 60 ft. high, gnarled trunks and branches rising to where in summer the foliage meets and intertwines overhead to form a high archway or lofty corridor of dignified beauty like the nave of some vast cathedral.

This stately avenue, planted 300 years ago, was once the main approach to the House, and records tell of a substantial avenue of

[1] A stone built into the foot of a gable to receive the downward and outward thrust of the gable-copings.

beeches, with associated planting, even at the beginning of the 15th century. At this time practically the whole of the Howe and the coastal area was denuded of trees progressively from the 12th century onwards, a situation fairly general in lowland Scotland. This process was retarded in the case of the king's forests and round the lairds' houses where hardboard plantations for shelter and amenity seem to have been retained.

A Garden of Great Variety

Everywhere in the seven acres of grounds in which the historic mansion nestles is beauty to be found in a charming and attractive landscaped garden of great variety. First laid out as a formal garden in the 17th century, it has always been treated as an extension of the House itself, no attempt having been made to divorce the House from it, as was customary.

The Neolithic Long Cairn of Hillhead

Before we turn for home, let us visit the second of the five long cairns and barrows which are to be found in Kincardineshire, especially when it is so near. We must continue along the B967 for almost exactly half a mile and take the first turning to the right at Parkneuk where survives in part to wall-head height a 19th century Episcopalian mission chapel, built in Gothic revival style. We leave our car after only 350 yards where a Forestry Commission track descends the hill to meet our road on the right. Up this track we climb through the former plantation of Hillhead for 560 yards, at the end of the wood bearing half left through the heather moorland. A further 430 yards (it's a walk of only a little over half a mile in all) will take us to

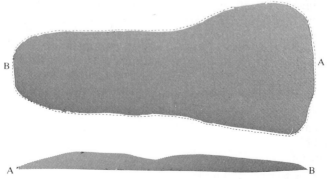

Plan and elevation diagrams of the long cairn in the former plantation of Hillhead.

The Neolithic long cairn of Hillhead. On the 9 ft. high flat-topped east end an Ordnance Survey triangulation station has been erected.

the long cairn of Hillhead plantation on the skyline of its isolated hill from which it is visible from various directions.

The Hillhead cairn has an overall length of about 170 ft. and is 73 ft. wide at the maximum. It is aligned ENE-WSW with, in the former direction, as is usual, the wider and higher end with a flat-topped mound 9 ft. high. Miss Audrey Henshal, who visited Hillhead on April 10th, 1968, tells us that this eastern mound, which contains the interments

> *is divided from the western part of the monument by a wide, shallow ditch some 70 ft. to 85 ft. from the eastern end. The bottom of the ditch is about 5 ft. above ground level. In plan the sides contract fairly sharply from the wide eastern end as far as the ditch and then run parallel to near the west end which is rounded. The east end of the west part is 6 ft. 6 ins. high and drops very gently towards the west end until near the end the drop becomes steeper. In cross-section the west part is rounded, not flat-topped. The sides [of the barrow] rise steeply from the ground, and the edges can be defined with fair precision though with less . . . along the south side where they tend to merge with a slight dip in the ground level. Although there are stones in the mound, there also seems to be earth and gravel in two or three places.*

The cairn appears to have been hardly disturbed at all except for probable superficial interference indicated by the very slight dishing on the flat top of the mound. It is now covered with a deep growth of heather, and on it an Ordnance Survey triangulation station has been erected.

On a slight spur 185 yards west-south-west of the long cairn is a cairn measuring 16 ft. in diameter and just under a foot in height. You may care to descend that way.

Arbuthnott School

Homeward now, and quietly through twelve or thirteen miles of some of the back broom-clad roads of the Mearns, a route, however, with varied points of interest in plenty. We begin by returning along the B967 towards Inverbervie. In a mile and a quarter we pass Arbuthnott School in a little school-room of which the foundations of Lewis Grassic Gibbon's life were laid. *Many would remember him*, writes his old schoolmaster, Mr Alexander Gray, *as the boy who looked after the defective drinking well at Arbuthnott School*, and it was with Mr Gray that Leslie Mitchell made a friendship that was to be lifelong: to him he later dedicated his greatest work of historical research, *The Conquest of the Maya*. Leslie read incessantly, sometimes even during the school intervals, his back against the play-ground dyke, and, although her apparently ne'er-do-weel son's talent impressed his country mother but little (*Ay, but look how his brother's got on*), the story of Leslie Mitchell's childhood finds an echo in almost everything he wrote. Vivid memories of his schooldays here were carried with him all through his life for from his childhood Mitchell was determined to be a writer.

Recumbent Stone-circle on Mont Goldrum

In another fifth of a mile is the road to Pitcarles Farm where was found a brown flint leaf-shaped arrow-head which was donated to the Meffan Institute, Forfar, and about 275 yards south of the farm, on the summit of the Cot Hillock is a cairn, measuring 46 ft. in diameter and 3½ ft. in height. In the Den of Pitcarles is said to have been a chapel or cell. In just short of 600 yards we turn left opposite the road we originally took to Arbuthnott Church. This we follow for just under 1½ miles until we reach on the right a farm road which leads us after 260 yards to the farm of Montgoldrum.

Leaving our car here, we must now follow the farm road to the east round the foot of the hill from which the farm derives its name, a hill sometimes (erroneously) called Camp Hill. After 480 yards a gate indicates that we have reached the end. We now climb the hill for 135 yards, following the edge of the field to the gate at the top. Thence 80 yards will take us to the left to what the Ordnance Survey calls an *ancient earthwork*, in fact a possible Bronze Age recumbent stone-circle known as 'The Camp': the large shattered boulder is probably a displaced recumbent, and there had been a ring cairn in the centre of the monument. The circle, now in a state of considerable dilapidation, measures some 58 ft. in diameter. There still is evident a kerb or low 'wall' of small stones, some 14 ft. in breadth, and there still remain fifty and more large stones, visible in whole or in part, forming a ring of cairn material reduced by robbing to a height of 2½ ft. The hole in the centre of the hollow in the middle betokens an early attempt at 'excavation'.

There are evidences of five smaller cairns on the hill. About 28 yards away to the north-east on the actual summit is a cairn measuring 60½ ft. by 2¼ ft., and placed in a line to the north-north-east of 'The Camp' are three cairns up to 18 ft. in diameter, within kerbs and 1¼ ft. in height. What may be a cairn, 13 ft. in diameter and just under 10 ins. in height, lies 5 yards north-west of 'The Camp'.[1]

From our vantage point of 430 ft. there is, of course, a superlative view. One cannot miss Bruxie Hill with its wireless transmitting mast to the north. Three-quarters of a mile nearer us, and to the north-east, is Mitton Hill with a round cairn awaiting our visit, while to the south-east and on the skyline is Gallow Hill along the shoulder of which we recently drove.

The Lonely Croft of Bloomfield

Returning to the main road, we continue north on to the windy uplands until, in three-fifths of a mile, we reach the little wind-swept cottage of Bloomfield where young Lewis Grassic Gibbon spent eight years of his boyhood. You will remember that we visited his grave in Arbuthnott churchyard. When he was eight, his family moved south into the Mearns to this lonely croft above which the moor called the Reisk mounts to the Hill of Bruxie which, with its snipe-haunted lochan, overlooks the main road from Stonehaven to Laurencekirk. This croft his father tenanted from 1909 until his death in 1937, the Mitchell family struggling to earn a chancy living from the coarse, grudging soil and the hungry acres making heavy demand on them. The old pre-War look of the cottage has, of course, been swept away with its extensions as have the three beech trees and honeysuckle with which the summer garden hedges were bedecked. Yet here is still the very heart of the Mearns, the land of *Sunset Song*. Surely it is not without significance that it is almost within sight of Clochnahill where William Burness, the father of Robert Burns, was born and grew up.

[1] Yet another cairn, measuring 54 ft. in diameter and 3¼ ft. in height is situated 380 yards east-north-east of the group of cairns mentioned.

The lonely, wind-swept cottage of Bloomfield where young Lewis Grassic Gibbon spent eight years of his boyhood. His father struggled to earn a chancy living here from 1909 until 1937.

'Long Rob of the Mill' and Rebecca

The Mitchells' nearest neighbours across the field at Hareden, the now modernised cottage just over quarter of a mile away to the north-east, were the Middletons, and Robert Middleton was the original of one of Leslie Mitchell's strongest characters, Long Rob of the Mill, while his daughter, Rebecca, born in Glasgow, was to become the author's wife. With her and other children from the neighbouring crofts the young Mitchell daily plodded his way up and down the two-mile hilly road to Arbuthnott School.

An Unusual Boy, Completely Different

The other pupils (there were between seventy-five and a hundred at the time) soon realised that this new boy was completely different, and few got to know him well. Even at the age of nine he was an unusual boy, quiet and sensitive, distant in manner, lonely and introspective by nature, a thinker who kept to himself. Yet Leslie was fond of talking, too, when he could find someone to take him seriously. Often he would be seen discussing politics with the road-man who became Chae Strachan of *Sunset Song*.

Bright and eager, he had a passion for learning and an insatiable appetite for books. He worked through every volume of the school's 'Coats Library', not even shirking titles like *Origin and Growth of Cities*. He borrowed an armful of books from the manse and returned them, read, within a day or two; he was given access to the schoolhouse books; he read British, Greek and Roman history and practically exhausted the authors of fiction popular at that time; he had already a considerable knowledge of the stars and the sea. As any books he borrowed from the schoolhouse had to be criticised afterwards, the pupil kept the teacher on the alert. He read anything anyone could lend or procure for him and still came back for more. Ivor Brown, later commenting on the width of Leslie Mitchell's reading, wondered how he ever found time for it. There were times when he read all the way to school, sometimes pausing, lost in the depths of a book, forgetting that a day's work awaited him. He even attempted to use the handlebars as a book-rest while cycling.

Farm Work in the Fields

When he was not reading, he was working on the hungry acres of Bloomfield. On his older brother and on him fell much of the farm work, and to him this work did not come easily. Often when he reached home from school by the old track over the hill, he was kept busy in the fields till darkness came. There was work, too, on Saturdays. Yet, when work and reading came in conflict, the reading usually won. Many a time you might have seen the two horses waiting patiently at the rig end near the plantation while, unknown to his elders, the youthful ploughman lay devouring a book beside them. Sometimes he even attempted the surprising task of hoeing turnips with an open book in his hand.

'Blawearie, Lonely on the Brae'

To this cottage of Bloomfield Leslie Mitchell returned for a few months at the age of eighteen to recuperate after an illness, during which time he doubtless re-absorbed the atmosphere which he knew so well and which later found its way into his books. For time and again he referred to it in his novels. It was the little farm high on the Reisk that Chris visited in *Cloud Howe*; it was the house in *Grey Granite* that Ewan craned his neck to see as he passed in the bus; it was the thinly veiled Blawearie of *Sunset Song*, his masterpiece of 1932 about the humble farmers who peopled the land from Arbuthnott up to Bruxie Hill.

How often in his happy home in Welwyn Garden City must he have seen his cottage home in the windswept Reisk of Arbuthnott and caught the sweet fragrance of honeysuckle! At times he must have remembered the sharp sting of the east wind blowing over Auchendreich. But insistent beyond all else he must have heard the *immemorial plaint of the peewit flying lost*, symbolic of his own tempestuous life.

The Mearns called him again, and in October, 1934, he came to Scotland alone, driving his first motor car. The first week he spent with his parents at Bloomfield, driving them here and there and doing his best to entertain them. But they had not forgotten that he had failed according to Arbuthnott standards, and had aggravated his previous imperfections by writing a 'dirty' book which made them the speak of the place. The next year he was dead.

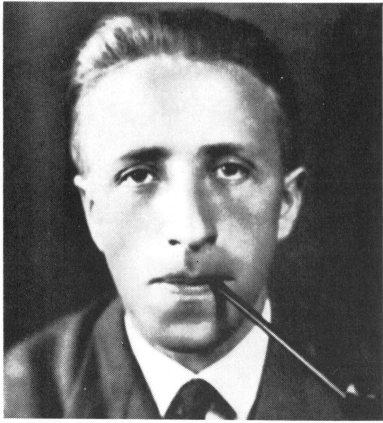

Lewis Grassic Gibbon (1901-1935).

'Sunset Song' a Symbol of Bitter-sweet Days

Sunset Song tried to set down from the author's own recollections the courage and the squalor and the pain and the glory that was the history of the folk of the windy Howe in the beginning of his day and generation. It was, it seemed, a kind of symbol of the bitter-sweet days of his own childhood by Arbuthnott here, a Valentine decked with his love for the sullen acres of Kincardine and the men who slaved on them, yet weighted with his hatred for man's inhumanity to man,

> *... and faith! it was coarse land and lonely up there on the brae, fifty-sixty acres of it, forbye the moor that went on with the brae high above Blawearie, up to a great flat hill-top where lay a bit loch that nested snipe by the hundred; and some said there was no bottom to it ... but there the spleiter of water was, a woesome dark stretch.*

The farms all along the hill slopes – Upper and Nether Craighill, Pitcarles, the Milton and the rest – are all in *Sunset Song*. And the blunt, couthy characters who lived in them were very real people in their day, so real and unflattered that the name of James Leslie Mitchell was none too popular in these parts for a time.

Round Cairn on Mitton Hill

As we have said, there are ancient recumbent stones and the remains of stone-circles on the moorland around Bloomfield, and these too we find in *Sunset Song* with a brooding sense of the supernatural,

> *As he went over an open space of the vanished Standing Stones, he saw right in front of him a halted cart; and a man had got out of the cart and knelt by the axle and looked at it. And Chae thought it some carpet billy from the Netherhill taking the near cut through the moor, and steered out to go by and cried, 'Good night, then'. But there wasn't an answer, so he looked again, and no cart was there ... and Chae's hackles fair stood up on end.*

Let us look at some of these antiquities for it is time we were on our way. At the road fork at the farm of Nether Pitforthie in 1¹/₅ miles we turn right and proceed for exactly one mile to the cross roads at Cothead of Barras. Let us follow the farm track to the left and at its extremity in about 320 yards pass through a gate towards Mitton

Hill on our right. A short, easy climb of 160 yards to the top of the hill will take us to a Bronze Age round cairn which has been robbed. It is 2½ ft. high and its diameter (55.7 ft.) is almost exactly the same as that of the stone-circle on Mont Goldrum. It is in a state of some dilapidation, about twenty of the boulders which originally formed the kerb lying haphazardly around.

A Vigorous Beaker Community

The remains of the Mont Goldrum stone-circle one clearly sees just a mile and a third away to the south-west. Almost directly south and about 2²/₅ miles away are the remains of the other stone-circle and the huge standing-stone on the lower slopes of Gallow Hill, while just over 1¾ miles away to the south-east are the knolls on the farm of Largie in which short-cist burials were found. In a short time we are to refer to the cairn on St John's Knap. All this, together with the Moray Stone on Murraystone Hill (it measures 4¼ ft. by 1½ ft. at the base and 5½ ft. in height), the finding of a cist on Grieve's Knap, a tumulus on St John's Hill and so forth makes one realise with awe something of the large community of vigorous Beaker folk[1] who walked these hills and cultivated their little fields in the valleys below for six miles around Arbuthnott parish some 3,600 years ago.

Just three-fifths on the way towards Mont Goldrum and 300 yards north-west of the top of Murraystone Hill was found a sandstone spindle whorl with incised radiating lines. It is now in Dundee Museum.

Influence of the Knights Templars

Continuing on our way, we turn to the right at the next fork in just under half a mile and carry on for another half mile to the farm of Chapel of Barras. This, together with the various Chapeltons and Temples throughout the county, the name of the farm of Chapelton 2⁴/₅ miles away and the site of the actual chapel nearby it (we shall shortly see exactly where it was) indicates an ancient cell or church, very often a sacred well as at Glenbervie, St Ninian's etc. The chapel and burial-ground are said to have been situated just over 100 yards west of Chapel of Barras farmhouse. They are first mentioned in the 17th century but may have been of mediaeval origin.

[1] Intrusive people and perhaps the first Indo-Europeans who came to Britain at the beginning of the Bronze Age *c.* 2,200 B.C. They are so named from their characteristic reddish pottery. See *Highways and Byways Round Stonehaven*, pp. 109-110 and 197.

We are reminded, too, that in days gone by a considerable portion of these lands of Barras belonged to the Knights of St John. You will recall that we commented on this when we passed the farm of Temple and the old church of Catterline earlier in our journey. The influence of the Knights Templars is seen, too, in the names of the two small hills both to the east and west of the road that travels south-east from the Chapel of Barras to join the A92 at Roadside of Kinneff. To the west is St John's Hill, part of the Templar lands in Kinneff and Catterline; to the east is St John's Knap.

St John's Knap

On top of St John's Knap is quite clearly visible on the skyline and only half a mile away the remains of a mound or round cairn about 82 yards in circumference and 26 yards in diameter. The stones of which it is formed are to be seen in places protruding through the grass. This cairn was opened about 1820 when there was uncovered a little below the surface a stone cist or coffin constructed of long, flat stones for the sides and cover, a short stone forming each end. In this, states the 1843 *Statistical Account*,

> *was contained nearly a cart-load of rich black earth, having a mixture of half-burnt bones and bits of oak charcoal, without any kind of urn.*

It is not unlikely that on St John's Knap still remain unexplored tumuli bearing mute but expressive testimony to the ideas which prehistoric man had concerning religion and a future state.

If you have time to deviate from the homeward road to visit this site, I suggest that you travel by car along the road for just over half a mile until you reach a gate on the left almost exactly at the top of the hill. (There is a turning place available a little farther on.) You will see the cairn quite clearly on the skyline on your left, some 620 yards away, and it may be possible to reach it if the field is fallow. The choice is yours. From the top can be seen to the south, in the valley below, the tops of the trees round Fawsyde House at Roadside of Kinneff. One recalls that coins of the reign of Antoninus were found there in the 19th century, not far from the main road. Two bronze bars and a piece of bronze like the clasp of a strong-box were found at the same time.

Through the Lands of Barras

And now towards home again! We return to Chapel of Barras and take the fork to the right from which we arrive at crossroads in four-fifths of a mile. Turn right here again, continue for three-tenths of a mile, turn left and then (for the third time) right again in 320 yards. Some 340 yards along this new road, that is opposite the middle of the second field on the right, there was found while ploughing just over 100 yards from the road a small leaf-shaped arrowhead of brown flint, ¾ in. long and of the same maximum breadth. There is a photograph of it in Aberdeen University Library.

Three-fifths of a mile farther on we arrive at a T-junction near which is the farm of East Mains of Barras. The lands of Barras through which we have been travelling, you will have noticed, represent one of the most thriving agricultural regions in the county, but of old they formed an estate of some importance the homesteads of which extended over the south of Dunnottar and the greater part of Catterline. The area is rich in historical associations as we have seen, and what interests us now is not the farm of East Mains of Barras itself, the drive to which is only 50 yards away, but a ruin in a neighbouring field.

The Ancient Place of Barras

The field to the north-east of the farm is the site of the barest vestiges of the ancient House or Place of Barras as it used to be called ('placed on the barr or ridge-top'), a tower-house which belonged to the latter part of the 17th century. It was the home of the Mearns Ogilvys. A considerable stretch of wall now flanking the north-east side of the farm garden was, amazingly enough, once standing parallel to its present position fourteen or fifteen yards out in the field beyond and moved by a farmer many years ago to be rebuilt, stone by stone, in its present place so that he might gain a greater area for his crops. That this wall originally bordered the garden of the House of Barras is made evident even today by the fact that the soil of that part of the field which was once garden is considerably richer than that elsewhere. Remains of the House of Barras itself are still to be seen behind the present farmhouse where thirty yards of mouldering wall still stand, some of it seemingly part of what was the south-east frontage of the building with, in all probability, a door and a window now filled in. The house wall, we note, was 3 ft. thick. At right angles to this is another ten or eleven yards of what was quite obviously the wall of the house which would seem to have been L-shaped. Behind it on the ground are several dressed stones.

In a flower bed outside the front door of the present farmhouse is part of what I am told was an ornamental gate-post of the old House of Barras with inscriptions of some kind on the stone ball on top. On an adjacent wall is a small part of yet another pillar, again surmounted by a stone sphere about the size of a football, this time a fragment of a 17th century globe sundial. Beside the wall lie parts of an old stone fireplace. In the field to the north of the farmhouse, and amid the trees, is a spring which is still surrounded by many chiselled stones, one of them circular in shape, which had once walled in the well of the House.

All that remains of the 3 ft. thick wall of the ancient House or Place of Barras, the home of the Mearns Ogilvys and of the Lieutenant-governor of Dunnottar Castle who in 1651 and 1652 defied the efforts of the Cromwellian forces to capture the castle and the Regalia of Scotland. It will be seen that a door and a window have now been filled in. It was in the garden wall here that part of the Regalia, the Sword-belt, was discovered in 1790.

Mysterious Retention of Scotland's Sword-belt

What is far more interesting is that it was in the garden wall here as we have seen (page 96) that part of Scotland's Regalia, the belt of Scotland's sword, was discovered in 1790 when the wall was taken down prior to being moved nearer the farm steading. For the House of Barras was the home of the Lieutenant-governor of Dunnottar Castle who from 1651 until May 24th, 1652, defied the efforts of the Cromwellian forces to capture the castle and, more important, the Regalia of Scotland.

The Governor had earlier removed the Sceptre from Kinneff to offset the machinations of the Countess Marischal, the mother of the Earl Marischal, whom he distrusted because of the clamour of his friends and their insistence that she was attempting to betray him. Indeed, she had written Charles, the king, six days before his arrival in London in 1660, assuming all responsibility for the Regalia and requesting to be favoured with his personal instructions as to their disposal. This probably accounts for the mysterious and unexplained retention of the Sword-belt. Fearing that the Earl Marischal might refuse to grant him a receipt, Ogilvy was constrained, we take it, to appropriate the belt that he might still have something to produce in proof that he alone could render the Regalia intact to the king. This is a mere assumption, but it affords a reasonable explanation of the fact that the Sword-belt was retained and subsequently found at Barras here.

The Place of Barras was eventually used as a farmhouse which, about the year 1862, was demolished by the Governor of Donaldson's Hospital, Edinburgh, into whose possession it had come. Only a bell, some stones of the belfry and an old gateway were preserved. The bell, latterly mounted on the gable of the present farmhouse, fell down and was broken; part of the gateway we have already seen in the flower bed near the farmhouse; the other part rests in a garden at Cheyne.

The tale of the successful defence of the Regalia under the very eyes of the besieging host is told elsewhere.[1] But perhaps one may digress for a moment to note the repercussions on the family of Ogilvy. After the gallant garrison of Dunnottar had marched out with drums beating and colours, borne by the Governor's son, flying, George Ogilvy and his wife were rigorously dealt with despite an agreement that they were to enjoy personal freedom. The estate of Barras was sequestrated, and the Ogilvys were closely confined in a room in the stronghold they had so stoutly defended and denied even the services of a servant. This state of affairs lasted for approximately a year until, on the bond of Sir Robert Graham of Morphie and James Anderson of Uras, they were permitted to go home on condition that they would not go above three miles from Barras, that they would engage in nothing prejudicial to the Commonwealth and that they would be prepared to present themselves as prisoners if called upon to do so. Within a year of their return to Barras Mrs Ogilvy died but, with the restoration of the monarchy in 1660, her husband got his reward for services rendered and was made a baronet, obtaining at the same time a grant from the Crown

[1] See *Highways and Byways Round Stonehaven*, pp. 142-145.

converting his feudal tenure of the lands of Barras from *ward-holding to Blanch*, that is, acknowledging his superior only by a mere nominal payment annually.

Lumgair

The next farm on the left, three-tenths of a mile along the road, is the farm of Lumgair or Lonkyr as the word was rendered in the days of William the Lion. The name literally means 'the church by the fort'. Lumgair was one of the first important places in the county, held during the centuries by the Glaysters or Glosters and the Raits. It also had associations with the Lindsay family and was the original seat of the Falconers of Haulkerton whose representative married Catherine, elder daughter and heiress of the second Earl of Kintore. Lumgair was also the first estate of the Ogilvys of Barras. In this connection it is recorded that William, second and surviving son of Ogilvy of Balnagarrow and Chapelton sold his ancestral estate in Angus and had a wadset or mortgage right of the small barony of Lumgair from the Earl Marischal. This particular Ogilvy by his marriage with a niece of Strachan, laird of Thornton, was the father of the brave Governor of Dunnottar (see above) who defended it against the forces of Cromwell for eight months, from a military point of view no mean achievement. It is gratifying to know that the enemy acknowledged its heroic character in the honourable terms they conceded.

Law of Lumgair

After travelling another three-tenths of a mile, we reach a side road branching off to the left. This we should follow for just under quarter of a mile until we arrive at crossroads. The road to the right will take us in around 230 yards to the farm of Law of Lumgair, named from the law of 492 ft. in height which stands behind it amid the trees. This eminence, too, has a place in the lore of the county for near its summit there was found in an excavation of 1860, under what previously had been a cairn, an ancient kiln, probably mediaeval, entered by rude steps on the west side. The kiln, 7 ft. deep, 8½ ft. in diameter at the top and 4½ ft. at the bottom, was lined with stones and small boulders bearing the marks of fire. At the bottom were rudely shaped, decomposed bricks under which was a layer of clay 2 ins. thick. At the bottom, too, were found large quantities of black, unctuous earth, charcoal and a small quantity of burnt oats and barley. There is now no trace of what for some inexplicable reason was called the Pict's Kiln except for the excavation hollow on the south-west side of the law. Although the mound may have been a prehistoric cairn, no burials from it are recorded, and it may have been built to support the funnel of the kiln.

Site of Chapel of John the Baptist

Having returned to join our main road by exactly the same route, let us again turn northwards towards Stonehaven. But let us stop for a moment just before we leave the straight part of the road and veer slightly left exactly three-tenths of a mile farther on. On the crest of the seemingly artificial knoll in the middle of the field 335 yards to your right and some 60 yards beyond the end of the fence which you see plunging into the dip once stood the chapel of which we spoke earlier, a chapel on lands belonging to the Knights Templars as at Johnshaven and Inverbervie. Dedicated to St John the Baptist, it was called *capellaria de St John in Kinneff vocatae Barras* (the chapel of St John in Kinneff, called Barras) and was undoubtedly proprietory, the owners being the barons of Barras and formerly the barons of Lumgair, and the patronage went with the lands. Like its church, the chapel was in the diocese of St Andrews, the church and chapel being rated together at 40 merks.

It is believed that the chapel was in use up to the year 1641 when the advowsons (rights of patronage or presentation to a church benefice) of the chaplainries of Kinneff and Barras together with the kirk-lands of Kinneff were given to William Gray of Pittendrum. There was, however, at least one other chapel in the district as, in a deed of reversion at Kinneff, granted by Alexander Straiton of Key to Andrew, Lord Gray, in 1493, mention is made of a croft of land *lyand at the bridgend beside Saint Martin's Chaple* between the lands of Dullachy and Discluse.

Although no trace of the existence of the chapel now remains, cropmarks reveal a rectangular enclosure, measuring 131 ft. by 98 ft. within a ditch 10 ft. broad. Furthermore, the hill opposite to where it stood is known as St John's Hill, and further evidences of there being an ecclesiastical establishment in the vicinity are seen, of course, in Lumgair, in Lampool a mile to the north-west (llan, a church, and poll, pond or lake – the pool beside the cell) and in the name of the neighbouring farm which we shall pass in just over quarter of a mile, styled to this day Chapelton or Chapel of Barras.

Kittlenakit

In just under half a mile turn right past Brackmuirhill School and, on the left, Brackmuir Hill itself on the slope of which, 270 yards to our left, two cists, one of them containing a beaker, were discovered early in the century. We turn left again at the end of the road at North Gallaton Farm on the Barras Estate or, as it was once known, Kittlenakit, the name, too, of an adjacent hamlet in bygone days. 'Kittle' is probably from 'cuthail', a place for drying corn, the same as Quithel. With 'naked' the second part of the word the whole place-name means a bare height where corn was dried. It seems not unlikely that on the eminence behind North Gallaton Farm, 400 ft. high and some 200 yards long by 100 yards wide, crofters of Dunnottar once spread their grain to dry, removed from the danger of a coastal haar below.

Found at North Gallaton in 1923 and now in the Museum of Antiquities, Edinburgh, was a stone whorl or disc, decorated on both sides with interlaid work and dating from the Roman period onwards. The whorl would have been slipped on to a spindle used for spinning thread by hand for the purpose of continuing the rotary movement imparted to the spindle by a finger or hand.

Smiddymuir

In around 270 yards we reach the farm of Bourtreebush in the field beyond which, 180 yards past the farm and 100 yards from the road on the crown of the ridge, there once were Bronze Age cairns where stone implements were found. Before 1865 *several small cairns* were removed from moorland nearby. After a further three-quarters of a mile we pass on our left the headquarters of Dunnottar Quoiting Club, the only surviving club in the Mearns where the near forgotten art of quoiting is still practised. The Club was formed at Brackmuirhill School, which we have just passed, on 10th July, 1890. A sharp turn to the left reveals that the house in the grounds of which quoiting continues was an old smithy (now quite converted) which gave its name to the neighbouring farms of West Smiddymuir and Smiddymuir. The smiddy was an ancient one which ceased to exist early in the 19th century when the tenants and crofters of the hamlet of Smiddymuir removed to the old town of Stonehaven. The work was transferred to the smithy on the site of St Bridget's opposite the Sheriff and District Court Buildings, a smithy which had existed there probably for a century or two.[1]

Continuing down the hill, we are soon at Glaslaw Bridge and in one and three-quarter miles in Stonehaven Square where we started. The round trip, including our various small walks, has covered in all just 46 miles.

[1] See *Highways and Byways Round Stonehaven*, p. 6.

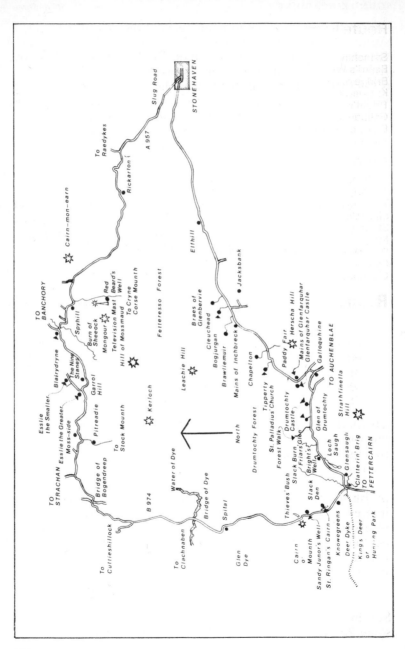

Route Four

Stonehaven Square – Rickarton – Television Mast – Cairn-mon-earn – Red Beard's Well – Blairydryne – The Nine Stanes – Esslie Greater and Smaller – Bridge of Dye – Spitalburn – Clochnaben – Thieves' Bush – Cairn o' Mounth – Knowegreens – Clatterin' Brig – Deer Dyke – Slack Burn – Loch Saugh – Bright's Well – Friars' Glen – Glen of Drumtochty – Drumtochty Castle – Galloquhine – Glenfarquhar Castle – Paddy Fair – Herscha Hill – Tipperty – Braes of Glenbervie – Mains of Inchbreck – Brawliemuir – Jacksbank – Bogjurgan – Cleughead – Elfhill – Stonehaven Square.

Distance: 44¾ miles, 43 by car and 1¾ on foot.

Additional suggested excursions are of the following total lengths:
The original Bogjurgan – 0.8 miles by car
The original Brawliemuir – 1.2 miles (1 mile by car and 0.2 miles on foot)
Slack Den – 1.5 miles on foot
St Mary's Well and Chapelton – 1.5 miles (0.6 miles by car and 0.9 miles on foot)
Deer Dyke to Glen Muchrae – 3 miles on foot
Cairn-mon-earn – 4 miles on foot
Clochnaben – 5.2 miles on foot.

Round the Cairn o' Mounth, the Glen of Drumtochty and the Braes of Glenbervie

concerning Hogs and pigs and a pigsty with Burns associations, concerning a school with cock-fighting and one opened by the King of Norway, and concerning the abode of a witch, a ravine of evil repute and a stone with the Devil's wife beneath it.

This particular car run is intriguing in that it follows the most famous hill route in Kincardineshire and one of the best known passes traversing the lower Grampians. On our way there is much of varied interest to see.

Doubtless with surprise we shall end by visiting a most attractive parish at the edge of the Grampian moors which has an outstanding interest and importance to Scotsmen the world over in that it was for well over a century the cradle of the family of Robert Burns, Scotland's national poet. It is even said that the ancestors of Burns had their little farms around this area for 300 years, but this has never been proved.

The Slug Mounth

Starting from Stonehaven Square, we proceed up Evan Street for some 260 yards, taking the third turn on the right, the A957 to

Banchory. This is the well-known winding and picturesque Slug Road or Slug Mounth (from sloc, the throat, or slugan, the gullet) which penetrates a region of remarkable grandeur and isolation although so near centres of population. The Slug Road is an ancient drove road which intersects the parish as it passes over the hills to Deeside, and there must have been a road of some kind here from very early days. Points of interest at the Stonehaven end of the road, Arduthie Camp, Mackie Academy, Ury House, the Barclay family and the rest have already been dealt with in *Highways and Byways Round Stonehaven*, pages 167-181.

Rickarton

Let us therefore join it at the middle reach of the Water of Cowie, at Rickarton with its tightly knit little community just under five miles from Stonehaven where the shop, the school and the church (the last two both now closed) line the south side of the Slug Road. The church owes its foundation to the Rev. George Thomson, minister of Fetteresso, who made a bequest of £3,237 for its erection. It was built in 1871, and in 1872 Rickarton became a *quoad sacra* parish, taking in parts of Fetteresso and Glenbervie.

Well over a century ago the population of 'The Glen' was far greater than it is today, and to find evidence of this one has only to survey the remains of one-time homesteads and holdings that are scattered from the borders of Netherley and Durris to those of Glenbervie. How steep the decline in population has been is shown in the roll of Rickarton's little country school which once housed between 100 and 130. Even in the 30's of this century there were between sixty and seventy pupils.

The answer to the evacuation is that the soil, not the most productive at any time, yielded only an existence when cultivated in small units by the primitive tools which our ancestors possessed. Perhaps it was a happy enough existence according to the standards of other days, but it was not enough to persuade following generations to stay. They drifted off to larger communities, and the land which had supported their forebears reverted to heather. A benefactor, however, has been found in the shape of the Forestry Commission. Acre upon acre of barren hill-side has been reclaimed, ploughed and planted, and today the scene is a complete transformation from what it was some thirty years ago or more. The assistant forester's house, Sylvan View, is, incidentally, built on the site of a former POW camp.

Some two miles or so farther on the road enters upon a fine

stretch of moorland from various points on which the views on both sides and of the North Sea behind are magnificent.

Television Mast

On the left near the top of the bleak heather-clad Hill of Mongour about a mile and a quarter to the south-west is the 1,005 ft. high Grampian and BBC television mast of Durris, a prominent feature of the landscape. With the start given by the 1,232 ft. high Hill of Mongour it is the highest mast in Great Britain and about the fourth highest in the world. It serves Aberdeenshire, Deeside and Kincardineshire.

The mast weighs at least 140 tons, and the movement at the top is something like 7 ft. The concrete base on which it is poised is sunk 16 ft. on to solid rock, and the mounting is of the ball and socket type. The steel 'ball' on which it rests and on which it depends for its 'truth' is only 1½ ins. in diameter.

Such a colossal mast requires to be securely 'stayed', and this is done by a series of guy ropes fixed to the mast at different levels and to concrete bases – also sunk on to solid rock – at varying distances from the base. The top stays are naturally the longest and strongest, and their anchorages are each 1,000 ft. away from the foot of the mast. As they fade upwards, they look like threads, but an inspection of them on the ground reveals that they too are of great strength.

The Durris transmitter has been beaming colour television pictures and sound signals to 1,000,000 North-east viewers since 1961. Some twenty-five workers maintain costly equipment there, monitoring the quality of pictures and keeping an eye on a chain of twenty or so relay transmitters strategically sited throughout Grampian and Tayside Regions and the Northern Isles. So powerful are the 625-line colour transmitters at the station that they have to be cooled by a constant stream of water which is, of course, converted to steam by the intense heat.

Red Beard's Well and Cave

Near the television station is Red Beard's Well, a chalybeate spring (i.e. one impregnated with iron) and reputedly mediaeval well the waters of which, unfortunately now contaminated by reeds and decayed vegetable matter, were supposed to resemble the waters of Harrogate! This watery lair was named after a robber who headed a band specialising in freebooting and cattle thieving, lying in wait, according to tradition, for travellers. Red Beard's cave was on

Craigbeg (1,054 ft.), the hill half a mile to the south-west surmounted by two small cairns.

Cairn-mon-earn

Opposite on the right is Cairn-mon-earn (1,254 ft.) on the west shoulder of which the road rises to a height of 757 ft. as it crosses the throat through the eastern continuation of the Grampians. Here is the last prominent hill of the Grampian range, dominating miles of country. The name possibly means 'quharn-na-quharn', the cairn of cairns (for it occupies a commanding position and the top is even shaped like a cairn), or 'fearna', cairn of the alder trees, and 'nan-earann', of the divisions of land.

The summit is surmounted by a somewhat dilapidated Bronze Age cairn about 60 yards in circumference, now regrettably topped by an Ordnance Survey triangulation point and a wooden hut! The masts are for the use of Grampian Region police and fire services and are linked with the Region's ambulance and Hydro Board radio systems. From this vantage point there is a fine view of the most easterly portion of the great range of the northern Grampians, tapering off by gentle slopes to the pasture lands along the coast, all of considerably lower elevation than Cairn-mon-earn itself and, viewed from it, having perhaps little appearance. Immediately to the north is Mundernol (1,035 ft.), separated by a slight depression. It is rather flattish topped and from some points of view is indistinguishable from Cairn-mon-earn. There are fine views, too, of the lovely valley of the Dee (now generally regarded as the Deva of Ptolemy), so richly endowed by nature.[1]

About 1841 a considerable quantity of copper Scots pennies of the reign of Mary Queen of Scots and Francis II, her husband, was found lying on the surface of the earth on Cairn-mon-earn by a carter who was removing some stones to build a new tollhouse. F and M were imprinted on one side, a lion rampant on the other with the motto, *Veritas vicit* (Truth hath conquered).

The Cryne Cross Mounth

The road continues over the high ridge of Cairn-mon-earn with a steep bend to the right just under 9½ miles from Stonehaven and, interestingly enough, just 9 miles too from Banchory as is proclaimed on a mile-stone round the corner near Spyhill Farm. From here a road has been carved due south uphill to the transmitting

[1] One may climb Cairn-mon-earn on foot, entering Durris Forest by a Forestry Commission road exactly half a mile past the seventh milestone. The distance to the summit and back is 4 miles.

station for in the depths of winter Mongour can be a most desolate spot. While nobody lives at the station permanently, provision has been made for emergencies, and during severe snow-storms the staff may expect to work long shifts!

We may not drive to the transmitting station, as can be seen from the notice at the end of the road, but if another day we were to walk there, we could continue over the east shoulder of the Hill of Mossmaud to the south-east of Mongour and behind the television station. Then due south through Fetteresso Forest and across the Cowie Water to the Braes of Glenbervie (which we shall see before the end of this outing) between the farms of Cleughead on the east and on the west Bogjurgan. We would then be following the old right of way called the Cryne Cross Mounth. Sir James Balfour of Denmilne (1600-1651) spells the name as Craiyin Crosse, while on Gordon's map of Kincardine in 1776 it is named Crine Cross Road. This Mounth pass is also marked as a road on Roy's map of 1755.

Cryne's Cross Mounth was much used in history. It is the probable route taken by Edward I on July 13th, 1296, when he travelled from Glenbervie to Durris. It was also used repeatedly in the time of the Covenanting troubles by Montrose who, knowing well how to take advantage of routes as well as ground in his campaigns, came to be very familiar with all these passes over the Mounth.

The name, Cryne's Cross, is most probably a personal name. There was a noted family called Cryne in Aberdeen in the middle centuries when boundary crosses were in use to distinguish particular lands. It is not unlikely that a boundary stone of the Cryne family gave the name to this route over the Grampians.

The distance from the Spyhill Farm corner here to Quithel on the Braes of Glenbervie and thence to the Stonehaven-Auchenblae road is only 5$^{1}/_{5}$ miles, and I recommend this second Mounth pass as a most pleasant and historic walk for a sunny afternoon. From this point of the Slug Road, too, is to be had what is perhaps the best view of Crathes Castle in its woodland setting just under 3¾ miles away on the other side of the Dee valley. Far in the background can be seen the Mither Tap, the volcanic tip of the hill of Bennachie nearly 30 miles away to the north. The journey across the Slug Road is one we shall not readily forget.

Blairydryne

In just over another 1¼ miles we arrive at the early 19th century Bridge of Blairydryne with its corbelled parapets, crossing the Burn of Sheeoch which rises on the east side of Kerloch and has a course of nearly 12 miles, in some parts rather picturesque. Leaving the

Slug Road here, we must turn sharply left towards Strachan (pro-nounced Stran!). At the junction is the farm of Blairydryne the lands of which along both sides of the Sheeoch Burn are first mentioned in the 15th century as part of the ancient barony of Dores (Durris) when they were owned by William Keith, 2nd Earl Mari-schal. In 1478 the Earl Marischal's tenant of the property was one Andrew Hog whose family of Scandinavian origin had been tenants on Durris lands for several generations. They had established themselves in the Lothians some time during the 13th century, but it is not known when they first settled in Kincardineshire.

It was in Blairydryne early in October, 1537, that King James V, 'the poor man's king', and his party were made welcome for the night and entertained lavishly on country fare. He loved to travel the country incognito and, following the death of his consort, Queen Madeline,[1] he was returning from a pilgrimage to the shrine of St Duthus in Tain. He had forded the Dee at Mills of Drum and had been visiting Ashentilly, a place some five miles to the north-east on the route traversed by Edward I. (To distinguish it from a similarly named place which belonged to a subject, it was thereafter named Ashentilly Regis.) On his way south towards the Grampians via the Cairn o' Mounth he and his party encountered a sharp thunder-storm which compelled them to seek shelter at the farm of Blairydryne, then tenanted by the generous Monane Hog who, quite unaware of the identity of his guest, slaughtered several hogs which he served the king at table.

So impressed was King James by the friendly hospitality towards travellers that, when he was leaving, he enquired the farmer's name and shook his hand, saying, 'Your name is a good one, Hog, especially for a farmer! Always remember a good name gives strength'. That was not the end of the incident for the king informed the Earl Marischal how well he had been treated so that not long after the worthy Monane Hog was granted the farm and lands of Blairydryne by the Earl Marischal (who had a proprietory interest in Durris) in recognition of his courtesy to his sovereign. Thus a Kincardineshire farmer became a laird.

With the passing of the years the Hogs of Blairydryne prospered and married into several well-known Deeside families. About 1680 a James Hog, the great-great-great grandson of Monane. married

---

[1] It is interesting to note that this sad event (the queen died barely eight weeks after her arrival in Scotland) marked the introduction of 'dool weeds' – mourning dress – then used for the first time in Scotland.

Margaret Skene, only daughter and heiress of Robert Skene, 5th laird of Raemoir, whose father, James Skene, the 4th laird, had built the old Ha' Hoose there. Hog's coat of arms can be seen above the entrance doorway, reminding us of a fascinating story.

Alexander Hog's 'Mortification'

Although the family of Hog have died out, the name has been perpetuated in the parish as, in 1787, a Mr Alexander Hog, a native of the area, entrusted to the kirk session of the parish bequests for educational and other purposes. In the *Statistical Account* of 1843 the *mortification*, as it is called, is stated to have been *£500 three per cents reduced, yielding £15 a year*. The *Account* continues that it was later sold for £420 and *placed at interest in this country*, the money being devoted to several benefactions. The sum of £5 was given yearly to the headmaster of Mr Hog's charity school whose income was augmented by the interest on a further legacy of £100, fees from pupils at the rate of 3/6 per quarter and the tenancy of a small croft, gifted by the proprietor of the estate. The remainder of the yearly interest was disbursed as follows: £1 to the kirk session for their trouble in managing the fund, 10/- to the session-clerk for keeping the books, £9 to poor householders not on the poors'-roll, and 10/- to the herds round the hill of Cairnshee. This last allocation, a considerable sum in those days, is possibly the most interesting feature of the bequest.

The Nine Stanes

We must now continue westwards along the Strachan road with on our left the bare, exposed northern slopes of the Grampians. After $2^1/_{10}$ miles we reach a woodland area on our right and the first of three stone-circles in the area, evidence that this region was inhabited long before the Christian era. Further proof is supplied by the many small cairns dotted on the neighbouring moors.

On the summit of Garrol Hill stop at the red Fire notice at the end of the Forestry Commission road which leads into Mulloch Wood. There is easy pedestrian access through a swing gate. 100 yards along this road there is seen very obviously on the right, most picturesquely situated in a clearing, an impressive recumbent stone-circle (see page 24) with the remains of a ring cairn inside. Almost entire, with only part of one of the uprights broken, it is known locally as The Nine Stanes: it has seven uprights varying between 3 ft. 2 ins. and 6 ft. 6 ins. in height and two huge boulders which have fallen. A bank of earth and stones runs between the stones of the circle the diameter of which is 56 ft.

The recumbent stone with its flankers (one of which has fallen) of the Nine Stanes stone-circle three miles east of Strachan. Three other stones of the circle can be seen in the background. Recumbent stone-circles, peculiar to North-east Scotland, belong to a period from 1800 B.C. to around 1500 B.C.

This stone-circle differs from classic sites in having the recumbent set 12 ft. inside the outer stone-circle. Since the centre of the circle is the centre of the ring cairn, this has the effect of tending to distort the shape of the ring cairn and of incorporating the recumbent and flankers on the ring cairn's circumference. At Aquhorthies, too, just under 11½ miles from here as the crow flies (see page 26) the recumbent is also set well within the line of the circle. The kerb of the ring cairn (which was no more than 3 ft. or 4 ft. high) is connected to the flankers of the recumbent. Here at Mulloch Wood there is a marked asymmetry, and the same feature occurs at more normally circular sites. This variation in plan suggests that this circle was built late in the sequence of recumbent stone-circles.

Within the outer circle is an inner concentric circle of upright boulders varying in height from about 1 ft. to 3 ft. and delimiting an open circular area between 11½ ft. and 13 ft. in diameter, a feature of several of the recumbent stone-circles of North-east Scotland. The middle of this central area was slightly hollowed out of the natural subsoil when the site was carefully excavated in 1904 by an archaeologist named Coles who found at its centre a slab-lined, funnel-shaped cist or pit (2 ft. 2 ins. in diameter at the top and 10 ins. in depth), filled with charcoal and comminuted burnt bone. Round about were four pits or scoops with cremation deposits, each apparently representing a single person, a charcoal deposit and several fragments of undiagnostic pottery.

There is some evidence that the central ring might have stood as an independent feature within the recumbent stone-circle before the addition of the covering cairn. The uprights of the ring cairn have been carefully supported from behind by a second ring of large boulders with smaller stones between the two rings.

Burial by cremation, possibly at more than one time at Mulloch Wood and Eslie the Greater (which we have yet to visit and where there may have been inhumation also) seems to have been part of the function of the sites. It is, however, unnecessary to ascribe a purely sepulchral function to recumbent stone-circles (as we have already seen on page 28).

Eslie the Greater and Eslie the Smaller

When we have returned to our car, we continue along the Strachan road, admiring the wonderfully panoramic view of the hills of Deeside which unfolds itself after we turn the corner in only one-tenth of a mile. In just under half a mile we must take the first turning to the right which leads us to our next circle, Eslie the Greater, 100 yards off the public road in a field to the left just 130 yards farther on. A gate and a path lead to it. There are ten stones in the outer circle (it seems originally to have had twelve) and twelve in the inner circle which is 20 ft. 7 ins. in diameter. There is evidence of there having been two if not three and perhaps four inner circles originally in this elaborate structure which is much larger than the other circles and which excellently illustrates cinerary purpose and method.

Here, 2½ ft. down, a rough stone cist was found of common boulder stones, 8 ins. to 10 ins. in diameter, *in which were found black marks and pieces of bone but no more.* Round this, we are told by those who excavated the grave, there seem to have been another three or four bodies buried, *laid so as to form a circle*, a most unusual form of burial.

Just short of half a mile farther on, past the road on the left to Eslie Farm, is the third stone-circle of West Mulloch or Eslie the Smaller, again very obvious about 100 yards to the left of the public road. Although in this case most of the stones have toppled down and have been misplaced, it is clear that here there were originally two circles, the outer with a diameter of 45 ft. or 48 ft. and the inner of smaller stones of about 34 ft. Only five of the larger outer standing-stones remain in position. Irregularly placed slabs, the only find from the ring at Eslie the Smaller, are more likely to be displaced kerbstones than the remains of a cist.

Stock Mounth

Back to the Strachan road. A further half-mile takes us to the farm of Mosside, just under a quarter of a mile beyond which (and just past the corner) a path leads off to the south, uphill to the farm of Pitreadie. From there a track goes south-east across the hills, about a mile east of Kerloch, the conical hill in the distance, descends to the Well of Monluth and crosses the Cowie Water and the east side of Leachie Hill, again reaching the Braes of Glenbervie and Bogjurgan Farm in which we shall later be interested. This is yet another interesting pass across the long range of hills between Deeside and the South, this time known as the Stock Mounth. One day you may care to walk it: now a poor track, but easily distinguishable the whole way, it *contains sex myles of mounthe* or, to be more exact, is only 7¹/₅ miles over to Bogjurgan and thence to the Stonehaven-Auchenblae road. Eleven of these Mounth passes were listed in the 17th century by Balfour. They are printed in the Spalding Club *Collections on the Shires of Aberdeen and Banff*, published in 1843.

Cairn o' Mounth

We now proceed gradually into the charming valley of the Feugh with the village of Strachan appearing on our right, and in just over a mile join the B974. Here we are to turn left on to the romantic Cairn o' Mounth road, the most westerly of the historic passes over the Mounth, a steep and barren hill which even from Pictish times has been a great highway.

Kincardineshire being on the direct route between the north and south of Scotland, the earliest of the main roads in the country ran generally in these directions, leading to the Highlands and Lowlands. Where much of the land was ill-drained and boggy, the making of suitable roads was often a difficult and tedious matter. The high roads, being dry roads, were of necessity the first to be followed, while the straight line as the shortest distance between any two given points was, where practicable, preferred. In olden times posts were stuck into the ground at suitable intervals over the Cairn o' Mounth to direct travellers over an irregular course, but whatever improvements are made on it, the road is still liable to be blocked by snow in winter.

Snow fences are stark reminders of less clement days. We have seen them as early on in this journey as Rickarton, and we shall certainly see them on the Cairn. Erected by Kincardine County Council in the late 1950's in an effort to minimise blockages on the road, they stand out against their background, attracting a great deal of attention and giving rise to considerable conjecture. Strangers who see them on a warm, sunny late-summer day cannot visualise the possibilities of the area in deep, dark winter!

The importance of historic passes such as the Cairn o' Mounth has been fully shown by Dr Douglas Simpson in his various works and in the *Proceedings of the Society of Antiquaries*. The Cairn o' Mounth has echoed to the tread of the army of Malcolm Canmore who in 1057 gradually drove north beyond the Mounth the fleeing Macbeth who for seventeen years had with the help of Thorfinn, the Scandinavian (whose name may be seen in the Deeside town of Torphins), usurped the kingship of Scotland. Canmore overtook Macbeth in Lumphanan across the Dee where Macbeth was slain. Edward I, too, crossed the Cairn o' Mounth during the Wars of Independence when he passed through the Mearns on his triumphal march northwards in 1296. From Montrose he directed his course to *Kincardine in Mearns Manor*, then to Glenbervie Castle where he stayed a night, next over the Cairn to *Durris manor among the mountains*.

Montrose and Claverhouse also used this pass in the lower Grampians as did the red-coated regiments of King George II under that renowned road-maker, General Wade, the last of whose military roads this was. After the defeat of the rebels at Culloden not a few of them fled in the direction of the Mearns, coming down over the Cairn o' Mounth and molesting the peacefully disposed inhabitants of Fettercairn who were generally loyal to the House of Hanover. A number of these, acting in accordance with a proclamation of the Duke of Cumberland and on the authority of the sheriff of the county, armed themselves as a guard to watch the Cairn road day and night to prevent the destruction of life and property.

The road was also one of the great drove roads in the North of Scotland, used for many years by Highland drovers on their way via Banchory, Fettercairn and Brechin to Falkirk Tryst (by 1770 the greatest cattle market in Scotland) and the great annual fairs and markets south of the Grampians with cattle in their thousands from all over the northern counties. There they would meet dealers from the south. Let us follow the line of this very ancient track from our T-junction here over the Mounth to Glen Dye and the Clatterin' Brig, for it generally followed the line of the present roadway.

155

Bridge of Bogandreep

Our first point of interest is when we cross the Water of Dye at the Bridge of Bogandreep. Here is an extremely beautiful spot, quite as attractive as that where we shall later cross the stream at the Bridge of Dye. Passing through magnificent pine woods for 1¾ miles, we soon reach the AA box at Glen Dye where a fork bears off to the right. A little over a mile and a third along this road is Cuttieshillock where once stood one of the well-known inns of the North-east; but that is for another day.

Ascent of Clochnaben

Exactly 1½ miles beyond the AA box are some cottages on the left-hand side of the road. Opposite is an estate road leading into the woods, and here is the nearest possible point from which to ascend Clochnaben (1,944 ft.), the striking hill on the right the principal interest in which is the massive and very impressive granite tor on its summit. The estate road should be followed until, after about half a mile, the woods end. Turn left and follow the road down the hill until it crosses a small burn where a rough track leads off to the right. Follow the track until you come to a wood, continue through it and eventually follow the floor of a deep ravine. At the top end of this the path runs south-westwards directly to the summit. The rock on the top looks very unclimbable but can easily be ascended by going round the back. The distance to the summit, if you are so minded one fine day, is around 2³/₅ miles, the ascent from Feughside being a little longer.

Bridge of Dye

Another mile or so farther on is the entrance to Glendye Lodge, a beautifully situated shooting-box, and, 90 yards farther on again, in the heart of the delightfully wooded Glen Dye and just four miles short of the summit of the pass, our road ultimately crosses the Dye by the narrow, picturesque Bridge of Dye, a very old structure and one of particular interest. Under Ministerial care as a fine example of an early humpbacked bridge with a pointed, ribbed arch, it is the oldest bridge in the whole valley of the Dee, except the Bridge of Dee at Aberdeen. Prior to the erection of this bridge the Ford of Dye was at the spot and was evidently well known as we see from the new *Statistical Account* of Scotland:

> *In a remote and rude age the Cairn o' Mount road . . . was haunted by a lawless banditti. . . . About a century and a*

half ago (about 1692) *a highlander passing to the south was obliged to stop at a smith's shop at Ford of Dye near where the present bridge stands.*

The narrow, picturesque Bridge of Dye which, built in 1681, is the oldest bridge in the whole valley of the Dee. It is a fine example of an early humpbacked bridge with a pointed, ribbed arch. Sockets survive in two pillars on the bridge, opposite each other, from which at one time was hung a chain that spanned the causeway in order that tolls might be exacted for keeping the bridge in order.

Authorised Tolls for Repairs

The Bridge of Dye was built in 1681 by Sir Alexander Fraser of Durris, assisted by *mortification*, an archaic usage of the word which we have already met. By Scottish Acts of Parliament tolls were authorised to be charged for keeping the bridge in repair. The first, dated 1681, of the reign of Charles II reads:

> *The Kings Majestie and Estates of Parliament, having considered a Petition presented by Andrew ffrazer of Kinmundie Representing That wheras by the liberal and charitable contribution of the deceist Sir Alexander ffraser of Doores Baronet ... ther is ... Ane stonebridge of Asclerwork of a large extent of ffyftie foot diameter erected over the water of Dye upon the public road that crosseth the Cairne of Mounth, Which Bridge standeth upon one of the most impetuous waters within the Kingdom wher many have perished, And as this bridge was a most necessary work, so lykways it is subject to great and sudden Innundations and danger of being spoyled by storms, And therefore ther is a necessitie of a yearly supplie and continual attendance to prevent its ruine, Wheras there is no stock to that end, ffor the money mortified by the said Minister was only Two Thousand Merkes, which scarce served to pay the Maisons builders of the said Bridge, Albeit at their entry the stones were all hewin, And all other materials and service laid to their hands; ... The Kings Majesty and Estates of Parliament ... Doe hereby grant, ordor and Warrant to the said Andrew ffraser, Petitioner to exact and vplift at the Bridge of Dye, for vpholding of the said Bridge, the small customs vnder-written for the space of Nynteen yeers after the date hereof, viz, for each sadled horse and his ryder, or each horse with a Burden, Eight pennies scots money, And for each man or woman, or each horse, ox, cow (four sheep) or other small beast, ffour pennies money foirsaid, With power to the said Petitioner to appoint a Collector for vplifting thereof, He having found sufficient Caution that what shall be so vplifted shall be employed to the use above mentioned.*

The uplifting of the toll on the Bridge of Dye proved, however, unexpectedly difficult. Persons using the roads and bridges in 1681 were no more willing than their successors in the days of turnpikes to pay toll if they could avoid it. Accordingly, instead of using the new bridge over the Dye and paying the toll, travellers on the Cairn o' Mounth road forded the stream when it was at all possible and evaded their just charges. In 1685, therefore, Sir Peter Fraser of Durris, son of Sir Alexander who provided the bridge, petitioned Parliament to the following effect:

> *And now seeing that, by experience of collecting at the said Bridge, the yearly toll forsaid doth not amount to tuentie pound Scots by reason the Water is but small, except at extraordinary times, And the Bridge, lying in a mountain-ous place is not so much frequented except at certain Seasons and when there is no speat of waters it is easily fordable, albeit the water when in speat is a great torrent and Damnefies the bridge exceedingly, It being therfor requisit that for the supply of the said Bridge the toll foirsaid be perpetual As to other bridges in the same case And that the samen toll should, after expyring of the nynteen yeares for which it was first granted be therafter payable to your suppliant, his aires and successors, heretors of the Lands upon which the said bridge stands to be by them expended for the use of the said bridge.*

This petition, like the other, was granted, but for how long the toll was exacted nobody can tell. Quaint structural evidence survives in two pillars opposite each other, built into but rising above the low parapets of the bridge. In each is a socket from which was hung a chain that spanned the causeway in order that the tolls might be exacted.

The Cairn Road 'Spital'

From the Bridge of Dye the road by hill-side and moorland in just short of 1¼ miles reaches the farm of Spitalburn where it enters the valley of the Dye[1] about 2¾ miles north of the summit of the Cairn. Here, too, it crosses the Spital Burn which, after uniting with the Cran Burn, joins the Dye.

As the name implies, there existed on this spot from remote antiquity the 'spital' of the Cairn road, a hospital or hospitium for accommodating travellers and much frequented by cattle drovers. A very ancient ale-house or inn, aptly called Muirailhouse, suc-ceeded the hostelry long before the cattle trade began. It too

---

[1] In Glen Dye was found a Late Bronze Age hoard. Two leaf-shaped swords and two spear heads are to be seen in Montrose Museum.

159

disappeared as the drovers took to the railway. Here at the beginning of the 17th century lived a notorious witch, so far-famed that two ladies of quality travelled all the way from Montrose for a deadly potion. This they gave to the laird of Dun, their young nephew. When the boy's skin turned black, however, after death, the two ladies and their brother, who nearly became laird, were hanged. At one period this public house, like that at the Clatterin' Brig, had an indifferent reputation as may be inferred from an intimation once made in Strachan church,

> *The Cairn o' Mount road is quite safe now: there's honest folk at the Spital.*

Clochnaben

During the long and gradual ascent of 1 in 6½ in places with no difficult gradients and bends a fine view is obtained on the right of Clochnaben, with the possible exception of Mount Battock the most noticeable hill in the range between the Aven and the Dye. This peak may be properly designated the last of the Grampian range on the east. Clochnaben signifies 'stone of the mountain'. The 'stone' to which it refers is a mighty perpendicular projecting mass of granite, a crag 100 ft. high that has been produced by the wearing away of the softer material around it. Granite is the backbone of these 'grand old hills' and may be observed on Mount Battock and all the central heights eastward to Cove where it was extensively quarried.

Clochnaben is clearly visible from many different points: from its shape it is readily recognisable – which doubtless adds to its popularity – and it is so situated that it is seen far out to sea like a watch-tower or the ruins of a fortress. An old seaman's rhyme states,

> *Clochnaben and Bennachie*
> *Are two landmarks o' the sea*
> or
> *Are landmarks far upon the sea.*

There is a tradition, embodied in a poem written by Rev. George Kennedy, the minister of Birse near Aboyne who died in 1789, that the stone perched on top of the mountain originally lay *low in a plain* whence it was taken by the Devil to be hurled at his dame who has lain since entombed beneath it.

Range of Volcanic Hills

Clochnaben is part of a hilly range between the Waters of Aven and Dye, culminating at the upper end in Mount Battock (2,555 ft.), the highest mountain in the Mearns on top of which the three counties of Angus, Kincardine and Aberdeen meet.

The striking hill of Clochnaben (1,944 ft.) with a massive and very impressive granite tor on its summit. From its shape Clochnaben is readily recognisable from many different points – which doubtless adds to its popularity.

161

Between Mount Battock and Clochnaben, a distance of about four miles, the ground is much broken up by 'moss-hags' so much so that walking between these two points of the range is not very agreeable. North-eastwards from Clochnaben, at a distance of seven-eighths of a mile, is Mount Shade (1,662 ft.), the deep, narrow gorge between the two hills – visible from considerable distances – being locally known as The Devil's Bite. Still farther to the northward the range may be said to end in Craigangower (892 ft.) between the Dye and the Burn of Greendams, a small tributary of the Feugh.

It is of interest to note in passing that on the Cairn o' Mounth we are on a great line of volcanoes the lava and ashes from which spread eastwards over the countryside. There is another line away to the east off the village of Crawton.

Thieves' Bush

Five hundred yards from the top of the Cairn o' Mounth, on the left-hand side, is a ravine of evil repute called The Thief's Bush or Thieves' Bush or Lair which reminds us that the Cairn road was at one time infested by robbers who did not hesitate to murder on occasion. In this lonely place not a few old-time drovers were severely mauled and relieved of all they carried. On the southward journey the sturdy drovers had to guard against any of their cattle being stolen, and on the way back they were liable to be attacked and robbed of the price of the beasts they sold.

The kings of Scotland seem to have been solicitous about the perils to which this road exposed travellers. In the Lord High Treasurer's accounts there are frequent entries of the experience of messengers beyond the Mounth and to other parts of the kingdom. In March, 1497. for example, we read that a messenger named Currie received his expenses for a journey to an eyre or circuit court in the royal burgh of Bervie. And on April 15th, 1504, the king

> *for the singular favour he bears to Adam Hepburn of Craggis and for the good service of the said Adam, and for the common convenience of the lieges crossing the Mount of Fethercarn, erected the lands and town of the kirk-toun of Fethircarn, belonging to the said Adam and Elizabeth Ogstoun, his spouse, into a free burgh with the right of having a market cross, a weekly market and a public fair annually.*

The Summit

After a twenty-eight mile car journey from Stonehaven we find the cheerless summit of the pass (1,488 ft.) a fine view-point. With its cairn[1] which has stood from time immemorial (50¾ ft. in diameter by nearly 11½ ft. in height and surmounted by an Ordnance Survey Triangulation point) it provides a glorious, expansive view of the surrounding country: one looks far down to the south and east over the Kincardine coast and the fertile Howe of the Mearns and beyond the far-spreading, rolling stretches of Kincardineshire and Strathmore in Angus to where the distant waters of the North Sea glisten in the sunshine. On the west side are mountain-chains and valleys and wild, bleak moorland spread towards Mount Battock, Mount Keen (3,077 ft.) and the dark, blue outline of the Cairngorms. Mountains and upland forests are all around, and the healthy tang of the heights will doubtless be tempered even on the most beautiful day by a breeze from the distant sea and the soft freshness of the Howe of the Mearns beneath us.

The Descent

And now we wind downwards for two miles over a wide stretch of moorland high above the valley. From the summit there is a descent of 1,000 ft. and more, the gradient in places being as steep as 1 in 5½. But the fact that the road is in good condition helps the motorist immeasurably. For variety of scenery and expanse of mountain landscape the long and interesting descent of the Cairn o' Mounth with its intriguing and at times deceptive gradients is unequalled in Scotland; for those travelling in the opposite direction it is a popular and exhilarating climb.

Sandy Junor's Well

Seven hundred yards from the summit we pass on the left a well, so welcome to travellers of old. It was the handwork of one Sandy Junor whose object in constructing the fountain is thus told upon a polished granite panel fixed in the structure:

> *This fountain was erected in memory of Captain J. N. Gladstone, R.N., who died in 1863, by his grateful friend, Sandy Junor.*

The labour of collecting and rolling down, even with occasional help, the large quartz boulders off the hill-side to form the sides of

[1] Just over 50 yards east-south-east and immediately west of the road there is a second Bronze Age cairn 32¾ ft. in diameter and just short of 1 ft. in height.

the fountain overtaxed his strength and brought on the illness of which he died. A headstone to him, erected by the late Sir Thomas Gladstone, stands near the north-east corner of Fetteresso kirk-yard.

Pictish Stone and St Ringan's Cairn

Just 90 yards short of half a mile from the well you will arrive at the entrance to a small quarry on the left-hand side of the road. If you care to park your car here (the view is delightful in any case), you will find it rewarding to walk only 140 yards across the heather, eastwards up Redstone Hill, until you arrive at a height of just over 1,000 ft. at a fence where you will see you are on a portion of the old Cairn military road. By following the fence for only 150 yards downhill you will reach St Ringan's Cairn, a felsite intrusion measuring 28 ft. in diameter and 1¼ ft. in height. Stone-robbing in 1964 revealed a small fragment of the bottom of a Pictish cross-slab, carved in high relief, along with its slotted base. Was there a Cairn road in use then, even in Pictish times? One might reasonably assume so.

Knowegreens

Three-fifths of a mile farther on, and just before beginning the final steep descent to the Clatterin' Brig we pass on the right-hand side a sunny knowe on which stand the ruins of Knowegreens, for many a day an inn which was a place of call for drovers along this highway across the Grampians. It was built between 1789 and 1807 and abandoned between 1864 and 1901. Temperance legislation killed it.

Situated some 75 yards west of the ruinous inn there is a farm-stead comprising three rectangular buildings, all reduced to the lower courses of their stone walls and one incorporating a probable kiln. Immediately to the north are the remains of a slurry-pit or pond, and 40 yards to the east-south-east the stone wall-footings of a small square structure. The farmstead is depicted on a map of 1774 and, like the inn, was abandoned between 1864 and 1901.

Clatterin' Brig

And so at last we reach the Clatterin' Brig at the foot of the Cairn, in itself an interesting name, derived from 'clacharan', stepping-stones. It is literally the bridge which took the place of a row of stepping-stones, the brigs being stones or clods. In old days soft ground was made up by embanking, and the embanking here was done to carry the Cairn road over wet ground in the hollow where the Clatterin' Brig now stands. In the same way passages made across mosses or moors were called Heathery Briggs as at White Hill on the Netherley Road from Stonehaven to Deeside.

The picturesque 18th century bridge is a simple semi-circular arch, and at this famous beauty-spot road and Devilly Burn criss-cross. The stream in July is like a rock-garden with richly coloured dwarfish mimulus and wild thyme.

The ruins of Knowegreens, once an inn and stopping-place for drovers along the Cairn o' Mounth road for some 80 years and more.

Clatterin' Brig Restaurant

The Clatterin' Brig Restaurant on the hill-side above, built of stone
and cedar-wood, was opened on May 23rd, 1958, by Prince Georg
of Denmark. It has restaurant accommodation for 74 and, adjoining
it, a tweed shop selling woollens, fancy goods, Celtic jewellery and
pottery. These ventures were founded by Miss Diana Bowes-Lyon,
now Mrs Somervell, a cousin of the Queen. Another of the directors
is her sister, Princess Anne of Denmark, who spends part of each
summer with her husband, Prince Georg, at Fettercairn House. The
third is their mother, the Hon. Mrs Bowes-Lyon.

The Deer Dyke

One hundred and twenty-five feet above the Clatterin' Brig Restaurant, on the ridge of Arnbarrow Hill (1,060 ft.) and to the west of
the little ravine nearby, will be seen a Forestry Commission plantation, quite easily reached after a climb of only some 125 yards up the
path from the back of the restaurant. Quite a distinct path, too,
follows the northern side of the wood for some 300 yards after
which, at the end of the plantation, you must follow a diagonal
course to your left. After walking only a further 55 or 60 yards you
will arrive at an interesting object of great antiquity. This is the
remains of the mediaeval Deer or King's Dyke which enclosed the
Royal Hunting Park of the Palace of Kincardine the ruins of which
are just two miles away from where we stand. The lands of the farms
of Lammersmuir, Arnbarrow and Bogendello are within its boundaries. Scott, incidentally, uses the name of the last-named farm in
Guy Mannering when he is describing the place where Dandy
Dinmont was attacked.

A long stretch of the northern boundary of the Deer Dyke is quite
well defined as it climbs 475 ft. along the northern shoulder of
Arnbarrow Hill, running westwards more or less continuously and
in a straight line for just under two miles. It appears as a raised
bank, varying from about 9¾ ft. to 14¾ ft. in thickness, and
standing to a maximum height of 4¼ ft. above the bottom of an
internal ditch 6½ ft. to 9¾ ft. broad. The ditch from which the earth
was originally removed is still most obvious as indeed is the whole
length of the dyke from the Cairn o' Mounth road if one knows
where to look.

A gentle climb of 350 yards up the ditch to the top of the hill will
reward you with a magnificent view of the dyke stretching away into
the distance. Alternatively, a pleasant afternoon may be spent

following the dyke farther along the slopes of the hill, descending some 120 ft. at the end of two miles to the hidden little Loch of Muchrae nestling delightfully in the minute and unexpected glen of the same name only some 300 yards long. Those so disposed can follow the dyke for 125 yards farther on, 150 ft. up Longside Hill (1,264 ft.) in front and then down to the south-west where it disappears in the head-stream of the Burn of Cardowan.

An aerial photograph, taken in 1961, showing the Clatterin' Brig at the junction of three roads, the road to Fettercairn leading off to the south, the road to the Glen of Drumtochty on the right and, leading off to the north-west, the Cairn o' Mounth road. Slack Den with the Slack Burn can be seen in the top right-hand corner. Most interesting is the Deer Dyke (some 1,250 yards of it) in a direct line with the white rectangle of what is the Clatterin' Brig Restaurant. It is most obvious as it leads off across the top of the field and crosses the old King's Deer or Hunting Park of Arnbarrow Hill, disappearing off the picture to the left and almost dividing the picture in two. The Dyke also continues down the east side of the field above the Restaurant.

167

A Hut-circle Settlement Some 2,700 Years Old

On a south-facing slope 165 yards west-south-west of the Loch of Muchrae, and at a height of about 900 ft. is an unenclosed settlement comprising three hut-circles with walls 5 ft. thick and measuring 32¾ ft., 29½ ft. and 23 ft. in diameter respectively.

Their interiors have been dug into the slope, and one is occupied by a circular enclosure 17¼ ft. in internal diameter. Nearby is an oval enclosure (19½ ft. by 16½ ft. internally) and also two other enclosures with interiors levelled into the slope, one D-shaped and 35½ ft. by 28¾ ft. internally, the other rectangular and 32 ft. by 25 ft.

These stone hut foundations and low rectangular walled enclosures indicate the beginning of settled farming life, perhaps to some extent forced on the population by gradual climatic deterioration after 1,000 B.C. and during the Middle and Late Bronze Ages although such farmsteads continued into the Iron Age around 450 B.C. The low circular walls, 3 ft. or 4 ft. high, sometimes with porches to give added protection from draughts and driving rain at the door, supported timber rafters that rose to a point like a wigwam.

On the slope around the settlement is a scatter of small cairns.

A Hunting Park of Five Square Miles

The Deer Dyke[1] enclosed within its western boundary the Garrol Hill (1,025 ft.), seen across the valley of the Burn of Garrol to the south-west, and of this western dyke a trace still remains in Crichieburn Wood behind the Garrol Hill at the source of the Crichie Burn, stretching 400 yards until it disappears on reaching the arable lands above Fasque.

The eastern boundary, which included inside it a third hill, the 600 ft. high Hunter's Hill, was formed in part by the rocky banks of the Knowegreens Burn, tributary of the Devilly Burn, and followed more or less the line of the road to Fettercairn for three-fifths of its way. On this eastern boundary about 180 yards of the dyke are still visible on the west side of the Clatterin' Brig – Fettercairn road directly opposite Green Castle earthwork (see page 362).

The length of the Deer Dyke all round had been not less than eight miles, and it had enclosed, perhaps in winter only, a deer or hunting park of about five square miles. Along the patches of boggy and grassy ground as well as at the crossing of burns no traces of the dyke appear. A stockade of felled trees probably formed a fence in

[1] See frontispiece aerial photograph.

these watery hollows and on top of the dyke as well: an ordinary bank would be no obstacle to animals of the chase.

Royal Visits for Five Centuries

This deer park in what used to be the forest of Kincardine, together with the forests of Cowie and Durris, the three Mounth forest centres, without doubt shared royal visits from the beginning of the 12th century to the end of the 16th for the kings of the time were great hunters in imitation of the Norman monarchs of England. One can picture the sporting equipages or cavalcades as they issued from Kincardine, Dunnottar or Cowie or from any of the intervening castles to hunt those wastes in those far-off times – the usual royal retinue of the great barons and their ladies, the Frasers, the Keiths, Barclays and Strattons from the coast castles, the Strachans and the Durwards from the Mounth and the Wisharts from the Howe, all emulating the style of their princes. There would be the kinsmen and bailies, tenants and attendants, and all would be waited upon by the forester whose duty it was to take care of the game for his master's favourite sport.

In the 12th century David I appointed sheriffs to the territorial divisions of the Mearns, and it was this officer who was also called the Forester of the Mearns, exercising jurisdiction in offences against forest laws over the forests of Kincardine, Cowie, Durris and Garvock where there was a similar deer dyke. The office was also held by the Frasers and Keiths.

The dykes were made probably to enclose the deer and in a way to protect them from the wild beasts which still roamed in the neighbouring forests. We are left in no doubt as to the antiquity of the hunting park when we read in the writing of the more imaginative of the old chroniclers (Holinshed and Boece for example) that Kenneth III who met his death at Fettercairn in 994

> *lodged in his Castell of Fethircarne where there was a forest full of all manner of wild beasts that were to be had in anie part of Albion.*

And in an account of the parish of Birse occurs the following:

> *On part of the farms of Deerhillock and Kirkton, on the estate of Aboyne, and between the church and Marywell, there appears a narrow strip of ground which is said to have been fenced with a deer dyke by order of King Kenneth III for confining deer to stock his park near his Palace of Kincardine in the Brae of The Mearns.*

Two and a half centuries later, when Alexander III was king, a

169

charge of seven marks was made for *fencing a new park* at Kincardine. The park, however, may have been established by William the Lion (1165-1214).

When you return from your walk, if you follow the eastern side of the wood towards its extremity before descending to the restaurant, you will find yourself at the north-east corner of the hunting park. From here you will be able to follow a further portion of the deer dyke along its eastern side for some 400 yards or more beside the ravine and parallel to the main road alongside which, as we have seen, it appears just three-quarters of a mile farther on.

The Hamlet of Clatterin' Brig

At Clatterin' Brig in the early part of the 19th century was a hamlet of some importance with, on the hill-sides around, a number of homesteads, now in ruins, where the business of lime-burning was long and vigorously carried on. For limestone crops up in this area as it does in Drumtochty and Glenfarquhar, at Tilquhillie and Whistleberry, at Mathers near St Cyrus and at Kirktonhill, Marykirk. The remains of what was once a thriving limekiln can clearly be seen at Clatterin' Brig. The limestone quarry, becoming unworked, was given up in 1732.

The School

Also in the heyday of the village was a unique school of excellent repute at the foot of the hill road where about 1833 the children of lime-burners and crofters of the glen were taught to read and write at one end of his biggin by 'Dominie Young', a schoolmaster with a wooden leg who lorded it over his pupils and neighbours in inimitable style. He had a reputation of being a good teacher, but his discipline was of the severest kind. With a short stick, flat at one end, he hammered the Ten Commandments into the boys in a way which the great lawgiver had not prescribed.

The school is now chiefly remembered as one where cock-fighting was encouraged, and the dominie, an enthusiastic patron of the 'sport', used to arrange an annual fight, with himself as umpire, which people from all over the countryside came to see. His pupils brought the cocks and, as he collected the slain, he had thus an excellent reason for endeavouring to secure a good entry. The dead he strung on a rope in the ben-end of his biggin until he found means of turning them to remunerative account. To end the day of a fight with celebration the dominie adjourned with all interested cronies to a favourite well or pool near the school into which, cleared of its debris, they allegedly poured upwards of a dozen bottles of whisky according to the amount of water. Squatting round with their jugs and other utensils, they drank until there was no more to drink or as long as they were able to lift their hands to their heads. This custom continued at least till 1826.

The Inn

In addition to teaching in his school the enterprising Mr Young ran a public house in the other end of his biggin in opposition to the inn of Knowegreens the ruins of which we passed a little higher up the road. Drinking went on to such an extent, and the public house gained such an unsavoury reputation that a Dr Leslie of Fettercairn had the licence withdrawn. But this did not effectually put a stop to the drinking: Mr Young was in office at the time of the passing of the Reform Bill, and he turned out with his bibulous band of habitués to witness Fox Maule's (Lord Dalhousie's) memorable march across the Grampians via Clatterin' Brig in celebration of that event.

Slack Den

Before you leave Clatterin' Brig, if it is a pleasant day and you are disposed to linger, you may care to cross the road to follow the path of the small Slack Burn a little to the north for three-quarters of a mile or so. Overlooked by historic Strathfinella Hill (1,358 ft.) with its thriving plantations – it has been described as a *cheerless, dark-faced hill* – the burn issues from Slack Den, a gorge in the hills 60 ft. deep.

This is because at one stage of the Ice Age the ice, moving north, pushed in behind Strathfinella Hill which is formed of Old Red Sandstone. Through this the glaciers ploughed their way, leaving what now look like huge river-beds in which the tiny streams are misfits. The ice did not surmount the Cairn o' Mounth but dislodged melt-water to cut numerous valleys and gorges (like this one) which are now almost dry. The gorge of one of the streams draining the Cairn, about 250 ft. deep, is one of the most spectacular melt-water channels in Scotland, giving some indication of the amount of water that passed that way in the Ice Age. In the miniature Grand Canyon where we are now the Slack flows for some distance underground – or rather under a tremendous accumulation of debris of quartz and felspar.

Glensaugh, Loch Saugh and Bright's Well

From Clatterin' Brig, instead of continuing along the B974 to Fettercairn (which we shall see another day) let us take the very picturesque route to the left round by the famous and richly wooded Glen of Drumtochty, one of the most popular circular tours in the district. Here there is a little of everything – hills and glens, woods and moorland and the purple of rhododendron in bloom in the early summer.

Cross the Burn of Slack and climb up the hill for just short of half a mile to Glensaugh Research Station on part of which, following a 1969 conference, organised jointly by The Highlands and Islands Development Board and the Rowett Research Institute, Aberdeen, an experimental red deer farm has been established by the Hill Farming Research Organisation. It is argued that red deer, if managed intensively, could produce meat directly from the grazing resources of a hill farm without requiring large quantities of brought-in feed. The argument has clear relevance as a possible alternative to sheep-farming in many areas. Officials of the land development division of The Highlands and Islands Development Board foresee the day when venison could take its place alongside beef, mutton and pork in the butcher's shop. The rent of this experimental farm about 1725, we learn from a tenant's rent-book, was £52 Scots together with £4 10/- Scots and half a boll to the minister! The rent in 1744 was £93 Scots and a boll of meal!

The hill Loch Saugh among the trees on the right a little farther on has certainly now little appearance of being artificial. Made by residents of Auchenblae many years ago, it has wooded islets, the haunts of wild-duck and other water-fowl. At the present time this loch is the preserve of the Brechin Angling Club, and local people must ask permission to fish here. On the left-hand side and opposite the second Passing-Place sign 316 yards after the end of the loch is Bright's Well, a bubbling spring once reputed to have medicinal qualities.

Friars' Glen

Two-fifths of a mile farther on is the entrance to Friars' Glen, protected on the north by the Grampians and on the south by Strathfinella. The name of this secluded glen is derived from the tradition that a small priory or hermitage once stood here, surrounded by mountains and watered by a transparent brook. Certain it is that, by a charter dated 1st May, 1402, James Frazer of Friendraught granted the property with a small annuity to the Carmelites (White Friars) of Aberdeen. Ten years later, by another charter, the lands of little Glensaugh were conveyed absolutely to the Carmelites who continued to draw the revenues and in whose hands the lands appear to have remained until 1565. Of the site of a religious house, however, if indeed one ever existed here, there are no records whatsoever. A mistake had obviously originated with the writer of the old *Statistical Account* of 1843 who, writing of the 1402 charter, thought the remains of a dwelling house, barn and byre standing in a corner of the glen were *the ruins of a small priory*.

On 26th September, 1592, King James VI granted to George, 5th Earl Marischal, *an annual rent of £3 arising from Friars' glen in Mernis*, which sum the Earl Marischal made over to Marischal College. In Principal Howie's rental of the College of 1598 among the *annuals to be pursued* is *£3 out of freres glen, or the landis of Littil Glansache*, while 42 years later the stipend of the Third Regent[1] includes *Item, the Laird of Pitarrow* (near Fordoun), *his lands of Easter glensaught, alias friers' glen in the Mernes qlk holds few of ws £3-3-4d.* On May 29th, 1644, *the lands of Frier Glen alias Eister Glensauch* were bought by Sir Alexander Carnegie of Pitarrow to be held by him from the superiors (Marischal College) in perpetual feu, for 4 merks 6s 8d. In 1806 Aberdeen University disposed of its interest in the Glen, the superiority passing for the sum of £45 to George Harley Drummond who built Drumtochty Castle.

If you walk some 430 yards up the glen, you will notice on your left, just where the path turns westwards at right angles, a spring of clear water known as the 'Priest's Well', said to be *one of the most copious flowing in Scotland*. You may also notice the presence of slate and limestone in Friars' Glen. This indicates that Drumtochty lies upon two very distinct geological formations, the Old Red Sandstone to the south-east and the Dalradian metamorphic schists and gneisses to the south-west, clearly separated from each other by the Highland Fault the line of which passes in a north-east to south-west direction through the area as it crosses Scotland from Stonehaven to Helensburgh.[2]

John of Fordoun

Now, what is of interest is that Friars' Glen is allegedly the glen where John of Fordoun, early chronicler of Scotland and the oldest authority on the subject of Scottish history, did his work. Born about 1350 and dying in 1385, he was the first to arrange in something like chronological order the facts and fables which earlier writers had recorded or tradition brought down. His important

[1] An instructor of the teaching staff who tutored undergraduates.
[2] See *Highways and Byways Round Stonehaven*, pp. 66-67.

Chronicles of Fordoun embraced five books of consecutive annals, complete down to the death of David I in 1153, but he had collected very full notes relating to public transactions during the reigns of several of that monarch's successors, the last date of his history being 1385. It is generally admitted that his work forms the basis of the history of Scotland prior to the death of James I, his annals of the fourteenth century being of enhanced value as a contemporary authority as far as they can be relied on as the genuine work of the chronicler himself and not of any credulous continuator. Before his time materials were crude and scanty, consisting chiefly of short chronicles and lists of regal names with the fabulous and artificial mixed with fragments of true history. On the basis of his system later historians reared their fictitious superstructure.

John of Fordoun is traditionally supposed to have been born in the parish of Fordoun, supposedly assuming his name from the village. Camden (died 1623), Goodall in his edition of 1759 and Chambers in his *Picture of Scotland* (1837) state that the historian was born in the ancient Kirkton of Fordoun itself, *ab ingenuis parentibus oriundus* (sprung of honest parents) according to the second named. The writer of the old *Statistical Account* records that

> *he was thought by some to have been a man of property in the parish, by others, with greater probability, a monk who resided here,*

while the new *Statistical Account* of 1843 states that he was

> *either a native of the parish or resided in it when he wrote his history of Scotland.*

According to Dr Marshall (*Historic Scenes*, 1880)

> *perhaps the most illustrious son whom this parish has produced was John de Fordon, the father of Scottish history. He is supposed to have been a native of the village of Fordoun and a priest of the church of the parish.*

The Royal MS in the British Museum styles him *Capellanus Ecclesiae Aberdonensis*, and Skene in his *Historians of Scotland* concludes that he was a *chantry priest* or chaplain of that cathedral.

That John of Fordoun in the discharge of his duties as presbyter may have had a connection with the parish is not at all improbable: this could explain how his name has come to be associated with Fordoun. It is said, indeed, that he was an incumbent of Fordoun in

1377. On the other hand, to substantiate the positive statement that he was born in the parish is merely an inference from his name. The surnames Stirling or Aberdein prove nothing at the present day, and surnames were well established in Fordoun's time. Furthermore, the identical name of John de Fordun is met with in other parts of Scotland, both before and after the historian's time. It would seem that Dr Skene's statement is the most reliable.

The name *Scotichronicon* has been applied both to the continuation of Fordoun's work by Walter Bower, abbot of Inchcolm, who interpolated the five books of Fordoun with additional matter covering the period up to 1437, and also to Walter Goodall's edition of John of Fordoun's work, published in 1759.

Glen of Drumtochty

Our road now descends via Strath Finella into the narrow and richly wooded Glen of Drumtochty (not Ian Maclaren's),[1] the glen that carries the upper reaches of the Luther Water from Loch Saugh through the wooded defile in a great semi-circle between the main body of the foothills of the Mounth and Strathfinella Hill. It is certainly one of Kincardineshire's most popular and strikingly beautiful glens and, possibly, one of the more romantic and picturesque spots in Scotland.

Drumtochty Glen owes its origin to the movement of huge glaciers during the Ice Age when Strathfinella and the Cairn o' Mounth stood out as bastions in front of the ramparts of the Highlands, composed as they are of particularly persistent rock of the Old Red Sandstone type. The ice front at one time stood above the Glen of Drumtochty, and the melt-water flowed down the little valleys already cut by the burns, widening them and enlarging them as we have seen. Hence we have a deep valley – 2,000 ft. or 3,000 ft. deep – but only a trickle of water.

The restoration of beauty and new life in Drumtochty Glen is largely due to the Forestry Commission which acquired and planted Drumtochty Forest in 1926-27, covering in all 3,294 acres, and the Glenfarquhar Hills in 1953. The fifteen or twenty men employed may not seem a great force, but the difference they have made to the landscape is profound.

[1] John Watson (1850-1907), Free Church minister of Logiealmond, Perthshire, and novelist and short-story writer. He wrote as 'Ian Maclaren' and in his stories of rural life called his area 'Drumtochty'.

Forest Walk

Seven-tenths of a mile from the entrance to Friars' Glen and immediately opposite a cottage on the right is the entrance to a large
car park in which there is a Picnic Area. There is, too, with its
signpost, a delightful, circular Forest Walk, just short of a mile in
length. On the way one follows the tumbling Luther Water which
issues at one point from a small sylvan wildlife pond, much favoured
by the birds and animals of the forest and, when the author last saw
it, literally the *haunt of coot and heron*. Time spent on this walk
will be most pleasurable.

Near the car park there is a remarkable sitka spruce specimen
tree believed to be one of the largest in Britain: its age is estimated
at over 120 years, and its height now exceeds 120 feet.

Drumtochty Castle

Only three-fifths of a mile along the road is the entrance to Drumtochty Castle on the left (the drive is just short of half a mile in
length). A stately mansion in castellated neo-Gothic style with twin
angle towers, it was erected around 1830, incorporating an earlier
more modest building, at a reputed cost of £30,000, a large sum for
those days. The castle, which stands in some 60 acres of wooded
policies, was designed for George Harley Drummond of the well-
known banking-house of the time in Charing Cross by James
Gillespie Graham, the famous architect who was also responsible
for the steeple in Montrose.

It is beautifully and romantically situated, occupying an ideal
tree-thronged site, hardly anywhere excelled, on a richly wooded
plateau above the brawling waters of the Luther and commanding a
view of the glen. To see the superb setting when the rhododendrons
are in bloom is to behold an Arcadia that would charm even the
most fastidious. Taste also characterises the extensive planting that
was done, and land improvement and reclamation enhance the
already attractive amenities. Drumtochty became the show-piece of
the area.

The Drumtochty estate has a long history, and it is uncertain
when a dwelling first stood on the site. By a charter of 1457
Archibald Rate received the western portion, but his successors
were dispossessed in 1559 by the Crown, the lands being given to Sir
James Keith whose son appears as Sir George Keith of Drumtochty
in 1618. The next owners were the Carnegies, but at the death of Sir
James Carnegie of Pitarrow the estates were purchased by Dr John
McKenzie in 1767 and the name of the earlier house changed to
Woodstock.

His widow survived until 1810, and Dr James Leslie, Minister of Fordoun, tells in the *Statistical Account* of 1843,

> *She inhabited a snug and unpretending cottage on the site of which the present mansion stands. Situated on a steep bank on the north side of a narrow valley, enveloped by planta-tions of considerable extent in which the graceful birch predominates, and surrounded by lofty mountains, it may be questioned if the view of the present lordly mansion ever gave half the pleasure to one possessed of sound judgment and taste which the former humble cottage afforded.*

Hospital, Interrogation Centre and School

In 1822 the castle and estate of 12,000 acres were purchased by the Gemmell family of Countesswells, Aberdeen, who retained posses-sion until about 1922, renting it to shooting tenants. The estate was then split up, and the castle itself during the first World War became a Red Cross hospital for wounded soldiers many of whom were Belgian. During the 1939-45 War it was modernised and adapted for use as an interrogation centre for Norwegians who had escaped from their own occupied country in small boats bound for Scottish shores. Latterly it served as a residential primary school for the children of serving Norwegians, opened for this purpose by King Haakon before a distinguished gathering in the huge banqueting-hall on November 2nd, 1942, and visited by Crown Prince (now King) Olaf for a short informal holiday in the following year. During his visit King Haakon planted at the front of the castle a Norwegian spruce which is now about 60 ft. high. The Norwegian children returned home in 1946. From May, 1947, until the summer of 1971 Drumtochty Castle was a preparatory school for boys.

Drumtochty Castle was latterly owned by Mr and Mrs W. Victor Ogley, the public rooms along the south front of the building serving since 1976, after extensive restoration, as an exclusive lux-ury restaurant which looked over the wooded den to the tree-clad slopes of Drumtochty Forest and Strathfinella Hill. The stately restaurant suite was most beautifully decorated: the banqueting-hall with its three tall Gothic windows had a formal magnificence while in the drawing-room the elaborate and beautiful cornices and the lovely fireplace with its classical overmantel had been perfectly restored. The morning-room with its large bow-window was also a work of art.

In June, 1981, the castle was offered for sale, and the following year Kincardine and Deeside District Council Planning Committee gave permission for the building to be converted to a private house again.

We may note in conclusion that during the month of May (and only then) the ghost of a Green Lady appears, we are told, on the main front staircase of the castle.

St Palladius' Church

Fifty yards farther on, in the middle of the Glen, is a small, ornate Gothic episcopal church with a circular bell tower. Dedicated to St Palladius who was closely associated with the parish of Fordoun, it was built for the Reverend J. S. Gammell of Drumtochty Castle and opened for public worship on November 1st, 1885. It was consecrated by the Bishop of Brechin on 29th July, 1886. The architect was Arthur Clyne of Aberdeen.

Galloquhine

In just under half a mile turn left where the sign points to Auchenblae. A further three-quarters of a mile takes us to the farm of Galloquhine, seen nestling in the valley at the road junction.

Galloquhine was at one time from a historic point of view perhaps one of the more important meal and barley mills in the parish of Fordoun, well provided as it was with grinding power. Other mills were sited at Denmill at the southern extremity of Auchenblae and Pitrennie (see page 331). To all these by agreement with the superior the feuars, farmers and crofters of every district were thirled. The mill was situated immediately below the steading of the farm and was, in fact, an adjunct of it. It derived its water supply from the West Burn which rises in Drumtochty Glen, and it was to this mill that the tenants on the barony of Glenfarquhar and those feuars in Auchenblae who were vassals of the baron gave their custom.

The house of Galloquhine in earlier days was not only the farmer's residence but a licensed inn. It stood then (as it stands now) facing the road that leads to the ford below the mill. Crossing at this ford, that road ascended zigzag-wise to a spur of the Grampians opposite the parish church, then turned in a westerly direction to pass via Fettercairn, Edzell and Brechin into the vale of Strathmore. Much of this ancient roadway has now been obliterated, but it was in former days a road frequently traversed by dealers from lower Deeside and other northern parts en route for the southern markets. On going to and returning from these, pilgrims and others would often halt to find shelter and refreshment at this wayside inn which was a comfortable and convenient resting-place.

Associated with the name of Galloquhine is one outstanding personage, the stalwart figure of miller William Beattie, a man of considerable strength renowned throughout the district for his physical powers. To swing with 'the miller's lift', as it was called, a sack of oatmeal over his left shoulder on to his back and transport a bag of corn, no matter what the weight and what the distance, was child's play to him.

Mains of Glenfarquhar

And now, avoiding what used to be called 'The Miller's Road' from the mill to Auchenblae, turn sharply to the left and continue for quarter of a mile to the Give Way sign at the T-junction. Another mile to the left brings us to the farm of Mains of Glenfarquhar, once the chief farm on the Barony of Glenfarquhar although not perhaps the largest or even the most productive on the estate. On the steading today may be seen two inscribed stones, one 'F.A.E.K. 1857 M.L.C.K.' and another, erected by Sir Alexander Falconer, 'S.A.F. 1674 D.H.G.' (perhaps, Mr Jervise says, for Lady Graham). At Mains of Glenfarquhar during the 1745-46 Rebellion a certain David Campbell

compelled one James Eddie to drink the Pretender's health as Prince of Wales, holding a drawn cutlace over his head.

Glenfarquhar Castle

We should stop, however, about 30 yards before the right-angle bend at Mains of Glenfarquhar and just before the sign to Stonehaven where there is a rough track to the left. If you follow this for just over 20 yards, enter the gate on the right and cross the field for some 80 yards, you will arrive at the rectilinear site (up to 45 yards across) where in ancient days stood the old baronial and embattled Glenfarquhar Castle. Mention of it as Glenfirkaryn is made as early as 1214. Traces of its foundations are barely traceable for by the beginning of the 19th century the castle had been demolished, almost every stone having been appropriated as material for other buildings; on the west side, however, there are the footings of a wall which originally may have continued around the perimeter. Especially noticeable are the remains of the moat that surrounded the castle, quite clearly extending round three-quarters of the little eminence on which the castle once stood, each side being about 50 yards in length.

For several centuries the lands of Glenfarquhar were in the possession of a representative of the Falconers of Haulkerton (near Laurencekirk), an ancient and powerful family (see page 387) who are said to derive their origin from Walter who obtained a grant of certain lands in the Mearns from David I. His son, Ranulph, was appointed 'Falconer' by William the Lion, by royal favour having the properties added to the family possessions (vide Chalmers' *Caledonia*, vol. 1, p. 54). It was at Glenfarquhar Castle that Sir David Falconer of Newton, Lord President of the Court of Session, was born. His son, David, became 5th Lord Falconer; his daughter, Catherine, the mother of David Hume, the famous historian.

Ornamental Stone Balls

In 1893 two pieces of glass bottle, inscribed 'Glineferqr 1707' in raised letters on the glass, were found on the site of the castle. There was also found at Glenfarquhar an ornamental knobbed hard sandstone sphere the size of a cannon-ball. There are traces of five circles slightly indented or cut in outline over its surface, and the diameter is about $2^5/8$ ins. The stone ball is in an excellent state of preservation and is now in the National Museum of Antiquities in Edinburgh.

Stone balls such as this one have been found only in this part of Scotland. They belong to the Secondary Neolithic period (around 2,400-1,800 B.C.) and are not associated with particular sites, being found by chance in fields. It is thought that they were symbols of authority, bound to the end of a stick or carried perhaps in the hand of a chief.

Paddy Fair

And now let us carry on northwards. Just before the corner, less than half a mile farther on and about 33 yards after the double bend sign, a track leads off to the right by the copse[1] up the lower slopes of Herscha Hill.

The field into which this leads was once a long stretch of dreary waste, covered only with heather, whins and broom, the appearance of which years had done little to change. From time immemorial this field (or deserted moor as it was) presented an animated spectacle on the first Tuesday in July when there was held Paldy or Paddy Fair (so called in honour of the patron saint, Palladius). The fair, the largest annual market in the district and the most famous of

---

[1] You may simply prefer to climb the necessary 50 yards alongside the fence.

the many animal fairs in the Mearns, was originally held in the open piece of ground, larger than at present, in front of Fordoun Church but through changing proprietorships was eventually established on the moorland here.

When the town of Fordoun was made into a barony by Queen Mary in 1554, the charter of erection, made in favour of Robert Beaton of Creich, Captain of the Palace of Falkland, granted that there be three fairs annually on St Palladius' Day and the octaves thereof. The fair here continued for four days. Tuesday was the sheep market; Wednesday was the weavers' day when they came from miles around with all kinds of home-made clothes and cloth to tempt you; Thursday was the big cattle-market when the number of cattle which came down the drove roads from the north might be between 2,000 and 3,000 and when even more people milled around. It was the busiest day of all. Friday was the horse-market for which school-children always received a holiday – and 'Paddy' was reputed to be one of the best horse-fairs in the North-east. If, however, all you wanted was the fun of the fair, then any day would suit you.

Dealers in sheep, cattle and horses congregated from every corner of the county, from Angus and across the hills from the upper regions of Deeside. Young men resorted hither to engage for harvest work, and there was commonly a winding-up of accounts between farmers and corn-dealers with respect to the preceding crop. Shoemakers, saddlers and other craftsmen also collected accounts, while dealers in turnip seeds and other specialities solicited fresh orders. Men are socially inclined, and it was but on rare occasions that such an opportunity presented itself. On this market one formerly relied for the Whitsunday rent!

A Variety of Entertainment

To accommodate this assemblage of people from far and near there was always plenty of entertainment and ways of spending surplus money. Whole streets of tents were erected. With the regularity of a military encampment were set up vintners' tents where all kinds of liquors and spirits were to be had and gills and half-mutchkins (two gills) were measured out as taste required. Behind were blazing fires with broth pots suspended from tripods. In her day Betty Gordon of the Chestnut Inn in Auchenblae (long since out of existence) always had a tent – it would be termed a marquee today – and a goodly supply of hot soup and a special supply of her own special liquid refreshment was always welcome. There were available, too, sweetie stalls and, for dinner, plentiful supplies of ready-dressed meat of various kinds to whet the hungry appetite, provided by the different inn-keepers from the neighbouring towns who, acting as sutlers for the occasion, did a great deal of business.

To amuse the heterogeneous crowd a variety of entertainers used to assemble. Here were acrobats, poets like Homer of old reciting their own compositions, blind fiddlers and pipers, clad in the garb of Rob Roy, and minstrels playing such music as they could through their tin whistles. Here were sellers of Belfast Almanacs, then an essential article in every country household, shooting-galleries with a bag of hazel nuts as the alluring prize, and the usual sprinkling of legless, defective and misshapen flotsam of humanity who, by hook or crook, had got themselves transported thither, some in their carriages drawn by a couple of panting dogs. There were also the police under the direction of a magistrate who presided in the tent of the Justices of the Peace with a strong guard armed with rusty halberds to enforce his decisions and, if necessary, to apprehend and punish delinquents on the spot. It was rare, however, for him to exercise the latter part of his executive powers although stocks appeared regularly at the market; yet he had frequent occasion to judge between parties and to give a summary judgement which was understood to be final. Despite this, however, it is little wonder that before sunset various other methods of settling accounts had been adopted and that some veterans were left for the time being hors de combat on the field. Such was Paddy Fair.

The Stocks

When the Earl of Kintore, who resided at Inglesmaldie, succeeded to the barony, it was the duty of his baron bailie to take charge of the stocks outside the Justices' tent at the fair. Many a poor fellow who had committed some misdemeanor found his way into them, and these stocks were the last of these instruments of incarceration and ridicule to be employed in Scotland, finally used in July, 1841. On this date Superintendent Weir, then Chief of Kincardineshire Constabulary, visited the Fair and found a man confined in them. He immediately ordered his release, and the stocks passed from the realm of usefulnesss for ever.

One might note that the Earl's stocks were used also at Lammas Fair (Arnbarrow near Clatterin' Brig), Laurence Fair (Crookieden, 2½ miles north of Laurencekirk), the Pasch Fair for cattle at Auchenblae, which was particularly well attended, and, for grazing cattle, Cammock Fair (between Laurencekirk and Fordoun) on the second Wednesday of June. The stocks were purchased about 1880 at a sale at Inglesmaldie and created considerable interest when they were exhibited shortly afterwards at the Glasgow International Exhibition in 1901. On their return to Kincardineshire they were handed over to the County Council to be retained at County Police Headquarters at Stonehaven. There they certainly were in the late 1950's; now, alas, they have disappeared and cannot be found.

The Decline of Paddy Fair

In common with other similar historic markets the importance and character of Paddy Fair declined as 'communications with other parts of the country were improved and the transport of cattle, horses and sheep became easier, particularly when the railway line was extended through the Mearns in 1850. Gradually it became a mere one-day event with ever decreasing numbers of live-stock on display. It is recorded that in 1901 the Fair still showed something of its former glory, but within a matter of twenty years after that it lapsed completely. 'A good Paddy Fair', once a standing toast in the Mearns, was heard no more.

There were once as many as twenty fairs in the county besides weekly markets at Stonehaven on Thursdays, and at Auchenblae on Fridays. The Auchenblae market was held from the beginning of November till the end of April in what is now known as the High Street but was then rightly termed The Market Square. Cattle, grain and other farm produce were sold. Feeing markets when farm servants were engaged or fee'd for the following six months were on May 26th and 22nd November. Other fairs which have vanished, in addition to the six already mentioned, included the mid-Lenten fair for cloth at Banchory, St Anthony's Fair, Gardenstone Fair and Louran Fair at Laurencekirk, St Mark's Fair at Fettercairn, Bervie Fair, Michael Fair at Drumlithie and St James's Fair at Garvock.

Herscha Hill

Paddy Fair was situated, as we have said, on the lower slopes of Herscha Hill (725 ft.), the hill on the eastern side of the road northwards from Mains of Glenfarquhar. Here the monks of Arbroath at one time had a right to pasture, and here many stone-circles and two cairns once were to be found. None now remain. One circle, 25 yards in diameter and consisting of six large boulders, was carefully searched in 1855, says Mr Andrew Jervise, but no trace of burial urns was found within it.

About 50 yards west of the site of this circle, and some three-fifths of a mile south-east of where we are standing now, there used to be a knoll near the centre of which during gravel-digging in 1865 an immense, rough block of stone, some 12-15 tons in weight, was found to lie. When it was blown up, it was discovered that it had been acting as the cover of a well-constructed cist the rough slabs of the sides of which had been cemented together with clay, said to bear the imprints of the fingers of the builders. The bottom of the grave was of baked clay, and in one end lay a quantity of black, clammy earth. Nothing now remains of what may have been a barrow.

Tipperty

Three-fifths of a mile farther on from the track leading to the Paddy Fair field, and just before we cross the Bervie Water, a road leads off to the left to the farm of Tipperty. Near here is St Mary's Well, the name of the farm (Tiobartach – well place) showing that this very ancient fountain, sanctified in the Christian period, refreshed wayfarers over the mountain in Pictish times. Tipperty was known, it seems, even long before that for four yellow flint arrow-heads were found here, one leaf-shaped, the other three with barbs and stem. These were given in 1874 to the Society of Antiquaries in Edinburgh.

St Mary's Well and Chapelton

St Mary's Well, actually, is on the land belonging to the farm of Chapelton which (like Herscha Hill) can be seen from the Tipperty road end, half left and on top of the rise. From it are to be seen telegraph poles descending the hill towards Tipperty. It is in the hollow to which they lead that the well is to be found, a bubbling spring, gushing forth soon to lose itself in the Bervie Water nearby.

If you have any particular interest in seeing this so-called well, you must turn up the Chapelton farm road at which we arrive in 370 yards and proceed another 500 yards to the farm itself. If permission is granted and the appropriate field is fallow at the time, a walk of 180 yards through the steading and another 310 yards down towards Tipperty Farm will take you there.

Chapelton is so named because of the existence nearby at one time of St Mary's Chapel. The site? Proceed for some 350 yards in the opposite direction, northwards towards Bogton Farm. The chapel was built almost half-way down the fence demarcating the end of the first field on your left where an extra stoney piece of ground was pointed out to me as the foundation. Jervise, however, places the site of the chapel near St Mary's Well.

Braes of Glenbervie

And now, as we proceed homewards, we see for the first time in front of us and on our left the Braes of Glenbervie, the fatherland of Robert Burns and where the Grampians end. The upland parish of Glenbervie is the apex of the Mearns Howe where the lush fat lands of the great inland valley of Strathmore – the northern extension of which is the Howe of the Mearns – run into the coarse, wet lands of the foothills of the Mounth. Thus from a hill-top in Glenbervie one can survey the two worlds, a world of rich red loam to the south and, to the north, the world of difficult clay hillsides, the hard, unkindly land farmed by the Burneses and the parents of Lewis Grassic Gibbon. It is somewhat coincidental, is it not, that the valley of the Bervie Water is the cradle of the ancestral origins both of Scotland's national bard and her great novelist of recent times?

Devotees of Robert Burns immediately associate him, we suppose, with Alloway and the southern counties of Ayr and Dumfries. Few pilgrims to the 'Land of Burns' ever think of any other part of Scotland. They may have heard, but know nothing of another land of Burns lying at the head of Strathmore, under the shadow of the Grampians. Who even among students of Robert Burns ever dreams of associating him with the Bervie and the Carron and the small upland farms on which his forefathers dwelt? Let us, at any rate, make sure that we are familiar with some of these. And the first is the farm of Mains of Inchbreck, almost exactly 2½ miles from the Tipperty road end.

Mains of Inchbreck

At the Mains of Inchbreck with its most interesting sign – a Highland Games 'heavy' throwing the hammer – Burneses even in 1547 were found among the roll of tenants when the Stuarts acquired Inchbreck from Sir Alexander Douglas of Glenbervie. Evidence has been found of a family of the name of Burnes living in Ury even farther back than that, and it may well be that Ury was the cradle of the family of the poet. Who knows?

It should be noticed that the earliest form of the family name appears to have been Burnes, and Burnes is the way the name is invariably spelt in the Glenbervie kirk session records. The poet spelt it Burness for a time and ultimately Burns, but Burness was the form usually adopted in Kincardineshire in the early part of the 18th century, and probably before that time.

Robert Burns' Kincardineshire Relations
A Genealogical Tree pruned to include only relatives mentioned in the text

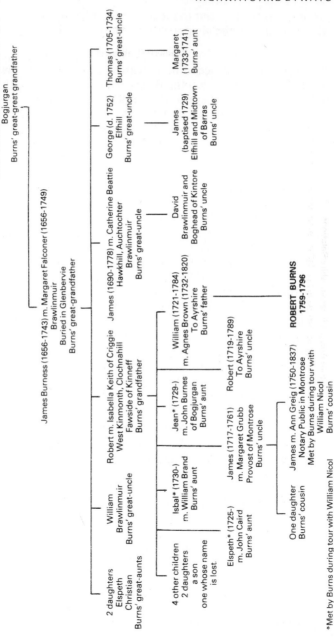

Walter Burness (d. 1670) m. Isabel Greig
Bogjurgan
Burns' great-great grandfather

James Burness (1656-1743) m. Margaret Falconer (1656-1749)
Brawlinmuir
Buried in Glenbervie
Burns' great-grandfather

Robert m. Isabella Keith of Criggie
West Kinmonth, Clochnahill
Fawside of Kinneff
Burns' grandfather

James (1690-1778) m. Catherine Beattie
Hawkhill, Auchtochter
Brawlinmuir
Burns' great-uncle

George (d. 1752)
Elfhill
Burns' great-uncle

Thomas (1705-1734)
Burns' great-uncle

William
Brawlinmuir
Burns' great-uncle

David
Brawlinmuir and
Boghead of Kintore
Burns' uncle

James
(baptised 1729)
Elfhill and Midtown
of Barras
Burns' uncle

Margaret
(1733-1741)
Burns' aunt

William (1721-1784)
m. Agnes Brown (1732-1820)
To Ayrshire
Burns' father

Robert (1719-1789)
To Ayrshire
Burns' uncle

**ROBERT BURNS
1759-1796**

Jean* (1729-)
m. John Burnes
of Bogjurgan
Burns' aunt

James (1717-1761)
m. Margaret Grubb
Provost of Montrose
Burns' uncle

James m. Ann Greig (1750-1837)
Notary Public in Montrose
Met by Burns during tour with
William Nicol
Burns' cousin

Isbal* (1730-)
m. William Brand
Burns' aunt

Elspeth* (1725-)
m. John Caird
Burns' aunt

One daughter
Burns' cousin

2 daughters
Elspeth
Christian
Burns' great-aunts

4 other children
2 daughters
a son
one whose name
is lost.

*Met by Burns during tour with William Nicol

Robert Burns' Kincardineshire Relations
A Genealogical Tree pruned to include only relatives mentioned in the text

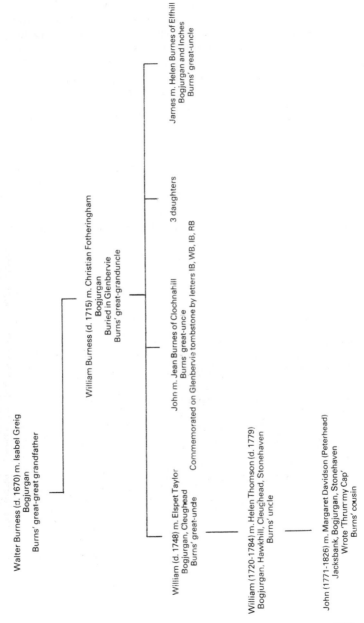

Walter Burness (d. 1670) m. Isabel Greig
Bogjurgan
Burns' great-great grandfather

William Burness (d. 1715) m. Christian Fotheringham
Bogjurgan
Buried in Glenbervie
Burns' great-granduncle

John m. Jean Burnes of Clochnahill
Burns great-uncle
Commemorated on Glenbervie tombstone by letters IB, WB, IB, RB

3 daughters

James m. Helen Burnes of Elfhill
Bogjurgan and Inches
Burns' great-uncle

William (d. 1748) m. Elspet Taylor
Bogjurgan, Cleughead
Burns' great-uncle

William (1720-1784) m. Helen Thomson (d. 1779)
Bogjurgan, Hawkhill, Cleughead, Stonehaven
Burns' uncle

John (1771-1826) m. Margaret Davidson (Peterhead)
Jacksbank, Bogjurgan, Stonehaven
Wrote 'Thrur my Cap'
Burns' cousin

Brawliemuir

Almost exactly quarter of a mile farther on, and in the foothills of the Mounth where it faces the Howe of the Mearns, is the ancient 150-acre farm of Brawliemuir (or Brawlinmuir as it was once spelt), the road to it leading off at right-angles to the left. Although the now deserted, plain, two-storey farmhouse can be clearly seen from our present position (it is an early 19th century building), Burns enthusiasts may wish to view the ruins of the humble cottage which local tradition proclaims to be the original Brawliemuir. One can travel towards it by car on the farm track alongside the trees for exactly half a mile, but when the road finally turns to the left towards the farmhouse, one must continue for 220 yards straight on up the hill on foot to the top of the line of trees. (It's only a mile and a third there and back.) Here you will see the very little that remains of this interesting but-and-ben which will soon completely crumble away and disappear if steps are not taken to arrest further decay.

All that remains of the original farm of Brawliemuir high on the Braes of Glenbervie, the road in the distance leading to the village of Glenbervie itself. Brawliemuir was once owned by James Burnes (1656-1743), Burns' great-grandfather.

The ruin which confronts us was once tenanted in 1697 by James Burnes, Robert Burns' great-grandfather, and occupied by Burneses down to 1807 when the farm passed from David Burnes to a John Kennedy. James Burnes, born in 1656 and the eldest son of Walter Burnes of Bogjurgan and Isobel Greig, married a Kincardineshire woman, Margaret Falconer, and had five sons and two daughters, dying on 23rd January, 1743, aged 87. He and his wife are buried in Glenbervie churchyard.

The sons bore the names of William, Robert, George, James and Thomas. William, the eldest, who succeeded his father at Brawliemuir, died at an early age and left no issue, being succeeded at Brawliemuir by his brother James who had been previously farmer at Hawkhill just over two miles to the south. This second James in Brawliemuir was twice married. His sons succeeded him in turn and remained in the farm until 1807 when the long connection between the Burnes family and the estate of Inchbreck terminated. Thomas, the youngest son of the original James of Brawliemuir, also died a youth, and it was the second son, Robert, grandfather of the poet, brought up in Brawliemuir, who became tenant of West Kinmonth outside Drumlithie and later of Clochnahill, 3¾ miles from Stonehaven on the Laurencekirk road. The remaining brother, George, also left the paternal lands on the Braes of Glenbervie and became a leaseholder of Elfhill of Fetteresso which we shall later see.

James Burnes a Man of Sagacity

James Burnes, Burns' great-grandfather, paid £300 sterling as tenant of Brawliemuir, but under his will the sum total of his bequests did not amount to more than about £25 sterling. The Burneses certainly had neither wealth nor position: they had at times a hard struggle to live.

Traditionally James Burnes was a person of sagacity. Once when Highland freebooters were in his neighbourhood, he concealed his money in the hub of a cartwheel in the midden of his house. The robbers left without suspecting the existence of the treasure they trod upon. Glenbervie was almost in the direct line of these freebooters, and Highland raids were not uncommon, sometimes leading to great desolation.

Of James Burnes Grassic Gibbon writes:

> *His folk had the ups and downs of all flesh till the father of Robert Burnes grew up, and grew sick of the place, and went off to Ayr, and there the poet Burns was born, him that*

lay with nearly as many women as Solomon did, though not all at one time.

There is in existence an inventory of Brawliemuir and Inchbreck, dated 1759, the year of Burns' birth. The following is the part applicable to Brawliemuir:

Imp.[1] *– The Dwelling-House Wall, wh. stone midd-wall valued at Eighteen Pounds Scots*	*£18*	*0 0*
The roof and door of sd. House, valued at Nineteen Pounds Scots	*19*	*0 0*
2d – The Barn walls valued at fifteen Pounds Scots	*15*	*0 0*
The Roof Door etc. of sd. Barn valued at fifteen Pounds and one merk Scots	*15*	*13 4*
Sum total of Brawlinmoor sixty seven Pounds and one merk Scots	*£67*	*13 4*

The dwelling-house and barn at Brawliemuir – it could be described as little better than a hovel – are therefore valued at a little more than a £5 note in sterling!

Brawliemuir is a farm which is now 'merged' and farmed by a neighbouring farmer to the west. The empty farmhouse on this historic Burnes holding, *lonely up there on the brae* as Lewis Grassic Gibbon introduces it in his book, the BBC were able to use as the setting for the Guthrie farm of Blawearie in their TV film dramatisation of *Sunset Song* in 1970 because it was one of the very few three-storey farmhouses available. It was refurnished with 'bygones' collected from the Angus Folk Museum and many items loaned by the farming folk of the Braes of Glenbervie.

There is some evidence that Burns may have visited his father's cousin David at Brawliemuir during his Highland tour in 1787. Provost Burness, Montrose, a grandson of Burns' uncle, stated to Peter Livingstone, the Dundee poet, that when Will Nicol and the poet were returning from their Northern tour,

My father and myself went out as far as Marykirk to meet them. Among the first words Robert said after kindly embracing us was, 'I have been at our paternal farm in the Mearns'.

[1] Imprimatur – let it be printed.

There is still another statement allegedly on record to show that Burns was at Brawliemuir, this time from the lips of a member of the Burns family who became a Mrs Strachen of Auchenblae. Asked what she thought of the poet, Mrs Strachen, then a servant at Brawliemuir, is supposed to have said,

Weel, naebody could pit up wi' him ava. He wis ower cliver and said ower mony smairt things for puir country folk.

Jacksbank

If you take the turning to the right at the Brae School corner only some five hundred and twenty yards or so past the Brawliemuir road end, you will reach the farm road to Jacksbank on the left in just a third of a mile. But you will probably think it unnecessary to drive so far for the farm can be seen perfectly clearly from just past the school. Here once worked John Burness, born March 23rd, 1771, the son of William Burness of Bogjurgan and the author of *Thrummy Cap* (see page 271).

In the lower part of this farm two leaf-shaped swords of the Bronze Age were found on 30th April, 1880, lying together about 3 ft. from the surface between vegetable or mossy matter and a bed of sand across the bottom of a drain which was being cut. In the course of removal the sword which was first seen and which till then had been entire was broken into three pieces. The second sword, which was removed with care, weighed a little over 20 ounces and measured $25^7/_8$ ins. including a 4 in. handle plate. The breadth of the leaf was $1^5/_8$ ins. There was no appearance of wood, bone or horn attached to the handle, but the pins there protruded on either side, breaking off at once when touched. The blade, considerably oxidised, was greatly bent. The entire sword and the three pieces were presented to the National Museum of Antiquities in Edinburgh. At Jacksbank, too, an arrow-head was found. For a long time it used to be seen in a case of specimens in Auchenblae Public Hall.

On the same estate and between the Jacksbank farm road and the Auchenblae road along which we have been travelling is a stretch of ground named the Muir of Germany where tradition has it that a battle was fought. But I have been able neither to trace the origin of the name nor tell if and when a battle took place.

Bogjurgan

The next road end, 190 yards farther on, is more important for it leads to a place of peculiar interest to Burnsians, all that remains of the original sixty-acre farm of Bogjurgan (most likely from deargan, a red spot – from iron oxide on the hill), once owned by Burns' great-great-grandfather, Walter Burnes, in 1640 and tenanted by Burneses for four generations from the 16th century onwards. Where the Burnes family originated no one knows, and speculation on the subject will take us nowhere. We do know, however, that there were Burneses farming in the neighbourhood in 1547 in the days of Mary Queen of Scots (as we have seen) and that after a blank of more than a century we can trace Robert Burns back in a direct line to Walter Burnes on the Braes of Glenbervie here, the first paternal ancestor whom we know by name. He married Isobel Greig and had five sons and two daughters. As far as we are concerned, it is from Bogjurgan that the family now rendered famous by the genius of Robert Burns sprang. The original building, once thatched, later a pig-sty, and now, most sadly, merely a rickle of stones, can still be seen. Yet the enthusiast will doubtless not grudge the four-fifths of a mile journey there and back to ask permission to see it.

After the death of Walter Burnes in 1670 the farm passed to his son, William Burnes, Burns' great-grand-uncle who died in 1715 and who, with his wife, Christian Fotheringham, is buried in Glenbervie churchyard. Before his death William Burnes surrendered the farm to his sons, William and James. These, after holding it on a joint lease, separated in 1705, James to farm Inches, near Glenbervie, and William remaining at Bogjurgan where he died in 1748. The next owner was his son, yet another William Burness (but notice the new double 's' in the surname) who lived from 1720 to 1784 and who was the father of John Burness (mentioned above) who decided to quit the place and move to Stonehaven. On the death of this third William, Bogjurgan ceased to be farmed by the Burness family, but it is interesting to know that from this branch of the family there are descendants named Burness living in Stonehaven today.

An Inventory of a Clay Biggin

A very interesting document is a copy of the inventory of the homestead at the time of the separation of the sons of the first William in 1705. I quote from Chambers' *Life and Work of Robert Burns* to show how simple it was:

> *Ane note of the biging off Bogjorgine, belonging to William Stuart, heritor thereoff. given up be William Burnasse,*

*present tenant of the said rowm, and James Burnasse, late
possessor of the halff thereoff, upon the seventainth day of
July, 1705 years.*

*Imp (a ffyr) houss, consisting of three couplles, ffour
horses, two tail postes ane midle wall with ane post ffrom
the ground, with ane rooff, two pares in the syd with ane
door bandet, locked, and bared, and with ane window off
two lightes, bradet, bandet, and snecked, with ane loume,
all to be sufficient.*

*Item, ane barne, consisting of ffyve couplles, four horses,
two taillpostes, and rooff, thrie pares in the syd, with ffor
door locked, and handed, and back door bared and
steepled, all to be sufficient.*

*Item, ane byre, consisting of four couplles two in the syd,
ane roof, with door and door cheikes bandet, all to be
sufficient.*

*It is declared be both parties that if thar be no other
inventur ffound betwixt this and Whytsonday nixt, 1706
years, that this shall be ane tr(ue) inventur off the said
William Burness at his removell from the said roum. In
witness . . . beffor these witnesses – Robt. Middletoun in
Broombank, and David Watson in Polburn, wryter hereof.*

R. MIDLETONE, *witness.*   WILL STUART,
   D. WATSON, *witness*   1705,
      and wryter.   W.B.

It thus appears that the original auld clay biggin of Bogjurgan
consisted of a barn, a byre and a dwelling-house with an earthen
floor which had only one room, divided by a wooden partition, one
door, one window and one chimney. It had open rafters and a
thatched roof. A middle-class farmer of today would consider it
little better than a hovel. Its estimated value is not stated.

Cleughead

It's very slightly more than a third of a mile farther on along this
same road before we pass our next farm with Burns associations. I
refer to Cleughead on our left, away up on the heather-clad slopes
of the Braes of Glenbervie. This was tenanted for a time in the 18th
century by William Burnes of Bogjurgan. On a declivity 300 yards
from Cleughead in February, 1878, an Early Bronze Age cist was

found, containing calcined bones and a perforated stone hammer. They are now in the National Museum of Antiquities, Edinburgh.

Elfhill

The last farm with Burns associations on our route is 2½ miles away, past the farms of East Town, Quithel and Annamuik, the farm named Elfhill. Elfhill was once owned by George Burnes, the great-uncle of the poet or, if you like, the brother of Robert Burnes, Burns' grandfather, and uncle of the young William Burnes of Clochnahill who was to become the father of the poet. George Burnes farmed here from 1729 until his death in 1752 to be succeeded by his son James who removed to the farm of Midtown of Barras, Kinneff, in 1785 when the connection of the Burnes's with Elfhill ceased.

The name, Elfhill, has always been associated with fairies and, indeed, the glen of the Carron is here beautiful enough to be a fairy glen. But the name really springs from the wooded hill behind. Within such hillocks in olden times elves or fairies were believed happily to dwell.

About 1850 what was probably a cremation in a cinerary urn was found when a track was being widened some 240 yards south-west of Elfhill farmhouse.

Gate-post of Place of Barras

In just short of 2½ miles we pass on the right what used to be one of the lodges to the Fetteresso Castle estate. And in just under half a mile farther on, round the corner at the top of the hill, have a peep at the garden on the right as you pass. The ornamental pillar there, topped by a stone ball, is in fact part of one of the gate-posts of the old House or Place of Barras to which I refer in some detail on page 138.

Soon, beyond the Forestry Cottages in the middle distance, is seen quite clearly in Ury Estate the hillock with its clump of trees concealing The Howff,[1] the burial-place of the Barclays. There follows a good view on the left of the ruins of Ury House as we descend the hill to reach in a third of a mile or so the farm of Farrochie. On the right is the wooded knoll that is Malcolm's Mount,[2] and in just under a mile, under the railway bridge, along Arduthie Road, past Arduthie School and down Evan Street, we end our journey where we began it – in Stonehaven Square.

[1] See *Highways and Byways Round Stonehaven*, p. 175.
[2] Ibid., pp. 104-109.

A view of Galloquhine, at one time a wayside inn on an ancient roadway traversed by pilgrims and dealers from Deeside and the north en route for southern markets. Immediately below the farm steading stood an important meal and barley mill beside which was a ford over the West Burn.

The meeting of the Cairn o' Mounth and Glen of Drumtochty roads at the Clatterin' Brig which is seen on the left of the picture. On the extreme left is the Restaurant on the hill while top left is the Forestry Commission plantation along the side of which one must proceed to reach the Deer Dyke. In the field in the foreground once stood the hamlet of Clatterin' Brig.

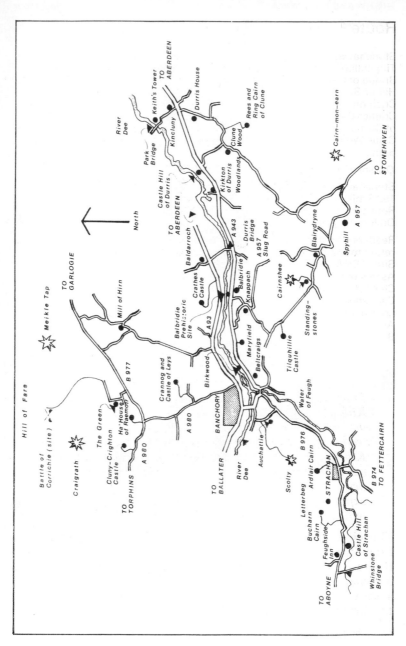

Route Five

Stonehaven Square – Slug Road – Blairydryne – Standingstones – Cairnshee –
Tilquhillie Castle – Knappach – Balbridie – Maryfield – Birkwood – Beltcraigs –
Bridge of Feugh – Strachan – Feughside Inn – Whitestone – Bucharn – Castle
Hill of Strachan – Ardlair – Scolty – Banchory – Loch of Leys (site) – Cluny
Crichton Castle – Raemoir Hotel – Site of Battle of Corrichie – Mill of Hirn –
Crathes Castle – Baldarroch – Nether Mills of Crathes – Wester Durris – Kirkton
of Durris – Castle Hill of Durris – Keith's Hill – Keith's Stone – Durris House –
Clune Wood – Woodlands – Calladrum – Inchloan – Slug Road – Stonehaven
Square.

Distance: A total of 79¾ miles, as follows:

Stonehaven Square to Blairydryne and back (from top of Slug Road) by car
19.18 miles
Round trip from Blairydryne by car 49.62 miles
On foot 11 miles.

Readers who do not wish to travel far on foot may find it helpful to know the
return mileage of walks a quarter of a mile and more in length:
Site of Battle of Corrichie 4.36 miles
Ascent of Scolty 2.67 miles
Clune Hill 1.40 miles
Cairnshee .93 miles
Loch of Leys (site) .74 miles
Ardlair cairn .25 miles
Bucharn cairn .25 miles

Round Strachan, Banchory-Ternan, Durris and Deeside

*in which we read of a fairies' mound, the Kew Gardens of
Kincardineshire and Edward I's 'manour among the
mountains'. We discover the earliest known piece of architecture in the British Isles and the earliest human presence in
Kincardineshire, the most visited of North-east estates and a
mansion distinctive of that area. Finally, we learn about
Scotland's finest painted ceilings, a laird's lug, the greatest
exponent of Scottish violin music and a poltergeist's pranks
with potatoes.*

This circuit of 49½ miles really starts at Blairydryne, 10½ miles
from Stonehaven along the A957, and to this point we must follow
Route 4. At the Bridge of Blairydryne we turn left along the road to
Strachan, turning sharp right again in 190 yards. At the crossroads
at the top of the hill, in two-thirds of a mile, we reach the road end to
the farm of Standingstones[1] 280 yards away on the right. Here is the

---

[1] In the 19th century a stone-circle at Standingstones Farm was removed.

point from which to climb the small, wooded hill of Cairnshee (725 ft.) which has been in our view since Spyhill Farm corner. A walk of 400 yards round the perimeter of a field will take one to the hill itself the top of which is only a little over 700 yards away as the crow flies. The walk is an arduous one over pitted, rough terrain and should be attempted only by the most resolute and enthusiastic.

Cairnshee, the Fairies' Mound

On the summit of Cairnshee (in Gaelic Cairn Sithe, 'the fairies' cairn or mound') a large Bronze Age cairn stands, 70 ft. in diameter. As, however, it may well be that many readers will not attempt the ascent of Cairnshee to see it, I think it advisable to postpone what there is to be said about such monuments until we visit the very much more accessible Bronze Age cairn of Bucharn later in this tour. It is, after all, only five miles away. On Cairnshee it was the custom for well over 100 years for sheep and cattle-herds annually to burn a huge bonfire on midsummer-eve to exorcise evil spirits and ensure the safety and prosperity of their flocks during the ensuing twelve months. Though there is no actual record of when this rite originated (the event is of much greater antiquity than Stonehaven's fireball festival), we know that it was in existence for many years before 1787. This ancient ceremony therefore linked even the late 19th century with the days of Baal and fire – and sun-worship.

It was because his memories of the fire ritual were so pleasant that Alexander Hog, a native of the area (see page 151), earmarked a sum in 1787 to be donated annually to ten young cowherds in the neighbourhood of the hill to ensure its survival and in remembrance of the fact that he himself once herded cattle there as a lad. Each herdsman received 1/- for his part in the ceremony.

The spectators who flocked to Cairnshee from all over the district were regaled with bread, cheese and ale. By the year 1900 the ancient ceremony had taken place 112 times and, perhaps unfortunately for the picturesqueness if not the safety of the district, finally lapsed in the third or fourth decade of the present century when the legacy would not bear the march of time.

The ancient Celtic festival on Mayday, the beltane, was also quite an established festival all over the Mearns at one time. The last traces of it were found in the Mayday walks to saints' wells, the girls carrying bouquets and wearing crowns, the boys bearing sticks.

Tilquhillie Castle of 'Four-hoose Hicht'

Continuing our journey to the north-west, we make our way to the old castle of Tilquhillie (the name may mean 'Bubbling Spring') which we see quite distinctly a little over a mile away in front of us on high ground, dreaming amid its trees. Its position was very well chosen for it stood on one of the old-time Mounth routes to the north that led down to the Dee at Banchory. It also commands an extensive eastern prospect, backed up in the distance by the mountains at the head of Glen Dye conspicuous among which is Clochnaben. Let us turn up left at the farm road end opposite a ruined gable and have a look at it: it is only 350 yards away in a field.

Tilquhillie is a fine and imposing example, albeit plain and unusual, of the semi-fortified smaller Scottish mansion or tower house of the period. Built on the stepped or Z-plan, a design that is peculiar to this part of the country, it has a massive, central keep rising to *four-hoose hicht*, including a garret. In the main re-entrants there are two semi-circular turrets diagonally opposite each other at the north-east and south-west angles, probably of later date. One is a slender stair-turret, unusually corbelled out above the first floor; the other admits of a square staircase between the south-west tower and the main block. At the foot, in the shade of the trees, is the door above which is a worn heraldic panel.

Architecture Both Functional and Beautiful

The two echeloned towers are both square, and there are no angle turrets. The corners of the building are unusual in that they are all rounded off and at all angles corbelled out to the square near the eaves, presumably for better roofing. Kitchen, larder and storehouses were on the ground floor off which opened the withdrawing-room and 'best bedroom' of the house. All the basement rooms were vaulted.

From the point of view of defence against siege the castle was almost impregnable. Loopholes in the towers and on the 7 ft. thick walls of the basement were so arranged that the whole of the walls, on every side of the house, could be swept by gun-fire. Supposing some intrepid enemy did reach the only door, defying the loopholes on each side, there were traps waiting for him even beyond the threshold. Coming down stairs, the defenders could stab him in the flank, and if he got beyond that point, there would not be enough room for him to draw his sword.

One has nothing but admiration for the marvellous ingenuity of the masons who built the stronghold. The windows are mainly small, yet one admires the fine lighting of the rooms by windows on two walls. Although the masons had probably a rough plan mapped out on a piece of wood, they had not the services of an architect and 'improvised' when they came to ticklish work like the construction of the staircases. One extols, too, the common-sense way in which the builders designed the castle at ground level. It was built on a better plan in that respect than many more modern houses with their basements. We are accustomed to hear a great deal nowadays about 'functional architecture', and there are some who believe that so long as a building perfectly fulfils its function, it is bound to be beautiful. But to be beautiful a building has to be built with a sense for form, and it can be said of Tilquhillie Castle that it both perfectly fulfilled its original function and has beauty of form as well.

Tilquhillie Castle, a plain yet imposing specimen of a semi-fortified mansion or tower-house of the late 16th century. Built on the Z-plan in 1576, it has a massive central keep and two square echeloned towers. It was the seat of the Douglas family.

'And the Name of the Douglas is There'

The estate of Tilquhillie Castle originally belonged to the Abbey of Arbroath. At the Reformation it passed to the family of Ogstoun, and about 1479 became the seat of the Douglas family when Jane, the heiress of Walter Ogstoun of Tilquhillie, married David Douglas, second son of Sir Henry Douglas of Lochleven and a grandson of the second Lord of Dalkeith. In the Douglas family, with the exception of a short break, it remained:

> *'Tilquhillie stands on the old, red lands,*
> *And the name of the Douglas is there'.*

The building of the present castle was begun after the Renaissance on the foundations of an earlier structure by John Douglas, a great-grandson of David Douglas, the first laird. The architectural features suggest that it was not finished until the 17th century.

Fourteen years before he built the castle, John Douglas fought under the banner of the Earl of Huntly against Queen Mary at the Battle of Corrichie on the Hill of Fare in 1562. Under the Great Seal he was later pardoned by King James with the consent of his Douglas relative, the powerful Earl of Morton, the Scottish Regent, who in the days of his later adversity is believed to have lived incognito at Tilquhillie for some time under the name of James the Grieve. He built the present castle in 1576 (so states an inset stone over the door), *a plain but massive specimen of a Scottish house at the end of the sixteenth century*. Later 17th century lairds, the brothers Archibald and Robert Douglas, who were sons of John Douglas, received knighthoods from Charles I for bravery and succeeded to the estate in turn. The latter, a militant Royalist, was commissioned in the Royalist forces but, ruining himself in the Royalist cause, had to sell all his lands. In his time Tilquhillie Castle was garrisoned by Covenanters.

In Tilquhillie was born in 1868 Norman Douglas, novelist and essayist. His reminiscences, *Looking Back*, state that he spent little time on the estate after leaving to study in Karlsruhc (*c*. 1886). He lived in Capri when he left the Foreign Service and wrote there his most successful novel, *South Wind* (1917). He died in 1952. The owner of Tilquhillie at the beginning of this century, Mr John W. E. J. Douglas, was married to a daughter of Baron August de Reuter of Reuter's Agency.

An Exciting Discovery at Balbridie

In just under half a mile we follow the road to the right along which in four-fifths of a mile is the farm of Knappach. In a further quarter of a mile we cross thc Slug Road (A957) and in a few moments reach the South Deeside road (A943). Here we turn left to reach on our right in 170 yards the site[1] of one of the most important and exciting archaeological discoveries of the century.

[1] As all evidence of excavation has now disappeared because of cultivation, the enthusiastic reader may wish to know that the centre of the site is 27 yards before a gate on the left, inside the field on the right and just short of 12 yards from the edge of the road.

For at Balbridie on an undulating area of terrace beside the River Dee, and standing on its own with no other building near, were the remains of what is the first really substantial Neolithic house, the earliest known monumental piece of architecture ever found in the British Isles although it is only a matter of time before Balbridie is no longer alone. Timber buildings of this nature have been discovered in Central Europe, Czechoslovakia, France and Scandinavia but not previously in Britain. Moreover, the pattern here differs markedly from Continental examples.

The discovery was first made during the drought of 1976 when archaeologists from the Royal Commission on the Ancient and Historical Monuments of Scotland made an aerial survey of the eastern Lowlands. The drought created ideal conditions for the formation of particularly fine 'crop-marks' above archaeological features – damp patches which can be clearly seen from the air. The large rectangular shape at Balbridie was visible for the first time, and another similar site across the Dee in the grounds of Crathes Castle, still to be excavated, was located at the same time. The quality of the Balbridie mark was especially remarkable as the field in which it was positioned was in pasture, and grass is not renowned for showing such marks. Excavations took place between 1977 and 1981.

A Unique House, Older than Stonehenge

The shape of the Balbridie building recalls descriptions of the vast chieftains' timber halls in *Beowulf*. But the outstanding feature was its size. It measured 78 ft. long by 39 ft. wide, and the roof would have risen to a massive height of almost 30ft. Previous early 'houses' in Shetland, for example, go back to Mesolithic times (around 6000 B.C.) but were little more than shelters. The Balbridie building was a substantial structure of oak beams, at least as sophisticated as the 'long houses' of Europe which were used to house several families and their animals, and apparently devoid of ancillary structures.

Other rectangular Neolithic houses known in Britain are all much smaller. Balbridie was at least double the size of all others in both dimensions so that it was at least four times the area. The width was especially remarkable for, although there are continental Neolithic long houses that are longer, none of them are anywhere near as wide. The roof of the Balbridie hall had to span a width nearly twice that of the largest of these (over 39 ft.) and would have required considerable building skill. Furthermore, beams of up to approximately 11¾ ins. by 19½ ins. in cross-section had been used, and stains on these showed that some at least of the major vertical posts holding up the roof had been neatly squared and jointed with pegs. The axial ridge pole of the building must have stood at least 26 ft. above the floor level and must have been sufficiently strong to support a sizeable portion of the roof's considerable weight. All of this suggests that pioneering farmers from the Continent who moved north to Scotland brought with them techniques which were then improved and developed.

The main doorway is believed to have been in the east end of the building which appears to have had V-shaped or curved walls at both gable ends. Complex features inside included traces of roof-supports and major 'partitions' or cross-walls. The fact that enough daub was found to fill three match-boxes suggests the walls might have been covered in this way. The hall was probably used for storage and lived in by a complete, settled farming community – it could have accommodated thirty to sixty people – and it is likely that the settlers had sheep and cows. But no evidence of animals could be found since bone does not survive in acid soil. The type of ground on which the building was located was, indeed, very suitable for primitive farming, and certainly, to the early settler coming up the river valley, this well-drained flat ridge well above the flood plain must have seemed very attractive. The first farmers came to Britain from the more accessible parts of the Continent: one would expect them to bring their type of house with them. *But as far as we know at present*, says Professor Leslie Alcock of the Department of Archaeology at Glasgow University, *though there are large wooden houses on the other side of the North Sea, there is none quite like this.*

Advanced Agricultural and Architectural Development

Archaeologists believe that the building experienced several phases of rebuilding or repair with strengthening posts and was finally burnt down, having stood for several hundred years. Some of the timber posts appear to have been pulled out – perhaps in an attempt to stop the fire. The carbonised material from the site is significant for our consideration of the hall's chronology which is provided by four consistent carbon datings of charred timber fragments which indicate that on average the timbers used in the construction of the huge hall were felled around 3500 B.C. and that the building therefore was erected around 5,500 years ago, firmly in the middle of the Neolithic period – and much older, for example, than Stonehenge. People lived here, therefore, in the late 4th and early 3rd millenia B.C.

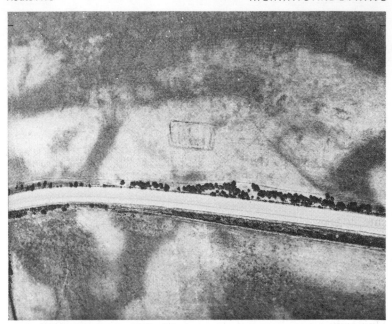

An aerial picture, taken in 1976, of the large rectangular shape, 78 ft. by 39 ft., of the Balbridie timber hall on the north side of the South Deeside Road. What seems to be the main doorway appears in the east end of the building which is seen to have curved walls at both ends. Below: *an artist's impression.*

An advantage conferred by the conflagration of the building was the incidental preservation of other organic substances which had either been deliberately transported by man into the hall or had arrived there, as it were, under their own steam. To the second category belong a few insect remains, including a weevil; to the first category food remains, principally hazelnut shells (indicating that gathering was practised) and cereal grains. Preserved principally near the road, relatively free from plough and tractor interference and representing the crops raised in the vicinity of the site, were quantities of seeds of barley and of emmer wheat, the earliest domesticated wheat in the world. Such substantial amounts of wheat and barley grains were recovered that the building must have served at least partially as a granary. Carbon-dated about 2764 B.C., these seeds vindicate the date of the wood samples and also indicate, together with pollen and other evidence, that the climate was more favourable than at present in the valley of the Dee. Clearly, too, the society of the time was one of the first in the North-east of Scotland to practise the new skills associated with an agricultural economy at least partially based on cereal cultivation. Here lived a Neolithic community which had already reached an advanced stage of development when, as archaeologist Ian Ralston of Aberdeen University reminds us, *people were supposed to be fumbling with the rudiments of agriculture.*

The bulk of the pottery evidence consists of small characterless fragments of body sherds which are not typologically distinctive. However, about a dozen sherds of Unstan Ware, a pottery type characteristic of the early Neolithic period in the Orkney Islands, were found on the site and in one of the post-holes of the building. These support the radio-carbon analysis given above. Apart from this, the small finds include one hammerstone and a small quantity of flint chips. All this is evidence of a sophisticated farming and stock-raising community with a high level of architectural sophistication too. This suggests specialist expertise and may force archaeologists radically to revise their conceptions of Stone Age man in this part of the world.

The remarkable structure which stood on the site before you could have been produced only by a society far more civilised than the Neolithic people of the North-east were thought to be. *Nowhere in Europe is there this level of sophistication,* says Nicholas Reynolds, Inspector of Ancient Monuments in Scotland. *It is possible that this technology developed independently in Scotland and was a native creation.* The Balbridie Hall is thus of considerable significance for Neolithic studies at both national and local level. It seems extremely unlikely, however, that such a building is unique in the Dee valley or elsewhere in Britain: therefore we may expect aerial photography to reveal further potential examples in the years to come. Indeed, aerial photography has already identified crop-marks of a similar rectangular building 550 yards east-south-east of Crathes Castle which we are to visit later. The building, at least 65½ ft. by 32¾ ft., is sited in the middle of the open field between Castle Wood and the lake.

Birkwood and Kincardine's First Settlers

Let us now turn westwards towards Banchory along the A943. In half a mile we pass the tollhouse of West Balbridie at the end of the Slug Road (a good example of a semi-circular ended building of the first period, *c*. 1798) and in another quarter of a mile or so a farm road on the left to Maryfield. A second most interesting site is to be found two-thirds of a mile farther on where a drive on the right-hand side of the road leads to Birkwood House. At the entrance to this drive we should park our car. Thirty-eight yards along the road is a gate into a field. If you proceed down this field for 80 yards or so towards the red-roofed fisherman's hut, you will find yourself near the south bank of the River Dee. In this area in a molehill in the pasture of the alluvial terraces, about 300 yards above Birkwood House itself and on corresponding terraces across the river, were found between 1903 and 1906 by Miss Hilda Paterson of Birkwood what are probably the earliest traces of human presence in Kincar-dineshire, and the first sign of man in Scotland for which we have evidence. (The population of Scotland at the time would be under 100.) Here were made the first discoveries in the area of so-called microliths or pygmy flints, beautifully made miniature tools of delicately worked flint, and here too was found a camping site of Mesolithic food-gatherers where charcoal and fire-cracked stones revealed the presence of a hearth.

The story of these first settlers in Scotland is a romantic one. With the final retreat of the ice-sheets a moister and milder climate began to prevail with a resultant change of vegetation and animals. Forests with an increasing predominance of oak and alder spread over the clay lowlands, cutting back the pastures, and great peat-bogs developed in which the stems of ancient forest trees, blown down by westerly gales, may still be found embalmed. Larger creatures gave way to the fleeter elk and deer, the wild pig and the early cattle called aurochs, together with smaller game. Hunting methods and equipment had to be drastically revised, a variety of adaptations made to a somewhat bleak way of life, and new sources of food exploited. The result was the Mesolithic or Middle Stone Age culture, a period of transition between Palaeolithic or Old Stone Age and Neolithic or New Stone Age times.

One of the terraces above the River Dee at Birkwood, a mile east of Banchory, where between 1903 and 1906 were found delicately worked pygmy flints or microliths belonging to the Mesolithic period, 3000 or 4000 years B.C. These are the first signs of man in Scotland for which we have evidence and, of course, the earliest traces of human presence in Kincardineshire.

Mesolithic Pygmy Flints

The pygmy flint people after the last glaciation spread over those higher and more open parts of Britain which were free from thick forest cover, and undoubtedly reached Scotland by the eastern route, coming up from northern England where their camping sites and pygmy flints are found in Yorkshire, Durham and Northumberland. It possibly took them 3,000 or 4,000 years to get as far north as Banchory. Indeed, since the charcoal found on the Birkwood Mesolithic site was oak, it may be presumed that these wandering primitive craftsmen were camping and making their little implements on Deeside 3,000 or 4,000 years before the birth of Christ. The brae on which Banchory stands today would probably have been part of a vast oak forest where wild boars grunted their satisfaction as they cracked acorns, and giant wolves saluted the moon.

The microliths which were found here on the banks of the lower Dee are characteristic of the Mesolithic period during which they were extensively used. Some of these chipped or pressure worked tools were only half an inch long. A thin blade or flake of flint was notched on one side. Top and bottom were then snapped apart, leaving below a remainder or reject piece called a 'microburin'. The upper part of the sliver of flint was then worked into exact geometric shapes of many forms – elongated triangles, crescents, tapering or narrow rods with battered edges, penknife forms, etc. Often several microliths were mounted like teeth in slotted implements of wood or bone, one edge finely chipped to prevent the wooden haft splitting, to form a composite tool to be used perhaps like a primitive sickle for cutting edible grasses or to provide saws, darts, awls, core-scrapers, non-geometric blades, spears and tanged arrow-heads to tip and barb the arrows with which their owners hunted small animals and birds. It is from this time that the attachment of wooden handles to all sorts of tools and weapons became general. The bow became the major weapon, and the dog first joined forces with man as a hunting ally. Some microliths were blunt-headed to kill small fur-bearing creatures by the force of the blow without damaging the pelt. Upon edible grasses, nuts and berries and such small game as they could collect amid the primeval forests these early men contrived to maintain what must have been a wretched existence.

Pygmy flints of the Mesolithic period have also been found in great quantities on the alluvial and fluvio-glacial terraces at Knappach, at Maryfield and at some three or four dozen sites on the banks of the Dee. In Balbridie Farm, indeed, is a collection of 24,000 picked up between Balbridie and Banchory! Microliths from Birkwood may be seen in the Museum of Antiquities, Edinburgh.

A Mesolithic Settlement

On your return journey to your car you will be fascinated to realise that in 1935 trenching revealed part of an actual Mesolithic settlement only some 100 yards farther west from where you are now and midway between the A943 and the Dee. Artifacts of flint, schist and quartz (some burnt) were found with charcoal at depths of between

2 ft. and 3 ft. These are preserved in the National Museum of Antiquities of Scotland with flints from two lower terraces of the Dee on the farms of Beltcraigs, Birkwood, Maryfield and Knappach, and microliths from Inchmarlo Cottage, Banchory. Preserved in Aberdeen Art Gallery and Museum, too, are Mesolithic flints from a site 220 yards north of Balbridie farmhouse, 1¾ miles away to the east, on the South Deeside road.

But we must be on our way towards Banchory. In two-fifths of a mile is the farm road to Beltcraigs where, yet again, great quantities of pygmy flints have been found. What an industrious community must have lived within an area of one and a half miles on the south bank of the Dee in the 3rd and 4th millenia B.C!

The Picturesque Bridge of Feugh

In a further third of a mile we arrive at the Bridge of Feugh, erected about 1790 by Mr Russel of Blackhall, a plain narrow structure, built of granite, with three arches and one of the most noted sights on Deeside. It derives its reputation and picturesqueness from the fact that it stands in a romantic setting and spans, both above and below it, a beautiful rocky channel of the fast-moving Feugh where the vast volumes of cascading waters tumble and roar over the rocks from a height of 18 ft. into the deep basin below, presenting a never-failing source of interest and admiration.

But there is something even more intriguing and irresistible to the onlookers: the Feugh is a noted salmon and trout stream, as many as fifty salmon having been caught in one day in the pool below the bridge. Here is a famous salmon-leap, and when the water is high, the bridge parapets are frequently crowded with visitors watching dozens of salmon and sea-trout making their exciting and unceasing efforts to surmount the seemingly unscaleable rocks of the falls to make their way upstream – a wonderfully fascinating sight as they leap many feet only to be dashed against the rocks and swept back to where they started.

Especially when in flood, the Feugh is one of the finest sights among the tributaries of the Dee. The old tollhouse nearby was flooded out in the 'muckle spate' of 1829 which caused terrific havoc. The result of an unprecedented cloud-burst on upper Deeside on August 3rd, the River Dee at Banchory rose to 27 ft. above its normal level. But in any circumstances the Falls of Feugh are well worth a visit and, except perhaps in the dead of winter, one seldom finds the Bridge of Feugh deserted.

The Church and Village of Strachan

At the west end of the Bridge of Feugh is the tollhouse of which we spoke. Built in 1790 along with the bridge, it has a design unique among the tollhouses of Deeside. Here we turn left along the B974 and in a little over 2½ miles find ourselves in the village of Strachan, an old-fashioned kirkton lying in the centre of the parish of Strachan and sheltered on the north by the Hill of Scolty. The name is a corruption of Strath Aven, and it is spelt Straen on a tombstone in the churchyard of Banchory-Ternan. But it will be seen from old charters that the name was hardly every spelt twice alike.

The strath or valley of the Feugh from which the village is named is, of course, the origin of the personal name of Strachan, as well as of the parish: by as early as 1100 the family of Strachan were probably in possession of the village and took their name from the strath and river Aven where they were located. Ultimately, and partly through family alliances, they descended into the Howe and occupied Thornton.

The mediaeval church of Strachan was dedicated to St Mary on July 16th, 1242, by Bishop de Bernham who had crossed the Cairn o' Mounth to do so. It formerly belonged to the cathedral of Brechin, the minister of Strachan being archdeacon, and in 1574 was served along with the churches of Nigg and Maryculter. The minister of Strachan was once entitled to receive the sum of £3 16/- Scots yearly for certain services which, prior to the Reformation, had to be performed by him in the cathedral of Brechin. It was a dangerous distance the worthy man had to travel right over the Mounth – and little enough money for his pains. The old church stood within the burial-ground in or near the site of its late 18th century successor, but a new building was erected in 1837 on the north side of the road. In front of it is a fountain, dated 1866 *in remembrance of William Burnett Ramsay of Banchory Lodge.*

At the manse (the present one was built in 1777) was born the learned Dr Thomas Reid (1710-1796), parish minister of New-machar in Aberdeenshire and Professor of Philosophy at King's College, Aberdeen. He wrote a renowned book, *An Inquiry into the Human Mind on the Principles of Common Sense*, and created the Scottish school of philosophy opposed to David Hume. He succeeded Adam Smith in Glasgow. Two of his ancestors who were eminent, one a philosopher and the other a physician in the time of Charles I, were sons of the minister of Banchory-Ternan. Also a native of Strachan was the Rev. Andrew Cant (1590-1663), a stout upholder of the Covenant. Dr George Campbell, the great Presbyterian divine, was translated from Strachan parish church to the Principalship of Marischal College at Aberdeen in 1759.

Feughside Inn, an Ancient Hostelry

In a little over two miles we reach Feughside Inn or, as it was once known, Whinstones, for centuries a great halting-place for cattle dealers and drovers in pre-railway days as it was on the road running south to Forfar and Perth and north to the Highlands. Many hearty and glorious nights were spent here in the good days of old. The inn is mentioned as early as 1549, and one can infer that there has been a hostelry here near the Cairn o' Mounth road throughout recorded history.

At one time there was here over the Feugh a bridge of five arches which was swept away by the flood of 1799. On the Cairn o' Mounth road from Fettercairn to Potarch, it was erected at the expense of the Rev. Dr Gilbert Ramsay of Barbadoes, a native of the district.

Whinstone Bridge in an Area of Beauty

260 yards beyond the inn is Whinstone Bridge which ends our travelling farther to the west for this picturesque wooden structure marks the boundary between Kincardineshire and Aberdeenshire and is half in one county and half in the other. In the area, despite the barrenness of the Grampian district, there are many places which the sight-seer will find of interest and of great beauty. Only some 550 yards above Whinstone Bridge the Feugh is joined by a considerable tributary, the Water of Aven, which we have already mentioned, while the Feugh and Dye conjoin about half a mile above the village of Strachan. The valleys of all three rivers are charming, and the river scenery in the neighbourhood with the pine forests of Feugh and Birse (the only deer forest in the county and the most easterly deer forest in Scotland) form the background of many of the most beautiful paintings by Joseph Farquharson, R.A., the laird of Finzean from 1880 to 1906. He was famous for his glorious paintings of, among other things, the rushing waters of the Feugh with the trees of Deeside in their gorgeous autumn dress of crimson, gold, lemon and orange.

The Gaunt Bronze Age Burial Mound of Bucharn

On our way back towards Banchory there are three places of great interest to see. The road to the first is just short of a mile from Feughside Inn. It is on our left, a single track road with passing places. In just under half a mile we turn sharp right towards the farm

211

of Bucharn, again turning right when at a T-junction in 370 yards we meet another farm road. In a further 180 yards we arrive at the farmstead where we leave our car. 220 yards away to the east and along the side of a field stands an excellent Bronze Age cairn, gaunt and forbidding on the top of a hill which it has dominated for over 3,500 years.

Round barrows or round cairns like the one before us, with an extraordinary variety of content and structure, are the standard tombs of the Bronze Age from about 1800 B.C. to 550 B.C. No monument is more typical of our Kincardineshire countryside than these great burial mounds which surely mark the resting-places of Bronze Age chiefs, the graves of humbler folk being smaller and on lower ground, one presumes.

The Bronze Age barrow or cairn of Bucharn, gaunt and forbidding on the top of a hill and exactly one mile from Strachan. The barrow, formed of round boulders as heavy as a man can carry and about 100 ft. in diameter and 30 ft. in height, was the standard tomb of the Bronze Age from about 1800 B.C. to 550 B.C.

By far the majority of round barrows or cairns are of the simple 'bowl' form, like an inverted pudding basin. It is of interest that in this case, instead of being made of earth, the Bucharn barrow, circular in form and thirty feet in height, is formed of boulders, round and smooth and as heavy as a man can carry. This is, of course, quite usual in the rocky soil of a highland area. The barrow still remains entire, or nearly so, and is about 320 feet in circumference or about 100 in diameter, about 20 feet less than the largest diameter known.

Cists in a Sacred House for the Dead

The contents of the barrow may be guessed with some accuracy from the fact that another barrow once stood some 430 yards away above the farm of Letterbeg in a direct line between the barrow at Bucharn here and the barrow at Ardlair which we have still to visit. It was, we are told, about 100 ft. in diameter, about 30 ft. high and formed of huge, round stones. Shortly before 1914 the cairn disappeared, three hundred cart-loads of stones being removed by some hard-working farmer of the time. (One is tempted to think that most of these may have formed the huge consumption dyke, some eighteen to twenty feet wide, which is to be found, the width of a field away, to the east of the Ardlair cairn.) Enclosed underneath were discovered two cists formed of oblong stones set on end, flags being under the bottom and over the top. All that remained of the cremation burials were small heaps of ashes and bones which crumbled on being touched. Presumably very much the same kind of inhumation burial rests underneath the two remaining cairns. Many such barrows have, indeed, several burials, although the normal rite in the Bronze Age burial is a single burial as opposed to the collective burials of the long barrow.

One must remember that round barrows are not tombs as such but only the final coverings of a sacred area where the dead were laid and where ritual was carried on. Generally speaking, a circular area was marked out (ditches are absent on the rocky soil of this area). Here the dead were laid, sometimes on a platform of stones or wood, long enough for the flesh to decay. Sometimes the primary burial was in a stone cist in a pit dug in the ground at the centre of the circle, but quite often the body was laid on the natural surface. (Professor Childe has pointed out that pastoral people do not like digging!) When the time came and the body or bodies had been variously disposed of, the sealing rites were held. These included a funeral feast held outside the sacred area, fire and the digging of pits, possibly for libations to the spirits in the earth. Some days later the barrow mound was contructed from turfs or baskets of soil brought from some distance or, as in the stoney country here, made of heaped stones. A ring of posts, lintelled together, may have been placed round the barrow to keep the stones in postion or, alternatively, to delimit the extent of the sacred grave mound – but not necessarily so.

It is a curious fact that the Bronze Age roundhead man built a round barrow while that of the Neolithic long-head was long. An interesting sidelight on the belief of those days is also shown by the provision of these monuments. It suggests that in Bronze Age times, when cremation slowly replaced inhumation, the spirit was freed at once to go to the spirit world, whereas in Neolithic times the spirit was tied to the earth for some little while.

Castlehill of Strachan, a Norman Motte

Back on the B976, we have to travel only some 170 yards to see our second place of interest. For on our right-hand side is a fine specimen of a severed spur, 21 ft. high, the only remaining portion on the left bank of the Feugh of a gravel shelf left behind by the retreating ice after the Ice Age. Another severed spur cut off by the action of the river in its tortuous course is visible on the other side of the stream. The former knoll or spur, subsequently 'trimmed' to a level summit of up to 26¼ yards across to suit military requirements, was later to be known as the Castlehill of Strachan, a fine example of a motte or conical mound of earth on the flat top of which stood a strong wooden tower or castle, in its day practically secure from capture in its isolation and remoteness. The top of the motte was originally ringed with a stout palisade with a platform on the inner side, and wooden steps led up one side. Attached to a motte there was normally (but not here) a banked and palisaded enclosure called a bailey or lower mound on which were erected the subsidiary buildings necessary for horses and food storage. Usually it was surrounded by a ditch. The rapid building of mottes began after the Norman invasion. There are about 100 mound sites in the North-east, three of them in Kincardineshire, one of the other two being within the grounds of Banchory House and the other to the east of Kirkton of Durris. The latter we shall visit later.

Castlehill of Strachan was excavated in 1980 and 1981. This was largely a rescue excavation as the mound was in danger of collapse because of erosion from former quarrying on the west and south-west and from the work of animals. Evidence of a stone and timber superstructure, thought to have been a single-storey hall, was revealed on top, with unique stone settings for a palisade. Revetment walls were also discovered, constructional rather than defensive, with, at the foot of these walls, good examples of drainage features. Discovered on the site were pottery, metalwork, a fine key and a whetstone – probably from the 13th century – together with bronze strap ends, a silver pin, a bronze bracelet and a very fine silver ring which had only slight corrosion. A hearth and three domestic ovens were also found, proving that a good deal of cookery was carried out on the mound for the associated castle. A ditch was revealed on the north, south and west.

Castlehill of Strachan, one of the three mottes in Kincardineshire which was from the 12th century onwards in the possession of the powerful Durward family, the most famous of whom was Alan Durward. On the top originally stood a strong wooden tower or castle, ringed with a stout palisade. Wooden steps led up one side.

The Powerful Durward Family

The motte of Castlehill of Strachan was from the 12th century onwards a fort in the possession of the powerful family of the Durwards who probably supplanted the Strachans as lords of the valley, driving them south to what is now the Howe of the Mearns. This stronghold dominated the northern end of the famous Cairn o' Mounth pass, then the main highway to the north. It was one of a chain to which belonged Green Castle near Kincardine.

The Durwards were the descendants of doorwards or sergeants who before 1300, under the direction of constables, guarded the body of the king. Twelve took their meals while the other twelve guarded, and all were on duty at night. When the court moved, these doorwards, as ushers, ran on foot before the constable in place of sergeants-at-arms or mace-bearers.

The office of doorward was first conferred by David I on one Walter, the son of Alan and, as it became hereditary in the family of Durward of Coull in the Forest of Birse by grant of Malcolm IV in 1158, the office was intimately connected with Kincardineshire. How many Durwards were in possession of the forest fortress of Strachan cannot now be ascertained, but the family was a prominent one up to the War of Independence.

Alan Durward a Prominent Statesman

The most famous member of the family and one of the most powerful Scottish magnates of the 13th century who occupied, amongst other castles in his many estates, that on the Castlehill of Strachan was Alan the Doorward or Durward who had doubtless raised himself above his position as a doorward through character and ability. While the origin of the Durwards was probably no higher than their office indicates, they had made alliances of importance before the reign of William, and Alan was the first, after the days of the maormors, to rise from local knight to great statesman. A cunning diplomatist and accomplished and fearless knight in the reigns of Alexander II (whose daughter, Marjory, he married), his successor David and Alexander III, he was the first to revive a position in the fastnesses of the Mounth analogous to that held a century or two before by the maormors or 'earls' of the Mearns, transferring the exercise of their dangerous power first to Strachan and then to Coull, both situated in the heart of the mountains, seven miles from each other and extremely difficult to approach. He built a wooden bridge over the Dee and a hospital on his own property at the end of it.

Alan Durward was the leader of a party of earls and lords, all leaning upon the fickle and foolish Henry III of England and opposed to a national or Scottish party of the time, headed by Walter Comyn, Earl of Menteith, against whom he unceasingly turned Henry's attention. So was Durward brought into the high favour and confidence of the English king because of his military ability. It was Durward who, when made one of the governors of Scotland in 1258, came north under certain obligations to Henry who promised aid and counsel so long as the governors ruled according to the laws and customs of the country. And it was Durward who, with Buchan and Mar, upon the retreat of King Haco of Norway from Scotland, was given by the king of England the task of punishing Highland chieftains who dared shelter him, a task which he pursued with the barbarity characteristic of the age.

It was in the disorders of the reign of the eight-year-old Alexander III that Durward became a prominent statesman, being one of the barons appointed by Henry to take his daughter to Scotland to marry the young Scots king. Durward was at the marriage ceremony in 1263 and seems to have taken part in frustrating Henry's claim to homage from the kingdom of Scotland. It was the leading men of Durward's party who, as the result of a little revolution, assumed the regency over the young king and queen, Durward as a consequence becoming justiciary of all Scotland north of the Forth. Accused by Pope Innocent IV of removing the counsellors of the late king, Alexander II, from his son, Durward and his followers were excommunicated, the sentence against him being repeated as a warning with bell, book and candle in every church and chapel in the land.

A Time-server's Family Falls into Obscurity

Durward was an unscrupulous time-server with only selfish interests at stake and did not seem to mind much what the king of England did so long as he, Durward, was at the helm. He died in 1275, and Fordoun says of him that he was

> *vir dapsilis et strenuissimus in armis ac Regie et regno fidelissimus* and *tanquam flos militiae reputatus.* (a bountiful man, most vigorous in battle and faithful to king and country and considered the flower of the soldiery.)

His character is illuminated by an incident given in the *Lanercost Chronicle* which tells of him, on one of his rent days at Coull or Strachan, informing a tenant he had received an offer of a higher rent. The tenant, choosing to remain, paid up but required the assurance this would not happen again. *My right hand on it*, answered Durward, and the bargain was sealed. When this cunning transaction was repeated throughout the succeeding years, the farmer eventually exclaimed when once more offered his lord's right hand,

> *The left hand this time, my lord: the right has so often deceived me.*

The descendants of Alan Durward do not appear to have figured prominently in subsequent history except perhaps for the fact that his grandson, Nicolis de Soulis, in 1291 made a ridiculous claim to the crown of Scotland because his grandmother, the wife of Alan, was a natural daughter of Alexander II. The family seems to have fallen into comparative obscurity: it is not improbable that the office of doorward had begun to yield in importance to that of the constables' and marischals' men. So it is that here on Castlehill, Fraser, Thane of Cowie, was later to have a stronghold in 1351. Sir William Keith of the Marischal family appears to have succeeded him, occupying Castlehill before he rebuilt Dunnottar in 1394.

Ardlair Cairn on its 'False Crest'

After travelling a mile and a tenth, we return to the village of Strachan and, just opposite the B974 across the Water of Feugh, arrive at the farm of Bowbutts the name of which is derived from three circular mounds which once stood in the field behind, each about a third of an acre in extent, recalling the time when local bowmen practised archery. The mounds were ploughed up during World War II.

By following the road behind Bowbutts (at first sight it does not seem a public road) we can reach Ardlair Cairn, another Bronze Age cairn similar to Bucharn Cairn which we recently visited. First, in three-quarters of a mile we reach Ardlair Farm where we leave our car. Then we must walk 125 yards past the steading along the road to Upper Shampher Farm and a further 100 yards through a field where the cairn is easily seen.

The Ardlair cairn is not quite so entire as and slightly smaller than its neighbour, being only about 250 feet in circumference and some 79 feet in diameter. It is, moreover, slightly below the actual top of the hill on what is called a 'false crest' so that, when seen from the settlement which was presumably lower down the slope, it would be on the skyline.

Splendid Views from the Hill of Scolty

And now (if you feel fit) for the ascent of Scolty (983 ft.), the hill with the prominent monument which we have been seeing off and on for most of our jouney. Here is an easy family walk.

From Ardlair Farm itself a walk of little more than two-thirds of a mile would take us to the top of the hill. We could proceed through the farm and on to an uninhabited cottage where, because of a gate, we can go no farther. From there the walk is an easy one of some twenty minutes to the summit, following the cart track uphill and through a perceptible gap in the dyke ahead.

Perhaps, however, it would be better if we chose the more usual path up Scolty. This requires us to follow the Strachan-Banchory road for two miles and a tenth, turning left along the road to Auchattie Farm which in just under half a mile takes us to a corner on which stands a house named 'Oakleigh'. We leave our car here by a Fire notice where a gate on the left leads into Craigloch Wood. The rough track into the forest we must follow for 400 yards, turning right (west) through the usually open gate into a plantation of mixed pine and larch. Keep straight along the road, ignoring a turning to the right, until you pass through another gate, then immediately take the left road for 150 yards, keeping a lookout for a footpath to the right. This path leads up the hill through open woodlands of birch interspersed with a few Scots pine, with the fenced forestry plantation on the left.

The heather-clad hill is surmounted by a familiar circular tower, devoid of its staircase, erected in 1842 by his tenantry and friends to the memory of General William Burnett of Banchory Lodge, an officer in the Napoleonic Wars and local laird who was born on 19th February, 1762, and died on 7th February, 1839. This tower, a notable landmark seen from considerable distances, was restored by public subscription in 1964.

From the top of the hill splendid views are obtainable of the scenery of Aberdeenshire on the north and of the Howe on the south. A wide view opens out, showing the town of Banchory with the Dee and Feugh valleys immediately beneath. In its woodland setting Crathes Castle, General Burnett's home, is clearly visible across the Dee to the east of Banchory. To the south the fine tor of Clochnaben is readily recognised, and to the north-east and north-west respectively the characteristic tor shape of Bennachie and the cone of the Tap o' Noth, both the sites of ancient forts.

Blackhall Castle and the Thirsty Wood-floaters

Having completed our climb, we continue on our way, reaching the South Deeside Road (A943) in just over half a mile. Here we turn sharply left and reach the Dee in a mere 180 yards, passing on our left the principal entrance gateway to Blackhall Castle, demolished in 1946 but once a beautiful grey granite structure on a splendid secluded site. Probably comprising a tower-house and at least one later extension, it was originally the stately home of the ancient family of Russell and later owned by Mr Archibald Farquharson, M.P., and others. The artistic façade of the entrance used to be surmounted for many generations by the life-size stone figure of a goat, the crest of the Russells, with the motto *Che sara sara* (What will be, will be) before being removed to Finzean towards the turn of the century.

The approach to the castle is about two miles in length, and it is difficult to imagine one more picturesque with the river flowing closely alongside the avenue and, on the south side, the high wooded ground sloping from Scolty.

Above the site of Blackhall Castle, on the south side of the Dee, there still stands the remains of a famous old howff, well-known to the wood-floaters who in the 1840s, when the water was high, piloted rafts of timber down river from the upper reaches of the Dee, often all the way to Aberdeen. Until the Deeside railway was built in 1853, there was considerable traffic in timber, and quaint old river songs could be heard echoing far through trees and fields. Ferrying the logs down river was thirsty work as the men would be constantly shouting to one another while they balanced precariously on their rafts, and at the howff the 'gude-wife' did a roaring trade in whisky with the floaters and was never caught by the Excise Officers. The remains of this shebeen are difficult to determine with exactitude today, but there are by the roadside two possible ruins 100 yards and 120 yards respectively east of what is now the Blackhall Research Station of the Institute of Terrestrial Ecology. The choice is yours.

The old stones with iron rings for tying up the timber rafts can still be seen on the river bank below the Silverbank sawmills which were opened in 1854 with sidings on the newly formed railway.

A Dee Ferry at Coble Heugh

We cross the river by an iron truss bridge of 175 foot span which has also three stone arches. Here in 1798 a wooden bridge was erected by public subscription, this being replaced after flood damage by the present structure in 1829. Originally the crossing of the Dee was accomplished by a ferry at Coble Heugh, the ferry-man's house standing on or near the site of Banchory Lodge the entrance to which is the second opening on the right beyond the bridge. The name of the ferry and the house denoted the croft or parish of land granted to the ferry-man who kept a coble or long shallow boat.

At Blackhall, too, in the old days before the bridge, a ferry-boat crossed the Dee, and the boatman there, as at Coble Heugh and at Boathole of Durris, had weird tales to tell of the water kelpie that lured folk to their death on stormy nights when the river was running in spate.

St Ternan Civilises the Banchory Community

In a third of a mile we find ourselves in the High Street of Banchory, the popular, progressive and attractive little capital of Lower Deeside, standing on the southern slope of a ridge overlooking a beautiful stretch of the river and sheltered from the cold wind of the north by the great bulk of the Hill of Fare. With its superb and sheltered setting, natural amenities of hill and river, woodlands and meadow and abundant attractions, the burgh has long been renowned as a pleasant health and summer holiday resort. Its southern exposure also contributes to its advantages.

It was in the 5th century, we are told, that the primitive Pictish natives of what is now Banchory-Ternan were converted to the Roman Catholic religion by the saintly St Ternan, one of the early Scottish missionaries who, according to the Breviary of Aberdeen, is believed to have been born in the Mearns of noble parents, although the date of his birth is uncertain. He was baptised by St Palladius (who is said to have been directed to the child by an angel) and instructed by him in the rudiments of the faith.

Early in life St Ternan became a pupil of St Ninian at Candida Casa in Whithorn, was trained at Fordoun and eventually studied under Pope Gregory the Great in Rome. So favourable an impression did he make that he was appointed *Pictorum Archipresulis* or what Bishop Forbes calls *High President or Bishop of the Picts*, planting churches in Findon and Arbuthnott. A progressive and civilised Banchory community resulted as St Ternan also taught arts and crafts and the cultivation of the soil.

St Ternan's Bell and Gospels

He received from the Pope a marvellous hand-bell, a so-called Celtic Ronnecht (or Songster) which will always be associated with

Banchory's legendary lore. It is said miraculously to have followed him from Rome and to have accompanied him on all his journeys. Preserved at Banchory-Ternan, it was a much venerated relic up to the time of the Reformation when it disappeared. About 1889 a small square bell, alleged to be St Ternan's, was unearthed in Bellfield Park (off Dee Street on the right as we entered the town and behind the car park) by workmen making the path from Banchory Lodge to the railway station. It is now preserved in Banchory-Ternan East Church.

St Ternan's Book of the Gospels was

Quator voluminibus metallo inclusis, argento auro texto in superficie fabricatis.
(Four volumes encased in metal and with covers bound with gold and silver intermixed.)

It is asserted that part of this book, the copy of the Gospel of St Matthew, encased in a wonderful shrine of silver and gold, was also preserved in Banchory until the Reformation.

Ternan died at Banchory-Ternan, and it is said a church was built over his remains. His head was allegedly preserved there, the skin of the tonsured and anointed part which had received the episcopal consecration existing for 1100 years afterwards so that it was seen by the compiler of the Aberdeen Martyrology about 1530!

The Lands of Banchory-Devenick and the Kirktown

Banchory was later to embrace two different properties, Banchory-Devenick and the Kirktown of Banchory, each of which had a separate history up to 1618 when the proprietor of the former purchased the latter and merged both lands into one. The lands of Banchory-Devenick were granted to the Abbot of Arbroath in the 13th century by Alexander II, and the lands of Kirktown of Banchory were also originally church lands, granted again to the Abbot of Arbroath but in this case by William the Lion. In 1163 the lands had been granted to the see of Old Machar by Malcolm IV, thereafter being kept in the hands of the Church for four centuries until 1571. The Kirktown, an ancient burgh of barony, has as its centre St Ternan's kirk the ruins of which can be seen in the old kirkyard.

Two and a quarter centuries later Banchory-Ternan was still an entirely rural and, indeed, backward parish. The newer section of the burgh really dates from 1805. For a considerable time this was known as Arbeadie Village from the estate on which it was mostly built, the higher ground immediately to the west of where the railway station used to be. It was not until 1805, 1807 and 1809 that the land of the Banchory we know today was feued by three persons who in turn sub-feued.

Feuars and Founders of Banchory

The first feuar was one William Shaw, postmaster, who was granted land at 2/- per acre by the laird of Tilquhillie and whose feu extended from Arbeadie Terrace to the Douglas Arms on High Street. In 1805 the first house of stone and lime was erected at Bellfield on Dee Street where, too, stands a granite obelisk to the memory of Dr Francis Adams, some 75 yards down the hill from High Street. Dr Adams was the first resident doctor in Banchory. He married the only daughter of William Shaw and was a brilliant surgeon and classical scholar whose name extended even beyond Britain.

The second feuar was John Watson, a farmer from Braemar and for some time tenant of the farm of Mills of Drum, who in 1807 invited tradesmen and merchants to settle in his land. This was originally part of Arbeadie which formed a rough square, the four corner points being Corsee Road in the west, the east end of Arbeadie Terrace, the east end of Watson Street, and Mount Street. His name is preserved in Watson Place, Watson Lane, Watson Cottage and Watson Street near to Airy Castle where was once the Wyvers' Shed where many old fabrics were woven. To the enthusiasm and vision of John Watson the development of Banchory was to a great extent due. Convinced that in time the town would become a popular holiday and residential resort, he anticipated its foundation into a burgh by founding a Town Council, all village residents being eligible for membership on payment of an entrance fee of 2/6 and thereafter an annual payment of 1/-. He alone gifted for all time a piece of land around the public well, the free income of which was to be spent in beautifying the village.

In 1810 the lands of Arbeadie, stretching from Arbeadie or Ewan Place, north by Schoolhill and Ramsay Road (all to the east of the town in the area of Arbeadie Road) were feued by William Ewan who is interesting because his ancestor, Ewan MacDonald, was one of the men who escaped the Massacre of Glencoe and came to Deeside. His surname was dropped for self-protection. The surnames of these founders of the burgh of Banchory are now household words, enshrined in the names of streets and houses in the town.

Development of Banchory as a Residential Centre

By 1840 about fifty houses had been erected in Banchory together with a chapel, a post-office, a prison, two schools, three inns and a branch bank; in 1841 the population had reached 2,240. At this early period Banchory became attractive to summer visitors, and feuing land had rocketed from £1 an acre to as much as £120. The arrival of the railway brought added prosperity and further development (ready access being afforded to Aberdeen). By 1881 the population of the parish had passed the 3,000 mark, and the two villages of Arbeadie and Townhead eventually adopted the Lindsay Act in 1885 and merged as a Police Burgh under the name of Banchory-Ternan in commemoration of the life and work of the saint, the two parishes being sometimes distinguished as Upper and Lower Banchory. In this year the present West Church was opened for worship. Thereafter, in contrast to the previous century when the rural population had been drawn to Aberdeen, Banchory developed as a residential and dormitory centre, first on the lower ground between the Dee and the adjoining main road and later in the hill terraces above. Successive development has linked the original Kirkton with the newer section.

Queen Victoria, Scott Skinner and an Early Christian Stone

Before we leave the High Street, let us look at two things. First, the Burnett Arms Hotel concerning which we recall the issue of *The Scotsman*, dated Wednesday, 20th September, 1854, with its comments on the annual journey of Her Majesty, Queen Victoria, from Aberdeen to Balmoral Castle. It reads,

> ... *and, followed by the Royal children and suite, Her Majesty, leaning on the arms of the Prince, walked to the refreshment rooms where luncheon was served in very elegant style by Mr Grant of the Burnett Arms Inn.*

Second, inset into the wall of the garden of the office block next to the business of a family grocer (just where we originally joined the High Street) may be seen a commemorative grey granite memorial, marking the birth-place of the famous Scottish violinist, J. Scott Skinner, who was a native of Banchory. The inscription reads,

> *James Scott Skinner, the Strathspey King, the greatest violin exponent and composer of Scottish national music, was born near this spot on 15th August, 1843.*

His marvellous playing of reels and strathspeys will long be remembered. Scott Skinner died in 1927, and in 1931 a fine memorial was erected over his grave in Allenvale Cemetery, Aberdeen. It was unveiled by his old friend, Sir Harry Lauder.

The fine memorial erected over the grave of the famous Scottish violinist, J. Scott Skinner, in Allenvale Cemetery, Aberdeen. It was unveiled by Sir Harry Lauder.

225

But the most historic area in Banchory is three-quarters of a mile along the Aberdeen road to the east. As this is our route in any case, let us travel three-fifths of a mile to the fork where the A980 road to Raemoir joins the A93. Here we could leave our car on the A980 (for we are to go that way) and continue on foot for 220 yards towards Aberdeen.

In 60 yards, in a wall on the left-hand side of Station Road, opposite the manse of Banchory-Ternan, we reach an engraved slab of red granite built into the dyke in a hollow left by a stone cist. A beaker in the Anthropological Museum, Marischal College, Aberdeen, may have come from the cist found by workmen in 1801 when they were making the North Deeside Road to Aberdeen. It contained *some ashes* and an *urn* of the drinking-cup type, 6¾ ins. high by 6¼ ins. across the lip, and with rectilinear ornamentation. The inscription brings to our notice a delicately carved Celtic wheel-cross stone built into the north wall of the East Parish Chuch manse exactly opposite. The stone dates from the early Christian period although its exact date is not known.

St Ternan's College for Novices on the River Bank

The site of the East Church, however, 160 yards farther along the Aberdeen road, is one of the most historic in Banchory for it was most probably in this area or on the river bank below that St Ternan, directed by his old teacher, St Palladius, founded his chapel or college for novices in the 5th century. To this time one can trace the recorded history of the town. Certain it is that near this church was once situated a Dominican or Black-friars church to which, in January, 1363, the king by charter granted an annuity of 100 shillings from the barony of Banchory-Devenick for the endowment of a chaplain to serve in their church *at the altar of the Blessed Virgin or of St Michael*. James III, by charter, dated 30th September, 1477, confirmed this annuity. Opposite the East Church, too, is the old school of St Nicholas which served the parish until the Disruption of 1843. Each pupil was required to bring a peat for the school fire!

Tradition, however, points to the bed of the river opposite the East Church as the site of St Ternan's 5th century academic cloisters! The Dee has always been a picturesque and desirable river and, from a monastic point of view, no part of it, indeed, more desirable than at Banchory. A reasonable deduction seems to be that St Ternan's supervision extended over both northern and southern Picts within easy reach of the river. He had become head of his master's foundation at Whithorn when he died in 440 A.D.

The chapel of St Ternan was a seat of instruction, a Divinity Hall of the infant church, and subsequently a monastery or training-school during Celtic times. It was missionary zeal that directed the training of the Pictish students, and it was from Bangor in Ireland that so many missionaries came to civilise the Picts. The most notable feature of such institutions was their choral service, their *laus perennis* or perpetual praise, an exalted form of service of song of vast influence among the heathen people whose conversion the missionaries sought to accomplish. So it is that some think it likely that the name Banchory is just a modification of the name of the great seat of learning at Bangor, signifying 'High Choir' or 'College'. Certainly it was this 'Bangor' here on the banks of the Dee that was St Ternan's *magnum opus*, the accomplishment which gave him claim to a place in the calendar of saints. Here he found his spiritual home; here he finished his course; here, it is believed, he was buried.

The importance and permanence of the religious colony established by St Ternan is attested by the great variety of saint names such as St Machar (another great worker among the Northern Picts), St Arnaud, St Nicholas and St Duthac which still linger in or near Banchory. The name of St Machar is preserved in a house opposite the East Church, and at Kilduthie, about a mile from the Loch of Leys, was once, it is believed, a chapel or religious house ascribed to St Duthac who had several dedications in Scotland. Furthermore, the site of the colony later became that of the original parish church for Banchory-Ternan.

The Original Kirktown of Banchory-Ternan

It was in the kirk lands below the East Church near the site of Kirkland House on what is now the Garden of Rest, and near the area some 230 yards to the west where the railway station used to be, that the original hamlet of Kirkton of Banchory-Ternan (known as the Kirkton and subsequently Townhead) sprang up. Through it the North Deeside Road formerly passed. It was not until 1324, however, in an old charter, that Banchory was first mentioned as a village, and a considerable one it must have been for the time with its schools, its church and manse, its hospital, its inn for travellers, and several labourers' cottages. A fragment of its historic old Market Cross, where weekly and annual markets were held, was discovered centuries later when the main road was being made and is preserved in front of the East Church already mentioned.

The village was given to the Burnett family in 1638, and here in old times the Barony Court was frequently held under the overlordship of the Lord of Leys. It was Sir Thomas Burnett, the laird, who erected in or near the present churchyard a new and spacious grammar school in Townhead, with its accompanying school-house, endowing it with 5,000 merks on October 29th, 1651. It was later endowed by the Reids, the first ministers of Banchory after the Reformation. The sons of James Reid, Thomas and Alexander, became, the one Greek and Latin Secretary to James VI and the other physician to Charles I. They left funds for the Aberdeen colleges and for the poor and the schools of the parish.

A similar *woman's school*, the Lady Burnett School or, latterly, the Reid and Burnett School, was opened about the same time. Sir Thomas Burnett had on January 15th, 1614, been with his father a party to a grant of annual rent of 200 merks to six poor men of the parish. In the *Family of Burnett of Leys* (Spalding Club) we find in the *Private Register of Sir Thomas Burnett*, 1651-2, the following interesting details of accommodation for the poor and aged of Banchory in those olden days,

> *the four waults under the school of Banchorie built be me ... for the sustentation of ane old persone and a young body to attend them in every one of the four waults, hous or chamber under the said school; and it is expresslie provydit be thir presents that the young persones attending the old as said is goe a part of the day, for sex houres at least, either to the man's school, if males or boyes, or to the woman's school, being females and maids, to be instructed and educat, and the rest of the day all the night tyme to waite upon the old persones.*

No forty-hour week for these *young persones*! One wonders when, with a twenty-four hour day, they were supposed to sleep?

A Safeguard Against Body-snatching

Before we depart, you may be interested in the quaint little watch-tower (or mort-house) which you can see in the cemetery below: it was built as a safeguard against the notorious custom of body-snatching which flourished from 1711 onwards and is a good example of this type of building. Circular in plan, it is furnished with a fireplace and a belfry. The local watch would fire with blunderbusses from towers such as this upon the 'Resurrectionists' who used to perform their gruesome and profane work of robbing graves, selling bodies to anatomy demonstrators who, not too particular about where they had been found, would use them for dissection. As Aberdeen was the centre for the study of anatomy, burial-grounds located near the town were considered more suitable for this activity.

The venerable bell on the watch-tower once hung on the old church preceding the present parish church which dates only from 1824. On it is an ornament of a small rose and leaves, a figure of a recumbent ox and the inscription,

> *Petrus Ostens, Rotterdami me fecit Ao 1664. Soli deo gloria.* (Peter Ostens *or* Peter of Ostend made me at Rotterdam in 1664. To God alone be the glory.)

In the churchyard, too, is the Douglas aisle which was built by John Douglas in 1775.

The Ancient Castle of Leys in the Loch

Let us now continue our journey. We proceed along the A980 (Raemoir) road for just over a mile and take the first side road to the right at the house named Woodfield. Soon this side road swings to the left and, three-tenths of a mile after leaving the highway, as the road swings right again, you should park your car where a path leads off to the left along the side of a dyke. Follow this track for some 260 yards. You have now reached the well-defined basin of the drained Loch of Leys which covers about 140 acres but at an earlier date was four or five times as large and had a circumference of between two and three miles. You will recognise the area in question by the profusion of common sallow (*salix oleifolia*).

If you proceed through the gate on your right and walk eastwards about 400 yards, you will see on your left, immediately opposite the second derelict rifle-range platform and about 100 yards from where you are, a small knoll surrounded by sallow and high reeds, once an oval-shaped islet which still stands out in the middle of the now drained lake. It measures nearly 200 ft. in length by about 100 ft. in breadth and is elevated about 10 ft. above the bottom of the loch. You can easily reach it, but wellingtons are essential because of the boggy ground.

Here is traditionally said to have been a 14th century fortalice of the Wauchopes and, latterly, the ancient Castle of Leys (or the 'Gow' or 'Goo' house), the first Crathes Castle as it were, and the first stronghold of the famous family of Burnett of Leys which, according to a plaque in Crathes Castle, they occupied from 1323 until 1550. It was a substantial building, some 30½ yards by 16¾ yards according to a plan drawn before it was removed in 1850, but originally, no doubt, primitively constructed of wood, earth and stone. Regrettably, the timber substructure of the building was destroyed by excavation. It is interesting that in a charter of 1324 the grant of King Robert I to Alexander de Burnard, the ancestor of the Burnetts, includes *lacum de Banchory cum insula* (the lake of Banchory with the island).

The oval knoll, surrounded by sallow and reeds, which was originally a mediaeval crannog or lake dwelling, the idea for the first of which was brought to Britain probably some time after 200 B.C. Surrounding it was at one time the Loch of Leys, drained in 1850, although to reach it one must still cross very boggy ground. On the crannog is traditionally said to have been the first stronghold of the Burnetts of Leys which they occupied from 1323 until 1550.

A Mediaeval Crannog or Lake Dwelling

When the lake was drained in 1850 and digging operations became possible, it was found that the island which had been the site of a mediaeval castle was artificial, a specimen of a mediaevel crannog or pile dwelling originally used for lakeside houses in Central Europe. The idea was brought to Britain by settlers from the Continent in Iron Age B, as it is called, probably sometime after 200 B.C. when, according to the latest view, the use of iron became general in Scotland.

All through the later Bronze Age and the earlier part of the Age of Iron, indeed, Scotland had been receiving constant fresh streams of racial immigrants, and in the 60's and 50's of the 1st century B.C. there was a flow of small groups of refugees from Caesar's conquest of Gaul with as many of their possessions as they could save. Quite possibly it was these settlers who brought with them the idea of the crannog or lake dwelling, a type of habitation certainly very characteristic of the Scottish Iron Age when for the first time we are confronted with such a formidable work of defence, the lake constituting a natural barrier.

And yet the crannog must not be construed too narrowly in terms of defence although doubtless in most cases the defensive advantages of lake dwellings would not be wholly absent from the minds of their founders. In those early days the mountain slopes were densely clothed with forest, and along the lake margins the narrow strips of land were liable to flood. The inhabitants, therefore, erected their settlements on piles, by which ingenious device they were enabled to use the whole available area of flat land for stock-breeding and corn raising as well as to engage in fishing in the lake and hunting in the woods.

The crannog was composed of succeeding layers of clay, brushwood, sand and stone. Eventually the whole structure sank of its own weight and formed the foundation of the island which was then surrounded by oak piles projecting some two or three feet above the ground to prevent its being washed away. Within a palisaded enclosure on the surface of the crannog the lake dwellers built their huts of wattle and daub. Of these lake dwellers Dr Simpson tells us in *The Province of Mar,*

> *They were an agricultural population, tilling the soil and tending herds of oxen and swine and flocks of sheep and were possessed of a high standard of practical and artistic skill. Iron was used for many of their weapons.*

The lake dwellers were in no sense an uncivilised folk, and in the construction of their abodes they developed a high degree of engineering skill too; yet the reasons which impelled the inhabitants of Scotland to erect such amazing structures provide us with some of the most difficult and fascinating problems of prehistory. Scottish crannogs had a long life from Iron Age times onwards, and some were still in use in the 16th and 17th centuries.

When the lake was drained, the bones and antlers of a huge deer were found, as also were a millstone, two small canoes which the crannog dwellers must have used and a rough flat-bottomed boat about 9 ft. long which had been hewn from one piece of oak. Mediaeval cooking utensils were also found: a brass pot (11 ins. by 9½ ins.) and a flagon (9 ins.) with handle and spout are in the National Museum of Antiquities, and four bronze cooking pots, reputedly from the Loch of Leys, are at Crathes Castle below the plaque mentioned above.

Cluny-Crighton Castle, a Striking 'House-of-fence'

Returning to the main Raemoir road (A980), we continue our journey to the north and in a little under a mile and a quarter find ourselves at a T-junction, facing the drive to the Raemoir Hotel. Here we turn left along the road to Torphins, in two-thirds of a mile following the first road on the right to Cluny Farm on the lower slopes of the Hill of Fare and on the estate of Raemoir. Just in front, close by the crest of the field, is romantic Cluny-Crighton Castle which for some reason, among the numerous ancient castles and mansions of Deeside, seems to have been curiously disregarded to a certain extent. It has been uninhabited for a very long time. Despite the fact, however, that it is rapidly falling into complete dilapidation, it retains something of its former dignity and is deserving of something more than the fate that is fast overtaking it.

This small castle was built in 1666 by George Crighton of Cluny who in the previous year had married the only daughter of Sir Robert Douglas of Tilquhillie (see page 201) who was obliged to retire to the Continent in Jacobite times. Between two recesses above the entrance door is a third one for the family coat of arms and a finely carved panel which reads

$$16 \quad \begin{array}{c} CLU(NIE) \\ CRICHTO(UN)E \end{array} \quad 66$$

The castle was never in fact completed, probably owing to lack of funds, but its ruined and shattered towers still stand out boldly from the surrounding agricultural land, a striking landmark on the hill, commanding an extensive view of the surrounding country.

The tower house is an interesting example of a Scottish laird's 'house of fence' of the 17th century. It stands to a height of three storeys, and there was probably a garret. The material used in building had been rough granite stones gathered from the hill-side on which it is situated, and these have weathered to a fine warm pink. Originally the castle would have been surrounded by a wall enclosing a courtyard and necessary subsidiary buildings. They have long since disappeared.

The small castle of Cluny-Crighton, an interesting example of a Scottish Laird's 'house of fence' of the 17th century. The castle, built in 1666 by George Crighton of Cluny, still retains something of its former dignity, and its shattered towers still stand out boldly some 2½ miles from Banchory.

An L-plan Building of Fine Workmanship

Cluny-Crighton Castle is an L-plan type of building but with the addition in the re-entrant angle of a rectangular staircase-tower in the west side of which is the entrance doorway cunningly defended by three shot-holes. Inside the badly damaged door, bar-holes, seven inches square, are situated, while the bar-hole proper penetrates five feet into the wall. All dressed stone-work, quoins or corner-stones, lintels and jambs of doors, windows and fireplaces have been removed in course of time to repair farm buildings. Any dressed stones left are of fine workmanship. The entrance door gives access to a small barrel-vaulted passage off which are three rooms, while at its extremity was situated a circular newel staircase, no longer in existence, although traces of stone steps can be seen.

To the north-east and south-west of the passage are two store-rooms, both about 17 ft. by 15 ft., and to the south-east is the kitchen, 17 ft. by 17 ft. Between it and the south-west wall is an ambry 18 ins. by 18 ins. by 11 ins.

An unusual feature is that, with the exception of the entrance passage, the basement was not vaulted. Joist holes remain to indicate the various floors, and none of the upper floors are accessible except with the aid of a ladder. On the first floor a well-lit hall, measuring about 17 ft. by 15 ft. and housing the remains of a stone fireplace, leads through to a 17 ft. square withdrawing-room. In the north-west angle of this room was the strong-room measuring about 4 ft. by 5 ft., a feature of castles of the period: being above the vaulted passage, it would be practically fireproof. In the north-east wall of the withdrawing-room is a doorway into a private room, 17 ft. by 16 ft., and there is a window and ambry.

The second storey is in rather a dilapidated condition, but would appear to have consisted of three bedrooms, each of which has open fireplace and garde-robe, and the north-west one a mural cupboard. There is no trace of any doorway to the newel staircase, and the manner of access to the second floor is a matter of speculation – probably a wooden staircase.

The Magnificent Little Ha' Hoose of Raemoir

We must now retrace our steps to the impressive mansion-house of Raemoir, now a hotel, the drive to which, two-thirds of a mile away, we passed earlier. The hotel, built in 1817 and added to in 1844, is finely situated in spacious grounds, well wooded and sheltered from the north wind by the wide-based Hill of Fare. Tucked away behind the hotel as a detached annex is the picturesque Ha' Hoose of Raemoir, one of the most charming and interesting old houses on Royal Deeside to students of Scottish architecture and probably the least known.

The Ha' Hoose (Hall-like-house) is one of a unique group of buildings erected during the 17th century on what was known as the 'hall plan' – the simple, rectangular, hall-like plan which succeeded the castellated, Z-planned tower-house and which caused a house so designed to be called a Ha' Hoose. Of this distinctively North-east form of mansion it is a magnificent and splendidly preserved example.

The picturesque 17th century Ha' Hoose of Raemoir, one of the most charming and delightfully attractive dwelling-houses on Deeside. It is a magnificent example of a distinctively North-east form of mansion which succeeded the castellated Z-planned tower-house.

This delightfully attractive little dwelling-house was built by James Skene, 4th laird of Raemoir, and about 1680 became the property of James Hog of Blairydryne who married James Skene's heiress grand-daughter, Margaret. High above the entrance doorway can be seen a time-worn panel bearing the old coat of arms of Margaret Skene impaled with those of her husband – for the Hogs, as landed proprietors, had recorded arms when Blairydryne became their property. These armorial bearings naturally commemorated the romantic meeting with King James described elsewhere – three hogs' heads distilling blood as a reminder of the animals slaughtered for the royal repast (and a pun on the family name), the crest, a right hand (King James'?) and the motto, *Dant vires gloriam* (a good name gives strength). The Ha' Hoose was restored in 1923.

The Site of the Battle of Corrichie

When we leave Raemoir Hotel, we turn left along the B977 on which we remain for only four-fifths of a mile before following the road to the left to the farm called The Green. Just under half a mile along this road (which latterly is not in too good condition) we reach a gate by a 'No Tipping' notice. Here we leave our car. If we pass through the gate and follow the Forestry Commission road for just under 2^1/$_5$ miles, we reach a hollow on the south-eastern slopes of the great flat-topped granite tableland called the Hill of Fare (1502 ft.), the most outstanding mountain mass in the landscape, where took place the saddest and most momentous event in the history of the parish – the Battle of Corrichie. The path is an easy one, and the reader who is prepared for a total return walk of 4^1/$_3$ miles in the hills will find the site of the battle easily enough. It was fought in the hollow on the left just 300 yards after crossing the Burn of Corrichie and only some 70 yards below the crossroads which one sees in front where the road begins to climb towards a ruined cottage on Greymore Hill. One might add that this is true at the time of writing in 1980; when the trees reach maturity, nothing of the battlefield will be seen.

'The Bluidy Fecht' between Mary and Earl Huntly

The Battle of Corrichie took place on October 28th, 1562. Because religious fanaticism was combined with feudal or clan rivalry, the civil war between the factions assumed an aspect of peculiar savagery: the battle was a contest between the forces of Mary under the powerful Lord James Stewart (half-brother of the Queen, who championed the Reformed Church) and George, the proud 4th Earl of Huntly and a loyal supporter of Catholicism, who was to lose his earldom to Stewart at a time when the great nobles were contending for power.

The Queen had offended Huntly by creating her brother Earl of Moray and by declining to visit him at Strathbogie Castle during her tour to Inverness when she was making a progress through the northern shires. On her return Huntly marched south with a considerable army and met her at the Howe of Corrichie, a fact which was represented by Lord James Stewart as an act of rebellion although Huntly vigorously protested that he had no such intention, having gathered together his followers only for his own protection. He had, however, largely through Moray's intrigues, been declared an outlaw and rebel, along with his sons, at a meeting of the Privy Council in Aberdeen only a few days previously.

Atholl and Moray were ordered to intercept him at all costs before he reached Aberdeen. At Corrichie, where Huntly encamped, he took the offensive and drove back the vanguard of the royal forces. The Gordons, however, hopelessly outnumbered, were totally defeated by the Queen's army and at last compelled to surrender. Huntly died of apoplexy, it is said. Another report states that he fell from his horse and died immediately, while *The Ballad of the Battle of Corrichie* (written considerably after the event by Forbes, the schoolmaster at Maryculter) speaks of a fatal sword wound at the height of the struggle on the hill-side. Huntly's sons, the intransigent Sir John Gordon and Adam (the former an aspirant for Mary's hand and a rival of Lord James Stewart), were taken prisoner and executed three days later at the Castlegate in Aberdeen. We read, too, in the ballad of the sons of Sir John Wishart of Pitarrow, the Queen's Comptroller, although it distinctly stated elsewhere that Huntly had only twenty-six men slain and mentions no persons of rank:

> *Erle Murray lost mony a gallant stout man,*
> *Th' hopefu' laird of Thorniture,*
> *Pitterra's sons, an' Eglis' far fearit laird,*
> *An' mair to mi unkend, fell doune.*

It was a great tragedy that the Earl of Huntly, a man of culture and a great pillar of the Royalist cause in the north, was forced into a rising which ended in the ruin of his power and the wreck of the ancient faith for which he fought. There is no doubt that the balladist's sympathies were with him:

> *I wis our quine had better friends,*
> *I wis our countrie better peice;*
> *I wis our lords wid na' discord,*
> *I wis our weirs at hame may ceise!*
> *Murn ye highlands, and murn ye leighlands*
> *I trow ye hae meikle need;*
> *For thi bonny burn o' Corichie*
> *His run this day wi' bleid.*

Tradition states that Queen Mary viewed the progress of the *bluidy fecht* from a hollow in the rock just under 1½ miles away on the lower slopes of the hill called Meikle Tap (the one with the mast), a spot still known as the Queen's Chair. She is also said to have been a spectator of Gordon's execution. A spring between the stone and the site of the battle is known as the Queen's Well.

Cuimhnichibh La Coire-Fhroichidh

Back on the main B977 road, we continue to our left for a further 1⁴/₅ miles until a fork to the right indicates the road to Hirn. This is our road. But before we take it, would you care to see a monument commemorating the Battle of Corrichie about which we have been talking? The return journey will take you only half a mile out of your way for a quarter of a mile farther along the B977, and just off the road, is a huge granite block erected by the Deeside Field Club in 1951 and thus inscribed:

> *Cuimhnichibh la Coire-Fhroichidh*
> (Remember the day of Corrichie)

The Picturesque Mill of Hirn

Back to the Hirn road. At the T-junction in just under a mile farther on we turn right again, in some 530 yards reaching the picturesque crow-stepped, gabled Mill of Hirn which still stands in all its glory, much photographed and well cared for. Although meal milling has not been carried on at the Mill of Hirn for some time, Mr Norman Duncan, the farmer at the mill for the last 47 years, still used it until 1977 for corn-dressing and hashing and bruising.

Renown came to this parish landmark when Scott Skinner named one of his most famous compositions *The Miller of Hirn*, a schottische or strathspey.

Crathes Castle Transferred by Parliament to Kincardine

We take the right-hand fork towards Banchory and in 2¼ miles arrive at the North Deeside Road (A93) where we turn left towards

The huge granite monument which commemorates the Battle of Corrichie (1562) and which was erected by Deeside Field Club in 1951.

Aberdeen and one of the best loved and most interesting attractions of Deeside. For in another mile and a half we reach the entrance to Crathes Castle, one of the most famous of the stately homes of Scotland and, next to Balmoral Castle, the most visited of all the estates in the North-east of Scotland. Let us drive up to the castle in its excellent position among fine trees overlooking the River Dee.

Interesting is the fact that Crathes is included in Kincardineshire: an odd little kink on the northern boundary of the county crosses the Dee to bite defiantly into Aberdeenshire, folding round the large Crathes estate to the Hill of Fare and Banchory, and then crosses back again to the south. The cause for the enclave of twenty-six square miles is an old one, resulting from the fact that the very old Aberdeenshire family, the Burnetts of Leys, had one of the longest continuous tenures of occupation in the land and took a prominent part in much of Scottish history. As far back as March 28th, 1324, Alexander de Burnard or Burnett received a charter from King Robert the Bruce, granting him certain lands in Drumoak together with the lands of Leys in Banchory *with his forest of 'Drom' and within the park of the said forest.* So it was that, as Crathes Castle had been continuously the seat of the Burnetts of Leys since 1553 and as Sir Thomas Burnett, 1st baronet and 13th laird of Leys, inherited the extensive barony of Muchalls south of the Dee in the Mearns, it was solemnly decided by Act of Parliament in 1646 that the lands of Crathes should be transferred from Aberdeenshire to Kincardineshire.

In the royal forest the castle was a place of importance. It is said to have been built on the site of a Pict's house, and a daughter of the castle was the heroine of an ancient 15th century ballad:

> *And many a flower by the silvery tide*
> *Springs up by the silvery water,*
> *But the fairest flower on all Deeside*
> *Was the baron's youngest daughter.*

The baron was Robert Burnett of Leys.

The Charm and Glory of Castellated Architecture

Crathes Castle, built of granite and rising to four storeys and an attic, is one of the finest and most beautiful examples of ancient *third period Scottish castellated architecture* (to quote Messrs McGibbon and Ross). It is a superb example of the 16th century Scots baronial style, similar to the Castle of Muchalls, what Dr Simpson calls *one of the most spectacular architectural conceptions in Scotland.* During what was perhaps the most troublous yet romantic and colourful period in Scottish history the structure was begun in 1553 by Alexander Burnett, the 9th laird, and completed in 1596 by his great-grandson, another Alexander. The original portion of the castle is the tremendous double square tower in the traditional form of a keep, enhanced by a small but dignified projecting east wing of three storeys, added in Queen Anne's reign in an unpretentious Georgian manner by another Alexander, the 4th Baronet, and giving a re-entrant angle to the south-east. This wing was burnt down in 1965 but later rebuilt.

Crathes Castle, built between 1553 and 1596 is one of the finest and most spectacular examples of Scottish castellated architecture. The original portion of the castle, seen here, is a tremendous double square tower in the form of a keep. Crowning the high walls is the usual flourish of Flemish characteristics – dormer windows, sky-pointing pinnacles and multifarious parapets. There is, too, a rich profusion of picturesque turrets with quaint finials and other decorations.

The ground-plan is on the traditional L-shaped keep form, and the lower storeys for the sake of safety exhibit the old precautionary style of building, conspicuously plain and dark. The solid appearance of the exterior and the noticeable lack of windows near ground level, except for more modern alterations, are a reminder of the days when self-defence was the prime consideration in building a house.

Crowning the very high walls with their rounded corners below, on the other hand, the upper part of the castle shows the usual flourish of Flemish characteristics – a number of dormer windows, a wonderful cluster of sky-pointing pinnacles and multifarious parapets. Of particular interest, the castle is one of the few Scottish houses to alternate a rich profusion of picturesque and spectacular square and gabled turrets, almost watch-chambers, with slated roofs, quaint finials and other decorations, with the normal circular angle turrets at eaves level. Notice the fashion of squaring off a stair turret to form a clock tower and crenellated look-out platform. Notice, too, directly above the main door of the keep, guarded by its original 'yett' of interlaced iron bars, and three storeys high, the machicolated dormer window for the casting down of missiles, boiling oil and pitch to discourage uninvited guests. The castle carries the typical northern extravagance of corbelling and turreting to a marked degree, the crow-stepped gables with their beautiful carving and ornamental mouldings being of a very elaborate character.

Fantastic gargoyles at impossible places, applied as mere ornaments, also occur in profusion. Carved at the top of the castle is a curious effigy of an early Scot with a gold-laced coat and three-cornered hat, and immediately above the large window inserted in the south wall of the castle about 1830 are three coats of arms – in the centre the Royal Arms of Scotland, denoting that the lands of Leys were a gift from the Crown, flanked on either side by two shields with the arms of the Burnett lairds who began and finished the house, with appropriate dates.

All these features add to the charm of the castle and show the unique glory of Scottish castellated architecture which here reaches its fullest flowering, marking a period when wars had ceased and Scotland had entered its second Golden Age under James VI. The period shows magnificent taste in design and a higher standard of domestic comfort and accommodation in imitation of that south of the Border as a result of the Union of 1603 after which many of the nobility followed the Court to London. It is indeed a house that inspires the love of long-descended things, continuously inhabited down to the present day by the descendants of those who built it and

retaining the very furniture with which they surrounded themselves when the harl was still damp upon its walls.

This furniture forms an outstanding collection, mostly from the reign of James VI: thus is preserved intact, with family relics and portraits and contemporary decoration, the home of a 16th century Scottish laird.

The Ancient Magnificence of the Great Hall

On the first floor is the barrel-vaulted Great Hall, its original stone lighted by a high window at the south end. The outlines of three former windows on the west side, filled up years ago, can still be traced on the outer wall, and the original fireplace was at the northern end, not on the west side as now. Above a blocked window over the fireplace and above a window in the south-west corner are painted decorations. These are but fragments of the original decoration of the ceiling and all that the restorer's art could retrace, but they give a glimpse of ancient magnificence. Fine examples of armorial carvings are seen in the old stone pendants hanging from the lofty stone ceiling. The Great Hall, too, contains some good oak carving, for which the castle is famous, part of the original plaster and some of the magnificent family portraits including that of Sir Thomas Burnett, the 1st Baronet, by the eminent Scottish painter, George Jameson (painted about 1632). Another treasure is a portrait of Bishop Burnet which reminds us of the great ecclesiastic's link with the family of Leys. In the corner adjoining the outside staircase is the laird's lug, a primitive form of hidden listening-post used by the laird during his absence from the dinner table to keep in touch with the current trend of loyalty or treachery among his guests.

The Precious Horn of Leys

Among the antiquities preserved is the most precious of all the family treasures, the wonderful ivory and jewelled Horn of Leys, said to have been presented in 1323 with the original grant of lands by King Robert the Bruce, fluted, with four silver gilt rings (the two centre ones containing a carbuncle) and three pieces of transparent crystal. Attached to it is a tasselled scarf or baldric of green silk of the time of Charles II which is now so frail that it would crumble to dust if touched. The horn is believed to have been the badge of office of Alexander Burnard, the first laird of Crathes, who in return for the gift of land was required to serve as Royal Forester or custodian of the Forest of Drum. The 'service of the horn' was employed in early days to mark the handing over of lands, the possession of such a 'horn of tenure' quite often requiring no additional charter. The Horn is the only one of its kind owned by a Scottish family and remains to this day an inalienable heirloom of the Burnetts. It was not included with the castle and gardens when they were handed over to the care of the National Trust for Scotland.

Adjacent to the Great Hall is the ancient withdrawing-room or Stone Hall, simply and beautifully furnished. A single lamp hangs from its great vaulted stone ceiling, and a narrow-backed armchair, a Scottish version of a French design, bears the date 1597 and the initials K.G. for Katherine Gordon, wife of Alexander Burnett.

The Finest Painted Ceilings in Scotland

There are other features of Crathes that you simply must see. If you ascend the circular stone staircase that runs inside a turret right to the top of the tower, you will find – on the second and third floors – noteworthy bedrooms with remarkable ceilings with the best of the castle's decorative painting (for, when the castle was built, painted tempora walls and ceilings were fashionable). All were decorated from 1599 to 1602 by Jacobean artists on the same principle – no doubt to the order of Alexander Burnett – and all are considered to be the finest in Scotland. On the boards between the joists are gaily painted symbolic figures, while on the sides of the joists themselves there are inscribed wise saws and descriptive jingles explaining the pictures and delivering little homilies in the way beloved of mediaeval rhymsters.

The Chamber of the Muses on the second floor gets its name, of course, from the nine classical goddesses who inspired the arts, but the Five Christian Virtues are there too as large as life in pictorial allegory. Here are famous, glowing ceiling paintings with a real Scots renaissance flavour in their rhymes. The Chamber of the Nine Worthies (or Nobles), also on the second floor, shows representations of nine heroes such as Hector of Troy, King David, King Arthur, Charlemagne and other *worthy men* from Biblical, national and international history (each with a traditional coat of arms assigned him). The quaint, almost mediaeval whimsy in the figures provides an absolute feast of colour and deeply touching charm. Who was the pietistic poet who wrote the running commentary, one wonders?

244

These wonderful ceilings were discovered in 1877 when layers of lath and plaster were removed, and the lustre of the colours and the printed captions have retained all their original clarity without retouching. Almost certainly there are more paintings of this kind hidden in other rooms which have not yet been investigated.

The Mysterious Green Lady, the Family Ghost

On the panels of the third bedroom, the mysterious Green Lady's room on the third floor, are painted eleven figures, and on the joists various proverbial inscriptions such as the following gems of wisdom:

The slothful hands maketh poore but the hand of the diligent maketh riche.

Wine, women taken insatiable
Has brocht gryt kings to miserie.
Therefore my God I pray to this:
Keep me from crymes and harlotrie.

Thryce happy is that man indeed
That weids ane vertuis wif:
She is the blessing of his seid
And comfort of his lyff.

The bedroom takes its name from the family ghost of Crathes: the room is allegedly haunted by a girl in a green dress or shroud with a child in her arms, and it was here that the skeletons of a woman and child were discovered last century when the fireplace was being altered.

The apparition of the Green Lady, it seems, originally haunted the ancient island stronghold on the Loch of Leys but moved to better quarters when the present castle was built! She has apparently not been seen in the room since the far-away days of the fourth baronet. Some sceptics say she was, in fact, never seen at all. One version of the story tells that the Green Lady was the last of the line of the Norman De Bernands from whom the Burnetts of Crathes were derived. During a time of trouble and upheaval in France she was brought to Scotland by a French relative and left in charge of the then Lady of Crathes and her son, the baron. Fearing that the young baron might dismiss a desirable Scottish alliance for love of the Green Lady, his mother sought to remove the 'intruder'. The young baron returned after an absence to find his De Bernand ward at death's door. When she died, this fair lady returned to take her revenge.

The Long Gallery with its Unique Roof

Another feature leaving an indelible impression is the stately Long Gallery at the top of the castle, extending the whole length of the tower from east to west and popularly known as The Chapel. There is a characteristically Scottish open fireplace, and the walls and ceiling which extends into the roof (the shape of which is seen on either side) are finely oak-panelled. The room houses a great display of splendidly carved heraldic shields and ornate coats of arms in the bosses, including the Royal Arms of Scotland, and charters such as the original one from David II to Alexander Burnard, dated 17th November, 1358, and confirming that granted by Robert I thirty-five years earlier. In this famous gallery the barony court was frequently held, and this beautiful room was also used for occasions of state. Such long galleries are not uncommon in the castles of the period, frequently on the top storey like this one, but a roof panelled in oak in Scotland is unique. And yet, in an *Inventory and Apretiation* of the household furniture, dated 1760, the contents of 'The Gallery' are valued at three shillings and sixpence!

Magnificent Walled Gardens

Sir Thomas Burnett did much to improve the surroundings of Crathes, and there are beautiful grounds and magnificent and picturesque walled gardens close to the castle itself. Originally planned and laid out in the early 18th century, these are known to botanists everywhere. The massive and unique yew hedges, more than 12 ft. high to their ridged tops, date from 1702 and partition the grounds to the south of the castle into a number of individual gardens, all attractively named after their central feature. There is a Camel Garden with its small hump in the middle, a Pool Garden with a colour scheme of yellow, purple and red, a Trough Garden laid out round an old farm trough, and an exquisite Rose Garden. There is an unusual Golden Garden and a fairly new Red Garden, and in the Fountain Garden planting has been confined to blue flowers laid out in geometrically cut beds with box hedge borders. To the west of the noted mighty Lime Avenue, which now stands over 100 ft. high, lies the Crathes Wild Garden. Tucked away on the left of the main drive, it can be seen when one approaches the castle. This little bay-shaped garden is backed by a 50 ft. cliff of bare rock, and its rhododendrons, azaleas and other plants have a look of indiscriminate nonchalence which only an expert gardener could visualise and produce.

The Kew Gardens of Kincardineshire

Travelling round the world as a soldier, Sir James Burnett made the study of nature in the garden and forest one of his hobbies. Rare ornamental wintering shrubs and trees were a particular interest, and the herbaceous borders are widely renowned, giving carefully planned displays of colour throughout the summer. A White Border runs from the distinctively clipped Portuguese laurel to the west boundary wall, and from the Portuguese laurel to the dovecot at the southernmost tip of the formal garden stretches diagonally a June Border, consisting entirely of June-flowering plants and flowers. This dovecot was formerly hidden in the trees near the stables and was re-erected stone by stone in its present position in 1938. It is surrounded by a small Spring Garden. Sir James collected from all parts of the globe rare plants, attractive to enthusiast and layman alike, from New Zealand, Chile, California, Tasmania, India, South Africa, China, Australia and the Himalayas, and the result is that today the grounds of Crathes Castle are the Kew Gardens of Kincardineshire. Here is to be found as cosmopolitan an assembly of plant life as would be found anywhere in a private botanical garden.

Sir James had been assured by expert botanists that the rigorous Scottish climate would be too severe for many of these delicate foreigners, but he was confident that with special care they could be made to survive and to flourish so far north near the east coast of Scotland. He has proved that the experts were wrong. Practically every square inch along the boundary walls is occupied by uncommon shrubs many of which it is surprising to see thriving in such a hard climate, even with the protection of a wall. Alas, the woodlands were devastated by the storm of January, 1953.

Link with a Gracious, Historic Past

The visitor to Deeside finds it a richly rewarding experience to visit this lovely place. All the paintings, weapons, silver and original decorations and furnishings are a sheer delight, a direct link with a gracious and historic past, telling the story of 400 years of unbroken family occupation for, since 1951 when Crathes Castle was gifted to the nation by the late Major-general Sir James Burnett, Bart., and Lady Burnett of Leys with an upkeep endowment, the Burnett family still retain a connection. With its harling glinting in the sun, the castle is a living symbol of the best in Scotland's heritage, one of Scotland's special treasures.

The castle is open to the public from May to September at a moderate charge, its fine grounds and gardens all year. The entrances are well signposted on the main Deeside road. Knowledgeable guides await the visitor, and the round horse-mill on the rising ground behind is now a delightful tea-room.

The De'il at Baldarroch

And now we are on our way home. In just under half a mile along the A93 we reach a crossroads with the turning south to Stonehaven across Durris Bridge. Before we take this road, however, let us deviate along the opposite road to the left for only 300 yards to have a look at the farm of Baldarroch which created a panic throughout the parish in 1838 when strange poltergeist outbreaks appeared there. William Walker described these poltergeist pranks in his poem, *The De'il at Baldarroch,*

> *Afore the fire folk couldna sit for fear*
> *For peats and clods cam' bunging ben the fleer;*
> *The parson cam' and gained the house wi' prayer,*
> *But still the clods were thuddin' here and there.*
> *The spoons an' dishes, knives an' forks,*
> *They frisked aboot as light as corks,*
> *And cups and ladles joined the dancing,*
> *An' thro' the house they a' gaed prancing.*

As so often happens in such cases of poltergeist activity, the immediate cause turned out to be an adolescent girl. The parish minister and the brother of the laird of Crathes, on visiting Baldarroch, found the 'kitchie deem' washing potatoes in a tub on the kitchen floor. As they watched, they saw that by a quick movement she made the potatoes squirt through the fingers and scatter over the floor. The minister ordered the girl to take her fingers from the tub, and instantly the commotion ceased. The girl and an accomplice in raising alarm and despondency were summoned to Stonehaven to answer for their tricks, and the whole incident was allowed to fall into the limbo of forgotten things. The circumstances were, however, referred to in a pamphlet, *The Dance of Baldarroch*, the concluding words of which are,

> *This is placed here to point out Baldarroch as the spot where superstition and witchcraft were last believed in Scotland, anno 1838.*

Further Evidence of Mesolithic Man

On now across the Dee to the South Deeside road. We should, however, note when we are about 200 yards away from Durris Bridge that we are in the midst of another area in the County which was inhabited by Man in the earlier part of the 4th millenium B.C. Between 1972 and 1974 820 flints were discovered 230 yards to our right and 580 yards away on the bank of the Dee. These are preserved in Aberdeen Art Gallery and Museum. Two fields away to our left, at a distance of 600 yards and at the edge of the river, excavation in an area of flint scatter south-east of Nether Mills of Crathes farmhouse (which we can see) has revealed pits and post- and stake-holes of another Mesolithic settlement, exhibiting several phases of use, possibly for winter occupation. Flint scatters have been noted, too, farther north in the same field and in the field immediately east of the road.

When we reach the A943, we turn left. In exactly a mile we pass a pylon in a field on our left: a little to the west of it and in the middle of a field a stone cist was found in 1829. The minister of Durris was removing some stones from a large round cairn which stood on the rise before the field falls away towards the Dee, assisting in preventing future encroachments of the Dee after a flood which had occurred in that year. The hillock which the stones covered, upon being broken up, yielded sharp flint flakes and, at a depth of 3 ft., a grave, 7 ft. long, built of slabs which contained calcined remains and, at one end, a skull.

The Wooded Lands of Durris

From now on and, indeed, until we rejoin the Slug Road in 11½ miles, we are in the lands of Durris, once a chapelry of the Knights Templars and spelt Duires in old MSS, said to signify 'a rising ground near a water' or, more probably, 'a mouth or entrance'. The scenery in the neighbourhood is finely wooded, and numerous little dells and streams give added beauty to the windings of the Dee.

Kirkton of Durris

In a third of a mile we arrive in the village of Kirkton of Durris with its picturesque (but now disused) mill just south of the main road on the Burn of Sleoch, the largest tributary of the Dee in the parish. One of its most famous natives was Cosmo Innes (1798-1874) who was trained as a lawyer. In 1846 he was appointed Professor of Constitutional Law and History in Edinburgh University. He is best known for his two historical works, *Scotland in the Middle Ages* and *Sketches of Early Scottish History*.

At the crossroads let us follow the road to the left from the village shop towards the Dee for it takes us in only 370 yards to the church, a plain structure erected in 1822 by the 5th Duke of Gordon. Dedicated to St Congol, it was originally in the diocese of St Andrews before the Reformation. Before 1717 it was in the presbytery of Fordoun, but in that year was attached to Aberdeen. A part which remains of the old parish church (which was *under great decay* by the late 17th century) bears the date 1537. The bell is inscribed,

> *Iohn Mowat, Old Abd. Fe. 1765*
> *In Usum Ecclesiae De Durris*
> *Sabata Pango, Funera Plango.*

(I record the Sabbath for the Church of Durris and I lament funerals.)

At the east end of the church is the burial-aisle of the original Frasers of Durris, the oldest inscribed date, beside the family crest, being 1594. In the aisle may be seen a massive iron mortsafe, about a ton in weight, which was used in the 'Resurrectionist' days to prevent the recently buried corpses of the parishioners being lifted: the coffin was buried inside the coffin-shaped chest which was removed after a few weeks by means of sheers.

A short distance below the church of Durris in 1829 the Rev. Robert Copland, when removing a large round cairn of stones, discovered underneath an artificial stone-capped mound of earth in which some *bones, partly burnt*, and a *number of sharp flint stones* of different sizes were found. Afterwards, 3 ft. under the surface of an adjoining field, a stone cist over 7 ft. in length was discovered, containing human bones mixed with charcoal.

Edward I's 'Manour Among the Mountains'

Continuing our journey eastwards along the South Deeside Road, we reach in three-fifths of a mile a farm track leading off to a small, tree-covered hillock occupying a commanding site 120 yards away on the north side of the road. It is 23 ft. high on the south with a level summit 45 yards by 33. On the west is a length of ditch, and on the north a steep slope to the Dee. This interesting spot is now known as Castle Hill: it is a motte on which, when the lands were mostly forest, stood in early Scottish history the ancient stronghold of Dores (Durris), a hunting-seat of the kings of Scotland which exercised authority over the surrounding district. It was, it seems, a place of some strength as formerly evidence was not altogether wanting that it had been protected by artillery.

The earliest mention of the building is contained in the Chamberlain Rolls of King Alexander III who used it as a residence in 1260, 1279 and 1282, and it is recorded that certain sums were paid for repairs to the house of Collyn (Cowie) and the vessels and bridge at the house of Durris. (It is thought that the bridge referred to was a drawbridge to the castle which historians surmise was surrounded by a moat in its heyday; but some would have us believe that in the reign of Alexander III a bridge crossed the Dee here.) The Castle of Durris guarded the north-eastern passes over the Mounth on the Aberdeenshire side just as Cowie and Kincardine did on the southern side. However, it never enjoyed a distinctive military position like Cowie and Kincardine, and comparatively little is known about it. It was later supplanted by the stronghold of the Douglasses of Tilquhillie.

Originally the castle was the residence of the thanes or stewards who collected the rents of the king's lands in the area which, in the time of Robert I, together with the royal forests of Drum and Leys, formed a royal hunting-ground. That it must, however, have been a reasonably prominent castle in the 13th century is proved by the fact that this *manour among the mountains* was visited by Edward I of England on Friday, 13th July, 1296, when he was welcomed by the Cumin family to whom he had previously granted the forest and castle for faithful services in those troublous times and when he received the homage of the neighbouring barons prior to his easy day's march to Aberdeen.

From Glenbervie the royal party had crossed the mountains by the Cryne Corse (see page 148), to this day a dreich and swampy path, and in the pleasant Glen of Mergie first cast their eyes on the Cowie Water. Edward and his army then forded the Cowie near Stonehouse of Mergie. Today there is a bridge built by the Forestry Commission, but the ford still exists, adjacent to the chief source of the water supply of the burgh of Stonehaven. They next struck the line of the modern Slug Road via Red Beard's Well and finally breasted the shoulder of Cairn-mon-earn to the Castle of Dores. The great army accompanying 'the hammer of the Scots' included 30,000 men-at-arms and 5,000 mounted mail-clad knights.

Castle Hill of Durris and the Frasers

Of the history of the castle subsequent to 1296 very little is known, but here and there throughout the remaining years of its existence certain interesting facts emerge which are well worth recording. After the expulsion of the English the castle with the lands of Durris was gifted by the Bruce to Sir Alexander Fraser, his chamberlain and brother-in-law who probably lived in Cowie and who was so instrumental in placing Bruce on the throne. He it was who became the first Baron of Durris. Sir Alexander's son, Sir William Fraser, who fell at the Battle of Durham in 1346, was later granted the lands by King David II.

Castle Hill of Durris, the motte on which once stood a stronghold which was a hunting seat of the kings of Scotland and which Edward I of England called his 'manour among the mountains'. It was visited by 'the hammer of the Scots' in 1296 when, accompanied by a great army of 30,000 men-at-arms and 5,000 mounted knights, he received the homage of neighbouring barons.

In 1373 King Robert II granted to John Fraser, son of the deceased Sir William Fraser, a cadet of the original family and ancestor of the House of Philorth, the land of Wester Essyntoly for the *blench ferme* or rental of a silver penny yearly at the castle hill of Durris – *apud castri montem de Durrys*. The lands of Durris continued in the possession of the Frasers until almost the end of the 15th century although in 1413 the knight of the period, because of extreme financial embarrassment, agreed to sell the property to Hay of Erroll, Constable of Scotland, reserving only the liferent interest of his mother-in-law. The Deed of Disposition, confirmed by the Regent, Robert, Duke of Albany, on May 14th, 1415, quaintly states that he sold

> *all the landis of the baronyis of Cowy and Duryss wid tenand and tenandryis, and service of the tenand for euirmare for a sowme of sylure before hand in my mykyle mistre* (great necessity) *to me payit.*

Despite the apparent conclusiveness of that document, it would appear, as we have said, that the Frasers continued to hold some sort of interest in the lands of Durris for in 1494 the Bishop of Brechin raised an action before the Lords of Council alleging that William Fresale withheld from him and the kirk of Brechin *the secund teynd of his relief of the landis of Durris* which, he claimed, belonged to his bishopric.

The Castle of Durris Burnt by Montrose

In the 16th century yet another monarch visited Durris. His visit, as far as is known, was not directly connected with the castle although, since records are so meagre, it might well have been. Tradition says that King James V, travelling incognito, visited Ashentilly, a place on the route traversed by Edward I and a mile or two east of the castle, and that, in return for kindness shown to the king, the Earl Marischal, who had a proprietory interest in Dores, gifted the farm of Blairydryne to the tenant. But it was not until the wars of Montrose that the castle itself again figures in the pages of history, and then only for a short twilight period prior to total eclipse. At that time it was occupied by Forbes of Leslie who is described by Spalding as *a gryte Convenanter* and who lived in constant fear of an attack by the Royalists. So great was his apprehension that he had the greater part of his effects hidden or carried away to a place of greater safety. As events proved, his presentiments were well founded. In 1639 the Gordons of Lord Aboyne descended like

253

wolves on the fold and, although the treasures of the castle were safely stowed away, they did not find the cupboards bare: history says they regaled themselves upon *beir and aill* and

> *bruk up girnellis* (granaries or meal-chests) *and book* (baked) *bannockis at good fyres, and drank mirrellie upone the lairdis best drink, syne careit away with thame also mekill victuall as they could beir, whilk they culd not get eitin and distroyit.*

Five years later the castle was subjected to a similar raid and garrisoned by *ten soldiouris* under the command of one, Robert Irvine, who *leivit upone nolt and scheip and vther commodeteis.* Meanwhile, however, the Marquis of Montrose had espoused the Royalist cause, in October, 1644, marching through the Mearns with his whole army and crossing the Dee at the Mill of Drum. On Sunday, March 17th, 1645, in pursuance of his vengeance on the Covenanting gentry, he halted on his march southward to Dundee and plundered the lands and burned the Castle of Durris – which we shall be visiting in a short time – in the Royalist cause. In the words of a chronicler he set fire to

> *the place, lauche bigging, and haill cornes, and spolzeet the haill ground of horse, nolt, scheip and other goodis.*

The Lands of Durris for 200 Years .

Although that was the end of the Castle of Durris, the lands around continued to find a place in history. After the War of Independence Durris was granted to the Frasers who remained in possession for over 400 years with the complication in 1669 of a John Burnett, son of Andrew Burnett *of Dooris, merchant burgess of Aberdeen*, being declared heir to the estate. It is considered by several authorities that Burnett held a mortgage over the lands which passed, by a charter from Charles II, to Sir Alexander Fraser, the most learned and progressive of the Fraser lairds and for many years physician to the royal household. It was he who built the older part of the present House of Durris.

Sir Alexander, who was twice married, had by his first wife a daughter and two sons the younger of whom translated Plutarch's *Lives.* By his second wife he had a son and daughter, the former, Sir Peter, being the last Fraser of Durris. His daughter, Carey, a maid of honour to Catherine, Charles II's queen, married Charles Mordaunt, Earl of Peterborough and the famous general of William

III and Queen Anne. Their only daughter in 1706 became the wife of the 2nd Duke of Gordon. So it was that in 1825 the lands of Durris passed to the ancient family of Gordon when the 4th Duke, as next heir of entail, won them after a protracted lawsuit, Keith's Tower – which we shall be visiting in a short time – commemorates his legal victory. But his possession was short-lived for in 1834 the property was sold again to Anthony Mactier, a Madras merchant who was suspected by some of having been a pirate. Mactier extended Durris House which his son disposed of in 1871 for no less than £300,000 to James Young, the discoverer of paraffin. In 1890 Durris House was acquired by Henry Robert Baird of the family of the Bairds of the Gartsherrie iron works.

Durris House Originally a 17th Century Castle

In exactly a mile and a half (and only 100 yards before the crossroads) we pass on the right the drive to the present Durris House, an elegant, imposing and very substantially built mansion house, standing on the high ground overlooking the valley and on the edge of the steep bank of a stream. It is pleasantly situated in the large and ancient estate of which we have been speaking, unique in respect of the number and variety of old shrubs and trees which have grown to great height. Nowhere in the northern half of Scotland is there a finer or more varied collection of foreign conifers – both useful and ornamental – than in the policies of Durris House: almost every known species of pine is represented, and there are also specimens of rare and beautiful elms, ashes, beeches, sycamores and planes. A giant of the woods, a huge Douglas fir, 126 ft. in height and 16 ft. in circumference, measured breast-high, is the finest example of Oregon pine in the country.

The House itself, harled and yellow-washed, consists of a picturesque L-shaped tower of a large courtyard type of castle, built in the early part of the 17th century, to which has been added a more modern and larger granite house of considerable character. There have been so many modern additions (even as late as 1980) that it is difficult to realise that the building is much older than it seems. Much of the original vaulted basement foundations are now below ground level, the roof-level is somewhat altered and the re-entrant angle of the tower has been filled in with later work so that each floor now contains an extra small room. Tranter in his *Fortified House in Scotland* thinks that the tall square building at the eastern extremity, directly across from the old tower, might represent at least the base of a former courtyard tower. Furthermore, the original entrance is now inside the building at the foot of the stairway as was usual, and the ceiling of the ground-floor room has been raised, the corbels for the former joists still projecting. The taller stair-wing with its tiny turnpike stair culminates at the stair-head in a little watch-chamber, built out on simple, individual corbels and with an unusual stone seat at one side of one of its little windows. Also unusual are the two very small angle turrets at the western corners and the fact that the moderately sized Hall on the first floor has two fireplaces, a large one near the door and a smaller opposite.

The Peculiar Green Lady of Durris

Associated with Durris House – but not the present building – is the Green Lady of Durris (Green Ladies were a common phenomenon a century or two ago!) whose rare appearances were always out of doors and whose peculiarity was that she never manifested herself to her own sex. The legend was once firmly established in the parish, and well into this century there were people firmly convinced that they had seen her.

The story of her origin goes back to Covenanting days when the Marquis of Montrose was sent north to the Mearns and Deeside on what was really a punitive expedition. Calling on his erstwhile Covenanting friend, the laird of Durris House, he became involved in violent political arguments, and the charming and beautiful lady of the house at first unavailingly attempted to intervene and bring about some degree of harmony as Montrose was now their implacable enemy.

She is reputed, finally, to have called him a traitor and a turncoat and to have put upon him a curse. The immediate result, you remember, was that the House of Durris was razed to the ground and horse, cattle and sheep slaughtered. It is said that the lady of the house (whose taste in dress ran to green and who usually wore an emerald necklace and head-dress) wandered over the ruins of her home, wringing her hands and wailing. In the end, lured by the sound of the friendly stream which runs through the romantic den at the back of the house, she sought rest in its quiet bed!

Keith's Tower and St Congol's Fair 'at the Kirk of Doors'

The turning to Park Bridge, 100 yards beyond the drive to Durris House, passes through a peninsular-shaped piece of land known as Kincluny within a peculiar bend of the River Dee where it first flows north-west and then south-east. If we proceed along this road for just under half a mile, we arrive at a bend where there is a cottage on the right. Let us park here. A path behind the cottage takes us in 135 yards to the top of a small eminence known as Keith's Hill, surmounted by the octagonal Keith's Tower, about 80 ft. in height, a familiar landmark erected in 1825 by the Duke of Gordon to commemorate his winning possession of the estate of Durris. There is an inside staircase with sixty-two steps. Some hold that it marks the spot where a young member of the Keith family was slain by the Irvines of Drum because, ignoring a family feud, he had loved one of the ladies of the latter family. Surprised during a stolen meeting, young Keith had fled and swum for the south bank of the Dee, being shot by his pursuers while resting on a rock in the middle of the river. Of this romantic episode Keith's Stone, 280 yards below the bridge, and Keith's Pot between the two are pointed out as conclusive proofs. Keith's Tower and Keith's Stone are however erroneously named, a skirmish between the Keiths and the Irvines of Drum having taken place on the north bank of the Dee near the spot in the 13th or 14th century, the outcome being that the Irvines drove the Keiths over the river.

A further 260 yards takes us to Park Bridge itself from which we are able to see Keith's Stone down river. We are also able to see, on the flood-plain alongside the river, the Market Stance where St Congol's Fair used to be held *at the kirk of Doors in Mernshire*. Congol, who was born in Magheramorne in Northern Ireland in A.D. 517, came from the great monastery of Bangor in County Down and may have continued Ternan's work among the Picts.

On the western side of the bridge, 200 yards away on the north bank of the river, a concentration of 662 flints was found in 1973. These are preserved in Aberdeen Art Gallery and Museum.

As you approach the crossroads on the A943 on the return journey, take a look to the left where, 430 yards away, may be seen a mound called Gallow Hill. The eminence may be reached from the South Deeside Road by walking 200 yards across a field.

The Rees and Ring Cairn of Clune

And now we are really on our way home. We cross the A943 and turn right almost immediately, in nine-tenths of a mile turning right again until, in just under a further half mile (that is some 470 yards before Woodlands School) we arrive at a Forestry Commission road on our left into Clune Wood.

Here we leave our car and follow the woodland path for 750 yards up to the top of Clune Hill, deviating neither to right nor left until we reach the third main fork to the right near the crest of the hill from where we can just discern fields in front through the trees. Just under 300 yards along this fork we shall find on our left a narrow path through the wood which takes us in a further 120 yards to a clearing on the hill crest (563 ft.) where we find the Bronze Age recumbent stone-circle (see page 24) known as the Rees of Clune (from ree meaning an enclosure).

The impressive Bronze Age stone-circle, known as the Rees of Clune, which stands on the top of Clune Hill. Pictured is the recumbent stone, 10 ft. in length, with its two flankers still in an upright position.

The circle, with a diameter of some 40 ft., is an impressive one: it still possesses eight of its large monoliths, five of them, including the flankers, remaining in an upright position, their heights varying from about 4 ft. 5 ins. to 5 ft. 8 ins. The recumbent stone is 10 ft. in length. Eight or nine feet inside is an inner circle with a diameter of some 23 ft., showing a dyke, now reduced to a low bank, joining the uprights. One of the stones of the outer or larger circle which lies prostrate is marked by a number of incisions made by the chisel of some mason who had begun to cut it up.

Immediately beside the recumbent stone-circle is the ring cairn of Clune Hill. As it is now largely overgrown with heather and bracken, I feel it advisable merely to reproduce verbatim the description written by Miss Audrey Henshal after her visit to it in 1957:

> *The diameter is about 41 to 45 ft., but there is no kerb to be seen and the edges are rather indefinite. The cairn material of irregular rounded stones remains to a height of about 3 ft. 6 ins. In the centre is exposed a roughly circular setting of upright split stones enclosing an area about 9 ft. in diameter. The stones are carefully set with their vertical edges fitting closely, and in one place where the lower parts of two stones do not meet the space has been neatly filled with a thin vertical stone. The top edges of the slabs are almost level and generally square, the stones on the N side being slightly lower. The stones are exposed for 1 ft. 3 ins. to 2 ft. which seems to be about half their real height. There is a gap in the setting on the S side but there is no sign of a passage leading to the cairn edge.*

When you return through the forest clearing to the forestry road, you might care to continue along it, before returning to your car, for only a further 80 yards. On your left is a typical Bronze Age cairn similar to those you have already seen on Cairnshee, at Bucharn and at Ardlair but, unlike them, in a great state of dilapidation.

Return to Stonehaven Square!

And now we return to our car, our next stop Stonehaven. We continue past the village of Woodlands, turning left towards Cairn-mon-earn at the fork which we reach in 1³/₅ miles. In just under 1²/₅ miles we rejoin the Slug Road and in a further 8½ miles reach Stonehaven Square.

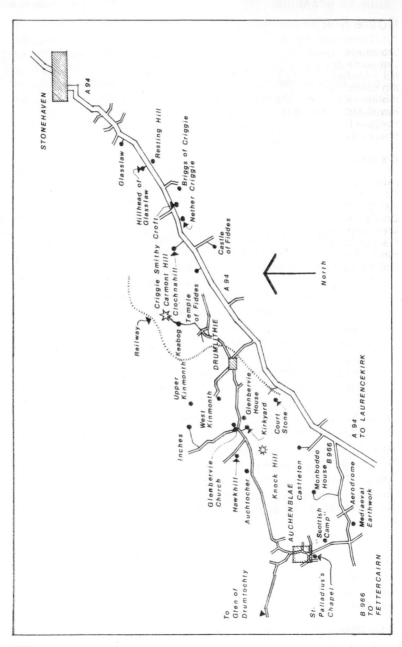

STONEHAVEN

A 94

Glasslaw

Resting Hill

Hillhead of
Glasslaw

Briggs of Criggie

Nether Criggie

Castle
of Fiddes

North

A 94

Criggie Smithy Croft
Carmont Hill
Clochnahill

Temple
of Fiddes

Keabog

A 94
TO LAURENCEKIRK

Railway

Upper
Kinmonth

DRUMLITHIE

West
Kinmonth

Glenbervie
House

Inches

Kirkyard

Glenbervie
Church

Court
Stone

Hawkhill

Monboddo
House B 966

Auchtocher

Knock Hill

Castleton

Aerodrome

AUCHENBLAE

Mediaeval
Earthwork

To
Glen of
Drumtochty

"Scottish
Camp"

St.
Palladius's
Chapel

B 966
TO
FETTERCAIRN

260

Route Six

Stonehaven Square – Glasslaw Farm – Hillhead of Glasslaw – Resting Hill – Lampool – Briggs of Criggie – Criggie Smithy Croft – Nether Criggie – Clochnahill – Castle of Fiddes – Temple of Fiddes – The Bogs – Drumlithie – West Kinmonth – Glenbervie House – Glenbervie Church – Inches – Upper Kinmonth – Knock Hill – Old Church of Glenbervie – Glenbervie Churchyard – Hawkhead – Auchtochter – Auchenblae – Gilbert's Hill – Kirkton of Fordoun – Fordoun Parish Church – St Palladius' Chapel – Drumsleed Hill – Monboddo House – Castleton – Court Stone – Stonehaven Square.

Distance: 26¾ miles (25.5 by car and 1.2 on foot).

Additional suggested excursions are of the following total lengths:
Carmont Hill – 4.54 miles (3.46 by car and 1.08 on foot)
Inches 1.89 miles by car
Bruxie Hill long cairn – 1.78 miles (1.7 by car and 0.08 on foot)
West Kinmonth – 1.76 miles by car
Blackhill Wood long cairn – 1.01 miles by car
Hawkhill – 0.81 miles by car
Drumsleed earthwork – 0.09 miles on foot

Round Glenbervie, Auchenblae, Fordoun and Mondynes

in which we talk of a hearse house, the theft of eighty loaves, the mother church of the Mearns, Burns' only poem with Kincardineshire associations, a midnight game of football with ghosts, a steeple taken in during rain and monkeys with tails worn off by constant sitting!

Leave Stonehaven Square and travel southwards along Allardice Street, taking the right-hand fork at the old tollhouse on the outskirts of the town and following the road to Laurencekirk up the hill. To those acquainted with the district this will be known as the 'high woods', a title reminiscent of the days when trees were more plentiful. In just over a mile we pass Gallow Hill,[1] clearly visible on our right and, after a further quarter of a mile, we cross Glasslaw Bridge, built in the early 19th century.

Glasslaw Farm

Three-tenths of a mile farther on is on our right the road to Glasslaw Farm where there was at one time a number of what used to be termed sepulchral tumuli, the old name on Ordnance Survey maps for what are now termed cairns or barrows.

---

[1] See *Highways and Byways Round Stonehaven*, pp. 88-90.

Hillhead of Glasslaw

After proceeding just short of three-quarters of a mile farther on, one reaches the road end to the farm of Hillhead of Glasslaw where at one time a number of Bronze Age barrows existed as well.

Resting Hill

Exactly opposite Hillhead of Glasslaw and only 300 yards or so from the road is a raised eminence in the field about 700 yards in length. It is called Resting Hill, and the mound in the middle was formerly crowned by a stone called the Resting Stone. When trenching at the south-west end of this tumulus on 21st January, 1864, the farmer found a cist pointing north and south and consisting of four large slabs of freestone, the side ones 3 ft. long, the ends 2 ft. The grave contained a beaker 6 ins. high and 4 ins. in diameter at the brim which was broken when the stones were being removed. Another stone cist and urn were found 240 yards to the north-east, some 35 yards from the edge of the rise. Yet another, exactly similar and containing an urn with elementary ornamentation, was found on the adjoining farm in the spring of 1859.

Lampool

A little under half a mile away we see on the left, behind the trees, the farm with the name of Lampool, one of the few instances of Welsh nomenclature in the county. The name, it would seem, is derived from llan, a church, and poll, a pond or hole – the pool beside the cell. Here is only one of the remaining indications of ecclesiastical establishments in the vicinity. There are to the south Chapelton nine-tenths of a mile away, Lonkur or Lumgair one and a third miles distant and, just under a mile and a fifth, Druidsdale, once thought to have been a Druid retreat. Yet again, another farm, the Chapel of Barras, is just over three miles away, and in two and two-third miles we shall pass the Temple of Fiddes. Quite a cluster of names of religious significance!

Briggs of Criggie

The next farm we pass on the left in some 350 yards is one with the interesting name of Briggs of Criggie, situated at the spot where once were briggs – a kind of causeway over boggy land. At one time there was a lochan at what became the briggs, and indeed marshy land is still in evidence on the west side of the farm even today.

Criggie Smithy Croft

In 130 yards or so on the right is the road end to the farm of Newlands a quarter of a mile north-west of which was formerly a *small but very perfect Druidical circle.*

A third of a mile farther on is Criggie Smithy Croft on the left. Here on a knoll on August 30th, 1954, two farm workers, operating a mechanical excavator, uncovered a short stone cist, 3 ft. in length, 2 ft. in width and 18 ins. in depth. It was constructed of slabs of Old Red Sandstone for which the area is famous and floored with what Professor O'Dell of Aberdeen University described as a form of crazy paving.

The cist contained the bones of a woman and child (all in a remarkable state of preservation), three urns, intricately patterned and kiln-baked, and some small implements or scrapers, including a 'thumb scraper', used for cleaning and indicating that the occupants of the cist had been members of a tribe of herdsmen. The child had died at birth and the mother, aged between 22 and 25, at delivery.

The period around which death had occurred, indicated by the nature of the cist, the method of burial and the implements and urns – or beakers – was in the early Bronze Age, between 3,000 and 4,000 years ago, certainly not more recently than 1500 B.C. The skull of the woman showed her to be a member of the broad-headed race of Western Goths who, under pressure from the peoples of the east, found their way to Britain in those far off times.

Nether Criggie

In yet another third of a mile, and past the farm of Upper Criggie, we reach the road end to the farm of Nether Criggie on the left. William Falconer, a cotter here, once stole four score loaves, a whole batch of bread from the ovens of Glenbervie House. So horrified was he of the consequences that he fled the county!

More recently, in 1964, earth-moving operations revealed a cist set into a 5½ ft. deep pit in a gravel hillock 525 yards east of Nether Criggie farmhouse. It contained a crouched inhumation and the fragmentary skeleton of a new-born child, accompanied by three beakers. Two flint scrapers and other stone objects found nearby probably came from the cist. The bones and finds are preserved at Marischal College, Aberdeen.

The lands of Nether Criggie, however, have a greater call to fame: they were once settled on the Countess Marischal (the mother of the Earl Marischal) in the mid-17th century to be enjoyed by her after her husband's death. They were also closely associated with the Ogilvys of Barras, a family honourably connected with the leading branches of the noble family whose name they bore. It was George Ogilvy (later to be Governor of Dunnottar Castle at the time of the defence of the Regalia) who secured these lands on lease. Like many other Scotsmen of his time he had been a soldier of fortune in which capacity he had served with credit and distinction in the German wars. Prior to 1630 he married Lady Elizabeth, daughter of John Douglas of Barras, fourth son of William, Earl of Angus, and although possessing a small property in Angus, seems to have preferred to live within his native county. His purchase of Barras some years later did not interfere with this arrangement, and Criggie Manor Place in the immediate neighbourhood here (of which there is now no evidence) remained the residence of the family until 1679.

Manor Place of Criggie Searched

So it was that one night in 1652 the Manor Place of Criggie was surrounded by the troopers of Colonel Morgan to whom Dunnottar Castle surrendered on 24th May, 1652. They were intent on seizing William Ogilvy, the father of George Ogilvy, the ex-Governor of the Castle. But they were unsuccessful: Ogilvy was constantly upon the move wherever and at whatever time convenience dictated. Thrice, too, was this same Manor Place searched in the delusive hope that there might be found in it some trace of the much coveted Regalia which for eight years lay concealed in Kinneff Church[1] only a little more than four and three-quarter miles away, under the guardianship of Mr Grainger, the minister, and his wife, and visited at stated intervals by George Ogilvy himself who brought fresh linen to preserve them from the ravages of dust and mildew.

Clochnahill

On the right this time – again in round about a third of a mile – is the road end to the farm of Clochnahill, the site of the small, wind-swept farm once owned by Burns' grandfather, Robert Burnes, who was born, lived and died in the Mearns with his wife, Isabella Keith of Upper Criggie, an adjoining farm. (Hogg, the Ettrick Shepherd, thinking possibly of this marriage, went the length of calling the Burnes family cadets of the Earls Marischal, meaning that they were members of a younger branch of the Keith family.) With the neighbouring farmers Robert Burnes built a school at Clochnahill and supported a teacher. He had ten sons and

[1] See *Highways and Byways Round Stonehaven*, pp. 144-145.

a daughter, and it was probably at Clochnahill that William Burnes, the father of Robert Burns, was born on 11th November, 1721. He is now commemorated, as we shall see, by a cairn farther along the A94 Stonehaven-Laurencekirk road.

Glenbervie Inhabited by Relatives

To the young William, descended from pure Kincardineshire crofting stock, it must have seemed that the whole district from Clochnahill to Glenbervie and round by the braes of Glenbervie was inhabited by his relatives. His grandfather and grandmother still lived at Brawliemuir, and so did his Uncle William. His Uncle James was at Hawkhill beside Glenbervie, and his Uncle George at Elfhill to the north. There were other Burneses, relatives on his father's side, at Bogjurgan and Inches, as we have seen. And when all the connections by marriage – the Falconers, the Brands, the Greigs and the rest – were added to the list, their number must have seemed legion. As a young man in his early twenties he would have attended the funeral in Glenbervie churchyard of his grandfather, the farmer of Brawliemuir, and many a time he must have seen the gravestone which was erected to the old man's memory.

Ruined by Winter Frosts

The family was ruined by the atrocious winter and spring of 1740 which was long remembered. The early frost continued long and intense to the end of April, no seed being sown till May and vegetation suffering severely. Ridges were then formed high in the centre as a protection against moisture and, the frost having penetrated into the soil and the season being advanced, the sunny side was ploughed first and the other side only when the thaw was complete. Because of this and the continuance of rough weather the crop was useless, and Robert Burnes and his sons abandoned Clochnahill where they never had a chance of prospering. One by one the sons were compelled to proceed elsewhere for employment.

James Burnes of Montrose

The first to go was the eldest son, James, who settled in Montrose where he became a burgess and a town councillor. He died in 1761 at the age of 44 and left a son and daughter. The son, who was a notary public in Montrose, has been greatly applauded by the various biographers of the Bard for his (James') response to the appeal of his, at that time, needy cousin. He it was who met the poet by appointment at Stonehaven in 1787 and introduced him to the northern branches of the family while Burns was on a tour with his friend, Mr Nicol. James Burnes died in 1837.

Burns' Father Leaves the Mearns

Then Robert went south and finally Willam, Robert Burns' father, the youngest of the three who, when but 19 years of age, left his native county to try his fortunes in the south of Scotland. Today this may not seem to be anything out of the ordinary, but to the early 18th century youth it was a great decision and a great wrench as his own words to his children testified. To them he was wont to describe how he took a sorrowful farewell of his brother on the summit of the last hill from which the roof of their lowly dwelling could be descried. In a letter Gilbert Burns, the poet's brother, writes,

> *I have often heard my father describe with anguish when they parted on the top of the hill on the confines of their native place, each going off in search of adventures, scarcely knowing whither they went.*

So did the poet's father soon after 1740 (one can, I think, be more accurate in date than the memorial cairn indicates) with only a poke of beans to sustain him, leave Clochnahill and the Mearns. He went first of all to the Edinburgh district where he was employed as a gardener, but soon forsook the east for the west, taking up his abode in Ayrshire. In 1757 he married Agnes Brown, and two years later

> *a blast o' Janwar' wind*
> *Blew hansel in on Robin.*

Or, as Lewis Grassic Gibbon puts it when writing about James Burnes, the poet's great-grandfather,

> *His folk had the ups and downs of all flesh till the father of Robert Burns grew up and grew sick of the place and went off to Ayr, and there the poet Robert was born, him that lay with nearly as many women as Solomon did, though not all at one time.*

Misfortune of the Poet's Ancestors

Robert Burnes himself, son of James in Brawliemuir and the poet's grandfather, in arrears with his rent, unsuccessful as a farmer in Clochnahill and in various other difficulties, removed on Whitsunday, 1745, to Fawsyde of Kinneff of which he took a seven year lease. In 1747, owing to an accumulation of financial difficulties, not least being the inability of his successor in Clochnahill to pay him for crops already sown because the farm had been pillaged by Prince Charlie's army on its way to Culloden, he left Fawsyde a ruined man, and nothing further is known of him. No record has been found of his death, and he lies in an unmarked grave, some say in Dunnottar churchyard.

Burns, the poet, claims for his ancestors (Robert, his grandfather, and George, Robert's brother, both of whom left Brawliemuir to become leaseholders on the domain of the Keiths Marischal) the honour of having shared the misfortunes of William, 6th Earl Marischal, a privy councillor to King Charles I in whose misfortunes and those of his family the Keith family were destined largely to share. In a letter to Dr Moore, dated August 2nd, 1787, he writes,

> *My ancestors rented lands of the noble Keiths Marischal and had the honour of sharing their fate. I mention this because it threw my father on the world at large. They followed boldly where their leaders led, and welcomed ruin and shook hands with infamy for what they believed to be the cause of their God and their King.*

A Wet, Unproductive Countryside

In the time of the Burneses the whole countryside must have been wild and uncultivated. Even the names are suggestive of wet and unproductive land and of the original character of the soil – Bogjurgan, Brawliemuir, Bogandriep, Moss-side, Spittalmyre and many others. The name Clochnahill itself is supposed to indicate a stone-circle which stood on the eastern part of the ridge to the north until about 1864 when the stones were removed to form the foundation of a neighbouring threshing-mill. There were, indeed, numerous pillar stones all over the district, and about 1841 a cist containing fragments of bone and two urns was found 165 yards south-west of Clochnahill farmhouse.

The Castle of Fiddes

In exactly quarter of a mile we reach on the left a road to Roadside of Kinneff. This we should follow for only 670 yards until we reach the private drive to the delightful Castle of Fiddes on the lower slopes of Bruxie Hill with its cairns and barrows and, on top, a television booster station. It should be possible to pick out the castle if we walk but a few yards from our turning-point to enable us to see along the side of the field.

The Castle of Fiddes is a most striking example of a moderately sized 16th century tower-house or feudal stronghold. From the high ground on which it stands, upwards of 400 ft. above sea level, it commands a wide view of the country to both east and west.

The Castle of Fiddes built in 1592. Notice the circular tower on the right with the picturesque roofed chamber at the top, supported by corbels, and notice, too, the tall circular stair tower, corbelled out from midway on the north side of the first floor.

Traditionally an Arbuthnott Dower-house

Little is known of its history. As far back as the end of the 13th century the lands of Fiddes were owned by the Arbuthnott family whose home, Arbuthnott House, stands five miles to the south, and Fiddes Castle was traditionally a dower-house set apart for the widow of a deceased Arbuthnott laird. The lands were transferred elsewhere for some 200 years, but historians record that a Sir Robert Arbuthnott again became the owner during the reigns of James III and IV with both of whom he was in favour. In 1553 one Andrew Arbuthnott, second son of the laird of Arbuthnott, was granted a charter of the lands by Queen Mary of Scots and, 100 years later in the time of Charles I, another second son of the Viscount was designated Andrew Arbuthnott of Fiddes, having bought the castle from a cousin. It was his second son, John, who sold Fiddes Castle to James Thomson of Arduthie. To this day can be seen on an inside doorway in the east wall of what was an addition to the castle the inscription, 'I.A. – H.B. – 16-73', the initials of John Arbuthnott and Helen Burnett, his wife who, it is thought probable, restored the castle at this time.

Architectural Elegance with Unusual Modifications

The castle with its three storeys, attic and basement, is a most elegant and interesting composition architecturally, possessing some good specimens of late 16th century architecture which make the building significant. It was built in 1592 as is proved by the presence of that date on the pediment over the top dormer window on the south-east face of the wing. Although the castle is built on the L-plan, that is a tower with a wing appended to the long side of the main building, there are several most unusual modifications of old forms which prevailed at that time. For example, the staircase normally in the 're-entrant angle' as it is called – tucked in, so to speak, between the projecting limbs of the building – is housed in a large circular tower projecting beyond the main building. A second exceptional feature is the fact that this tower has an open platform roof which was at one time covered. It has, too, over the door, a projecting, galleried parapet supported by elaborate corbels and with an opening through which molten substances might be poured upon an attacking force beneath. On this projection is an empty panel space.

Towers and Angle Turrets

Another unusual feature is a second circular tower occupying the angle on the second side of the main building, thus narrowing the gable considerably. The square, pack-saddle roofed chamber at the top (which would have served as a small watch-tower) is extremely picturesque, being set diagonally and supported by corbels. A third tall stair tower, also square on the top, is corbelled out from roughly midway on the north side of the first floor, while a fourth very small one rises between the main stair tower and the south gable of the main block. On the south-west tower and the north turret there is a free use made round the windows of dripstones or projecting mouldings characteristic of this part of the country, and two corbelled angle turrets are two storeys high.

The Interior of the Castle

Regarding the interior of the castle I quote from *Castellated and Domestic Architecture of Scotland* by MacGibbon and Ross:

> *The main staircase is 4 ft. wide and leads to the first floor only. On this floor are the Hall (26 ft. by 16 ft.) and a private room with a small chamber off it over the entrance. From the Hall a stair in the south-west corner leads to the second floor. The turret in the centre of the north wall also contains a stair leading to the upper floors. From the second floor a small stair is corbelled out next to the south-east turret which leads to the attic, and also gives access to a balcony or bartizan over part of the south-east tower.*

The arrangement of this balcony and small overhanging turret projecting from an angle in the top of the tower makes the southern face of the building most pleasing. To the north, however, the castle is somewhat forbidding and formidable.

Several other points about the design and layout of the castle are worthy of note. In the east wing, on the ground floor, the kitchen with its oven and large fireplace arch is barrel-vaulted like the cellar. That is, they have both semi-cylindrical roofs. The cellar has its own private stair from the Hall. At the side of the Hall fireplace is an ambry or cupboard for victuals, and the tiny chamber off the Hall which has already been mentioned has a fine decorative ceiling. The castle is well supplied with shot-holes dotted all over the building, the arrangement in the turrets on the ground-floor being such that every side is commanded.

For many years the castle was used as a shelter for animals and for stores, but happily it is now restored, in excellent condition and in full use as a dwelling-house with walls seemingly in no way impaired by the ravages of time.

The Legend of 'Thrummy Cap'

One of the chief interests for us in the Castle of Fiddes lies in the metrical tale of *Thrummy Cap* which is based on a legend associated with the castle, for it was here the incidents of the story were enacted. The author was John Burness, the son of William Burness of Bogjurgan and later of the neighbouring farm of Cleughead and a cousin of Robert Burns who was, incidentally, a great admirer of his work. John Burness was a talented writer with, among his master-pieces, not only *Thrummy Cap* but *The Ghaist o' Garron Ha'*. His name and works were once almost as well-known throughout Scotland as those of his more distinguished kinsman which have, of course, always overshadowed them, but they have been allowed to drift almost to oblivion. His plays were produced on the provincial stage all over Scotland and even in England, Burness himself often taking a part.

John Burness not Destined for Fortune

John Burness, born at Bogjurgan on May 22nd, 1771, and orphaned while still in his teens, became a shepherd after a year's schooling. He gave early proof of his ability as a rhymester and often inscribed verses on stones erected to the memory of sheep or lambs which died in his care. For some reason his father had to leave his farm and became ill while John was working at Jacksbank. Dutifully he visited his father almost nightly, and on one occasion when he seemed very frail, John was advised to return to work on the understanding that he would be summoned if there was any change for the worse. This, however, his relations failed to do, and the first John heard of his father's death was an invitation to the funeral. This unfortunate incident had a lasting and unhappy effect on his mind.

John gave up farming and was apprenticed to a baker in Brechin where he worked until 1794. He afterwards enlisted with the Angus Fencible Volunteer Corps of Infantry after four years' service with which he commenced business as a baker in Stonehaven. Restless in disposition, however, he joined the Forfar Militia with which he served until 1815, thereafter again attempting bakery unsuccess-fully in Stonehaven. Like his cousin he was not destined for worldly fortune partly on account of an injudicious marriage and partly on account of a love for intoxicating liquor. He ultimately became a packman, hawking books (and possibly his own compositions) round the countryside for a publishing house. One stormy morning in January, 1826, he left Stonehaven to trudge to Aberdeen and after a life of penury and hardship met with a tragic death when he perished in a blizzard near the church of Portlethen. His body was dug out of the snow and interred in St Peter's cemetery in Aberdeen where a rugged block of granite was erected to his memory in 1912.

A Popular Ghost Story

It was when the Angus Fencibles were in Dumfries that John Burness wrote his *Thrummy Cap* which he showed to his cousin, the poet, whom he met there in 1796, shortly before Burns' death. Burns thought it *the best ghaist story in the Scottish language that I am acquainted with*. The story, popular in its day, takes its title from one of the two men who *forgather'd o' the way* about *a hunder miles ayont the Forth* on a stormy winter day and who

> *on his heid had got*
> *A thrummy cap, baith large and stout,*
> *Wi' flaps ahint, as weel's a snout.*

(A thrummy-cap is a cap made of 'thrums' or weavers' ends.) Overtaken by a snow-storm, they eventually were directed to shelter,

> *Gin ye'll gan but two miles forrit,*
> *Aside the kirk dwalls Robbie Dorrit,*
> *Wha keeps a change-house, sells gude drink;*
> *His hoose ye may mak' oot, I think.*

The *kirk* is the old kirk of Glenbervie (which we are soon to visit), and Robbie's *change-house* (an ale-house or tavern), now no longer there, stood on the left-hand side of the road leading from Drumlithie to the kirk. There Thrummy *at the footba' played* with two ghosts after midnight, for his boldness eventually gaining fifty guineas because he thereby freed the laird from a complicated lawsuit. For details of the connection between football and a lawsuit, and of who handed over the fifty guineas, the reader must consult the poem itself!

The manuscript of *Thrummy Cap* was bought in 1933 by Dr Charles Murray ('Hamewith') and generously presented to the library of the University of Aberdeen.

A Bruxie Hill Long Cairn Rim

It would seem a pity when we are so near not to drive to the top of Bruxie Hill – for there is an excellent road to the summit – to see the remains of the third of Kincardineshire's long barrows and cairns, in this case, because of robbing, a mere rim of cairn material just over 2½ ft. high. Indeed, if you have already seen the long cairns of Gourdon and Hillhead, it is hardly worth a visit; yet it may be that you have time and that the day is a pleasant one.

You must continue onwards towards Roadside of Kinneff for only half a mile to the farm of Ferniebrae, turning right at the road to the top of Bruxie Hill. Stop at the pile of stones on your left just over a third of a mile up the hill and you will find the remains of the long cairn 75 yards away on your right on the north-east flank of the hill. It measures 114¾ ft. from east to west by 39 ft. at the west end and 65¼ ft. at the east end. To the east of the cairn there are several other heaps of stones but they, like the pile at which we have left our car, appear to be recent. Just over 100 yards north-west of the Television Link Station, however, and on the edge of a scarp, is a cairn belonging to the Bronze Age, 19½ ft. in diameter and just over 1¼ ft. in height.

And now let us retrace our steps to meet the main road in just under three-tenths of a mile from the gate to the Castle of Fiddes. As we curve right, however, prior to joining it, have a look at the field in front of you. Here again stone cists and urns were found – three this time – at the end of the fence stretching in front and 500 yards away in the corner of the field which is part of the farm of Clochnahill on the lower slopes of Carmont Hill.

The Temple of Fiddes

Turning left, in 280 yards we pass on our right a cairn with the following inscription:

> *This Memorial Cairn overlooks CLOCHNAHILL from which, between 1740-50, William Burnes, the Father of Scotland's National Poet, left for EDINBURGH, and then AYRSHIRE.*
> *Erected by Wm. Coull ANDERSON, Esq., Florida, U.S.A., a family descendant – 1968.*

Only the chimneys of Clochnahill, however, can be seen from here.

In a further quarter of a mile we pass, again on our right, the farm of Temple of Fiddes, a name already mentioned and derived from the fact that the ground was at one time owned and cultivated by the Knights Templars who had once much to do with the neighbourhood of Inverbervie, nearly five and three-quarter miles away. Formerly the turnpike left the present main road here, passing by Drumlithie and coming to the village by the farm of Fallside. Hence

Drumlithie was one of the places of call for the stage-coach, the only means of communication with the outside world in the days before the railway the arrival of which was an event of some importance.

The Bogs

On now until in a mile and three-quarters we turn right to Drumlithie at Candy corner (ceann, head, and dubh, dark), well-named because the half mile between here and Drumlithie was once known as 'The Bogs', a number of low-lying and swampy fields which formed at one time a kind of huge common on which the crofters' cows were allowed to graze on payment of an annual rent of 7/6d. A herd boy whose wages were paid proportionately by those employing him blew a horn to intimate his departure, and the hue and cry when any of the animals became 'laired' in the Bogs resulted in neighbourly assistance being readily given by the weavers of the village. The names of different parts of The Bogs were very suggestive, like The Muckle Meadow, Fit o' the Parks, John Smith's Loch and so on. Out of Foggie Moss peats were cut.

Drumlithie Shaken from the Clouds

And so, after a journey of exactly eight miles, we find ourselves in one of the quaintest and most picturesque places in the Mearns, the famous and irregularly built old-world weavers' village of Drumlithie. This, the only village in the parish, has been in existence for a very long period, dating back at least to the beginning of the 17th century. It stands on a gentle slope at the end of the Howe of the Mearns and is said to have rivalled Stonehaven in size in the days when that town was a village itself. It has been suggested that, as 'lithie' is the same as 'Leith' which means water, the name had its origin in the slope leading towards the village which is still known as 'The Watery Backs'. The name Drumlithie is also said to mean 'the ridge at the end of the valley', and its situation would answer to this description as well.

Of Drumlithie it has been said that the only regular feature about it is its irregularity and that a bird's eye view of it would almost convince one that the houses had been shaken from the clouds! Certainly the long tradition of the village is evident in the very alignment of its intimate High Street and, indeed, in all its narrow old-fashioned streets. The High Street is like no main street you've ever seen – merely a narrow lane which bends and twists with the houses and leads you down even narrower lanes. You're constantly discovering yet another quaint cottage in some unexpected place.

Away back in 1329 Drumlithie became an independent burgh of barony, and the village for a considerable period retained not only its position as the principal community in the area but also a strong adherence to the Episcopalian faith, even through the troublous times of the Reformation. Its chapel, first mentioned in 1536 and formerly a dependent unit of the kirk of Glenbervie, kept the flag of Episcopacy flying until 1746 when the building was razed to the ground by order of 'Butcher' Cumberland. Even that did not quench the fires of the chapel-goers, and the minister of the time, the Rev. John Petrie, suffered imprisonment with others in the county tolbooth in Stonehaven.[1] Chapel Street in the village, behind the present Episcopal Church of John the Baptist, com-memorates the old building a part of which is allegedly still to be seen forming part of a wall nearby.

In Every Ben-end a Loom

One of the chief industries used to be the manufacture of linen and other similar goods, and Drumlithie was originally a village of long, low thatched cottages with in every ben-end a loom shop with its raftered roof and dusty walls in which a hand-loom weaver worked from morning to night. These cottages extended considerably west of the village (several stood on what is now the school-house garden) to the present Dencroft Cottage which is built on what was then the village common, known as the Ba' Green and used as the parish school playground. The market to and from which goods were taken by carrier's cart was either Stonehaven or Montrose.

But the power-loom put an end to all that. By 1838 Drumlithie's weaving industry was in depression and decline although even until 1860 the population of the village of between 200 and 300 were still mostly weavers, the agricultural land around being worked in rather primitive fashion. By 1879 we are told only

> *a single hand-loom weaver still continues to maintain an unequal struggle against the superior power of steam.*

Today Drumlithie is a dormitory village which depends for its existence largely on its up-to-date and fruitful agricultural sur-roundings.

The Steeple a Village Feature

In a prominent place in the centre of the High Street the most characteristic feature of the village is a unique and isolated circular

[1] See *Highways and Byways Round Stonehaven*, pp. 33-35.

sandstone tower or miniature steeple on a stepped base, incongru-
ous in its setting and visible above the houses wherever you stand in
the village. Built in 1777 and renewed in 1880, it is surmounted by a
belfry which was presented by Robert Dyce Smith, postmaster and
unofficial 'provost' of the village in the days when the Amenities
Committee was a thorough-going village council with 'provost',
'town clerk' and six 'councillors', elected by popular vote after a
lively heckling meeting. The council was to continue until the late
1930's.

This celebrated steeple the villagers regard with much pride: the
Drumlithie Hotel has a Steeple Lounge, and the local tailor makes
Steeple Badges to adorn his blazers which members of the village
committee are proud to wear. The local poultry factory even sells
Steeple Chickens. The steeple has always been a source of fun and
envy to the rest of the county. By now the villagers are used to the
taunt sometimes levelled at them that it has to be taken in on a rainy
day! In the 1920's one 'provost' even had hundreds of postcards
printed, showing himself with an umbrella in his hand and with the
steeple under his arm and the caption, *I doot it's to rain. It's time we
had in the steeple!*

*A picture of the original postcard sold by Provost Mowat of
Drumlithie, a cobbler, to raise funds for a new Drumlithie
Hall which was opened on 16th April, 1927.*

The unique, circular miniature steeple, built in 1777, which is the most characteristic feature of the village of Drumlithie. The steeple bell once summoned weavers to their work and indicated meal times. The villagers are now used to the taunt that the steeple has to be taken inside on a rainy day!

The steeple bell was possibly taken with the church plate from Glenbervie Church for use at the Episcopal Church here after the 1688 Revolution. It was broken by Cumberland in 1746 when he destroyed the predecessor of the present Episcopal Church and recast by the villagers most of whom were episcopalian. Prior to 1777 it was hanging on a large ash tree in the village, ultimately being transferred to the steeple when it was built to summon the weavers to their work and to indicate meal times. Since then, all down the years, the steeple has had its official bell-ringer, and today the bell is still pealed but only to celebrate the occasional wedding of a villager either here or abroad or to ring in the New Year.

The Famous Michael Fair

One or two other features in the village may merit attention. Half-way along Croft Road (and near the swings) is Main House, once the village stage-coach post. Notice the hitching-ring on the wall. Farther along and next to the church at the end of High Street is St John's Cottage, once an episcopal school of the early 19th century, while round the corner to the right is Harvey Well with its cold spring water, standing on the Water Backs and part of the original coach road. Dated 1887, this is the oldest remaining well in the village, the others having disappeared. Most interesting perhaps is what used to be the field between the school and the Glenbervie road (now the site of a housing development): here was once held annually the famous Michael Fair of Glenbervie when it eventually moved to Drumlithie where it was held until auction marts put fairs out of fashion at the beginning of the century. The site is still called Michael Fair, now partly occupied by the poultry-packing station of E. Watson and Son which, with around sixteen workers, is the largest single employer of labour in the village.

Seggat and Skite in 'Sunset Song'

Drumlithie is often thought to be the original of Seggat, the village that features in *Sunset Song* and *Cloud Howe*, the first and second books of the trilogy subsequently published under the title of *A Scots Quair*, commenced in 1932 and ending with *Grey Granite*. The author is Lewis Grassic Gibbon (see page 120) who writes satirically of Drumlithie but with genuine affection hidden in his laughter, as is seen in this passage from *Sunset Song*:

> *. . . There to the left rose Drumlithie at last . . . some called it Skite to torment the folk and they'd get fell angry at that in Skite. No more than a rickle of houses it was, white with sunshine below its steeple that made of Skite the laugh of the Howe, for feint the kirk was near it. Folk said for a joke that every time it came on to rain the Drumlithie folk ran out and took in their steeple, that proud they were of the thing. . . .*

A Scots Quair is a Scots classic, without question the finest work yet written on the Howe of the Mearns, and *Cloud Howe* is about the blunt, couthy weavers and others who lived in what was once Burnes country between Drumlithie and Carmont. *Sunset Song* is a celebration of the sweetness of the Scottish earth and a memorial to a particular class of men who tilled it – the men of the crofts and small farms who gave their lives in the first of the Great Wars.

It was this race of indomitable crofters and smallholders, producing large, struggling families, who filled the hill lands of Scotland in the first agricultural revolution of the 18th century. It is the second farm revolution in the 20th century which is emptying the hill farms, merging them into larger units and turning the old peasant into the modern mechanic. Because this process is still going on, *Sunset Song* which describes its beginning has its continuing relevance and topicality today: this is why it will live as the classic statement of the death of the 'old Scotland' and as a memorial to the Burneses and, indeed, all farm labourers of the Mearns – to what they were, how they lived, and to every thread in the pattern of their existence.

Blackhill Wood Long Cairn

If ample time is available, the reader, before leaving Drumlithie, may wish to journey to the top of Carmont Hill nearby (774 ft.) from the summit of which an excellent view is obtained and on top of which is a dilapidated Bronze Age cairn. The round journey is one of exactly 4½ miles. En route one passes near the fourth of the five Neolithic long cairns and barrows in the county (in this case also in a state of dilapidation) which, of course, it is possible to visit without climbing Carmont Hill at all.

You must travel north-east along the road opposite Drumlithie Hotel for just under a mile until a road intersection is reached. Now turn immediately to your left along the road to Carmont Station at a sharp angle for only 175 yards and you will see the long cairn on the crest of a low rise in the field on your left just east of the north-east corner of Blackhill Wood. It measures 52 ft. in length and tapers from nearly 18 ft. in breadth at the east end to about 5¼ ft. at the west end. The central portion has been severely robbed, but at the east end the cairn survives to a height of over 1¼ ft. The west end of the cairn is apparently overlain by a round cairn nearly 28 ft. in diameter by 1¼ ft. in height, and about 33 yards east-north-east of the east end of the long cairn is at least one other small cairn some 15 ft. in diameter by 1¼ ft. in height.

Yet another is just over 100 yards away on a low rise south-south-west of the long cairn and immediately within the fence of Blackhill Wood. It measures 46 ft. in diameter and 2¼ ft. in height.

Ancient Tribes on Carmont Hill

If you wish to climb Carmont Hill, you must return the few yards to the road intersection and thereafter follow the road to Keabog Farm a further three-quarters of a mile away. An easy walk of just over half a mile takes you to the summit. It is highly probable that this was the place from which ancient tribes kept outlook against inroads from Deeside via Durris and Fetteresso, and from the south. The cairn on top is some 52 ft. in diameter, but most of the stones have been removed throughout the centuries doubtless for purposes of building, until the height is now no more than 2½ ft. In it, around 1852, were found a short cist *level with the surface of the ground*, a small urn and black unctuous earth.

It may be of interest that in the gravel quarry at the road intersection and at the road end to Keabog Farm two Bronze Age cists have been found during digging. The first was disturbed but had contained an adult inhumation (radiocarbon dated *c* 1780 B.C.), accompanied by a beaker. The second, discovered on 24th January, 1977, was a cist of grey, schist-like stone, measuring 35.4 ins. by 28.3 ins. by 23.6 ins. It contained the crouched, partially decayed skeleton of a young adult, probably male, lying on its left side (radiocarbon dated *c* 1745 B.C.) and with a triangular flint flake knife at its hips and portions of the neck and rim of a beaker behind its head. The cist can now be seen in the Tolbooth Museum, Stonehaven.

West Kinmonth

But we must be on our way from Drumlithie along the Glenbervie road. In three-fifths of a mile we are opposite the farm of West Kinmonth, 750 yards or so across the fields among the trees on the hill on our right. We could, indeed, have visited it from Drumlithie (the journey is only one and three-quarter miles there and back if one continues along High Street past the Scottish Episcopal Church), but perhaps one must be an enthusiast to do this. For West Kinmonth has associations with both Robert Burns and Lewis Grassic Gibbon.

The farm was once tenanted by Robert Burnes, second son of James Burnes of Brawliemuir, the poet's great-grandfather, who must have looked down with interest at the time on the growing village of Drumlithie which had been in existence for about a century. In West Kinmonth he married Isabella Keith whose father farmed Upper Criggie which we passed earlier, and it is to be presumed that the third son, William Burnes, who was to be the father of Robert Burns, was possibly born here too on November 11th, 1721. He is likely, however, to have been born at the more considerable 60-acre farm of Clochnahill where the family moved around 1721, but this cannot be positively asserted as the date of the removal is not known.

Glenbervie House — a Famous Stronghold

Another quarter of a mile along the road in this delightful foot-hill country and we reach the entrance to Glenbervie House which nestles under the shadow of the Knock Hill on a high triangular cape of land where meet in a picturesque wooded dell the Water of Bervie which comes down by an ancient ford still in use and the tributary Pilketty Burn.

It is believed that there must have been a castle of some kind here as far back as the 10th century — or the 12th century at least — occupying the same site as the present elegant and capacious three-storey mansion. Certainly the lower part of the present mansion-house dates from the 16th century. The castle is built on an unusual plan with two massive round towers projecting at either end of the symmetrical east frontage of the main block, originally the flanking-towers of a courtyard type of castle of early date with some of the curtain-walling still traceable. The north tower is comparatively new and is surrounded by an extinguisher-shaped roof with a vane at the top, dated 1762. The south-most was remodelled with a bartizan in 1854 when the House was much altered and the west wing added. It was, however, restored to its original form in 1965. Both towers have slit windows and wide-mouthed gun-loops so disposed as to cover the approaches and rake with fire the front of the building. Another ancient feature, the basement, together with the two towers, is vaulted throughout and, owing to the falling away of the ground level southwards, semi-subterranean. There is an iron yett in a basement window near the present front door.

Although most of Glenbervie House is ancient, modern features tend to dominate the aspect. The gable on the south side was probably built in the 17th century while the upper parts of the main block were altered and rebuilt in the 18th and 19th centuries. To modern times, too, belong the entire roof line and north frontage, altered in pseudo-baronial style. Above the doorway the family arms are sculptured, the motto on the scroll being *Nil sistere contra*

(Nothing stands against us). Originally a famous stronghold, Glenbervie Castle possibly succeeded the stronghold of Malpeder, Thane of the Mearns in the 11th century, as the habitation of the Lord of Glenbervie.

The elegant mansion-house of Glenbervie the lower part of which dates from the 16th century. Notice the two massive round towers projecting at either end of the east frontage, originally the flanking-towers of a courtyard type of castle of early date. Edward I of England spent the night of July 12th, 1296, in Glenbervie House during his journey through Scotland to receive the submission of Scottish chiefs.

A Walled Garden and Fine Old Trees

There is a walled garden with fine herbaceous and annual borders, and the glass-houses provide one of the most brilliant displays in Scotland of interesting and unusual plants. Fine old trees adorn the lawn in front of the House, very prominent being two large, knarled larches, curiously branched, which originally came from the Tyrol. The principal entrance to the mansion is flanked on each side by more splendid old trees with towering branches forming a natural archway of great beauty. The other approach to the House and the whole policies are enclosed by beech hedges, well-trimmed and kept, which gives them a pleasing look. Indeed, the whole area round Glenbervie House is one of the most attractive in the parish, the landscape being diversified by wood, river, meadow and hedge-row.

It was a gardener of Glenbervie House, Mr David Gairns, who developed the famous 'Glenbervie Early' potato, an agricultural distinction which enjoyed a splendid reputation from about 1850. The potato was acknowledged a leading favourite, especially in north-eastern counties, although the original character of the variety is doubtless now considerably altered.

Original Proprietors of Norman Lineage

The original proprietors are said to have been the Olifards or Oliphants as the name is now written, Norman colonists who were given lands by King David 1. Osbert Olifard was Sheriff of the district in the time of Malcolm IV. His only daughter became the wife of Hew, the lord of Arbuthnott, and thus was the female progenitor of the noble family of that name and title.

How much reliance can be placed on the story on the mural which is in the burial-aisle of the Douglasses in Glenbervie churchyard it is hard to say (see page 290), but records, accepted by historians, show that the Olifards were followed in Glenbervie Castle in the 12th century by a baron named Melville whose family reputedly settled in the Lothians in the reign of David I. This view is taken by Chalmers in his *Caledonia*: he avers that the family was of Anglo-Norman lineage, originally surnamed 'Male'. The name of Melville he derives from 'Maleville', the title given to their special domains. In Crawford's *Peerage*, however, the Hungarian origin (see page 291), attributed to them on the mural, is accepted. During the reign of William the Lion the family held lands both in Angus and in the Mearns.

Philip, called by some chroniclers the founder of the Mearns branch of the family, and certainly one of its earliest members, is said to have been the son of Galfrid of Melville, a prominent personality in the reigns of David I and the two succeeding monarchs. Some years prior to 1200 A.D. he married Eva, daughter of Walter, the son of Sibbald, and from her received the lands of Monethyn (Mondynes) in the parish of Fordoun. Their son, Philip, in 1222 became Sheriff of the Mearns, holding that post until 1240 and a year later becoming joint justiciary of Scotland with Richard of Montealt. In the official records he is referred to as Philip of Maleville of Mondynes.

King Edward Spends the Night

On July 12, 1296, King Edward I left the Castle of Kincardine on his journey north through Scotland to receive the submission of the Scottish chiefs and, in the words of his *Diary of his Journey*, passed to the *mountagne of Glowberwy*. Although there is no definite record of the point, it is generally assumed that it was at the Castle of Glenbervie that he spent the night. The Castle at the time was the property of a descendant of Philip de Maleville, one *Johannes de Maleuil miles*, probably *John de Malevill, Chevalier, the laird of Glenbervie*, who paid homage to Edward at Lumphanan in Aberdeenshire on July 21st, 1296, nine days after the monarch's visit to his castle. Sir Francis Palgrave records that John of Stowe, parson of Glenbervie kirk, followed the example of his laird on the same day. The minister was apparently determined to convince the king of his loyalty for he followed him southwards to Berwick-upon-Tweed and again took the oath of allegiance. History does not, however, record if his fealty was attended by any great material or spiritual reward!

Melvilles, Auchinlecks and Douglasses

The original Mearns branch of the Melville family survived in the male line until 1468, and it was one of these later lairds, the luckless John Melville, who in 1420 was the unpopular Sheriff of the Mearns who was *sodden and suppit in bree*, traditionally boiled alive as he was upon the Hill of Garvock by four of his obstreperous neighbour barons who were thereafter outlawed for their crime.

By the marriage in 1468 of Elizabeth, only daughter of Alexander Melville, to Sir Alexander Auchinleck, the old family of Auchinleck succeeded to the estates, and in like manner in 1492 the lands of Glenbervie came to the son of Archibald, Earl of Angus, Sir William Douglas of Braidwood, who married Sir Andrew Auchinleck's grand-daughter. So started a long succession of Douglas lairds, and it was ultimately through the Glenbervie branch of the Douglasses that the line of the Earls of Angus was carried on. Of interest, too, is the fact that a grandson of Sir William Douglas of Braidwood, also Sir William Douglas, became ninth Earl of Angus and was the progenitor of many of Scotland's famous families including that of the Dukes of Hamilton and Douglas.

The castle in its rural seclusion seems to have escaped the violence which often erupted around it. But there was one exception. During the troublous times of the latter half of the 16th century Glenbervie, in common with many other places, suffered from the violence of the redoubtable Adam Gordon of Auchindoun (the 'Edom o' Gordon' of the ballad) who, *playing King Herod in the north upon the King's friends and gude subjects*, made an incursion into the Mearns on behalf of the deposed Mary Queen of Scots in 1571. At the head of a force of infantry and *a fyne trowpe of chosin horsemen* he besieged *the castell of Glenbervie in the Mernis*, laid waste the Douglas lands and carried off their goods and chattels. The owner, Sir William of Douglas, was absent at the time. This and other successes reaching the ears of the Regent, the Lords of the Privy Council granted a commission to Robert, Earl of Crawford, Patrick, Lord Lindsay, the Earl of Buchan and others *to conserve the lieges* of Kincardine *in warlike manner* at the kirk of Fordoun *to resist the treasonable attempts of the said traitor*.

The estate was briefly in the hands of the Burnetts before it was sold in 1721 to the Nicolsons one of whom, Sir William, became a father at 93 when his daughter was 66. Today Glenbervie House is the centre of a 2,500 acre estate employing ten people and is the home of Mrs Patience M. Badenoch-Nicolson. Around 1,000 acres of the estate are leased to tenant farmers, and much of the rest of the land in the parish is owned by private farmers.

Glenbervie Church

And so on to reach in just under half a mile the church of Glenbervie standing alone on a cheerless site at the fork to Brae School. It was built in 1826 and dedicated to St Michael. Although somewhat barn-like perhaps, it is quite a handsome structure, with pinnacled angles and belfry and Gothic perpendicular buttresses. It retains inside its handsome old lighting standards and oil lamps although the building is now supplied with electricity. One of the pews bears a carved plaque from the old kirk with the date 1620. Glenbervie is now a joint charge with Fettercairn and Fordoun, the minister, the Rev. Kenneth Tyson, having a huge rural parish to cover.

Inches

Burns enthusiasts may care to deviate along the fork to the right for just under two miles, there and back, for nine-tenths of a mile brings us to the road end to the farm of Inches (where we can turn), yet another Glenbervie farm with Burns associations.

Inches was once in the possession of James Burness, son of William Burnes, Burns' great-grand-uncle who took it in 1705. The name Inches, as does the name Inchbreck, indicates that at one time the farms were built on rises in the bogs, high and dry in the surrounding watery country. Farms which have the word 'Inch' as part of their names figure all over the county, and one is reminded that a thousand years ago and more from the North Esk to Drumlithie and from the Grampians to Garvock was a morass. In prehistoric times the Howe of the Mearns must have been almost covered by water which in the course of countless ages was drained away by the Esk, the Carron and the Bervie.

Facing Inches on the other side of the road is Droop Hill (732 ft.) disposed around the OS triangulation station on the summit of which there are at least thirty cairns ranging from 5 ft. to 21¼ ft. in diameter by up to 1¼ ft. in height.

Upper Kinmonth

About 800 yards beyond Inches to the east can be seen the farm of Upper Kinmonth which could have been, and probably was, the Blawearie of Gibbon's *Sunset Song*. Remember?

> '*Out of the World and into Blawearie' they said in Kinraddie, and faith! it was course land and lonely up there on the brae, fifty – sixty acres of it, forbye the moor. . . . The biggings of it stood fine and compact one side of the close, the midden was back of them, and across the close was the house, a fell brave house for a little place, it had three storeys and a good kitchen and a fair stretch of garden between it and the Blawearie road. There were beech trees there, three of them, one was close over against the house, and the garden hedges grew as bonny with honeysuckle of a summer as ever you saw; and if you could have lived on the smell of honeysuckle you might have farmed the bit place with profit.*

Not that that describes Upper Kinmonth exactly, but it is a marvellous transcript of a Mearns farm.

A Successful Factory Enterprise

Those of us who wish to continue with the main route, however, face at the Glenbervie church fork low, attractive factory buildings of Macphie and Company, established in 1973 to make special additives for commercial baking. The enterprise is a successful one, employing ninety people and with a turnover of £4½ million. In 1981 the company won a *Sunday Times* 'Enterprising Britain' award.

As the wife of the owner, Mr Stewart Macphie of Knockhill House (the old manse of the parish of Glenbervie), is a niece of Mrs Nicolson of Glenbervie House, one day she will inherit the castle and, with her husband, be called upon to run the estate. His sound business skills will stand him in good stead.

The Knock Hill

In front of us is the Knock Hill from which an extensive view can be obtained. Occupying a remarkable position, it is visible from the upper end of Strathmore and commands the valley more effectively than any other hill at the north-east end of the Grampians. Furthermore, it blocks the way to the north by the coast route on the east and also the bridle-paths by Glenfarquhar. The Bervie Water sweeps round the eastern base of this interesting hill.

What are probably the remains of a cairn, measuring about 20 ft. in diameter by 1 ft. in height, are situated some 40 yards east of the summit. It is also just possible that an ancient fortress stood on the Knock Hill, the seat of Malpeder or Macpender MacLean, Thane or Earl of the Mearns in the 11th century, although it is unlikely to have been his principal stronghold. Certainly names in the immediate neighbourhood are significant of former greatness – King's Croft and, in connection with religion, Killhillock, Killfield, Monk's Park and Abbeyton. It was on the Knock Hill, according to tradition, that the ecclesiastical authorities in a remote age had intended to build the parish church but, having been repeatedly counselled by unseen powers to desist, they wisely did so.

Each night, the legend tells us, the stones were knocked down, kelpies and warlocks being heard to chant,

> *Gang farrer doon*
> *Tae Fordoun toon*
> *And big yer kirkie there.*

On the Knock Hill was found a round stone the size of a tennis ball and dated 1500 to 2000 B.C. It is now in the National Museum of Antiquities, Edinburgh.

The Old Church of Glenbervie

Resuming our journey, in only ninety yards we turn left along the 130 yard drive to the old parish kirk of Glenbervie, now an ivy-clad ruin, which once belonged to the diocese of Brechin. All that remains are the east end, now adapted for use as a burial-aisle, and a small portion of the south wall, now used as a family memorial. The old kirk was partly rebuilt and enlarged in the late 18th century. The ruins are situated on a plateau near a bend in the Bervie Water and under the dark shadow of Knock Hill, bounded on one side by the approach to the Manse by which it is overlooked, on the other, at the foot of the slope, by a prattling burn which runs cheerily through a short glen to join the Bervie.

In this lovely wooded country stood the ancient Kirkton itself, erected a barony in 1326 by the Douglas family and once the centre of the parish amid all the essentials of a mediaeval manorial centre – the kirk on the green haugh, the manse, the laird's doocot, the mill and, on the other side of the stream and across the tree-lined gorge formed by the Pilkettie Burn, the castle overlooking the ford at the junction of the two streams. What a magnificent view of it we obtain from the kirkyard! The old kirk was abandoned in 1826, and while the present one was being built, it was in this kirkyard that the Rev. James Drummond preached throughout what was fortunately a dry summer and began a line of ministers which continued to 1948 when his grandson, the Rev. Patrick Lindsay Gordon, died.

Glenbervie Kirkyard

In the quietness of this ancient kirkyard of Glenbervie are, dotted all around, the tombstones of Burns' ancestors and relatives by blood and marriage. Two famous ones are of special interest only some thirty-five yards away, erected by North-east Burns Clubs in an enclosure to protect them from weathering. They mark the graves of two brothers who worked for upwards of a hundred years the two small farms we have visited on the Braes of Glenbervie. The elder was William Burness of Bogjurgan, the poet's great-grand-uncle, while the younger was James Burness of Brawliemuir, his great-grandfather, the direct ancestor of the poet. The gravestone of the latter, under the conventional death's-head, hour-glass, mattock, spade, etc, bears the inscription:

MEMENTO MORI

J.B.   *M.F.*
Here under lyes the   *Also the body of*
body of James Burness   *Margaret Falconer,*
who was Tenant in   *his spouse, who*
Bralinmuir, who   *departed this life the*
died ye 23 of January,   *28th of December, 1749,*
1743. Aged 83 years   *aged 90 years.*

Altho' our Bodys worms destroy – Our
reins consumed be,
Yet in our flesh and with our eyes – Shall
our Redeemer see.

Here is the grave of Thomas Burnes, son to the above, who departed this life June ye 8th, 1734, aged 29 years. Also his lawful and only daughter Margarett, who departed this life March ye 24th, 1741, aged 8 years.

The enclosure erected by North-east Burns Clubs to protect the graves of two brothers of special interest in the ancient kirkyard of Glenbervie. One was James Burness of Brawliemuir, the great-grandfather of Robert Burns; the other was William Burness of Bogjurgan, Burns' great-granduncle. In the background is Glenbervie House.

The neighbouring decorated tombstone names William Burnes, tenant in Bogjurgan and great-grand-uncle of the poet, and his wife, Christian Fotheringham. On the upper part of the stone are the initials W.B. and C.F. beneath a heart, richly sculptured. Beneath are the words, *Here under lies ? Burnes 1715.* At the base is the date 1719 between sculptured cross-bones.

It was over a hundred years ago that these stones were found close together, crumbling and half buried in the churchyard. In 1885 they were lifted from the ground and fastened side by side to sandstone tables with iron bands and cement. In less than five years the surface of the stones started to flake off, and at last, in 1951, after various methods of preservation had been explored in vain, the stones were enclosed in casings of cement with an inscription on the outside. In 1968 they were placed under a canopy, as we have said, and protected by a grille.

Burial-aisle of the Douglasses

Also in Glenbervie kirkyard and within a few yards of the tomb-stones of the ancestors of Robert Burns can be seen the interesting burial-aisle of the Douglasses which provides an excellent starting point for a brief survey of the rich historical associations of this part of the Mearns. Among the memorials in the aisle is a curious mural tablet, described by Jervise as

> *a renewed monument of date 1680 with some curious mortuary ornaments and the armorial bearings of the ancient families of Hassa, Olifart, Melville, Auchleck and Douglas.*

A feature of this tablet is a lengthy inscription in old contracted Latin which describes the many brave deeds and the matrimonial alliances and records of the lairds and ladies of Glenbervie from the year 730 A.D. Although the tale unfolded in this inscription is not accepted as being wholly correct historically, certain parts of it are worthy of mention as authentic records of a later date can to some extent be reconciled with them.

Origin of the Arbuthnott Family

According to the tablet Hew Hassa, a German, came to Scotland around 730 and married Germunda Dervisa, the heiress of Glen-bervie. The male line from that union ended in 1012 when a Hassa fell at the Battle of Barrie in conflict with the invading Danes. Helen, last of the Hassas, is recorded as having married Duncan Oliphard, a captain of the Mearns (*Merniae Decurio*), and it is said that from Margaret, their great-granddaughter, the present family of Arbuthnott is descended. It was a great-granddaughter of Helen Hassa and the gallant captain who married James Melville, a Hungarian noble. Hew, the son of this marriage, wed the daughter of Malpeder, Thane of the Mearns, who murdered King Duncan II in 1095. The fact that Malpeder figures on this mural tablet might seem to indicate that Mondynes was probably the original of Glenbervie.

Two Thriving Institutions

Before we leave Glenbervie, let us remember a thriving local institution, founded in 1917, that still continues – the well-supported Glenbervie Ploughing Association which maintains with its annual matches that pride in the straight furrow that is bred in the bone in the Mearns. The social gatherings which follow are eagerly looked forward to. Let us also remember the Glenbervie Amateur Hortus Club, founded in 1887. The Club's annual show in August still continues with unabated vigour.

Hawkhill and James Burness, Boxmaster

230 yards along our road is a fork to the right which leads in only two-fifths of a mile to another farm with Burns associations – Hawkhill. As with West Kinmonth Burns enthusiasts may wish a closer inspection by deviating for three-quarters of a mile and more, but for most of us it will be sufficient to carry on our way for in just less than half a mile from the fork of which we speak we shall be able to see Hawkhill quite clearly on our right through an opening in the trees.

Hawkhill was the farm once owned by James Burness, son of William Burness of Bogjurgan and uncle of the young William Burnes of Clochnahill, later to be father of the poet. James Burness was so highly esteemed in the Glenbervie of his day as to be *elected Boxmaster by a majoritie of votes*. So are we informed by the Glenbervie Kirk Register of Discipline and Accounts, dated June 20th, 1746. The office of Boxmaster or Treasurer seems to have been of some consequence in those days. Nor is this to be wondered at when he held kirk session money. On October 22nd of the following year the session again met and

> *verified all their accounts since their last meeting on that account, and found them all right, at which time James Burness of Hawkhill resigned his office as Boxmaster after*

> *he had given a clear account and reckoning to the rest of the members. The elders hold themselves content and well satisfied and oblidged themselves to pay to the said James Burness the sum of nine pounds thirteen shillings and four pennies Scots, he having disbursed so much more to the poor than he received on their account. It was then put on the Leit whether John Hog, James Burness or Archibald Reith should be Boxmaster, and James Burness was chosen by a majority of votes.*

This would seem to indicate that James Burness not only performed all the duties of Boxmaster with exactness and care but also gained the confidence of the kirk session in this important position in the parish. Indeed, another entry, dated October 31st, 1747, reveals that Burness retained this office for over twenty years.

> *This day the Session, being met and constitute, granted a discharge to James Burness in Hawkhill for faithfully discharging the office of Treasurer from the time of his incumbency to this present time.*

From entries quoted above and from frequent references to his *distributions* throughout the Glenbervie Register during the time he was Treasurer it would seem that James Burness not only justified the confidence placed in him by the kirk session but also inspired such a trust in his prudence and knowledge of human nature as to be allowed to spend money from the session funds on the poor of his own accord, as is illustrated by the following entries:

Given out to sundry poor by Hawkhill	£14	12	2
Hawkhill's expenses for going to Aberdeen	3	12	0
Disbursed by Hawkhill	33	8	7

It is to be remarked that Hawkhill generally paid out more than other members of the kirk session.

The Causeway of Auchtochter

Three-quarters of a mile past the fork to Hawkhill we pass the farm of Auchtochter on our right, once farmed by James Burness of Hawkhill and great-uncle of Robert Burns. Here early last century there existed a large causeway, made of stones, stumps and tussocks, which some used to believe dated from Roman times, arguing that legions followed this route to Raedykes. There were other such causeways in the parish at the time, one being discovered leading from the Forthie Water towards Bankhead, 3¾ miles to the east, when the bogs of Thriepland were drained.

Picturesque Auchenblae

In just under a mile we crest the shoulder of Herscha Hill to be rewarded with a wonderful panoramic view of Auchenblae, nestling picturesquely below in a superb situation at the northern end of the great wooded ridge of the hill of Strathfinella prominent on its western side. Conspicuous in the foreground are the farm of Myreside[1] and the distinctive golf course seventh hole Fa' Hillocks mound on the south side of which in 1862 or 1863 a cinerary urn was found containing burnt ashes and fragments of bones. Another mile and a quarter and we find ourselves in the middle of the old-world village of Auchenblae.

The only village in the parish of Fordoun, Auchenblae lies between the foot-hills of the Grampians and the Howe o' the Mearns, standing on gently rising ground on the north bank of the Luther. Local scenery was described by Dr James Beattie (1735-1803) in his Spenserean poem, *The Minstrel*. A native of Laurencekirk (see page 447), he was parish schoolmaster here from 1753 to 1758. The following lines, it is said, he composed in the romantic dell of Fordoun.

> *Thy shades, thy silence, now be mine,*
> *Thy charms my only theme;*
> *My haunt the hollow cliff whose pine*
> *Waves o'er the gloomy stream.*

Some seventy years later Auchenblae was again described in the second *Statistical Account* as *a clean and thriving place* which contained many substantial houses. The government was rested, we are told, in a bailie appointed by the Earl of Kintore who was the superior, and the population amounted to 550 persons, partly employed in manufacturing linen and linen yarn, in the retail trade and as artisans and occupiers of croft land adjoining the village.

Gone are the outstanding Hortus Club Flower Show and the Highland Games held in the heyday of Auchenblae in its five-acre park just outside the village (now used as a football pitch and picnic spot), gone is Johnny Logie and his brass band, but the village is still the village beautiful with obvious attractions, ushering the modern tourist into such beauty spots within easy reach as Strathfinella and the lovely, wooded glen of Drumtochty.

[1] The cropmark of what may be an oval enclosure, measuring just over 100 yards from east to west, is revealed around the north and west sides of a knoll immediately north-west of Myreside farmhouse.

A History from Early Times

Auchenblae, along with Fordoun, inherits the traditions of what was once the most important district in the Mearns. It lies in an area steeped in history. Fordoun parish with its links with St Palladius was the cradle of Christianity in the Mearns and that at a time when the greater part of Scotland was still pagan. Auchenblae boasted, too, two important hiring fairs at Whitsunday and Martinmas. Once it was the ancient ecclesiastical centre of the court of Kincardine and, although it was founded and laid out in its present form by the Earl of Kintore about 1770 (the population was only 100 in 1791!) the history of Auchenblae, like that of most Kincardineshire villages, goes back to early times, doubtless originating from its proximity to the kirk of Palladius. It is repeatedly mentioned in deeds dating back some 470 years, and there are on record leases of the place, granted by the powerful barons of the barony, the abbots of Aberbrothok, long before the time when, as part of the barony lands, it came into the possession of the Falconers of Haulkerton, the hereditary keepers of the royal falcons. Thus, by lease dated September 29th, 1506, George, the Abbot of Arbroath as superior, assigned to John Strathquhyn (Strachan) and Mariot Martin, his spouse, *our new town of Auchinblay* for the whole period of their life upon condition of their paying three pounds, six shillings and eightpence of Scotch money on the festivals of Pentecost and St Martin, with a *rynmart weddyr* (the carcass of a wether) and all the other burdens of husbandry. *And if they shall be found remiss in paying, or acting rebelliously, it shall be in our* (the Abbot's) *power to dispone*. In 1510 the same parties had a renewal of their lease to which was added *le Awrne Aylhous* within the barony of Newlands. In 1525 John Strachan and his spouse, Egidia Gardin, and her son, James Gardin, had a lease of the same and some other adjoining lands from Abbot David, afterwards the celebrated Cardinal Beaton.

Auchenblae was quite a centre, it seems, for rebels during the 1745-6 Rebellion. William Brand, merchant, William Walker, *residenter*, and Robert Wylie, brewer and merchant, were all concerned in proclaiming the Pretender at Fordoun Cross, Brand offering money to anybody who would read his manifesto. The two first named were also guilty of ringing the kirk bell!

A Village in the Forefront of Progress

By old-time standards Auchenblae was once a place of some consequence, and certainly a place of activity. About 1840 private enterprise put the village in the forefront of progress for it was one of the first places in the north to have its own gas-works. At a time when gas as a means of light was a rare thing in country towns, an enterprising bank agent, named James Farquharson, startled the inhabitants of the village by equipping a spinning-works which he owned with gaslight at his own expense and by proposing to extend the benefit of this progressive step to the village in general.

The economic difficulty under which the project was launched met with a considerable measure of prejudice. The villagers of the Mearns had been familiar even up to this time with nothing more complicated than the old-fashioned oil crusie, a black iron lamp with a rush wick, augmented on special occasions such as Auld-Yule etc, with tallow candles. They did not therefore at first take kindly to this newfangled means of illumination. Indeed, a few of the more conservative who never became reconciled to what they regarded as a dangerous innovation would not hear of its admission to their homes. The disadvantage of being far from the coal producing districts was even more acute in those days than it is today. And since Auchenblae had not the advantage of railway communication, it was a matter of considerable expense to transport the necessary raw material to the spot. Nevertheless, the gas-works maintained a state of efficiency although in subsequent years, when transferred to new ownership, this was not so. With the coming of an improved type of paraffin lamp the use of gas in Auchenblae gradually died out. (Thirty years later Auchenblae, also by private enterprise, acquired its first piped water-supply, drawn from a spring on the farm of Newlands.)

A Venture in Flax-spinning

In its earlier years Auchenblae was designed as a manufacturing or 'mill town', and one of the earliest attempts of another kind in Scotland also took place in the village – a venture in flax spinning. The mill, established in 1795, was equipped with all the latest appliances, and its owner, besides having the necessary capital, possessed a liberal measure of enterprise and energy. As water-power was the only means of generation for industry in the district at the time, the site chosen for the factory had natural advantages. The ground lay on the right bank of the West Burn which, rising in the romantic glen of Drumtochty, flows through the valley, known as the Den, skirting the western side of the village. From this the factory was assured of ample supply, and a dam was built to conserve the water in abnormally dry seasons. Within the following half century, however, steam came into its own.

Apart from a few local women and girls skilled labour was drafted in, chiefly from the larger manufacturing towns of Angus; the influx of people of both sexes is reflected today in the survival of names in the district which were unknown before this time.

Maledictions and a Bullock's Horn

The factory was surmounted with a belfry fitted with a bell the function of which was that of a modern factory hooter – to summon the spinners to work at the appointed hour, to herald meal hours and to announce the end of the working-day. But this was not the only precaution taken to ensure that there were no sluggards; it was the duty of the mill overseer to rouse the workers from their slumbers. With a huge bullock's horn he used to make a morning round of the village. There were always some whom the most vigorous blasts of the horn failed to arouse, but for the benefit of these William Herries (for many years the head of the works) used to apply the heavy end of the horn to doors and windows where the slumberers were quartered. This had the desired effect, but needless to say it also wakened irate householders who had nothing to do with the factory. Despite the maledictions of some of those villagers treated to such a rude awakening, however, William Herries was remembered as an honest and conscientious man who never willingly gave offence. The spinning-mill kept going until the end of the 19th century when it was converted into a distillery where was produced the fine blend of Auchenblae Highland Whisky.

'So Glory's Thrill is O'er'

Eventually came the railway, however, and Auchenblae was suddenly off the beaten track. Its glory began to depart, thanks to the ease with which larger centres could be reached by man and by stock. Paldy Fair continued to be quite an event until the days of the drover and the country track were superseded and then, like many more similar markets, it too began to decline. In the 'twenties' of this century the last bones of the skeleton ceased to rattle.

To add insult to injury the mill had been closed since 1843, and the depression of the 1930's decreed that the trump-card of the village, the distillery, should close too. Eventually it was sold to a demolition agent. The very little that is left now to show where the distillery and the spinning-mill once stood may be seen today in the Den of Auchenblae for in fact both of them (and for good measure the gas-works!) stood more or less on the same site, the gas-works and the spinning-mill operating at the same time in the first place and, after additions and alterations, later becoming the distillery. Beside the ruin stands 'Mayfield', commonly called 'Distillery House' and built originally for the manager of the spinning-mill while the dam (now dry) which provided the power supply for the distillery may be seen at the top of the Den.

With ever-increasing transport facilities and the desire which came with them to seek relaxation farther afield, the village has become a quiet backwater for the few whose livelihood means they have to reside in the area and a casual stopping place for tourists who have deviated from the usual routes. Already helping the village, however, is Drumtochty Forest where the Forestry Commission have established themselves well and truly. In years to come the Forest should provide considerable employment and bring to the area possibly greater prosperity than it has ever enjoyed before.

The picturesque village of Auchenblae as seen from the top of Gilbert's Hill.

297

Gilbert's Hill

Let us now proceed to the south end of the village until we reach the T-junction at the foot of Gilbert's Hill which with its War Memorial commands a fine view of the Market Square and other portions of the village. On the left shoulder about 1843 there existed a mound called the 'witch knap' to which every schoolboy who had any superstition left in him contributed a stone in passing, believing in witches or warlocks or even, it may be, in the worricow (the devil) himself!

> *Haud the Bible till his e'e;*
> *Ding him doon and gar him flee,*
> *For he's a fause deceitfu' loon*
> *Wi' reekit ribs and riven taes.*

An easy climb of some 200 yards will take you to the top if you start along the Fordoun Station road. From the top you will be able to see, quarter of a mile away to the north-east, Castle Hill, a steep-sided promontory between the Burnie Shag and the Hodden Burn. Here a castle is said to have stood.

The Ancient Kirkton of Fordoun

Turning right at the T-junction, we again fork right in a moment up the Laurencekirk road towards the prominent parish church of Fordoun, commandingly situated on its knoll. About this historic area there is still, indeed, an old-time atmosphere for, dominated by the church, something of the ancient Kirkton of Fordoun is still to be seen. The old 18th century inn, a pleasant two-storey block with attic gable, is now occupied as a home and renamed Kirkton of Fordoun farmhouse. In this inn Robert Burns spent a night in a box-bed with doors on it, now converted into a wardrobe. The window of the room in which our national bard slept is at the extreme left-hand end of the upper floor as one faces the building. Also dating from the 18th century is the old single storey parish school with its tiny belfry in the middle of the roof. It is now used as the meals centre kitchen for Fordoun school. A later school which was enlarged in 1851 and closed in 1891 had a playground laid out in the open space between the churchyard and the old inn. Of this school no trace is left. Also in a corner of the kirk square is the old soup-kitchen (now the school canteen) opened in 1894 for children who had to walk a long way to school. A plate of soup cost one halfpenny a day. You are in a different world today for, up until the beginning of the 19th century, the ancient mediaeval settlement of

298

Fordoun formed a complete square here with, in front of the church, its market cross in the middle.

Queen Mary Creates Fordoun a Free Burgh

The name Fordoun – anciently spelt Fotherdun or Fordun – has existed from the earliest date of which there is record and is normally thought to be of Gaelic origin. By some it is said to signify 'the anterior or prominent hill' or 'the promontory hill or headland', a significance not inappropriate to the position occupied by the church at the foot of historic Strathfinella. The parish, or at any rate the district adjacent to the church, was at one time known as Palladius or Paldy Parish. This fact is attributed by Auld Kirk historians to a subterfuge of the Catholics who, according to them, wished it to be thought that the parishes wherein they had built churches were placed under the patronage of the saints to whom their places of worship were dedicated.

The village was created a free burgh of barony *for ever* by Mary Queen of Scots on June 22nd, 1554:

> *which town lies at the foot of the Mounth and woodlands called Crynecors, and where the Queen's lieges coming over the said Mounth have received entertainment – for their better entertainment and for the government of the said town, she erects the town of Fordoun and the lands thereof into a free burgh and barony for ever, and granted to the inhabitants liberty to buy and sell, etc. and that there be free burgesses, with power to elect baillies, etc. annually, with power to have a market cross and a weekly market on Saturday, with three fairs annually, on St Palladius day and the octaves thereof, with tolls etc. and with power to the said Robert* (Beittoun or Beaton of Creich, Captain of the Palace of Falkland) *and his heirs to set in heritage the said lands in burrow roods.*

In a charter to Wishart of Pitarrow on April 7th, 1603, James I *de novo* erected Fordoun into a free burgh of barony, giving the power of buying and selling to the inhabitants and other benefits as listed above. The free fair was to be on July 6th and *the whole above-written into the free barony of Pitarro.*

Queen Mary also sanctioned the marketing of wools, skins, hides and salmon within the county. This is interesting because, as these goods were discharged at Stonehaven, Gourdon, and other coastal harbours and marketed daily at Fordoun, Fetteresso and Fettercairn, the town of Montrose had as far back as 1506 petitioned the king against loss by this attack on their monopolistic practices. Even in 1351 King David II had made an *inhibitioun for halding off mercats of stapillhand* (staple-ware[1]) *at Fordoune*, it being found in the previous justice ayre (court of circuit judges) held at Montrose that common markets were held thereat to the king's prejudice and the loss of the burgh of Montrose. The king strictly forbade the sale of wool, skins etc, at Fordoun thereafter or in any other place *within the marches and bounds of our burgh of Monros*.

Fordoun Parish Church

Let us enter the churchyard of Fordoun Parish Church with its associations with St Palladius and Paldy Fair. It was erected in 1830 from plans by John Smith of Aberdeen and is built in the Gothic perpendicular style, battlemented, pinnacled and with a handsome, square bell-tower 93 ft. high. The church is the successor to a small church of considerable antiquity which occupied the present site and was demolished in 1787. At this church encamped Montrose when he had crossed the Dee and the Grampians after the battle of Alford, and in the vicinity too, annually on July 6th, a fair called Lady Market was held in the 18th century.

Curious Sculptured Stone

In the vestibule of Fordoun Church, fixed to the north wall with iron hooks, is preserved a fine sculptured slab of freestone of undoubted antiquity which was discovered in 1787 acting as the base of the pulpit of the old church which was being demolished preparatory to its being rebuilt. It had probably been hidden there for safety at the time of the Reformation. Thought to be of little account, it was thrown aside in Palladius' chapel where it remained until placed in its present position.

The curious stone, about 6 ft. in length by 2 ft. 11 ins. in breadth, and fully 4 ins. in thickness, bears various figures of armed horsemen and animals of the chase together with quaint emblems, cut deeply and with some degree of elegance. In his *Account of Some Sculptured Pillars in the Northern Part of Scotland* (1846) Professor Stuart describes it thus:

---

[1] Such goods as wool, leather, lead and tin which were the monopoly of the Staple, that is the town or place appointed by royal authority in which was a body of merchants who had the exclusive right of purchase of certain classes of goods destined for export.

On the top there is ... some animal resembling a serpent, and on the left side ... some written characters so ... defaced as to be ... illegible, and which may have been continued on the right side now ... broken off. Under these have been three squares filled with very pretty tracery, the first and third probably similar, the last being wanting, while the one in the middle is of a different form but equally well executed. The centre compartment appears to contain the principal figure of the group, being placed in a separate square, and represents a warrior on horseback with a spear in his hand. On either side is another horseman with a spear in the same attitude, but who appear in dress and otherwise to be of inferior rank to the chief figure. Above the horseman on the left is seen the figure of some wild animal, but so rudely drawn that it cannot be distinguished. Below on the left is distinctly seen the hinder parts of the body of a large dog, and opposite a very fine representation of two circles, joined together like a pair of eyes or spectacles, and filled with ornamental carving. And last of all, through the centre passes the connecting line of the three before noticed, the upper line terminating in a point like a spear, while the under one is somewhat different.

A Monument to Commemorate Kenneth III?

Professor Stuart and local tradition assert that this strange and interesting stone with its warlike symbols was a monument to commemorate the death of Kenneth III while hunting in 994 A.D. (see page 355). The slab is supposed to have marked his grave near the shrine of the saint. In the hunt which is portrayed the mutilated figure below, it is argued, is plainly a greyhound, and the animal above either another or the quarry. Might the principal figure be the king, the two other horsemen his murderers? Stuart knows of no other event in early Scottish history and connected with this part of the country which would justify such a memorial. And if the figure at the top really represents a serpent, might it allude to the art of Finella? Certainly the engraving seems of the antiquity required.

But of all this there is no evidence whatsoever. To begin with, some chroniclers relate that Kenneth and certain early Scottish kings who met their death in this part of Scotland were buried in Iona and, despite the fact that the stone differs from the great majority of similarly sculptured monuments by being carved only on one side, one cannot believe that originally it might have been placed horizontally to cover the grave of some old Celtic saint of the district. Nor is it an example of a well-known class of monument of the Celtic church although many of the devices on it are similar to those of other Scottish sculptured stones not only in the character of the pictures but in the type of scroll, and the style of ornamentation is the same as the ornamentation on illuminated pages of Irish manuscripts of the Gospels of the 8th, 9th and 10th centuries.

A Pictish Symbol Stone

The stone is, in fact, a good deal earlier than Kenneth's time and is a rather early example, part incised, part relief, of a Pictish symbol stone, belonging, according to Professor K. H. Jackson, to the middle of the 8th century and one of only eight Pictish stones found in Kincardineshire. Another is at Auquhollie;[1] the remainder, found at Dunnicaer, at Banchory House (see page 10).

Pictish sculptures were classified at the beginning of the century by J. Romilly Allen into three main categories. Class I stones, dating from 650 A.D., comprise simple, roughly dressed stones and boulders with characteristic symbols incised upon them. These predominate north of the Mounth, mostly in Aberdeenshire and the North-east. For the Mounth acted as a kind of artistic and cultural boundary between the Picts of the North and those of the South that cannot be ignored.

But the Fordoun stone reveals the budding of a more mature and quite distinctive Pictish art in that it is an example of a Class II stone which is more frequently found south of the Mounth. Of this type of stone that at Fordoun is the most northerly example. The stone Latin cross, carved in relief with deep hollows between the arms and interlace in the centre, shows the elaborate double disc and spear or Z-rod symbols (note the ornate ends of the Z-rod) together with the achievements of a most original development in Pictish art where the stone is used as a great page to portray a pictorial scene, in this case a hunting scene with dogs and warriors with their ornaments and equipment, on a scale and of a kind unknown in Western Europe at the time. The inspiration may have come from wall-painting in France or late Roman narrative manuscripts. A Class III stone omits symbols altogether, portraying only an elaborate scene or an early Christian cross.

The precise significance of symbol stones like this at Fordoun constitutes a long-standing problem in Scottish archaeology: were the symbols badges of rank or indicative of family or clan? All one

---

[1] See *Highways and Byways Round Stonehaven*, p. 200.

can say is that the controlling purpose behind such a stone apparently required monuments that could be erected at selected places in the open air.

The fine sculptured slab of freestone, 6 ft. by 2 ft. 11 ins. which is housed in Fordoun Church. The stone is the most northerly example of a Class II Pictish symbol stone. It belongs to the middle of the 8th century and portrays a hunting scene with dogs and warriors together with the elaborate double disc and spear or Z-rod Pictish symbols and with interlacement at the top.

A Fascinating Inscription

In 1893 an inscription of Irish type was discovered incised on the edge of the stone, written in Roman letters in a script of the 8th century current in early Christian Scotland – 'pidarnoin'. It is the well-known name, Idarnoin or Idarnon, which seems the same as other names which have appeared in historical sources, Edarnon or Ethernan or Itharnan, the founder and first bishop of Rathin in Buchan, and Itharnan, a Pict who died in 669 according to *The Annals of Ulster* and who may be the same person. One cannot believe it to be the same as Ternan. The Fordoun stone has a word 'ipe' prefixed to Adarnoin which is quite unknown: from the context it might mean 'and' or 'son of' or 'nephew of' or the like, but these are guesses.

Also suggested by Diack in his *Inscriptions of Pictland* is that the P stands for P(ax), an example of Christian piety which can be paralleled elsewhere, so that, as Idarnoin is dative, the translation might be 'Peace (be) with Idarnon'. A point which he mentions in confirmation of this reading is that the P and I are much the biggest letters in the line. It is to be assumed, therefore, that in the scene on the stone Idarnoin, whom the stone commemorates, is supposed to figure.

P Idα ᴘNOIN

A tracing of the fascinating inscription of Irish type, written in 8th century script, which is incised on the edge of the Pictish stone in Fordoun Church. The inscription may mean 'Peace be with Idarnon', Idarnon possibly being a bishop in what is today Buchan.

Monument to George Wishart

In the churchyard is the family burial-vault of the Carnegies, lairds of Pitarrow, and, near the entrance gate on the left, an impressive and tasteful monument, erected in 1850 to the memory of George Wishart, one of Scotland's seven Reformation martyrs. Burned at the stake as a heretic on March 1st, 1546, at the early age of thirty-three, he was one of the Wisharts of Pitarrow and probably worshipped in St Palladius' Chapel as a boy. The monument consists of a neat, polished granite column with a massive pedestal, flaming urn and appropriate spiral inscription.

The 'Mother Church' of the Mearns

The most interesting and historic building in the churchyard is, of course, the small, ancient chapel which is claimed to be the first Christian 'Mother Church' of the Mearns. Here in 431 A.D. the Celtic saint, Palladius, is traditionally said to have settled and to have introduced Christianity into the Mearns, ministering to the Pictish peoples of the district.

St Palladius – Mysterious and Misunderstood

There has long been a great deal of mystery and misunderstanding about the career of St Palladius, and much that has been written about him is fanciful and romantic. Some say he was a foreigner or a Roman missionary while, according to other sources, he was probably a Briton by birth, having sprung from the Gaulish family of Paladii. The first and almost the only authentic record regarding him was given by Prosper of Aquitaine in Gaul, a contemporary of the saint, who recorded that Palladius, a deacon of the Church, was ordained by Pope Celestine about 430 and sent by him two years later to the believing Scots as their first missionary bishop,

(ad Scotos in Christum credentes, ordinatus a Papa Celestine Palladius primus episcopus mittitur).

Much critical discussion has arisen as to whether the phrase, *ad Scotos*, relates not to Scotland but to Ireland which was known as Scotia in all documents prior to the 6th century. Again, the word *primus* ambiguously might signify first in dignity as well as in time (the sense taken by John of Fordoun and other writers).

The author of *Secunda Vita* in Father John Colgan's collection of saints' lives, *Acta Sanctorum*, writing about 900 A.D., certainly believes, as do the authorities collected in the calendars of Scottish saints, that Palladius led a wandering life, spending some time in Ireland and founding several churches. Rejected by the natives of Ireland, he allegedly sailed northwards and was accidentally swept by a great storm round Cape Wrath to find a resting-place on the eastern slope of the Grampians in the bleak, inhospitable region of the Mearns at a time when it was little more than a succession of bogs. You may say, of course, that this tale of so perilous and adventurous a voyage must be dismissed as pure fiction, and a myth it probably is.

Some say that Palladius, after a short time among the Picts, *was crowned with martyrdom there* (in Fordoun) a few years after 430, which is not impossible because the Picts, after their first conversion, now and again lapsed into heathendom so that even St Patrick himself speaks of *the apostate Picts*. There is, however, no positive proof as to where Palladius died or was murdered. According to the *Aberdeen Breviary* he is said to have died at Longforgan, near Dundee, while Jervise in his *History and Antiquities of the Mearns* (1858) asserts, *There is no reason to doubt that he died in Fordoun*. Others specify more exactly that *he died in the Plain of Girgin in a place which is called Forddun*.

His Association with Fordoun

Various theories are propounded regarding the associations of St Palladius with Fordoun: whether Christianity came to Fordoun with the saint himself between 400 and 500 A.D. or was brought by others in memory of his life and work is still a matter of conjecture among historians. John of Fordoun, writing nine centuries afterwards, claimed the saint entirely for Scotland, had no doubt but that St Palladius himself planted his cross here and, it is interesting to note, urged the Scottish church to commemorate him by keeping his festival. Yet, originator of Scottish history as he was (see page 174), Fordoun's account of Palladius must be set aside as altogether legendary, being influenced by the Romanising zeal so characteristic of the time.

Certainly zealous upholders of the reformed kirk were inclined to scoff at Palladius' dissemination of the gospel among the men of the Mearns and doubted the authenticity of the relics of the saint, questioning their method of arrival. Rather did they revere George Wishart and honour his father, James Wishart of Pitarrow, Justice-clerk under the sovereignty of King James V and his family, for throwing off the yoke of the Church of Rome soon after the martyrdom and *embracing the doctrine of the glorious Reformation*.

A Tradition Entitled to Consideration

St Palladius may indeed have been dispatched to convert the Picts, however, and perhaps a tradition that has come down to us through so many centuries is entitled to some consideration. The probability is that, finding the chief seat of tribal government of the northern branch of the Southern Picts at Fotherdun or Fordoun, as a matter of policy and by permission of the chief – who had probably begun to have an inkling of and a sneaking affection towards Christianity – he selected a site for his cell in the neighbouring glen and from there did most of his proselytising.

On the other hand, amid so much dubiety it is just as probable that Palladius died in Galloway on his way back to Rome and that he never set foot in the parish, his relics being brought to Scotland, as some would have us believe, by his disciple Ternan, a native of the Mearns. A whole misunderstanding may have arisen through confusion between Palladius, an emissary from Rome, and another missionary named Paldoc or Paldy, a disciple of St Ninian. Whatever version is correct none can say for certain, but it cannot be denied that the influence of the saint and the faith which we hold today took very firm root indeed in the soil of Kincardineshire in an age when pagan gods still held undisputed sway over the greater part of Scotland. Tradition, if it cannot be wholly substantiated through lack of authentic records, cannot be discounted for a similar reason.

That a Palladius was the patron saint of Fordoun, that his name has from time immemorial been indelibly associated with the chapel here by the Luther, with the well-known well in the manse grounds, and with the annual Paddy Fair which used to be held nearby in July are facts that cannot be left out of account. There were Christians in Caesar's household. Long before Palladius' time Roman troops had marched through the Mearns to their marching camp within a mile of this sequestered spot. Is it a thing impossible that he should have found his way hither as tradition asserts he did? What do you think?

The Original Church or Cell

The present-day roofless and rather inconspicuous ruined chapel of St Palladius (38 ft. 2 ins. by 18 ft. 2 ins.), dedicated to the saint and erected on the site of the shrine is, naturally, not the original one. There can be no doubt, however, that it is a structure of considerable antiquity despite its various architectural peculiarities and restorations from many different periods.

We shall never discover when the original church or cell here was built and dedicated to St Palladius, but it was probably somewhere between the 8th and 12th centuries and doubtless long before the 13th century. There are records of pilgrimages by many notable figures in the ancient history of our land in addition to Kenneth III who met his death journeying to or from this sacred spot. It is presumed that these pilgrims throughout the ages refreshed themselves at a well which stands in the manse grounds near the shrine and which itself bears the name of the patron saint. It is 24 ins. in diameter and 5 ft. 5 ins. in depth. A building which stood near the entrance to the churchyard and was pulled down in the first half of

the 19th century to make room for additional interments was reputed to be the abode of the monks who tended the chapel.

Oldest Parts of the Fabric

The oldest part of the present fabric which we see now is in all
probability part of what was the mediaeval church of Fordoun
belonging to the Archbishop of St Andrews, David de Bernham,
who dedicated the building on Monday, 17th October, 1244. The
chapel at this time was called a 'mensal church' as the teinds of the
parish were allotted for the support of the prelate's table. Parts of
the 13th century structure are, unquestionably, two deeply recessed
holes, about 9 ins. square, slightly above the eaves in the gable.
Their purpose is unknown, unless they are reminiscences of small
openings for light in the original Celtic oratories.

Ancient, too, may be the most mysterious feature of the chapel,
the small burial vault or crypt beneath with stone steps leading from
about the middle of the floor of the chapel, but this is difficult to
determine. It seems not unlikely that the supposed sacred relics of
the saint would be kept in this vault which is admirably adapted for
veneration by companies of pilgrims who would pass in at one door
and out the other. In the crypt are buried the families of Haulkerton
and Monboddo to the latter of whom there is a monument with a
quaint Latin inscription, and here is said to have been the burial-
place of the lords of Glenfarquhar on one side and the incumbents
of the parish on the other, the last incumbent to be buried here
being, it is said, the Rev. William Forbes in 1771. There is no trace,
however, of any tomb or memorial within its walls.

Restorations and Insertions

The widely divergent and often strongly expressed views of those on
different sides of Scotland's religious fence burst into active flame in
the 16th century. Roman Catholic writers describe how Archbishop
Shevez of St Andrews, when he made his pilgrimage to St Palladius'
Chapel half a century before the Reformation restored and decorated the building. One of his restorations in the 15th century Gothic
style was what is now a small mutilated piscina in the east wall,
terminating in a rude pointed arch hewn out of a single stone. In the
north wall towards the east end is another arched recess with
projecting sill measuring 6 ft. 8 ins. by about 2 ft. This would have
been a simple ambry in which the sacred vessels were kept although
it has been suggested that it may have been for holding the supposed
relics or ashes of the saint at some time. His bones Archbishop

Shevez is said to have collected as they were apparently *scattered about* at the time and put into a new silver shrine or, alternatively, as Butler puts it, *had the old shrine enriched with gold and silver stones.* (The revered remains of the saint were, however, destined again to be scattered to the winds when James Wishart of Pitarrow, father of the martyr, later seized the holy casket to enrich, so it is said, his own coffers. One writer of old adds a rider – *from which time the family never prospered.*)

Other later insertions in the chapel, probably in the 17th century, are the three rectangular windows in the north wall, the only windows of the chapel, splayed outside and with segmented rear arches inside. The masonry is similar to that of both the west and north doors. These have round-headed arches, the west one with a single splay and the north composed of two abutting stones in the true Gothic fashion which obtained in Scotland throughout the development of Gothic styles and which could not possibly have been earlier than the 12th century. It is likely that a large portion of the south wall was rebuilt in the 17th century too.

The ancient, historic chapel of St Palladius in the churchyard of Fordoun Parish Church which is claimed to be the first Christian 'Mother Church' of the Mearns. Here in 431 A.D. the Celtic saint Palladius is traditionally said to have settled and introduced Christianity into the Mearns. The original church or cell here was built probably somewhere between the 8th and 12th centuries, and the oldest part of the present fabric is in all likelihood part of the mediaeval church of Fordoun dedicated in 1244.

This restored edifice ascribed to Archbishop Shevez is reputed to have given way in 1787 and to have been replaced a year later by yet a third structure which in its turn fell into decay – leaving the chapel as we see it now. The roof collapsed around 1828 when the new parish church took its place. In 1837 the chapel was used as a joiner's shop, and it was allegedly used later as a dames' school – or so we are told. Perhaps the weather was more clement then.

Honesty requires me to record as a tailpiece that in 1978 three saints from the early days of Christianity in Scotland were struck off the list of saints by the Catholic Church because of doubts over their existence! After an intensive search which tested their historical basis and relevance to the diocese St Comgan and St Bean were excluded together with – you've guessed it! – St Palladius!

An Intriguing Coffin-slab

In 1872, when the chapel was being repaired, workmen came upon a slab which had been used, time out of memory, as the inside lintel of the north door of the chapel. It is about 4 ft. 10 ins. long by about 20 ins. in breadth. The figures are all incised, and (as shown by the accompanying woodcut) two of the objects represent a sword and a stringed bow and arrow. The shaft which runs up the middle of the stone, with a curious bulging base and ornamented circular top, is a common feature in coffin-slabs and possibly represents nothing else than simply a cross.

The bow and arrow may have reference to the office of a forest ranger, but it is likely that these objects adorned the tombs of others who had a taste for field sports: such attractions had been much greater in early times when there was but little cultivation in the Fordoun area. Records inform us that the monks of Arbroath employed their territory of Glenfarquhar for the pasture of cattle and swine, etc.

There is no knowing to whom the coffin-slab had belonged. It had probably covered the grave of some person of local importance, and it is just possible that it may have belonged either to the Wisharts or the Strachans who were contemporary lairds in Fordoun. The slab is presently in Inverurie museum.

Ministers 'Strak Vpoun the Heid'

Fordoun Church manse with its handsome Tudor Gothic south front and the manse garden are prettily situated on the summit of a steep bank skirted by a deep den in the bottom of which runs the Luther Water. The building of the original manse resulted in a criminal trial in 1601. Adam Walker, assistant and successor to the first Protestant minister in the parish, a Mr Patrick Boncle, was engaged with others in designing *ane manse* when he was *sett vpoun and invadit* by Sir David Wod of Craig,

> *knycht who wuth vtheris his complices to the number of twelf personnis or thairby strak him with the gaird of his sword vpon the heid, put violent handis on him and with his sword behind his back strak att him and flung him to the eird and with their drawin swordis hurt and woundit him in baith his hands to the effusion of his blude in grit quantitie.*

To another former minister a more amusing story is credited. Meeting a shepherd who for some time had been conspicuous by his absence from church, he expressed his grief at this lapse in attendance.

'*I dinna doot that,*' was John's reply.

'*And have you not been at church all this long while?*' the minister further persisted.

''*Od, aye hiv I. I've bin antran times* (occasionally) *in the kirk o' Fettercairn.*'

'*Well,*' rejoined the minister, '*I'm a shepherd myself and never like to see my sheep wandering into other folds and among other pastures.*'

'*Well,*' said John, '*that's a' the difference, ye ken. I niver min' far they gang if they're gettin' better girse.*'

Hearse House and the Inconvenience of Dying

Before we enter our car, let us walk a mere 150 yards up the hill on the Fettercairn road to see a building with a story which must have few parallels in the parochial history of the North-east. This is the square, ivy-clad building described as Hearse House. It is the story of a time when the inhabitants of Auchenblae and district were not so much concerned with the cost of living as with the inconvenience of dying because there was nothing more suitable in the immediate district to convey them to their last resting-place than a cart or wagon. So did two of the leading men of the parish in 1864 – Mr Edward of Nether Coullie and Mr Kidd of East Cairnbeg – raise a public subscription to provide a hearse for the community. Such was the response that they were able not only to purchase a one-horse vehicle, with harness, but also to build a shed for it. The bereaved family were expected to provide only a horse. The old hearse, of course, fell into disuse with the coming of the motor-car. For a number of years it lay in its shed, which with its contents was sold to the farmer of Kirkton about 1922. The hearse has long since been broken up, and Hearse House is now used as a garage.

A Bogus 'Scottish Camp'

And now back to our car. We should return to the foot of the hill below the church and turn right. In just about three-tenths of a mile, opposite the house called Whinhill on the other side of The Den and overlooking the Luther Water, was what the Ordnance Survey map called 'earthworks', situated perhaps 80 yards away through Drumsleed Wood on the top of the steep slope of Drumsleed Hill on our left. The site consisted of a low bank with a ditch about 100 yards in length from east to west, and in breadth just under half that extent. I deliberately use the past tense because, although the bank and ditch were once quite evident, I could not find them in 1978 as considerable ploughing and levelling of the ground had taken place.

By tradition this structure was thought to have been in ancient times an entrenchment, generally known as The Scottish Camp, capable of containing a large body of men and later to be magnified by Knox (*Topography of the Basin of the Tay*) into the remains of a fortification which had accommodated a large British strength. It was even alleged to have been a Roman camp. Now it is generally accepted that the remains were not suggestive of fortifications at all and that the bank was probably the western boundary of a mediaeval arable field the ridges of which, ten yards broad, ran off eastwards at right angles. It would be difficult to find a better example of the untrustworthiness of the so-called tradition which turns a ploughed field into a 'Scottish Camp' within a century or two of its disuse.

A flanged axe of bronze, 5 ins. long, and a bronze dagger were found nearby, the latter in 1840. The axe is now in Arbroath Museum. A stone hammer was found in Auchenblae. The name Drumsleed (Dronsled at the time of Robert I) is almost certainly derived from the word sled, a vehicle without wheels used by the ancients for taking wood or peat down steep hills or slopes. Sled roads are often clearly visible on hillsides. Drumsleed therefore means the ridge of the sleds.

In another half mile we arrive at crossroads when we meet the B966. Our road is to the left. First, however, a point of interest. We should note that 200 yards along the road which leads straight on, just off the road on the left and at the bottom of Fir Hillock, a Bronze Age stone cist was found about 1848. It contained an inhumation accompanied by a jet necklace.

An Oblong Encampment

And now let us turn to the left and head homewards along the B966. Our first stop is only two-fifths of a mile farther on, by the garden of the house on the right. If we follow the edge of the field southwards for some 220 yards and then some 80 yards to the west, we arrive at the remains of an oblong encampment, still reasonably intact and with the outline of the earthwork clearly marked by trees. Only some 250 yards from Fordoun House, it is internally about 82 yards long from east to west and about 46 yards broad, the enclosed area being about 3,760 square yards. Very near the south-west corner is the gate, 22 ft. wide, and the very distinct moat or ditch or fosse is about 23 ft. wide and, even now, some 8 ft. deep, but it was formerly deeper. There is no rampart on the inside of the moat, but some traces of an outer one on the east, up to 11½ ft. thick and 1½ ft. high.

Allegedly a Roman Praetorium or Castellum

In this 'fort' in the early centuries of the Christian era, it is alleged by the writer of the old *Statistical Account* and others, the Romans entrenched themselves for protection in their incursions northwards, it being directly in line with the northward march of Agricola by whom, according to Chalmers, it might have been occupied. It is supposed to be the praetorium (or site of the general's tent) of an *extensive Roman camp*, capable of accommodating a large army of 26,000 men, or what General Melville describes as the *very distinct remains of a Roman castellum*. We know, of course, that the Romans, having crossed the Esk at the King's Ford, marched straight through the valley of the Luther Water for about 8½ miles to a camp below Kair House at Fordoun (see page 399), *commodiously placed*, says Chalmers in his *Caledonia* (1807), *on the rise of the valley known by the appropriate name of the Howe of the Mearns*. But were there two Roman camps, as Chalmers asserts, or only one? If two, is this 'fort' at which we are now looking the praetorium of the 'West Camp', so called, as opposed to the Fordoun camp?

The Earthwork Mediaeval

No, it is not, for the earthwork is plainly of mediaeval origin. It has sharp, not rounded corners and has a wide moat, probably formed for an artificial stream entering it at the north-east corner – both features of mediaeval homestead moats in the south of England. Whoever the bold intruders were, with what feelings must the natives from the uplands have witnessed the earthwork take form, for one must preclude the idea of its being in itself a camp at all, or even part of one. What intercourse they had with the foe or whether the only intercourse consisted in efforts to harass him and bar his further progress is now only a matter for imagination.

One of the 84-yard sides of the oblong mediaeval homestead near Fordoun House, marked by trees. The 18 ft. wide ditch or fosse, even now some 8 ft. deep, is very distinct and was originally a moat, probably formed for an artificial stream. The traces of a rampart outside the moat can readily be seen.

Varied 'West Camp' Sites

What, then, of the 'West Camp', for a camp of some kind west of the Kair House camp there certainly seems to have been for of it there are reliable descriptions. Knox in his *Topography of the Basin of the Tay* states that the ramparts and ditches were *nearly entire* about the middle of the 18th century, and the Rev. Alexander Leslie, minister of the parish, made minute measurements of the camp in 1799 although in 1792 the entrenchments were *scarcely discernible in many places*. He states that some of his information was given him in his younger days by

> *old people who could trace a considerable part of the outlines of the camp which were most extensive and which had been defended by triangular forts at the different corners, by outposts and by a deep morass at the lower extremity. These outworks have been levelled, and the morass at the lower extremity* (probably towards the south) *has been drained.*

The *outposts* may have been the banks of traverses, for that was how they were formerly regarded and described. Parts of two of the sides still remained in 1801:

> *these run at right angles to one another and seem to have composed the west and north side of the camp.*

By about 1864 the greater part of the ground had been brought into cultivation so that, although the shape of the camp must have depended somewhat on natural features, there is now complete absence of visible remains.

A Prima Facie Case for a Roman Marching Camp

Where then was the exact location of the 'West Camp'? Views on the site are varied. We read that the *extensive camp* near the mansion-house of Fordoun was about a mile south-south-east of the church of Fordoun, so that what would appear to be the middle of the camp is only 70 or 80 yards south-west of Fordoun House and only some 330 yards west of the oblong earthwork where we stand. Professor Stuart wrote in 1819 that there could still distinctly be traced some appearance of a large camp *surrounding* the mediaeval site or what he called the praetorium. Cramond in his *Annals of Fordoun* stated, in agreement with Chalmers, that the west side of

315

the original camp was bounded at Pitrennie Mill by the Luther Water, which ran formerly through the west side of the camp, and on the east side by several springs. As we have seen, part of the fortification was said to have been a large, deep morass. Robertson, on the other hand, in his map of Aberdeen, Banff and Kincardine, published in 1822, shows an oblong marked *Remains of a Camp* farther to the east, extending in length for about 600 yards from Crossroads towards the House of Redhall with its north-west side of about 300 yards long at right angles to the Luther Water, nearly following the present Fettercairn road, the road to Fordoun station intersecting the site almost in the middle.

I think we may decide that a strong *prima facie* case has been made out for an extensive Roman marching camp, which could well be Agricolan, on the low ground of the Luther valley between Pitrennie Mill and the Luther Water and the road from Crossroads to Redhall House. All we can say with certainty is that it was somewhere in the 194 acres surrounding the mediaeval earthwork which, on the evidence, would seem to be sited more or less in the centre of it. Mr Ian Shepherd, Grampian Regional archaeologist, is of the opinion that the corner triangular forts mentioned above are best explained by the fact that the camp was a two-phase one, one rectangular site overlapping the other so that triangular areas resulted at the corners. All this aerial photography will doubtless one day reveal. But how curious is the likelihood that Agricola and Severus, 127 years apart, should camp on sites so close to each other, for the Kair House site is only 1⅓ miles away as the crow flies.

Bronze Age Finds

In the late 18th and early 19th centuries in various places south of the mediaeval earthwork native sepulchral remains which fell to dust when exposed to the air have been found in a number of rough, unhewn stone chests or cists belonging to the Bronze Age, some buried under cairns and several laid in the open fields where they were accidentally turned up by the plough. In urns which were found entire there was generally a considerable quantity of calcined or half-burned bones. The urns themselves were of very rough clay manufacture, retaining the marks of the strings with which they had been bound when being made.

A fine example of a dagger was unearthed about 1842 in the boundary ditch between Mains of Fordoun and Marchburn. Nine inches in length, with three rivet holes and nearly black in colour, it was evidently intended to be rivetted to a wooden handle and was apparently composed of mixed metals resembling bronze with sharp edges having a decidedly brazen look. It had a prominent mid-rib on each side of which were two bands of two lines. On each side, towards the centre, it swelled out about an eighth of an inch. A gold ring was found with it. Both belonged to the Early Bronze Age.

Monboddo House and its Lairds

Let us now resume our journey along the B966. At the crossroads which we reach in half a mile we must continue straight over, and in a further third of a mile, at the corner, we reach the drive to Monboddo House, the birth-place and family seat of James Burnett, Lord Monboddo (1714-99), the son of James Burnett of Monboddo and Elizabeth, only sister of Sir Arthur Forbes, Bart. of Craigievar. He was a descendant of the founder of the family of the Burnetts of Leys, Alexander de Burnard, who obtained from King Robert the Bruce in 1324 a charter of certain lands in the Forest of Drum. Lord Monboddo's great-grandfather, James Burnett of Lagavin and Monboddo (who died in 1683) had united the families of Burnett and Monboddo when he married Elizabeth, daughter of Colonel Robert Irvine of Monboddo.

From the 13th century onwards, however, Monboddo was Barclay property, and by 1593 the laird was James Strathauchin or Strachan. Soon afterwards it passed to the Irvines, and it was Colonel Irvine, a cadet of the House of Drum, who founded the family of Monboddo. Colonel of a Scots regiment which served with the great Gustavus Adolphus, King of Sweden, Colonel Irvine distinguished himself on several occasions and particularly at the Battle of Lützen (1632) where Adolphus perished. In 1634 he retired to Monboddo, and in 1635 built the *manor place* of Monboddo, a simple oblong residence, two storeys and an attic high, on the site of an older building (possibly a tower), according to the fashion he had seen in Flanders.

A Modern 'Development'

This plain, unpretentious country dwelling-house has recently undergone a transformation. To it had been attached a handsome modern Scots baronial mansion which was enlarged and improved in 1866-1867 at a cost of £2,000 after a design by Mr James Matthews, ex-Lord Provost of the City of Aberdeen. Altogether a serene and elegant residence, it was shaded by thriving plantations. In 1977 this

Monboddo House in the process of 'development' in 1977. Although now converted to a self-contained private house, the shell of the original building mercifully remains. In the picture we see one of the two small corner turrets crowning the northern angles and, in the middle of the west gable, the heraldic panel bearing the date of the building and the arms and initials of the builder. The most famous person who lived here was, of course, Lord Monboddo, judge, scholar, soldier, agriculturist. He played host to Dr Johnson and Boswell in 1773. Burns also visited Monboddo House.

19th century addition was demolished, its gardens in front to the south destroyed and (alas) its woods and orchards to the north and west cut down. The steadings have been converted into three houses, and in the policies another seven houses have been built.

We must be thankful, I suppose, that Monboddo House was more interesting historically than architecturally and that the shell of the original building remains at all, presently converted to a self-contained private house. The ancient well-proportioned Hall on the first floor (with its two garde-robes) where many distinguished guests were entertained with lordly hospitality is in its original form no more. The old kitchen in the western end of the basement has become a dining-room, the very large fireplace arch there being retained as a feature. But, on the other hand, the chimneys and roof-line have been altered to approximate to what they originally were while we can still see the fairly large and regular windows and the two small corner turrets crowning the northern angles. In the middle of the west gable remains, too, the inset heraldic panel bearing the date of building, the arms of the builder impaled with those of his wife, Elizabeth, third daughter of Sir Robert Douglas of Glenbervie, and the initials R.I. and E.D.

Lord Monboddo — Brilliant and Illustrious

Quite the most famous person who was born and lived here was, of course, Lord Monboddo, illustrious as a judge, soldier and agriculturist, a keen 'improver' who made great alterations in the appearance and value of his farm. He was, moreover, the most upright of men and one of the most remarkable and celebrated scholars of that time. He studied first at Aberdeen and Edinburgh where he distinguished himself by his proficiency in ancient literature his enthusiasm for which in later life became his ruling passion. He used to give once a week what he called his 'learned' suppers, and his list of guests was a distinguished one, his table being open to all votaries of literature and of the fine arts.

Designed for the bar, he went to study civil law, as was the custom of the time, to Holland where he spent three years in the University of Groningen. Passing his examinations on February 12th, 1737, he was admitted a member of the Faculty of Advocates. In course of time his practice grew to be very considerable indeed, and he eventually rose to distinction at the Scottish bar, first coming into prominence as counsel for the Douglases in the celebrated Douglas peerage case between the two sons of the duke's sister and the Duke of Hamilton.

He was three times in France, leading the proof taken there. About 1760 he married Miss Farquharson, a relative of Marshal Keith, and in 1764 was appointed Sheriff of Kincardineshire. On February 12th, 1767, he was, through the interest of the Duke of Queensberry, then Lord Justice-general, raised to the Bench of the Court of Session when he assumed the title of Lord Monboddo. This position he held for thirty years.

— and Eccentric

Lord Monboddo was accounted brilliant but eccentric as his original thinking was far in advance of his time. A prolific and very talented writer and a man of great literary taste, he was the author of *Ancient Metaphysics* and *The Origin and Progress of Man and Language* in which he anticipates the Darwinian theory. The latter work, although very learned and acute, is very whimsical as Monboddo held, for example, remarkable opinions about men being monkeys whose tails had worn off by constant sitting. This led to some good-humoured banter with some of his fellow Law Lords.

A favourite recreation during vacations was an annual visit to London which he made until he was well over 80 years of age. While there he often visited Court, and the king was said to have taken great delight in his conversation. All his journeys to and from London were accomplished on horseback, with a single servant attending him, not in a carriage as Lords of Session were wont to move about the country. He considered a carriage an effeminate conveyance, and to be dragged at the tails of horses instead of being mounted on their backs seemed to him a ludicrous degradation of the dignity of human nature. Lord Neaves, for example, a versatile successor in the Court of Session, sings of him,

> *His views, when forth at first they came,*
> *Appeared a little odd O!*
> *But now we've notions much the same,*
> *We're back to old Monboddo.*
> *Though Darwin now proclaims the law,*
> *And spreads it far abroad O!*
> *The man that first the secret saw*
> *Was honest old Monboddo.*

His patrimonial estate was small, producing during his lifetime only about £300 per year, but he would never dismiss a poor tenant for the sake of obtaining an increase from a new one. It was his boast to have his lands more numerously peopled than any estate of equal size in the neighbourhood. When in the country during vacations, he wore the dress of a plain farmer and lived on a footing of familiarity with his tenantry which greatly endeared him to them. His private life was spent in domestic bliss and in the practice of all the social virtues. Rigidly temperate himself, he took a delight in convivial society. 'Balloon' Tytler,[1] the miscellaneous writer, who, it is believed, experienced his kindness even in a more tangible form than by being a frequent guest at his 'learned suppers' thus affectionately sums up his character:

> *If wisdom, learning, worth, demand a tear,*
> *Weep o'er the dust of great Monboddo here,*
> *A judge upright, to mercy still inclin'd,*
> *A gen'rous friend, a father just and kind.*

---

[1] So called because in 1784 he made an ascent to a height of 350 ft. in a fire balloon at Comely Gardens, Edinburgh, and was the *first person in Great Britain to navigate the air.*

Lord Monboddo aged 84. A portrait by John Kay.

Lord Monboddo died in Edinburgh on May 26th, 1799, at the advanced age of 85. His remains lie in an unmarked grave in Greyfriars Churchyard, Edinburgh.

Dr Johnson and Boswell Visit Monboddo

Lord Monboddo was a great patron of merit and a friend of the learned Dr Johnson and his companion, Boswell, who dined at Monboddo House in the autumn of 1773 when passing through the Mearns on their famous journey to the Western Isles. Johnson thus briefly refers to the visit:

> *Early in the afternoon Mr Boswell observed that we were at no great distance from the house of Lord Monboddo. The magnetism of his conversation easily drew us out of our*

321

way, and the entertainment which we received would have been a sufficient recompense for a much greater deviation.

Boswell in his *Journal*, dated August 21st, 1773, is more expansive:

I knew Lord Monboddo and Dr Johnson did not love each other, yet I was unwilling not to visit his Lordship, and was also curious to see them together. I mentioned it to Dr Johnson who said he would go two miles out of his way to see Lord Monboddo. I therefore sent forward Joseph with the following note:

'Montrose, 21st August. My dear Lord – Thus far I am come with Mr Samuel Johnson. We must be at Aberdeen tonight. I know you do not admire him as much as I do, but I cannot be in this country without making you a bow at your old place, as I don't know if I may again have an opportunity of seeing Monboddo. Besides, Mr Johnson says he would go two miles out of his way to see Lord Monboddo. I have sent forward my servant that we may know if your Lordship be at home. – I am ever, my dear Lord Monboddo, sincerely yours.'

Johnson, on his visit to Monboddo, writes of the Mearns

that the hedges were of stone for instead of the verdant thorn to refresh the eye we found the bare wall or dyke intersecting the prospect. It was wonderful to see a countryside so divested, so denuded of trees'.

This, of course, was the overall picture at the beginning of 'improvement' when, during the late mediaeval period and the 17th century, areas of woodland suffered as the areas of outfield and common land increased apart from the Caledonian Forest on Deeside and the existence of sparse planting round some of the lairds' houses.

Boswell goes on:

We stopped at Laurencekirk where our great grammarian Ruddiman was once schoolmaster. We respectfully remembered that excellent man and eminent scholar ... About a mile from Monboddo where you turn off the road Joseph was waiting to tell us my lord expected us to dinner. We drove over a wild moor. It rained and the scene was somewhat dreary. Dr Johnson repeated with solemn emphasis Macbeth's speech on meeting the witches ... Monboddo is

> *a wretched place, wild and naked with a poor old house,*
> *though if I recollect aright, there are two turretes which*
> *mark an old baron's residence. Lord Monboddo received*
> *us at his gate most courteously, pointed to the Douglas arms*
> *upon his house and told us that his great-grandmother was*
> *of that family. 'In such houses' said he, 'our ancestors lived*
> *who were better men than we.' 'No, no, my Lord,' said Dr*
> *Johnson, 'We are as strong as they and a great deal wiser.'*
> *This was an assault upon one of Lord Monboddo's capital*
> *dogmas and I was afraid there would have been a violent*
> *altercation in the very close before we got into the house.*
> *But his lordship is distinguished not only for 'ancient meta-*
> *physics' but for ancient politesse, 'La vielle cour', and he*
> *made no reply. His Lordship was dressed in a rustic suit*
> *and wore a little round hat, told us we now saw him as*
> *Farmer Burnett and we should have his family dinner, a*
> *farmer's dinner. He said, 'I should not have forgiven Mr*
> *Boswell had he not brought you here, Dr Johnson.' He*
> *produced a very long stalk of corn as a specimen of his*
> *crop, and said, 'You see here the laetas segetes'* (the richness
> of the crop) *and observed that Virgil seemed to be as*
> *enthusiastick a farmer as he, and was certainly a practical*
> *one.*

Boswell then proceeds to reproduce their conversation on emigration, Homer, the decrease of learning and so on.

Robert Burns and 'Fair Eliza'

Lord Monboddo was a friend of Robert Burns who had been introduced to him by the Hon. Henry Erskine (all being Free-masons) and who frequently visited him at his residence at 13 John Street, Edinburgh, in 1788. Burns visited Monboddo House, later writing an elegy on the death of Elizabeth, *Fair Eliza*, the younger daughter of Monboddo who was much attached to her father and continued to keep house for him until her death. *The heavenly Miss Burnett* as Burns used to call her, or *Fair Burnett* (as she is called in Burns' *Address to Edinburgh*) was a charming, intellectual and gifted young lady with fine literary taste. Burns writes to his friend, William Chalmers, on December 27th, 1786,

> *There has not been anything like her in all the combinations*
> *of beauty, grace and goodness the great Creator has formed*
> *since Milton's Eve on the first day of her existence.*

She died of consumption in 1790 at the age of 25.

Here are two stanzas from the beautiful and touching *Elegy on the late Miss Burnett of Monboddo*, the only poem Burns ever wrote with Kincardineshire associations:

> *Life ne'er exulted in so rich a prize*
> *As Burnet, lovely from her native skies;*
> *Nor envious death so triumph'd in a blow,*
> *As that which laid th'accomplished Burnet low.*
>
> *In vain ye flaunt in summer's pride, ye groves;*
> *Thou crystal streamlet with thy flowery shore,*
> *Ye woodland choir that chant your idle loves,*
> *Ye cease to charm – Eliza is no more!*

Fordoun a World War II Fighter Command Station

And now, having retraced our way along the drive (three-fifths of a mile long), we turn left on the B966 and in 700 yards find ourselves crossing a runway 1,500 yards in length in the middle of what used to be the World War II aerodrome of Fordoun, opened in 1941 as a satellite Fighter Command station for use by RAF Peterhead with a Spitfire squadron, a Fleet Air Arm squadron of Sea Hurricanes and an anti-aircraft co-operation flight of Oxfords and Defiants. On October 1st, 1943, it was transferred to Flying Training Command as a satellite of RAF Montrose with a Flying Instructors' School. On 21st August, 1945, Fordoun was transferred to Maintenance Command as an ammunition depot. It became totally inactive in June, 1951. The aerodrome is now used by Fordoun Flying Club. In another 700 yards we cross the second of the runways (this time 1,100 yards long) and soon join the A94 where we turn left.

The Cushnie Cist of a Bronze Age Youth

In exactly three-tenths of a mile we arrive at a road on our left which would take us, if we were so minded, to the farms of Cushnie and Castleton of Mondynes just over half a mile away. We can just catch a glimpse of them. In a sandhill on the farm of Cushnie on the left a rough, unhewn red sandstone cist was found about one foot under the surface of the ground. Placed east and west, its inside measurement was 5 ft. 1¾ ins. in length, 11 ins. in breadth at the head and 9½ ins. deep. 20 ins. from the head it was 14 ins. broad, and 8 ins. broad at the foot. The stones, set on edge, varied from 1 in. to 3½ ins. in thickness. Inside were the remains of some bones, very much decayed, and part of the skull with a fine set of teeth. From the size of the coffin and the bones found, it is surmised that the body interred was that of a youth.

Castleton, Home of the Thane of the Mearns?

Castleton is named after a castle which once stood just over a hundred yards beyond the farm on what the Ordnance Survey calls Castlehill, the low, rectangular forested eminence on one's right 21 by 18½ yards in size. But no remains of any kind are to be seen now except for a defence ditch on the east 22¾ ft. broad and over 1½ ft. in depth. The ancient castle of Monachedlin once stood here, commanding the eastern route to the north – the route the Romans probably took – and may have been the home of Malpeder MacLeon, Thane of the Mearns. Two stone cists were found on Castleton fields about 300 and 350 yards east of the farmhouse, 6 ft. and 4½ ft. respectively in length and 3¼ ft. broad. The long cist contained an extended inhumation, the other bones and ashes. A stone-circle once stood 700 yards away in the same direction.

At the farmhouse of Castleton[1] (dated 1746) was born in 1751 John Stuart of Inchbreck who was Professor of Greek in Marischal College, Aberdeen, for forty-five years. He attended the parish schools of Glenbervie and Arbuthnott, was licenced by the Presbytery of Fordoun and preached occasionally in the church of Fordoun. He died in 1827.

The Lands of Abbeyton

Just under half a mile farther on is a road on the right to the farm of Abbeyton which is of interest insofar as its lands were gifted to the Abbey of Arbroath in 1178 by Philip of Melville who received them when he married Eva, daughter of Walter, the son of Sibbald. Before this time the land was owned by one Richard of Freuill, a family introduced among the people of the Mearns by King William I.

The Lands of Mondynes

Now we are approaching the area of Mondynes on the Water of Bervie, once all forest and moss. From the eastern part of Drumlithie round by the Bervie Water there existed in bygone days an extensive pool or morass. It is noteworthy that 104 acres of land in this area were granted to the Abbey of Arbroath in its foundation

---

[1] According to the title-deeds the owner of Castleton has the right to cut peats at Inchbreck.

charter by William the Lion. The land was measured by the king's command by *Willus de Munfort et Umfridus de Berkeley et Walterus Scotus et Alanus, filius Symonis.* Four-fifths of a mile from the Abbeyton road end is a road on the right to the Mill of Mondynes from which rebels of the 1745-6 Rebellion, Thomas Kemlar, miller, and his son, Alexander, *went in arms to Stonehaven to assist the French sloop against the British man-of-war.* What resulted we know not.

The Solitary Court Stone

Of greater interest, however, is the farm road exactly opposite, leading to East Mondynes 300 yards away over the railway for on a knoll in one of its fields has stood from time immemorial a solitary white monolith, without letter or sculpture of any kind. It is evidently intended to perpetuate some remarkable local occurrence and is possibly the remnant of a stone-circle. The fact that it stands on a hillock with a wide view all round strengthens the presumption that it marks the site of a burial. When paganism gave way to Christianity, the large, unembellished boulder may have continued to be regarded as the emblematic centre of authority in a steward-ship, thanedom or barony. It is called The King's Stone or The Court Stone, a name which seems to imply that it had been used as the site or the judgement-seat of the barony of Mondynes which was gifted by William the Lion to one of his Anglo-Norman followers. But there is no evidence to connect the stone with any judicial or other function.

To reach it we leave our car at the farm and carry on along the road for some 185 yards. Then we strike off at right angles to our left for 200 yards[1] along the side of a field to reach 'the ridge of the watery place', that gives its name to Drumlithie. And there stands our monolith, leaning towards the north-west and about 6 ft. in height with a circumference of 10 ft. at a height of 2½ ft. from the base and 7½ ft. at a height of 4½ ft.

Duncan's Shade Where a King was Slain

As this great stone is also called Duncan's Shade, it is no unusual stretch of the imagination in the light of the evidence to assume that it may mark the spot where ill-fated Duncan II of Scotland met his death, and perhaps lies buried. For it would seem that here in 1094 a great battle was fought as two rivals had arisen against the king to

---

[1] 250 yards at right angles to our right from this point is a hillock where about 1855 a cist was found containing *fragments of bones and a great quantity of burnt ashes.*

claim the Scottish throne because Duncan II was the bastard son of
Malcolm Canmore's first wife and not of Queen Margaret. He had
been left in England as a hostage, had served William Rufus as a
knight and had obtained the English king's permission to invade

*The King's Stone or the Court Stone, the solitary white monolith, 6 ft. in height, which
is also known as Duncan's Shade and which, standing on a hillock, may mark the spot
in Mondynes were ill-fated Duncan II of Scotland met his death in 1094 and perhaps
lies buried. The name, Court Stone, seems to imply that it marks the site of the
judgement-seat of the barony of Mondynes, but there is no evidence of this.*

Scotland in 1094. His uncle, Donald Bane, Malcolm's brother, had
been expelled from the throne and he, Duncan, had reigned in his
stead.

One of the claimants was Edmund, son of Malcolm Canmore and
Margaret and the only bad son of his mother, so it was said. The
other was Donald Bane with whom Edmund covenanted for a
portion of the kingdom. They were backed by the Earl of the
Mearns, Malpeder MacLeon, whose train-band in all probability
would have consisted largely of the men of the Mearns from his
headquarters at Fettercairn who presumably were largely responsible for ensnaring the king.

Who Malpeder was nobody has discovered, but the name of this noble is of greater antiquity in the Howe than that of the Keiths, the Hays, the Falconers, the Durwards, Wisharts or Carnegies. He was probably an incomer who, receiving a gift of the forfeited estates of Finella, waxed strong in the fortresses of the Grampians and became able to defy royal authority as former maormors had done, for the population of Scotland had even then begun to be turbulent and masterful towards their kings. He probably dwelt in the Castle of Kincardine, either as owner or as steward for the king, although it is possible that an ancient fortress stood on the Knock Hill nearby or at Castleton (already referred to) where an immense cairn of loose stones once existed.

It was by Malpeder, state our oldest chronicles, that Duncan was said to have been assassinated at the instigation of Edmund and Donald Bane – just a century after the murder of Kenneth III. And so it was, says Skene, generally a reliable commentator, that the Scots

> *took to them a second time his* (Duncan's) *paternal uncle, Donald, for King, through whose machinations and incitement he* (Duncan) *was betrayed to death.*

The scene of the tragedy, Monathyne, Monathechyn or Monythyn (as are some of the variants in old chronicles and in the foundation charter of the Abbey of Arbroath, granted by William the Lion less than 100 years after Duncan's death) is a place evidently identical with the modern Mondynes in Fordoun parish of the Mearns where we are now.

Diverse Accounts Recorded

Of the circumstances in which the death of the king occurred diverse accounts are recorded by the historians. Some would have it that he was treacherously assassinated during a very stormy night while he lay asleep. Wyntoun says he was killed in open warfare between him and Donald, his uncle, assisted by Malpeder:

> *The Erle than*
> *Of the Mernys a manly man*
> *Agayne Duncane wyth hys powere*
> *Ras wyth Downald in-to were*
> *And slwe this Duncane swne to dede.*

But an ancient chronicler states with certainty that

> *Donekan MacMalcolm who reigned for six months fell by*
> *the hand of Malpeder MacLeon at Monachedin in the*
> *Mearns,*

while the historian, Fordoun, adds,

> *Qui cum per unum annum et sex menses regnasset avunculi*
> *sui Dovenaldi dolo quem saepius bello vicerat per admini-*
> *culum cujusdam comitis de Mernis nomine Malpetri,*
> *Scotice Malpedir, apud Monathethun caesus interiit et in*
> *insula Iona sepultus.*
>
> When he had been king for a year and six months, he was
> killed at Monathethun because of the scheming of his
> uncle, Donald, whom he had often defeated in battle, and
> through the agency of a certain thane of the Mearns, called
> in Scots Malpeder. He was buried in the island of Iona.

He also quotes from an earlier monkish writer,

> *Mensibus in regno sex regnavit Dovenaldus*
> *Malcolmi regis frater in Albanis.*
> *Abstulit huic regnum Duncanus Malcolmides*
> *Mensibus tot anno rex erat in Scotia.*
> *Hic fuit occisus Mernensibus in Monathethyn*
> *Malpedir comitis plebs premit omnis cum.*
>
> After Donald, the brother of King Malcolm, had reigned
> in Albany for six months, Duncan, the son of Malcolm, in
> as many months took his kingdom. And he was slain by the
> men of the Mearns in Monathethyn, assisted by the retain-
> ers of Malpeder.

Whichever version is correct, it would seem that here at Mondynes
Duncan II was defeated and slain, Edmund and Donald Bane
dividing the kingdom between them and reigning for three years.

Back on the main road, in only a third of a mile we find ourselves
on the Bridge of Mondynes and, immediately we are across it with
the Pade or Path o' France road leading off on our left from the old
toll-house of Mondynes. Between this road and the railway on our
left, in a mound in a field of Broombank Farm, a considerable
number of stone coffins were unearthed while the track was in
course of construction. Soon, in under a mile, we again find ourselves at Candy Farm where some time ago we left the A94 for
Drumlithie. We have travelled full circle. When Stonehaven Square
is reached in a little over 6½ miles, we shall have completed a
journey of nearly 27 miles in all.

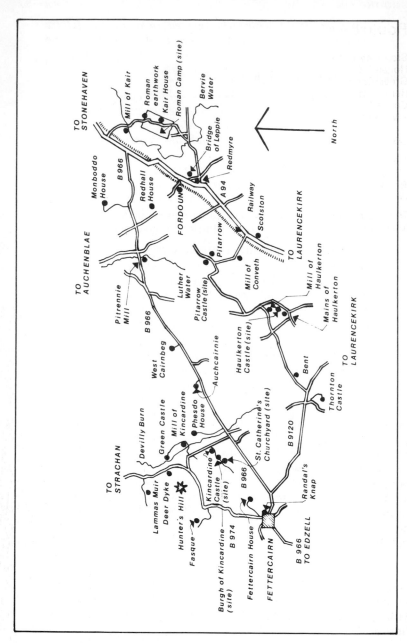

North

TO STONEHAVEN

TO AUCHENBLAE

TO STRACHAN

TO LAURENCEKIRK

TO LAURENCEKIRK

TO EDZELL

Mill of Kair
Roman earthwork
Kair House
Roman Camp (site)
Bervie Water
Bridge of Leppie
Redmyre
Monboddo House
B 966
Redhall House
FORDOUN
A 94
Railway
Scolston
Pitarrow
Mill of Conveth
Luther Water
Pitarrow Castle (site)
Mill of Haulkerton
Mains of Haulkerton
Haulkerton Castle (site)
Pitrennie Mill
B 966
West Cairnbeg
Auchcairnie
Bent
Thornton Castle
Devilly Burn
Green Castle
Mill of Kincardine
Phesdo House
St. Catherine's Churchyard (site)
B 9120
Lammas Muir
Deer Dyke
Hunter's Hill
Kincardine Castle (site)
B 966
Randal's Knap
Fasque
Burgh of Kincardine (site)
B 974
Fettercairn House
FETTERCAIRN
B 966
TO EDZELL

Route Seven

Stonehaven Square – Pitrennie Mill – West Cairnbeg – Auchcairnie – Phesdo House – Castleton of Kincardine – Kincardine Castle – Mill of Kincardine – Green Castle – Fasque – Fettercairn House – Fettercairn – Thornton Castle – Bent – Mains of Haulkerton – Haulkerton Plantation – Pitarrow – Mill of Conveth – Redmyre – Fordoun – Bridge of Leppie – Bridge of Kair – Kair House – Mains of Kair – Shepherdshaugh – Stonehaven Square.

Distance: A total of 48¼ miles as follows:

Return journey from Stonehaven Square to the junction of A94 and B966 – 17.50 miles
Round trip by car from junction of A94 and B966 – 28.96 miles
On foot 1.74 miles

There is an additional suggested excursion to the Cairn of Arthurhouse with a total return length of – 1.78 miles (1.30 by car and 0.48 on foot)

Round the Howe of the Mearns –
A Five Castle Tour

in which we read of the 'marvellous and pleasant jest' of a king's demise, hangings from Queen Victoria's bed, a squirrel-like witch and an important literary find. We learn of a county town which disappeared, of a king's head brought to Kincardine, of the first farmhouse floored with deal and of Adam wearing shorts in Eden.

Our Starting-Point the Junction of the B966 and A94

To embark upon this circular journey we must drive for nearly 8¾ miles from Stonehaven, south along the A94 to our starting-point, the fork where the Laurencekirk road is joined by the B966 road to Fettercairn. This part of our journey has already been covered, of course, in Route No. 5. Indeed, when we turn right at this starting-point with its interesting mile-stone, we are still on a familiar road as, again in Route No. 5, we have also travelled the next two miles to the crossroads to Auchenblae. But here we are ready to cover new ground as we continue on this occasion straight across towards Fettercairn.

Pitrennie Mill

Our first stop is after only some 200 yards at the road which leads off to the left by the side of the Luther Burn. This leads to Pitrennie Mill, 180 yards away, which once manufactured oatmeal, at one time a staple article of food in this part of the county, drawing grist from the homesteads on the surrounding plains. The original small 18th century mill, now a farm outhouse, can still be clearly seen. But the undershot mill-wheel has gone, and the weed-choked Luther Burn which once supplied the motive power falls idly by a gaping hole in the wall where once it was. Even after the beginning of the 19th century, driven by a clumsy arrangement of wooden wheels which only ground or crushed the grain, these mills were no better than the large quern-stones some of which still stand stacked outside. The miller's function was simply to grind; customers had themselves to see to the process of sifting and cleaning by hand.

A Miller Assoilzied

A William Mollison of the Mill of Pitrennie was once accused of stealing from John Arbuthnott of Fordoun a piece of oak, from James Farquharson in Fordoun or Robert Smith in Auchenblae four horn spoons, *thrawen tailled*, and a flaughter-spade (a two-handed spade for cutting peats and turfs), from John Wishart of Cairnton a quantity of corn and meal and from John Arbuthnott of Fordoun and Margaret Falconer, his wife, and others *when thou wast miller at the ... Milne of Pitrennie* from 1701 to 1708. Isabella Watt, his spouse, was also accused. Being found innocent by the *assize* (jury), however, they were *assoilzied* (acquitted) by the sheriff.

The Howe of the Mearns

In just under three-quarters of a mile past Pitrennie Mill we reach Charterstones at the road fork (so named from boundary stones being placed there) and in just under another half mile the farm road to East Cairnbeg on the right of which, and half-way to the farm, cropmarks reveal an oval enclosure measuring about 62 ft. by 42½ ft. and within double grooves. In yet another half mile we reach the farm of West Cairnbeg, the scene of the notorious Garvie murder of 1968. We become more and more conscious of why the surrounding country through which we are passing is called the Howe of the Mearns: the low-lying saucer-like depression – or hollow – that is really a continuation of the great Vale of Strathmore becomes increasingly obvious, its 50 square miles sheltered by the Grampians on the right and the Garvock heights on our left. In prehistoric times it must have been almost covered by water which in course of countless ages was drained away by the North Esk and the Bervie to the south and north respectively, and by the Carron.

A general idea of the Howe in past ages is afforded by place names like Whitemyre, Redmyre, Gyratesmyre and a score of others which remind us that a thousand years ago and more there was a number of bogs and meres throughout the county. 'Main' in Balmain and 'Mon' in Monboddo signify mosses and swamps, 'Drumforber' and 'Drumlithie' etc, mounds or ridges, and 'Inch-gray' rising ground or islands in the morass. Indeed, the Howe was for hundreds of years so marshy as to be incapable of agriculture except in 'inches' or 'drums'. On the uplands of the Howe a dense forest, interspersed with lochs, existed down to a comparatively recent period.

Auchcairnie

In three-quarters of a mile we pass the farm of Auchcairnie (or Auchincarny as it was in 1309), the scene of conflicts in the past. In 1323 King Robert the Bruce granted six acres of arable land in this property *adjacent to our manor of Kincardine* to his faithful follower, Sir Alexander Fraser of Cowie and Kinnell, *and the heirs legitimately procreated betwixt him and Mary Bruce, his wife, our beloved sister*. The land was to be held *in unum liberum hostilagium* (for a place of free entertainment), and to be used as common pasturage in the king's thanage of Kincardine for two horses, ten oxen, twelve cows and one hundred sheep till these should be a year old, with freedom to dry peats and turfs within the same thanage.

On January 8th, 1473, Auchcairnie features again in a charter of William Earl Marischal, Sheriff of Kincardine, to Master John Spalding, Den of Brechin:

> *We have granted to Master John Spalding a toft[1] and croft lying in Kincardine, commonly called the toft and croft of Auchkarne, with their pertinents, to be held by the said John Spalding and his heirs in fee and heritage as a free hostelry with liberty to brew and bake, buy and sell, and do any else recognised by use and wont as belonging to a free hostelry, with fuel and common pasture within the commonty of Kincardyn and Auchcarne. Paying one penny yearly of silver if asked. Sealed at Dunnottyr, 8th Jan., 1473.*

Auchcairnie was one of the pendicles or crofts first granted when the royal demesne of Kincardine was broken up (see page 349).

---

[1] Dwellings with the adjoining lands appropriated to their households.

Phesdo House

In exactly one mile we pass on our right the long tree-lined drive at the end of which stands the magnificent two-storey classic mansion of Phesdo House. Built of Aberdeen granite around 1830 and surrounded by tall, splendid trees, the house stands in its own grounds. The frontage with its impressive pillared porch is reckoned to be architecturally the finest example of a front elevation in this part of the country.

The old manor-house of Phesdo stood on rising ground adjoining the Auchcairnie lands with a fine view of the Howe of the Mearns. We first hear of it in the 14th century when King Robert the Bruce gave its temporalities or revenues to the Abbey of Arbroath. The first recorded lay proprietor of Phesdo and Auchcairnie was Alexander Lindsay who in the 15th century married Elizabeth, daughter of Falconer of Haulkerton, and whose family held the lands of Phesdo (and perhaps those of Auchcairnie as well) till about the middle of the 17th century. In 1682 Sir John Falconer committed suicide at Phesdo House on being charged with corruption in his office of Warden of the Mint. His son, Sir James, Lord Phesdo of the Court of Session, was a lawyer of great eminence, one of the Privy Council of King William and Queen Anne and one of the first negotiators for a Union. When Lord Phesdo's last son died in 1764 without issue, the succession devolved on the Hon. George Falconer, Captain RN, son of David, 5th Lord Haulkerton, who died Commander of the *Invincible* man-of-war in 1780.

The estate of Phesdo was later in the possession of the grandson of Sir John Gladstone of Fasque, Baronet, who purchased it about 1845. He was the nephew of William Ewart Gladstone, the statesman. Latterly Phesdo House was the home of shooting parties and other guests to Fasque a mile away to the west before it fell from grace. The building was occupied in 1945 by German POW's who worked on the agricultural land surrounding it. On June 4th, 1949, it was opened as a hostel of the Scottish Youth Hostels Association.

About 1970 Phesdo House was purchased and renovated by Col. J. W. R. Woodroffe, extensive alterations being made to the grounds a⹁d drive. His wife, who died in 1978, was an aunt of Lady Gladstone, wife of Sir William Gladstone, Bart. of Fasque. Mrs Woodroffe was also the sister-in-law of the late Right Hon. Andrew Elphinstone, a cousin of the Queen.

Kincardine Castle a Fortress of Strength

Three hundred yards farther on at the hamlet of Land's End we turn right along the wide road signed Cairn o' Mount and Banchory. It seems odd to find Land's End among the fertile fields of Kincardine-shire, and I do not know how the hamlet got its name. Nothing seems to end there as far as I can see. In a further two-fifths of a mile we reach on the left a wooded eminence on the farm which bears the imposing name of Castleton of Kincardine: behind the farmyard and on the wooded knoll is what little remains of the once famous castle and palace of Kincardine, a residence and hunting-lodge of kings of Scotland for many years. The windows of the farmhouse, moreover, overlook the site of Kincardine, the county capital which withered and disappeared as we shall see.

Kincardine Castle, the parent stronghold of the Mearns and believed to be the oldest castle in the county of which any remains exist, is said (together with its park) to have been enlarged by Bruce. Doubtless many alterations and enlargements were made upon it from time to time.

That this great fortress dates back to an obscure period of Scottish history there can be no doubt. There are no authentic records to show when it was originally built, but it doubtless occupied the site of previous royal palaces of wood and wattle (and of palisaded earthworks in more primitive days) where Pictish and Scottish kings held state, probably being maintained as a fortified castle of rough stone by successive kings following the unification of Scotland *circa* 844-860. That it was a residence of Kenneth III in 994 when, according to history and tradition alike, he was murdered in the neighbourhood, seems well attested (see page 355), and the prob-ability is that soon after Kenneth's death it was rebuilt two or three times. As a royal residence it remained for at least 300 years more.

The castle the ruins of which we see dates from the beginning of the 13th century and was of the Edwardian type, an example of the earliest castle to be built of stone and lime in the county with grouted walls after the Scottish style and bearing traces of Norman ideas of castle building. That it was a structure of great strength is evidenced not only by the ruins of its foundations yet remaining but by the fact that its battlements stood erect through varying feuds and fortunes of so many war-like generations of men.

Watch-towers, Walls and Courtyard

Now very little can be seen of this once royal edifice as we can see for ourselves if we approach it from the top of the field adjacent to the farm. A roadside gate will give us access if permission is granted. The ground-plan was still traceable towards the end of the 19th century, and around the beginning of the first World War the foundations were still substantial, the walls then standing 6 ft. high or more. From a survey carried out on the instructions of Crabb Watt it seems that the castle was in the form of a great square with a side of some 44 or 45 yards,[1] defended by two round watch-towers projecting 20 to 30 ft. from the main building and placed to the greatest strategic advantage on the south front, one at the south-west corner and the other, larger and of superior design and work-manship, to the east. This served as a keep and afforded considerable accommodation for garrison and inmates. The great enclosing curtain walls, or walls of enceinte, constructed of chisel-hewn, hammer-dressed, hard, durable sandstone (and now heavily robbed), were of great strength and enormous thickness. The outer walls, which were probably 20 to 30 ft. high, were between 8 and 10 ft. in thickness, and some parts of the front walls as much as 12 ft., those on three sides of the building being constructed on the same principle as harbours and fortifications, sloping outwards at the base to keep diggers away and to make their task more difficult by exposing them more clearly to the defenders on the top of the walls. Even the inner walls were 3 or 4 ft. thick.

The principal gateway (where there was a gatehouse), about 9 ft. wide and with a drawbridge over a moat, was on the south between the two round towers. From this gateway the royal train issued forth in quest of pleasure or on its way to Cowie in the north or Brechin in the south. Behind the gateway were many doors, a portcullis and a pend 21 ft. long, leading to the courtyard. Certainly, as long as provisions and munitions lasted, the castle could be bravely de-fended and difficult to capture. There seems also to have been a secondary postern some 8 ft. wide in the north wall, in all probabil-ity also leading to the court through another arched pend past offices or cellars. Yet another door, about 5 ft. wide, was on the east.

The inner courtyard, 90 ft. by 82 ft., was more or less filled with ranges of buildings, accommodation being augmented by additional structures against the walls on all sides except the west. Inside the east wall, on each side of the door, were two spacious apartments measuring about 14 ft. by 50 ft. and 14 ft. by 35 ft. Two other apartments on the south were 22 ft. by 60 ft. and 22 ft. by 14 ft., and the front wall, though mostly composed of watch-towers, embraced

---

[1] According to the Royal Commission on the Ancient and Historical Monuments of Scotland about 38¼ yards.

several compartments of various sizes. At the north-east corner of the ground floor was a grande-robe in the wall. As late as the end of the 19th century the sides of the great fireplace were complete as were the lower steps of a staircase leading to an upper storey. Probably there was a hall above and doubtless cellars on the ground.

The ancient Palace or Castle of Kincardine, just over 1½ miles from Fettercairn, as it would have been in its heyday from the 13th century onwards. The drawing is from a survey carried out on the instructions of J. Crabb Watt, K.C., author of The Mearns of Old. *A structure of great strength with a permanent garrison, the castle was for centuries a place of resort for kings of Scotland, a stopping-place for military expeditions and for royal excursions and a favourite hunting-seat of the Scottish court.*

Important Strategic Position

Even a glimpse through the trees that cover the knoll on which Kincardine Castle stood suffices to show that the tremendous importance in early times of the castle and the county town that grew up around it was due to the fact that it was located in a place of strategic importance. A safe distance from the sea, it occupied a key position at the southern end of the Cairn o' Mounth pass, guarding the direct road from the Mearns and the south, via Clatterin' Brig, to Deeside, Donside and the Moray lands. From a remote period invaders, merchants, noblemen and travellers of all descriptions had to cross the hills by either this pass or the Cairnwell. The route, therefore, became important and had to be strongly fortified according to the methods of the time.

Except at a part to the north-west the projecting eminence on which the castle stood was surrounded by a morass across which no army could safely venture and on three sides by the waters of the Devilly Burn which was not wholly drained off until the beginning of the 19th century, giving place to fertile meadows. In addition, the castle was surrounded not only by a moat but by terraced defensive earthworks. Standing 281 ft. above sea level on a natural hillock nearly 60 ft. high, it commanded the whole of the Howe and about half of the valley of Strathmore: from its watch-towers vigilant watchmen could descry the approach at a considerable distance of friend or foe.

Lordly Cavalcades

For centuries Kincardine Castle was a regular place of resort for many a king of Scotland. When there was strife, it was a stopping-place for military expeditions, and when peace prevailed, it was a favourite hunting-seat of the Scottish court for large surrounding areas were reserved for falconry and the chase, and to the west of the Clatterin' Brig the remains of the great royal deer park can still be seen. The King's and the Chancellor's Parks and other places with relative names around it attest to its ancient glory. Thanks to Anglo-Norman influence and the spread of Christianity, wise and progressive kings may be presumed to have kept a close watch on this, their *Manor of Kincardine*, unquestionably the key to the north. Moreover, it was only a day's march from the seat of Scottish monarchy in and around Perth.

The castle was also a resting-place where royal excursions with retinues of high officials, nobles and knights in coloured cloaks and proclaimed by banners halted in the Mearns. Cavalcades would cross the North Esk at Dalbog or Stracathro, following the old causeway from the King's Ford northwards towards the tract of forest and marsh that was then the Howe. Avoiding the swamps between the Esk and Drumlithie, they would keep to the higher ground of the Balbegno ridge with Balfour on the one hand and Balmain on the other until the towers of Kincardine Castle were seen rising over the woods of Fettercairn at the eastern end of the ridge. And when the lordly company came to the castle, the granary, the forest and fields, breweries, mills and dovecots yielded abundance of sustenance. There would be assembled the neighbouring barons and thanes to render account of their thanages. And the king in his great hall would dispense justice among his subjects high and low. When business was ended, the cavalcade would depart down the slope from the great gate flanked by its sullen towers and, under the direction of the falconers and foresters, would hunt in the hills within and beyond the Deer Dyke or hawk in the vast morass drained by the Luther and its tributaries amidst which stood the tower of the chief falconer at Haulkerton. The visitation lasted sometimes for weeks. Then the king passed over the Mounth to Kildrummie or by Glenbervie to Cowie, Dunnottar or Durris.

A Place of Resort for Kings

Even as early as the reign of Alexander I (1107-1124) the castle was obviously a place of note for the first charter granted by him to the town of Stirling was dated *at Kyncardyn, 18th August, 1119.* David I favoured Kincardine and its sport, and it was probably he who instigated amongst his royal tenants in the Mearns the agricultural industry which made Scotland during the last fifteen years of his reign the granary of England. Successive sovereigns, notably Alexander III in the 13th century and Robert the Bruce, occasionally resided here. Alexander II, also, when he had to go north to call a northern rebel, Earl John, to account, probably stopped at Kincardine, and the castle is also associated with Macbeth whose head was brought here to the waiting Malcolm after the defeat of the former at Lumphanan.

William the Lion made several journeys to the north, during one of which the Moray pretender, MacWilliam, was caught by William Comyn, Earl of Buchan, and taken to Kincardine.

The Earl had already reached Kincardine with his prisoner whom he was in haste to present to William before death

> *robbed him of his prize – for Guthric had resolutely re-*
> *fused all nourishment since his capture.* (The earliest ex-
> ample of a hunger strike?) *He was met by a significant*
> *message from the king that he had no desire to see his*
> *enemy; and the unfortunate MacWilliam was at once be-*
> *headed and hung up by the feet lest starvation should antici-*
> *pate his doom.*

William was in the north again in the summer of 1214 to receive at Kincardine the submission of Earl John who, however, yielded speedily.

It is not improbable that during the long reign of William the Lion alterations and possible reconstruction took place at the castle. It was certainly during his occupation of his *house at Fettercairn* that all the offices common to a royal household of the period were attached. Royal castles were usually under the care of a constable, and William's constable, as far as is known, was the first of the Carnegies of the noble house of Southesk for which service he received the lands of Phesdo and Pitnamoon nearby. Similarly, William granted a charter of land to Gulielmus Auceps, that is William the Falconer, and the first Falconers were called Falconers or de Haulkerstoun. William's first hawksman or falconer was progenitor of the noble family of Kintore, and at the Castle of Kincardine Ranulph, the king's falconer, son of Walter of Lumgair (see page 387) was granted by his master a charter of the lands of Luthra, said to be along the north side of the Luther, including Balbegno.

Alexander III was, we know, at Kincardine on 19th August, 1252, and on 27th January, 1276, when he declared his burgesses of Aberdeen to be under his protection and their goods to be free from poinding (in Scots law the seizing and selling of a debtor's goods). One of the witnesses to the deed was Simon Fraser who had prob-ably come over from Cowie to be the king's guest or to make one of his Council. In 1277 Alexander was again at Kincardine when he wrote to Edward I about the division of the lands of the Earl of Wynton.

Edward I and his 'Faiour Manour'

Kincardine was one of twenty-three royal castles Edward I of Eng-land ordered his captains to seize, and more than once on his journeys to and from the north he halted at what he calls in the diary of his journey this *faiour Manour*. On 18th November, 1292, he ordered sasine (legal possession) of the castles of Aberdeen and Kincardine to be given to John Balliol when he, Edward, awarded the kingdom of Scotland to him. And, when he came to Scotland during his triumphant tour in 1296 with 30,000 foot soldiers and 5,000 mailed and mounted men-at-arms (whose fighting power was enhanced by the superstition that they were invincible), he arrived on his northward journey at *Kyncardyn en Mernes meynor* (i.e. an estate with a house upon it belonging to the king in the Mearns) on 11th July, 1296, and took up his quarters for the night. Lord Hailes records in his *Annals* that it was in the great hall of Kincardine Castle nine days prior to this that the helpless and ill-fated John Balliol, the *toom tabard* of the Scottish monarchy, signed his scroll of abdication, humbly resigning to the Bishop of Durham and the English lawyers the Scottish crown in favour of the hated king of England from whom he had received it four years before.

When Edward left Kincardine Castle with his army, he travelled north-eastwards along the more lowland route of the Mounth via the base of Strathfinella Hill in preference to crossing the Cairn and halted after a very short journey at the *Montaigne of Glonberwy* or *Glombervy* where there was an ancient castle near the Bervie Water on or near the site of the present House of Glenbervie. This was the probable seat of the distinguished laird, *Dns Johannes de Maleuil, Miles*, (see page 284), who succeeded ancient chiefs at Mondynes and who submitted to Edward, curiously enough, at Lumphanan on 21st July, 1296 (nine days later), along with John of Stowes, the Glenbervie minister. On the following day the king proceeded to *a Manour among the mountagnes*, Durris on Deeside.

On August 4th Edward, on his southward journey, again spent some time at Kincardine Castle when he received the homage of Ranulph of Kynnard, chief of a noble Perthshire family, and it was when he was returning to England from this expedition that he took the Stone of Destiny with him. In the account of Walter de Langton for the year, November 1290 to November 1291, amongst the expenses while Edward was in Scotland are recorded:

> *To John des Guideford for keeping the castle of Kyncardyn at a merk per diem.*

A similar receipt appears for 1292. Again, in 1307 a certain Robert de Kethe got 70 merks from Edward for repairing Kincardine and Dunnottar Castles. On August 17th, 1343, the king again visited the castle.

Queen Mary of Scots the Last Royal Visitor

In 1341 when David II and his queen, returning from France, were driven ashore at Bervie, they visited Kincardine Castle and Fettercairn where these royal visits must have created no small stir. The marriage of David's sister, Margaret, to William, Earl of Sutherland, took place at the castle, Margaret receiving a grant of the lands of Fettercairn. In 1369 Robert II, when at Montrose in October and December, would probably visit Kincardine. He presided at jury courts there in December 1375 and January 1383 (for in the progress of affairs the principal fortress in the county naturally developed into a seat of local government and centre of judicial and administrative jurisdiction) and issued charters from it, dated 1371, 1375, 1382 and 1383, perhaps the date of the last royal charter from the castle, one to Thomas Rait, his shield-bearer, concerning certain portions of Lumgair. James IV, the founder of King's College, Aberdeen, and Margaret, his queen, when on their way to and from Aberdeen, paid visits to Kincardine in 1507 and 1511; James V was perhaps at Kincardine in 1526, and Queen Mary of Scots who halted here on her northern tour in 1562 was perhaps the last monarch to visit the castle.

Although it had a permanent garrison, the ancient Castle of Kincardine was by no means occupied constantly by the Court, but only at intervals, particularly because of the opportunity for sport it afforded the Scottish kings. While the influence of the Court would undoubtedly foster local craft and husbandry in its vicinity, reservation of large surrounding areas, as well as areas near Durris and Cowie, would inevitably retard agricultural and rural development. For example, cattle straying in the parks could be confiscated.

Crofts for Officials and Artisans

Kincardine Castle, as you will have seen, at an early stage of its history came to be surrounded by officials and court retainers who for many centuries had the care of the castle in their keeping and lived in small dwellings surrounding it, basking in the protective shadow of this great stronghold. To these officials, artisans and labourers necessary for the upkeep of a royal establishment, the community was for many years confined. The list of crofts and curious tenures attached to the castle was a long one, many of the holdings retaining names indicative of their owners and of who and what the subordinate officers were.

The Fettercairn Charter Chest shows several dwellings named after pages, palfreymen and tire-women or ladies'-maids as well as after higher attendants on royalty. Palfreyman's Croft, for example, was named after George Palfreyman who formerly possessed it. Jervise in his *Memorials of Angus and Mearns* states,

> *Traces of the ancient greatness of the place are the names of adjacent fields such as the King's and Chancellor's Parks, the Chancellor's and the Dean's Crofts, the Deer or Hunting Park, the Countess' Croft, and the Earl's Inns, as also the Lorimer's, the Archer's and the Palfreyman's Crofts. These names, it will be seen, differ from the Duray, Bakehouse, Brewhouse, Gardener's, Hen and other Crofts which, common in the vicinity of baronial establishments, are also to be found at Kincardine. As for the most part these places are described as marching with lands belonging to some of the more ancient and powerful lords of the Mearns, the persons from whom these names were derived may have filled, in connection with the Court, the offices indicated by them.*

Traces of these names will be found in old charters, and the same remarks apply to the crofts surrounding Cowie Castle, the southern guardian of the Causeway.

Obviously, in the service of the Court a large number of people were employed. Charters show that many of the lands of the parish of Laurencekirk were granted as the result of proximity to the abode of royalty. Favourite servants, and in one case a brother-in-law, were selected for gifts of land in possession of the Crown and near the residence of the king.

Justices in eyre (judges who went to circuit) were appointed to visit Kincardine in 1526, probably by James V, and on January 27th, 1531, this same king in a charter to William, 4th Earl Marischal, who held the lands adjacent to Kincardine Castle

> *granted for good service and for composition paid, the lands, town, tenements and crofts of Kincardine, Gallohilstoun, Palframanstoun with advowson of the Chapel of S. Catherine which formerly belonged to William and his predecessors past memory of man, and the said town was of repute a free burgh and the Sheriff Courts of Kincardine were held in the same, and the charters of the said town being lost in the time of pest and troubles, he* (the King) *de novo created the said town a free burgh and gave the inhabitants the power to pak peile* (conduct business) *and*

343

> *sell with power to make baillies, burgesses, sergeants, and*
> *of having a market cross and a weekly market on Friday,*
> *and a free fair twice a year, on the day of S. Catherine the*
> *Virgin in winter, and on the day of S. Catherine of Senis in*
> *summer with tolls, etc. paying annually 26s 8d of blench*
> *ferm* (nominal rent in acknowledgement of superiority)
> *and burgh maill* (rent) *whereas they paid nothing to the*
> *King aforetime.*

On March 11th, 1531, the king confirmed to William, 4th Earl
Marischal, the lands in the charter above, creating the burgh of
Kincardine the *principal and capital burgh in the county.*

The Town at Best a Regality

Where exactly, then, was this capital burgh with its small crofts and
tofts, this small town which had grown up by the year 1532 under the
protection and basking in the shadow of Kincardine Castle? Rather
like the Royal Mile in Edinburgh it stretched from the castle on the
hill along the road which passes the farm of Castleton of Kincardine, and it will surely be pleasant nostalgically to wander there
awhile. Being the seat of a royal manor, of course, Kincardine never
did grow to any extent as a community, its development being
discouraged as the Mearns was marked out chiefly for sport and as a
royal playground. At the best the town was a regality instead of a
burgh under a baron, never, indeed, much more than a long row of
straggling crofters' holdings and wattled, clay dwellings, occupied
by farm servants and originally thatched.

The East Port was sited at a small farm or croft, called The Cross,
immediately below the farm of Castleton, and historians are at
some variance over the dimensions of the township. Some assert
that the street extended to near Fettercairn House, a distance of a
mile and more, this view being based on the fact that from time to
time the foundations of cottages have been unearthed on the old
highway between Kincardine and Fettercairn. Others say it
stretched westwards from the East Port near the Castle only to the
site of the West Port (where also was the small farm or croft of
Chapelton) a distance of almost exactly half a mile. This is much
more likely.

Heralds at the Market Cross

Mid-way along the street and some 320 yards from the West Port the
Market Cross was erected. From its steps heralds would have made
proclamations for this was the only way in which laws were made

known to the lieges. On 18th June, 1572, for example, it was proclaimed that William, Master of Mareschal, the leading baron, was to display the sovereign's banner in war-like manner against the rebels and traitors of the north. In 1577, during James VI's reign, proclamation was made to convene all persons between sixteen and sixty to put down what Crabb Watt calls *the broken men of the Highlands and other parts.* And on 9th November, 1571, all persons in the sheriffdom between sixteen and sixty were charged to assemble with six days' victuals at the kirk of Fordoun to put down the traitors under Adam Gordon of Auchindoun who had committed barbarous cruelty on the *honest and peaceable subjects of the Mearns.*

A Graveyard the Sole Relic

A third of a mile west of the castle and about 80 yards south of the road, situated in a field in the Chapelton Park, is the sole relic of the town, the oblong burying-ground of St Catherine's Chapel, dedicated to St Catherine of Sienna and with, until recently, the foundation of a mediaeval chapel still visible in it. The lonely little graveyard which ended the strange story of Kincardine is now an island of weeds surrounded by a low rude wall and preserved from the plough by an edging of tall beech trees planted by Sir John S. Forbes, Bart. It is recorded that just before the middle of the 19th century there were people alive who could recall burials within its precincts: cortèges went from Fettercairn, preceded by a bellman, there being neither church nor bell available at the kirkyard or, indeed, in the village. There is now only one small, humble tombstone left, the only trace of the ancient greatness of the place that remains. It bears the names of William Taylor, M.A., of Land's End (the hamlet at the crossroads beside the school) and some members of his family. The Master of Arts, I am told, was the schoolmaster of Land's End. He died in 1786, and his lonely grave, standing there among nettles, seems to me a monument to the simple but effective system of Scottish education personified by able but ill-paid dominies of long ago.

Corporate Life in Kincardine

There would have been cultivated areas adjoining the king's castle in the more readily drained area of the Howe and on the uplands, particularly the Garvock hills, and the cattle of the town no doubt grazed on these hills and on patches of clear ground nearby.

345

The whole half-mile length of the main street of what was once 'the principal and capital burgh in the county' which has now completely disappeared – the small town of Kincardine. It winds between the squared-up fields of the farm of Castleton of Kincardine. In the wooded eminence in the foreground stand the ruins of Kincardine Castle, the parent stronghold of the Mearns; in the copse of trees at the top of the picture is St Catherine's burial ground with its one small tombstone.

The market cross of Kincardine stood on the roadway just where it is met by the wall between the field containing the burial ground and the adjacent field nearer the farm. The East Port of the town was sited immediately below the farm of Castleton, the West Port at the top of the picture, just where the curve of the road straightens out by the solitary tree over halfway up the field.

The old road, winding among the fields of Castleton Farm which, apart from the disused kirkyard of St Catherine's Chapel, is the sole reminder of the once famous burgh of Kincardine. In 1600 the burgh ceased to be the capital of the shire, leaving the county only its name. The picture shows the street along which was once a long row of straggling crofters' holdings and wattled clay dwellings, the West Port of the town being once situated between the trees.

The lonely little burial ground of St Catherine's Chapel, 1½ miles from Fettercairn, the sole relic of the burgh of Kincardine. There is only one tombstone left, the only trace that remains of the ancient greatness of this county town that has completely disappeared. Nearby the gate shown in the picture once stood Kincardine's Mercat Cross, possibly the cross now to be seen in Fettercairn.

In the town itself, with its monopoly of trade in the surrounding district, there must have been some kind of corporate life. It was the last major shelter for the traveller to the north and the first where he could eat and sleep after coming over the Mounth from Deeside. Because of its proximity to the royal seat Kincardine was the centre of law and order in the county. Here the muster of the shire was called by the sheriff and here, between the visits of the king, justice would be done by sheriff, thane and baron although the jail or thief's hole was such that any prisoner there immured was not secure a single night from rescue by raiding accomplices. It must have been a sorry building, hardly fit to retain the species of male-factor proclaimed in these times when the county was infested by murderers and rogues. Ale would be made on the spot and sold at taverns, and there may have been a shop or two – sheds or veran-dahs in front of traders' dwellings. But after the 13th century the merchant had little or no security against attack and plunder by Highland robbers.

The Necessity of Administrative Change

For a century or two Kincardine remained the centre of local authority, being frequently visited by the sovereign for business and pleasure. But with the consolidation of the monarchy, the growth of civilisation and the emergence of national interests elsewhere per-haps it was not surprising that from 1531 onwards the Keiths desired the substitution of Stonehaven for Kincardine as the county town. Cowie, which had never been in the possession of the Keiths, was quite out of the running for the leadership of the county (in any case by 1531 its prestige had waned) while Bervie, the only chartered burgh, never enjoyed the patronage of nobles sufficiently powerful or interested to effect its elevation.

In the time of Queen Mary Kincardine Castle was finally relin-quished by the Crown, and at the end of 75 years the honour of the Earl Marischal was withdrawn. (He had been granted, you remem-ber, the adjacent lands in 1531.) Justice seems to have been system-atically neglected in the local tribunal, and the state of the country just before and after 1600, which obviously pointed to the necessity of administrative changes, is shown by the Privy Council and other Registers. Kincardine as a county town was rapidly becoming inef-ficacious from, amongst other things, its inability to deal with crime. The unsettled state of the county was due to the proximity of the hills where outlaws lurked, the fact that the whole district was a prey to the depredations of Highland freebooters, the prevalence of lawless vagabonds who came into the Howe from both sides of the Mounth, and the licence of the gentry, one of the reasons why the town was degraded. Furthermore, after the lands in the Kincardine area were granted to vassals and the justices in eyre called more infrequently, the administration of justice, although partly in the hands of the sheriff, was more and more controlled by the barons even in the sheriff's court. With regard to smaller offences in particular necessity arose for another set of administrators.

Kincardine and its Castle Finally Decline

The importance of Kincardine declined finally as a royal residence and then as a hunting park. The importance of the castle's position, commanding the southern entrance to the main pass to the north, had diminished, too, probably owing to the growth of the hamlets of Fettercairn and Auchenblae and of Aberdeen as a city with which there were more frequent communications. This caused improvement of the road or causeway through the Cowie Mounth from Stonehaven so that the passes became neglected and traffic began to go round by the coast. By the latter half of the 16th century Kincardine Castle had become the common plunder of the neighbourhood.

Whatever the cause of its decay, by charter of Queen Mary's son, James VI, the Strathauchins or Strachans of Thornton occupied the castle from 1601 and, when Alexander Strathauchin de Thornton succeeded his grandfather in 1616, his lands *near the town of Kincardine* included

> *the croft called Hill Croft, the aiker riggs thereof, Weal (Well) Croft, Chancellor Croft, Den Croft, two crofts called Calsey Crofts, Lonie Croft, Bakhouse Croft, Lorimers Croft, Burne Croft, Hals Croft, half of Boigs Croft and Coryismanis, Beatties Croft, Annabadies Croft, four crofts of Craigisland, of which two are called Hall Croft and Hen Croft, and two Hill Croft and Archer Croft, James Petterscheidsland, Countess Croft, Countaishauch Croft, crofts called Lochietraist, Blaikindennis, Dewresunis, Weal Croft with (?) shady half of Bowmanis Croft, all lying in the town and constabulary of Kincardine, lands, crofts, and tenements of Gallowhillstoun, Palframanstoun, Langhauche, Suitter Croft, Temple Croft, Skinner Croft, Gois Croft, twa chaippell Crofts, Lonie Croft, aiker and Newlandis. Old extent 20s; new extent 33s. Also two crofts in villa de Fettercairne. O.E. 3s 4d; N.E. 6s 8d.*

The castle was burnt down at the end of the Strachans' tenure and finally reduced to ruins by John Middleton, afterwards Earl Middleton, on March 16th, 1646. Its prestige as a royal residence had disappeared, its Crown lands and hunting park were cut up and gifted to vassals of the Crown or dispersed amongst Court favourites and various local subjects. Kincardine itself was in course of time split up into many ordinary holdings, and ultimately the walls became a quarry to supply stones for houses and, at a later date, for the dykes and drains of the farm of Castleton. Beyond some fragments of the foundations nothing now remains of this ancient stronghold.

'Courtis at Stanehyve in All Tyme Heirefter'

Simultaneously with the decline of Kincardine and its castle the power of the hereditary sheriffs increased in Stonehaven. The Burgh of Barony of Stonehaven was becoming progressively more important, and the hamlet of Kincardine in 1600 ceased to be the capital of the shire which it had been from the time when division into counties took place, the county courts being transferred to Stonehaven. An Act of Parliament in 1607 provided that

> *the haill lieges within the schire should compeir to persev and defend in their courtis at Stanehyve in all time heirefter.*

One of the prominent reasons assigned for the transference was the curious one of lack of proper accommodation and security:

> *the Schiref of the Mernis alias Kincardine, and his deputtis, hes bene in use this mony zeris to sit at Kincardine, quhair thair is nather ane tolbuth nor any hous to pairties to lodge into for thair intertenement, quhairby the lieges are greatulie damnifeit.*

This degradation when Stonehaven became the head burgh of the sheriffdom of Kincardine and the chief seat of local administration did not assist the fortunes of the decaying burgh. The market-cross was removed from the market-place of Kincardine to nearby Fettercairn in 1670 (see page 375), and by 1730 Kincardine had dwindled so much that the annual Fair of St Catherine was removed there too. By 1790 only a few houses and *seventy or eighty souls* remained. In 1807 Robertson in his *Agricultural Survey* remarks that

> *the only remains to be seen are the ruins of the County Hall which was probably entire till the County Courts were removed to Stonehaven.*

A Dead County Town

Now nothing marks the site of this once famous burgh except the old road winding between the squared-up fields of Castleton Farm, the park behind called the Castle Park or the King's Park, the Deer or Hunting Park, and the disused kirkyard of the vanished St Catherine's Chapel. Kincardine had flourished, declined and disappeared completely. It had never measured up to the requirements of the county town though it manifestly gave the county its name. Perhaps it is this that has led local people in the North-east to refer to 'The Mearns' rather than to Kincardine. The Mearns is a more meaningful title than that of a shire named after a dead county town, buried in the remote past.

Let us now return to the major road beside Kincardine Castle and turn northward to the left for we are to visit another remarkable fortification only a mile and a quarter away. In just under half a mile we reach a T-junction. Here we turn right towards the disused Mill of Kincardine. In a further quarter of a mile we pass right through the farm steading until, just before the dovecot on the right, we reach a turning to the left alongside the garden of the farmhouse. This is our road, and we must follow it uphill for 540 yards. There is no reason why you should not take your car unless it is low-slung (there is turning room available), but you may prefer to walk. At the top we must continue to the left towards the trees through the open gateway and along the obvious pathway at the top of the field. In 320 yards we shall have arrived at the knoll enclosed by the earthwork of Green Castle.

Green Castle a Remarkable Fort

Green Castle is a high, trapezoidal earthwork which in ancient days had been a small water-guarded earthen fort at a time when forts were not roofed and when the buildings inside were of wood. Evidence of its obvious strategic importance at the earliest times is seen in the fact that it is advantageously placed in the strongest site that could have been chosen for the guarding and fortifying of the principal passage through the Grampian mountains, the well-known Cairn o' Mounth pass into the valley of the Mearns and the low lying country to the south. It also acted as a place of safety or retreat from the depredators who frequently came down from the Highlands to carry off cattle belonging to lowland inhabitants.

This remarkable fort was surveyed by Chalmers in May, 1798. It stands on a precipitous bank, its sides formed into a broad terrace of perhaps an acre in extent. Surrounding the enclosure rises a massive earthen rampart up to 45 ft. thick, 8 or 9 ft. broad on top and about 10 ft. above the interior with an opening towards the north-east which would have been heavily strengthened against attack. The height of the rampart above the interior is peculiar and seems to imply that the fort must have been defended from the broad top, probably from behind a palisade. The breadth of the fort within the rampart is 147 ft. 9 ins. at the north-east end and 82 ft. 6 ins. at the south-west. The length is 262 ft. 6 ins. Green Castle is fortified not only by its rampart but by a ditch or fosse 51 ft. 9 ins. from the top and 37 ft. 6 ins. in breadth with a counterscarp 3 ft. to 8 ft. in height. It is also naturally fortified against the south by an almost perpendicular slope of 170 ft. from the top of the ditch and by the Devilly Burn. These are dimensions rarely if ever equalled in Scottish forts.

The high oblong mound which is Green Castle, an acre in extent and standing on a precipitous bank a little over a mile south of the Clatterin' Brig. It is a native British defensive ring fort, dating between 400 B.C. and 125 A.D. during the Iron Age. Traditionally the fort is also known as Finella's Castle where Finella, wife of a maormor of the Mearns, allegedly assassinated King Kenneth III of Scotland about 995 A.D.

Plan and Section of Green Castle

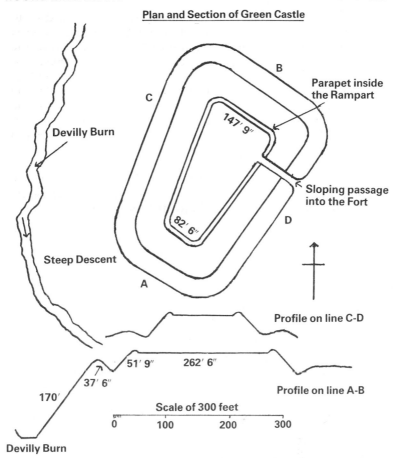

B

**Parapet inside
the Rampart**

C

147′ 9″

Devilly Burn

**Sloping passage
into the Fort**

82′ 6″

D

Steep Descent

A

Profile on line C-D

51′ 9″   262′ 6″

37′ 6″

170′

Profile on line A-B

Scale of 300 feet

0   100   200   300

Devilly Burn

Roman or Pictish Stronghold

Of the origin and early occupation of this marvellous structure no record exists. Chalmers states that it was a Roman fort, and many used to incline to the view that it was one of the outposts which the Romans established along the base of the hills as a defence against Caledonian attacks. Crabb Watt, again, speculates that the fort at a later date may be synonymous with the Dunfother or Fotherdun in the Mearns mentioned in *The Annals of Ulster*, one of the principal forts, if not the chief fortress, of the Southern Picts on the south side of the Mounth. The parish of Fordoun, he thinks, was probably named after the stronghold. If Green Castle was indeed originally

353

Dunfother or Fotherdun, then it was besieged twice, we learn from *The Annals of Ulster*, first in 681 by Brude, king of the Picts who led an army south of the Mounth, and again in 694 in the reign of Taran, his successor. Crabb Watt believes Green Castle, too, to have been a royal seat and the principal seat of barbaric government in Cirig (the Mearns), one of seven Pictish provinces. The name, Green Castle, in his view, may be simply a corruption of Cairn Castle (the fort on the way over the Cairn to the north). The fort was also called Cairngreen, a Celtic word meaning the sunny hill or favourite spot, suitable for a royal residence.

An Iron Age Fort

Green Castle is probably the remains of an early mediaeval castle, before that doubtless being a native British ring fort, dating between 400 B.C. and 125 A.D. during the Iron Age, a defensive structure which was possibly not lived in permanently but which may have been a temporary place of refuge from marauders or invaders in time of danger and political unrest, being left unoccupied in peace-time. One recalls that this was the period of Roman military action and, as the essential feature of this fort was defence, every effort was made to make it difficult to attack and to take advantage of natural features. There can be little doubt as to the serious nature of the local engagements with the Roman troops when we read that the Emperor Severus in 209 A.D. lost 50,000 soldiers in the North-east of Scotland. We may safely assume that a certain proportion must have fallen within the bounds of the Mearns because no doubt every inch of their progress would be disputed by the natives.

Traditionally Finella's Castle

The fort, also known as Queen's Castle or Finella's Castle, is traditionally believed to have been before the days of thanes the ancient early-mediaeval seat of the maormor of the Mearns, the 'earldom' comprising the territory lying between the North Esk and the Dee or what eventually formed the county of Kincardine. The term maormor, literally 'great officer', was the Celtic title of honour conferred upon the chief or civil ruler of a district. His power was such that he could not be deposed by the king, and he governed very much by the laws which he himself enacted. This led to frequent broils and open hostility, and in the Mearns to the deaths of three kings of Scotland.

Now, the wife of the maormor of the Mearns was Finella, daughter of Cunecht or Connacher, also known as Cruthlynthus, the maormor of Angus whose rebellious only son Kenneth III had executed at Dunsinnan. Let *The Buiks of the Chroniclis of Scotland* (1532) tell the story:

> *Ane lord of Angus callit Cruthlynthus*
> *Ane dochter had wes callit Finella,*
> *Quhilk had ane sone Cruthlynthus hecht alsua.*
> *Lord of the Mernis in the tyme wes he,*
> *So hapnit him with his grandsire to be*
> *Into the castell then of Dalbogy.*

As a result of a quarrel Cruthlint or Cruthlynthus, following his mother's advice, led the men of the Mearns *quietlie ane nycht* in a concentrated assault on the Castle of Dalbogin on the south bank of the North Esk about seven miles from Kincardine, slaying all in it, his grandsire included, and carrying off the spoil.

> *The castell syne gart cast down to the ground.*

King Kenneth Assassinated

Cruthlint was then convicted of treason, and it is said that it was because King Kenneth suppressed the insurrection, captured Cruthlint and his companions and ordered them to be killed for conspiracy that in revenge he was treacherously assassinated in the year 994 at Fettercairn through the contrivance and stratagem of Finella. He was at the time on a pilgrimage from Kincardine Castle to the shrine of St Palladius at Fordoun to do penance for his share in the murder. St Palladius' shrine was credited with many virtues, and Kenneth knew it well.

> *In pilgramage syne to Palladius,*
> *Into the Mernis, my author sais thus,*
> *In Fordwy quhair that his banis lyis,*
> *As he befoir was wont to do off syis,*
> *With great devotioun to that halie santt.*
> *Beseikand God thairof his grace to grant*
> *Fre indulgens of all things less and moir,*
> *Aganis him committit wes befoir.*

There is no real authority, however, for this tradition, and how Kenneth was murdered is not certain. Tighernac says merely that he was slain by his relatives or subjects,

A.D. 994 Cinaeth mac Malcolaim Ri Alban a suis occisus,

to which *The Ulster Annals* adds *by treachery*. *The Chronicle of the Picts and Scots* simply states that 'he was slain by his kindred at Fothercairn through the treachery of Finvela, daughter of Cunchor, Earl of Angus, whose only son Kenneth had killed at Dunsinnan'.

> *Interfectus est a suis hominibus in Fotherkern per perfidiam Finvelae filiae Cunthar, comitis de Engus cujus Finvelae unicum Filium predictus Kyneth interfecit apud Dunsinoen,*

and Spottiswood's *History* tells us,

> *As King Kenneth was visiting the grave of Palladius, being invited to lodge in the Castle of Fettercarne where there was 'a forest full of all manner of wild beasts that were to be had in any part of Alban' he was there treacherously murthered.*

This not unlikely version is adopted by Burton who speculates,

> *From the Tay to the Dee are the districts of old, called Angus and Mearns ... These ... were under Maormars, and among these Kenneth 'suppressed an Insurrection'; he asserted his authority where it had not been acknowledged before ... A young man was slain, whether the son of Maormar of the Mearns or the Maormar himself is not clear ... His mother, Finella, ... was strong enough to avenge his death on the King. She got him by force or guile into her stronghold of Fettercairn and slew him there.*

An Ingenious Theatrical Account

The accounts of the regicide by John of Fordoun and Hector Boece are, however, much more highly theatrical, spectacular and picturesque for, according to legend, Lady Finella committed the murder in a most ingenious manner. The story is indissolubly linked with the history and the traditions of the district. First, John of Fordoun:

> *This wily woman, ardently longing for the king's death, caused to be made in an out-of-the-way little cottage a kind of trap such as had never been seen before. For the trap had attached to it on all sides crossbows always kept bent by their several strings, and fitted with very sharp arrows, and in the middle thereof stood a statue fashioned like a boy, and cunningly attached to the crossbows so that, if anyone were to touch it and move it ever so little, the bowstrings of the crossbows would suddenly give way, and the arrows*

would straightway be shot forth and pierce him through. Having thus completed the preparations for perpetrating the crime, the wretched woman, always presenting a cheerful countenance to the king, at length beguilded him by flattery and treacherous words. The king went forth one day with a few companions into the wood to hunt, and while pursuing beasts hither and thither with his dogs ... happened by chance to put up hard by the town of Fettercairn where the traitress lived. After he had alighted from horseback, she took his hand and quickly led him alone to the house where the trap was concealed. 'If,' she said, 'the top of the head of this statue (the lever of the whole trap) be touched and moved, a marvellous and pleasant jest comes of it.' So, unconscious of hidden treachery, he gently with his hand drew towards him the head of the machine, thus letting go the levers and handles of the crossbows, and immediately he was shot through by arrows sped from all sides, and fell without uttering another word.

Fanciful 'Improvement' by Boece

Hector Boece (the most credulous of historians), in accordance with his custom of 'improving' with prolific fancy on the writings of those who went before him, has embellished the story by creations of his own invention, painting a strange and vivid picture with all the minuteness of an eye-witness and, like Holinshed, introducing a curiously skilful and complicated mechanical device which would have done credit to a 20th century inventor. He states that the king was received by Finella in her castle with lavish hospitality. Within she had caused to be constructed, fitted with rich furnishings, a tower *quhilk*, to use the words of Bellenden's Scots version of Boece,

> *was theiket with copper and hewn with mani subtil mouldry of sundry flowers and imageries, the work so curious that it exceeded all the stuff thereof.*

Boece talks of the same infernal and wonderful machine, invented by Lady Finella, but tells that in the centre of the room was a brass statue of the king in armour, an excellent likeness, which held in one hand a golden apple ornamented with six different gems and so artfully devised that, if anyone took hold of it, the crossbows would discharge their shower of arrows upon him with great force. When Kenneth arrived at the castle (yet another version says it was after dinner!) he was invited into the chamber. He admired the rich tapestries and furniture and asked what the flattering representation of himself signified. Finella smilingly and courteously requested him to accept from the hand of the image the apple which (so Kenneth was told) was a gift for himself. To avoid danger she artfully drew aside. The king no sooner took hold of the apple in all innocence than a secret spring caused the crossbows to discharge their arrows, and he fell mortally wounded. When, after a short time, his servants forced their way in, they found him dead on the floor.

In this case the motive is given as resentment at the king's efforts to end the complicated Pictish system of descent in the female line which half a century later gave Macbeth a better right to the throne than the *gentle Duncan* whom, according to Shakespeare, he supplanted. Other early historians have repeated Boece's marvellous tale though with hardly the same minuteness of detail.

Honest Andrew Wyntoun

George Buchanan, on the other hand, though a follower of Boece in many matters, found this story so fanciful (as did other historians) that he hesitated to accept it. It is not probable, says he, that in Scotland in those barbarous days any statue could have been so ingeniously contrived – and scarcely within the walls of a feudal castle. And we agree! He thinks it more likely that the king, who engaged in hunting the deer, the wolf, the badger and the bear in the pleasant and shady groves near Fettercairn, was slain in an ambush prepared by Finella because

> *when he* (Kenneth III) *came to Mearns to do reverence to the bones of Palladius, he turned a little out of his way to go and take a view of a neighbouring castle called Fettercairn.*

Skene in his *Celtic Albion* quotes from *The Pictish Chronicle* of St Berchan and states that Kenneth was slain on the moorland plain at the foot of the Mounth,

> *He will bend his steps, no neighbourly act*
> *To Magsliabh at the great Monedh;*
> *The Gael will shout around his head;*
> *His death was the end of it.*

And honest Andrew Wyntoun in the 15th century simply makes the sober statement in his *Rhyming Chronicle* that the king was killed while riding near Fettercairn by some of his courtiers and supposes

that he was waylaid or lured into a hunting match at the instigation
of Finella who

> *had ay in thowcht*
> *To get this kyng to dede be browcht;*
> *And for scho cowth noucht do, that be mycht,*
> *Scho made thame traytowyrs by hyr slycht,*
> *That the kyng befor them wend*
> *For his lele legis hade bene kend.*
> *As throw the Mernys on a day*
> *The kyng was rydand his hey way,*
> *Off hys awyne curt al suddanly*
> *Agayne hym ras a cumpany*
> *In to the towne off Fethyrkerne;*
> *To fecht wyth hym thai ware sa yherne,*
> *And he agayne thame faucht sa fast;*
> *But he thare slayne was at the last,*
> *And off this mak and rehers*
> *Owth hym wryttyn ar thire wers.*

The King's Hillock

Bishop Leslie, who wrote a century later, tells us especially that it
was while returning *from* a pilgrimage to St Palladius' shrine that
the king met his fatal accident. And the authorities quoted by
Jervise conclude that Kenneth unwittingly came by his death by the
swords of a band of hired assassins. Tytler and some other historians
are of opinion that Kenneth fell in the forests of Stracathro in Angus
in this way. The parishes of Fettercairn and Stracathro are separated only by the North Esk, and a knoll in a field a little to the
westward of the kirk of the latter parish has long borne the name of
the Re or Rye (King's) Hillock. Whether the spot is the burial place
of Kenneth III or the Earl of Moray or any of the other leaders who
fell in the battle which was fought at Stracathro in 1130 is a matter of
doubt. But it is certain that in the middle of the 19th century, when
the knoll was being reduced in size, a carefully constructed stone
coffin was found in the middle of it, about 2 ft. below the surface,
containing human remains and the figure of a fish, apparently of
gold, about the length of a man's finger.

Recorded Historical Fact

The details of the varying stories and how vengeance was accomplished vary according to the tellers. They are conflicting and not

altogether accurate for the vast majority of so-called traditions, directly traced to falsifiers of Scottish history like John of Fordoun, Boece and Buchanan, are all historically valueless. If we sweep away much of the romance of Fordoun's original story, the only certain historical fact that can be recorded is that about 995 (*Irish Annals*) at Green Castle, *Fenella's Castell of Fethircarne, the chiefest fortress of all the Mearns*, or nearby, there was slain Kenneth III, an enterprising warrior who had enlarged the bounds of his kingdom to comprise everything north of the Forth. And all historians agree that the king's untimely end was engineered in some way or another by the hand or treachery of the irate Finella. Some doubt exists even as to where the vengeful lady lived, and some historians record that the colourful episode of the assassination of Kenneth III is associated with Kincardine Castle while Buchanan asserts that the Castle of Fettercairn (Green Castle), 1½ miles south-west of the village, is the more likely locus.

Finella's Witching Flight

Some maintain that Finella was captured, taken back to her castle and burned, together with the building, while Holinshed relates that she took horse, escaped from her pursuers and, with the help of Constantine, Kenneth's successor, landed in Ireland. But Mearns legend, which sees Finella as a witch, avers that, attempting to escape by sea or to the fortresses on the cliffs by taking the nearest cut across country, she fled across the Howe and over the hill of Garvock, concealing herself for some time in the tree-tops on the hill of Strathfinella and leaping from branch to branch through the dense forest like a squirrel. When overtaken by her pursuers near the coast in the wooded rocky ravine of Lauriston, St Cyrus, called after her to this day the Den of Finella,

> *She leapt from the rocks to a wild, boiling pool*
> *Where her body was torn and toss'd.*

When overtaken in the Den, Finella is said by other chroniclers to have been apprehended and executed. This, of course, is mere tradition. Her memory is preserved locally in the name of beautiful Strathfinella, a continuation of the equally beautiful Glen of Drumtochty.

Kenneth's body was carried to Iona and buried with other kings and nobles. His subjects deeply lamented his untimely death, and in Perthshire, where he defeated and drove off the Danish invaders, the very name of Fettercairn became a byword and a reproach. Of

Green Castle after the murder of Kenneth the only record is that of John of Fordoun who relates that

> *the King's companions, missing him, broke into the house and, finding that he was murdered, consumed the* town *with fire and reduced it to ashes.*

Whether the castle was ever afterwards restored or occupied is a matter of conjecture. It may not be unreasonable to assume that for the slaughter of King Kenneth Green Castle as a residence was very likely doomed, forfeiting its territory to the king, and that from the date of the tragedy the manor was removed to Mondynes or to Kincardine the story of which as a royal residence may have begun at that time. The two hundred years that elapsed before the grant of Balbegno lands by William the Lion to Ranulph the Falconer are a complete blank in history and, indeed, Balbegno as the little new town might have become the manor. Over three hundred years elapsed before the building of Belbegno Castle (see page 406), and whether during these five centuries the seat of the feudal superiors was at Green Castle, Balbegno or elsewhere cannot now be determined.

And now back to the Mill of Kincardine and the T-junction to Kincardine Castle. Only some thirty yards along from the T-junction a stone cist was found on the top of a slight rise on the north side of the road during road construction shortly before 1863. It measured about 3 ft. in length and contained *unctuous earth and bones*. We should proceed straight on for a little over a quarter of a mile to join the Fettercairn-Clatterin' Brig road.

Hunter's Hill

Before we continue on our journey southwards to Fettercairn, however, one or two points of interest command our attention to the north, and you may consider it worthwhile to turn right towards the Clatterin' Brig for a short distance. To begin with, only 340 yards along the road, another Bronze Age stone cist was discovered in 1871 at a sand pit some 30 ft. up Hunter's Hill on our left. The sides and ends were formed of rough slabs placed on edge and the top of three flat stones each 6 to 7 ins. thick. Its length was 3½ ft., breadth 2½ ft. and depth 2 ft. It contained a bent up skeleton of large size, probably that of a chief or leader, buried where he fell. The skull and thigh bones were fairly entire but they crumbled on exposure to the air. On the right side and near the head was an empty clay bowl of rude workmanship, 6 ins. wide and 6 ins. deep, with a black streak round the interior, showing that it had been half filled with the food which, according to the custom of the time, was one of the things laid in the tomb beside the dead body.

Deer Dyke and Lammas Muir

A little over a quarter of a mile farther on we reach on our left a reservoir for the East of Scotland Water Board almost exactly opposite Finella's Castle on the other side of the Devilly Burn. And from here a wood extends along the left-hand side of the road for 140 yards. Immediately inside and parallel to the road (you can see it quite easily in some places) are the remains of part of the Deer Dyke which we discussed more fully on pages 166-170. A third of a mile farther on we reach on our left the road to Arnbarrow. If you drive up it for 700 yards or so, you will see on your left something of Lammas Muir where the famous Lammas Market was once held every July, horses and droves of cattle travelling north and south to it over the Cairn. Auction marts were eventually to supersede such old markets held periodically all over the county, Michael Fair at Drumlithie, Paddy Fair at Fordoun, St James's at Laurencekirk, Muchalls Fair at Cookney and Megray on Megray Hill.

If you have time, you may be able to see something of the seventy small cairns on Lammas Muir, varying between 16½ ft. and 5 ft. in diameter. The best preserved examples are situated near the west corner. Three small rectangular structures at the south corner are probably associated with the market-place depicted here on estate plans of 1789 and 1807.

Fasque

Now we are ready to resume our journey southwards. Let us turn to the right when we regain the Fettercairn road and drive for a mile and a half to the farm of Craigmoston where a food vessel was found in a Bronze Age short cist. (It is to be seen in Montrose Museum.) Over Craigmoston Bridge is an entrance to Fasque,[1] a superb, castellated mansion in the English baronial style with towers, battlements and a stately central dome. Elegant and very commodious, it faces the south on gently rising ground and commands from its elevated situation a most extensive and magnificent view of the Howe of the Mearns and the surrounding country as it peers from the woods that skirt the green and pleasant foothills of the Grampians around Fettercairn. For long a seat of the Ramsays, barons of Balmain, it was built by Sir Alexander Ramsay in 1809 at a cost, it is said, of £30,000, and some idea of its dimensions may be formed

[1] Fasque means 'a shelter'.

from the fact that the masons' and builders' wages were only 1/6 per day. The House was almost ready for occupation when Sir Alexander died in May, 1810. At midnight on 23rd October, 62 years later, a fire threatened to destroy the whole of the mansion, but by prompt action it was happily kept from extending to the main building. Again in 1937 an outbreak of fire destroyed three rooms in the east wing.

A Second Sir Alexander a Pioneer in Arboriculture

We have no idea exactly where the original 18th century mansion-house of Fasque was although a possible site is the flat space west of the present House where a fine flower garden requiring five gardeners used to bloom (it is now more or less derelict) and where a bowling-green and, from about 1900, a tennis court were once laid out. The old house, demolished by Ramsay, is pictured for us in Francis Douglas's *East Coast of Scotland*, 1780:

> *The house faces south and make   hree sides of a square. There are many good apartments in it, especially the dining-room and library. Just by the west end there is a den or hollow with a Chinese bridge thrown over it, and a small brook in the bottom. It is planted and laid out in serpentine gravel walks. The house is well sheltered on all quarters, especially on the north and south-east.*

There are few spots in this part of the country that could be of greater interest to students of arboriculture for Fasque has been famous for its trees for centuries. As far back as the early years of the 18th century the extensive grounds were enhanced by grand old beech and ash trees planted by David Ramsay who died in 1710. Like his father and grandfather before him, he was M.P. for the county. His brother, Sir Alexander Ramsay of Balmain and Fasque who succeeded him, was one of the chief landowners in St Cyrus where he owned the estate of Snadon. There he made his improvements as well as on his larger estates farther inland. He was a pioneer in the draining of the marshes and was one of the first people in Scotland to introduce summer fallow. It was he, too, who introduced the sowing of grass seed, the building of stone dykes to enclose his fields and the application of vast quantities of lime, transported in creels on horseback over the rough roads of Garvock, as he reclaimed acre after acre of moorland. His most notable work was as a pioneer in the planting of trees, and he it was who planted in 1730 the famous avenue of stately beeches leading to Fasque.

His nephew, Alexander Ramsay Irvine, carried on in a remarkable manner the improvements begun by his uncle. Not only did he plant larches, spruces and silver firs in the den already mentioned but he also introduced the cultivation of turnips and, with the making of roads, the use of wheel carriages hitherto locally unknown. Few men of his day did so much for the science of agriculture.

Magnificent Rhododendron

The pride which the Ramsays had taken in fine trees was shared by the Gladstone family who purchased Fasque and estate from them in 1829. An instance of how highly the fine specimens in the policies were prized is furnished by a story of an incident which occurred in 1838. A group of fine beeches near the house were uprooted by a storm, but Sir John Gladstone had the top branches lopped off and the trees raised again to their original positions by means of block and tackle. They took root and flourished magnificently – only to be levelled again by a storm in 1839! No further attempt was made to raise them. Features of the lovely grounds are the shady walks, the verdant lawns and everywhere the magnificent show of rhododendron boasting profusion and variety of colour. Sir John Gladstone made a special hobby of cultivating these shrubs, and the result of his enthusiasm is seen today in the masses of blooms which vary from the common rhododendron colours to delicate shades of yellow and pink.

Sir John Gladstone – the First of a Line

Sir John Gladstone, the first of a line of baronets whose names have become inextricably linked with the annals of the Mearns, was born in 1764. Endowed with exceptional business ability, he became a partner in a Liverpool firm of grain merchants and gradually extended the business to many parts of the world. In the course of his career he amassed a huge fortune, disposing of part of it in a manner which made him noted for his munificence in the Mearns and other parts of the country. In Parliament from 1820 until 1827, he contested Dundee at the General Election after William IV's death in 1837 but was defeated by Sir Henry Parnell. He was made a baronet in 1846 and spent his later years at Fasque where he died in 1851 aged 87.

Improvement of Fasque Estate

Soon after purchasing the estate Sir John energetically set about improving it. It was he who transformed the Bog of Foda nearby, nearly twenty acres in extent, into a beautifully picturesque artificial lake stocked with fish and fowl. Its banks are prettily clothed with trees and foliage, and it has two wooded islets in its placid waters. It was also he who built St Andrew's Episcopal Church, one of the loveliest buildings in the county, which stands a little to the eastward of Fasque and which is well worth a visit. Services are held weekly. The original building, consecrated on 28th August, 1847, was greatly improved by the erection of a new chancel which was consecrated by Alexander Forbes, Bishop of Brechin, on 15th April, 1869. It is in the Early English style of architecture with deep splayed lancet windows. The east window which contains representations of St Andrew and the four evangelists is a fine work of art.

Sir John also added the portico and facade which appears to be the top storey of the central tower of the present stately home. To the house he constructed a long new approach with a Gothic lodge and picturesque bridges over the burn. He built the walled garden, the stable block, an Episcopal school and almshouses and encouraged improvement of agriculture by bringing in new and better seed corn. He carried through a scheme with his tenant farmers to improve the houses of their labourers many of whom were living in very sordid conditions. And it was Sir John who erected the graceful spire of the parish church of Fettercairn where he was for many years a regular worshipper.

William Ewart Gladstone – Prime Minister

The eldest of Sir John Gladstone's four sons by his second wife was Sir Thomas, an able and scholarly man. In the affairs of the county he took a keen and active interest and was appointed Lord-lieutenant in 1876. His father had acquired the estates of Balbegno and Phesdo, and by the purchase of Littlestrath, Glendye, Strachan and Balnakettle Sir Thomas became the largest landed proprietor in the county. It was he who established the high traditions of the prize-winning Aberdeen Angus herd which was gradually phased out from the farm with post-War modernisation. The youngest of Sir John's four sons was the Right Hon. William Ewart Gladstone, born in 1809 and later to be four times Prime Minister. He spent 20 years of his early manhood at Fasque – until his father's death in 1851 – and, as many entries in his diaries testify, he was very fond of it. Fasque is now the home of Mr Peter Gladstone, great-grandson of the Victorian Prime Minister, who looks after this stately house for the present owner, Sir William Gladstone Bart., the Chief Scout. He it was who opened Fasque to the public in 1978 and introduced a herd of deer and some Soay sheep to the park in front.

The Finest Collection of Victoriana in Scotland

Fasque in all its spacious elegance is now presented to the public as it was, full of the domestic articles and furniture of the last century. An outstanding feature is the magnificent cantilever double stair-case, soaring past windows 'double glazed' with attractive engraved glass. Each step relies on the ones below for its support with only about six inches of stone inset into the wall – work which not many would be prepared to undertake today. It is certainly one of the finest stairs of its type existing. The public rooms are magnificent. The white and gold drawing-room (two rooms knocked into one) is a storehouse of most beautiful treasures, inlaid tables, games tables, a grand piano and other beautiful 18th and 19th century furniture, while the dining-room is hung with family portraits, including two by Raeburn. The library houses books collected by William Gladstone, the statesman, whose bedroom has become a place to display Gladstone memorabilia, particularly the illumin-ated scrolls sent from all over the country by a grateful electorate. There is, too, the bedroom of the Prime Minister's gifted sister, Helen, with its Gothic windows and sombre religious painting. In a nearby bathroom is one of the earliest versions of the modern loo, a flush commode disguised discreetly by its wooden box. Even the domestic rooms illustrate the lives and work of the staff in former times. In the vast kitchen there is an impressive collection of copper cooking ware.

Fasque, indeed, houses what some experts believe to be the finest collection of Victoriana in Scotland and possibly in Britain – orna-ments, knick-knacks, workaday tools, sporting equipment, house-hold requisites – all trivia mirroring the Victorian age and its people in a way which possibly cannot be matched elsewhere and the personal possessions of three generations of owners, Sir John Gladstone who bought Fasque in 1829, his elder son, Thomas, and Sir Thomas's only son, the late Sir John who died in 1926, together with members of their families. The house also illustrates the lives and work of the many servants who contributed to the community of a great household.

Fasque is open to the public daily (except Fridays) from 1.30-5.30 p.m. from May to September.

'Reminiscences of Scottish Life and Character'

At Fasque was born in January, 1793, The Very Reverend Edward Bannerman Ramsay who in 1846 became Dean of Edinburgh and who died in 1872. A handsome memorial to him in the shape of a tall, granite cross stands near St John's Church at the west end of Princes Street, Edinburgh. Of his many publications the most popular is his *Reminiscences of Scottish Life and Character*.

A Perfect Bronze Age Round Barrow

In just under half a mile we reach on the right another entrance to Fasque. But what is noteworthy for us this time is the drive on the opposite side of the road to another famous Kincardineshire mansion – Fettercairn House – and, incidentally, only 170 yards farther on, a perfect Bronze Age round barrow,[1] situated on a gravel ridge in a plantation immediately on our left-hand side. It is 55¾ ft. in diameter and 6½ ft. in height. In 1941 gravel digging on the south-east revealed a beaker.

Fettercairn House — Partly Ancient, Partly Modern

If you drive slowly, a glimpse of Fettercairn House can be caught through the trees almost exactly half a mile farther on. Although the origins of this partly ancient, partly modern building are obscure, the oldest visible part facing the south, and with the flower garden in front, was originally a plain three-storey building, long and narrow, but commodious for its time and midway in dimensions between a cramped, old castle and a modern country house. It was built shortly after the Restoration in 1666 by John, 1st Earl of Middleton, who incorporated the little that remained of an even older and much smaller building on the site. A plaque bearing his initials and those of his wife, Grizel Durham, together with the date of the erection of the house, can be seen over the lintel of the front tower door on the garden side. At the time the name of the estate was changed to that of Fettercairn, but a hamlet on the property still retains the name of Middleton. Lovely but decaying laburnums in the grounds show that they are at least as old as the south part of the mansion.

The Earl of Middleton, Lord of Fettercairn

The Middletons, a family of great antiquity, were by far the earliest lay proprietors in the district. William the First confirmed a donation charter to one of them of the lands of Middleton (Midtown) in

[1] Fuller details about round barrows will be found on page 423, where Witch Hillock is dealt with.

the parish of Fettercairn which had been granted by King Duncan. They were certainly here in 1221 for Humphrey of Middleton then bestowed a grant of the lands of Pittengardine to the Abbey of Arbroath.

John, Earl of Middleton, (who built Fettercairn House and who gifted the Mercat Cross of Fettercairn) was born about the year 1619 and, because of his brilliant talents, had a most eventful career. He entered the army as a 'pikeman' but was a captain under the leadership of Montrose as early as 1639. When Montrose espoused the side of the king, General Middleton was his most resolute opponent: in 1645, as brigadier and second in command to Sir David Leslie, he led his army through the Mearns in pursuit of Montrose when he found that the house of his cousin, James Strachan, had been burnt and his aged father, Robert Middleton, murdered as he sat in his chair at his own fireside in Caldhame Castle, long since razed to the ground. Whether out of revenge or as part of the campaign, Middleton proceeded to attack Montrose's house and to burn the Castle of Kincardine.

After a few years he, too, became a zealous Royalist. In 1648 he obtained a royal grant of the barony of Fettercairn, and in 1656 was created Earl of Middleton, Lord of Claermont[1] and Fettercairn, by Charles II whom he joined in exile in France after being taken prisoner while fighting in the Royalist cause at the Battle of Worcester. These titles were confirmed by letters patent at the Restoration in 1660 when the king appointed him Lord High Commissioner to the Parliament of Scotland. One of his daughters, Helen, married Patrick Lyon, Earl of Strathmore and Kinghorne, from whom the present owner of Fettercairn House is descended.

Later Owners, Enlargements and Alterations

In 1777 the estate was sold to Sir John Belsches Stuart of Inverness, M.P. for Kincardineshire and later a Baron of the Exchequer, whose only child, Williamina, had James Mill, the philosopher, as her tutor and was engaged to Sir Walter Scott, although with the disapproval of her parents. She finally married Mr William Forbes, son of the 6th Sir William Forbes of Pitsligo, the Edinburgh banker who on his father's death became Sir William Stuart Forbes, the 7th baronet of Pitsligo and Fettercairn. Of most of this family, from Alexander, 1st Lord Forbes of Pitsligo onwards, there are portraits in Fettercairn House. Still preserved, too, is a brooch, a gold St Andrew

[1] Part of Fettercairn estate on the hillside, east of Arnbarrow, was named Claermont.

cross, given by Prince Charles Edward to the 4th Lord, a great Jacobite figure who fought in the 1715 and 1745 risings and raised the men of Buchan to the Prince's support. Fettercairn House was enlarged in 1829 by the 8th Baronet, Sir John H. Stuart Forbes, Bart., an elegant frontage to the north-west being added in the Elizabethan style. In 1877 a small wing was built on the east side by his son-in-law, the 20th Lord Clinton, adding a handsome and convenient suite of rooms and offices. The 21st Lord Clinton, who succeeded to the Fettercairn estates in 1869, made some alterations to the interior and built the library, and now Fettercairn House is perhaps, with the exception of Fasque, the most commodious in the county. It is interesting to note that it was the 21st Lord Clinton who set up the Forestry Commission of which he was Commissioner from 1919 to 1929 and who in 1957, when he died aged 94, was engaged in the unusual task of felling timber which he himself had planted. It is to his granddaughter, Mrs Peter Somervell, that the estate now belongs. She is a cousin of our present Queen.

Fettercairn House, partly ancient, partly modern, and from the 17th century the home of the Middletons, a family of great antiquity. It now belongs to Mrs Peter Somervell, a cousin of the Queen. Here were discovered in 1930 the 'Fettercairn Papers', including around 1,100 letters written or received by Boswell, three journals of Boswell and 119 letters from Samuel Johnson – one of the most important literary finds of recent years.

James Boswell's Manuscripts Discovered After 135 Years

One of the most interesting stories concerning Fettercairn House has its beginning with one of Mrs Somervell's ancestors, Williamina Stuart, mentioned above, who was wooed by Sir Walter Scott when he paid a visit to Fettercairn House in his youth. Instead, however, she married a friend of James Boswell who by his will nominated her husband and two other friends, W. J. Temple and Edward Malone, as his literary executors. Now, Boswell died in London in 1795, and for many years it was supposed that his manuscripts had been destroyed immediately afterwards. But not so. It was to become clear that Boswell's papers and collections of manuscripts had been brought to Fettercairn House after his death by Sir William Forbes in his capacity of executor. Yet he was unfortunately to survive Boswell by only three months so that the three executors never met and no settlement was ever made of Boswell's papers. They were to lie in a number of chests in Fettercairn House for 135 years before their discovery in 1930 by Professor Claude Collier Abbott while he was lecturer at King's College, Aberdeen.

Discoveries Which Preserve Boswell for Posterity

While there are a few breaks in continuity, the 'Fettercairn Papers' were one of the most important literary finds of recent years. The discovery of these manuscripts went far to fill in the gaps in the collection of Boswell's papers and to give further success to Boswell's attempt *to preserve himself for posterity*. They undoubtedly enlarge our knowledge of Boswell and give a far clearer insight into the manners and customs of the 18th century Scotland in which he lived. The Boswell Papers were purchased by Yale University and published in 1950 in a series of fascinating volumes, including the *London Journal* which covers the period from 1762-3. just after Boswell had attained his majority.

The principal discoveries made at Fettercairn House were as follows. There were over 1,000 letters received by Boswell over the greater part of his life. They included the lost half of his correspondence with the Rev. William Temple, amounting to no fewer than 160 letters. Secondly, there were forty-one letters written by Boswell to Sir William Forbes, the aforementioned preserver of this mass of documents, and drafts or copies of some fifty others written by Boswell to various friends, including Burke, Malone, Wilkes, Langton, Oglethorpe, Paoli, Sir John Pringle, Anna Seward, the Bishop of Killaloe and Lord Hailes. A corresponding number of letters from these friends appear in the first category. Thirdly, there were 119 letters from Samuel Johnson, some of them hitherto unpublished, written to Langton, Reynolds, Mrs Porter, Windham and others, and collected by Boswell when working on the *Life* though not wholly included in it. Fourthly, there were three journals of Boswell, one of which covers the period of his first acquaintance with Johnson and described by Professor Abbott as *in some ways the most interesting and revealing of all Boswell's Journals.* Lastly, there were various miscellaneous Boswelliana which included a register of letters sent and received from 1769 to 1782, some Johnsoniana and a number of letters which passed among several members of the Boswell Johnson circle.

Fettercairn Linked with a Remote Past

In just under three-quarters of a mile we arrive in the Square of the picturesque and neat old-world village of Fettercairn, perhaps one of the most attractive villages in the county. It occupies a delightful situation in a pleasant and interesting countryside on the western fringe of the fertile Howe of the Mearns. Set amid rich woods and lush fields and within easy reach of the Cairn o' Mounth pass to Feughside and Deeside, it is a charming place for a quiet holiday amid beautiful surroundings. The present village, which is really quite tiny, dates from the middle of the 18th century when it consisted mostly of clay thatched huts which were replaced about 1750 by the strongly built two-storey houses round the historic market square. These fine old cottages possess considerable character and form a pleasing architectural group. They are unique in having two farm steadings as part of the built-up area and form one of the community's chief assets. But Fettercairn has several links with a much more remote past. It was once a burgh of barony on the estate of Fettercairn or Middleton and is a place of great antiquity. Archaeologists have found a wealth of sculptures, stone slabs and coins in the neighbourhood. It was upon the decay and extinction of this older Fettercairn on the one hand and of Kincardine on the other that the modern village flourished.

Fethyrkerne Mentioned in 'The Brus' and Domesday Book

According to the old chroniclers the ancient *towne* of Fettercairn existed about the year 1000, ranking in antiquity with Dunnottar. While some authorities maintain that *Fotherkern* was the original name, the oldest form as written by Wyntoun, Prior of Lochleven and the rhyming chronicler who gave us the story of Finella and the murder of Kenneth III, is *Fethyrkerne.* There have been no fewer than twenty different forms of the word from the 10th century to the present time. The 'cairn' retained in the name, descriptive of the hillocks and heights lying about the village and Green Cairn, possibly suggests that the village originally stood not at Kincardine or Green Castle but south-west of the present village, alongside the north side of the knoll on which the fort of Green Cairn stood. As with the town of Kincardine not a trace remains. Fettercairn is mentioned in Barbour's *Brus* and also in the *Domesday Book*.

The Throng of the Market from 1504 Onwards

On April 15th, 1504, James IV granted the first charter to the village to suit his subjects crossing the Cairn o' Mounth and likewise to honour for his good service Adam Hepburn of Craggis (Inglismaldie). In it he

> *fefts and creates the lands and toun of the kirktoun of Fethircarn in the shire of Kincardin, pertaining heritably to* (i.e. belonging to) *Adam Ogstoun and Elizabeth Ogstoun, his spouse, a free burgh for ever; granting to the inhabitants the usual privilege of buying, selling, and being burgesses, and that the said Adam and his heirs shall have the power of electing bailies and other officers; and that the burgesses shall have a market cross and a market every week on any day the said Adam may appoint with public yearly fairs on the Festival of St Peter ad vincula and during the octaves thereof, with tolls, etc.*

So was Fettercairn for the first time in history created a free burgh of barony with a Cross, the right to hold an annual public fair on August 1st and a weekly market. Following the superiority of the Woods of Balbegno, this licence was renewed to John, Earl of Middleton and Claermont, superior of the village and proprietor of the mansion of Fettercairn, in 1670. These markets were originally held on the ground now occupied by the school and its playground, in former days known as the Market Park, where cattle, sheep etc, were sold. Hiring markets were held regularly in the village at the terms of Whitsunday and Martinmas. While the main object, of course, was servant-feeing, these days were observed as general holidays in the parish. Even as late as the 1860's the village street all the way from the bridge to the Cross used to be lined with stalls selling sweets and all kinds of wares. A few cattle used to appear for sale, huddled together in small groups to the east of the Cross, and near the Cross itself were displayed for sale tubs, butter kits, milk cogs and tee-totums for the youth of the village. In the throng of the market cheap Jacks did a roaring trade. From a subsequent charter to the burgesses of Montrose it appears that wool, skins, hides, salmon and other merchandise also were sold at Fettercairn markets.

Fettercairn Often Visited by Royalty

Although Fettercairn is one of the most peaceful looking villages in the Mearns, it was not always so for in olden times the main route from the south to Aberdeen used to lie, not along the coast as it does nowadays, but through the south-west corner of the Mearns and over the Cairn o' Mounth. Situated as it was, therefore, at the eastern end of the Grampians on a natural highway between north and south, and, furthermore, adjacent to the ancient Castle of Kincardine, Fettercairn was often visited by kings and queens. Later royalty passing through on some if not all of their visits to Aberdeen were King James VI and Mary Queen of Scots, the former in 1582, 1589, 1592, 1594 and 1600, the latter on 26th August, 1562, when she journeyed northwards, accompanied by her nobles, attendants and men-at-arms, to quell the Huntly rebellion.

Fettercairn a Focal Point in History

Fettercairn was also the focal point for some stormy moments in history. The many armies which poured through the village left traces of themselves and their movements. Through the Howe of the Mearns the Romans passed northwards to the Moray Firth, and in 1303, by almost the same route, Edward I with his forces passed through the village on his conquering journey to Aberdeen. Wallace's men fought here, and Robert the Bruce won a great victory close by so that the county thereby became a battleground for Romans and Britons, Scots and English. It is indeed a fact supported by eminent authorities that few districts in Scotland have witnessed to a greater degree scenes of battle and bloodshed than the neighbourhood of Fettercairn. From the loopholes of its church spire at least six battlefields can be viewed.

The Presence of the Marquis of Montrose

In no place more than in Fettercairn was the presence felt of the Marquis of Montrose, his erratic marches and sudden victories throughout Scotland reading like a romance of history. We first hear of him as an ardent Covenanter on 12th February, 1639, riding with a chosen company of 200 men through Fettercairn and over the Cairn o' Mounth to support a meeting of Covenanters at Turriff when the Committee of the Tables had given him command of their forces. In the autumn of 1644, having turned Royalist, he passed twice through the village. And what an amount of suffering the helpless inhabitants of Fettercairn were subjected to later in the year because of him! According to Spalding, a regiment raised by the Earl of Argyle in opposition to Montrose landed with their wives at Old Aberdeen and so plundered the country to compensate for small pay, or no pay, that 800 of their number were paid off with 4,000 marks at Drum and took the high road south. Their wives were sent by the citizens to overtake their husbands at Fettercairn which was consequently plundered by this wild, lawless and hungry army with their followers.

After his defeat by Argyle at Inverlochy on February 2nd the following year the ill-fated Marquis of Montrose again visited Fettercairn with a number of Highland chiefs and their followers, routing a party of Covenanters at Haulkerton and laying waste the neighbouring countryside. Marching southward from Aberdeen, he pillaged and burnt Stonehaven,[1] Cowie, the estates and lands of the Earl Marischal, who took refuge in the Castle of Dunnottar, and the lands of Drumlithie and Arbuthnott as well as the Howe of the Mearns which was left *black with fire and red with blood* amidst the tears and lamentations of the wretched inhabitants. Spalding relates the following incident of the army of Montrose in 1645:

(Montrose) *cumis to Fettercarne ypone Frydday, quarteris his foot army, and sendis out quarter maisteris to quarter sum trovperis in the countrie. Bot Generall Maior Hurry, lying in ambush within the planting of Halkertoun by thair knouledge, issues out suddantlie, with ane gryte cry and ane schout vpone thir trovperis, who returnit bak to Montroiss camp schortlie. And he directlie sendis out ane better number of trovperis. But how sone Hurry seis thame he takis intil ane vther buss hard besyd; bot he is rousit out, and routit throw the north water, who fled, with gryter skaith nor he gave, to Livetennant Generall Major Ballie, lying nar hand with his army. Montroiss trovperis returnis back to the camp, quhair Mr James Strathauchin's* (the minister's) *hous in Fettercarne was brynt. Montroiss stayit at Fettercarne, Frydday, Setterday, Sonday, and marchis thairfra vpone Mononday, the 25th of Merche* (1645) *with his foot army.*

[1] See *Highways and Byways Round Stonehaven*, pp. 19-20.

Processions of Different Character

It would appear from Spalding's account that General Blake and his Covenanting army passed through Fettercairn on April 11th en route to Aberdeen and

> *syne merchis throw the heidis* (hillsides) *to Fettercarn, and vpone Setterday, 10th of May, he cums and campis in the Birss, plundering the countrie quhair euer he gois, eiting the grein growing cornes, scarss cum to the blaid, with their horssis. He wes estimat aboue 2,000 foot and sexscoir trovperis.*

Five years later, in 1650, the people of Fettercairn saw the great and high-handed Montrose, sadly humbled, after his betrayal by MacLeod of Assynt being led along on horseback, a prisoner bound hand and foot with straw ropes, to his execution in Edinburgh.

At the end of the same year another procession of a different character passed through Fettercairn. The Earl of Errol, journeying from Slains Castle to Scone where he had to officiate as Lord High Constable of Scotland at the coronation of Charles II on January 1st, 1651, arrived in Fettercairn from Muchalls on December 26th and lodged there for the night. In a Household Book of the Errol family the following record of discharge occurs:

> *For supper and breakfast at Fettercarne in Harie Balfour's*
> *£7-0-0 (11/8 stg.)*
> *For corn and stra for 7 horse, one night there £5-4-0 (8/8)*
> *To the servants in drink money   £0-8-0 (8d)*

the whole amount of the bill being 21/- sterling.

An Ancient Mercat Cross

Of particular interest to visitors is the ancient Mercat Cross, an octagonal column, 10 ft. high, set upon a flight of six concentric octagonal steps, each 1 ft. in height, which have been several times renewed. The shaft is surmounted by a four-sided capital, its markings forming a link with ancient Scottish history and custom. On the west side is the Scottish lion rampant with a double tressure, the arms of one of the Lords of the Barony, John, the celebrated first Earl of Middleton. On the east side are the coroneted initials of this nobleman, on the south a sundial, and on the north the date 1670.

Attached to the pillar is an iron hasp or rivet and two links to which criminals and scolds in the olden days used to be chained by the jougs, an instrument of punishment consisting of an iron collar placed round the neck of the wrongdoer with another part called the branks, a sort of iron halter or cage over the head with a 'bit' for the mouth – the latter a special punishment to silence and punish unruly tongued termagents who had there to suffer the indignities of the crowd. The marks of the chains can still be seen on the shaft of the Cross, evidence of frequent use. On another side is notched a line showing the measurement of the old standard Scottish ell (37 ins.). Here traders had their measure adjusted and bargainers came to clinch a deal. Handfasting or betrothal at this spot was no light matter either, for the Cross was an emblem of the Church which had reached the market-place to impress men with the sacredness of a bargain.

The Cross is believed to be part of the original, old Mercat Cross

Part of the historic market square of the picturesque and old-world village of Fettercairn, one of the most attractive villages in Kincardineshire. In the background are shown the strongly-built two-storey houses erected about 1750; in the foreground is the ancient Mercat Cross, an octagonal column set upon a flight of six concentric octagonal steps. Attached to the pillar is an iron hasp to which the jougs used to be chained. On another side is a line showing the measurement of the old Scottish ell.

of the extinct county town of Kincardine (new *Statistical Account*, 1837), said to have been removed from there to Fettercairn in 1730 by the Earl of Middleton. Biscoe, however, in his *Earls of Middleton* asserts that the first Earl erected it in 1670 in Fettercairn in memory of his wife, Grizel Durham, when he was granted in that year by Act of Parliament a renewal of the royal licence to hold weekly markets and to erect a Cross in the town, a licence originally granted in 1504. Long before 1670 St Mark's Fair (named doubtless in honour of the saint to whom the kirk was dedicated) was a market of considerable importance. The probability is, certainly, that the capital with the date 1670 was made for Fettercairn and not for the decaying town of Kincardine from which the county headquarters of judicial business had been removed to Stonehaven in 1607. But whether the present shaft was the original shaft of a Cross erected in Fettercairn in 1504 or the original shaft of the Cross erected in the county town of Kincardine which lay a mile and a half north-west of the village (which seems more likely) cannot be determined. It certainly looks very much older than its capital. Fettercairn Cross, a physical token of an old burgh of barony, is scheduled as an ancient monument in the care of HM Office of Works. This ensures the preservation for all time of this most historic landmark in the Mearns. It is surely time that Fettercairn, along with several other old-world spots in the Mearns, was designated a conservation area.

Church and Ministers

Several other features in the village attract attention. The splendid parish church which dominates the village from the east on its storied kirkyard ridge was built in 1803, a tall, handsome spire being added in 1878. It was originally a mensal church of the Archbishop of St Andrews. In old times the bell was suspended from a tree which stood upon 'Bell Hillock' at the west end of the old church and now no more. The first minister of the parish, as far as can be found, was *Maister David Setone, persone de Fethyrcarne* whose name appears in minutes of the Council Register of the Burgh of Aberdeen in 1491. He was also designated *Rector of Fethyrcarne* and held office at least till 1514. In 1567 the minister (Patrick Bouncle) was also minister of the three adjoining parishes of Fordoun, Newdosk and Conveth (Laurencekirk) at a salary of 24 pounds *with the support of the Prior of St Androis*. Other ministers included David Strachan, afterwards Bishop of Brechin, and William Chalmers who presented a congratulatory address to Queen Anne from his brethren in the Episcopal Church.

The predecessor of the parish church of Fettercairn, *a very old house, too narrow for its length*, stood immediately to the south.

Adam Wears Shorts in the Churchyard

In the churchyard, standing by itself 16 yards from the church door, may be seen an interesting 5 ft. high gravestone which is an unusual example of local 18th century sculpture. On the upper part of the stone, which is dated 1737, there is a carving of Eve tempting Adam with the forbidden fruit from the laden Tree of Knowledge. Both are headless, and Adam is depicted as wearing a pair of short trousers. Surrounding this representation of our first parents (who symbolise the mortality of mankind) is the couplet,

> *Adam and Eve by eating the forbidden tree*
> *Brought all mankind to sin and misery.*

Carvings of an hour-glass, skull and cross-bones and a sickle with an arrow through the handle cover the foot of the stone. The other side is also elaborately carved. It depicts a crowned figure surmounted by two angels with, underneath, a heraldic crest containing the monogram Dm.

Hall, Fountain and Distillery

The fine Public Hall, built in 1890 by public subscription and sur-mounted by an elegant tower, is English in style with a leaning to Scottish neo-baronial, and the neatly carved and turreted fountain-tower memorial to Sir John Hepburn Stuart Forbes, Bart., of Pitsligo and Fettercairn (1804-66) was erected in 1869. Twenty feet high, the memorial is of polished Redhall (Edinburgh) freestone and is in the early English Gothic style, richly ornamented. The drinking basin is of polished Peterhead granite. There is also a widely-known distillery which was established at Nethermill on the outskirts of the village in 1824 and which, although burnt down in October, 1889, still functions actively. Because of its well-known quality whisky the name 'Fettercairn' once commanded the highest price in the home and foreign markets. The distillery produces 'Old Fettercairn', its own brand of Highland malt whisky, but most of its output is used for blending. The fifteen employees of the distillery work a three-shift system, and output is in the region of 295,000 gallons a year. Perhaps one should add that the Burn and Fetter-cairn House Curling Club, formed in 1848, is the oldest in the Mearns. Its curling pond, as also the beautiful expanse of ice on Fasque Lake, have been the scene of many a well-contested bonspiel. Moreover, Fettercairn Farmers' Club is the oldest provincial agricultural society in Scotland, being established in 1826.

Handsome Triumphal Archway

Attracting most attention, however, and greeting the visitor at the entrance to the village where it spans the roadway at the west end of the bridge crossing the Cauldcots Burn is the picturesque and very handsome stone triumphal archway in all its Rhenish Gothic splendour, erected in 1864 at a cost of nearly £250 to commemorate the visit on 20th September, 1861, of Queen Victoria and Prince Albert.

The picturesque archway erected in Fettercairn in 1864 to commemorate the visit three years earlier of Queen Victoria and Prince Albert. They stayed in the Ramsay Arms Hotel, appropriately enough immediately adjacent.

The semi-circular memorial arch, rather more than 18ft. in the span and upwards of 16 ft. in height to the keystone, is flanked by two massive octagonal battlemented towers, each about 7 ft. in diameter and supported by buttresses 60 ft. high. Above on one side is inscribed 'Visit of Victoria and Albert 1861' in round letters of Old English character; on the other side the date of erection. On each side, above the cornice is a royal crown and, cut in high relief, the national emblem. Mr John Milne, a St Andrews architect and native of Fettercairn, superintended the whole work without fee.

The Ramsay Arms a Historical Puzzle

The impressive arch stands, appropriately, right in front of the Ramsay Arms Hotel where the Queen and Prince Albert, on one of their Highland tours, with a few members of the Balmoral house party (Princess Alice, her husband, Prince Louis of Hesse, and others of the suite) spent a night incognito as *a marriage party from Aberdeen*. The Ramsay Arms Hotel, enlarged and modernised several times, has been changed out of recognition from the tiny village inn which it was then. The room in which the Queen dined is now a drawing-room, and upstairs one can still see part of the small but well-furnished room in which she slept, still used as a bedroom. The hangings from the Queen's bed, which were rescued from a jumble-sale by a farmer's wife, can be seen in the Glenesk Folk Museum.

The hotel is the centre of a historical puzzle for, although the Queen called the inn the Ramsay Arms, its present name, it seems it was then known as the Eagle Inn and consisted of the two-storey portion at the back of the present hotel with the Queen's bedroom upstairs in the projecting gable facing the street. Sir Alexander Ramsay of Balmain was the proprietor and Charles Durward the landlord. A brass plaque with these details engraved upon it is still held by the lessees, but it has never been actually fixed to any part of the fabric.

The Queen's 'Great Expedition'

The Queen had left Deeside that morning, crossed the shoulder and 'ladder' of Mount Keen on a hill pony to Invermark Lodge to pay a visit to Fox Maule (Lord Dalhousie). In the afternoon she drove down Glenesk in a carriage. But the journey, which in Her Majesty's *Journal* is termed a *Great Expedition*, is best described in her own words, faithfully and minutely as follows:

*We had three miles further to drive to Fettercairn, in all 40
miles from Balmoral. We came upon a flat country, evidently much cultivated, but it was too dark to see anything.
At a quarter past seven o' clock we reached the small, quiet
town or rather village of Fettercairn, for it was very small,
not a creature stirring, and we got out at the quiet little inn,
'Ramsay Arms', quite unobserved, and went at once upstairs. There was a very nice drawing-room, and next to it a
dining-room, both very clean and tidy _ then to the left,
our bedroom, which was excessively small, but also very
clean and neat, and much better furnished than at Gran-
town. Alice had a nice room, the same size as ours; then
came a mere morsel of one (with a 'press-bed') in which
Albert dressed: and then came Lady Churchill's bedroom
just beyond. Louis and General Gray had rooms in an hotel
called the 'Temperance Hotel', opposite. We dined at eight,
a very nice, clean, good dinner. Grant and Brown waited.
They were rather nervous, but General Gray and Lady
Churchill carved, and they had only to change the plates
which Brown soon got in to the way of doing. A little girl of
the house came in to help, but Grant turned her round to
prevent her looking at us. The landlord and landlady knew
who we were, but no one else except the coachman, and
they kept the secret admirably. The evening being bright
moonlight, and very still, we all went out, and walked
through the village, where was a sort of pillar or town cross
on steps, and Louis read, by the light of the moon, a
proclamation for collections of charities which was stuck up
on it. We walked on along a lane, a short way, hearing
nothing whatever, not a leaf moving, but the distant barking
of a dog! Suddenly, we heard a drum and fifes! We were
greatly alarmed, fearing we had been recognised; but Louis
and General Gray who went back, saw nothing whatever.
Still, as we walked slowly back, we heard the noise from
time to time; and, when we reached the inn door, we stopped, and saw six men march up with fifes and drum (not a
creature taking any notice of them) go down the street and
back again. Grant and Brown were out, but had no idea
what it could be. Albert asked the little maid, and the
answer was, 'It's just a band,' and that it walked about in
this way twice a week. How odd! It went on playing some
time after we got home. We sat till half-past ten working and*

Albert reading, and then retired to rest. Saturday, September 21st. Got to sleep after two or three o' clock. The morning was dull and close and misty, with a little rain; hardly any one stirring, but a few people at their work. A traveller had arrived at night, and wanted to come up into the dining-room, which is the 'commercial travellers' room'; and they had difficulty in telling him he could not stop there. He joined Grant and Brown at their tea; and on asking, 'What's the matter here?' Grant answered, 'It's a wedding party from Aberdeen.' At 'the Temperance Hotel' they were very anxious to know whom they had got. All, except General Gray, breakfasted a little before nine. Brown acted as my servant, brushing my skirt and boots, and taking any message; and Grant as Albert's valet. At a quarter to ten we started the same way as before, except that we were in the carriage which Lady Churchill and the General had yesterday. It was, unfortunately, misty, and we could see no distance. The people had just discovered who we were, and a few cheered us as we went along. We passed close to Fettercairn, Sir J. Forbes's house; then, farther on to the left, Fasque, belonging to Sir T. Gladstone, who has evidently done a great deal for the country, having built many good cottages. We then came to a very long hill, at least four miles in length, called Cairniemonth, whence there is a fine view; but which was entirely obscured by a heavy driving mist. We walked up part of it, and then for a little while Alice and I sat alone in the carriage.

Randal's Knap

We leave Fettercairn by the Stonehaven (B966) road and travel east for only 330 yards until we stop by the Fettercairn road sign. On our left across the field can be seen a prominent knoll, measuring about 72 ft. in diameter and 6½ ft. in height which may be a prehistoric barrow and which was probably the mod or mote-hill of the Earl of Middleton in olden times. Since the middle of the 18th century it has borne the name of Randal's Knap because of the weird tale that upon it an Irish soldier, Randal Courtney, who resided in Luthermuir, was hanged. He had broken into the *stane hoose o' Cadam* (Caldhame Castle) and stolen a watch and other articles, the property of the laird of Caldhame. Caught in a weaving cellar at the 'Townhead' of Fettercairn (he was identified by means of the watch he had stolen) and tried before the Justiciary Court on 6th August, 1743, he was sentenced to be hanged at Fettercairn on 21st September following.

Thornton Castle

Quarter of a mile farther on we leave the B966 to take the right-hand (B9120) fork towards Laurencekirk. In three-fifths of a mile we see immediately on our left the old farmhouse of Middleton. Here in the 18th century the *blythe-meats* were being enjoyed by a few neighbours when a party of the Duke of Cumberland's soldiers entered and cleared the festive board! In a further mile and three-tenths we reach on the right at the crossroads the entrance to Thornton Castle, a fairly small but excellently preserved example of a late 15th or early 16th century castle to which a more modern mansion is now attached. There are various additions of later date to the northern and eastern parts of the building: the oldest of these ends in a round flanking tower on the north-east which is claimed to be a 13th century structure. Much alteration was done in the 19th century.

The castle is an old L-shaped keep, four storeys in height, together with a renewed garret storey. On the main block a renovated panel gives the date 1531 although some parts of the building are probably earlier. A stair-wing is attached. The structure has a crenellated parapet with open rounds at the corners carried on a chequered corbel-table. There is a parapet walk round the building, drained by the usual cannon-like spouts projecting as a half round to give access past a chimney stack on the east front.

Many original features remain inside including the vaulted basement, now the vestibule, and the wide, roomy turnpike stair. Behind the panelling of the Hall on the first floor traces of tempora painting remain.

The Lairds and Lands of Thornton

The lands of Thornton were at one time named Pitgarvie; Thornton is an English name and the best example in the county of a change from a Gaelic to an English name as early as the 14th century. These lands, in fairly low-lying parkland, originally belonged to the family of Thornton of that Ilk but passed in 1309 by marriage to Sir James Strathauchin or Strachan who came from the original home of the family in the strath beyond the Cairn o' Mounth. In the Strachan family (*the belted knichts o' Thornton*) the lands remained for thirteen generations until the 17th century. Their names appear on a handsome heraldic panel on the flanking tower on the north-east side of the castle. In 1460 John de Strathachin was a receiver of rents for the Crown, and in 1590 another Strachan of the same name, a good Protestant it would seem, was appointed to a commission to act against Jesuits and seminary priests. In 1616, because of trouble between a later laird, Sir Alexander Strachan of Thornton, and Sir Robert Arbuthnott of that Ilk, the former was required to pay 10,000 merks caution to the Privy Council to keep the peace, and two years later was politely exiled by being required to travel abroad for three years. Despite this, however, four years after his return he was created a baronet! The 6th baronet, Admiral Sir Richard Strachan, CBE, was a distinguished naval commander of the Napoleonic period.

The estate of Thornton in 1683 passed by marriage to Robert Forbes of Newton whose family owned it for three generations. The Fullartons then became the owners, and after them Lord Gardenstone and, in the 19th century, the Crombies. After a gap of five and a half centuries the castle returned to the Thornton family when in 1893 it was bought back by Sir Thomas Thornton, Town Clerk of Dundee, a descendant of the baronial family of the Thorntons who first appeared during the Wars of Independence. The present laird is Mr Nigel Thornton-Kemsley, the son of the former M.P. for North Angus and Mearns.

The castle is noted for its rock-gardens and rhododendrons and is occasionally open to the public.

A Remarkable Discovery at Bent

We turn right now towards Laurencekirk along the B9120 but take the first turn left in only a little over 200 yards. In two-fifths of a mile we arrive at the farm of Bent. Here in the course of draining bogs in 1862, some 400 or 500 yards on our right, a remarkable discovery was made. A large accumulation of the bones of horses, cattle, deer and a human skeleton were found in what had probably been a 'wal-ee' ('well-eye'), the part of a quagmire most likely to prove fatal to unsuspecting man or beast. The animals had probably met their fate, at long intervals between, when on the way to quench their thirst at a neighbouring stream. A number of the bones were transferred to Montrose Museum, and the following account is extracted from the records there:

The bones were found beneath 3 ft. or 4 ft. of peat, lying in a quicksand through which a strong spring of water arose, and belonged to man and the following animals – viz. the

*horse, the dog, the red deer and the roe deer; and three
varieties of oxen – Bos primigenius, Bos longifrons and a
hornless animal resembling the existing Angus breed.*

Mains of Haulkerton and Ancient Stones

Straight on now for just under a mile to the crossroads at Kilnhill.
Here we turn right and drive for just over half a mile until we reach
the T-junction at Mains of Haulkerton. Here we turn left. It is
interesting to note that the present Mains of Haulkerton was the
first farmhouse in the parish to be floored with deal, carpets and
hearth-rugs being unknown even in 1805 when it was built. (The
first sofa that came to the parish did not appear till twenty years
later.)

The name of the present farmhouse still bears witness to the past
existence of Haulkerton Castle nearby although the stones of which
it was built were taken chiefly from the ruins of Pitarrow Castle, just
under one and three-quarter miles away as the crow flies. Still
prominent on the farm buildings are two stones which had done
service on the walls of Haulkerton Castle, one of them bearing the
date of (15)56 – the first two numbers were destroyed in a fire –
and with the head of a female carved on it, perhaps that of Elizabeth, only daughter of Sir Archibald Douglas of Glenbervie who
married Sir Alexander Falconer, founder of the first part of the old
castle. Another stone bears the initials L.A.F. and the date 1648
when an addition may have been made to the castle in the time of
another Sir Alexander Falconer, a Lord of Session who was afterwards created the first Lord Falconer of Haulkerton in 1647.

The Cowies of the Mains

For a century and a half before 1805 an earlier building was tenanted by successive members of the Cowie family who had occupied
the farm for five generations. The first of whom there is authentic
record is Alexander Cowie (1630-1709). His wife was a daughter of
David Beattie, probably the progenitor of the leading Beattie families in the parish.

There is in existence a lease of the farm of Mains of Haulkerton to
another Alexander Cowie in 1710 from which it appears that the
annual rental was under £40, paid in kind. If the other lands were
rented in proportion, the whole rental of the parish at the time
would have been rather less than the present rent of the Mains.
There is available, too, the valuation of the same farm in 1756, the
farm consisting of 300 acres. The prices are given in sterling:

10 young cattle	*£15*	*0*	*0*
7 kine	*14*	*0*	*0*
6 car (calves)	*4*	*0*	*0*
16 oxen	*48*	*0*	*0*
11 horses	*55*	*0*	*0*
carts, ploughs, harrows etc.	*27*	*1*	*8*
Sowing of the town	*80*	*0*	*0*
A year's maintenance	*36*	*6*	*8*

The entire value of the stock thus amounted to £276 8s 4d, while the buildings, including the farmhouse, were valued at less than £30.

The first Alexander Cowie's great-great-grandson who in 1862 retired from the farm is of interest because, after winning two gold medals from the Highland Agricultural Society for the best plans for large and small farms, he was selected by the editors of *Encyclopaedia Britannica* and *Chambers' Encyclopaedia* as a contributor on various agricultural subjects. On these he was a prolific writer, and his works include *Rabies or Madness in the Dog, Farm Buildings Past and Present, An Address to Farm Labourers* and *A Sketch of Seasons, Crops and Prices from Early Times.*

Haulkerton Castle – the Royal Mews

Three hundred and fifty yards farther along the road we arrive at a few cottages and the beginning of Haulkerton Plantation. Let us leave our car here and cross into the plantation by the stile 20 yards away by the side of the cottages. A walk of 150 yards or so at an angle of 53 degrees from the road by the cottages will take us to the westmost point of the plantation and the site of Haulkerton Castle which was probably a tower. Indentations in the ground and the obvious presence of buried stones clearly show traces of the building even today. By the public road may be seen along the margin of the wood what might have been part of the carriage-drive.

In the first decade of this century one could still observe signs of the foundations of Haulkerton Castle. The building itself gradually fell into ruin until about 1790 when the walls were demolished and the stones utilised in building dykes around the plantation and in erecting the parish church and the farmhouse and outbuildings of the Mains of Haulkerton. The fruit-trees continued to bear until that date, and the last remnant of the fine old trees which adorned the grounds was cut down towards the end of last century. It was a beech, said to be the largest in the county, overspreading half an acre of land.

Haulkerton Castle was the ancient residence of the Falconers, ancestors on the female side of the noble family of Kintore which has the distinction of uniting two illustrious names, Keith and Falconer. The Falconers were the keepers of the royal falcons of Kincardine Castle, looking after the royal sport when Kincardine was a palace and the Howe of the Mearns the favourite hunting-ground of the Scottish kings at and after the consolidation of the monarchy. There is little doubt that at Haulkerton were the royal mews where the king's birds and all the paraphernalia of sport were kept. The close proximity of Haulkerton to the royal castle is significant.

In times not so very remote both sides of the Luther Burn formed an entire morass: the countryside abounded in wild-fowl such as herons, ducks, snipe and other species of bird which were regarded as the proper quarry of the hawk or falcon. It is not surprising, therefore, that this was a fitting neighbourhood for the king's hawker or falconer who had charge of the old marshy forest here when the kings of Scotland came to enjoy the royal game. The Hill of Johnstone nearby was in all probability named Falconleys from its having been the place where the huntsmen on the lower ground were accustomed to see the falcon fasten on its quarry.

The Falconer Family

Haulkerton, Halkerstoun or Hawker's Town (a burgh later to be included in the name of Laurencekirk) is, of course, one of the earliest names in the history of the parish. The first mention of hereditary hawkers or falconers to the kings of Scotland is in the 12th century at the Palace of Kincardine when Gulielmus Auceps, i.e. William the Hawker, is named in a charter (as we have seen on page 340). He was probably the founder of the family of Falconer. As William the Hawker he gave a piece of land to the kirk of Maryington (now Marykirk) in token of which gift, as was the fashion of the period, he had a turf cut from the lands which are described as lying near to a stone bridge that crossed the Luther Water and laid it upon the altar of the church.

There is no evidence, however, that 'Lachra' or Luther, under the new name of Haulkerton, was in possession of the family until some years later. Robert le Falconer of Haulkerton, who swore fealty to Edward I of England in 1296, was the first to have his name associated with the estate, and Haulkerton from its excellence as a sporting place was occupied by Falconer and his family for generations before being gifted to them as vassals. David Falconer, godson of King David II, seemed to have been high in favour at court according to a charter, dated *2nd April, 1365*, which granted *filiolo nostro dilecto quem de sacro fonte levavimus* (our loving son whom we have exalted from the sacred spring) a yearly sum of £8 sterling for his support when he chose to visit his royal godfather at his Court, and the connection of the family of Falconer with Haulkerton can be clearly traced from the 15th century onwards. On July 28, 1612, for example, the king granted to Sir Alexander Falconer of Haulkerton the lands and barony of Haulkerton also the lands and barony of Glensauch, the reddendo or rent for the latter being payable at the manor-place of Kincardine. On April 21, 1619, Alexander Falconer, eldest son of Sir Alexander, and his heirs were granted the lands and barony of Glensauch. The king also ratified at this time possession by the said Sir Alexander and his predecessors of the lands and barony of Glenfarquhar of an annual free fair from 1st to 7th July and a weekly market on Saturday in Auchenblae.

Malignancy of 'Brave Halkertone'

Many years after the removal of the King's residence from Kincardine Castle the first Lord Haulkerton already mentioned for his service to the two Charles's was rewarded by his elevation to the peerage and by other marks of royal favour. He was on terms of friendship with the Marquis of Montrose who paid him a visit at Haulkerton about 1630 when on his way from Aberdeen, shortly before his marriage to Magdalene Carnegie who was a cousin of Lord Falconer. Whatever difference may have been between their political sentiments then, they were both staunch promoters of the royal cause before the year preceding the execution of the Marquis, when Lord Falconer was superseded from the office of Lord of Session for malignancy. The only historical events connected with the castle or lands had some relation to the Earl as soldier of the Parliament or the Marquis as an ardent Royalist. Spalding mentions that

> *tuo cartowis, or quarter canons, haueing the bullet about 24 pund wecht*

were ordered to be sent to Aberdeen after Montrose's army in 1639, and that subsequent

> *directioun wes given to stay the tua cartowis, quhilk wes cum no forder nor Halkertoun, on cum farrer northe.*

And we have already read the story by the same old writer concerning the incident of Montrose's army in 1645 routing a party of Covenanters at Haulkerton and making the Howe *black with fire and red with blood*.

Lord Falconer's removal from office in 1649 was not the only sacrifice he had to make in the interests of the king. The following sonnet by Drummond of Hawthornden portrays his character and laments his misfortunes:

> *I feare to me such fortune be assign'd*
> *As was to thee, who did so well deserue,*
> *Braue Halkertone! even suffred here to sterue*
> *Amidst base-minded freinds, nor true, nor kind.*
> *Why were the Fates and Furies thus combined*
> *Such worths for such disasters to reserue?*
> *Yet all those euills neuer made thee swerue*
> *From what became a well resolued mind:*
> *For swelling greatnesse neuer made thee smyle,*
> *Despising greatnesse in extreames of want;*
> *O happy thrice whom no distresse could dant!*
> *Yet thou exclaimed, O Time! O age! O Isle!*
> > *Where flatterers, fooles, baudes, fidlers are rewarded,*
> > *Whilst Vertue sterues vnpitied, vnregarded!*

It was the great-great-grandson of this *brave Halkertone*, Alexander the 4th Lord Falconer who died in 1727, who was the last to occupy the Castle of Haulkerton as a residence. The 5th Lord Falconer, marrying Catherine Margaret Keith, eldest daughter of the 2nd Earl of Kintore in 1703 (the bride was only 13 years and 5 months old) united the family with the Keiths-Marischal and opened the way of succession to the earldom of Kintore.

The Mill of Haulkerton

And now to continue our journey. In 440 yards our road veers to the left (we avoid the right-hand fork) and, after a further 360 yards, we arrive at a side road to the left. Let us follow it for the same distance again to arrive at the now disused Mill of Haulkerton, its name still bearing witness to the existence of a castle nearby. Here for a number of years Laurencekirk Episcopalians met for divine service as regularly as possible, the baptismal registers showing baptisms performed there from September 1747 to December 1759.

For, together with the churches of Drumlithie and Stonehaven, the Episcopal Church at Laurencekiek was committed to the flames when the Duke of Cumberland was on his way north, suppressing the Rebellion of 1745, or on his return, either by his express orders or at the instance of his more zealous soldiers. Episcopacy was disestablished in Scotland in 1689, the national church becoming Presbyterian, and congregations were therefore driven to such resort as was most convenient.

At Mill of Haulkerton, too, on 4th June, 1753, a declaration was drawn up by the *mannagers of the Episcopell congragation* in

> *consideration that there appointed meetings have no hitherto been regallarely attended by severals of the members thereof*

and containing an obligation to attend the future half-yearly and other meetings or

> *forfeit two shillings and sixpence sterling for the first offence and three shillings forsaid for the second and subsequent offenciss*

provided a reasonable excuse was not sent and sustained by the managers present. In November, 1755, the attendance still being irregular, the obligation was renewed.

Pitarrow Castle and the Manor-place Tower

Returning to the road-end, we see straight in front of us, half a mile away across the fields, the farm of Drumforber where a small stone hatchet was found. The farm reminds us that agriculture was in such a backward state about the time of the '45 that prospective tenants for farms were obtained with the greatest difficulty. Drumforber was to be let about that period. As no tenant was forthcoming, the proprietor was obliged to stock it himself. Even then he succeeded in inducing a tenant to enter only on condition of his receiving half of the profits.

And now, turning left, we proceed on our original route, in a third of a mile turning to the right and continuing on this new road for one and two-fifth miles until we reach the farm of Pitarrow one hundred yards and more past a right-hand fork. Let us stop in the courtyard of the farm from which a lane leads to our left. About 140 yards down this lane stood Pitarrow House, a large mansion described as

> *a fine specimen of an ancient baronial castle which might have lasted for centuries to come as it had lasted for many bygone centuries.*

Around it was a great amount of fine old timber.

Pitarrow Castle was the seat of the distinguished family of the Wischarts or Wisharts who once held large possessions in the Mearns and elsewhere. Now only the farmhouse remains, the old castle, in a dilapidated condition, having been sold for a few pounds in 1802 and pulled down to build dykes, etc. A fine old tower (the manor-place tower it was called in a grant under the privy seal by Charles I to David Lord Carnegie in 1631), long a well-known landmark in the Howe, shared the same fate. In the garden at the farm, however, there remain from the castle an initialled dormer-window-pediment and a skewput, probably dated 1672.

Interesting Religious Paintings

The great hall of Pitarrow House had been adorned with paintings of religious subjects, afterwards covered with wooden panels, and some interesting paintings were found on the plaster of the wall when it was demolished. There is reason to believe that they were executed by George Wishart, the martyr. Of these Dr Leslie gives a detailed account in the new *Statistical Account* of 1843. Below the paintings was an inscription in Latin verse, thus translated:

To the Pope: thy merit, not thy craft, thy worth, not thy ambition, raised thee to this pitch of eminence. The Papal curia, as we well know, gives freely to the poor, nor grudges its gifts.

The writer, however, at the close states that his verses are to be read by imitating crabs, i.e. backwards, which brings out a very different meaning:

The Papal curia, as well we know, grudges its gifts, nor bestows on the poor freely. To this pitch of eminence thy ambition raised thee, not thy worth, thy craft, nor thy merit.

Almost exactly half a century after Pitarrow House was demolished, several oak panels carved with the armorial bearings of the Wishart family came into the possession of a Montrose cabinet-making firm to be worked into a cabinet which was purchased by a Mr Patrick Chalmers of Auldbar in Angus. He writes:

The coat of arms is three passion nails meeting in a point; the shield has a narrow ledge around it and is surmounted by a tilting helmet having for its crest what seems to be a feather; supporters two horses, saddled and bridled.

The Family of Wishart and Wishart Lairds

The family of Wishart has been traced to various sources. One account states that the first Wishart was a nephew of William the Lion, named 'Guishart' because he inflicted heavy slaughter on the Saracens. Another holds that the family was descended from a distinguished Norman, so-called from the cunning of his disposition, while it is also believed that the first member of the family, distinguished for his wisdom, was named 'Wise-heart'. Still another possible origin is that the name is derived from the French huissier – usher.

The first member of the family whose name is on record was *Johannes Wischard, vicecomes de Mernez*, a sheriff of Kincardineshire who was knighted by Alexander II and who obtained the lands of Conveth in 1246 from Adam, Abbot of Arbroath. A later relative, one of the most acute churchmen of the age, was Bishop of St Andrews and Lord High Chancellor of Scotland in the time of Alexander III. But it was the fifth baron, *Dominus Joannes Wishart*, who was the first to be designated *de Pittarro*. It was his son who was one of the barons engaged in the murder of the sheriff on the Hill of Garvock (see page 63) and who had previously been in the suite of Princess Margaret when she married the Dauphin, afterwards Louis XI, in 1434.

In the 16th century another laird of interest, again a Sir John Wishart, was closely associated with the names of Knox and Erskine of Dun in Reformation times. It was he who was instrumental in procuring the return of Knox from Geneva and in bringing Protestantism to the Mearns. He was a Member of Parliament who ratified the Confession of Faith in 1560, was Comptroller and Collector-general of Teinds, and one of fourteen persons to whom the government of the state was entrusted. For opposition to the marriage of Mary Queen of Scots and Darnley he was declared a rebel and suffered forfeiture, and a common saying among the Reformed clergy whose stipends were not of the highest was,

> *The good laird of Pitarro was ane earnest professor of Christ, but the meikle Devill receave the Comptroller.*

His nephew who succeeded him, yet another Sir John, was nominated at a parliament in Stirling in 1578 one of the Commissioners to examine the *Buik of the Policy of the Kirk* with a view to its ratification. He was also one of those *that subscribed the band anent the religioun at Aberdeene* in 1592. Regrettably, his good reputation was short-lived as he later became a braggart whose character is said to have suggested to Sir Walter Scott the unamiable Captain Craig-engelt in *The Bride of Lammermuir*. He was the last of the family to possess Pitarrow estates which were sold in 1631 to David, Lord Carnegie of Kinnaird, for 59,000 merks or £3,277 15s 6d sterling. The Carnegies were to hold them for exactly 200 years.

Two Illustrious Carnegies

Lord Carnegie's fourth son, Sir David, may be regarded as the founder of the Pitarrow family. *The illustrious merits and rare virtues of his lovit David Carnegie* having commended themselves to King Charles, he was created a baronet in 1663. Twenty-seven years later he was commissioned by the Privy Council with Robert Burnett of Glenbervie to raise 100 men for a month's service to resist the depredations of rebellious Highlanders who, ill-disposed towards the Government, were at this time making incursions into the Mearns. These he spiritedly dispersed with a force of 400 men at Cuttieshillock (see page 156), but the Highlanders in resentment retaliated with their whole army of more than 3,000 men who, camping at Pitarrow, plundered the mansion and

> *destroyed Sir David's corn, wasted his lands and robbed his tenants, doing damage to the extent of £422 8s Stg.*

For that he was never fully recompensed by the Government. Two of his three wives were the dowager of the second Lord Arbuthnott (whom he married in 1684) and Jean Burnett, daughter of James Burnett of Lagavin, great-grandfather of Lord Monboddo and the laird of Kair. Sir David lies buried

> *in our burial place at the back of the Church of Fordoun where my father, severalls of my brothers and sisters and of my owen children are buried.*

Sir James Carnegie, the third baronet who succeeded to the title in 1729, was elected Member of Parliament for Kincardine in 1741, 1747, 1761 and 1765, and saw a good deal of military service with the Duke of Cumberland in Flanders at the battle of Fontenoy in 1745 and with great bravery at Culloden the following year. There his younger brother George, espousing the cause of rebellion, was fighting on the opposite side, having accompanied Prince Edward to England after the battle of Preston. When his *friend Frank Garden* became Lord Gardenstone, Sir James Carnegie expressed great satisfaction and used his influence to favour his kinsman, James Burnett, afterwards Lord Monboddo, for the sheriffdom of the county.

Birth-place of George Wishart, Martyr

Pitarrow Castle is probably best remembered because it was here in 1513 that was born a younger son of this ancient house, George Wishart, the illustrious Protestant martyr whose cruel death at the stake on March 1st, 1546, at St Andrews, did so much to hasten the Reformation by being the first effective blow to Papal supremacy in Scotland. Beaton, the future cardinal, is understood to have been related to him – a circumstance which probably increased the bitterness of his hatred against the youth whose popularity he feared and whose influence for the reformation of religion he sought with unparalleled cruelty and folly to extinguish by a wicked and illegal decree.

Admiral Sir James Wishart, C.-in-C.

A linear representative of the Wisharts, by a female line, was Sir John Stuart Forbes, Bart. of Pitsligo and Fettercairn, whose ancestors possessed the lands of Fettercairn since the time of the decline of the Middletons. The Wisharts are also identified with the neighbouring parish of Fordoun which from the last years of the 14th century until the beginning of the 18th century belonged almost entirely to the several branches of the family. One such distinguished parishioner was Admiral Sir James Wishart, Commander-in-chief Mediterranean until 1714. A model of his flagship, HMS *Ripon*, can be seen in the Scottish United Services Museum at Edinburgh Castle bearing the following inscription,

Dockyard Model of H.M.S. Ripon 1712-1729.

The model belonged to the Admiral who about 1727 left it at the manse of Fordoun where it remained until it was deposited in the Museum about 1935.

The Mill of Conveth

Let us now return to the road fork which we passed 160 yards or so before the farm, turning south towards the Laurencekirk-Fordoun road. In two-fifths of a mile we arrive at the Mill of Conveth, even as late as 1934 one of the few surviving links with a number of mills that stood on the banks of the Luther and Bervie Water in the 1890's, proclaiming at a dozen different points the prosperity of miles of fields in every direction. Day after day the machinery could be heard humming and grinding, swallowing up the abundant crops of the Mearns and disgorging them again for the great markets of the country, reward for a year's labour on the land. At the same time they provided the livelihood of a small section of the community.

In earlier halcyon days of milling the water of the Luther turned six or seven water-wheels. Upstream from Conveth was Denmill of Auchenblae and the Mill of Pitrennie with which we began this journey. The Blackiemuir and Thornton establishments had closed down even earlier, and the Mill of Haulkerton and Nethermill, Fettercairn, were never rebuilt since they were razed to the ground by fire.

A stone in front of the dwelling-house at Mill of Conveth has the inscription, 'S.D.C.', for Sir David Carnegie. Others have '1679' and '1703'. A corner-stone built into the mill has '00', probably part of '1700'.

Scotston a Reminder of Pictish Inhabitants

In just under half a mile we reach the A94 where we are to turn left on our homeward journey. Let us for a moment, however, diverge southwards for only 350 yards to the farm of Scotston with its interesting name. For its origin takes us back to the days when the inhabitants of these parts were not Scots but Picts and when the Scots (who were originally from Ireland and who established themselves in Argyll during the 6th century) gradually extended their dominion northwards, after the lapse of centuries penetrating into the north-eastern part of the country. Individuals and families from time to time came and settled in Pictland, and the holdings which they acquired by right or might were called by the Picts 'Scottistowns'.

Who the stranger may have been who settled here in the immediate vicinity of the lands of Conveth cannot, of course, be known. Perhaps he may at once have become a vassal of the kirk for the earliest record shows that Scottistown was the property of the Abbey of Arbroath and was conferred, along with Conveth and Haulkerton, on Sir John Wishart of Pitarrow about 1246. It probably found its way before long into the possession of the Keith family, but the earliest certain notice of it after that date is in the second half of the 15th century when it formed a constituent part of the barony of Scotston.

Some 380 yards behind Scotston farmhouse you will see the low promontory of Chapel Knap to which reference is made at the beginning of Route 9 as the probable site of the original Kirkton of Conveth near Laurencekirk. In the 19th century a circular mound of stones and the foundations of a building were removed from Chapel Knap. Although there were ashes in the mound, no burials were found, and it was thought to have been a 'kiln or cooking place'.

There is no evidence to support the suggestion that the building was a chapel.

A large mound on Erskine's Knap, about 250 yards behind the site of the Chapel of Conveth, is probably a barrow. It measures 130 ft. in diameter and some 6 ft. in height.

The Stuarts of Redmyre

And now we are on our way home. A further mile and a quarter and, where the B967 forks to Inverbervie, we arrive at the village of Redmyre. Though there is now no trace of a mansion-house, here at Redmyre was once a seat of the Keiths Marischal and, later, of the Irvines of Drum. From them the estate passed as a gift to the Stuarts of Inchbreck which had been part of the barony of Glenbervie, David Stuart being so rewarded for his invaluable attention to Sir Archibald Douglas when he lay wounded upon the field of Pinkie. It was this same David Stuart who was with Queen Mary's forces at the Battle of Corrichie (see page 236) where, it is alleged in the old ballad, he killed the Earl of Huntly with his own hand:

> *The Murray cried, 'Tak' the auld Gordoun',*
> *An' mony ane ran wi' speid,*
> *But Stuart o' Inchbreck had him stickit,*
> *And out gushit this fat lurdanes* (worthless man's) *bleid*.

David Stuart's son, Captain James Stuart, after serving in Holland, enlisted under Lord Ogilvie in the cause of the Pretender and was present at Culloden whence he escaped to France where he died in 1776, having been created a Knight of St Louis. One of his grandsons, John Stuart, an able writer and devoted antiquary, from 1782 onwards occupied the Chair of Greek at Aberdeen University for nearly forty years.

Episcopalian Mission at Redmyre

It was to East Redmyre that the Episcopalian mission house already referred to in connection with the Mill of Haulkerton was transferred in 1760 – and under the same clergyman, John Strachan, a native of Gourock, who had officiated in the parish for the previous eight years and who was, incidentally, also the farmer of Bush, St Cyrus. At Laurencekirk on the 16th August, 1744, he had been recommended to the Bishop *as a person fit to be entered into holy orders*. Later, in 1788, he was consecrated Bishop of Brechin.

Despite the change to a Redmyre meeting house the congregation of the Episcopal Church continued practically the same as is evidenced by lists of the regular recipients of alms. Evidenced, too, by the fact that seventy-one persons were confirmed at East Redmyre in 1765 compared with fourteen and nineteen at Mill of Haulkerton in 1755 and 1758 respectively, and forty-eight in 1752, probably at Laurencekirk. Episcopacy, of course, was still under proscription, and the utmost secrecy had to be observed in administering the rites of the Church. Information, indeed, was lodged against Mr Strachan's successor in the Redmyre mission, a Mr Spark, who resided in the House of Kair and discharged the twofold duties of pastor and schoolmaster. He was tried at the circuit court for having performed the marriage-rite, but the case fell to the ground.

When he was called to be minister at Drumlithie, the mission at Redmyre was discontinued, the congregation being divided between Drumlithie and Laurencekirk where at the instance of Lord Gardenstone a new church had been erected in which, we are told in the *Laurencekirk Episcopal Register*,

> *were collected the scattered members of the old loyal Jacobite congregations of St Cyrus, Redmyre, Luthermuir and Conveth.*

Fordoun a Development of the Railway Age

Let us now proceed for a third of a mile to the village of Fordoun which is essentially a development of the railway age, consisting of a nucleus of older houses and a shop or two scattered in the vicinity of the railway station and the main road. Kilns for limestone burning (an industry now entirely given up) existed here. Natives of Fordoun were Sir John Wishart, judge, who died in 1576, and Dr John Brebner (1833-1902) for twenty years head of the educational system of the Orange Free State. Professor James Beattie (a nephew of the poet) of the Department of Civil and Natural History, Aberdeen (1767-1810), was also a member of the parish.

Local Prehistoric Remains

In Fordoun and district have been found a number of Stone Age flint tools and arrow-heads. The arrow-heads, which have been presented to the Society of Antiquaries in Scotland, vary from ½ in. to 2½ ins. in length. Seventeen have barbs and stems, three have stems but no barbs, and five are leaf-shaped. Two examples of flint-cutting instruments, one $3^3/_8$ ins. by $3^3/_4$ ins. and at its thickest part less than ½ in. in thickness, are now in the National Museum of Antiquities in Edinburgh. Found near Redhall House in 1892, and also in Edinburgh, is a finely polished and very heavy chisel-like Stone Age axe of dark flint, 8 ins. in length and 1¾ ins. across the cutting face. It has been chipped from both sides over the whole surface except for the part immediately above the perfect cutting edge. A ridge left running up the centre gives the cross-section in the middle of its length an irregular, lozenge-shaped outline. The butt is tapered to a point, and the edge more flattened on one side than on the other. A portion of a jet necklace found in Fordoun is now to be seen in Montrose Museum.

A Jovial Bridge of Leppie Howff

We must turn right just before Fordoun village where the B967 to Inverbervie is signposted. In 350 yards we pass on the left the road to the Bridge of Leppie, some 270 yards away, where during the 18th century stood the Chance Inn, one of Scotland's most important country inns, the only place between Brechin and Stonehaven at which post horses could be procured. This fact in itself indicates that it was a house of some account in the district. In 1792 the landlord was James Andrew who had succeeded his father in the occupancy. Besides giving temporary accommodation to travellers on the road in days when the post-chaise was the only conveyance of the rich and walking on foot the resort of the poor, it was a favourite meeting-place of farmers and others in the district. The howff must have seen many a jovial evening.

The Cairn of Arthurhouse and Waterlair Antiquities

Although we are eventually to turn left along the B967 Inverbervie road 320 yards farther on, you may care, if you are so minded, to deviate for a return journey of only 1¾ miles (1¼ miles by car and half a mile on foot) to visit the Bronze Age Cairn of Arthurhouse. You must cross the B967, pass the old school of Redmyre and proceed up the hill for just over half a mile until you reach the wood on your left. A walk of 300 yards through this wood (parallel to the edge of the field), followed by a 130 yard walk at right angles to your right, will take you there. The cairn, measuring 68¾ ft. by 61¼ ft. and 10¾ ft. in height is now completely overgrown with grass and somewhat dilapidated, three-quarters of it having been used for the making of road metal. If you have already seen a similar cairn at Bucharn, Ardlair or Cairnshee, a visit is not very warmly recommended unless you have time to spare.

Yet the cairn is not without interest. Surrounded by a kerb of large granite stones 2 ft. or 3 ft. high, set close together on edge, the cairn originally covered the stones of the ring and extended 4 ft. beyond them. Within the ring was found a coffin; outside amid the stones a variety of mediaeval silver coins, worn and corroded but sufficiently well-preserved to be identified. One was coined in the reign of Alexander I in 1107 and another in that of Robert the Bruce in 1320. A silver brooch of ancient workmanship was also found. Such ancient burial places were often selected in later times as places of deposit for hoards of valuables, probably because they were easily recognised by the depositors and in many cases were protected by the superstitious fear of the neighbouring population.

On your way down the hill afterwards have a look at the farm of Waterlair on your left. In a field here a small cairn was opened about 1860 and a bronze vessel found. In the same field were found flint arrow-heads. Also unearthed here 2 ft. below the surface, when trenching was being carried out, was a greenish stone ball, 2½ ins. in diameter, covered with small rounded projections in low relief.

The Roman Camp of Fordoun

Back to the B967 Inverbervie road which, however, we leave in two-thirds of a mile just after we cross the Bridge of Kair. This road to the left we follow for only some 300 yards until we reach crossroads, but we must carry straight on for just under half a mile until we are opposite Kair House on our right, occupying a pleasing site among the trees just within the boundary of Arbuthnott parish. Let us stop a moment. Kair House is an early 19th century classic mansion-house of considerable beauty. A portrait of Dr Patrick Sibbald, Professor of Divinity in Marischal College, who died on November 14th, 1697, and who was said to be *descended of a lawful brother of Sibbald of Kair* is in the possession of Aberdeen University.

What is of greater interest is the fact that our car is presently parked more or less exactly in the centre of what was the site of a 120-acre rectangular Roman camp which straddled the summit of this prominent hill all round Kair House and Mains of Kair farmsteading, the sides facing north-east and south-east being some 1,970 ft. in length, the other two sides being 2,850 ft. Here was the Roman camp of Fordoun, the second marching camp to be set up in Kincardineshire by the Romans on their northern march into Aberdeenshire and on to the Moray Firth, a classic example of a temporary camp built by the Emperor Septimius Severus during his second campaign in 210 A.D. or thereabouts and possibly the most

northerly of the series associated with his campaign. Although most
of the perimeter was first discovered in 1945 from crop markings,
the north angle and considerable portions of the adjacent sides can
still be traced as earthworks in a conifer plantation. The only gates
to be definitely identified are those on the north-north-east and
south-south-west sides, each guarded by a titulum, a traverse or
short earthwork.

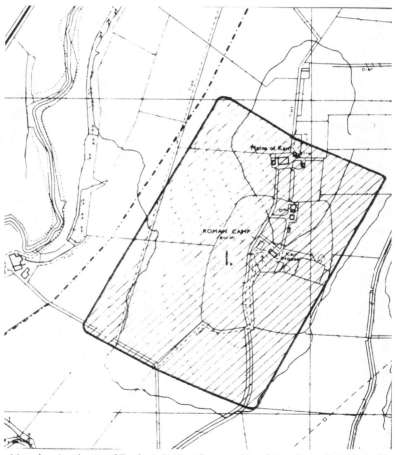

*Map showing the site of Fordoun Roman Camp and its relationship to Kair House (in
the middle of the site) and Mains of Kair (at the top). It is interesting to compare the
diagrammatic outline of the north-west corner of the camp with the cropmarks shown
on the adjacent picture.*

The Romans would enter the Mearns by crossing the North Esk at its junction with the West Water at the passage called King's Ford. As the greater part of the Howe from Redmyre to Luthermuir was at that time bog and moss, their most easy and direct route from

An aerial view, taken in 1977, of cropmarks showing the outline of part of the temporary Roman Camp which occupied the eminence round Kair House, a mile and more from Fordoun. In the bottom right-hand corner is the Mains of Kair. The picture shows the north-west corner (typically rounded) of the camp and half of the top short north-west/south-east side. Just off the picture on the right and across the road seen running north from the Mains of Kair is the only minute part of the camp still actually remaining – some 20 yards of the turf rampart (much dilapidated) and a continuation, of course, of the line of the cropmarks shown.

Strathmore was by Fordoun. They would thus find themselves at the usual interval of about 12 miles or a day's march from Stonehaven in the bay of which with its natural harbour it is reasonable to conjecture their fleet lay.

A Tired Roman Legionary's Earthen Wall

Now let us carry on up the hill to the steading of the Mains of Kair. Here we turn right and left again, past the dwelling-house, until in just under quarter of a mile in all we reach two small huts on the right. Between them you should stop again for you are parked on the site of the porta praetoria or general's gate, the main entrance to the camp, placed as was always the case in a slight re-entrant angle in the middle of the north-east side of the camp, the side facing the enemy. Between the two small huts can still be seen the remains of about 20 yards of the turf rampart or agger which, originally 7 ft. high, had once surrounded the camp surmounted by a palisade (vallum) of sharpened wooden stakes. How fascinating that the earthen wall built by some tired legionary nearly 1800 years ago should show today where the line of the defence once continued for another 280 yards down the field on our left!

Redhall and the Imported Hedger

As we descend the hill towards the Mill of Kair, we can see across the railway and one and a third miles away to the left the ancient mansion-house of Redhall which with its estate was mentioned as early as 1296 when Sir John Wishart granted ten merks out of Redhall and Balfeith to St Thomas the Martyr in the cathedral of Brechin, an endowment which, it seems, was continued for centuries. About 1747 the lands and barony were bought by Sir John Carnegie from George Wishart of Kemnay, and seventy-eight years later was sold by G. F. Carnegie of Pitarrow to Rev. Alexander Carnegie, minister of Inverkeillor, whose wife was Elizabeth Skirving, daughter of the author of *Johnnie Cope*.

When around 1826 all the hardwood about Redhall was planted, and all the hedges on the main roadsides, as well as those on the estate, hedges were not common in this district, and consequently few men seem to have had any special knowledge about them. A professional hedger had therefore to be imported all the way from Northumberland to do the planting on the property.

Redhall has given no fewer than three senators to the College of Justice, one of whom was sometime the Lord President.

Home Again

Shortly after passing Mill of Kair, we find ourselves crossing the Bervie Water[1] (an intriguing experience!) after which we have for some inexplicable reason a stretch of appalling unsurfaced road to cover. Yet it lasts for only 520 yards. We use the crossover which faces us, turn right and in under ten miles, having again passed the B966 road-end where we started our circuit, we are back at Stonehaven Square. We have covered, all in all, just over 48 miles.

The magnificent cantilever staircase is an outstanding feature of Fasque. This is the view from the entrance hall up the staircase to the windows which, even then, were 'double glazed' with attractive engraved glass.

[1] If you consider it unwise for your car to cross the bridge, then you must return to Fordoun, travelling to Stonehaven therefrom. This will add 3½ miles to your journey.

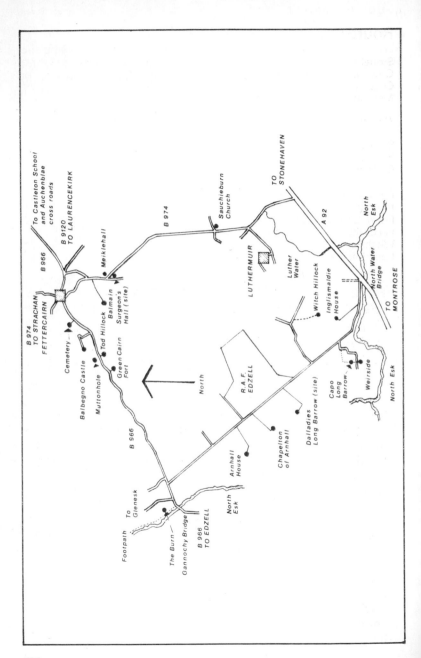

Route Eight

Stonehaven Square – Fettercairn – Balmain – Balbegno Castle – Tod Hillock –
Green Cairn – Gannochy Bridge – The Burn – Arnhall House – RAF Edzell –
Chapelton – Witch Hillock – Capo – Inglismaldie – Luthermuir – Sauchieburn –
Meiklehall – Fettercairn – Stonehaven Square.

Distance: A total of 56½ miles as follows:

Stonehaven Square to Fettercairn and back by car – 34.63 miles
Round trip from Fettercairn by car – 17.12 miles
On foot – 4.83 miles

Readers who do not wish to travel far on foot may find it helpful to know the
return mileage of three walks:
From Gannochy Bridge along the bank of the North Esk (but there is no
necessity to travel the whole distance) – 3.36 miles
Witch Hillock – 0.69 miles
Capo long barrow – 0.59 miles.

Round the Head of the Vale of Strathmore via the Burn, Inglismaldie, Luthermuir and Sauchieburn

*in which we read of Scotland's first Sunday school and last
hand-loom weaver, of the ghostly origins of a bridge and
the largest barrow in Scotland. We also learn that plumes
and gaiters are fashionable in Heaven.*

We Start from Fettercairn

For this excursion you must begin by following in reverse Route No.
5 from Stonehaven to the Auchenblae crossroads on the B966 and
thereafter Route No. 6 from this point to Castleton School.
Another mile and four-fifths along the B966 (the only part of the
road not already traversed elsewhere) takes us to Fettercairn which
we have already visited. There our journey starts.

Balmain – a Gaelic Reminder

And now let us follow the B966 road towards Edzell. Just short of a
half mile from Fettercairn Square we reach on our right the lichgate
to the churchyard. Exactly opposite and 800 yards away on our left
is the farm of Balmain (baile, town, and main, middle), a Gaelic
reminder of the midtown once lying between Balbegno and Esslie
which later produced the modern name of Middleton and also the
family name of the Middletons of Fettercairn. We are reminded
that once on the occasion of a birth in the old farmhouse of Middle-

ton the 'blythe-meats' were being enjoyed by a few neighbours when a party of the Duke of Cumberland's soldiers entered and cleared the festive board!

Balbegno Castle and the Woods

Another half mile takes us to the handsome and attractive old castle of Balbegno, set back on our right some 300 yards from the road. It was built in 1569 by John Wood, Thane of Fettercairn, and his wife, Elizabeth, the daughter of Sir Alexander Irvine of Drum. The carved heraldic panel above the highest front window in the watch-chamber on the south side gives the date and depicts the figures of two males and one female with the inscription, *I. Wod and E. Irvein*, below a shield with the Wood and Irvine arms. As Thanes of Fettercairn the Woods bore, in addition to the parental coat of arms, an oak tree, two keys fastened to a branch. It is said that the cost of building the castle impoverished the Wood proprietors and became a burden on the estate.

John Wood was the son of Sir Andrew Wood of Over Blairton, a famous admiral whose family, originally of Norman descent, had been hereditary constables of the royal castle of Kincardine since they appeared in the Mearns in the time of James IV. By this king in 1488 Balbegno was granted to Sir Andrew. Six generations of Woods were to follow, the last laird being a companion-in-arms of the royalist Earl of Middleton who built Fettercairn House. Before entering the field of battle on one occasion, they agreed, in the event of one of them being killed, that the other should return and give the survivor some account of the other world! Balbegno fell, and one day while Middleton, a prisoner in the Tower of London, had just finished reading a portion of Scipio, Balbegno's ghost appeared and, taking him by the hand, said, 'Oh, Middleton, do you not mind the promise I made to you when at such a place, such a night on the Border?' Prophesying Middleton's future greatness, the ghost vanished from view, giving the illuminating description:

> *Plumashes* (plumes of feathers) *above, gramashes* (gaiters reaching to the knees) *below,*
> *It's no wonder to see how the world doth go.*

Although Cromwell confirmed by a precept, dated at Edinburgh in 1657, to another Andrew Wood the lands of Balbegno and the thanedom of Fettercairn, the Woods in 1687 ceased to be feudal owners of Balbegno: it was sold to Andrew Middleton, brother of the notorious Earl of Middleton, passing later to the Ogilvys who made an addition to the east side of the castle in 1795 by which the original entrance and front were covered up and considerably spoiled. Now the ancient portion is practically unused while the modern commodious extension is occupied as a farmhouse.

A Castle on the L-plan — with Modifications

Balbegno Castle is another fine and highly interesting example of a castle on the L-plan of the old Scottish baronial style into which various modifications have been introduced. Containing many late mediaeval features, it was a manifestation of the Indian summer of mediaeval art.

The attractive old castle of Balbegno, three-quarters of a mile from Fettercairn, which was built in 1569 by John Wood, Thane of Fettercairn. The freestone roof is the castle's most striking feature for it is one of the few Scottish castles which have a ribbed and groined vaulted ceiling over the Hall.

407

The castle is four storeys high with a garret, double oblong roof and an open bartizan. The parapet along the top and around its east side and corner previously continued right round the house at this level, traces of it remaining in the eastern gabling. As at Crathes the whole of the re-entrant angle is filled up instead of there being a turret inserted in the angle. This is to give provision for a wide corbelled staircase to the first floor. This stair wing finishes at the top in an elaborately decorated watch-chamber, provided with an angle turret with oversailing roof – this having been formerly one of the open rounds of the parapet. At ground level the re-entrant angle was filled in with a modern porch, masking the original entrance which was in the usual position at the foot of the stair wing. On the first floor is a private room in the wing; the floor above is divided into four bedchambers, each with a garde-robe; above again is further domestic accommodation. Upon the bartizan, boldly carved in freestone, are three circular ornamental medallion heads, one male with a hat, and two females, perhaps the founder and his family; and upon other parts of the walls are several shields with arms, again possibly those of the founders of the castle. The roughcast walls of the building are five to six feet in thickness and well pierced with splayed gunloops and circular shot-holes, significant of the time when the castle was built. The basement containing the kitchen and cellars is vaulted and was entered from a back passage by a massive oaken door with heavy bolts and strong locks and studded with large-headed iron nails.

A Splendid Vaulted Ceiling

Balbegno Castle is one of the few castles in Scotland which have a splendid ribbed and groined vaulted ceiling over the large interesting Hall on the first floor, the groins springing from grotesque corbels. Certainly the freestone roof is the most striking feature, some of the bosses presenting ornaments, some grotesque and others floral, one of them bearing the Irvine arms. The ceiling has two shields, one with the Scots lion and the other with the Wood arms. After the Union of the Kingdoms the sixteen vaulted severies or compartments were painted in tempora with fine plaster armorial bearings of some of the principal families in Scotland (the sixteen representative peers in Scotland), most of them unfortunately now so defaced by damp and decay that the names and titles have been obliterated. Over the door on the right, however, can still be seen the coats and mantlings of Lauderdale (or Wemyss?), Montrose,

Earl of Orkney, Gordon? Earl of Moray; on the south side those of Bothwell, Argyle, Crawford, Errol and Eglinton.

The Scottish Nelson in the Garden

Over a side garden door is a carved figure showing a male bust with the face bearded and the head with morion or helmet. The left hand is erect, three fingers extended. It probably represents a hero of the family, Admiral Sir Andrew Wood of Largo, the Scottish Nelson and commander of the first Scottish navy. He humbled the English in a great sea-fight in the Firth of Forth in 1488 when he and his two brothers with two ships captured three which Henry VII of England had sent to make an end of Scots power at sea. The sculpture had no doubt a more honourable place originally in the east front of-the castle and must have been removed by the Ogilvys when they built the plain and homely addition to the castle. Some stones bearing the Wood and Barclay arms were also removed to Caldhame where they may be seen stuck up in the wall of an outhouse.

The carved head of Admiral Sir Andrew Wood of Largo, the Scottish Nelson and commander of the first Scottish navy.

Tod Hillock

Quarter of a mile farther, on the left of the roadside, is a wooded knoll with a name which bespeaks the lingering grimness of times past – Tod Hillock. Here was no doubt the tribunal court or mote-hill (mod, a court) where, during the long ages that preceded the erection of Balbegno Castle and the sway of the Woods, the feudal baron held his court and judged all civil and criminal cases arising in his district. The heritable right of jurisdiction was abolished after the Rebellion of 1745. On these mote-hills (now known as gallow-hills) men were hanged so that Tod Hillock is also known as Executioner's Knoll.

The Balbegno Muttonhole

The Balbegno muttonhole (from the O.E. gemythan, a junction of two roads or streams) was about 100 yards away in the springy hollow of the field across the road from Tod Hillock. Until about 1869 on this spot there was a group of old cottar houses known as Muttonhole. Occupying the adjacent roadside corner of the park nearer the castle, and demolished about the same time, once stood a small croft called Taed's Nest or hangman's dwelling.

The Fort of Green Cairn

In a further quarter of a mile we reach on our left traces of the small, very fragmentary but well-defined vitrified fort of Green Cairn, a turf-covered oval depression measuring 55 yards by 20. Vitrified masses and occasional large boulders are visible round the edges. One of the few vitrified forts in Strathmore, it is 130 yards or so from the road on a fluvic-glacial mound with its top trimmed off. A path opposite the cottage and alongside the field leads one to it. The site, which is in an advanced stage of destruction, commands an extensive view over the Howe of the Mearns as far as the Garvock Hills to the south-east, the hills of Finavon to the south-west and the Menmuir ridge to the west. It also is in a position to command two crucial trans-Mounth routes through Glen Esk – the Firmounth route and the Cairn o' Mounth.

The site of the fort was partially excavated in 1973-4 and 1977 and had apparently suffered little from the attentions of early excavators although it has clearly been used as a quarry for many generations, rampart foundation stones being removed even to this day. As there were no finds, dating must rest on the basis of radio-carbon tests of charcoal from three samples. A totally carbonised timber beam resting against the inner revetting foundation of the rampart, and consequently used in the construction of the fort, gave a date of

540 ± 90 B.C. A second date obtained from a pile of charred twigs at the base of the destruction debris was 180 ± 100 B.C. while carbon material from a post hole gave 390 ± 95 B.C. While C14 dates are no more than a guide without supporting find material, we can hazard a rough average date for the building of the fort as something like 470 B.C. in the early Iron Age. Then refugees of mixed Celtic and Teutonic blood from Gaul or north-east France and Belgium were peopling the Mearns when Western Europe was invaded. The fort stood (apparently maintained in good condition) for 300 years, and it was destroyed just before the beginning of the Christian era.

The small very fragmentary vitrified fort of Green Cairn, 1¼ miles south west of Fettercairn, which is in an advanced stage of destruction. The earthwork, which in all probability was not lived in permanently, was originally excavated by Sir Walter Scott in 1746 when he was visiting Fettercairn House to woo Williamina Stuart-Belsches, the daughter of the laird.

A Defensive Structure with Vitrified Walls

Like other strongholds of the same character the fort consisted of a central building with vitrified walls, in this case varying from 19 ft. to 30 ft. in thickness. There remains some little evidence of surrounding ramparts built of stone. The inner rivetting face of the south rampart proved to be of similar construction to that of the north. A series of trenches to the east end of the site, when excavated, revealed a gateway with a later blocking structure. An earlier phase of occupation, indicated by a large number of post holes, was discovered beneath the fort levels.

Aerial photography has revealed the previous existence of three outer works, protecting the easiest approach round the north-east shoulder of the knoll: curving lines of greener, higher growth were obvious in a crop of oats in the 1977 investigation. The line of the innermost outer work could be traced as a change of slope around the south-east side of the knoll and as a scarp round the south-west side; there was no sign of the other two continuing, but they may have terminated in what would have been a bog for the fort would have been built above the level of what at the time would be water. In each outer defence a possible entrance gap of just over 8 ft. was evident.

Apparently no structures were built inside so that the earthwork in all probability, like Green Castle, was not lived in permanently, being purely a defensive structure or encampment to which the native Britons in all likelihood retreated only in times of danger and political unrest – during the period of Roman military action for example. Protection and security would therein be afforded to the dwellers and their goods.

The fort, as we have said, was a vitrified one, being originally built of logs with stones in between, a kind of lattice arrangement. Whether it was set on fire by defenders or attackers is not clear, but lumps of stone had melted and fused together in tremendous heat. This has been proved to be possible in a successful experiment in the 1930's with a similar wall of stone and timber: if one piles heather and peat against such a wall and waits until the wind is in the right direction, a blast furnace effect is obtained. If this is kept up for a week, stones can, in fact, be fused together. Green Cairn Castle must have been a place of great strength but must have been uninhabitable for many ages. This is borne out by the state to which the collection of unhewn vitrified stones, hidden under whins and broom, have been reduced despite the durable nature of buildings of this kind.

Walter Scott Borrows a Spade

Information regarding the ruins is furnished by a letter of Sir Walter Scott, written from Kinross on May 6th, 1796 (when Scott was 24) to Rev. James Walker, minister of Dunnottar, after Scott's visit to Dunnottar and to Fettercairn House in April and May of the same year to woo Williamina, the lovely fifteen-year old daughter of the laird, Sir John Stuart-Belsches, who had then according to Scott's son-in-law and biographer, J. G. Lockhart, *for so many years been the object of his attachment*. Borrowing a spade, he seems, however, to have spent most of his time digging at Green Cairn and making many fascinating discoveries. Perhaps it is not surprising that some time in the early autumn he got his dismissal. Miss Williamina, though Scott suspected her mother's influence, had given her heart elsewhere and in January, 1797, married the banker, Sir William Forbes of Pitsligo, who thereupon took the name and arms of the Stuart family and at his father's death became Sir William Stuart Forbes of Pitsligo and Fettercairn.

Scott narrates in the introduction to *The Antiquary* the intended journey by coach of a young man – no other than himself – on a love expedition to the Mearns. In canto IV of *Rokeby* Miss Williamina, it is believed, stands in grace and beauty as the proto-type of Matilda,

> *Wreathed in its dark brown rings, her hair*
> *Half hid Matilda's forehead fair,*
> *Half hid and half reveal'd to view*
> *Her full dark eye of hazel hue.*

Scott's Letter to the Minister of Dunnottar

Part of Scott's letter is as follows,

> *I was detained at Fettercairn House by the hospitality of Sir John and Lady Jane two or three days longer than I expected, from which you will easily guess Miss Belsches was recovered and able to see company. Thus I had plenty of time on my hands which I employed in causing two labourers begin at the ring or vallum immediately without the main compact and cut down till they came decisively to the original soil. This outer embankment I found to consist of a mound of stones of no very considerable size none of which, as far as I could perceive, had suffered from fire. . . . We then continued opening our trench, still digging down to the soil, till we came to the very foundation of the main and innermost bulwark. You may guess my satisfaction when on laying this bare I found the most unequivocal marks of human industry, It consists of oblong flat stones from 4 to 6 feet long, piled above each other to the height of about 4 feet and breadth of 3, with symmetry more exact than could have been expected.*
>
> *This foundation formed a kind of casing within which were piled, apparently by the hand, large bullet stones which, I presume, were prevented from spreading inwards*

by a similar pile of large flat stones corresponding to that on the outside, and thus a firm foundation had been obtained for the mound to be raised above, which, as far as it now remains, consists of bullets, etc. diminishing gradually in size to the very top. Upon all this mass the effect of fire was very visible, and at the bottom I found quantities of charcoal, but these effects were much less remarkable below and appeared more and more strong upon the higher stones till you came to the top where the mass was completely vitrified. Thus the whole was probably constructed as follows:– First two walls of large flat stones were erected parallel to each other at a distance corresponding to the height of rampart of which this was to be the base; that rampart I take to have been composed of branches of trees and stones, the latter gradually diminishing in size from that of the large round bullets which occupied the interval between the two casing walls of the foundation to a size which could be more conveniently raised to the height of the top of the mound. Supposing such a fabric to be surrounded by 3 or 4 external ramparts of loose stones, it would compose such a fortification as I take the fort of Balbegno to have been when entire. Again, supposing it to have been stormed and set on fire, it is obvious that the lower part, being composed of huge stones, would suffer little from the heat, that the middle would suffer more and that the stones composing the uppermost part of the mass would, if their substance admitted it, be actually vitrified, both from their size and situation, the fire always penetrating upwards, for the same reason that charcoal found its way to the bottom of the mass would not be totally consumed; and thus I account for the appearances I have detailed above. My works are already filled up with rubbish and some of the foundation stones carried off, but I am convinced you will find upon examination that the appearances are uniform.

Additional Information

The obvious deficiencies in Scott's record regarding the dimensions of the fort are somewhat mitigated by additional information, given when Green Cairn was surveyed in May, 1798, by James Strachan, gardener to Lord Adam Gordon, as follows. I quote from Chalmers' *Caledonia*:

It (Greencairn Castle) *is of an oval form, and is surrounded by two ramparts. The outer rampart is built with dry-stone, without any lime or mortar, and without the least mark of any tool; and under the foundation are found ashes of burnt wood. The space betwixt the outer and inner ramparts measures 93 feet 9 inches. The inner wall is 30 feet thick and has all undergone the operation of vitrification. The area within this is 140 feet long; 67 ft. 6 ins. broad at the east end; and 52 ft. 6 ins. broad at the west end. The elevation (of the site) on the north side, is about 40 feet, and fully 60 feet on the south side, where it is all wet, mossy ground.*

In the early years of the nineteenth century parts of the wall stood a foot or two above the surface but, although some scattered fragments may still be seen, the stones were gradually removed to build dykes and farm steadings. Local residents can remember the interior of the fort being ploughed and cropped, and at least one farm track has been surfaced with vitrified fragments.

Gannochy Bridge

And now let us proceed straight on for two and three-tenth miles. past the road-end to RAF Edzell and North Water Bridge on the left, past the entry to Glen Esk on the right, until we arrive at Gannochy Bridge over the North Esk, the boundary of Kincardineshire. Connecting two tremendous rocks on the banks of the river, Gannochy Bridge consists of one large arch, 30 ft. high and 52 ft. in span, and was erected in 1732 at a cost of 300 merks (about £200 Scots money, and a large sum at the time) by a wealthy farmer, James Black, tenant of a farm in the vicinity. Mr Black also left 200 merks to the poor of the parish of Fettercairn and 50 merks for maintaining the bridge, both sums being left to the management of the kirk session.

James Black employed a man to prepare the materials and erect the stone-work of the bridge but built the parapets with his own hands. Although adequate, however, for the time when it ws built, the bridge was soon found to be too narrow for the traffic that passed along the roadway from Fettercairn to Edzell. It was widened in 1796 at the joint expense of the Hon. William Maule (Lord Panmure) and Lord Adam Gordon – £300. In the middle of the 19th century the structure was strengthened and the parapets heightened. Later on several landowners and others made additions to the bridge so that it is now entirely different.

Three Ghostly Visitations

The traditional origin of Gannochy Bridge is as remarkable as the engineering skill shown in the erection of the bridge itself. It is alleged that Black's friends and neighbours, inconvenienced by round-about roads and the dangerous nature of the fords of the North Esk, adopted a wily scheme, aware as they were of his credulity and of his great wealth. As several people had been drowned fording the river in the vicinity of Gannochy when it was in spate during the winter of 1731, they ingeniously contrived that three of their 'ghosts' would visit him on three successive nights to urge him to erect a bridge to prevent travellers from being swept to their deaths when the river was in flood. Unable to find peace of mind or withstand further appeals for his generosity, he erected the bridge at the very spot indicated by his nocturnal visitors. A variant to the story is that only one spirit of a drowned man made three successive midnight calls on Mr Black to implore him to build a bridge and save further loss of life.

Archibald Cameron, minister of Fettercairn kirk, gives a less sensational account of Black's motive, and this is probably the correct account of the circumstances. He states that owing to a serious difference with the kirk session of Edzell, Black attended Fettercairn church, crossing the river on horseback above the 'Loups Brig', a suspension footbridge farther up the river. Finding this very inconvenient and being himself a mason, he hired work-men and built the bridge which by his somewhat ungrateful neigh-bours was nicknamed 'Black's Grey Mare'.

A Wild, Magnificent View

The fine proportions of the graceful arch of Gannochy Bridge are enhanced by the view on both sides which is extremely beautiful. The gushing Esk spectacularly tumbles its way over cascades, foam-flecked and hemmed in by the huge rocks of a narrow gorge. It is recorded that this gorge, which measures about 30 ft. from the crown of the arch to the bed of the foaming stream, was filled during the great flood of August 4th, 1829. Fine old trees on the precipitous and lofty banks gracefully bend their luxuriant arching branches over huge lichen-covered boulders and deep, dark pools. Wild flowers adorn the banks, and beyond rise the mountains that form the gateway to Glenesk. It is a wild, yet charming scene, delighting alike geologist, botanist and the lover of the picturesque.

Riverside Policies to Explore

A gateway near Gannochy Bridge (where there is a fine lodge) leads to the elegant mansion of The Burn on the north-eastern bank of the River Esk but, like Alice popping down a rabbit-hole to look into *the loveliest garden you ever saw*, we should pass through the small, unpretentious gate in the wall immediately before the bridge to enter upon a most delightful and unexpected 'wonderland' walk along the shaded, wooded bank of the Esk. As the grounds of The Burn, contained within an oval-shaped piece of land between the Glenesk road and the River Esk itself, are just within Kincardine-shire and no more, the winding path continues for a little over a mile and a half to where it joins the Glenesk road, converging to meet it before the county boundary is reached. Thereafter one can retrace one's steps through the woods of The Burn or return by the main road. The walk is varied and picturesque in the extreme, and there are superb riverside policies to explore.

The sides of the path are covered with the richest and most varied of clustering woodlands of Alpine character, overtopped with sombre pines. In every crevice where soil will rest there is luxuriant vegetation. The magnificence of the walk lies not least, however, in the succession of charming and romantic views of the narrow ravine and of the peculiar tilted nature of the old sandstone through which the North Esk rapidly flows. On occasion, high above the river, a path has been carved at great expense out of the massive rocks from which wonderful views can be obtained. Little pinnacled eminences of various heights and shapes project into the stream which twists around to rest in spacious circular basins, and cauldrons have been worn out by eddies turning boulders round and round within them. In the rugged schist rocks masses of jasper, some red and some yellow, are embedded in several places. At all accessible points byways lead to the deep, rocky bed of the river or to places of vantage from which striking views can be seen.

Along these thickly planted banks walked Queen Victoria and the Prince Consort in 1861 when they visited The Burn on their way to Fettercairn.

> *We came to a wood* (the Queen recorded in her journal) *where we got out and walked along The Burn. The path winds through the wood, just above the most curious narrow gorge which is unlike any of the other lynns; the rocks are very peculiar, and the burn very narrow, with deep pools completely overhung by wood. The woods and grounds might be in Wales or even in Hawthornden. . . .*

417

Improvement and Reclamation

All this is the more remarkable when one realises that prior to 1780 the grounds of The Burn were

> *an expanse of bare heath without a single tree or any semblance of cultivation, its gravelly and water-worn stones showing that in ages far remote the North Esk ... overflowed the surface.*

It was only when Lord Adam Gordon, fourth son of the second Duke of Gordon, owned the estate that the work of improvement began to manifest itself. Within a score of years he created *an Arcadian grove* from *a dreary desert*: he planted 527 acres, converted much moorland into arable land, laid out pleasant grounds and planted some of the fine woods which are a feature of the estate. So completely did he change the appearance and increase the value of his land that it became a subject of wonder how much was effected in such a short time.

It was Lord Adam Gordon who in 1791 built the mansion-house of The Burn, one of the most interesting in the parish of Fettercairn, which we pass on our right after walking half a mile. He retired to it in 1798. Lord Adam had a distinguished military career and sat in Parliament for upwards of thirty years. After representing Aberdeenshire from 1754 onwards, he was member for Kincardineshire from 1774 to 1788. A year later he was appointed Commander of the Forces in Scotland. It was then he used French prisoners of war to make the popular walk to the Rocks of Solitude which we have described, to plant trees and to make paths on his estate.

Such was the extent of Lord Adam Gordon's improvements that on his death in 1801 *from violent inflammation produced by drinking lemonade while overheated* the estate which had been bought, it is said, for £300 was sold for £20,000 to Alexander Brodie of Arnhall who paid £1,000 for the furnishings of the house. Brodie continued the work of improvement for thirteen years, reclaiming from moss and moor over 400 acres, enclosing 125 acres with stone dykes, making five miles of roads and planting 220 acres of waste ground. In 1814 the estate was sold to John Shand, a West Indian merchant, whose brother and successor sold it to Major William McInroy, one of those who helped most to establish the great agricultural traditions associated with The Burn. On one occasion when he was presented by the Fettercairn Farmers' Club with a piece of silver plate, the presentation speech was delivered by Mr William Ewart

Gladstone. Major McInroy was also founder of Fettercairn Curling Club.

The Burn as Student Residence

During the Second World War The Burn was used as a hospital, and in 1943 Mr G. H. Russell who had bought the estates of The Burn and Arnhall from the McInroy family decided to sell the latter and part of the former, retaining only the mansion-house policies and part of the woodlands. The great country-house he gifted with a substantial endowment in memory of his son to the Dominion Students' Hall Trust as a Scottish residence at reasonable rates for parties of students from British universities and as a vacation home for post-graduate Commonwealth and US students so that they might have an opportunity of seeing Scotland.

The oldest part of the present mansion-house, the eastern portion, was built between 1791-96 by Lord Adam Gordon. The delicate relief decoration in the magnificent ceiling of the hall and stairway date from this time, and the Adam-style mantelpieces remain exactly as Lord Adam installed them. The large stable-yard clock in its domed tower is dated 1796. It is still in first-class working order although the original pillars of wood had to be replaced by modern zinc ones. In 1933 very large and undistinguished additions made to The Burn were demolished and a more convenient and compact building, designed to replace them, completed in 1935. The house today consists of a large drawing-room, dining-room, library, television-room, recreation room and eighteen bedrooms, twelve of them double. The house is open all the year round, and charges include fishing for salmon and trout for nearly two miles on one bank of the North Esk, tennis, squash and croquet.

The clear, sparkling rivulet which flows past the house originally crossed the glen road behind the walled garden and entered the river direct. Lord Adam deflected it and led it through the garden in front of the house – a typical piece of 18th century landscape-gardening. It was made to serve a useful purpose also as it was eventually continued under the public road and used to drive the water-wheel of the estate saw-mill.

Arnhall House

Back from our wonderland on the B966 Edzell road, we must now retrace our steps towards Fettercairn for three-tenths of a mile until we reach the long, straight road to North Water Bridge on our right. This we must take.

After one and two-fifth miles we pass on our right the road to Arnhall House, a pleasant building once owned by Sir William Ogg, honoured for his work in soil research in Aberdeen. It is built on the site of a much older Aurinhall House, dated 1506, and has above a mantelpiece a stone dated 1622, doubtless from this building. The 'hall' is now pronounced 'ha' ', and the derivation of the name is the Mearns 'ha' to signify a place and 'airne' (sloe) – the place of the sloe shrubs. At one time the estate of Arnhall included The Burn.

RAF Edzell

Another quarter of a mile takes us to the gates of the United States Navy Base, RAF Edzell, which during World War II was occupied from August 1st, 1940, onwards by No. 44 Maintenance Unit, an aircraft storage unit for the maintenance of damaged fighters and bombers. However, like Fordoun, Edzell was also used as a satellite airfield for No. 2 Flying Instructor School (Advanced) at Montrose and in addition provided a rest area for pilots. After the War, in June, 1950, Edzell was given a further lease of life with the formation of No. 63 Maintenance Unit: during this period a number of more permanent buildings, including married quarters, were constructed. However, with the cut-back in the Services in the post-Suez period, the station (still a maintenance unit in No. 41 Group Maintenance Command) was proved surplus to requirements and disbanded on December 1st, 1957. On February 11th, 1960, the Americans took it over.

The American Base has been a great boon to the western rim of Marykirk parish for a station with about 200 civilian employees, numbers of whom come from Luthermuir, cannot but add a new and very welcome dimension to the area. Single servicemen have a tour of duty of two years and married men three years, and there is a total population of around 1,500, men, wives and children. Servicemen's families, as you will have seen, are housed in a delightful residential village outside the perimeter of the Base itself.

The William F. Halsey Jr. American elementary school in the Base with its eleven full-time teachers and 150 pupils, is said to be the finest American elementary school in Britain. By comparison Luthermuir has only 100 pupils and Marykirk thirty-two. It is a single-storey structure with a glass-fronted entrance hall, constructed on the concrete floor of an old hangar. On one side is the administrative block with offices, multi-purpose hall, a magnificent carpeted library, a teachers' conference room and a teachers' sitting-room. In the office there is an inter-com system connected to every classroom. On the other side of the entrance hall is the classroom suite and a splendidly equipped audio-visual aids room. The equipment includes a film-loop and a portable science cabinet with its own sink and water supply. RAF Edzell also houses a very good library of some 8,000 books, a ten-pin bowling alley and a theatre to seat 325, opened by Douglas Fairbanks Jr. One must not fail to note in passing how well the American servicemen have integrated into the local community. They compete in Grampian and local basket-ball, tennis and darts leagues; they have organised Highland danc-ing lessons for children and Scottish country dancing classes for adults; several servicemen study piping, and a tug-of-war team competes at Highland gatherings.

Chapelton of Arnhall

Ninety yards farther on is the road on the right to the cottage of Chapelton of Arnhall. The name indicates that, besides a chapel, there was here a group of dwellings, forming a town in the old sense of the term. All that now remains is a heap of stones, evidently the remains of part of buildings long ago demolished, and a farm cottage on the site of or nearby an old proprietory chapel of the Carnegies of Southesk, dedicated to St Martin. The adjoining pool in the river is still called Linn Martin.

Parts of the thick outer walls of the cottage obviously belong to an older building. An ancient carved stone, now built into the front wall and probably from the original chapel, bears the date 'Anno 1668' and what might be the family crest of the Carnegies with possibly its outstretched wings still visible. On it is the legend, 'E 171 SO4' which perhaps has some association with the initials of some Earl of Southesk. The door lintel and a circular stone nearby, bearing what is still recognisable as a face, are, it would seem, from the same period. The original site of the chapel was immediately south-east of Chapelton cottage.

Separated from the cottage by a garden and now part of the field in front is the old burying-ground, about 21 yards by 17 in size and completely overgrown, with no grave stones visible. Parts of the old wall which enclosed it, however, with its huge corner stones, are still clearly in evidence. The boundary is still traceable from its soil being blacker and richer than the rest of the field and from its crop being heavier and more luxuriant, especially in a dry summer. Some of the tombstones from the burial-ground are now in Edzell old churchyard, Angus.

A Dalladies Ditch System

Just under two-thirds of a mile farther along the road known as The Lang Stracht is a rough road to the right, leading to the farm of Dalladies which gave its name to the long barrow, now no more, which we described on page 68. At the end of this road, four-fifths of a mile away, during quarrying operations on a gravel pit a few years ago, a system of ditches was uncovered. The larger formed a horseshoe about 50 ft. across, 6 ft. wide and 2 ft. deep, the bottom being 5 ft. 6 ins. below present ground level. It was filled with black loam, peaty in places, with some charcoal.

The smaller radiated inwards from the bottom of the horseshoe and was about 10 ft. long by 3 ft. wide. It appeared to taper in depth from that of the larger ditch to nothing at its inner end. Subsequent work (including destruction of the site by quarrying) revealed no trace of a habitation level, but since the first 2 ft. of soil was removed before investigation began, this may well have been destroyed.

In the smaller ditch part of a Red Sandstone artifact 8 ins. by 5 ins. by 3 ins. was found, broken along a line through an hour-glass shaped hole bored in it. This was retained by the Arbroath Antiquary Club. A short cist from Dalladies is to be seen at the bottom of the garden at The Retreat, Glenesk.

The site, it is thought, holds the remains of a complex of religious structures dating to the late Neolithic – early Bronze Age periods 4,000 years ago.

Witch Hillock

In another half mile we turn left and proceed for three-quarters of a mile past the croft of Gawloch until we reach a road fork at the edge of Inverury Wood. Here we take the right hand road for only 200 yards before turning sharp right along a Forestry Commission path into the plantation. This we follow for 470 yards until we meet a track which crosses at right angles, continuing on our way straight on for a further 150 yards. On our left is to be seen a tumulus, largely earthen, with a diameter of some 20 yards and 6 ft. in height. It is known as Witch Hillock – in effect a beautiful example of a Bronze Age round barrow. About 1856 excavation revealed several cists, calcined bones and a cremation in a clay cinerary urn.

Some 33 yards to the north-east are three earth-fast boulders, about 4¼ yards apart, forming an arc and unusual in an area with no large stones. Their purpose is obscure, but possibly they are survivors of a stone-circle around 8 yards in diameter. 21 or 22 yards to the

The author at Witch Hillock which is 6 ft. in height and has a diameter of 20 yards.

north-west is a beautifully constructed stone-lined circular well-shaft 1½ ft. in diameter, 5 yards deep – and mercifully covered!

Witch Hillock is an example of the most numerous of all field monuments and the standard tomb of the Bronze Age from about 1800 B.C. to 550 B.C. Indeed, barrows similar to these were used from Neolithic times onwards and survived into the early Middle Ages. No monument is more typical of our Kincardineshire countryside than these burial-mounds which surely mark the resting-places of Bronze Age chieftains or, it may be with such small barrows as these on lower ground, the graves of humble folk. For some great burial-mounds can be up to 120 ft. across and 20 ft. in height and are often sited on moors and open stretches of country or on hill-tops where they may be slightly below the actual top on what is called the 'false crest' so that, when seen from the settlement lower down the slope, they are on the skyline. They are often associated with hut-circles, stock pounds (circular defensive stone wall enclosures round a group of hut-circles), cultivation terraces and other signs of primitive occupation.

By far the majority of Bronze Age barrows are of the simple 'bowl' form, like an inverted pudding basin (as here), and Middle Bronze Age burials (1400 to 1000 B.C.) usually yield the cinerary urn of that period in a small pit in the centre of the barrow, closed with a flat stone. These pottery vessels containing human ashes are often inverted, for what purpose is not clear.

Aerial view of Dalladies long barrow (see page 68) during its excavation in 1970. The barrow at Dalladies was some 26 ft. 9 ins. shorter than that at Capo, pictured opposite, and 13 ft. narrower at its broadest point. The most interesting and most complex feature of the site was the Mortuary Structure at the north-west corner of the barrow (see page 433).

Capo Long Barrow

We now return to the Lang Stracht. Just over half a mile farther on and precisely at the end of Capo plantation we turn right where Weirside is signposted. This road we follow for 180 yards until we reach the Forestry Commission barrier. We continue on foot into Capo conifer plantation for a further 220 yards before turning left. Another 260 yards will take us to Capo long barrow, covered in trees and rough grass. It is 40 yards inside the wood.

Part of the magnificently intact long barrow in Capo plantation, 240 ft. in length and 72 ft. in breadth, the author standing at the 9 ft. high east end.

The barrow before us, like that at Hillhead, is between 5,000 and 6,000 years old, the mother and father of long barrows, the largest in Scotland, the highest in Britain and quite the most ancient prehistoric relic to be found in Kincardineshire. Trapezoidal in shape, it was built by the people who originally brought farming to the area. The long axis lies just north of east to just south of west – which is usual, for long barrows are generally placed east and west. It is 240 ft. in length, 72 ft. in breadth at the higher and broader east end which contains the interments and 39 ft. wide at the narrowest western end. The maximum height near the east end is between 8 ft. and 9 ft. The barrow is magnificently intact, and excavation has shown that it is composed of turfs and top soil, revetted by a dry-stone wall. The usual small ditches were found along each side about 9 ft. from the revetment, joining up in a curve or horseshoe. Many think that the shape and layout of the interior suggest that they were merely adaptations of megalithic tombs. Further details regarding the building and contents of long barrows are given, you will recall, on page 68.

In 1960 a disturbed cist, containing a stone axe, was discovered some 250 yards north-east of Capo long barrow.

Inglismaldie Castle

And now back to the Fettercairn – North Water Bridge road where we turn right. In seven-tenths of a mile, having passed half-way an interesting doocot on our left, we reach on our left the drive to Inglismaldie Castle (originally Eglismaldie or Ecclesmaldie, a cell dedicated to St Maldie or Mallie). Standing in forested grounds, it is erected on the site of the historic ancestral seat of the Earls of Kintore and of their ancestor, Baron Falconer of Haulkerton. Built partly of red stone, it was originally an L-shaped turreted and battlemented tower-house in the Scottish baronial style of the mid-16th and early 17th centuries with three storeys and an attic. To it has been added a large modern mansion. The castle has a distinctive charm of its own, heightened by its beautiful situation near the North Esk.

Notable and Peculiar Features

The castle itself presents a variety of peculiarities characteristic of the period: crowning the corners, for example, are the usual angle-turrets supported by highly finished label (or dripstone) corbelling the design of which is continued in the projecting horizontal band or course running round the building above the windows of the second

426

floor (and copied on some later extensions). This is unusual as is a third matching half-turret between the angle-turrets on the south frontage of this fine house. The turret roofs are, however, modern, being too steeply pointed, and modern too between the twin shot-holes at basement level are the fine front doorway and the heraldic panel with its earl's coronet above it. The original entrance on the west front can still be traced inside.

The interior of the castle, although greatly modernised, still retains many notable features chief among which is excellently carved woodwork and an exceptionally wide and handsome turn-pike stair to the first floor where the Hall would have been. The turret stair to floors above is no more since the re-entrant angle with its stair projection has been built in, and a chapel to the east of the frontage was converted into a kitchen. The basement of the castle is vaulted.

A Descendant of the Earls Marischal

The church lands of Over, Middle and Nether Eglismaldie were granted by James VI in 1588, after the Reformation, to John Living-stone of Dunipace who held them for forty-three years or more. In 1635 the owner became Sir John Carnegie, sheriff of Forfar, who by royal consent changed his title to Earl of Northesk and Baron Rosehill and Inglismaldie; in 1693 it passed to the son of Sir David Falconer, Lord Newton, President of the College of Justice, who became 5th Lord Falconer of Haulkerton and who in 1703 married a daughter of the 2nd Earl of Kintore when she was only thirteen. (His sister was later to be the mother of David Hume, the phil-osopher.) So did the castle become a seat of the Earls of Kintore until 1925 when it was bought by a cousin of the family, Major Adrian Keith-Falconer. Thus once again Inglismaldie Castle re-verted to a descendant of the Earls Marischal of Scotland. Major Keith-Falconer served with the 4th Oxfordshire Hussars from 1914-18. Later he became assistant private secretary to Lord Curzon. Inglismaldie is now owned by Mr Murray McBay.

A North Water Bridge Camp

A further third of a mile takes us to the main A94 Aberdeen road, a mere 80 or 90 yards from North Water Bridge over the North Esk, built by the famous reformer, John Erskine of Dun. Here, within the parapets, towards the end of May, 1685, a company of wretched Covenanters, numbering altogether about 167 men and women, were made to camp for the night in a rain storm with sentinels

427

guarding each end of the bridge. Barefooted and with hands bound behind their backs, the unhappy prisoners were in the charge of a band of rude soldiers who were under orders from the Privy Council to convey them from the prisons of the south and west of Scotland to the Castle of Dunnottar. Throughout the long and wearisome journey no shelter by day or night was provided.

At this point we immediately turn left and continue along the road to Fettercairn for just over a mile, taking the first turning to the right. A further half mile takes us to the village of Luthermuir. It is well worth a visit.

Luthermuir's Last Hand-Loom Weaver

Luthermuir, concerning which little is recorded in history (although a Neolithic stone axe-head was once found here), sits in the middle of a reclaimed moor near the Luther, formerly called the Muir of Drumquharibar. St Laurence Fair was for some time held upon it. The village grew out of a row of primitive little cottages known as Feus of Caldhame (the farm which we passed a quarter of a mile before the school bears the old name) into a scattered hand-loom weavers' settlement about 1800. In 1841 200 persons were employed as weavers when the population was 1,090 so that the centre of gravity of the parish, as it were, was removed from Marykirk to the north. By that time, however, decline had set in due to competition from steam operated mills in the large centres: weaving had become a struggle in which these 200 craftsmen laboured 14-17 hours a day to earn about 8/- a week, scarcely scraping a living. Now the total population has declined to a mere 182[1] (numbers of whom are civilian employees in the American Base), and the old weaving industry is long dead except for the remarkable initiative of Mr William Taylor, the last hand-loom weaver of fine linen in Scotland (and probably in Britain), the sole surviving representative of fine damask linen weaving, a craft that was once the mainstay of the Mearns economy of which he has been an exponent in Luthermuir since 1952. He has a steady trade in extremely fine unique products, and his cottage is 160 yards along the village street, on the left hand side. There is a sign on the wall.

A Forerunner of Computer Technology

Mr Taylor wove twenty-four linen table-cloths for the Queen Mother when she occupied Balmoral Castle. He had originally five looms, which stood side by side in a shed, all examples of the first

[1] 1971 census.

Jacquard machines, made in 1803. A large proportion of Mr Taylor's products have been exported to distant places, world-wide, and one of his main customers is an American contact who sends in a constant supply of orders. Working alone meant that he had to be his own 'tentor' or loom repairer, and the intricate and tedious task of 'setting' a loom occupied all his time for three months: there are 4,200 master threads to set for the Scotch Thistle design of the table-cloths he weaves, and such intricate traditional designs, woven into the damask cloth, are controlled by hundreds of cards with holes in them which, like punch cards, act as the 'memory' of the loom which could therefore be claimed to be a forerunner of computer technology! A one-man industry if ever there was one! In the New Year Honours of 1979 Mr Taylor was awarded the British Empire Medal for services to export.

Mr William Taylor, B.E.M., of Luthermuir, the last hand-loom weaver of fine linen in Scotland, with one of his 120 year-old Jacquard looms.

Mr Taylor retired from full-time work in 1981, and one of his looms was destined for Aberdeen Art Gallery. But with the remaining three the clatter of looms is by no means lost to Luthermuir. For in 1982 Ian Dale, who was brought up in the village and who learnt how the looms worked when he was still in his teens, became a partner in the business – Luther Hand-woven Linen. With one full-time worker and two part-time seamstresses engaged during the last two years, together with a grant to re-establish the craft, larger premises in or near Luthermuir are now essential. One should add that Mr Dale has recently built a complete Jacquard frame on the top of which he has fitted yet another Jacquard machine on loan from the National Museum of Antiquities in Edinburgh. The loom so constructed is probably the first complete single-twist Jacquard loom built this century.

Luthermuir is a village full of character, its long straight street being mostly single storey cottages. Following the Disruption a Free Church was founded here which, with a small hall, once formed the nucleus of the village. But, alas, no more.

Sauchieburn Church and Religious Liberty

Let us now continue along the road by which we reached Luthermuir, along past the school until we join the B974 to Fettercairn. Here we turn left. Another half mile on our way takes us to the Sauchieburn crossroads. At the junction and opposite the hotel is all that remains of the old church of Sauchieburn. It recalls the fight for religious liberty which was waged in the district over 200 years ago when Scotland was seething with religious discontent and which forms an interesting chapter in the history of the Mearns.

It all began in 1773 when, upon the death of the Rev. Anthony Dow, minister of Fettercairn Church, his assistant, the Rev, John Barclay (1734-98), was unanimously called to be the new minister, a petition in his favour being presented by the parishioners to the parish land-holders. These, however, considered Mr Barclay's antinomian principles[1] and his divergence from the Confession of Faith to be heretical and installed another candidate. The parishioners, deeply attached to Mr Barclay, protested by all the means in their power: they petitioned the Synod, the General Assembly and, finally, the king himself whom they addressed in no measured terms, as the following extract shows,

[1] that Christians are emancipated by the Gospel from obligation to keep the moral law.

*There are two thousand, five hundred, in the parish, old
and young, who would fight for His Majesty, George III,
till their boots were full of blood upon getting Mr Barclay
for their minister . . . if they are frustrated, unforeseen dis-
turbances may take place, the peace and quiet of families
broken up in flame and riot and disorder, the one against
the other.*

Foote's Wind and the Bereans

It says much for the self-control of the people in Fettercairn that
there was, after all, no rioting when their petition was turned down
and the Rev. Mr Foote of the Presbytery's choosing inducted to the
charge. The Presbytery, however, took the precaution of having
themselves escorted by soldiers to the church, and some of the more
hot-headed rebels threw a stone at the new minister as he dis-
mounted from his carriage at the church door. Furthermore, the
devout on both sides saw a visitation of God's wrath when a strong
wind sprang up and did considerable damage to the crops – for it
was harvest time: it was long before the Howe of the Mearns forgot
'Foote's wind'.

Meantime the parishioners had not let the grass grow under their
feet for they seceded from the parish church of Fettercairn in a body
and in 1774 built the church at Sauchieburn with the noted reformer, the Rev. James McRae, as their minister. There they founded
the next sect of the Bereans, the name adopted being taken from the
Bible, Acts 17, 11, where we read of the people of Berea deriving all
knowledge of God from the Bible. The Scriptures were the only
standard of religious teaching and doctrine, and so they searched
them daily, differing little from ordinary Calvinists. Adherents to
the sect were gained in Edinburgh, Glasgow, Crieff, Kirkcaldy and
many other places.

The First Sunday School and Bible Class

The Sauchieburn congregation flourished during Mr McRae's long
ministry of over forty years. He had the distinction of founding the
first Sunday school in Scotland, and his successor, the Rev. Thomas
McKinnon, was the first to hold Bible classes. In 1809 the church
adopted Congregational principles. Soon, however, the population
decreased so much in the neighbourhood that it was no longer
possible to maintain the church. For a period it was used for month-
ly services by the three Marykirk ministers, but this custom also was
dropped when the doors opened only once per year. That, too, is

gone, and the church of Sauchieburn with its tablet in memory of James McRae is, as a centre of religious activity, but a memory.

The Curious Matter of Surgeon's Hall

In just over 1¾ miles we arrive at the junction with the Fettercairn – North Water Bridge road, at which fork was once the site of a country smiddy with the curious name of Surgeon's Hall. Closed in 1921, the smiddy is now no more, and the place on which it stood has long since been ploughed up although the floor of what was the neighbouring farmhouse can still be seen inside the large outhouse where the roads divide: it is actually built on to the sandstone foundations of the cottage itself.

Did Surgeon's Hall derive its designation from the fact that the neighbouring farm was once tenanted by a doctor, the name being bestowed with a certain degree of relevancy? Or was it because the smithy was at one time occupied by a farrier, once one of the outstanding personalities in any small burgh or village of the time, ranking alongside the minister and the dominie? Children were taught to respect his powers, and he was blacksmith, veterinary surgeon and jack-of-all-trades, often called upon to cure the ailments of his neighbours. Whatever the reason, the name is now merely a curiosity that will soon sink into oblivion.

In a little over three-quarters of a mile we arrive back in Fettercairn where we began our circular journey. Another 17⅓ miles take us back to Stonehaven Square.

Bannock stone used for baking bannocks before an open fire. The stone, donated in 1873, is from Balbegno and can be seen in Montrose Museum.

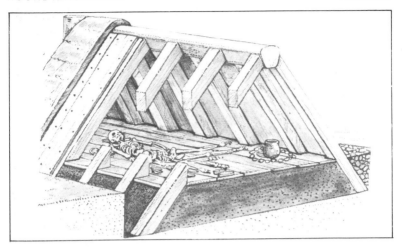

Houses of the Dead

Above: *Artist's reconstruction of a wooden mortuary chamber, supported by huge posts and built like a ridged tent. In this dead bodies were placed after being exposed to rot in the open air. Eventually, when enough bodies had accumulated, the barrow mound was heaped up over the mortuary house which was sometimes burned down first, scorching the bones inside.*

Below: *The remains of the mortuary house at Dalladies after excavation of the long barrow in 1971. The pre-existing timber building had been 26 ft. 2 ins. by 11 ft. 4 ins. and 4 ft. 9 ins. high, supported by nine large tree trunks (arranged in the pattern 1, 3, 3, 2) and roofed in pointed fashion with birch bark. There had been an imposing entrance facade and a crude surrounding boulder wall.*

It is to be assumed that the remains of a similar mortuary chamber exist inside Capo long barrow.

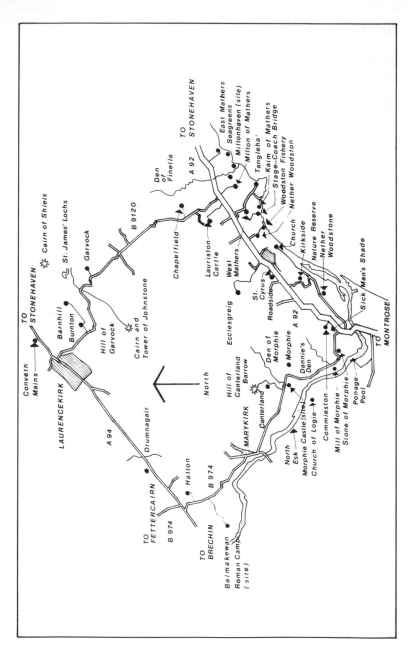

East Mathers
Seagreens
Miltonhaven (site)
Milton of Mathers
Tangleha'
Kaim of Mathers
Stage-Coach Bridge
Woodston Fishery
Nether Woodston
Church
Kirkside
Nature Reserve
Nether Woodstone
Sick Man's Shade

TO STONEHAVEN
A 92
Den of Finella
Chapelfield
Lauriston Castle
West Mathers
Ecclesgreig
St. Cyrus
Roadside
A 92

B 9120
Garvock
St. James' Lochs
Cairn of Shiels

Convein Mains
LAURENCEKIRK
Barnhill
Burnton
Hill of Garvock
Cairn and Tower of Johnstone

TO STONEHAVEN
A 94
Drumnagair

North

MONTROSE

Den of Morphie
Morphie
Dannie's Den
Commieston
Mill of Morphie
Stone of Morphie
Ponage Pool

Hill of Canterland
Barrow
Canterland
MARYKIRK

North Esk
Morphie Castle (site)
Church of Logie

Hatton
B 974

TO FETTERCAIRN
B 974
TO BRECHIN
Balmakewan
Roman Camp (site)

Route Nine

Stonehaven Square – Laurencekirk – Borrowmuirhill – Balmakewan – Mary-kirk – Hill of Canterland – Dannie's Den – Castle of Morphie – Stone of Morphie – Sick Man's Shade – Commieston – Nether Warburton – Ecclesgreig – Road-side – St Cyrus – Nether Woodston – West Mathers – Tangleha' – Kaim of Mathers – Milton of Mathers – Lauriston Castle – Hill of Garvock – St James' Loch – Barnhill – Laurencekirk – Stonehaven Square.

Distance: A total of 64½ miles as follows:

Round trip from Laurencekirk by car – 28.77 miles
Stonehaven Square to Laurencekirk and back by car – 28.46 miles
On foot – 7.46 miles

Readers who do not wish to travel far on foot may find it helpful to know the return mileage of the longer walks:
Cairn of Shiels from Hill of Garvock via St James' Loch – 1.78 miles
Seagreens from Tanglaha' – 1.64
Johnstone Tower from Hill of Garvock – 1.09 miles
Stagecoach Bridge from Rock Hall via Kaim of Mathers – 0.63 miles
Old Churchyard of St Cyrus from the Fishing Station – 0.60 miles
Bell-disc Barrow on Hill of Canterland – 0.47 miles

Round the Hill of Garvock via Laurencekirk, Marykirk and St Cyrus

in which we read of the first strike in the capital of the Howe, the minister who measures brides and a lord who slept with a sow. We discover a remarkable martyr who threw fish into the sea, a terrorist kelpie with sore bones, the spot where a poet blew his brains out and where a village disappeared in a night.

This journey starts at Laurencekirk. We therefore follow the last 11¾ miles of Route No. 5 along the A94 until it is joined by the B966. Thereafter we continue along the A94 for a further 4½ miles although, indeed, the part of the road from Redmyre to the Mill of Conveth turning has already been covered in Route No. 6. By the time we reach Laurencekirk only some 3¼ miles of road, therefore, are new to us. Let us park temporarily at the Boar's Head Hotel at the entrance to the town.

Laurencekirk, Ancient 'Capital of the Howe'

In Laurencekirk we are at the focal point of the finest agricultural area in Kincardineshire, its prosperity stemming from the fertile

Howe o' the Mearns with its rich, red soil. In consequence Laurencekirk has a character of its own – one that distinguishes it from
other towns – for it is the 'Capital of the Howe'. After rail access
was given to the burgh about 1850, it maintained its position as the
farming and shopping centre for the surrounding area and as a
market town of importance with an independent and very progressive weekly auction mart, established about 1920, which facilitated
the sale of cattle produced locally.

The burgh is named after St Lawrence, an ancient primate of
England who is said to have made a journey into Pictland some time
between 605 and 609 when it was under the Angles. It is thought to
have been visited by Ternan who no doubt was often in this district
where the church of Arbuthnott was subsequently dedicated to him.
The village is of ancient origin, the powerful family of Berkeley who
settled under William I possessing the lands of Monboddo, Glenfarquhar and Conveth, the original name of the village which means
either 'conveyed' (the Wisharts of Pitarrow having gifted lands to
the Church) or, more likely, 'the little head or promontory', a
translation of two Celtic words which a slight modification would
naturally merge into 'Conveth'.

Site of the Kirkton of Conveth Disputed

The *Kirk of Coneueth*, a rectory belonging to St Andrews, was
dedicated by Bishop David in 1244 and, in the old taxation of
Scottish churches, made about 1275, was rated at 30 marks. The
ecclesiastical superior at a very early date was the Prior of St
Andrews. Where the original church of Conveth was is a matter of
some dispute. Crabb Watt states that it stood *a mile to the east of
Laurencekirk*. Again, various records confirm the existence of a
parish church built much later, about 1625, dedicated to St Lawrence and thought by some to have been on the farm of Conveth
Mains half a mile to the north of the town. Yet again, Fraser in his
History of the Parish and Burgh of Laurencekirk argues that the
monks of ancient Conveth in all likelihood offered their devotions
exactly where the *present* church is today: the *Kirktoun of Conveth,
otherwise called St Laurence*, he argues, was probably situated on
the site of the present St Laurence Hall, the Clydesdale Bank and
the adjacent grounds. A point which gives credence to Fraser's
belief is that the earliest record of the village in a charter, dated 24th
June, 1646, annexes the Kirkton to the burgh of Haulkerton and the
lands of Diracroft or Bellakers which were situated a little to the
north of the railway station:

*Totas et integras predictas terras vocatas lie Diracroft alias
Belaikens cum domibus, edificiis, hortis, croftis, et omni-
bus suis pertinenciis, nunc vocatas lie Kirkton de Conveth
alias St Laurance.*
(The lands called Diracroft or Bellakers with houses, big-
gings, yards, lofts, crofts and whole pertinents thereof
called the Kirkton of Conveth or St Laurance.)

The probability is, however, that the site of the original Kirkton of
Conveth is one and two-thirds miles north-east along the A94, just
100 yards short of the farm of Scotston and 260 yards away to the
east. Here is a knoll still known as Chapel Knap, characteristic of
the Celtic definition above. Three-quarters of a mile farther away
on the rising ground to the east can be seen the farm of Haddo,
literally 'half davoch' (an ancient measure of land, averaging 416
acres). Haddo originally belonged to the Priory of St Andrews
before being owned by the Keiths in 1575.

The Name of Laurencekirk Familiar Before 1700

From 1646, then, the village of Kirkton of Conveth was called also
by its alternative name, 'St Laurance' and, although the name of
Conveth is occasionally found in ecclesiastical records during the
century which followed, it is reasonable to presume that the name of
Laurencekirk must have been familiar in the neighbourhood between 1695 and 1700 when Thomas Ruddiman, the renowned Latin-
ist, was officially connected with the parish as the first edition of his
Rudiments proclaims on the title page that he had been *sometime
schoolmaster at Laurencekirk*. The Burgh Muir within the Burgh of
Haulkerton had already identified itself with the name of the saintly
patron of the Church and become Laurencemuir and, probably as a
means of distinguishing it from the barony, the burgh of Haulkerton
itself came to be known by the same name for it is indeed remarkable that the parish should contain two burghs of barony, one
contiguous to the other.

Nevertheless, despite the fact that the first occurrence of the name
of Laurencekirk in the presbytery records is 10th September, 1701,
there is still evidence, even in the early years of the 18th century, of
two separate villages in existence – Laurencekirk and the Kirkton.
A kirk session minute, dated 25th March, 1712, records that

*James Nairn and Arthur Shepherd, Mert. att Laurence-
kirk, gave an oak plank to be a Bridge att the Kirktown, and
would have nothing for it.*

But eventually the original Kirkton on the border of the Haulkerton estate decayed, probably because of the abandonment of Haulkerton Castle and the removal of Lord Falconer's residence to Inglismaldie. Yet it was not until a quarter of the 19th century had elapsed that the last relics of the old village disappeared.

Lord Gardenstone's 'Regular Plan' Realises a Royal Charter

Most of 18th century Laurencekirk owed its being to Francis, Lord Gardenstone (1721-93), to whom the burgh's development and prosperity are due. Born Francis Garden, he was the second son of the laird of Troup in Banffshire, originally living in the parish of Fordoun. Appointed sheriff of Kincardineshire on 3rd July, 1764, he purchased the estate of Johnston on which he began to build a new village for which he did much, sparing no effort for the improvement of his property and the well-being of his tenants and servants. In the Preface to his *Letter to the People of Laurencekirk* he writes,

> *In ancient and heroic days persons of the highest ambition aspired at a character of being the founders of societies and cities. I have produced an elegant proof of this in a quotation from Vergil; and it is finely illustrated in a story related by Plutarch (I think) of Themistocles. A man of quality in ancient Greece, who seems to have possessed a modern taste of distinction and pleasure, asked Themistocles if he could play on the lute. 'No,' said he, 'I cannot, but I can raise a small village to be a flourishing city'.*

As early as 1772 his factor attended a kirk session meeting

> *to purchase the loft belonging to the poor in consequence of the increasing size of the village,*

and Lord Gardenstone had a *regular plan* prepared for the remodelling of the Kirkton, then a clay-built hamlet of fifty-four inhabitants. One of his fundamental principles was the giving of aid and encouragement to those of industrious habit who managed their affairs prudently and discharged their debts punctually,

> *I will make particular observation if your clothing and the furniture of your houses are produced by domestic industry or at least manufactured by some inhabitant of the village. This economy is both laudable and profitable to an industrious village and ought at least to be observed until they*

attain to some extent of foreign commerce when exchange of commodities may become a branch of trade and industry.

As encouragement was given to strangers settling in the village who were likely to promote its industry, it soon became a centre of attraction to craftsmen and others from all parts of the country.

On 27th August, 1779, the success of Lord Gardenstone's project was realised when a Crown charter was obtained, erecting the lands of Johnston and Laurencekirk into a barony

with all powers, liberties, privileges and jurisdictions whatsoever, belonging and competent, or which ought to belong or be competent, to any complete and independent burgh of barony.

When he presented the charter to the new burghers, Lord Gardenstone addressed a letter to them in which he gave them salutary admonitions as to their conduct, strongly exhorting them to cultivate habits of industry, frugality and sobriety. Defined in the charter, the boundaries of the burgh were

within eight hundred and thirty-eight yards on each side of the King's highway . . . as far as it passed through his Lordship's lands . . . which at present forms the street of the said town,

a distance of three-quarters of a mile. Now you see why Laurencekirk is called 'the lang toon'!

The Famous Hand-loom Weavers of 'Mearns Linen'

The election of a burgh council being thus facilitated, the feuars and all resident burgesses of full age were empowered every third year on the first Wednesday in June to elect a bailie and four councillors to whom the administration of the common good was entrusted, to collect customs and to hold weekly markets on a Thursday as well as an annual three-day fair on the first Wednesday of November. Several of these, of course, had already been held in the parish for the hiring of servants and disposal of cattle, and the annual fair on St Anthony's Day was probably originally held on the site now occupied by the Clydesdale Bank. Among his many activities Lord Gardenstone granted feus (on condition that every feu holder bought his own house) and, in addition, introduced to his new burgh rural crafts, a spinning-mill with a bleach-field on the Luther and the art of hand-loom linen weaving which took firmest hold upon the community and which added greatly to the trade of Laurencekirk for which it was long famous.

Referring to this period, the *Statistical Account* of 1843 records that

> *there was carried on an extensive domestic manufacture of linen which was commonly known in the markets by the name of 'Mearns linen', and the spinning of the yarn and manufacturing of the cloth* (in their cottages) *afforded employment to many hands in the families both of tenants and of crofters.*

The work executed was partly for family use, but the surplus found its way to the markets at which a day was specially appropriated for the sale of linen. By and by weaving at home was practically discontinued, and public weaving shops were built. For a while the linen was prepared to order or disposed of to private customers. But this process also came to be exceptional. Agencies for weaving companies, mainly in Aberdeen, were established, the weavers receiving so much a piece. According to the *Statistical Account* of 1836, when 147 persons were engaged in the parish in hand-loom weaving,

> *the number of pieces and yards made annually may on an average be as under: Pieces 5,812, yards 416,440, value £13,106. The average sum obtained for weaving at the rate of 1¼d per yard is £2,168 19s 2d. The weavers in general work about 15 hours a day.*

Towards the middle of the 19th century the population had risen to 1,391, including sixty-eight hand-loom weavers, but linen continued to be manufactured in the burgh on a steadily reduced scale because of the competition from power-mills built in larger centres of population. By 1880 hand-loom weaving, once the staple occupation, had declined to less than a quarter of its extent in 1836, giving employment only to thirty-four hands in all.

Whipping the Cat Causes the First Strike

The tailors of Laurencekirk gained publicity at the beginning of the 19th century when they called the first strike ever in the burgh to improve their working conditions. It was caused by the then general practice of 'whuppin' the cat', that is, going out to work in their employers' houses. At the time the tailors were paid the princely sum of sixpence plus their food for a day's work. Their dissatisfaction with everything – their meagre wages, long hours and poor food – reached a head at a meeting of burgh craftsmen when resolutions demanding better conditions were passed. Their efforts being unsuccessful, they went on strike. They weren't out long, however, for their employers, appreciating the threat to their own livelihoods, almost immediately conceded their demands

A Cumbersome Porcine Bedfellow

Lord Gardenstone, although a Lord of Session and Rector of Marischal College, Aberdeen, from 1788-89, was, like Lord Monboddo (see page 319) somewhat odd. His eccentricity assumed the strange form of a strong affection for pigs to one of which he was so attracted that he allowed it to share his bed. When good feeding and rapid growth made it too cumbersome a bedfellow, it still occupied comfortable quarters in his apartment. When David Cowie, Mains of Haulkerton, having occasion to see his lordship one morning, was shown into his bedroom, he stumbled in the dark upon it. A loud grunt was followed by a voice from the bed,

> *It is just a bit sow, poor beast, and I laid my breeches on it to keep it warm all night.*

Laurencekirk's Snuff-boxes Renowned World-wide

Towards the end of the 18th century Laurencekirk was renowned throughout the world for the manufacture of a special kind of wooden snuff-box the peculiarity of which was a 'secret' concealed hinge and wooden pin. In these days nearly everyone, both male and female, indulged in the luxury of snuff-taking, and Lord Gardenstone used to say that if he had half a dozen noses, he would willingly supply them all. His snuff-box he invariably carried in a specially made leather pocket in his waistcoat. It was customary for a bride to receive a box of snuff as one of her first wedding presents, and ladies of the highest rank enjoyed their pinch. So it was that these excellent snuff-boxes brought fame to Laurencekirk and are keenly sought after by collectors.

They were invented about 1780 by the ingenuity and creative ability of a genial Glenbervie man, Charles Stiven, who was born in 1753 and named after the Young Pretender, Bonnie Prince Charlie, by his father, a staunch Episcopalian and *gryte Jacobite*. When the Duke of Cumberland destroyed the Episcopalian Chapel at Stonehaven, the members worshipped in his sister's house. Stiven had become famous by ministering to the wants of the Glenbervie folk as a snuff-box maker for many years: his fame as a skilled and artistic craftsman spread, and he was persuaded to settle in Laurencekirk about 1783 by one of his customers, Lord Gardenstone, who first heard of Stiven's ability through his factor for whom Stiven had *executed some work of superior manner*. His workshop was part of the old Town Hall and the Masonic Hall where is now the business of Allan Gammie, ironmonger, next to the Boar's Head Hotel, and a thriving trade was carried on in the hotel itself (or inn as it was called then) next door.

Others followed Charles Stiven's example, and at one time there were no fewer than three establishments engaged in snuff-box manufacture in Laurencekirk. Firstly, Charles Stiven's son, Alexander, who succeeded his father in the parent establishment which not only survived the other two but far exceeded them in enterprise. Secondly, Robert Macdonald, an apprentice to Charles who married his master's daughter in Dick Whittington fashion and set up business for himself once he had acquired sufficient skill. The third establishment was owned by William Milne, another apprentice whose family had long connections with the parish.

Alexander Stiven, Boxmaker to the Queen

When the demand for snuff-taking waned about 1840, Alexander Stiven added other industries to his business, producing many useful and fascinating ornamental articles of all shapes and sizes, though still retaining his distinction as the prince of snuff-box makers. In those days the Defiance stage-coach and post-chaises halted daily at the Boar's Head which was the local booking-office. As Charles Stiven was for many years in charge of this office, he had ample opportunity to display his wares, capturing considerable attention and finding a ready and profitable sale among travellers. In due time, with such a reputation, it is not surprising that the firm was honoured, in some measure through the influence of Sir John Gladstone of Fasque, father of the famous politician, by being appointed Boxmakers to Queen Victoria, and more than once Alexander Stiven had the honour of bearing specimens of his craftsmanship for her inspection at Balmoral. Possibly a unique example of Stiven's work in yet another sphere is to be seen in the Bible stand on the Communion-table in Dunnottar Church, Stonehaven. A brooch and bangles made by Alexander Stiven may be seen in The Retreat in Glen Esk. Snuff-boxes may be seen there too, and in Montrose Museum is one with scenes from Beattie's *John o' Arnha'*.

Revival of Ancient Tee-totums

Stiven also gained a reputation when as a side-line he revived an ancient toy and became the maker of tee-totums with which the children of the district amused themselves at New Year festivities for the small charge of a halfpenny. The totum was a simple little cube with a stalk through its centre on which it was made to spin, the luck of the gambler depending on which of the four sides was uppermost when the top ceased spinning. A 'Yule preen (pin) or nut' was as like as not the humble stake. The origin of the totum was classical as Fraser explains in his *History of Laurencekirk*:

> *A Roman emperor ... commanded the wisest of his coun-*
> *sellors to find out some game whose freshness and ... ex-*
> *cellence would ... relieve him of his ennui. He invented*
> *the totum and was rewarded with all imperial honours. On*
> *the four sides were painted in Roman capitals the letters A,*
> *D, N and T respectively, the letters denoting four Latin*
> *expressions in a game of chance. A ... stood for 'Accipe*
> *unum' ... accurately translated in the vernacular, 'A, take*
> *ane'. When D appeared, 'Donato alium' was the disap-*
> *pointed remark in ... Rome, supplanted in Laurencekirk*
> *and Glenbervie by the still more expressive 'D, duntle doon*
> *ane'. N was a negative quality ... a contemptuous 'Nihil'*
> *from the imperial lips to be repeated with double energy*
> *by ... his modern representatives, 'N, nickle naething'.*
> *The most coveted of all letters was T. Success could no*
> *farther go, whether the stake was an emperor's crown or a*
> *'Yule preen'. 'T, tak' a'' was the exultant exclamation of the*
> *Scottish youth, which corresponds in meaning with the*
> *Roman 'T, totum'.*

Mrs Cruickshank of the Boar's Head Inn

Before we leave Laurencekirk, two things we should see. The first is The Boar's Head Hotel, originally The Boar's Head Inn, where we are now. The first lessee was one William Cruickshank who had some medical skill, his fame as a bleeder and blisterer bringing invalids from many parts of the country. His wife, whose portrait has a place among the famous sketches by Brich (a Dutch artist brought to the village by Lord Gardenstone) must have benefited by her husband's medical knowledge or been endowed with a like gift which she applied to some purpose as her skill was celebrated in the following lines, probably from the pen of Dr Beattie of whom we shall later write,

The gratefull village bless'd her name,
And all the country spoke her fame
For she of ev'ry herb and flower
Had learnt the wonder-working power,
And knew by secret art to drain
The juice that gives relief to pain.
In ready order rang'd around
The balm that soothes the throbbing wound;
Salves, cordials, balsoms, all were there
As various ills required her care.

The lines are on a print published in 1784 by 'John Walker, 148 Strand, near Somerset House, London', representing Mrs Cruickshank sitting beside a table on which stand a sand-glass, phials and scissors. She is looking earnestly through spectacles at the finger of a girl on whose face a painful expression appears. A small curly-headed girl is at her back gazing between the bars of a chair, evidently amused at the inspection. A lank cat at her feet surveys the scene with apparent unconcern.

Three Distinguished Visitors

An elegant, commodious inn, The Gardenstone Arms, the erection of which was sponsored by Lord Gardenstone, took the place of The Boar's Head Inn before it was renamed The Boar's Head Hotel. It had a museum and, for the benefit of travellers, *a very neat assortment of amusing books* which formed the Laurencekirk Public Library. This library was housed in a diminutive classic building protruding on to the pavement as an annex to the hotel. Sadly, this historic building was demolished many years ago, a wooden bar lounge now occupying part of the place where it stood.

The Gardenstone Arms was honoured in 1773 with a distinguished visitor in the person of Dr Samuel Johnson who, during his Hebridean tour, in the words of Boswell,

> *insisted on stopping at the inn at Laurencekirk when I told*
> *him that Lord Gardenstone had furnished it with a collec-*
> *tion of books that travellers might have entertainment for*
> *the mind as well as the body. The Doctor praised the design*
> *of the north end of the building but wished there had been*
> *more books and those better chosen.*

Though the terms are modified, considering from whose lips they came, and that they applied to a Scottish subject, they are probably

1. Sir Joshua Reynolds as President of the Royal Academy of Arts. A self-portrait.

2. Dr Samuel Johnson, a portrait by John Opie, painted in 1783. The day after this portrait was painted Johnson had a stroke. He died in December of the following year.

3. James Boswell, biographer of Johnson. This portrait was painted by Sir Joshua Reynolds in 1783.

The visit of Dr Johnson and James Boswell to Monboddo House is described in Route 6 and the discovery of James Boswell's manuscripts in Fettercairn House in Route 7.

to be interpreted as an expression of the highest praise. The Gardenstone Arms became one of the most flourishing posting establishments in the county.

In 1782 George Colman the younger, the English dramatist (1762-1836), when a student at King's College, Aberdeen, in his twentieth year, put up at The Boar's Head Inn. He amused himself by writing in the album of the inn some verses on Scottish characteristics which, like Dr Johnson before him, he despised. He *deposited upon a profane altar*, he said, his *virgin offering to the Muse*. This was a contemptible piece of doggerel. He had occasion to return soon after and, turning over the leaves of the album, found that his 'ballad' had elicited the following couplet, probably from the pen of the schoolmaster, Mr Scott,

> *I like thy wit; but, could I see thy face,*
> *I'd claw it well for Scotia's vile disgrace.*

The witty Englishman, not to be outdone, added these lines,

> *Is, then, a Scotchman such a clawing elf?*
> *I thought he scratched no creature but himself!*

A third distinguished visitor was Robert Burns who with his schoolmaster friend, Willie Nicol (the Willie who brewed an immortal *peck o' maut*), spent a night in the burgh in 1787 on his return from his tour of the Scottish Highlands and on his way to Montrose. Burns' *Journal* states,

> *Lie at Laurence Kirk – album – library – Mrs ... a*
> *jolly, frank, sensible love-inspiring widow – Howe of the*
> *Mearns, a rich cultivated but still unenclosed country.*

Burns' horse was housed in what is now partly the function room and partly the rooms of the proprietor, transformed out of all recognition from the stable it once was during the days of coaching. A large part of the present building, indeed, may have been in existence about 1770. A stone lintel over the front door (which may originally have belonged to another building) bears the initials P.B. and the date 1638. It may refer to the year of the birth of Peter Barclay, proprietor of the estate of Johnston and grandson of the David Barclay whose initials appear on a stone at Johnston Lodge. It may be of interest that Peter Barclay's father-in-law was one of a family of twenty-four children born of the same parents, John Gardyne and Elizabeth Arbuthnott.

Two stones, one taken from a cart-shed and the other from a stable, bear the dates 1774 and 1778 and indicate perhaps that the steading was a subsequent erection – but these are not now to be seen since the walls have been harled.

Of later interest is the fact that on 21st June, 1819, the bailies and councillors of Laurencekirk Council convened for the first time in an apartment in the western wing of The Boar's Head (at that time The Gardenstone Arms) called The Council Room. Previously they had met, first in Murdoch's Inn and afterwards successively in Cream's, Adam's and Downie's.

James Beattie, Laurencekirk's Illustrious Son

The second thing to be seen requires us to continue northwards along the A94 for only 30 yards until, immediately we cross the Kirk Burn, we turn right along the side of the stream. In 65 yards we arrive at the farm of Borrowmuirhills on the site of which, in a farm on which his father was tenant, was born on 25th October, 1735, James Beattie, the celebrated author and Laurencekirk's most illustrious son. His forefathers had farmed in the immediate area for several generations, Beatties connected with the Mill of Haulkerton and (on his mother's side) Watsons with Scotston. His father also had a small shop in Laurencekirk, at that time and for thirty years afterwards merely a cluster of straggling houses.

The youngest of six children, the poet was a shy, retiring boy, fond of solitude and reading. He received his whole elementary education at the parish school where he made rapid progress, his poetic talents and thirst for knowledge soon becoming apparent: even at that early age his school friends called him 'The Poet'. According to his intimate friend and biographer, Sir William Forbes, he had then

> *been accustomed to spend his playful hours* on *the banks of the rivulet* (the Kirk Burn), *beautifully fringed with wild roses which he delighted to contemplate each time he passed through Laurencekirk with that enthusiasm with which we revisit, in after life, the haunts of our boyish days.*

Alas, no wild roses now – only a scene of utter desolation, a place for the discharge of rubbish. How very sad!

Despite losing his father, from whom he inherited his love of poetry, when only seven years old, the young James was maintained at school by his mother who, assisted by her elder son, continued to manage farm and shop. He had mastered Homer and Vergil as well as the fiddle by the time he was ten, and from the first exhibited many signs of devotion to literature of which the following instance, which he frequently told in after life, may be recorded in the words of his biographer,

> *Having lain down early in the morning on the banks of his favourite rivulet adjoining his mother's house, he had fallen asleep: on awakening, it was not without astonishment that he found he had been walking in his sleep and that he was then ... about a mile and a half from the place where he had lain down. On his way back to the spot he passed some labourers; and enquiring of them if they had seen him walking along, they told him that they had, with his head hanging down as if he had been looking for something he had lost.*

Or, as Beattie later writes,

> *In truth, he was a strange and wayward wight,*
> *Fond of each gentle and each dreadful scene.*
> *In darkness and in storm he found delight;*
> *Nor less than when on ocean-wave serene*
> *The southern sun diffused his dazzling shene.*
> *Even sad vicissitude amused his soul;*
> *And if a sigh would sometimes intervene,*
> *And down his cheek a tear of pity roll,*
> *A sigh, a tear so sweet he wished not to control.*

Familiar Scenes in 'The Minstrel'

James Beattie is chiefly remembered for *The Minstrel*, a sentimental and descriptive poem in Spenserian stanza tracing the development of a poet. It is still read today, and from it the above stanza is taken. The work remained unfinished, Book I appearing in 1771 and Book II in 1774. Many of the most beautiful passages were due to impressions on Beattie's mind while he was a boy at school, and his love for nature and the beautiful Mearns countryside can be sensed throughout. Familiar scenes are referred to again and again, and local people can easily recognise his allusions to Garvock Hill, Strathfinella Hill, Drumtochty Glen and other spots which he has immortalised in verse of unusual beauty. Love for the simple life is an outstanding feature of Beattie's poems, but at the same time they reflect the philosophy of a brilliant scholar and thinker.

In the words of his biographer,

> *He used himself to tell that it was from the top of a high hill*
> *in the neighbourhood* (Garvock Hill?) *that he first beheld*
> *the ocean the sight of which, he declared, made the most*
> *lively impression on his mind.*

So it is that Beattie writes biographically,

> *And oft he traced the uplands, to survey,*
> *When o'er the sky advanced the kindling dawn,*
> *The crimson cloud, blue main, and mountain grey,*
> *And lake, dim-gleaming on the smoky lawn;*
> *Far to the west the long, long vale withdrawn,*
> *Where twilight loves to linger for a while;*
> *And now he faintly kens the bounding fawn,*
> *And villager abroad at early toil,*
> *But lo! the sun appears! and heaven, earth, ocean smile.*

The stanza of *The Minstrel* in which he feelingly describes the spot
which he envisages for his grave is so very exact a picture of the
churchyard of Laurencekirk which stood almost within a stone's
throw of his mother's house that he must certainly have had it in his
view when he wrote the following lines,

> *Let Vanity adorn the marble tomb*
> *With trophies, rhymes and scutcheons of renown,*
> *In the deep dungeon of some Gothic dome*
> *Where night and desolation ever frown.*
> *Mine be the breezy hill that skirts the down*
> *Where a green grassy turf is all I crave,*
> *With here and there a violet bestrown,*
> *Fast by a brook or fountain's murmuring wave;*
> *And many an evening sun shine sweetly on my grave.*

The 'Essay on Truth' and Sir Joshua Reynolds

After graduating MA with distinction from Marischal College in
1753, Beattie was appointed schoolmaster of Fordoun and precen-
tor in the parish church where he gained the friendship and favourable notice of Mr Garden (afterwards Lord Gardenstone) and of
the celebrated Lord Monboddo (see page 319). It was at Fordoun
that he enjoyed the contact with nature in all its moods that laid the
foundations of his fame as a poet. For example, the hollow between
the church and the rising ground opposite is clearly referred to in his
Ode to Retirement. Here the poet is said frequently to have mused.

In 1758 Beattie was appointed a member of staff in Aberdeen Grammar School and, two years later, when only 25 years of age, Professor of Moral Philosophy and Logic in Aberdeen University. His most famous literary work, his *Essay on Truth* (1770), written in defence of Christianity against Hume's attacks, would have kept its author from being forgotten although he had written nothing else. With five editions in four years and translations into several languages this masterpiece brought upon the author a series of bitter attacks from the sceptics. Yet it evoked world-wide interest and had a great contemporary reputation, resulting in his being honoured by a private interview with George III who, greatly pleased, granted Beattie a royal pension of £200 a year. The University of Oxford, in recognition of his qualities as a writer, later conferred on him the honorary degree of LL.D.

The *Essay on Truth* won him the firm friendship of many eminent men, among others Dr Samuel Johnson, Lord Lyttleton and Sir Joshua Reynolds, the distinguished painter, who presented him with an allegorical painting of himself. The following letter from Sir Joshua adds further details:

> *In this inestimable piece, which exhibits an exact resemblance of Dr Beattie's countenance at that period, he is represented in the gown of Doctor of Laws with which he had been so recently invested at Oxford. Close to the portrait the artist has introduced an angel, holding in one hand a pair of scales, as if weighing 'Truth' in the balance, and with the other pushing down three hideous figures, supposed to represent Sophistry, Scepticism and Infidelity, in allusion to Dr Beattie's 'Essay' which had been the foundation of all his fame and all the distinction that had been paid to him.*

This second letter from Sir Joshua Reynolds may be of interest:

> *London, 22d February 1774*
> *I sit down to relieve my mind of great anxiety and uneasiness, and I am very serious when I say that this proceeds from not answering your letter sooner. This seems very strange, you will say, since the cause may be so easily removed; but the truth of the matter is, I waited to be able to inform you that your picture was finished, which, however, I cannot now do. I must confess to you that when I sat down, I did intend to tell a sort of white lie, that it was*

*finished; but on recollecting that I was writing to the author
of 'Truth', about a picture of truth, I felt that I ought to say
nothing but truth. The truth then is that the picture probably
will be finished before you receive this letter, for there is not
above a day's work remaining to be done. Mr Hume has
heard from somebody that he is introduced in the picture,
not much to his credit: there is also a figure covering his face
with his hands, which they may call Hume, or anybody
else – it is true it has a tolerable broad back. As for Vol-
taire, I intended he should be one of the group.*

*I intended to write more, but I hear the postman's bell. Dr
Johnson, who is with me now, desires his compliments.*

*The 'inestimable' allegorical painting of Dr James Beattie by Sir Joshua Reynolds in
the possession of Marischal College, Aberdeen. The picture shows 'an exact resemblance of Dr Beattie's countenance' and an angel, weighing Truth in the balance and
pushing down the 'hideous figures' of Sophistry, Scepticism and Infidelity.*

451

A Life Clouded with Tragedy

As with many great men James Beattie's private life was clouded with tragedy. His wife, a daughter of the then Rector of Aberdeen Grammar School, inherited from her mother insanity which culminated in her removal to an asylum. To this sorrow was added the death at the early age of twenty-three of the poet's elder son. Beattie's health suffered as a result of these sad happenings, and when his younger son died of fever in 1796, it was more than he could bear. He died, a cripple, on 18th August, 1803, and was buried, according to his own wish, beside the remains of his sons in St Nicholas' churchyard, Aberdeen. He takes an honoured place along with his contemporary, Goldsmith, among the leading pastoral poets of Britain although the fact that *a prophet is not without honour save in his own country* may well be applied in his case. His works are little known in the Mearns.

James Beattie's grave in St Nicholas' Churchyard, Aberdeen. James Beattie, Laurencekirk's illustrious son, was Professor of Moral Philosophy and Logic at Aberdeen University and is chiefly remembered for 'The Minstrel', a descriptive poem in two books which appeared in 1771 and 1774.

The Illustrious Thomas Ruddiman

Before we leave Laurencekirk, we might with advantage walk a mere hundred yards from The Boar's Head Hotel, past the Royal Hotel and along Station Road. The site of the business on the right where agricultural implements are now sold (there once was a brewery there) is the site of the school where the renowned grammarian, Thomas Ruddiman (1674-1757), faithfully taught the children of the parish from April, 1695, until the beginning of 1700. The office was no lucrative one, the salary fixed by statute being from one to two hundred merks, ranging from £5-11-1⅓d to £11-2-2²/₃d sterling, and paid chiefly in grain. He sold his corn to his uncle, William Simpson, who gave him a high price for it during what were called the 'dear' years following upon the Revolution. Ruddiman's fame is chiefly identified with his work, *Rudiments of the Latin Language*, produced in 1714, which had great vogue for many years, for more than a century being almost the only entrance into Latin known in Scottish schools.

It is of interest that it is in connection with Ruddiman that we have our earliest intimation of an inn in the parish, the inn at Laurencekirk, the site of which there is no means of ascertaining, where he met the celebrated Dr Archibald Pitcairne, physician and one of the most illustrious literary figures of his time. Probably returning from Aberdeen where he had a degree conferred upon him by the University in August, 1699, Dr Pitcairne was detained by the weather at Laurencekirk, which had not yet a library at the inn, and felt the misery of having nothing to do. In the words of his biographer

> *he inquired if there were no person in the village who could interchange conversation, and would partake of his dinner. The hostess informed him that the schoolmaster, though young, was said to be learned and, though modest, she was sure could talk. Thus met Pitcairne at the age of forty-seven with Ruddiman at twenty-five. Their literature, their politics and their general cast of mind were mutually pleasing. Pitcairne invited Ruddiman to Edinburgh, offered him his patronage and performed in the end, what is not always experienced, as much as he originally promised.*

The Roman Camp of Balmakewan

But we have lingered long enough in Laurencekirk: we must be on our way. Let us continue straight down the A94 for almost exactly four miles without much to detain us until we meet the B974 Marykirk road on our left. Here we are to turn but, before we do, let us deviate just a little to see something of great interest. Proceed along the A94 for only four-tenths of a mile until you arrive at a gate on your left leading into Balmakewan Wood. Leave your car here and walk into the conifer plantation for 95 yards until you see a bank of earth and ditch on your left, parallel with the path, and, exactly on your right, a similar bank and ditch at right angles. You have arrived at what was the north angle of the temporary Roman camp of Balmakewan, the most southerly camp in Kincardineshire and probably one of those used in the campaigns of the emperor Septimius Severus (*c.* A.D. 208-11). From here the Roman legions marched to the Kair House camp at Fordoun, 9 miles away as the crow flies (see page 399) and from there to Raedykes[1] outside Stonehaven, another 9½ miles away.

Identified in 1967 and roughly trapezoidal in plan, the camp of which this is a part is situated immediately north-west of Balmakewan House at the confluence of the River Esk and the Luther Water, the centre of the site being 450 yards north-west of Balmakewan farmhouse. The proven lengths of the north-west and south-west sides (which are not parallel) are 2,185 ft. and 1,400 ft., and the longer axial dimension may be estimated at 2,785 ft. The area of the site is unlikely to be less than 120 acres so that Balmakewan automatically becomes one of the 130-acre camps.

Crop-markings and Air Photographs

Most of the perimeter was first identified from crop-markings. Generally speaking, the south-east side of the camp lies beneath the farm buildings and belts of trees, but the camp is delineated on its north-eastern half by a scarp where the ground drops steeply. The greater part of the north-east and north-west sides, and most of the south-west side, can be planned from air photographs, and the positions of three gates have so far been identified – the southernmost on the north-west side and central gates on the south-west and north-east. The last is guarded by a titulum – a traverse or short earthwork constructed across the line of entry to strengthen the entrenchment. The picture of the southern half of the site conveys a remarkable impression of its relationship to the North Esk.

[1] See *Highways and Byways Round Stonehaven*, pp. 181-190, where Roman camps are described in greater detail.

Considerable Lengths of Earthworks
As we have said, you are actually standing at the north angle of this Roman camp, and it is still possible to trace considerable portions of the adjacent sides as earthworks. The north-east side on your left you can follow for 90 yards until the path turns through a right angle to the left, the earthwork, however, being seen to carry on into the wood in front for a further 100 yards or so. From our position at the north angle it is also possible to enter the wood on our right and to follow the south-west earthwork by a parallel path for 135 yards until we reach a field where it disappears. It will be seen from the two or three hundred yards of rampart still clearly visible that the camp site was once entirely enclosed by a ditch (fossa) originally 7 ft. deep and 12 ft. broad and that the earth removed in the course of digging this, thrown inwards, was heaped up inside to form a turf rampart (agger), presumably 7 ft. high. Sometimes the ditch was of the kind which the Romans called fossa fastigata – V-shaped, about 15 ft. wide and with a vertical slit trench at the bottom. In addition to facilitating drainage such a trench was an important aid in the defence of the camp. Along the top of the upcast was set a strengthened palisade (vallum) of sharpened wooden stakes, every legionary carrying as many as seven as part of his marching kit. The labour involved must have been enormous, but the Romans had that type of genius which found nothing too much trouble.

The Fertile Parish of Marykirk
And now let us return to the B974 and enter upon the parish of Marykirk which embraces a large part of the gloriously fertile plain between the Mounth and Garvock hills that is the Howe of the Mearns. Except for its two hills, Kirktonhill and Balmaleedy on the flank of the Hill of Canterland, it is level, sloping very gently to the North Esk. By 1841 the parish had a total of 2,387 folk. It has never had so many since.

Horses in Clover at Balmakewan
In just under three quarters of a mile we pass on the right the road to the farm of Balmakewan to which we have already referred and which, together with farms like Balmanno, Hatton, Drumnagair, Mains of Luther and Thornton, is one of the great farms in the parish. About 8,000 of its 9,912 acres are good fertile land. Called Balmequien in 1320, as far back as the years 1329-71 Balmakewan was in the possession of a family who called themselves de Balmaquin. The tribes met here to dispute the passage of the Esk at or

near the King's Ford, and many a fight was fought on both sides of the River Esk only three-quarters of a mile away to the south-west.

It was at Balmakewan that the livestock of the county was first improved in 1754 by William Graham, laird of Morphie and the local pioneer of pedigree breeding. On this farm the first sowing of broad clover was made, a thing never seen in this part of the country before and doubtless followed up by Graham on his home-farm of Morphie. While the horses on the neighbouring farms fed at night on marsh plants and thistles from the corn-fields, his were indeed in clover, becoming noted for their beauty and power. When in 1775 he refused £80 for a pair of them, he finally proved to the surrounding farmers that in clover there was money. From horses he went on to cattle which were soon equally as sleek.

Perhaps a Square Barrow Cemetery

The site of the Roman camp is also remarkable for being probably the northernmost example on the East Coast of what may well be a square barrow cemetery. Traces of these newly identified structures or enclosures are visible in the photograph – three or four in all in this area and sited some 740 yards due west of Balmakewan farmhouse and about 180 yards north of the North Esk river. The significance of square barrows is that they have only recently been recognised as a class of Iron Age monument in Scotland whereas round barrows are, of course, quite common. Hitherto square examples have been known only in East Yorkshire. The first excavated barrow at Boysack on the Lunan Water in Angus has just produced a radiocarbon date of *c*. 2nd century B.C., and the distribution appears at present to extend from Fife to Kincardine although a variant type is known in Strathspey and the Great Glen.

A Wonderland of Colour

We are now entering a part of the Mearns which annually is transformed into a wonderland of beauty and colour because a relatively new industry has been brought to the county. For around you are daffodil and tulip fields which, if you've ever been to Holland, you'll recognise at once. If you're in the Howe in the spring and look down on the village of Marykirk from the high lands, your eyes will be dazzled by a blaze of colour more vivid and lasting than any rainbow. Although there is no suggestion of the Mearns rivalling Holland in acreage, the bulb fields here seem every bit as good as those in more widely publicised bulb-growing areas at home as well as abroad as far as appearance and colour are concerned.

Marykirk, an Ancient Village of Character

Soon we pass on the right the farm of Coblehaugh where Bronze Age stone cists with skeletons in them have been uncovered, and in very little over a mile we enter the small but very old village of Marykirk named after the Church of St Mary of Aberluthnott which was the name of the parish until around 1715. With the great curving line of the Hill of Garvock behind, Marykirk is beautifully situated on the left bank of the North Esk in the southern tip of the Howe of the Mearns (the Gaelic meaning of Aberluthnott is 'the meeting of the waters where the stream is swift'). All around, as we have said, are some of the finest and most fertile farms in Scotland.

A fragment of Marykirk's ancient market cross which till 1857 stood just within the gates of the churchyard is still preserved behind the telephone box in the village, and some of its older village houses have considerable character. The village is the most ancient populated place in the parish, but in historic times it certainly had more folk than it has now. In 1841 300 people lived here, and in 1793 208; in the 1971 census it had but 145 of a population. And yet in this old burgh ancient and modern are delicately blended. The old inn where we leave the B974 and turn to the right is now a modern hotel, and there is a splendid, bright new school, opened in 1968, with verandah and sunny classrooms, a functional, modern building planned for its job.

The Fascinating Thornton Aisle

It is the fascinating kirkyard and handsome church, however, 125 yards along the road, which sum up in themselves the whole story of the parish. Built in 1806 and dedicated to the Virgin, the present church has a fine screen, fine panelling and an elaborate timbered-ceiling. The original church of St Mary of Aberluthnott (which, incidentally, contained a ceiling of carved oak) was dedicated as far back as August 9th, 1242, by Bishop David de Bernham and belonged to the monks of St Germaine's Hospital, Tranent, and later to King's College, Aberdeen.

Of this church two substantial remains can still be seen in the kirkyard. The original north aisle, greatly overgrown with ivy and trees, has now become the burial vault of the Barclays of Balmakewan, showing the initials I.B. for John Barclay and the arms of the Barclay family under the ivy on the top right-hand corner of the ruin. The south aisle, now called the Thornton Aisle, is the burial vault of the Strachans of Thornton. This latter vault contains an ambry and a font and bears the Forbes and Strachan arms, a carved stone on the wall showing A 1615 S.

A superbly sculptured marble monument, flanked with pilasters, dates from 1661 and commemorates Dame Elizabeth Forbes of Thornton. This tall panel, extremely fine work indeed, can just be glimpsed through a small grating at eye level and from a window higher up on the east side. We learn from Andrew Jervise's *Epitaphs and Inscriptions* that the Latin inscription can be translated thus:

> *A funeral song to the memory of a most excellent woman: Dame Elizabeth Forbes, Lady of Thornton, who possessed all the merits that can adorn her sex and became a candidate for eternity on 10th Jan., 1661, in the 25th year of her age, having died prematurely in childbed. Although her worth is preserved by monuments more lasting than brass, her sorrowing husband, Sir James Strachan of Thornton, Knightbaronet, has caused this magnificent tomb to be erected to her most fragrant memory.*

After all this it is rather disillusioning to learn that this paragon among women left a son and two daughters who were brought up by their maternal grandmother who had to raise an action in 1665 against the baronet for having *abandoned his children*.

How tragic it is that enormous fungus streamers are allowed to obscure such a relic, that pigeons are allowed to perch and flutter there and that the authorities have taken no steps to expose and to restore such an elegant tomb. When the Scottish Ecclesiological Society in 1936 described these relics, their *Transactions* observed,

> *It is a pity that some restoration, or at least some examination of these now hidden features has not been done in order to expose and preserve whatever may be found to have survived the passage of time in this ancient spot.*

Worshippers in the northern and southern parts of the parish now form a single congregation, and services are held both in Marykirk and Muirton of Luthermuir each Sunday. The ecclesiastical parish has reverted to the old name of Aberluthnott.

The Potato — an Occasional Luxury

Marykirk is credited with having been the spot where in 1727 potatoes were first introduced into the Mearns on a limited scale. It appears that an old soldier who had travelled in Ireland lived temporarily in the village and turned to account some seed potatoes which he possessed by planting them for his private use. With no dyke round them, however, he failed to keep the sheep away from his crop which was not a success. The villagers, we are told, were *ready enough to steal* but, looking in vain *for seed from the stems*, had not the ingenuity to cultivate the crop for themselves! With the departure of the Irishman the art of potato-planting was suspended in the Mearns.

The next introduction of potatoes into the county did not take place until about 1760 when the villagers began growing them in earnest. But for several years after that the potato was such a rare production as to be, like apples or pears, distributed only as a luxury on special occasions. Till about 1775 few farms had over one-eighth of an acre of potatoes, but by 1807 there were 1,160 English acres of them in the county. It was not until after the great blight which swept Scotland and destroyed the potato crop in 1846 that farmers and crofters began growing them on a big scale.

Before we leave Marykirk, let us remember that, in the farm of Balmakelly, a mile and a third to the north-east was born David Herd (1732-1810) who collected and edited what Sir Walter Scott called the first classical collection of Scottish songs and ballads. Let us remember, too, that with neighbouring parishes, Marykirk was once rich in witch-lore. A parish record once read thus:

> *Nae sermon here this day – the minister bein' awa' at Fettercairn burnin' a witch!*

The Bell-disc Barrow of Canterland

Just 335 yards farther along the A937 we turn left at Marymill. In 300 yards we are able to see 1½ miles away on the hill on our left Kirktonhill Tower, built in 1880 or slightly earlier by one of the Taylor family who lived in Kirktonhill House nearby. The tower was used for shoots and for picnicking. In just under a mile and two-fifths we arrive at crossroads where Canterland Farm is sign-posted on our left. This is our road. Six hundred and twenty yards along it, and past Canterland Farm itself (famous for its herd of Aberdeen Angus), a farm track leads off to the left up Canterland Hill. A car may be driven 230 yards if desired; if not, a walk of only 420 yards takes one to the top of the hill.

Here, on the most prominent part of Canterland Hill, in a situation commanding the surrounding country and overlooking the estuary of the North Esk, are the remains of a circular earthwork some 40 or 50 yards in diameter which prior to 1842 was in tolerable preservation. The earthwork is now divided by a fence, a third of it being in a field, the remaining two-thirds, including the rough central cairn, some 70 ft. in diameter, in rough grassland and woodland. The mound itself is some 30 ft. in diameter by 2¼ ft. in height and is separated by a berm nearly 10 ft. broad from the usual fosse or ditch around the cairn. This in turn is separated from another concentric and intermediary ditch by an embankment or wall of turf and stone. The bank shows signs of disturbance, and the central mound is now unfortunately much reduced in height through natural levelling and excavation in 1850. This revealed an empty central cist which appears to have cut an earlier inhumation in a grave; on the east there was a second cist containing an inhumation and several flints.

The use of the earthwork has been much debated. It is certainly not big enough for a hill fort or camp although an ordinary Roman outpost and Danish and native forts have all been suggested. The fact that the earthwork is more or less circular and defined by a bank with an internal ditch leads one, too, to think of henge monuments used as sacred burial enclosures or for religious festivals and the worship of the sun. What we are looking at, however, is a Bronze Age barrow of an intermediate bell-disc kind and the only one to my knowledge in Kincardineshire. It must have been a monument to someone particularly important. Bell-disc barrows belong to a type which lies half way between the bell and disc barrows in that there is a central mound of moderate size together with a ditch, originally enclosed here by a double bank, now slightly mutilated. It is dated between 2200 and 500 B.C. and has been scheduled under the Ancient Monuments acts. One might add that the term, 'bell-disc', is not common in Scotland, the terminology being borrowed from Wessex in the south of England.

Fragments of a cinerary urn and part of an ornamental drinking-cup urn taken from the barrow at Canterland are to be seen in Montrose Museum.

The Lordly Grahams of Morphie Castle

Back at the crossroads sign to Canterland Farm, we proceed on our way after our diversion, in only 180 yards or so reaching the Den of Morphie Bridge which crosses a stream flowing through the den of the same name. Immediately on our right at the top of the hill is a triangular field, hemmed in between the Den of Morphie and a small ravine running from east to west. In the far western corner of this field, still called the Castle Park, once stood the ancient 14th century Castle of Morphie on a commanding site on the tip of a

promontory on the brink of the Den of Morphie and dominating
Angus across the North Esk. It was obviously a good place to watch
the approach of strangers for one of the main roads from the south
passed by to the north up the Den of Morphie, almost under the
castle walls. It was a fortress of strength with a wall, ditch and
drawbridge, all traces of which are now obliterated, the stones
having been carried off, even to the foundations, 200 years ago and
more to build field enclosures. It is alleged by some that the last
traces of the old paved road which once curved across to the
entrance gate have not yet finally disappeared.

Morphie Castle was the seat of a line of barons, the lordly
Grahams of Morphie, who gained their first footing here in the reign
of William the Lion and who intermarried with the first families of
the district in at least the time of James III. For upwards of five
hundred years they were among the greatest landowners in the
district. Sir Robert Graham, who died around 1630, was the
younger brother of the head of the family, the Earl of Montrose,
who owned half of Warburton and its salmon fishings. He was also
the uncle of the only son of the latter, James, who was later to
become the great Royalist leader – the famous Marquis of Montrose – and who, as might be expected, paid many visits to the
Castle of Morphie when he succeeded to the earldom at the age of
fourteen for he lived just a few miles away at Old Montrose near the
south-west corner of Montrose Basin and is said to have been
tutored by his uncle at the time. Then he became owner of half of
Warburton, Commieston, Stone of Morphie and the whole coastal
strip south of St Cyrus – Scotston and the former church lands of
Kirkside with the salmon fishings in the North Esk. Indeed, he
succeeded to more than that for his uncle a year before his death had
enlarged his estate still farther when he bought Canterland and the
Hill of Canterland where we have just been. For a very short time,
before both estates were broken up, Sir Robert and Sir Alexander
Straton of Lauriston owned almost the whole parish between them.
A later laird, William Graham of Morphie, was the county's first
improver of livestock at Balmakewan in 1745 (q.v.). The Grahams
of Morphie are buried in the old churchyard of St Cyrus where their
coat of arms can still be seen above the entrance to their burial
vault.

Exactly three-tenths of a mile away to the east and across the road
on which we have been travelling can be seen the farm of Morphie.
Its huge old steading once won a national competition as the best
designed steading in Scotland. The farm, which is visited by experts

from many lands, has been noted for many years for its famous herd of shorthorn cattle, the royalty of the shorthorn world and champions of many shows, which have in recent years been exported to America, Australia, Germany, the Argentine and the Soviet Union.

550 yards away to the south was the Cobler of Logie or Logie Ford across the North Esk, a place of ill repute. There a boat was kept to ferry across the river the retinues of the barons of Morphie after their ride down the hill past Logie kirk on the other side of the river. The ferryman was well recompensed for a busy time. There was no small stir, for example, when the Earl of Montrose set off again south after a fortnight spent in the castle in 1629 when he was sixteen. Three boats were required to take fourteen horses and all his baggage across the river, and the Earl's purse-bearer records:

> *Item: My Lord passing the water at the cobler of Logie, the*
> *boat having crossed the ferrie four of fyve tymes 19sh*
> *Item: That day at the ferries for two boats having twyse*
> *crossed the ferrie and carried fourteen horse 52sh*

A Terrorist Water Kelpie wi' Sair Banes

Few men dared to thwart the power of the lairds of Morphie Castle, and tradition tells us that even a water kelpie which lived in the North Esk and which terrorised the countryside for miles around had to do his bidding. When the Castle of Morphie was being built, it carried all the stones up from the river to the top of the ravine – but with a very bad grace, bearing a grudge against humanity as it did because of its earlier career as a draught-horse in service with the laird. Listen to the words put into Kelpie's mouth by Dr Jamieson, the celebrated lexicographer, in his *Minstrelsy of the Border:*

> *When Morphie's laird has biggin rear'd,*
> *I carryit aw the stanes,*
> *And mony a chiel has heard me squeal*
> *For sair birz'd* (bruised) *back and banes. ....*

Long afterwards, if you were bold enough to walk along the river bank at night, you might still have heard the water kelpie grumbling in the Ponage or Pondage Pool (perhaps pontage or the place of a ferry?) in which it had lived from time immemorial one and a quarter miles from Morphie Castle as the crow flies:

> *O sair's my back an' sair my banes,*
> *Leadin' the Laird o' Marphie's stanes;*
> *The Laird o' Marphie canna thrive*
> *As lang's the Kelpie is alive.*

The Ponage Pool was immortalised by George Beattie, born in St Cyrus in 1786, who became a prosperous Montrose lawyer, wit and author of the poem, *John of Arnha'*, his greatest triumph, written in his late twenties. The poem, which became an added sensational success when it was staged as a drama in a local theatre, is a saga about the kelpie in the pool and the fearless John who conquered it and Auld Nick as he had conquered so many greater fiends before:

> *When ye hear the Kelpie howl,*
> *Hie ye to the Ponage-pool;*
> *There ye'll see the Deil himsel'*
> *Leadin' on the hounds o' Hell.*

A highly imaginative picture of the Water Kelpie in the North Esk, rising 'streight frae out the river'. 'His legs were horn, wi' joints' o' steel, His body like the crocodile.' John speaks 'in daring accent, "stand aff, you fiend and dread my wrath, Or soon I'll steek your een in death" '. The picture is from the book John o' Arnha', *printed by Alexander Burnett of Montrose in 1883.*

The Battle in the Ponage Pool

In a description almost baffling the imagination the kelpie, according to Beattie, used to appear,

> *A stalwart monster, huge in size,*
> *Did straught frae out the river rise,*
> *Behind, a dragon's tail he wore*
> *Twa bullock's horns stack out before;*
> *His legs were horn wi' joints o' steel,*
> *His body like the crocodile.*
> *On smellin' John, he gie'd a scoil,*
> *Then plung'd and gar'd the water boil.*

It was a memorable fight. The bank that drops to the edge of the pool was even higher before the fight began. Beattie tells us that the kelpie

> *Raised sic a rutherair and clatter,*
> *The red brae tummelt i' the water.*

A thousand phantoms rushed to the kelpie's aid. Some witches cast a horrid spell, and the dead at Logie kirk rose out of their graves before the battle ended.

The Ponage or Pondage Pool in the North Esk near the Mill of Morphie in which lived from time immemorial a water kelpie, terrorising the countryside for miles around.

Today the Ponage Pool need hold no horrors for the visitor: its waters filter through to the wells at the waterworks nearby, and primroses in the spring-time sprinkle the banks that frame the distant hills with the conifers in the den not far away.

It may be that you wish to see the Ponage Pool. As this is not possible from the north side of the North Esk (without considerable difficulty), you must cross the river by Telford's bridge and continue on the A92 until, in just under quarter of a mile, you fork right. Follow this new road for a mile until you meet the A937, then turn right and, under the railway bridge, immediately right again for 400 yards until you arrive (yet again!) at the first turning to the right opposite Montrose Royal Mental Hospital. Three-fifths of a mile along a zig-zag road – it is possible to drive all the way – will take you to the river at a point overlooking the pool – a total journey of just over two and a half miles.

The Stone of Morphie

Let us now continue our journey. We proceed along our road to the south-east for a full mile until we reach the Mill of Morphie with its old mill-wheel still complete. One hundred yards before it we pass on the left the entrance to Dannie's Den, a ravine where stone coffins and bones were allegedly found. The den is said to have a Danish origin for tradition states that the Danes during the 10th and early part of the 11th centuries committed much havoc on the east coast. There is no evidence, however, to support the tradition.

From the Mill of Morphie another third of a mile takes us to the ancient commemorative monolith, the Stone of Morphie, an eight-ton block of white sandstone from the neighbourhood, 11 ft. 1 in. long, 3½ ft. broad at the base and 2 ft. thick towards the top. It stands in the stackyard of the farm of Stone of Morphie, the scene of George Beattie's ill-fated romance as we shall see. On this farm to which it gives its name it was once employed as the core of a corn stack. About 1850 it was overturned by a hurricane when it was thus enclosed in a stack of grain in the stackyard. Six years later, when it was re-erected on its former site, workmen came in the course of excavation on portions of a skeleton of *large dimensions* immediately underneath, but in no cist.

Local legend is rife about this huge monolith, usually attributing it to the local water kelpie (you can still see his fingerprint on the stone where he grasped it). There has been a persistent tradition, however, that here is the grave, marked by the Stone of Morphie, of the mythical Camus, a Danish leader or king who landed in Angus in 1010 at the head of an equally imaginary Danish army and who was defeated at the Battle of Barry by the Scots under Malcolm II. Camus was overtaken on his flight to the north, it is said, and killed by Keith, the founder of the Marischal family. As we have already said, however, there is no evidence to support this tradition, and the Stone of Morphie, in fact, belongs to the Late Stone Age (2000 B.C. – 1800 B.C.) of which it is characteristic, the men of the time being erectors of megaliths, leaving large stones such as this around the countryside, probably connected in some way with the religious ceremonies of the time.

The Stone of Morphie, an eight ton sandstone monolith which is characteristic of the late Bronze Age, 2000 B.C. – 1800 B.C.

Sick Man's Shade and Camustown

Continue the half mile to the A92 and then turn left. The next third of a mile between the turn and the farm road to Commieston on the left is an area with the curious name of Sick Man's Shade because so many Bronze Age cists containing inhumations were turned up by the plough last century. St Cyrus seems to have been quite heavily populated during the Bronze Age, and 'shade' just means a slope. Tradition has it again that here was a battle between Scots and Danes. The name of the farm 300 yards off the main road is appropriately Commieston (Camustown) to immortalise the Danish leader, Camus, said to be buried nearby, for Commieston is where the Danes were finally defeated, it is said, and where further large numbers of stone coffins have been found. Certain it is, too, that when a small bridge was being built near the farm of Pathhead 400 yards farther on along the A92, a large quantity of human bones were found in an irregular heap. There were no coffins or urns.

At Commieston is one of the oldest and finest Friesian herds in the country. The Mearns has played a significant part in the advancement of the Friesian cause and can, indeed, claim to be the real home of the Friesians which, in earlier days known as Dutch cattle, were originally brought across from Holland. The herd has quite a collection of cups won for herd championships, and numerous individual cows have also brought the county credit in this respect.

Telford's Bridge and a Welcome

Let us return now to the road junction where, after leaving the standing Stone of Morphie, we joined the A92. And let us continue southwards for some 280 yards: here we turn off sharply to the left to pass below the railway bridge. Notice Telford's Bridge over the North Esk on your right on the wall of which the stranger entering Kincardineshire by the coast road from the south is welcomed within its bounds by the words forming part of the inscription:

> *Travellers pass safe and free along this bridge built by the subscription to which the town of Montrose and the two adjacent counties contributes a large share. The foundation was laid on the eighteenth October, 1770, and the work was finished on the eighteenth October, 1775. The bridge and its approaches cost £7,500 sterling.*

An appeal for public subscription raised £6,500 including £800 which George III gave from the annexed estates to encourage an undertaking so useful.

Before the building of the bridge the main road into the parish from the south was across the ferry then up the long Den of Morphie to Denhead and Criggie.

A Cave of Scientific Interest

Just over a mile and a quarter down the road below the railway bridge and some 600 yards after we pass the farm of Nether Warburton was discovered in 1847 a most interesting cave situated on the face of the hill on our left 330 yards north-east of Nether Warburton farmhouse. The cave faced due south and overlooked one of the fields of the farm. About 15 ft. above high water mark, it had an entrance about 12 ft. wide and 5 ft. high. Originally it was 10 ft. high.

This cave, when found, was full of rich loam mixed with the shells of shell fish and teeming with thousands of bones of a wide variety of species, both domestic and wild, including ox, pig, sheep, deer, badger, hare, rabbit and other small rodents, all perfectly preserved. There were also a few bird bones (mainly gannet), a profusion of shell fish, the skulls of a wild cat and of rats, and the jaws of a fox or dog or wolf together with a pot and two bones definitely human. All were arranged in piles, as if by human agency, so that spadefuls could be lifted with scarcely any earth at all.

For two years at least, to improve cultivation, the farmer of Nether Warburton at that time, a Mr Walker, had happily spread the shells and bones on his fields as eleven years previously the East Mathers lime works, the last in the parish, had closed, unable to compete with imported supplies from the Forth and from England. Eventually, however, his discovery caused considerable scientific interest. Unfortunately, when workmen were engaged to clear the cave in the hope of gaining more information, the roof collapsed so that the entrance was blocked by the rock fall. Now, the only possible way to reach the inside, still part-filled with bones and shells, would be arduously to dig through the roof − if one knew, indeed, where the cave was sited, for not a trace remains!

Articles theorising about the Nether Warburton cave appeared in various scientific journals at the time, and a paper on it was read in 1859 at the British Association meetings in Aberdeen, attended by the Prince Consort. The cave had been occupied by hunting peoples probably in the Neolithic period (perhaps the 3rd or 4th millenium B.C.) and possibly as late as the Iron Age during the five or six centuries before Christ, the shells and bones being in fact a kitchen midden which had steadily increased in size over the years. According to an article of the time in the *Edinburgh New Philosophical Journal* there were found *an amulet formed rudely of the leg bone of an ox*, and another such bone which showed *evident traces of being sawn or ground flat*. Further evidence of human habitation was proved by the fact that long bones had been invariably split open by a tool so that the marrow might be extracted. And the final and most conclusive proof was, of course, found, as always, in two fragments of Early Bronze Age coarse pottery ornamented with a small cord pattern. One, charred inside, had been part of a vessel 10 ins. in diameter; the other, uncharred, from a vessel 7 ins. in diameter. In Montrose Museum some of the bones may still be seen. It could be that dunes or mounds in the Warburton area hide other kitchen middens yet undiscovered.

St Cyrus National Nature Reserve

Roughly a quarter of a mile farther on at the Fishery Station we arrive at the road fork to Kirkside and the main road which later we shall take. We may leave our car here if we wish for the track which we must follow to the churchyard three-tenths of a mile in front of us is somewhat rough. Yet it is quite passable.

After we have travelled 400 yards over the flat beach of fine sand bound together by sea grasses and other marine plants, we are reminded that the four miles along the coast from the mouth of the North Esk to just beyond the cliff-top village of St Cyrus, and two miles north-east and west of the Inverbervie Road to the Woodston Burn comprises the 227 acre St Cyrus National Nature Reserve. It was declared open in 1962 and embraces a sandy foreshore with rocks at the north end, a line of sand dunes, a salt marsh, sand flats, dune pasture and lava cliffs which are well covered with vegetation. Here is a good place to study nature for those who have an interest in plant life or uncommon birds. Of interest to the geologist, too, may be the fact that here is the only place in Kincardineshire where rocks of the Upper Old Red Sandstone system are found. Everywhere it is separated from the Lower Old Red Sandstone by lines of faulting. A vast epoch of time intervened between the deposition of the two formations.

A Dream World of Botanical Interest

For the botanist the Nature Reserve is a dream world of outstanding botanical interest for this coastal area has a remarkably rich flora because of its dry sunny climate and its remarkably fertile cliffs of andesite, a type of volcanic rock named after the Andes mountains. In the whole Reserve there are, remarkably enough, well over 300 different flowering plants of which, owing to favourable conditions, over 177 have been found on the slopes of these well-known St Cyrus braes, a large number not being found in other parts of the country. Here the volcanic rocks decompose into a light brown soil, extremely suitable for the growth of a rich variety of wild flowers. The exposure of the rocks, forming cliffs almost 200 ft. high, facing south and east, adds to the warmth afforded by the soil.

An aerial view of the coast at St Cyrus, looking north. The picture shows the sandy foreshore, sand dunes, salt marsh, sand flats and lava cliffs which go to make up St Cyrus National Nature Reserve. At the end of the strip of alluvial links and tucked under the shelter of the rocky cliffs can be seen the lonely little nether kirkyard of St Cyrus where once was a priory, ancient even in the time of William the Conqueror.

Unusual Plants and Insects, and Terns Undisturbed

Here during the summer may be seen in abundance the pretty little maiden-pink, the prolific rest-harrow, bladder-campion, bloody crane's-bill, hemp-agrimony, common cudweed, marjoram, goat's-beard, red poppy, field pepper-wort, soft-knotted clover, rough podded yellow vetch, field-garlic, wild sweet pea, wild liquorice and wood-vetch. On the loose sands along the banks of the North Esk and in the salt marshes at its mouth grow the lesser meadow-rue, the sea-rocket, the thrift or sea-pink, the prickly salt-wort and other similar plants. Close to the river, on ground liable to be flooded at high tides, may be found sea pearlwort, sand-wort spurreys, sea milk-wort, jointed glasswort, sea arrow-grass and several varieties of sedges. Grass wrack, one of the few flowering plants of salt water, grows in the mud at the old mouth of the river. It is the northern limit for many of them, and many are rare like the henbane, viper's bugloss, clustered campanula, Nottingham catch-fly and the hairy violet. Mostly they grow on the cliffs, but some of the rarest of all are in the salt marsh which stretches from the river mouth along the links.

An unusual variety of insects, too, is found on the cliff face, almost as varied as the plants. The cliffs provide nest sites for hundreds of gulls and fulmars. Eider-duck and jackdaws nest here, and here too is one of the few areas in Britain where terns can nest undisturbed. Seals and salmon are found along the coast and in the bay where they have been, as we shall see, since time immemorial.

The Lonely Nether Kirkyard

Our cart-track in another 140 yards across the dunes leads to the little churchyard of St Cyrus romantically situated on the fifty-yard strip of alluvial links, tucked under the shelter of the rocky cliffs and near enough to the beach to be swept by spray when the east wind blows. Dedicated to St Cyrus and to St Rule, the old kirkyard, surrounded by a rough wall, contains almost a square rood of ancient tombstones. The Register of St Andrews informs us that on the site was a priory which even in the time of William the Lion was called *ancient*. Its canons had probably been Culdees.

The old mediaeval parish church of Ecclesgreig stood within the burial-ground here. Although there was probably an ecclesiastical community here at an earlier date, the church comes on record between 1172 and 1178 and went out of use in 1632. It was attended by the young Montrose on Sundays when he was visiting Morphie Castle, and the churchyard continued to be the parish burying-

471

ground for more than two centuries after the church fell into ruins. It ceased to be used for burials about the time of the body-snatchers who according to local tradition did in fact come to this lonely graveyard at dead of night to open newly made graves and to ship corpses off to Edinburgh.

A Resting-place of the Illustrious

Here are buried the lairds of Kirkside and of Morphie whose coat of arms can be seen on their vault. A fine stone marks the resting-place of Sir William Fiddes Douglas, a former president of the Royal Scottish Academy. Here, too, is buried Arthur Straton, a relative of the laird of Lauriston to whom the Marquis of Montrose sold his lands on the coastal strip together with Warburton. There were Stratons at Kirkside for the next two centuries. At one time they owned the lands of Lauriston and Ecclesgreig. The grave of Arthur Straton in the Straton vault is marked by an ancient conical stone, covered with heraldic and mortuary devices.

One of his illustrious successors lies in the Nether Kirkyard, too, General Sir Joseph Straton of Kirkside, a hero of the Peninsular War and of the Battle of Waterloo who, when he died in 1840, left legacies for education and the poor of the parish. Entering the army at an early age, he had a distinguished military career a large part of which was spent on the Continent. The outstanding incident took place at Waterloo when he served under Wellington, commanding first his own regiment, the Sixth Dragoons, and later the brigade. In reward of his services he had various honours conferred upon him, becoming Commander of the Bath, Knight of the Guelphic Order of Hanover and Knight of the Order of St Vladimir of Russia.

Where a Poet Once Blew his Brains Out

And where else can one stand on the spot where a poet once blew his brains out? For beside the stile is the grave of George Beattie, of whom we have already heard, who, broken-hearted, shot himself for love almost at the exact spot where he lies buried. A herdsman discovered his body, propped against the wall close to the stile. His hands were resting on his chest, and a pistol lay with its muzzle on his lip.

It was in August, 1821, that a letter arrived at Stone of Morphie Farm from Beattie asking whether he could court the lovely William Gibson (the poor girl was thus named because her parents had wanted a son!). She was the only child of Robert Gibson who farmed there, and her 23rd birthday was not long past. Probably both her father and mother had a hand in the reply which stated that he could not though he would still be a welcome visitor. Soon, however, a new suitor was riding to Stone of Morphie, the wealthy corn merchant, William Smart of Cairnbank, whom William, now 25 years of age, had decided to marry. For her uncle (her mother came of a wealthy family) was Governor of Granada who, when he died, left her £10,000 – in those days a vast sum. As in the class-conscious days of the 19th century the sons of humble crofters did not marry heiress daughters of country lairds, Miss Gibson wrote to Beattie asking to be released from her promise of marriage. He refused.

The lonely mediaeval kirkyard of St Cyrus, tucked under the shelter of the cliffs and swept by spray when the east wind blows. George Beattie's grave is within the walled enclosure at the top right-hand corner of the burial-ground, the stile beside which his body was found being inset in the wall at this point.

His Record a Sensational Best Seller

In the history of unrequited love his was a suicide that can have few parallels. For on that fateful day before George Beattie went down the cliff path to the beach (having spent some time in the Kirkton inn), he had left a voluminous record behind, telling exactly why he did it and how he felt about it. Night after night in the months before he died, he wrote down his version of all that had passed between William and him – the letters they had written, the vows they had made, the thoughts that seethed through his head as he screwed up his courage for the final curtain. He recorded everything so that all who knew him would realise *I have been most cruelly treated*.

The final paragraph, written on Monday, 29th September, reads,

> *All is now over. I die in perfect good-will toward every human being. If my feelings may have led me to say anything offensive regarding Miss G. I am sorry for it. If I have erred in anything, I hope she will forgive me, and it will be wise in her to forget whatever may have passed betwixt us. If I could have done this, I would have been happy. There is no use in repining. I never did so before . . .*

A year later his friends erected a granite monument over his grave.

TO THE MEMORY

OF

GEORGE BEATTIE

WRITER IN MONTROSE

Who died 29th September, 1823, in the 38th year of his age

THIS MONUMENT WAS ERECTED

BY THE FRIENDS

WHO LOVED HIM IN LIFE AND LAMENTED HIM IN DEATH.

IN HIS DISPOSITION

HE WAS

JUST, CHARITABLE AND BENEVOLENT;

IN HIS PRINCIPLES

FIRM AND INDEPENDENT;

IN HIS GENIUS

FORCIBLE AND PATHETIC;

AND

IN HIS MANNERS

PLAIN AND SOCIAL.

HIS VIRTUES ARE DEEPLY ENGRAVED

in the hearts of those who knew him; and

his Literary Productions will be admired

while Taste for Original Humour and Vigorous Expression remains.

George Beattie's book, his *Statement of Facts*, *Supplement to State-ment of Facts*, *Additions to Supplement* and *The Last*, became a best seller and the graveyard a place of pilgrimage. It was a sweet revenge, a cry for sympathy, echoing from the grave. It was a suicide with a difference which was the sensation of the century for miles around.

The Original Hamlets of Roadside and Burnside

But now it is time to retrace our steps to the Fishing Station where this time we turn right up the hill to enjoy from the top of the cliffs a glorious view of the estuary of the North Esk with Montrose light-house in the background. Then past Kirkside which we have already mentioned (you will recall that it was once the home of the Stratons) and, after a journey of a mile in all, on to the main road. Here we turn right again. In 570 yards or so we pass on the left the road to the little croft of Whitehills two-thirds of a mile away at the foot of the Hill of Morphie where was born the lawyer-poet, George Beattie, of whom we have been reading. His home could hardly have been humbler with its walls of stone and turf, its thatched roof and earth floor. Beattie's father was a crofter and part-time salmon fisher.

In a further 200 yards we reach on our left a long row of cottages along the north side of the A92 where they began to appear im-mediately the new road to Aberdeen was constructed in 1820. Here are the original hamlets of Roadside and Burnside from which, with another hamlet, now extinct, a little to the west, and with the hamlet of Kirkton, once on the eminence a short distance ahead, the village of St Cyrus was eventually created. According to the parish school-master, writing in 1841, the united population of these four hamlets, inhabited by feuars and crofters, totalled 400 people, *about one fourth of the whole population of the parish*.

By 1840 Roadside and its neighbouring Burnside had merged into one, and it is interesting that the first house in the former hamlet is still to be seen, now joined to the neighbouring cottage. It is the twelfth house on the left-hand side, by the bus stop, for a time known as Genesis and later as Red Tiles. But the red tiles have been replaced by asbestos, and the age of the cottage hidden by new gray harling. Another half-mile takes us to the crossroads in the centre of St Cyrus itself.

Revolutionary Education in the Kirkton

The earliest reference to St Cyrus, which now tends to be a dormi-tory for Montrose, appears in the first *Statistical Account* of 1794.

> *The village stands beside the church, nigh the centre of the*
> *parish. It contains 144 inhabitants who are mostly mech-*
> *anics, salmon fishers or day labourers.*

The reference is, of course, really to the Kirkton, the first of the four
hamlets to which we have referred, situated on the old road to the
north round about the site of the old church which was built on top
of the cliff in 1632 or 1633 before the main road of today was made.
The independent tradesmen mentioned above seemingly disliked
living cheek by jowl with their neighbours if one can judge by the
cottages seen to this day. They almost invariably built their houses
to face in different directions from their neighbours', and it would
have to be a very tortuous road that served the front doors of such a
hamlet.

To the loose-knit huddle of cottages that was the Kirkton in
earlier days was added an ale-house where you could change your
horses on your journey south or north, an inn latterly known as The
Three Bottles and, even before the end of the 17th century, a
school. And here before another hundred years had elapsed, an
educational change, revolutionary for these early days, is to be
noted: for every three pupils learning Latin one was learning book-
keeping!

Quaint St Cyrus, the Place of Grig

In 1841 a somewhat jaundiced parish schoolmaster tells us that the
Kirkton

> *consists of about 40 houses, for the most part straw-*
> *thatched cottages, disposed without much regard to neat-*
> *ness or regularity around the parish church. The situation is*
> *exceedingly damp and exposed, and appears to possess no*
> *other advantage than that of showing off the church which*
> *has rather a respectable appearance when seen from a*
> *distance.*

Nevertheless, as none of the other hamlets could provide the amenities it possessed, it was inevitable that the Kirkton, although old-
fashioned by comparison with its neighbouring hamlets, should
gobble them up (especially when the salmon trade became a luxury
one) and turn itself into what is now the quaint little village of St
Cyrus, picturesquely situated on the brow of the headland overlooking the bay and the parish, a landmark from both sea and land.

Why the name St Cyrus? There is no satisfactory explanation beyond the fact that from about the first decade of the 13th century the parish and a village which once existed down at the foot of the heughs on the bank of the North Esk in the Kirkside area was called Ecclesgreig (eaglais and Grig or Ciric, the kirk of the chief Grig) because of their early associations with the name of a Pictish king of Scotland. The name which lingered on all through the Middle Ages in charters and church and civic records as the official name of the parish was finally dropped in the 1790's in favour of St Cyrus. The church of Grig was at one time the centre of the thanage of Ecclesgrig which extended from Morphie to Arbuthnott and as far inland as Garvock.

Ciric or Grig, according to Chalmers, was probably a Pict of the Mearns and probably ruler of what would be considered in those days a northern province between Dee and Spey, dominating the southern Picts. In 878, we are told by the *Ulster Annals*, he was appointed as a kind of governor when, after the last of Kenneth McAlpine's sons was slain in battle, the son of Kenneth's daughter, Eocha, was placed on the throne, by Pictish custom succession through female line being preferred. This king the Pictish Chronicle calls Ciricus from which name Cyrus is probably a corruption. In the Irish version he is called Giric, in the *Chronicle of St Andrews* he appears as Carus, and elsewhere the name is corrupted to Girg.

But why *Saint* Cyrus? We are told that King Grig won the title of *Liberator of the Scottish Church* in 877, and it is not impossible that he founded a cell amongst the Picts of Magh-Circin (the field or place of Grig or Circ). Or he may have built a church or endowed it.

Sir Alexander Straton's Cliff-top Church

Let us now turn right at the crossroads along the road to the beach. In just under quarter of a mile we arrive at the parish church with its lofty spire conspicuous on the summit (built between 1785 and 1787 and expanded in 1832), replacing an older narrow and dimly lit foundation erected in 1632 by Sir Alexander Straton of Laurence-kirk on the cliff-top to replace the mediaeval parish church of Ecclesgreig. The south aisle of Sir Alexander's church still survives at the highest point in the churchyard as burial vaults for the Stratons, the later lairds of Lauriston. High on the wall, on the corner-stone, can still be seen a monogram with the letters LS – EO, the initials of the eldest son of Sir Alexander and his widow, Euphame Ogilvy, daughter of the laird of Clova. Sir Alexander's son, indeed, laid to rest in 1631, was the first to be buried here instead of in the old churchyard of Ecclesgreig at the foot of the heughs for after a new church was built by Sir Alexander in memory of his dead son the ancient church went out of use.

In this upper churchyard, too, is proof that Miltonhaven ever existed! (see page 486). For you can read on an old gravestone:

Hier lyes David Brovn, layfull son to David Brovn and Effie Vill, indvellers in Miltovnhaven, who departed this lyf the 6 day of Febrvary, 1697, and of his age 12 yiears.

Rebels and Ruffians in the '15 Rebellion

It is recorded in the session records of St Cyrus parish church that on 5th February, 1716, the minister entered the pulpit (i.e. in Sir Alexander's church) at 3 p.m. and *lectured from the 3rd Psalm as long as the day would permit.* As the sun sets about 4.45 p.m. at that time of the year, he had a fairly long innings, but the inference to be drawn from the records is that he would have expected to preach for a longer time had circumstances permitted. The congregation, incidentally, was stated to be very sparse. In actual fact the minister was rather fortunate to be able to preach in his church at all on that day for these were stirring times in Scotland, and St Cyrus was not missed out of the picture. In September, 1715, the Old Pretender was proclaimed king in Aberdeen, and the Rebellion was on.

On 9th October, the records tell us, Mr John Lamy,

sometime prelaticall incumbent here, did violently intrud himself upon this church and parish, being assisted by ane armed band of ruffians brought in from other parishes who did violently deforce our minister when he was coming to perform divine worship as he had done twenty years before: but such was the fury of the mob that they would not suffer him to come near the churchyard, Mr Lamy meantime being possesst in the pulpit so that he was forced to retire to his own house where he preached to such as could have access to him.

'The Egyptians Ye Shall See No More'

Not unnaturally, in times of such unrest, there is a blank in the session records until 5th February when they state,

This day the rebells having all past by this church by about two o'clock in the afternoon, the minister ordered the bell to be rung, and repossest himself again of his pulpit to the great satisfaction of all present.

On the following week, although the rebels had gone, the good folk of St Cyrus were still rather afraid to venture to the church as the parish was *full of Swees and Dutch souldiers*. Those who did venture were some *Swees officers and some heads of families*. The minister preached that day from Exodus XIV, 13 and 14, *For the Egyptians whom ye have seen today, ye shall see no more for ever*. His discourse on this occasion was somewhat curtailed, however, for the brigadier in charge of the troops had sent word that he could not stay at church above *three-quarters of an hour*!

The Minister and His Measuring Rod

The present church of St Cyrus is today marked by a tradition. whereby most of the young wives in the parish start married life with a most unusual Ne'er Day dowry that keeps fresh the memory of a kind man's generous act. For the church is the only one in Scotland where after weddings of local girls the parish minister gets out a measuring rod to find out how tall the bride is. It is laid down that the bride must remove her shoes, stand in her stocking-feet and *undo her hair so that her tresses may hang loosely over her shoulder and add nothing to her stature*. The minister also makes careful note in a special register of the ages of all brides as evidenced by their birth certificates. To the youngest, oldest, tallest and shortest goes a money gift on the first day of the year. And, as there aren't many weddings in St Cyrus in a year, most of the girls qualify in one way or another for a dowry the following Hogmanay.

The money comes from the interest of a bequest of £1,000 left in the will of John Orr, laird of Bridgeton between St Cyrus and Johnshaven and, prior to his retirement, Paymaster-general to the forces in India, the benefaction dating back to August 26th, 1847. The interest accruing is divided into five parts. One part is to provide necessities and groceries and any other comforts which the clergyman might think proper to be given to the old and needy of the parish. The other four are to go to the girls specified above who are married in the parish church during the year. Each bride receives a share of the dowry amounting to between £8 and £9.

The bequest of Mr Orr was inspired by pity when, sitting by a blazing fire in his study one wintry December afternoon when the North Sea lashed the desolate coast and a piercing blizzard howled mercilessly from the North, he watched a humble country lad and lass, obviously rich in love but poor in worldly wealth, battling their way through the deep snow to the church of St Cyrus to be married. As he stood there in comfort, surrounded by a wealth of the good things of this world, he began to picture to himself the future lowly home of the young couple with its scant 'providing' and love the principal asset. His heart-strings were touched, and in gratitude to God who had dealt so kindly with him he decided to leave a portion of his wealth for the purpose to which it is now applied. It is recorded that Mr Orr gave the couple a 'little something' at the time to assist them to set up their home.

The church of St Cyrus is the only church in Scotland where the minister uses a measuring rod to find out how tall the bride is!

A Varying Number of Dowry Claimants

The number of claimants for the dowries varies from year to year and when there are fewer than four – some years there are none at all – the unclaimed dowries are added to the capital. Expenses amounting to £123.50 caused by legacy duties and the cost of process reduced the original capital to £876.50, and this was invested in Government Consuls.

Unbridgeable Gulf Between Rich and Poor

It must be remembered that, when Mr Orr made his will, the gulf between rich and poor had become almost unbridgeable because of the installation of spinning machines in Montrose. For many a long year the traditional employment of the women of St Cyrus had been spinning yarn for the sails of ships that put to sea from Montrose, 500 spindles of coarse yarn leaving the village for Montrose sailmakers weekly, except at harvest time. Travellers, we are told, used to marvel at the way the spinsters, famed for their skill, used to spin with both hands, two threads at a time, but as three spindles per week was as much as the average woman could be expected to produce, there must have been about 170 women at work with a steady income of 3/9 per week, enough to keep them independent. The Industrial Revolution stopped all that when no more coarse yarn was wanted. In 1840, seven years before Mr Orr made his will, thirty-six parishioners in St Cyrus were destitute, thirty of them women over sixty years of age.

Beautiful Five-mile Stretch of Golden Sands

And now let us leave our car in the park 140 yards along the beach road past the church and walk the remaining 100 yards to the top of the cliff from which a steep zigzag path leads down to the shore below. For here is a view that should not be missed: the long sweep of the heughs, the saltings, the sand-dunes and the beautiful golden sands stretch out magnificently before us, the best beach by far to be found in the county, reaching in a glorious unbroken sweep of five miles from the red rocks of Milton Ness to the mouth of the North Esk.

Probably the earliest known references to St Cyrus concern these sands below the village for they are mentioned in a charter of Sir George Keith of Drumtochty in 1618 which speaks of *the salmon fishings on the sands called Sanct Siras-sandes*. They are again mentioned in the following year with a different spelling, *the sands called Sanct Seirrece sands*. These sands must have been much smaller than they are today since at one time the North Esk took a different course, for over eighty years flowing parallel to the sea past the red church and churchyard at the foot of the cliffs for about two miles through what is now the Nature Reserve, and entering the sea almost as far north as the present village of St Cyrus or the Kaim of Mathers. All that remains to remind us is what we have called the saltings, a hollow in the links three-quarters of a mile along the foot of the cliffs from Kirkside to St Cyrus.

Ecclesgreig Castle, Gracefully Imposing

Back now to the crossroads on the A92, but before we continue on our way, let us go straight across and climb the rising ground to the west of the main road for a little over a mile, following the right hand fork through the pillared gate. For here is a modern mansion perpetuating the old name of the original hamlet of which we have spoken – Ecclesgreig House or Ecclesgreig Castle. It is modelled on the lines of a French château and was built in the years subsequent to 1845. Its steeply pitched roof and crow-stepped gables, surrounded by conical turrets, give it a graceful and imposing appearance.

Before the days of modern agriculture when stones still littered the countryside, the land around the present mansion had more than its ordinary share of stones and so was known in bygone times as Craigie or Criggie, the stoney place. Later its name was changed to Mount or Mont Cyrus which, according to local history, was the name of the mound on which the house is built. In the 17th century the lands formed part of the barony of Morphie and belonged to Sir Robert Graham of Morphie. Now, Ecclesgreig Castle has fallen on evil days: roofless and uninhabited, it is now used as a grain store, and the tastefully laid out policies with the exceptionally well planned gardens and fine old trees which once surrounded the House are, alas, no more.

The Remarkable Martyr of Nether Woodstone

Leaving St Cyrus, we return yet again to the A92, turn left and continue along it for only just under half a mile until we reach the turning on the right to the farm of Nether Woodston 400 yards away. The farmhouse is noteworthy because it was, nearly four and a half centuries ago, the home of David Straiton, one of the first and most remarkable martyrs of them all. The brother of two lairds of Lauriston, he was hanged in Edinburgh on 27th August, 1534. Strong-willed and stubborn, David Straiton owned the salmon fishings on the coast and, failing to see why a tenth of his fish should go to the vicar of Ecclesgreig, he started a private war of his own against the age-old right of the Church to levy teinds. Instead of giving the vicar a tenth of the fish he caught, he threw every tenth fish back into the sea! The vicar, he said, could fish them out for himself! When the vicar complained to the prior and he to the bishop, eventually a charge of heresy was brought against Straton. As he watched the shadow of death approaching, he was strengthened by works on the new religion of Martin Luther and, adopting Protestantism, argued passionately at his trial in the Court of Bishops against the Catholic conception of purgatory. It is not surprising that he was hanged and his body burnt as a warning to others.

At Woodstone, also, there died in 1823 one James McHardie, aged 95, who like the famous Barclay of Ury was noted for his walking prowess. Although a walker of ability, however, he never became as well-known as Barclay. A native of Crathie in Aberdeenshire, he came to St Cyrus a short time before the '45 as servant to the parish minister. One of his jobs in 1746 was to drive part of the Duke of Cumberland's baggage to Stonehaven! He visited Crathie once a year, setting out on Christmas morning and, after walking the 32 miles, dined and danced with his friends until daybreak the following day. He frequently walked from St Cyrus to Aberdeen.

London Discovers Fresh St Cyrus Salmon

If we turn right in the steading of the farm of Nether Woodstone, we shall find of great interest, too, the salmon station of Woodstone quarter of a mile farther on at the foot of the cliffs and owned by Joseph Johnston and Sons Ltd. A narrow coastal track of only some 560 yards leads to it from the St Cyrus road-end where we recently stood. Here where the oldest of local industries is salmon fishing, there has been an abundance of salmon throughout the centuries. In the Middle Ages the monks of Arbroath Abbey used to count their beads on the river-bank when they came for their regular supplies of salmon from the North Esk, while the vicar of Ecclesgreig got his share of the catch too as we have seen. On salmon the barons in the castles of Morphie and Lauriston fed their retainers until they were sick of the sight of it, and through most of the Middle Ages there was still plenty left to pickle or boil or pack in barrels for markets in the Baltic, the Netherlands, the Mediterranean and Venice in the far Adriatic.

The fishings along the St Cyrus coast and up the North Esk had always been a rich source of income to their owners, but in the late 18th and early 19th centuries the value of the fishings rocketed at an altogether phenomenal rate when for the first time a consignment of fresh salmon was sent to London packed in ice. As nobody in London had ever tasted fresh salmon before, the demand was tremendous, and by 1837 the fishings at Commieston and Kinnaber alone were said to have been let for about £3,000, an almost incredible figure.

The Dams and Underground Ice-house of Woodston

This revolutionary change involved great modifications at the salmon fisheries, and at the Woodstone station here is to be seen built into the cliff a huge, underground ice-house with a ground-plan of some 23 ft. by 20 ft. and perhaps 27 ft. in height. Here originally were stored through the summer blocks of ice which had been cut in the winter. Here also the salmon catch could be stored until ready for dispatch to England by a fast sloop. Donkeys carried the salmon from the foot of the cliffs until about 1950. Thereafter, for four or five years, Bergen, a Norwegian pony, filled the gap; now a more mundane caterpillar tractor is in use. It is of interest to see in passing that we are still within the area of the St Cyrus National Nature Reserve which continues to the point of the promontory immediately to the north with its Hen Rock guarding the point.

The remains of other salmon fishing modifications can be seen to this day if you wish to stop on the way back at the Woodston Burn, half-way between Nether Woodston and the main road. An adventurous walk of some 250 to 300 yards along the footpath on the west side of the burn will lead you to the remains of dams which had to be built, in days before refrigeration, to supply ice in the winter. These artificial ponds were filled by the Woodston Burn which went on to drive the wheel of the Mill of Woodston the ruins of which are some 300 yards farther on. The remains of the sluice, the old embankment and the old mill lade can still be clearly seen as can the site of yet another dam on the shore below St Cyrus.

The 'Lordlie' Kaim on its Sea-girt Rock

Once more we return to the main road where again we turn right, continuing along it for only half a mile until we reach the Tangleha' road on the right. This we follow past the farm of West Mathers until in just under three-quarters of a mile we reach a road junction. Here we turn right, reaching the end of the road in some 350 yards at Rock Hall on the south side of the promontory of Milton Ness.

A cliff-top track from here, varying in height from 50 ft. to 300 ft. and amid some superlative rock scenery with numerous caves and ravines, leads us eventually after two miles to the southern extremity of the braes of St Cyrus above the old kirkyard on the dunes. In parts some care is required. But that is for another day; our present purpose is to walk only some 300 yards along the cliffs until we see at close quarters the ruins of the mediaeval Kaim of Mathers, a stone fort or castle next to the ruins of Dunnottar Castle in antiquity and perched 60 ft. above the sea on top of a perpendicular and almost inaccessible sea-girt rock. It is separated from the land by a chasm 60 ft. deep. Sea and tempest have ceaselessly pounded at the rocks below this precipice top for centuries until more and more of the overhanging cliffs have come crashing down – and more and more of the castle with them. There is not much to be seen of it now: only a fragment of a tower measuring 8 ft. 2 ins. square and a small part of a 2 ft. thick wall remain on the seaward end of the promontory. Further remains of walling are visible across the neck 44 yards to the north-east.

David de Berkeley Defies the King's Wrath

The Kaim (the word means a fortress or pinnacle or ridge resembling a cock's comb) once consisted of a tower 40 ft. square and four

The ruins of the mediaeval and 'lordlie' Kaim (or fortress) of Mathers near St Cyrus, perched 60 ft. above the sea on a perpendicular and almost inaccessible sea-girt rock.

storeys high. It was built at the time of James I by the notorious David de Berkeley (the name Barclay had not yet been adopted), the laird of Mathers, as a stronghold and refuge after he had taken part in a conspiracy which shocked the country, the horrible murder in 1420 of the sheriff of Kincardine who was boiled upon the Hill of Garvock and *sodden and suppit in bree*. His accomplices took refuge from the king's wrath in Fife, but he preferred to stay at home and

> *Buyld a lordlie Kaim*
> *All onne the stonie rock*
> *Which mote defie the sovereign's arms*
> *And eke the tempest's shock,*

escaping the vengeance of the king who vowed he should never live on land or water. If you searched the world for a place that was neither on land nor sea, but poised between the two, you would find it hard to better this almost impossible eyrie on the cliff-top. He was safe enough. You approach the castle by an isthmus which was described two hundred years ago as narrow and almost inaccessible. Today it is even more so.

David de Berkeley was a descendant of the noble English family of Berkeley which came to Scotland with William the Lion and which was one of the most powerful and opulent in Kincardineshire.

Stage-coach Bridge and Bungytown

If you follow the cliff path for 250 yards beyond the Kaim of Mathers, you will suddenly arrive at a little old bridge still spanning the Woodston Burn like a forgotten monument. You may care to visit it: Stage-coach Bridge is its local name. Here is tangible evidence of the old coast road between Nether Woodston and the Kirktown. The road continued south by the cliffs and across the mouth of the Den of Woodston, hugging the coast all the way from Johnshaven. The steep slopes can still be seen down which the vehicles jolted and slithered before starting the steep climb up the other side. Today there are fields all around, but in 1804 the old dirt road still existed. Skirting the ice pond at the Mill of Woodston, the road went down the west side of the den and across the bridge at the mouth of the den. Midway between the mill and the bridge it passed through a hamlet with the intriguing name of Bungytown.

Miltonhaven – a Seaport in Decline

And now back to the road junction a mile away. This time we turn right and proceed for another quarter of a mile to the remains of the

Part of the lonely stretch of smugglers' coastline where at the beginning of the 18th century was the seaport of Miltonhaven. Miltonhaven, the largest village in the parish of St Cyrus and a burgh of barony, was 'carried away in one night' in 1795 by an inrush of the sea during a storm. The picture shows the low beach on which Miltonhaven stood with the remains of part of the massive wall built by the villagers in a vain attempt to save their village.

hamlet of Tangleha' ('tangles', an edible seaweed, and 'haven') with its landing-place among the rocks where now only four of its eight or nine houses remain occupied. Here is carried on a considerable amount of lobster fishing. In this lonely stretch of smugglers' coastline, and just 700 yards north of where we stand now, stood at the beginning of the 18th century a busy fishing village, by far the largest in the parish of St Cyrus. It was called Miltonhaven. Even in 1695, when the Stratons said good-bye to Lauriston, Miltonhaven was already a burgh of barony and a seaport with a weekly market and four-day fair each May and October – the hub of the whole parish.

Miltonhaven's line-fishing community was only a small one. When fishing along the rest of the Mearns coast was enjoying its heyday in the middle of the 18th century, there were only three boats in Miltonhaven, employing eighteen fishermen. Perhaps there was too much competition from nearby Johnshaven. There were probably never very many fishing boats anyhow not only because the people in the district ate little white fish but because people in those days lived in constant dread of being seized out at sea by press gangs as unwilling recruits for the Navy. They therefore reached the stage where they had neither the money nor the initiative to replace their boats. Perhaps there is significance in the familiar ring of the *Statistical Account* concerning Miltonhaven fishermen of the time:

> *Indeed, it is well known that scarce any but the children of fishermen follow the occupation of their fathers, and that they are a kind of distinct tribe by their manners and by intermarrying only with each other.*

French Gin, Dutch Brandy and the Finest China Tea

Prosperity and the comforts of life, indeed, were much more easily obtained by joining the ranks of the smugglers for smuggling was on this coast highly profitable and boomed as it had never done before. A man could earn much more by this means than ever he could from white fishing. Year after year, by dead of night, cargoes were landed along the rocky coast between St Cyrus and Johnshaven, and many a cottager around Milton of Mathers and many of the townspeople of Johnshaven took to French gin and Dutch brandy! One night in 1742, for example, two tons of tobacco were seized by Customs men in Miltonhaven, pushed overboard as the big tobacco ships neared Montrose, at the time the chief tobacco port of Scotland. Since those two tons were taken to a cottage in a cart, we can assume that the tobacco was in hogsheads dropped off some passing ship homeward bound from the American plantations, for that kind of thing did happen.

And with the tobacco, the gin and the brandy came the finest China tea, with sugar from the West Indies to sweeten it. Not a cottage could boast a teapot before the lime quarry opened, but by the end of the 18th century there was scarcely a house in the parish where the women didn't drink tea at least once a day. You could buy it in parcels of all sizes upwards from a halfpenny parcel, and a farthing one of sugar. It was reckoned that in the Mearns about 1807 the average farm labourer's wife was spending 7½d a week on tea and sugar, and the laird's wife 20 shillings!

Limestone Quarrying – and Disaster Strikes

The writing on the wall for Miltonhaven appeared when local landowners realised that a sprinkling of lime on their land increased the yield of oats and barley amazingly. In 1750 Robert Scott of Dunninald, M.P. for the county of Angus and agricultural pioneer, leased Lauriston estate and, in his search for the magical lime for his fields, chose Miltonhaven with its harbour and plentiful supply of labour as the first place along the St Cyrus coastline to work lime on a large scale. Knowing that the limestone in the area was of the highest quality, he built a kiln on the shore. Fortunes were made in the next few years, and the population doubled. In 1781 there was a population of 170 living in some fifty houses in the middle of this silent, shingly bay. The number continued to rise after that. All through the night the red glow in the sky over Miltonhaven shone like a welcoming beacon far out to sea to every ship that carried contraband so that soon the lime workers became involved in smuggling too. Eventually disaster struck.

The low beach on which Miltonhaven stood was protected by a natural breakwater, a projecting ledge of limestone rock that ran across the bay in front of the village. It was into this reef that the villagers, most of them lime workers (especially all the newcomers who arrived in the second half of the 18th century), began to quarry too deeply. As it gradually disappeared, the sea began to beat more violently on the coast. After some houses had been inundated in 1792, a massive wall was built by the villagers in an attempt to save the remaining part of the village. But the attempt was in vain; the digging for lime continued; they cut too far. In the words of a contemporary *Geological Journal*, during a storm when an easterly gale was blowing, an inrush of the sea at high tide

> *in 1795 carried away the whole village in one night and penetrated 150 yards inland where it has maintained its ground ever since, the new village having been built farther inland on the new shore*

– an account not altogether accurate as some houses had been carried away three years earlier. It was then that a much smaller village was built a little farther south on the new shore at Tangleha' where we are now. But it never remotely approached Miltonhaven in size. Some two-thirds of the inhabitants of the doomed village seem to have left the district, and from then onwards the Kirkton of St Cyrus became the largest village in the parish.

A Secret Passage to Lauriston Castle

Have you time for a stroll northwards along the footpath (sometimes not too well defined) which skirts the bay for only some four-fifths of a mile – a walk of only a little over a mile and a half in all? If so, you will see that the Miltonhaven disaster did not bring an end to lime quarrying in the district although, with production difficulties steadily increasing, it never really prospered again. In just over quarter of a mile we reach first of all the ruined salmon fishers' bothy on the point, thereafter proceeding over the Lauriston Burn to the caravan park. A narrow cleft beside the little stream was allegedly the seaward end of a secret subterranean passage to Lauriston Castle in olden days, covered, we are led to believe, during the spring tides. In it were once trapped (we are told) a blind piper and his dog so that the castle kitchen staff were disturbed night and day by the wail of the pibroch and the howling of the dog. Years later, so the legend goes, whitened bones were found to prove the truth of the tale.

Mute Evidence of a Doomed Village

A further 200 yards takes us to another stream – the Finella – at the mouth of the Den of the same name. Here were recognisable until fairly recently the foundations of the last of the Miltonhaven cottages. For on this low beach, a little to the east of the headland of Rockhall, stood the doomed village. Coastal erosion has been considerable over the years. The sea wall has disappeared under the sea and the pebbles and water-worn boulders of the beach although a fragment at the northern end is still in evidence to remind you that a busy little seaport, pulsating with life, existed well over 100 yards offshore. But the ruined limestone kiln, ironically enough, still disdainfully dominates the scene.

Seagreens Pier and the East Mathers Kiln

At the hamlet of Seagreens 600 yards farther on (which is as far as we shall go) one can still see the remains of the pier built in 1803 by a banker laird of Lauriston who with a staff of fourteen quarriers, six burners, six carters, eight labourers and six to eight sailors fetching coal from Fife for almost 20 years sold from the neighbouring farm of East Mathers 1,250 tons of lime (some 40,000 barrels) per year despite growing difficulties and rising costs. The price, once 1/6d for about a hundredweight and a quarter (and still only 1/10d in 1794) had risen to 3/4d by 1812. In 1820 competition arrived when English lime was brought in at Gourdon and Johnshaven so that latterly only one twentieth of the production of 1810 was reached. In 1836, when annual sales had dropped to a mere 2,000 barrels, the kilns were fired for the last time. It was at the lime works of East Mathers, still clearly seen in the field behind Seagreens, that the last of the limestone quarries operated although all surface quarrying along the coast had finished 24 years before because of uneconomic conditions.

Now along the shore between St Cyrus and Johnshaven only the ruined lime kilns remain as memories. Fragments can be seen between the one at East Mathers and Johnshaven, beside Girdle Craig road, once narrow and dangerous before lime burning began. One beside the ruined cottages of Tangleha' has now been bull-dozed away. More lasting monuments are seen in the green fields nearby where once was moorland.

George Carnegie's First Quarry Remains

On our return journey let us stop at the gate 200 yards from Seagreens and walk the 140 yards along the cleft to our right. We shall find ourselves in the remains of the first quarry which was opened by George Carnegie of Pitarrow, the developer of the East Mathers lime works when no more limestone remained close to the surface beside the shore. Indeed, 25 ft. of earth and rock had to be cleared away before limestone could be reached at all, two horses being required to work all day to pump out rising water. The quarry stretches back into the high bank to the west, a great hollow cavern on the hillside where with some expense the seam of limestone, scarcely 8 ft. thick, had been blasted out from a precipice face of 100 ft. and under a great depth of earth and rock. The field above has collapsed through subsidence.

Robert Scott, Milton of Mathers Pioneer

Now we must return to the A92 to proceed with our journey. But when you reach the top of the hill on the way back, after two-fifths of a mile, do have a look at the farm of Milton of Mathers half a mile away across the field on your right. For this farm, rented in the 18th century by Robert Scott of Dunninald, is associated with great land improvements in the Mearns. Having cleared his land of surface stones, Scott dug it deep and added a liberal dose of lime from his kiln at Milton of Mathers to the vast amusement of the neighbouring farmers who argued that the land would be ruined for all time. But they laughed less when they saw his crops and in the end decided to use lime as well.

On these fields, too, the first crop of turnips was grown in the Mearns in 1754, the solution of the previously unsolved problem of how to feed cattle through the winter months. Until then the vast majority of animals, fat or not, had been killed and salted in the autumn. The introduction of turnips led, too, to a big increase in the number of store cattle in the county and, later, to the selective breeding which eventually produced Old Jock, Old Grannie[1] and all the Aberdeenshire and Angus cattle that have sprung from them. In 1764 turnips found their way to Fordoun where they were grown on the farm of Wattieston in the east end of the village. Mr W. Lyall, the farmer, was content with half an acre at first and sold them for a penny a stone!

Also at Milton of Mathers potatoes were re-introduced by Robert Scott. But for many years they were to be seen only in gardens as they were considered as great a delicacy as apples and peas. The trouble from a commercial point of view was that the first variety had no keeping qualities.

Ruinous Lauriston Castle with its 18th Century Wing

At the main road we turn right and in 260 yards pass on the right the Bush Hotel. (If you look at an old map of 1822, you will find that The Bush had the more imposing name of Bourtree Bush – 'the elder bush'). But it is a turning on the left quarter of a mile farther on which interests us next for here a path in fairly poor condition leads us alongside the deep, wooded Den of Lauriston for a third of a mile to the ruins of Lauriston Castle, occupying a highly pictur-esque and strong situation on the brink of a deep ravine.

Perhaps the first thing we notice is that there is attached to the castle a more modern spacious mansion (still lived in) which was erected in 1789 by a prominent Montrose lawyer who bought the castle and incorporated it into his new home, a dignified, symmetri-cal and typically 18th century wing with a staid but restrained classical frontage, jostling with the mediaevalism of Lauriston Castle itself.

Surely we must be saddened by the extraordinary dilapidation which in less than half a century has befallen the main building which may date back, in part at least, some ten centuries although additions have been made at various times. Less well known than many other Kincardine 'fortresses', it was in bygone days on a par with Dunnottar.

---

[1] Old Jock and Old Grannie are, respectively, the first bull and the first cow in the Polled (hornless) Herd Book. Old Grannie lived from 1824 to 1859, had twenty-seven calves and was killed by lightning; Old Jock was born in 1842.

Corner Tower and Curtain Wall

The most obvious structure still defiantly rising from the empty shell of the castle is one of the original square corner towers seemingly growing from the living rock and dating from the 14th century. Three storeys high, unfortunately it has been heightened in an unsightly way above parapet level in modern times. This flanking tower which is corbelled out externally has a narrow turnpike stair from which a door at second floor level once gave access from a vaulted chamber to the parapet wall, parallel to the top of the ravine. At first floor level was a similar room. At the eastern end of the ruined castle is what appears to have been a later L-shaped gabled structure of the late 16th or early 17th century, probably erected on the foundations of the main keep.

Until recent years there was visible a fine section of a massive high curved curtain wall on the west side, dating from the 14th century and with small open rounds at the angles. This had once enclosed the courtyard. From a vaulted chamber at courtyard level steps once led down some 6 ft. to another vaulted chamber, belonging to the 14th century, which might have been the prison of the original keep. And from the parapet walk a few steps descended to a small vaulted basement chamber with an extraordinary gap in the stone flooring, opening on to a dizzy funnel-like shaft, some 4 ft. wide, cut in the cliff face right down to the floor of the den and possibly some kind of hidden exit.

Extravagant 'Romantic Revival' Landscape Gardening

How tragic, too, that in place of the amazing contrast that once existed between the architecture of Lauriston Castle and the surrounding landscape, dereliction now surrounds its remains. The grounds of the estate were once laid out in the most extravagant style of landscape-gardening popularised by the Romantic Revival with deep ravines, picturesque paths, tortuous streams and rugged bridges such as we can still see crossing the Den of Lauriston below the ruins and two-thirds of the way between the castle and the main road. In contrast to the wildly fanciful element once encountered in the grounds the frontage of the castle itself must indeed have seemed almost sombre!

The Remarkable Straitons of Lauriston

The Castle of Lauriston (named, perhaps, like Laurencekirk, after St Lawrence) from as early as 1243 belonged to the family of de

Strivelyn or Stirling, the first owners on record, who held the barony of Glenesk. Later in the 13th century it was the stronghold of a family who in their era played almost as prominent a part in the history of Scotland and the Mearns as the Earls Marischal – the family of Straiton or Stratoun who made their mark in many fields. They were a race of men remarkable for their size, their strength and their attachment to the family home. It is said that, so great was the last-named attribute, wherever they settled, they changed the name of the place to that of their erstwhile abode.

The first member of this family in the Mearns is mentioned as taking the oath of fealty to King Edward in 1296, and during the second War of Independence Lauriston Castle opened its gates to an English garrison but was captured and demolished by the Regent, Sir Andrew Moray, in 1336. The Straitons, however, re-built their home, and another member of the family, Alexander Straiton de Laurenston, *the knicht of Lauriston* as he was designated in literature of the period, was one of five hundred knights and burgesses who with several of his sons and many men from the Mearns fell at the Battle of Harlaw in 1411, defending Aberdeen for the Regent, Duke of Albany, against Donald, Lord of the Isles. In 1534 David Straiton, another member of the family, was hanged for the Protestant reformed faith on Calton Hill (see page 482).

George Stratoun, a descendant and one of the first persons of *rank and respectability* to embrace the reformed doctrines in 1540, 27 years thereafter represented Kincardineshire in Parliament. His son, Sir Alexander Stratoun, also sat in Parliament for his county, was a Privy Councillor and in 1605 was Lord High Commissioner to the General Assembly of the Kirk of Scotland which met in Aberdeen. He enlarged the estate by purchasing Woodston and the adjoining lands from Sir George Keith of Drumtochty. In 1695 the lairdship of the Straitons ended, and the barony was acquired by Sir James Falconer of Phesdo whose descendants held it until 1793.

In more recent times Alexander Porteous, a native of Crieff and latterly a successful East Indies merchant, bought the estate in 1849. Two years later he married Helen, a daughter of David Scott of Brotherton, and was the principal promoter of the Montrose and Bervie Railway Company. Mr Porteous died in 1872 and was succeeded by his son, Captain David Porteous of the Scots Greys. After his death in 1931, the Lauriston estate was exposed for sale at £14,000 two years later. It failed to find a purchaser although with improvements it is believed to have cost the Porteous family over £50,000.

The Awe-Inspiring Den of Finella

Back to the main road now where we turn left and travel for only some 330 yards until we see the sign to Laurencekirk which indicates the road we are to take. You may wish, however (but the decision is yours), to continue for a little over a third of a mile, and to stop at the road bridge over the well-wooded Den of Finella where traditionally Finella, who had contrived the death of King Kenneth III in the tenth century (see page 360), leapt to her death into the rocky gorge rather than allow herself to be captured by her pursuers:

> *And leapt from the rocks to a wild, boiling pool*
> *Where her body was torn and tossed.*

This romantic den rivals in grandeur the scenery of the North Esk at The Burn (see page 417) though not on so extensive a scale. Overhung with foliage, it is spanned by a high bridge a little above the still loftier arc of a railway bridge. It is one of the most awe-inspiring and weird beauty-spots in the Mearns, retaining to this day an air of danger, and to look down from the road bridge makes the heart flutter.

At the south side of the road bridge is an opening where at one time was a gate. A footpath leads down precarious steps inside, now treacherous and overgrown with moss and leaf-mould, which descend the almost precipitous south side of the den to two 'balconies'. So difficult of access is this part of the den that these points of vantage are set in the almost sheer cliff face overlooking a picturesque waterfall, some 110 ft. high, where the burn, taking a leap through a narrow cleft in the rocks, plunges into a deep cauldron in the dungeon-like den below to twist in the shadowy depths and rush by leaps and bounds for some distance down the glen. The descent is a dangerous one and is not recommended.

Above the road bridge the burn bubbles and froths through a fearsome gorge the bottom of which is pitted with holes and dark crevices. Here is a cave-like hole which, it is thought, may be the entrance to a tunnel leading to Lauriston Castle. In the 1900's, when horse and buggy were the order of the day, the den was the subject of considerable interest with people coming from far and near to view its beauty. Now its existence is known only to few except those conversant with the surrounding countryside.

St Lawrence's Chapel and the 'Wax Market'

And now we must be on our way back. We return to the Laurencekirk road, turn right and two-fifths of a mile up the hill pass the beautifully walled garden of Lauriston Castle on our left. Between this garden and the old castle was the site of a chapel, forming an interesting and valuable example of that association of church and castle which was characteristic of the Anglo-Norman penetration of Scotland in the 12th and 13th centuries.

Turning a corner immediately beyond the garden, we see the farm of Chapelfield on our right and reach the road-end to it in just under half a mile. The property takes its name from yet another chapel, standing within its burial-ground and dedicated to St Lawrence before 1243, which stood 530 yards to the east of the farm on the edge of Den Finella. From this chapel, which was a dependency on the church of Ecclesgreig, Alexander de Strivelyn settled an annuity on the prior and canons of St Andrews, binding himself and his heirs to pay yearly the value of a pound of wax at the market-place of Montrose. Thus one of the Lauriston owners was amongst the earliest customers in the 'Wax Market' there. Now the wax candle factory and the tallow-candle works have quite disappeared.

The Lands of Garvock and the Arbuthnotts

In two-fifths of a mile we find ourselves quite close to the attractive Den of Chapelfield on our right and in a further two miles at the end of the road to Garvock Church. There was a church at Garvock here in 1275, but there are no visible remains of the mediaeval building or its successor in 1678 which was replaced by the present church in the late 18th century.

This reminds us that at one period in history there was almost certainly connection between the lands of Garvock and the Arbuthnott family. Hugh Arbuthenoth, Le Blond and hero of the well-known ballad, according to Crawford's *Peerage* bestowed the patronage of Garvock on the Abbey of Arbroath *for the safety of his soul*. The exact particulars of the gift are:

To the Abbot and Convent of Aberbrothock in pure and perpetual alms of one oxengate[1] of land, lying adjacent to the Church of Garvock, with the right of patronage for 100 sheep, 4 horses, 10 oxen and 20 cows – Aberbrothock, 4 to nonas, Aug., 1282.

In a pretty dell some 85 yards to the north-east of Garvock Church was St James' Well. There is something pathetic as well as romantic about the fact that this copious spring with its cold clear water was

---

[1] A measure of land varying according to the nature of the soil.

496

once believed to work miraculous cures and that annual visitations were paid to it by the people from the Howe and other parts of the Mearns. Exactly half-way between the church and the well a prehistoric stone axe was found.

In a further two-fifths of a mile we arrive at the top of the Garvock Heights and would do well to pull in at the car park provided at this noted vantage-point to enjoy, if it is a clear day, a truly wonderful view, completely unparalleled in this part of the country.

Garvock — Forest and Hunting-ground

The Hill of Garvock, varying from 500 ft. to 900 ft. above sea level, runs in a south-easterly direction between the coast and the Howe of the Mearns and through the parishes of Arbuthnott, Garvock and St Cyrus. It is cultivated almost to the summit, and between it and the sea lie some of the best agricultural properties in the county, those around St Cyrus and Bervie being particularly fertile.

Garvock was a place of some importance in prehistoric days. Arrow-heads and flints from the area are to be seen in The Retreat in Glen Esk, and the parish has remains of stone circles. On the top of the hill are the remains of two large Bronze Age cairns. These had perhaps a judicial as well as a religious significance, and it is believed that they were used as the bases for fires on certain festival days. Apparently, as in other parts of the country, it was the practice of the heathen priests of the Mearns to exorcise evil and induce the blessing of their gods on crops by the conflagrations they raised, notably on the first days of May and November.

At one time Garvock was nothing but a vast forest used as a hunting-ground by the king and extending to the deer-dyke at Arnbarrow (see page 166). Of the pale of this mediaeval hunting forest there are no visible remains. It formed the boundary between the parishes of Garvock and Laurencekirk, and in 1836 it was stated that *the remains of a substantial fence along the north-west side of the parish, called the 'deer-dyke', are well remembered by old people although they have now nearly all disappeared under the plough'*. In 1880, however, traces of the dyke were still to be seen. The forest is reputed to have been part of the Earl Marischal property, and built into the walls of Garvock church (dedicated to St James the Apostle) are stones which obviously at one time had formed a monument to the Keith family. The dates thereon are 1666 and 1679, but some chroniclers are inclined to the opinion that they refer to scions of the family who were connected with the religious life of the parish rather than to the ruling line itself.

Panoramic View from the Tower of Johnstone

The most prominent ridge on the Garvock Heights is crowned by Johnstone Tower immediately above Laurencekirk, a conspicuous and commanding feature from all parts of the compass. As this is the best point of vantage, you may wish to walk to it southwards along the ridge, starting off at the gate beside which we have parked. The footpath gives no difficulty whatsoever, and the easy walk from gate to gate through four fields is a mile and some 160 yards in length. Your journey there and back should easily be accomplished within an hour. You will pass on the crest of the hill in just over half a mile a cairn measuring about 29½ ft. in diameter and just over 1½ ft. in height.

The Tower of Johnstone is a most singular building, circular and with wings to break the force of the wind. It is regrettably sadly in need of attention and stands on a mound of boulders, about 30 yards in diameter and 6 ft. in height, obviously the remains of a prehistoric Bronze Age burial cairn. It was built by an Aberdonian, James Farquhar, who became Member of Parliament for the Montrose and Aberdeen district of burghs. He bought the lands of Johnstone in 1805 and, to commemorate one of the great victories of the Peninsular War, erected this great tower, 30 ft. high, with a winding staircase inside to the top, to enable persons to enjoy the magnificent view, comprising hill and dale, stream and sea, green fertile fields, woods and cosy farmsteads and miles of fair farm land, stretching away to the Grampian foot-hills and dotted with township and village.

The panoramic view has few if any rivals in the county and has been minutely described in the second *Statistical Account*. The view embraces the Aberdeenshire coast, Fife and the Pentlands. Around and immediately beneath can be seen many parts of Kincardineshire while the valley of Strathmore opens out to the south-west where is visible a considerable part of Angus including the White Caterthun with its ruins of a prehistoric fort. An exceptionally fine view of the Grampian Mountains can be obtained to the westward, ranging from Lochnagar in the distance, Mount Battock and Mount Keen (all over 3,000 ft. in height) to the slightly lower hills of Kerloch, Clochnaben by the Cairn o' Mounth and Cairn-mon-earn. Farther away, and over the hills of Perth, the peak of the far distant Ben Lomond and practically all the eminences familiar to dwellers in Perth, Angus, the Mearns and Aberdeenshire are often visible. The view is equally extensive and intriguing seaward. Craig David at Inverbervie, and Montrose, seem just beneath you, and behind

on a clear day the eye traces the coastline from Lunan Bay and Red
Head to the Lammermuir Hills and St Abb's Head in Berwickshire,
and distinguishes among other objects of interest the tower on the
Bell Rock, the Isle of May, the Bass Rock and North Berwick Law.
Given good visibility, it is even possible to see the Cheviot Hills in
Northumberland. From few, if any, other hills that rise to a modest
914 ft. can such a range be covered.

The Howe Once a Prehistoric Morass

A view which is perfect is that of the whole of the low-lying Howe of
the Mearns, seen at a glance with its 50 square miles of ground
between the North Esk and the Bervie, sheltered by the Grampians
on the north and Garvock Heights on the east and really a continuation of the great Vale of Strathmore.

In prehistoric times the Howe must have been very largely covered by water which in course of countless ages was drained away by
the Esk, the Luther Water, the Bervie and the Carron. From the
North Esk to Drumlithie, between the foot of the Grampian hills
and Garvock was a morass. On the uplands a dense forest, interspersed with lakes, existed until a comparatively recent period.
Belts of moraines are prominent on the lowland floor with old lake
depressions and melt-water channels, that which breaches the
water-shed to reach the sea at Stonehaven being very prominent
and giving access for the railway line.

For hundreds of years the Howe was so marshy as to be incapable
of agriculture except in patches, and a general idea of what it was
like in past ages is afforded by place-names like 'Whitemyre',
'Redmyre' and 'Gyratsmyre'. A score of others remind us that a
thousand years ago and more there was a number of bogs throughout the county. 'Main' in 'Balmain' and 'Mon' in 'Monboddo'
signify mosses and swamps, 'Inchgray' rising ground or islands in
the morass, and 'Drumlithie', 'Drumforber', etc. mounds or ridges.
It was to Kincardine and Haulkerton in this successsion of swamps
in the centre of the Howe, before the encroachment of agriculture,
that kings came with falconers and falcons (whence Falconer and
Keith-Falconer) to have sport amid those areas of marsh gleaming
through dark pines and stately oaks. Into the heart of the kingdom
here, entering the forest through which the River Esk flowed, came
Bruce, overcoming all obstacles to overtake John Comyn, his
enemy.

Now, however, on any spring or summer day one sees the Howe
of the Mearns as Lewis Grassic Gibbon saw it in *Grey Granite*, the

third volume in his trilogy, *A Scots Quair*, for the land of the Mearns – of which the Howe is the heart – is as unchanging as the grey cliffs that gird its coast. This is what he says:

> *And then the road wheeled up and around and paused:*
> *there below the Howe of the Mearns, crowned, shod, be-*
> *belted in green and gold, silver chains where the Mearns*
> *burns wound and spun to the Forthie's flow, Stonehaven*
> *forward, Bervie behind, far off the shimmer where the*
> *Grampians rode, the farms gleaming below the bents,*
> *haugh on haugh, tumbling green long cornswaths under the*
> *wind.*

The Lofty Site of St James's Fair

Before we descend to Laurencekirk, you may care to have another walk (shorter this time) to see the lofty and windy site of Barnhill at St James's Loch which was the site of the great St James's Fair, deriving its name from the patron saint of the parish of Garvock in which it was situated. This largest of all fairs in the Mearns took place annually a fortnight after Paddy Fair and, like it, lasted four days. The fair began to decline with the introduction of feeing-markets and is now almost forgotten. The lake is, as the crow flies, only some 650 yards away to the north-east over the rise on the other side of the road, and one must start the walk through the open gate and along the track exactly opposite that used for the walk to Johnstone Tower. Probably the best way (for the ground is marshy) is to follow the fence for some 780 yards until one reaches a small clump of the last few straggling trees of Barnhill Wood which once covered some 47 acres here, and to explore from this point.

St James's Fair, which was moved from Garvock to Laurencekirk in 1846, was the only fair at the time which was recognised as the feeing-market for the area, being attended by all who wished to work at the harvest, and early one morning about the middle of July almost every man, woman and child, master, mistress and maid, dressed in all their finery, set out across the moorland in the direction of Garvock. Scarcely enough folk were left at home on the farms of the Mearns to keep the cattle out of the corn.

A Fair Resembling Saturnalia

Four or five hundred cattle were on show, of course, and there were long streets of tents with all sorts of tempting displays, clothes, household goods, shoes, jewellery and, most popular of all, sweets. There were great marquees, too, some seating almost a hundred, where the tightly packed crowds could get a meal almost as good as in the best inn in the country. For this you paid 1/- and for another 1/- you purchased enough ale to wash it down.

There was a justice tent and in it a magistrate whose main job was to act as arbiter when hard-headed business men could not come to terms. He might also deal, however, with the unwary pickpocket or drunk who would be dragged off by guards with rusty halberts for a healthy lesson in the stocks. Most of the people who had to spend an hour or two there were just country folk who had become fighting drunk. In almost every respect, it was said, St James's Fair bore a striking resemblance to the saturnalia, the greatest of all debauches of ancient Rome. The only saintly thing about it, some said, was its name!

It is asserted by some that permanent seating which accommodated the frequenters of the tents – long benches of turf in parallel rows of three, the middle one serving as the table – are still distinguishable. These the writer has failed to find. Nor has he located an oblong cairn near the site of the Fair which is said to commemorate a duel, fatal to both parties, fought by merchants who quarrelled at a gathering round about 1745. Perhaps the reader will be more fortunate.

The Bronze Age Cairn of Shiels

A further walk of half a mile or so to the north-east from the site of St James's Fair by the loch would take us, if we were so inclined, to what is called the Cairn of Shiels on the highest piece of land in the immediate area, 850 ft. above sea level and only some 90 ft. above where we are presently standing. Here is an oval bank or knap 17 yards long by 14 yards wide, and 3 yards in breadth, with on it a concentric ditch inside which is a Bronze Age cairn formed of earth and stones 67 ft. in diameter and some 5 ft. high. As it is, however, in a state of some dilapidation and as marshy ground and several fences must be negotiated, a visit to it is recommended only for the enthusiast. What may be the remains of a second cairn (measuring 16 ft. in diameter by less than a foot in height) are situated 9 yards to the east-north-east.

The Original Baronhill and its Jurisdictions

On your journey back to your car pause for a moment exactly 200 yards before you reach the B9120 Laurencekirk road, exactly on the top of the hill, 813 ft. above sea level. Here is an interesting spot. For here is the original Baronhill (the name of the farm Barnhill just over a third of a mile below is quite evidently a corruption) the centre at which justice was once administered and councils held in the barony of Garvock which, besides the lands in the parish itself, included those belonging to Conveth, Johnston, Burnton, Powburn, Scotston and Redmyre. The site was selected partly for its excellent position and partly for the admirable facilities which it offered for the safety precautions indispensable to such gatherings in those wild times.

Barons such as the Keith family who originally constituted and held this barony for many years had the hereditary right, granted by the Crown, of exercising arbitrary power over vassals and other persons within their domain. They could fine, scourge, imprison, and even put to death, without appeal to common law. It is significant that the name of the falling ground immediately to the east of where we are standing now is Gallow Bank! Those jurisdictions were abolished in 1747 when compensation amounting to over £150,000 was paid by Government to the proprietors whose interests were affected by the abolition.

Burnton Cabbages Foil Raiders

And now let us continue our journey. As we descend gradually to Laurencekirk, the slopes, as on the seaward side, are here and there dotted with patches of wood or grazing moorland which gives freshness and colour to a somewhat bare and monotonous district. On the right is the large farm of Burnton, visited by soldiers during the '45 when it was in the possession of a family named Christie. The soldiers demanded milk, which was not to their satisfaction when they received it: they therefore went into the dairy and emptied every basin of its contents. Against such a raid a daughter about to be married had her 'providing' well secured. It had been put into a chest and buried in what is still the garden attached to the farmhouse. To make detection impossible, and perhaps as a sly joke at the expense of the pilferers, the ground beneath which lay the valuables was planted all over with cabbages!

In just under two miles we arrive at the junction of the B9120 with the main A94, and our circuit is complete. Stonehaven Square is fourteen and one-tenth miles away.

Acknowledgements

I wish to acknowledge my gratitude and thanks to the very many people who have aided in all kinds of ways in the production of this book. I am particularly indebted to Mr Neil B. M. Fraser for again providing such excellent diagrammatic maps and to the following for substantial help in other respects:

The Viscount of Arbuthnott.

Aberdeen Art Gallery and Museum for the photograph on page 87.

Aberdeen Journals Ltd. for the photograph on page 403.

Aberdeen University for the picture on page 451.

Aerofilms Ltd., Boreham Wood, Herts, for the photograph on page 369.

The Cambridge University Collection for the photograph on page 346.

Mr J. S. Cardno for the photographs on pages 352 and 429.

Mr David Clark for the photograph on page 303.

Mr A. K. Cooper of Inverbervie.

Rev. James Gait of Laurencekirk.

Mr James Gammie of the Nature Conservancy Council.

Mr Peter Gladstone of Fasque.

Mr John Hogg for the photographs on pages 4, 5, 14, 15, 32, 42, 108, 115 and for other help.

Mr James W. Irvine-Fortescue of Kingcausie.

Mr James Lessells of Aberdeen.

Mr Gordon Maxwell and Staff of the Royal Commission on the Ancient and Historical Monuments of Scotland for the photographs on pages 111, 204 (top) and for other help.

Montrose Museum for the photograph on page 432.

Mr Alexander Murray of Drumlithie for the use of the postcard reproduced on page 276.

The Nature Conservancy Council, Edinburgh, for the photograph on page 470.

The Public Relations Officer, RAF Edzell.

Mr Ian B. M. Ralston of Aberdeen University.

The Staff of Renfrew District Council Museum and Art Gallery Service.

Mr Neil Robertson of Westfield House, Stonehaven.

Professor J. K. St Joseph, Professor of Aerial Photographic Studies, Cambridge University.

The Scottish Development Department for the photograph on page 167.

Mr Ian A. G. Shepherd, archaeologist, Grampian Region, for the photographs on pages 400 and 401 and for other help.

Mr Benjamin B. Smith for reading and checking the book while in typescript and for valuable suggestions.

Mrs Isobel Smith, St Cyrus, for the use of the photograph on page 480.

Wing Commander George D. Swapp, Stonehaven.

Mr W. A. Williamson, Kirkton, Arbuthnott.

Mr George Wood for the photograph on page 47.

Captain John Wood, Stonehaven.

Mr and Mrs J. G. Wood, East Mains of Barras.

And to my wife for her unfailing advice, support and help in ways too numerous to mention.